Lecture Notes in Computer Science 8538

Commenced Publication in 1973
Founding and Former Series Editors:
Gerhard Goos, Juris Hartmanis, and Jan van Leeuwen

T0183283

Vania Dimitrova   Tsvi Kuflik   David Chin
Francesco Ricci   Peter Dolog
Geert-Jan Houben (Eds.)

User Modeling, Adaptation, and Personalization

22nd International Conference, UMAP 2014
Aalborg, Denmark, July 7-11, 2014
Proceedings

 Springer

Volume Editors

Vania Dimitrova
University of Leeds, UK
E-mail: v.g.dimitrova@leeds.ac.uk

Tsvi Kuflik
Haifa University, Israel
E-mail: tsvikak@is.haifa.ac.il

David Chin
University of Hawaii, Honolulu, HI, USA
E-mail: chin@hawaii.edu

Francesco Ricci
Free University of Bozen-Bolzano, Italy
E-mail: fricci@unibz.it

Peter Dolog
Aalborg University, Denmark
E-mail: dolog@cs.aau.dk

Geert-Jan Houben
EEMCS, Delft, The Netherlands
E-mail: g.j.p.m.houben@tudelft.nl

ISSN 0302-9743   e-ISSN 1611-3349
ISBN 978-3-319-08785-6   e-ISBN 978-3-319-08786-3
DOI 10.1007/978-3-319-08786-3
Springer Cham Heidelberg New York Dordrecht London

Library of Congress Control Number: 2014942572

LNCS Sublibrary: SL 3 – Information Systems and Application, incl. Internet/Web and HCI

Typesetting: Camera-ready by author, data conversion by Scientific Publishing Services, Chennai, India

Printed on acid-free paper

Springer is part of Springer Science+Business Media (www.springer.com)

Preface

The 22nd International Conference on User Modeling, Adaptation, and Personalization (UMAP2014) was held in Aalborg, Denmark, during 7–11 July, 2014. UMAP is the premier international conference for researchers and practitioners working on systems that adapt to their individual users or to groups of users. UMAP is the successor of the biennial User Modeling (UM) and Adaptive Hypermedia and Adaptive Web-based Systems (AH) conferences that were merged in 2009. It is organized under the auspices of User Modeling Inc. The conference spans a wide scope of topics related to user modeling, adaptation, and personalization.

UMAP2014 submissions were invited from a broad range of issues faced by modern user adaptive systems, covering the following key areas: UMAP in the social era; UMAP in the era of big data; UMAP in the era of pervasive computing; infrastructures, architectures, and methodologies; human factors and models; personal and societal issues. The conference included high-quality peer-reviewed papers solicited from two areas: research and experience. The research papers present substantive new research results on user modeling, adaptation, and/or personalization. The experience papers present innovative use of user modeling, adaptation, and personalization, exploring the benefits and challenges of applying user modeling techniques and adaptation technology in real-life applications and contexts.

Leading researchers acted as area chairs who provided strategic help in selecting the Program Committee and conducting the review process. The international Program Committee consisted of 101 leading members of the user modeling and adaptive hypermedia communities as well as highly promising young researchers. They were assisted by 40 additional reviewers. There were 146 submissions, each submission received three reviews; a meta-reviewer facilitated consensus achievement when needed. In all, 23 submissions (16%) were accepted for long presentation at the conference, and another 19 papers were accepted for short presentation at the conference, i.e., the overall acceptance rate was 29%. Papers addressed well-established as well as emerging topics in user modeling, adaptation, and personalization. Among these are: large-scale personalization, adaptation and recommendation; personalization for individuals, groups and populations; modeling individuals, groups, and communities; Web dynamics and personalization; adaptive Web-based systems; context awareness; social recommendations; user experience; user awareness and control; affective aspects; UMAP underpinning by psychology models; privacy, perceived security and trust; behavior change and persuasion.

Three distinguished researchers gave plenary invited talks on related topics, illustrating prospective directions for the field. Elizabeth Churchill, Director of Human Computer Interaction at eBay Research Labs in San Jose, California,

USA, presented a framework for thinking about people-centered systems design. Kaj Grønbæk, Professor at the University of Aarhus, Denmark, and heading the Ubiquitous Computing and Interaction Research Group at the Department of Computer Science, gave an overview of methods being developed for mobile sensing and understanding user behavior in urban contexts. Gregory D. Abowd, Regents' and Distinguished Professor in the School of Interactive Computing at Georgia Tech, USA, and leading the Ubicomp Research Group, presented how a concrete application domain, such as autism and related developmental disabilities, could present a wide variety of opportunities for computing research.

The conference also included a doctoral consortium that provided an opportunity for doctoral students to explore and develop their research interests under the guidance of a panel of 18 distinguished research faculty. This track received 11 submissions of which five were accepted as full presentations and another three were accepted as poster presentations. The poster and demo session of the conference received 27 submissions, from which 17 were accepted.

The UMAP2014 program included the following workshops:

- Personalized Multilingual Information Access, organized by Ben Steichen, Maristella Agosti, Séamus Lawless, and Vincent Wade
- Personalizing Search - From Search Engines to Exploratory Search Systems, organized by Tuukka Ruotsalo, Giulio Jacucci, Peter Brusilovsky, Samuel Kaski, and Oswald Barral
- News Recommendation and Analytics, organized by Jon Atle Gulla, Ville Ollikainen, Nafiseh Shabib, and Özlem Özgöbek
- Personalization Approaches in Learning Environments, organized by Milos Kravcik, Olga C. Santos, and Jesús G. Boticario
- Personalization in eGovernment Services, Data and Applications, organized by Nikos Loutas, Fedelucio Narducci, Adegboyega Ojo, Matteo Palmonari, Cécile Paris, and Giovanni Semeraro
- Emotions and Personality in Personalized Services, organized by Marko Tkalčič, Berardina De Carolis, Marco de Gemmis, Ante Odić, and Andrej Košir
- Workshop on UMAP Projects Synergy, organized by Dhaval Thakker, Oliver Brdiczka, and Christoph Trattner

UMAP2014 also included the following tutorials:

- User Affect and Sentiment Modelling by Björn W. Schuller
- Social Information Access by Peter Brusilovsky
- Personalization for Behavior Change by Julita Vassileva and Judith Masthoff

We would like to acknowledge the excellent work and great help from the UMAP2014 Organizing Committee listed herein. We would like to acknowledge Marwan Al-Tawil's help with compiling the proceedings of UMAP 2014 and thank him for his efforts. We also gratefully acknowledge our sponsors who helped us with funding and organizational expertise: User Modeling Inc., U.S.

National Science Foundation, Microsoft Research, Springer, the Chen Family Foundation, and Aalborg City. Finally, we want to acknowledge the use of Easy-Chair for the management of the review process.

May 2014

Vania Dimitrova
Tsvi Kuflik
Peter Dolog
Geert-Jan Houben

Organization

UMAP2014 was organized by Intelligent Web and Information Systems at the Computer Science Department of Aalborg University, Denmark, under the auspices of User Modeling Inc. The conference took place during July 7–11, 2014, in Aalborg, Denmark.

Organizing Committee

General Co-chairs

Peter Dolog — Aalborg University, Denmark
Geert-Jan Houben — Delft University of Technology, The Netherlands

Program Co-chairs

Vania Dimitrova — University of Leeds, UK
Tsvi Kuflik — The University of Haifa, Israel

Doctoral Consortium Co-chairs

Francesco Ricci — Free University of Bozen-Bolzano, Italy
David Chin — University of Hawaii, USA

Demo and Poster Co-chairs

Min Chi — North Carolina State University, USA
Iván Cantador — Universidad Autónoma de Madrid, Spain

Workshop Co-chairs

Rosta Farzan — University of Pittsburg, USA
Robert Jäschke — University of Hannover, Germany

Tutorial Co-chairs

Judith Masthoff — University of Aberdeen, UK
Robin Burke — DePaul University, USA

Industrial Showcases Co-chairs

John Carney — Carney Labs, USA
Ido Guy — IBM Haifa Research Lab, Israel

Project Liaison Co-chairs

Oliver Brdiczka	Palo Alto Research Center, USA
Dhaval Thakker	University of Leeds, UK
Christoph Trattner	Know-Center, Austria

Publicity Co-Chairs

Ben Steichen	University of British Columbia, Canada
Nava Tintarev	University of Aberdeen, UK

Local Organizing Chair

Hanne Kristiansen	VisitAalborg, Denmark

Student Volunteers Chair and Web Chair

Martin Leginus	Aalborg University, Denmark

Program Committee

Area Chairs

UMAP in the Social Era

Kalina Bontcheva	University of Sheffield, UK
Werner Geyer	IBM Cambridge Research Center, USA

UMAP in the Era of Big Data

Bamshad Mobasher	DePaul University, USA
Wolfgang Nejdl	L3S Research Center, Germany

UMAP in the Era of Pervasive Computing

Keith Cheverst	Lancaster University, UK

Infrastructures, Architectures, and Methodologies

Bob Kummerfeld	University of Sydney, Australia
Owen Conlan	Trinity College, Ireland

Human Factors and Models

Elisabeth Andre	University of Augsburg, Germany
Cristina Conati	University of British Columbia, Canada

Human Factors and Models

Kaska Porayska-Pomsta	London Knowledge Lab, UK
Alfred Kobsa	University of California - Irvine, USA

PC Members for Conference Papers

Fabian Abel	TU Delft, The Netherlands
Kenro Aihara	National Institute of Informatics, Japan
Harith Alani	The Open University, UK
Omar Alonso	Microsoft Research, USA
Liliana Ardissono	University of Turin, Italy
Lora Aroyo	VU University Amsterdam, The Netherlands
Mathias Bauer	mineway GmbH, Germany
Shlomo Berkovsky	NICTA, Australia
Sara Bernardini	King's College London, UK
Pradipta Biswas	University of Cambdrige, UK
Oliver Brdiczka	Palo Alto Research Center, USA
John Breslin	NUI Galway, Republic of Ireland
Derek Bridge	University College Cork, Republic of Ireland
Peter Brusilovsky	University of Pittsburgh, USA
Susan Bull	University of Birmingham, UK
Robin Burke	DePaul University, USA
Iván Cantador	Universidad Autónoma de Madrid, Spain
Sandra Carberry	University of Delaware, USA
John Carney	Carney Labs, USA
Rosa M. Carro	Universidad Autónoma de Madrid, Spain
Federica Cena	University of Turin, Italy
Jilin Chen	IBM Research, USA
Min Chi	North Carolina State University, USA
David Chin	University of Hawaii, USA
Mihaela Cocea	University of Portsmouth, UK
Albert Corbett	Carnegie Mellon University, USA
Alexandra Cristea	University of Warwick, UK
Elizabeth M. Daly	IBM Research, Republic of Ireland
Paul De Bra	Eindhoven University of Technology, The Netherlands
Michel Desmarais	Ecole Polytechnique de Montreal, Canada
Ernesto Diaz-Aviles	L3S Research Center, Germany
Sidney D'Mello	University of Notre Dame, USA
Benedict Du Boulay	University of Sussex, UK
Casey Dugan	IBM T.J. Watson Research Center, USA
Jill Freyne	CSIRO, Australia
Cristina Gena	University of Turin, Italy
Bradley Goodman	The MITRE Corporation, USA

Alan Said   Centrum Wiskunde and Informatica,
                                    The Netherlands
George Samaras   University of Cyprus, Cyprus
Olga C. Santos   UNED, Spain
Shilad Sen   Macalester College, USA
Bracha Shapira   Ben-Gurion University, Israel
Amit Sharma   Cornell University, USA
Barry Smyth   University College Dublin, Republic of Ireland
Marcus Specht   Open University of the Netherlands,
                                    The Netherlands
Myra Spiliopoulou   University of Magdeburg, Germany
Ben Steichen   University of British Columbia, Canada
Loren Terveen   University of Minnesota, USA
Dhaval Thakker   University of Leeds, UK
Nava Tintarev   University of Aberdeen, UK
Christoph Trattner   Know-Center, Austria
Julita Vassileva   University of Saskatchewan, Canada
Yang Wang   Syracuse University, USA
Jian Wang   LinkedIn Corporation, USA
Gerhard Weber   University of Education Freiburg, Germany
Stephan Weibelzahl   Private University of Applied Sciences,
                                    Germany
Kalina Yacef   The University of Sydney, Australia
Michael Yudelson   Carnegie Learning, Inc., USA
Markus Zanker   Alpen-Adria-Universität Klagenfurt, Austria
Jie Zhang   Nanyang Technological University, Singapore
Ingrid Zukerman   Monash University, Australia

PC Members for Doctoral Consortium

Liliana Ardissono   University of Turin, Italy
Maria Bielikova   Slovak University of Technology, Slovakia
Peter Brusilovsky   University of Pittsburgh, USA
Iván Cantador   Universidad Autónoma de Madrid, Spain
Berardina Nadja De Carolis   University of Bari, Italy
Federica Cena   University of Turin, Italy
Fabio Gasparetti   Third University of Rome, Italy
Marco de Gemmis   University of Bari, Italy
Cristina Gena   University of Turin, Italy
Li Chen   Hong Kong Baptist University, Hong Kong
Eelco Herder   L3S Research Center, Germany
Pasquale Lops   University of Bari, Italy
Kathleen Mccoy   University of Delaware, USA
Melike Sah   Trinity College, Ireland
Olga C. Santos   UNED, Spain

Nava Tintarev   University of Aberdeen, UK
Marko Tkalcic   Johannes Kepler University, Austria
Ingrid Zukerman   Monash University, Australia

Additional Reviewers

Panayiotis Andreou	Shuguang Han	Rita Orji
Nicola Barbieri	Roya Hosseini	Viktoria Pammer
Marios Belk	Johnson Iyilade	Christoforos Panayiotou
Geoffray Bonnin	Shankar Kalyanaraman	Amon Rapp
Mehdi Boukhris	Hitoshi Koshib	Miriam Redi
Smitashree Choudhury	Dominik Kowald	Adem Sabic
Marco De Gemmis	Lukas Lerche	Lena Schwemmlein
Carrie Demmans Epp	Collin Lynch	Michiel Spape
Dimoklis Despotakis	Wookhee Min	Eduardo Veas
Stephan Doerfel	Priscilla Moraes	Huichuan Xia
Manuel Eugster	Juergen Mueller	Diego Zapata
Caroline Faur	Cataldo Musto	Yuxiao Zhu
Ruth Garcia Gavilanes	Zeinab Noorian	
Joseph Grafsgaard	Claudia Orellana-Rodriguez	

Keynotes

The ABCS: A Framework for Thinking about People-Centered Systems Design

Elizabeth Churchill

eBay Research Labs (ERL) in San Jose, California, USA

Abstract. Interactive technologies pervade every aspect of modern life. Web sites, mobile devices, household gadgets, automotive controls, aircraft flight decks; everywhere you look, people are interacting with technologies. This trend is set to continue as we move towards a world comprising Smart Cities built around the Internet of Things.

Unfortunately, much of the rhetoric surrounding this dawning age of ubiquitous and embedded computing fails to appropriately consider the people at the centre of it. These people are embodied social agents with motivations, emotions, capabilities, capacities, proclivities and predilections. Technological imaginings around the Internet of Things are often steeped in generalities or idealised scenarios of use. Such imaginings typically forget that design is always about meeting particular peoples' needs in particular contexts. From concept to ideation to prototype and evaluation, the design of interactive technologies and systems that are intended for people should start with some understanding of who the users will be, what tasks and experiences they are aiming for, and what the circumstances, conditions or context(s) are at play.

In this talk, I will discuss a simple people-centric framework devised with my colleagues and coauthors to inform the way we think about design, the ABCS of designing interactive systems. A descriptive guide rather than a prescriptive checklist, the framework draws on basic research in ergonomics, psychology and user modeling. It is intended to focus design thinking about people as the users of interactive, computational systems. It is intended to support us as the designers of interactive technologies as we scope, draft and iterate on the design space of imagined interactive experiences. Using examples from my own work, I will illustrate how this framework has been explicitly and/or tacitly applied in the design, development and evaluation of interactive, multimedia systems. In particular, I will consider how this framework is currently being applied to rethinking the concept of personalization.

Short Biography

Dr. Elizabeth Churchill is a an applied social scientist working in the area of social media, interaction design and mobile/ubiquitous computing. She is currently Director of Human Computer Interaction at eBay Research Labs (ERL) in San Jose, California. She was formerly a Principal Research Scientist at Yahoo! Research, where she founded, staffed and managed the Internet Experiences Group.

Until September of 2006, she worked at the Palo Alto Research Center (PARC), California, in the Computing Science Lab (CSL). Prior to that she formed and led the Social Computing Group at FX Palo Laboratory, Fuji Xerox's research lab in Palo Alto.

Originally a psychologist by training, throughout her career Elizabeth has focused on understanding people's social and collaborative interactions in their everyday digital and physical contexts. She has studied, designed and collaborated in creating online collaboration tools (e.g. virtual worlds, collaboration/chat spaces), applications and services for mobile and personal devices, and media installations in public spaces for distributed collaboration and communication. Her current focus is on developing principles for Human Centered Commerce. With over 150 peer reviewed publications and 5 edited books, topics she has written about include implicit learning, human-agent systems, mixed initiative dialogue systems, social aspects of information seeking, digital archive and memory, and the development of emplaced media spaces. She has been a regular columnist for ACM interactions since 2008. Her co-authored book, Foundations for Designing User-Centered Systems will be published by Springer in early 2014.

In 2010, she was recognised as a Distinguished Scientist by the Association for Computing Machinery (ACM). Elizabeth is the current Executive Vice President of ACM SigCHI (Human Computer Interaction Special Interest Group). She is a Distinguished Visiting Scholar at Stanford University's Media X, the industry affiliate program to Stanford's H-STAR Institute, and is on the advisory board for the Mobile Life Center in Sweden.

Computing and Autism: How a Real Problem Drives Computing Research

Gregory D. Abowd

School of Interactive Computing at Georgia Tech, USA

Abstract. In 2002, I had a fortunate collision of my personal and professional lives when I realized that work in ubiquitous computing, specifically the automated capture of live experiences for later access, could actually have an impact on the world of autism. I am the father of two boys with autism, and for the past decade I have seen many different ways that computing technology can address challenges faced by a wide variety of stakeholder communities linked with autism, from the individuals and their families, to educators, therapists, clinicians and researchers. In this talk, I want to explain how a concrete applications domain, such as autism and related developmental disabilities, can present a wide variety of opportunities for computing research.

Short Biography

Gregory D. Abowd is a Regents' and Distinguished Professor in the School of Interactive Computing at Georgia Tech where he leads the Ubicomp Research Group.

His research interests concern how the advanced information technologies of ubiquitous computing (or ubicomp) impact our everyday lives when they are seamlessly integrated into our living spaces. Dr. Abowd's work has involved schools (Classroom 2000) and homes (The Aware Home), with a recent focus on health and particularly autism.

Dr. Abowd received the degree of B.S. in Honors Mathematics in 1986 from the University of Notre Dame. He then attended the University of Oxford in the United Kingdom, earning the degrees of M.Sc. (1987) and D.Phil. (1991) in Computation from the Programming Research Group in the Computing Laboratory. From 1989-1992 he was a Research Associate/Postdoc with the Human-Computer Interaction Group in the Department of Computer Science at the University of York in England. From 1992-1994, he was a Postdoctoral Research Associate with the Software Engineering Institute and the Computer Science Department at Carnegie Mellon University. He has been a professor at the Georgia Institute of Technology since 1994. He is an ACM Fellow, a member of the CHI Academy and recipient of the SIGCHI Social Impact Award and ACM Eugene Lawler Humanitarian Award. Much more news about his research group, both personal and professional, can be found here.

Mobile Sensing and Understanding User Behavior in Urban Contexts

Kaj Grønbæk

Department of Computer Science, University of Aarhus, Denmark

Abstract. In the EcoSense project we strive to understand human activity in urban contexts and how it impacts the local environment and the climate in general. We develop methods that combine mobile sensing, mobile experience sampling, and qualitative ethnographic methods to understand behavioral patterns, their impacts, and the potentials to change behavior where needed. The methods involve dissemination of smartphone apps to the general public or specific user groups to sense and probe their activities in order to make analysis as well as to support the everyday life of the users. Examples of environmental domains for mobile sensing and analysis are transportation behavior, green transportation campaigns (e.g. promotion of biking and electric vehicles), pollution mapping, as well as sensing presence and energy related activities in large buildings. But the methods may also generalize beyond climate related behavior to e.g. safety mapping of city areas, and understanding participant behavior during large urban cultural events. The talk will give an overview of the methods being developed and examples of their usage. Finally I will discuss important challenges ranging from collection of data from a large number of heterogeneous devices, maintaining data collection, making sense of big data from mobile sensing, motivating users, preserving privacy, etc.

Short Biography

Prof. Kaj Grønbæk is heading the Ubiquitous Computing and Interaction research group at the Department of Computer Science, University of Aarhus, Denmark.

He is manager of the interdisciplinary Center for Interactive Spaces (2003 - present) that has developed a number of physically large-scale interactive systems, e.g. interactive floors for learning, interactive sports training equipment, and urban installations stimulating movement and social interaction. The research has lead to products being marketed by two companies the Alexandra Institute A/S and Redia A/S. He is a part time Research and Innovation Manager for Interaction at the Alexandra Institute.

He is currently research manager of two larger government funded projects: 1) The EcoSense project (Danish Council for Strategic Research) developing participatory mobile sensing and visualization methods and tools for personal environmental awareness and environmental decision making in companies and societies. 2) The PosLogistics project (Danish National Advanced Technology Foundation) developing logistics and service task management for hospitals based on indoor positioning and other context information.

His research areas span: Ubiquitous Computing, Interaction Design, Interactive Spaces, Hypermedia/Web, Augmented Reality, Context- aware Computing, Computer Supported Cooperative Work (CSCW), Participatory Design (system development with active user involvement).

Table of Contents

Long Presentations

Short Presentations

Doctoral Consortium

Modelling Long Term Goals

Debjanee Barua[1], Judy Kay[1], Bob Kummerfeld[1], and Cécile Paris[2]

[1] School of IT, University of Sydney, Australia, 2006
{debjanee.barua,judy.kay,bob.kummerfeld}@sydney.edu.au
[2] CSIRO Computational Informatics,
Cnr Vimiera and Pembroke Roads, Marsfield NSW 2122
cecile.paris@csiro.au

Abstract. Goals have long been recognised as important in user modelling and personalisation. Surprisingly, little research has dealt with user model representations for people's long term goals. This paper describes our theoretically-grounded design of user models for long term goals; notably, the theory points to the critical role of the user interface to this Goal Model, to enable people to set, monitor and refine their models over the long term. We report on a multi-study evaluation of the tightly coupled user model representation and Goal Interface, based on a preliminary lab study (16 participants), and a field trial (14 participants), starting with the lab study and then the in-the-wild use and the questionnaires. This provides multiple sources of evidence to validate the usefulness of our Goal Model to represent three long term health-related goals. It shows that the Goal Interface is usable and aids people in setting their long term goals.

Keywords: User Modelling, Long term User Models, Goal Setting, Intrinsic and Extrinsic Factors, Motivation, User Interface, Usability.

1 Introduction

User modelling and personalisation research aims to model people's *goals*, along with other such core aspects as knowledge, interests, traits and context [4]. Much of that work has dealt with inferring goals, to help interpret the user's actions [5,16,22], especially short term goals in a single session [14]. Surprisingly, there has been little work exploring how to define the user model *representation* of long term goals.

The need for user models that represent people's long term goals follows from both critical human needs and emerging technologies. There are huge potential benefits that personalised systems might offer if they can model long term goals for key aspects of people's lives, including health and wellbeing [6,8,10,13], sustainability [11] and learning [2]. Increasingly, it is becoming possible to create such models from rich and diverse forms of data captured by emerging technology; for example, sensors can unobtrusively capture data about a person's weight, activity, sustainable behaviours, the ways they use their computers and much more.

V. Dimitrova et al. (Eds.): UMAP 2014, LNCS 8538, pp. 1–12, 2014.

User models for long term goals need a *representation* that can be effective in providing a way to aggregate diverse streams of data from sensors, applications and the user. That representation should organise the data in ways that enable it to serve useful roles for personalisation and self reflection. This means that the representation must support relevant *user interfaces* for key tasks people need to do in relation to their long term goals. In particular, they need to set realistic goals, appropriate to their ability and preferences [15]. Interfaces should support the user in gaining an understanding of what is required to achieve each long term goal, and how to develop a plan and follow a strategy towards achieving the goal. The long term goal model can also support the key challenge of maintaining motivation [15]. In addition, there is the need for effective tools and interfaces that help people to monitor and self reflect on their progress towards long term goals. We can usefully draw on large established bodies of psychological theory (e.g., goal setting [19], social cognitive theory [3], and self determination theory [9]) to inform the design of the user model representation, and tools that use it to support people in setting, monitoring and achieving goals.

This paper contributes to the understanding of how to design a user model representation for lifelong goals. The next section reviews related work. We then explain how we drew on theory to design a Goal Model representation. We give an overview of the user view of our goal modelling system and its multi-study evaluation, followed by our conclusions.

2   Related Work

There are many health and wellbeing applications that aim to help people achieve healthier lifestyles. For example, some support goal setting[1], and sensor technologies[2] provide interfaces for goal setting and self reflection. Many of the commercial systems (e.g., Lifetick, HealthMonth) support SMART goals[3]. Lifetick, for example, even asks users to explain whether their goals are SMART. Some (e.g., HealthMonth, StickK) apply motivating strategies (e.g., games, challenges) for achieving goals. However, none has explored how to support users in setting and tracking long term goals along with intrinsic and extrinsic factors.

One important body of work comes from persuasive systems for wellness, with goal setting interfaces and validation in long term field trials. For example, some aim to motivate people to increase their physical activity [6,8,18,21], and others help people achieve a healthy diet [12,20]. These systems address various aspects of goal setting and motivation. For example, many give tailored feedback, and rewards/punishment reinforcement, as in Fishn'Steps [18], UbiFit [8], GoalPost [21] and the Family health living portal [6]. The effect of social support has been studied, both for competition [8,18,21] or collaboration [6]. Such work has

---

[1] Lifetick: www.lifetick.com, GoalsOnTrack: www.goalsontrack.com, Health Month: www.healthmonth.com, StickK: www.stickK.com

[2] Fitbit: www.fitbit.com, Nike+: www.nikeplus.com, Withings: www.withings.com

[3] Goal setting theory [19] suggests that effective goals should be "SMART": Specific, Measurable, Attainable, Relevant and have a Time-frame.

reported evaluations of usability and effectiveness in changing behaviour. However, we have found no work on the rigorous design and evaluation of a representation and interfaces for the very important extrinsic and intrinsic motivating factors.

User modelling research has a long history of work on goals and plans [4]. This used sophisticated machine learning for *plan recognition* [1,5,17], inferring the user's goals and plans, by reasoning from the user's actions or statements. For example, Lumiere [14] had a Bayesian network to infer the user's tasks as they used the system. The early user modelling shell, BGP-MS [16] aimed to provide a generic framework for reasoning about the user's **B**eliefs, **G**oals and **P**lans, based on observed actions and inferences. There has been considerable work in learning systems to represent learners' knowledge, and some of this has created interfaces to support metacognitive skills such as goal setting, planning, and self monitoring [2,7]. None of this work reported interfaces that would enable a user to see, manage and reflect on their goals as represented in the goal model.

While there has been much work reported on systems that draw on psychological theories for self regulation and behaviour change, none considered what information about goals is worth capturing in the long term, and how such information can be represented in a user model. In the next section, we draw on such psychological theory to do this.

3   Design of Goals in User Modelling Systems

This section describes the design of our Goal Model based on key psychological theories, for goal setting [19], social cognition [3], and self determination [9]. We used these theories to identify the important factors that help people achieve goals since these need to be represented in our Goal Model. Table 1 summarises the elements, with a short identifier in the first column, followed by a brief descriptive name and two illustrative examples. We describe each of them, and the reasons they are part of the Goal Model.

The first set of *SMART elements* (D1-D5 in Table 1) come from goal setting theory [19] as embodied in SMART goals. These have been shown to be effective in helping people set effective goals. While the elements of the Goal Model are domain independent, it is generally necessary to use domain-specific knowledge to define good *default values*, like the examples in the table.

The first element, D1 in Table 1, represents the **S**pecific target (the **S** of SMART goals). For the case where a person's goal is to have healthy levels of moderate intensity activity, a recommended target value from physical activity guidelines is 150 minutes a week, with 30 minutes most days, taken in bouts of at least 10 minutes [13]. The next two elements (D2, 3) cover the measurement of progress towards the goal target (**M** in SMART). The Goal Model represents the available set of **M**easuring tools (D2), where examples include various sensors, applications and logging tools that enable the user to provide data. That data is then used to create inference about the user's goal progress at each point in time, in the Goal Model element for **M**easured progress (D3). The table shows an example for a moderate activity goal, where the data from a device like a FitBit is stored in the D3 element. Inferences that are based on this, can determine how many minutes the user was moderately active. The second example makes a different inference from the same data; this time to determine the lengths of time the user was inactive.

The next element is **R**elevent subgoals (**R** in SMART), D4 in Table 1. This is needed to assess if subgoals are relevant to the user's parent goals. For example, to reduce weight, relevant subgoals include eating healthily and having enough physical activity. The **T**ime-bound aspect is (**T**ime in D5 of Table 1). a tuple, with a start date and duration for the goal. By default, a goal starts on the day it is set. The duration may be domain specific; but in many cases a default is 4 weeks, which has been proved effective for achieving changes in behaviour [19].

Table 1. User model representation for goals

ID	Goal represen-tation elements	Example values for the high level goal: being healthy and active
	SMART elements	
D1	Specific target	do 150 minutes moderate activity every week; avoid 30 minutes long inactive period
D2	Measuring tools	sensors (e.g., Fitbit, phone app); manual logging tool
D3	Measured progress	activity intensity level each minute; times user is inactive
D4	Relevant sub-goals	increasing moderate activity and avoiding inactivity are relevant subgoals for being healthy and active.
D5	Time	start from today, for 4 weeks
	Extrinsic elements	
E1	Reminder	email/tweet/SMS, every day at noon, triggered alerts
E2	Feedback	weekly report, most recent progress, overall progress
E3	Rewards or Punishment	scores, badges, messages
E4	Social involvement	competitive, cooperative, people involved, what to share, comparative performance
	Intrinsic elements (elicited)	
I1	Importance	Likert scale e.g., 1 (not at all) to 7 (very)
I2	Difficulty	
I3	Commitment	
I4	Self efficacy	
I5	Self satisfaction	
	Additional elements (elicited)	
A1	Notes	salient details about goals, e.g., "I was sick all day" in case one fails to achieve target

The next four elements are the extrinsic motivating factors [9] for goals: *reminder* (E1), which models the ways the user wishes to be notified about her/his progress; *feedback* (E2), for the user's preferences about the means and form of reports on her/his current and overall progress; *rewards/punishment* (E3), for the user's preferences for feedback on achievements and failures; and finally *social involvement* (E4), for the user's preferences associated with social support, in terms of the people involved, the information to share with her/his, and the information others have made available to this user. Social support is a key factor addressed in cognitive theories [3]. This can be either competitive or cooperative. This also represents whether the user wants a comparative performance evaluation (e.g., view a leaderboard).

Elements I1-I5 in Table 1 model the user's attitudes towards the goal she/he wants to set. These have proved useful in enhancing intrinsic motivation and so achieving goals [19]. These elements require explicit user inputs. The first two elements track the *importance* (I1 in Table 1) and *difficulty* (I2) of the goal from the user's perspective. These two elements affect a person's commitment [19]. Perceived *Commitment* (I3) is another internal factor that influences motivation. Theories suggest that higher commitment may lead to higher performance towards the goal [19]. *Self efficacy* (I4) is the person's confidence in achieving her/his goals. The stronger the self efficacy, the higher people set their target goals, and the firmer the commitment to them [3]. Finally, as people monitor their progress, the element for *self satisfaction* (I5) enables them to record an assessment of their progress and achievement and, this, in turn, can intensify efforts towards future goals [9]. These intrinsic elements might be measured using Likert scale rating, e.g., our implementation has a 5-point scale; Bandura had 9 points [3] for commitment and self satisfaction, and a 10-interval scale ranging from 0 to 100 for measuring self efficacy.

The goal representation has an element for the user's *notes* (A1 in Table 1). This enables the user to record arbitrary information about goals, such as the reason for failing to achieve a goal.

The elements of our goal representation are inter-related. For example, goal setting theory [19] suggests that goal importance, external rewards and incentives, peer influence, and self efficacy are determinants of goal commitment. Some of these factors need the users to explicitly specify what they perceive about them, while others can be set as defaults based on standard guidelines, or inferred based on the users' actions during goal setting and self monitoring. Some elements of the Goal Model need to be elicited from the user, notably I1-5 cannot be inferred any other way. When users set these, taking time to think about them, that process can help them set their own targets, revising the defaults. This points to the need for a user interface to these aspects of the model.

4   User Interface for Goal Setting and Self Reflection

Having defined the Goal Model, we needed to design accompanying interfaces to enable users to set and revise goals. We present a walkthrough of the Goal Interface in terms of a scenario:

Alex is an overweight young woman with a sedentary lifestyle. Her physician tells that she needs to become more active. She has a FitBit pedometer and wants to use this to help her achieve this goal. She uses the "Goal Interface" to set

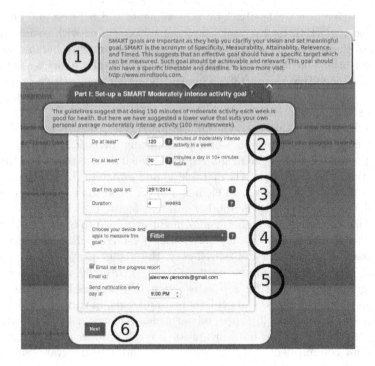

Fig. 1. Set Moderate Activity Goal: Step 1

SMART goals, linking her FitBit data to a goal, and so maintains a long term model of her progress towards her goal to be more active.

When a user like Alex goes to our Goal system, she first links in her FitBit, causing the system to offer her the list of associated goals. She selects one for *moderate intensity activity.* At that point the system creates a default Goal Model and sets her FitBit data in the Measuring tools element of the Goal Model (D2 in Table 1). This, in turn, triggers the access to her FitBit data which goes into the Measured progress element (D3 in Table 1) for this goal.

The system then interprets the raw FitBit data (an integer score for each minute) in terms of the recommended moderate activity levels. Figure 1 shows where Alex selected a goal to achieve healthy levels of activity. She may be unsure about SMART goals; hovering over the question mark gives the "Help pop-up" with the explanation marked with **1** in the figure. Then Alex can set her weekly and daily targets (2 in Figure 1). This goes into the *Specific target* element in the goal representation (D1, Table 1). The interface suggests that she should aim for 120 minutes of moderate activity a week. Here again, she hovers over the corresponding question mark to see the explanation shown. This has been personalised, based on her previous performance (from her FitBit data). So the explanation states the common recommendation of 150 minutes [13] but encourages her to set a more modest and realistic goal, based on the model of her performance to-date. As she has only achieved 100 minutes per week recently,

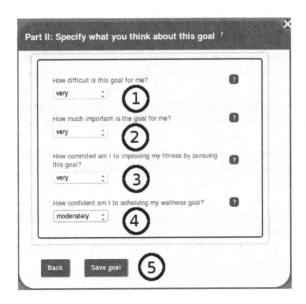

Fig. 2. Set Moderate Activity Goal: Step 2

it recommends 20% above that, suggesting 120 minutes as the target [23]. She can next set her daily target, here with the default of 30 minutes. Next, at 3 in Figure 1, she sees the default values for the *Time* element (D5, Table 1). Then, at 4 in Figure 1, she can see that FitBit has already been linked to the goal, as described above. This part of the interface enables her to add other sensors. She can see, and optionally revise, her *Reminder* (E1, Table 1) preferences (e.g., email, Twitter or none) (5 in Figure 1) in terms of the means and timing. Each input field has a "?" icon to provide explanations.

Figure 2 is the second phase for setting her goal. This interface is tightly coupled with several intrinsic elements (I1-I4, Table 1) in the goal representation. It appears when Alex clicks the "Next" button in the interface (6 in Figure 1). In particular, this interface seeks key perceptions related to her goal: its importance (1 in Figure 2), its difficulty (2), her commitment (3) and, self efficacy as her confidence in achieving it (4). Each question offers a drop-down list with the options *not answered*, *not at all*, *a little*, *moderately*, and *very*. For simplicity, and to avoid confusion, we used the same scale for all intrinsic elements. In our example, Alex indicates the goal is very difficult but very important, that she is very committed to it, and moderately confident in achieving it. Clicking "Save goal" (5 in Figure 2) updates this part of the Goal Model.

5   User Study

We designed a series of studies to evaluate 4 hypotheses:

- H1: Users can set SMART goal elements with our Goal Interface
- H2: Users can set extrinsic and intrinsic elements with our Goal Interface

- H3: Users find the Goal Interface easy to use to set goals
- H4: Users find the Goal Interface helps them *think* about their wellness goals.

H1 and H2 concern *performance* aspects of the usability of the interface, i.e., whether people can understand the interface readily and complete all the core tasks needed to establish the Goal Model. We separate direct elements from the extrinsic and intrinsic elements summarised in Table 1 because we anticipated more difficulties with the latter. H3 and H4 deal with user perceptions of the usability (H3) and usefulness (H4) of the Goal Interface.

Table 2 summarises the series of studies and their mapping onto the hypotheses. Broadly, we began with a formative laboratory evaluation of the Goal Interface. We used this to refine the interface. Then we began a field trial with participants coming again to the lab to do a think-aloud that was a key evaluation of H1-3. In Week 4, we asked participants to review their goals and collected data about this in-the-wild use as the final data about H1, 2. Finally, in Week 8, we asked participants to complete a questionnaire about their perception of the usability and usefulness of the Goal Interface (H3, 4).

Table 2. Studies designed (shown in rows) to test the hypotheses (columns)

Study – Hypothesis	H1	H2	H3	H4
Preliminary Lab Think-aloud	X	X		
– Associated questionnaire			X	
Start of Field trial, Think-aloud	X	X		
– Associated questionnaire			X	
Week 4 Field Goal review	X	X		
Week 8 Field Questionnaire			X	X

Preliminary Lab Think-Aloud Study and Questionnaire. We framed this as a formative usability evaluation of the Goal Interface. We asked users to take on the identity of a hypothetical user "Alex". Participants were initially given 5-10 minutes to explore the interface. We then asked them to do four sets of tasks, corresponding to Alex at the times:

- first use, setting several goals;
- after 1 week, to review progress and revise goals as needed;
- after 4 weeks, at the default goal deadline, to review and revise goals; and
- after 1 year (similar to above but for the long term).

We asked users to "think-aloud' as they completed each task so we could gain insights into any difficulties. The experimenter took notes and audio recordings. This design, around a hypothetical user and set goals, ensured a thorough evaluation. Each main interface tasks was done at least twice; if we needed to assist the user the first time, we could see if they could do this alone the next time. The design ensured that all participants did the same rich set of tasks, spanning a full (hypothetical) year. It also saved participants from needing to ponder about their personal aspirations. It concluded with an open-ended questionnaire about aspects liked/disliked. The study took 40-50 minutes. Based on this study we refined the interface.

Start of Field Trial, Think-Aloud Study and Questionnaire. This study was the beginning of the field trial. Participants collected a FitBit and spent 5-10 minutes exploring the interface. They were then asked to set their own goals for: steps walked each day; moderate activity per week; and levels of inactivity. For each of these, the defaults matched published recommendations, but participants were welcome to alter these. Notably, in light of the preliminary study results, we did not ask participants to define the intrinsic elements of each goal (illustrated in Figure 2) as we discuss below.

Week 4 Field Goal Review. At Week 4 of the field trial, we emailed participants to review their goal progress. At this time, the Goal Interface included the intrinsic elements. This part of the study aimed to gain in-the-wild evidence of usability and use of the Goal Interface (H1, 2).

Week 8 Field Questionnaire. At Week 8, participants completed a questionnaire on the usability of the Goal Interface (H3) and whether they found the interface helped them think about their goals (H4).

5.1   Results and Discussion

This section first reports on the preliminary usability study, explains how it informed interface refinements and then reports on the main field trial.

Participants Demographics. Sixteen participants did the preliminary study: 5 female, 11 male; age distribution 18-30 (5), 31-45 (10), > 46 (1) and education level undergraduate (7) and graduate (9). Participants were highly technical, 4 rating themselves just at the *competent* level, with the rest *expert*. Fourteen of these participants continued to the remaining studies in the field trial.

Preliminary Lab Think-Aloud Study and Questionnaire. All participants succeeded in all goal setting tasks on first attempt. P11 stated he really liked the simple way to add standard goals. P13 gave the "Help pop-ups" as the best feature of the interface. P2, P3, P4 and P10 wanted to be able set their own goals, rather than our set ones. Importantly, half of the 16 participants stated that it seemed hard to appreciate the usefulness of the intrinsic factors on first use of the system. Accordingly, we redesigned the interface, so that the Figure 2 interface does not appear the first time the user sets a goal. With this initial interface, all participants completed all the tasks successfully (H1,2) and generally considered it usable (H3).

Field trial and Questionnaires. We refined the design and invited the participants to take part in the think-aloud study at the beginning of the field trial. All participants were able to set their own goals as they wished, supporting H1, 2. Some chose to alter the default target values, as shown in Table 3. In the lab, P1, P5 and P7 lowered their target step count target (from the default of 10,000 steps). In week 4, P5 and P13 set this even lower, while P7, P9 and P11 raised their target. For the moderate activity goal, all participants kept the default in Week 1, but in Week 4, P2 and P8 increased it, while P13 lowered the target. For the inactivity goal, eight weakened the 25 minute target goal, P1 and P11

Table 3. Changes participants made in Lab (Week 1) and Field (Week 4) H1,2 (N=14), − was a decrease, + was an increase in the target

		Participant ID													
Goal	Week	1	2	3	4	5	6	7	8	9	10	11	12	13	14
Steps	1	−				−	−								
	4				−	+		+		+	−				
Moderate activity	4		+					+					−		
Inactivity	1	+				+		+	+	+	+				+
	4	−	+	+	+	+	+		+	+		−	+	+	+

increasing the maximum inactive period to 60 minutes, P5, P7-10 and P13 to 30 minutes. In week 4, we observed an interesting trend for this goal; except for P7 and P10, all participants changed their target and, P1 and P11 now set a harder target for them by lowering the amount of time they would be inactive to 30 minutes, while all others increased it.

No participant changed the default duration of 4 weeks. Two opted-out for the daily notifications. Five changed the time they wanted to receive the email reminders. In the final questionnaire, all participants agreed (4) or strongly agreed (5) that the interface was easy to use to set goals, supporting H3.

In week 4, participants set the intrinsic elements: importance, difficulty, commitment, and self efficacy. We found a strong positive correlation between participants' values for goal importance and commitment for all three goals (Spearman correlation coefficient: $r=0.69, p=0.003$ for step goal; $r=0.78, p=0.001$ for moderate activity goal; $r=0.93, p=0.0$ for avoid inactivity goal). This suggested that participants who saw a goal as very important also indicated high levels of commitment to it. We also found a positive correlation between self efficacy and commitment for the step goal (Spearman correlation: $r=0.68, p=0.008$) and moderate activity goal ($r=0.68, p=0.007$) but not the inactivity goal.

We found a negative correlation between goal difficulty and self efficacy for the step goal ($r=-0.11$), indicating that the more difficult this goal, the less confident the participants were of achieving it. For other goals, the very week positive correlation was not statistically significant (e.g., $r=0.24$, $p=0.46$ for moderate activity). However, there were some outliers, who were highly or moderately confident even though they rated the goal as difficult. But they indicated strong commitment which is strongly correlated to high self efficacy. Our findings are in line with goal setting theory [19], and this points to the validity and usefulness of these intrinsic factors (H2).

The results from the post-experiment survey strongly supported H1-H3. Participants considered they were able to easily set SMART goals (mean:4.22), supporting H1, and rated the interface easy to set goals (mean:4.22), supporting H3. Participants agreed the interface helped them think more about their goals (Strongly agree: 2, Agree: 9, Somewhat agree: 3, mean: 3.92), supporting H4. P12 stated: "...*definitely the options helped me think through my goals and plans in future. They put a challenge in front of me to monitor my behaviour. If I say I am committed and confident to achieve goals, but do otherwise... that means*

I am cheating myself." Overall, the results indicated that our participants saw value in SMART goals and in the intrinsic elements and successfully provided ground evidence for them.

6   Conclusion

In this paper, we presented the first user model for personal long term goals, in terms of a carefully designed representation that is based upon key psychological theories, goal setting [19], social cognitive theory [3], and self determination theory [9]. We designed tightly linked interfaces that are essential to populating and maintaining the goal models. These interfaces help users to set SMART goals and to think about several aspects: goal importance, difficulty, self efficacy, and commitment. To evaluate the usability and use of the goal setting interfaces, we conducted an 8 week-long field study with 14 participants. Our results indicate that participants were able to use the interfaces effectively (H1, 2), that they found the goal setting interface easy to use (H3), and that it helped them set SMART goals and see the importance of intrinsic factors (H4).

Our study has some limitations. First, our work involved just three goals, albeit important ones, that are in line with public health recommendations. We chose these as they are relevant to many people and readily understood. While our generic core of the goal representation is relevant to other long term goals, we have only demonstrated it for these three. Another limitation of this study was that our participants were highly educated and technically expert. However, we note that even our less technical users were well able to use the interfaces. We designed the studies with the user models not visible to us, except in consultation with users if they wished to do that. This gave privacy to the users and did not hamper testings our 4 hypotheses.

In the future, we aim to develop and evaluate interfaces for recent and long term self reflection that will take the intrinsic aspects into consideration to personalise feedback and motivation. Such interfaces will integrate metacognitive scaffolds to assist the challenging tasks of thinking about goal setting and revision and self reflection and monitoring over the long term data about health and wellness.

Acknowledgements. This work was supported by funds from CSIRO and the Australian Research Council Grant DP0877665.

References

1. Ali, R., Dalpiaz, F., Giorgini, P.: A goal-based framework for contextual requirements modeling and analysis. Requirements Engineering 15(4), 439–458 (2010)
2. Azevedo, R.: Using hypermedia as a metacognitive tool for enhancing student learning? The role of self-regulated learning. Educational Psychologist 40(4), 199–209 (2005)
3. Bandura, A.: Social cognitive theory of self-regulation. Organizational Behavior and Human Decision Processes 50(2), 248–287 (1991)

4. Brusilovsky, P., Millán, E.: User models for adaptive hypermedia and adaptive educational systems. In: Brusilovsky, P., Kobsa, A., Nejdl, W. (eds.) Adaptive Web 2007. LNCS, vol. 4321, pp. 3–53. Springer, Heidelberg (2007)
5. Carberry, S.: Techniques for plan recognition. UMUAI 11, 31–48 (2001)
6. Colineau, N., Paris, C.: Motivating reflection about health within the family: the use of goal setting and tailored feedback. UMUAI, 1–36 (2011)
7. Conati, C., Vanlehn, K.: Toward computer-based support of meta-cognitive skills: A computational framework to coach self-explanation. IJAIED 11, 389–415 (2000)
8. Consolvo, S., Klasnja, P., McDonald, D.W., Landay, J.A.: Goal-setting considerations for persuasive technologies that encourage physical activity. In: Persuasive, pp. 1–8. ACM (2009)
9. Deci, E., Ryan, R.M.: Self-determination theory. In: Handbook of Theories of Social Psychology, p. 416 (2008)
10. Dunstan, D., Kingwell, B., Larsen, R., Healy, G., Cerin, E., Hamilton, M., Shaw, J., Bertovic, D., Zimmet, P., Salmon, J., et al.: Breaking up prolonged sitting reduces postprandial glucose and insulin responses. Diabetes Care 35(5), 976–983 (2012)
11. Froehlich, J., Dillahunt, T., Klasnja, P., Mankoff, J., Consolvo, S., Harrison, B., Landay, J.A.: Ubigreen: investigating a mobile tool for tracking and supporting green transportation habits. In: CHI 2009, pp. 1043–1052. ACM (2009)
12. Gasser, R., Brodbeck, D., Degen, M., Luthiger, J., Wyss, R., Reichlin, S.: Persuasiveness of a mobile lifestyle coaching application using social facilitation. In: IJsselsteijn, W.A., de Kort, Y.A.W., Midden, C., Eggen, B., van den Hoven, E. (eds.) PERSUASIVE 2006. LNCS, vol. 3962, pp. 27–38. Springer, Heidelberg (2006)
13. Haskell, W., Lee, I., Pate, R., Powell, K., Blair, S., Franklin, B., Macera, C., Heath, G., Thompson, P., Bauman, A.: Physical activity and public health: updated recommendation for adults from the American College of Sports Medicine and the American Heart Association. Medicine and Science in Sports and Exercise 39(8), 1423–1434 (2007)
14. Horvitz, E., Breese, J., Heckerman, D., Hovel, D., Rommelse, D.: The Lumiere project: Bayesian user modeling for inferring the goals and needs of software users. In: Uncertainty in Artificial Intelligence, pp. 256–265 (1998)
15. Klasnja, P., Consolvo, S., Pratt, W.: How to evaluate technologies for health behavior change in HCI research. In: CHI 2011, pp. 3063–3072. ACM (2011)
16. Kobsa, A., Pohl, W.: The user modeling shell system BGP-MS. UMUAI 4, 59–106 (1994)
17. Lesh, N., Rich, C., Sidner, C.L.: Using plan recognition in human-computer collaboration. In: User Modelling, pp. 23–32. Springer (1999)
18. Lin, J.J., Mamykina, L., Lindtner, S., Delajoux, G., Strub, H.B.: Fish'n'steps: Encouraging physical activity with an interactive computer game. In: Dourish, P., Friday, A. (eds.) UbiComp 2006. LNCS, vol. 4206, pp. 261–278. Springer, Heidelberg (2006)
19. Locke, E.A., Latham, G.P.: Building a practically useful theory of goal setting and task motivation: A 35-year odyssey. American Psych. 57(9), 705–717 (2002)
20. Maitland, J., Chalmers, M.: Self-monitoring, self-awareness, and self-determination in cardiac rehabilitation. In: CHI 2010, pp. 1213–1222. ACM (2010)
21. Munson, S.A., Consolvo, S.: Exploring goal-setting, rewards, self-monitoring, and sharing to motivate physical activity. In: Pervasive Health, pp. 25–32 (2012)
22. Vassileva, J.: A task-centered approach for user modeling in a hypermedia office documentation system. UMUAI 6, 185–223 (1996)
23. Vogin, G.D.: http://www.webmd.com/fitness-exercise/features/lazy-persons-exercise-plan (last visited: April, 2014)

A Personalization Method Based on Human Factors for Improving Usability of User Authentication Tasks

Marios Belk[1], Panagiotis Germanakos[1,2], Christos Fidas[3], and George Samaras[1]

[1] Department of Computer Science, University of Cyprus, CY-1678 Nicosia, Cyprus
{belk,cssamara}@cs.ucy.ac.cy
[2] SAP AG, Dietmar-Hopp-Allee 16, 69190 Walldorf, Germany
panagiotis.germanakos@sap.com
[3] Interactive Technologies Lab, HCI Group, Electrical and Computer Engineering Department
University of Patras, GR-26504, Patras, Greece
fidas@upatras.gr

Abstract. Aiming to ensure safety of operation to application providers and improve the usability of human computer interactions during authentication, this paper proposes a two-step personalization approach of user authentication tasks based on individual differences in cognitive processing as follows: i) recommend a textual or graphical user authentication mechanism based on the users' cognitive styles of processing textual and graphical information, and ii) recommend a standard or enhanced authentication key strength policy considering the users' cognitive processing abilities. The proposed approach has been applied in a four month ecological valid user study in which 137 participants interacted with a personalized user authentication mechanism and policy based on their cognitive characteristics. Initial results indicate that personalizing the user authentication task based on human cognitive factors could provide a viable solution for balancing the security and usability of authentication mechanisms at the benefit of both application providers and end-users.

Keywords: Individual Differences, Cognitive Styles, Cognitive Processing Abilities, User Authentication, Efficiency, Effectiveness, User Study.

1 Introduction

User authentication tasks are performed daily by millions of users to access critical information and services on the World Wide Web. A high number of research works have been proposed aiming to improve the usability and memorability of user authentication mechanisms, and at the same time decrease guessing attacks by malicious software and users [1, 2]. Researchers promote various designs of authentication mechanisms based on text and pictures, biometrics and gestures, password managers and policies [2, 3].

Nevertheless, recent studies have shown that the same security and usability issues of user authentication mechanisms still exist [1, 4]. For example, an increasing number of minimum alphanumeric characters (with a combination of upper-case and

V. Dimitrova et al. (Eds.): UMAP 2014, LNCS 8538, pp. 13–24, 2014.

lower-case letters and special characters) are required by password policies to be entered by users, which hinder the memorability and usability of passwords. On the other hand, users proceed with work-around methodologies to support the memorability of their password key, such as writing down their password, using the same password key for multiple accounts, and thus decreasing the system's security.

Despite the fact that a very high number of user authentication mechanisms have been proposed over the last decade, the majority of today's systems still utilize text-based passwords as their sole means of authentication [4]. The same textual password mechanism and the same password key strength policy is provided to all users, without considering that users do not share common characteristics, cognitive abilities and preferences. In this realm, motivated by theories on individual differences, suggesting that individuals have different cognitive processing abilities and habitual approaches in processing verbal and graphical information, this paper proposes a two-step personalization approach of user authentication tasks based on individual differences in cognitive processing as follows: i) recommend a textual or graphical user authentication mechanism based on the users' cognitive styles of processing textual and graphical information, and ii) provide a personalized authentication key strength policy; standard or enhanced complexity, considering the users' cognitive processing abilities. The proposed approach has been applied in a user study of 137 participants interacting with a personalized user authentication mechanism and policy based on their cognitive processing characteristics.

2   Theoretical Background

2.1   User Authentication

A typical user authentication scenario requires from a legitimate user to provide specific information, used to prove identity or gain access to a resource. User authentication mechanisms consist of three main categories depending on the factors used for authentication: *knowledge-based* require from users to memorize specific information (e.g., password, passphrase, PIN code, sequence of images, etc.) to gain access to a resource, *token-based* require from users to provide a physical object (e.g., credit card) for authentication, and *biometric-based* require from users to reveal their identity based on biometrics (e.g., fingerprint, eye-gaze).

Knowledge-based user authentication mechanisms are currently the most popular mechanisms for authentication, primarily because they are very fast and less expensive to implement compared to token-based and biometric-based mechanisms that require additional hardware and development costs [2]. Researchers have proposed various approaches to improve usability and memorability, such as improving existing recall-based password approaches with recognition of text [5] and enforcing the creation of secure authentication keys through policies [6, 1]. Researchers also promote alternative designs of authentication mechanisms based on images that require users to recall and select pictures as their authentication key [2, 3].

2.2   Individual Differences in Cognitive Processing

Theories of individual differences in cognitive processing aim to describe and explain how individuals differ in cognitive processing abilities and styles. A number of researchers have focused on high-level cognitive processes such as *cognitive styles*, which explain empirically observed differences in mental representation and processing of information [9]. A particularly important cognitive style is the Verbal/Imager dimension that refers to how individuals process information and indicates their preference for representing information verbally, or in mental pictures [9]. *Verbals* prefer and perform more efficiently when hypermedia content is presented in the form of text and are better at recalling acoustically complex text. *Imagers* prefer and perform efficiently when the hypermedia content is provided in a graphical representation.

Various researchers also attempted to explain the functioning of the human mind in terms of more elementary cognitive processes. These include the *speed of processing*, which refers to the maximum speed a given mental act may be efficiently executed [7]; *controlled attention*, which refers to cognitive processes to identify and concentrate on goal-relevant information and inhibit attention to irrelevant stimuli [7]; and *working memory capacity*, which is defined as the maximum amount of information the mind can efficiently activate during information processing [8].

3   Motivation and Research Question

Based on the theoretical background, we suggest that the user authentication type (textual or graphical) might affect differently, in terms of performance, individuals that have a particular style of representing and processing information (verbally or visually). In the same line, the added cognitive effort that arises from password policies (e.g., that require users to memorize combinations of upper-case, lower-case, and special characters) might differently affect users with limited or enhanced cognitive processing abilities which are based on the elementary processes of the human mind.

Nowadays, textual passwords are provided to all users neglecting the fact that users might have particular cognitive styles toward processing and representing information in mental pictures (Imagers) and thus might benefit through a different authentication scheme. In addition, the same password policy is provided to all users without considering that users might have limited cognitive processing abilities and will be negatively affected by the added cognitive effort of applying the password policy.

To this end, we suggest that cognitive styles might affect the type of user authentication (textual or graphical), and cognitive processing abilities might affect user performance with different strength levels of authentication policies. In this context, the goal of this work is to improve the usability of user authentication tasks by recommending the "best-fit" user authentication type and policy to users with different cognitive styles and cognitive processing abilities. The following research question is investigated: *Does matching the user authentication type (textual or graphical) and policy (standard or enhanced) to users' cognitive styles and cognitive processing abilities improve task efficiency and effectiveness?*

4   Personalized User Authentication Based on Individual Differences in Cognitive Processing

This section presents the main components of the proposed personalized user authentication mechanism. It consists of three main layers; *the user modelling layer, the adaptation layer*, and *the user interface layer*.

4.1   User Modelling Layer

The user modelling layer entails the following phases: *user data collection, data processing* and *cluster analysis* for eliciting the users' cognitive styles (Verbal or Imager) and cognitive processing abilities (limited or enhanced), that are respectively related to a specific type of authentication (textual or graphical) and policy (standard or enhanced).

User Data Collection. Collecting data of users is the initial step for adapting and personalizing the user authentication task. Cognitive styles and cognitive processing abilities are considered the main factors in this work for personalizing the user authentication task. For eliciting the users' cognitive styles, Riding's Cognitive Style Analysis test (CSA) [9] was utilized that highlights individual differences in verbal or mental representation of information. An individuals' cognitive style is obtained by presenting a series of questions about conceptual category (e.g., *"Are ski and cricket the same type?"*) and appearance (e.g., *"Are cream and paper the same color?"*) to be judged by the users to be true or false. It is assumed that Verbals respond faster than Imagers in the conceptual types of stimuli, whereas Imagers respond faster than Verbals in the appearance statements. The response time and the given answer for each stimulus is recorded and provided to the next phase for data processing.

For eliciting the speed of processing and controlled attention of users, two Stroop-like tasks are used to measure simple choice reaction time of users [7]. The first task requires users to read words denoting a color written in the same or different ink color (e.g., the word "red" written in red ink color), while the second task requires users to recognize the ink color of words denoting a color different than the ink (e.g., the word "green" written in blue ink). The response time and the given answer for each stimulus is recorded and provided to the next phase for data processing. Furthermore, to elicit the users' working memory capacity, a psychometric test was developed that illustrates a series of geometric figures on the screen in which users are required to memorize the figure and then select the same figure among five similar figures. The total number of correct responses indicates the capacity level of working memory that is also provided to the data processing phase.

Data Processing. In this phase, all the users' responses to the psychometric tests are cleaned from invalid responses and inconsistencies are resolved in order to be used as input to the next phase of cluster analysis. During the first step of data processing, all users' responses to the psychometric tests are examined, and outliers are removed from the dataset. For example, in the case were users remain idle during a stimulus, data about that particular stimulus are removed from the dataset.

Responses of the cognitive style test are processed as follows: the average response time of all valid and correct responses is calculated on each of the two question types (conceptual and appearance) of the psychometric test, and then the ratio between the average response times on the verbal and imagery stimuli is calculated. It is assumed that users with a low ratio are considered Verbals, while users with a high ratio are Imagers.

For the three cognitive processing abilities' tests, a normalization by Z-score is conducted on the raw data, since speed of processing and controlled attention measure speed (average in seconds), whereas working memory measures capacity (total of correct responses). The pseudo code for eliciting the cognitive processing abilities is illustrated in Algorithm #1.

Algorithm #1. Calculate Cognitive Processing Abilities

Input : A set of all users' average response times to the speed of processing test s = { $s_1, s_2, ..., t_m$ }, a set of all users' average response times to the controlled attention test c = { $c_1, c_2, ..., c_m$ }, and a set of all users' total correct responses to the working memory test w = { $w_1, w_2, ..., w_m$ } where m the total number of users
Output : Cognitive Processing Ability – z

```
1:       procedure Calculate_Cognitive_Processing_Ability(s, c, w)
2:           for i := 1 to m do begin
3:               sop = ( s_i - mean(s) ) / stddev(s);
4:               ca = ( c_i - mean(c) ) / stddev(c);
5:               wmc = ( -1 ) * ( w_i - mean(w) ) / stddev(w);
6:               z_i = ( sop + ca + wmc ) / 3;
7:           end for
8:       end procedure
```

The final z-value indicates a user's cognitive processing ability, with a low value indicating an enhanced cognitive processing ability of that user, and a high value indicating a limited cognitive processing ability of that user.

Cluster Analysis. In order to elicit the users' cognitive styles and cognitive processing abilities, cluster analysis is performed to the users' cognitive style ratios and the z-values that were calculated in the previous phase, with the aim to divide the set of users into cluster groups that are different from each other and whose members are similar to each other according to the calculated ratios and z-values. Accordingly, in the case of cognitive styles, users having a small value of ratio are grouped as Verbals and users having a large value of ratio are grouped as Imagers. In the case of cognitive processing abilities, small values of z are grouped as users having enhanced cognitive processing abilities and large values of z are grouped as users having limited cognitive processing abilities.

We utilized the k-means clustering algorithm since it is considered one of the most robust and efficient clustering algorithms [10]. The k-means clustering algorithm requires a fixed number of k clusters to create before the algorithm runs. Given that the desired groups are known in our case (Verbal or Imager, and limited or enhanced cognitive processing), the algorithm is set to $k = 2$ in both cases. The algorithm initially sets the data point with the smallest value as the first cluster center (Verbal cluster and enhanced cognitive ability cluster) and the data point with the largest value as the second cluster center (Imager cluster and limited cognitive ability cluster). The distance between all other data points and cluster centers is then calculated, and each data point is assigned to the cluster whose distance from the cluster center is minimum of all the cluster centers using the Euclidian distance. New cluster centers are recalculated by measuring the mean of all data points of each cluster. Next, the distances between each data point and newly obtained cluster centers are recalculated in an iterative approach until no data point is reassigned.

4.2   Adaptation Layer

In this layer, based on the user modelling results, a two-step rule-based mechanism is applied to recommend a specific type of authentication and policy as illustrated in Algorithm #2. The applied rules are based on previous studies conducted which revealed an effect of users' cognitive styles and cognitive processing abilities on preference and performance of text-based and graphical user authentication mechanisms [11, 12].

Algorithm #2. User Authentication Recommendation for a Single User

Input : Cluster group of cognitive styles $vi = \{ verbal \mid imager \}$, cluster group of cognitive processing abilities $cp = \{ limited \mid enhanced \}$
Output : User authentication type $ua = \{ textual \mid graphical \}$, and authentication policy $p = \{ standard \mid enhanced \}$

```
 1:       procedure Recommendation(vi, cp)
 2:           if (vi == verbal) then
 3:               ua = textual;
 4:           else if (vi == imager) then
 5:               ua = graphical;
 6:           end if
 7:           if (cp == limited) then
 8:               p = standard;
 9:           else if (cp == enhanced) then
10:               p = enhanced;
12:           end if
13:       end procedure
```

During the first step of personalization, the mechanism recommends a textual password mechanism to Verbals, and a graphical authentication mechanism to Imagers since each type of authentication is best matched to the habitual approach of users' cognitive styles. In the second step, users with limited cognitive processing abilities are provided with a standard policy, whereas users with enhanced cognitive processing abilities are provided with an enhanced policy. A standard policy in the case of text-based password is considered a password that consists of eight alphanumeric characters, combination of upper-case and lower-case letters and special characters, whereas an enhanced policy needs a minimum of ten characters, entailing the same restrictions as the standard policy. In the case of graphical authentication mechanism, a standard and an enhanced policy respectively requires users to enter eight and ten images as their authentication key.

4.3   User Interface Layer

In this layer, depending on the decision made in the previous phase, either a textual password or graphical authentication mechanism is communicated to the user interface. The two user authentication mechanisms are described next.

Text-Based Password Mechanism. A standard text-based password mechanism was utilized in which users can enter alphanumeric and special keyboard characters. A minimum of eight or ten characters (depending on the policy) including numbers, a mixture of lower-case and upper-case letters, and special characters are required to be entered by the users during password creation. Password characters are hidden as being typed by the users to avoid bystanders reading the password.

Graphical Authentication Mechanism. A graphical authentication mechanism that involves single-object images was developed based on the recognition-based, graphical authentication mechanism proposed in [3]. During the authentication key creation, users can freely select a minimum of eight or ten images (depending on the policy), in a specific sequence out of a random subset of thirty images that are retrieved from a large image database. After the graphical authentication key is created, a fixed image set of sixteen images, containing the user-selected authentication images and system-selected decoy images are permanently attached to the username in order to increase security. During authentication, a four by four grid containing the user-selected and system-selected decoy images are presented. The image positions in the selection grid are randomly positioned in each authentication session. Thereafter, users have to select their images in the specific sequence, as entered in the authentication key creation process for accessing the system.

From a security point of view, text-based passwords and graphical authentication mechanisms provide similar security protection levels if they are encrypted properly on the service provider database layer and submitted securely on the transmission layer [2, 3]. Accordingly, aiming to defend against guessing attacks based on transmission sniffers, and brute force attacks at the database level, a cryptographic hash function is utilized in both authentication mechanisms that encrypts the given authentication key and transmits it through a secure channel (https), and stored in an encrypted format in the database. Furthermore, text-based and graphical authentication mechanisms entail similar threats with regard to guessing attacks on the client's side. Regarding capturing attacks (e.g., malware, phishing attacks, etc.), graphical authentication mechanisms are more immune than text-based passwords since additional spying software is needed to capture the screen as the user types. On the other hand, graphical authentication mechanisms are more vulnerable to shoulder surfing attacks and social engineering since the nature of the images used (single-object images) allows being easily described and thus easier to share with other users.

5   Experimental Evaluation

In this section we present and discuss our observations and experiences of applying the personalized user authentication mechanism in the frame of a four month ecological valid user study in which users interacted with personalized user authentication mechanisms based on their cognitive styles and cognitive processing abilities.

5.1   Sampling and Procedure

A total of 137 individuals participated in the study (54 males, 83 females, age 17-22) during September and December 2013, and were undergraduate students of Psychology and Social Science Departments. A Web-based system was applied within the frame of university courses. The user enrolment process was divided into two phases: i) participants were required to provide their demographic information (i.e., email, age, gender, and department) and interact with the developed online psychometric tests for eliciting their cognitive styles and cognitive processing abilities, ii) and participants created their authentication key that was used for accessing the courses' material (i.e., course slides, homework exercises) and for viewing their grades. During each course enrolment process, the personalization mechanism recommended a specific type of authentication (text-based password or graphical authentication mechanism) and authentication policy (standard or enhanced) based on the cluster each user was assigned according to the user modelling and adaptation process.

In order to investigate the added value of personalizing the user authentication task based on the users' cognitive styles and cognitive processing abilities, a matched and a mismatched condition was randomly assigned to the decision rules aiming to divide the sample into two groups; the one group being assigned a personalized user authentication mechanism (the matched condition that entailed the recommended user authentication mechanism), and the other group being assigned with a non-personalized user authentication mechanism (the mismatched condition that entailed the opposite type of user authentication to the one suggested by the system). The allocation was based on the users' cognitive characteristics so that the conditions were balanced across all user groups. Participants were not aware whether they were receiving a personalized or a non-personalized authentication mechanism.

Client-side and server-side scripts were developed to monitor the users' behaviour during interaction with the user authentication mechanism. In particular, the total time required for successful authentication (task efficiency) was recorded from the time users entered their username for identification, until they successfully completed the authentication process, as well as the total attempts required for successful authentication for each session (task effectiveness).

5.2 Hypotheses

The following hypotheses were formulated:

H_1. The time needed (efficiency) to successfully authenticate through a personalized user authentication mechanism is reduced compared to a non-personalized mechanism.

H_2. The total number of attempts (effectiveness) to successfully authenticate through a personalized user authentication mechanism is reduced compared to a non-personalized mechanism.

5.3 Analysis of Results

Clustering Results. The cluster analysis of the user modelling mechanism separated users into clusters based on their cognitive style ratios and cognitive processing z-values (Table 1). The main goal of the clustering algorithm was to minimize variability within the clusters and maximize variability between the clusters based on the ratios and z-values. The evaluation was focused on how similar the ratio and z-value of a particular user is to another user of the same cluster, and how different the ratio and z-value of users in clusters from the ones of the other cluster.

Table 1. Descriptive statistics of the ratios and z-values in each cluster

Cognitive Styles				Cognitive Processing Abilities			
Cluster 1 (Verbals)		Cluster 2 (Imagers)		Cluster 1 (Enhanced)		Cluster 1 (Limited)	
Mean (SD)	N	Mean (SD)	N	Mean (SD)	N	Mean (SD)	N
0.84 (0.13)	77	1.25 (0.09)	60	-0.93 (0.56)	89	1.04 (0.49)	48

Two independent-samples t-tests were conducted to determine mean differences on the cognitive style ratios between the generated cluster groups (Verbal/Imager) as well as the mean differences on the cognitive processing abilities z-values between the enhanced and limited cognitive processing cluster groups. Homogeneity of variances was violated in the case of cognitive styles, as assessed by Levene's test for equality of variances (cognitive styles: $p=0.032$; cognitive processing abilities: $p=0.216$). In this respect a Welch t-test was conducted for unequal variances of data.

Results indicated that there were significant differences among cognitive style ratios and among z-values between the clusters (cognitive styles: $t(128.892)=-20.694$, $p<0.001$; cognitive processing abilities: $t(135)=-20.193$, $p<0.001$), indicating that the user modelling procedure grouped the users into different clusters effectively, and could be thus safely used in the main data analysis.

User Authentication Efficiency. An independent-samples t-test was used to determine mean differences on the time needed to solve the personalized and non-personalized user authentication mechanism. Accordingly, if cognitive styles and cognitive processing abilities are of any importance, these two groups should have statistically significant different scores.

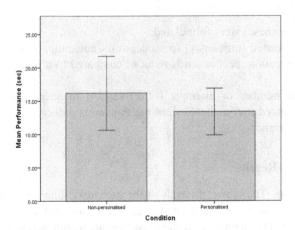

Fig. 1. Means of performances per condition

Data were normally distributed for both personalized and non-personalized data, as assessed by visual inspection of Normal Q-Q Plots. The assumption of homogeneity of variances was violated, as assessed by Levene's test for equality of variances (p=0.001). In this respect a Welch t-test was conducted that can accommodate unequal variances of data.

The analysis revealed that interactions with personalized user authentication mechanisms were more efficient (M=13.39, SD=1.75) than non-personalized user authentication mechanisms (M=16.19, SD=2.77). These results were statistically significant (t(2028.138)=-29.996, p=0.03). Figure 1 illustrates the means of performances of each condition. Accordingly, the results indicate that individual differences in cognitive processing could be a determinant factor on the adaptation of user authentication mechanisms as they improve task completion efficiency and supports Hypothesis #1.

User Authentication Effectiveness. Effectiveness was measured by the total number of attempts made for successfully authenticating in each condition. A Mann-Whitney U test was run to determine if there were differences in total attempts between the personalized and the non-personalized condition. Distributions of these attempts were not similar, as assessed by visual inspection (Figure 2). Total attempts for personalized user authentication interactions (*mean rank* = 1031.92) were significantly less compared to non-personalized user authentication interactions (*mean rank* = 1452.27) indicating that the personalized user authentication interactions improved task effectiveness, supporting Hypothesis #2. These results were statistically significantly different (U=517699, z=-14.898, p=0.01).

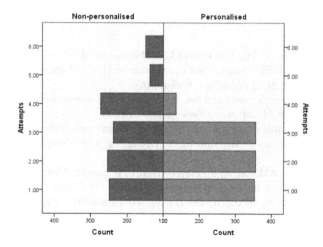

Fig. 2. Total attempts to successfully authenticate in each condition

6   Conclusions

The paper proposed a personalization approach for supporting the design and deployment of usable and secure user authentication tasks, driven primarily by the need to define more effective and efficient user-centered design techniques related to such tasks. The proposed approach was realized in a prototype Web-based system that provided personalized user authentication mechanisms based on individual differences in cognitive styles and cognitive processing abilities.

Our research revealed that personalizing the user authentication type (textual or graphical) and authentication policy to users' cognitive styles and cognitive processing abilities improves task performance, both in terms of task efficiency and effectiveness. These findings are consistent with previous studies that revealed an effect of human cognitive factors on task efficiency and effectiveness of user authentication [11, 12], and translating these findings into adaptation rules was at some extent successful. Limitations of the study include the limited sample size and participants of non-varying profiles (e.g., undergraduate students and age). In this context, bearing in mind that cognitive processing characteristics of users change and decline over time, the suggested approach could have stronger effects on older adults [13]. Although it is interesting and promising that results yielded statistical significant results, further studies need to be conducted in order to reach to more concrete conclusions about the added value and the effects of personalizing user authentication tasks based on individual differences in cognitive processing.

Acknowledgements. The work is co-funded by the PersonaWeb project under the Cyprus Research Promotion Foundation (ΤΠΕ/ΠΛΗΡΟ/0311(ΒΙΕ)/10), and the EU projects SocialRobot (285870) and Miraculous-Life (611421).

References

1. Inglesant, P., Sasse, A.: The True Cost of Unusable Password Policies: Password use in the Wild. In: ACM SIGCHI International Conference on Human Factors in Computing Systems, pp. 383–392. ACM Press, New York (2010)
2. Biddle, R., Chiasson, S., van Oorschot, P.: Graphical Passwords: Learning from the First Twelve Years. J. ACM Computing Surveys 44(4), Article 19 (2012)
3. Mihajlov, M., Jerman-Blazic, B.: On Designing Usable and Secure Recognition-based Graphical Authentication Mechanisms. J. Interacting with Computers 23(6), 582–593 (2011)
4. Zhang, J., Luo, X., Akkaladevi, S., Ziegelmayer, J.: Improving Multiple-password Recall: An Empirical Study. J. Information Security 18(2), 165–176 (2009)
5. Wright, N., Patrick, A., Biddle, R.: Do You See Your Password?: Applying Recognition to Textual Passwords. In: ACM International Symposium on Usable Privacy and Security, Article 8, 14 pages. ACM Press, New York (2012)
6. Komanduri, S., Shay, R., Kelley, P., Mazurek, M., Bauer, L., Christin, N., Cranor, L., Egelman, S.: Of Passwords and People: Measuring the Effect of Password-composition Policies. In: ACM International Conference on Human Factors in Computing Systems, pp. 2595–2604. ACM Press, New York (2011)
7. Stroop, J.R.: Studies of Interference in Serial Verbal Reactions. J. Experimental Psychology 18, 643–662 (1935)
8. Baddeley, A.: Working Memory: Theories, Models, and Controversies. J. Annual Review of Psychology 63, 1–29 (2012)
9. Riding, R., Cheema, I.: Cognitive Styles – An Overview and Integration. J. Educational Psychology 11(3-4), 193–215 (1991)
10. Wu, X., Kumar, V., Quinlan, J., Ghosh, J., Yang, Q., Motoda, H., McLachlan, G., Ng, A., Liu, B., Yu, P., Zhou, Z., Steinbach, M., Hand, D., Steinberg, D.: Top 10 Algorithms in Data Mining. J. Knowledge Information Systems 14(1), 1–37 (2007)
11. Belk, M., Fidas, C., Germanakos, P., Samaras, G.: Security for Diversity: Studying the Effects of Verbal and Imagery Processes on User Authentication Mechanisms. In: Kotzé, P., Marsden, G., Lindgaard, G., Wesson, J., Winckler, M. (eds.) INTERACT 2013, Part III. LNCS, vol. 8119, pp. 442–459. Springer, Heidelberg (2013)
12. Belk, M., Germanakos, P., Fidas, C., Samaras, G.: Studying the Effect of Human Cognition on User Authentication Tasks. In: Carberry, S., Weibelzahl, S., Micarelli, A., Semeraro, G. (eds.) UMAP 2013. LNCS, vol. 7899, pp. 102–113. Springer, Heidelberg (2013)
13. Schaie, W.: Developmental Influences on Adult Intelligence: The Seattle Longitudinal Study, 2nd edn. Oxford University Press, New York (2013)

The Magic Barrier of Recommender Systems
– No Magic, Just Ratings

Alejandro Bellogín[1], Alan Said[2], and Arjen P. de Vries[3]

[1] Universidad Autónoma de Madrid, Ciudad Universitaria de Cantoblanco,
28049 Madrid, Spain
alejandro.bellogin@uam.es
[2] Delft University of Technology, Mekelweg 4, 2628 CD Delft, The Netherlands
alansaid@acm.org
[3] Centrum Wiskunde & Informatica, Science Park 123, 1098XG, Amsterdam, The Netherlands
arjen.de.vries@cwi.nl

Abstract. Recommender Systems need to deal with different types of users who represent their preferences in various ways. This difference in user behaviour has a deep impact on the final performance of the recommender system, where some users may receive either better or worse recommendations depending, mostly, on the quantity and the quality of the information the system knows about the user. Specifically, the inconsistencies of the user impose a lower bound on the error the system may achieve when predicting ratings for that particular user.

In this work, we analyse how the consistency of user ratings (*coherence*) may predict the performance of recommendation methods. More specifically, our results show that our definition of coherence is correlated with the so-called *magic barrier* of recommender systems, and thus, it could be used to discriminate between easy users (those with a low magic barrier) and difficult ones (those with a high magic barrier). We report experiments where the rating prediction error for the more coherent users is lower than that of the less coherent ones. We further validate these results by using a public dataset, where the magic barrier is not available, in which we obtain similar performance improvements.

1 Introduction

Recommender systems aim to help people find items of interest from a large pool of potentially interesting items. However, when receiving these recommendations not all users are equally satisfied. One reason for this is, e.g. the choice of the recommendation algorithm. However, even when we account for this aspect, some users may receive better recommendations than others. Previous research has analysed this issue and characterised it as a matter of user inconsistency, that is, users have an inherent noise when interacting with the recommender system, which then affects the reliability of the recommendations produced. This concept is know as the magic barrier of recommender systems, a term coined by Herlocker et al. [9], referring to the upper bound on rating prediction accuracy: above it any further improvements on the evaluation metrics are meaningless [1, 18].

In this context, we aim to infer which users have a higher level of inconsistency *a priori*, that is, find the magic barrier without having the additional re-ratings as required

V. Dimitrova et al. (Eds.): UMAP 2014, LNCS 8538, pp. 25–36, 2014.

in the approaches suggested until now. We are particulary interested in predicting which users will have a low/high magic barrier using readily available information. We propose to measure how coherent a user's ratings are within an item's feature space. In doing so, we associate highly coherent ratings to users with a lower magic barrier.

Once the magic barrier – or any other measure of user's inconsistency – is successfully predicted, several applications to improve the recommender system's performance become available. One possibility would be to create separate training models for a subset of the users according to their predicted consistency.

Our research aims to answer the following two research questions: **RQ1)** is the rating coherence of a user a good predictor of the magic barrier? and **RQ2)** is it possible to cluster the user community into easy and difficult users – according to their coherence – so that the performance of the system is improved? We address the first question by measuring the correlation between our definitions of coherence and the magic barrier of each user. For the second question, we study how the error of the recommender system changes when considering different subsets of users (selected according to the proposed coherence values) to train and test the models.

The rest of the paper is organised as follows. Section 2 presents other research considering the concept of user inconsistencies, it also defines the magic barrier that we will use throughout this paper. Section 3 describes our approaches to measure the coherence of a user; then, in Section 4 the datasets and other experimental settings are introduced. Finally, Section 5 shows the results obtained, Section 6 provides additional works dealing with the problem of predicting the user's difficulty or the performance of a system, and Section 7 concludes the paper and presents some lines of future work.

2   Measuring User Inconsistency in Recommendation

One of the first works mentioning user-induced noise in movie ratings was presented in [10] by Hill et al., where the authors created an email-based movie recommendation service. The service asked its users to rate movies from a list of 500 pre-selected movies before attempting to create recommendations. The authors mention *The Upper Limit* as a bound on performance prediction based on the idea that a person's ratings are noisy or inconsistent. Based on statistical theory, the authors claim that it will never be possible to perfectly predict the users' ratings, instead they cite *the square root of the observed test-retest reliability correlation* as the optimal level of prediction due to the levels of noise in user-generated data. No attempt at estimating the level of noise was however performed in the scope of that work.

To our knowledge, the first mention of the *magic barrier*, the term currently in use for stating the practical upper bound on rating prediction accuracy (or lower bound on rating prediction error), appeared in Herlocker et al. in their seminal paper on recommender system evaluation [9]. In that work, the authors speculate whether recommender systems are hitting such a potential magic barrier, e.g. a point where *natural variability may prevent us from obtaining much more accurate predictions*. Additionally, the authors speculate whether minuscule rating prediction errors actually translate to a perceived improvement from the users or whether the increasingly smaller accuracy improvements have no effect on the quality as perceived by the end users.

Cosley et al. in [5] conducted an early study on the Movielens[1] website where a selection of users were asked to provide re-ratings to previously rated movies. Similarly, Amatriain et al. attempted to characterise the noise in ratings based on the reliability in the re-rating process [1, 2]. More recently, Kluver et al. addressed this problem from a different direction [12], where instead of measuring the level of noise in the dataset, the authors measure how much preference information is contained in a rating. To do this, the authors based their approach on Shannon's information entropy, which indicates how much actual information is concealed in a rating. Preference bits were then found through repeated re-ratings by users on the same items. Each re-rating can then be used to estimate the amount of preference bits in a rating.

In this paper, we focus on the definition of magic barrier as defined by Said et al. in [18] and [19]. This concept is derived as the lower bound of the Root Mean Squared Error (RMSE) that can be attained by an optimal recommender system. It is defined as the standard deviation of the inconsistencies (noise) inherent in the user ratings, as follows:

$$\widehat{B}_{\mathcal{X}} = \sqrt{\frac{1}{|\mathcal{X}|} \sum_{(u,i)\in\mathcal{X}} (r(u,i) - o(u,i))^2} \tag{1}$$

where $\mathcal{X}$ is the set of ratings for which we have re-ratings (opinions, in that work) available, $r(u,i)$ denotes the actual rating for user u on item i, and $o(u,i)$ is the opinion given by the user at a different point in time than $r(u,i)$. Note that this definition of the magic barrier actually is an estimation as it is not possible to directly determine the magic barrier because it involves an optimal rating function which is not usually available [18].

3   A Measure of User Coherence for Recommendation

Given a user u, her rated items $I(u) \subseteq \mathcal{I}$, and the ratings $r(u,i)$ assigned to these items, i.e., $i \in I(u)$, we aim to provide a score $\gamma(u) = \gamma(I(u))$ that measures how coherent a user profile is in terms of her assigned ratings. To compute this score we propose to use an external information source with which we can measure the inconsistencies of the user's ratings, by describing items in terms of specific features, e.g. genres. Although other measures could be available where no external information is required, such as the entropy of the ratings [12] or the Kullback-Leibler divergence between the user's preferences and the overall preferences [4], we believe that our formulation provides a measure that is easily explainable and justifiable, allowing for further feedback from the recommender system to the user. Furthermore, as we show in the rest of the paper, this measure obtains very good results, despite its simplicity.

3.1   Example

Before presenting the actual definition of the rating coherence of a user (or *user coherence*, for simplicity), let us first consider the examples presented in Figure 1. Here we

---

[1] http://www.movielens.org

have two users that have rated the exact same set of items, although their ratings are slightly different. Specifically, the user in Figure 1a gives more consistent ratings to items sharing the same features, which in this case corresponds to the movie's genres. In the long term we argue that such a user will have a more consistent (less noisy) behaviour, since her taste for each item feature seem to be well defined.

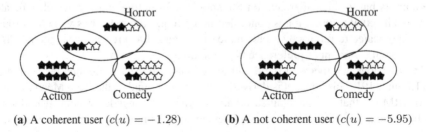

(a) A coherent user ($c(u) = -1.28$)   (b) A not coherent user ($c(u) = -5.95$)

Fig. 1. Example of a coherent vs. not coherent user. Our definition of coherence takes into account the rating's deviation within each item feature, which in this example consists of three genres: action, comedy, and horror.

3.2   A Simple Definition for User Coherence

Following the rationale presented before, we define the user coherence based on a set of item features $\mathcal{F}$ as:

$$c(u) = - \sum_{f \in \mathcal{F}} \sigma_f(u) \qquad (2)$$

where $\sigma_f(u) = \sqrt{\sum_{i \in I(u,f)} (r(u,i) - \bar{r}_f(u))^2}$ corresponds to the user's rating deviation within a specific feature f, having an associated mean rating for that feature $\bar{r}_f(u)$, which simply corresponds to the average rating within the set of items rated by user u that belong to feature f, denoted here as $I(u, f)$. We refer to this formulation as **basic coherence**.

With this formulation, the coherence $c(u)$ captures the variance of a user's ratings relative to the feature space in which the items are defined. Moreover, it also incorporates a negative sign to indicate that the larger the variance, the less coherent (or more incoherent) a user should be.

The key aspect of this function, hence, is that we are accounting for the rating deviation of the user with respect to a particular feature space. Besides, such definition allows for a more general case, where the space $\mathcal{F}$ could be – instead of (textual) item features – any embedding of the items into a space $\mathcal{F}$, such as an item clustering or the latent factors of the items, and also other functions apart from standard deviation to statistically summarise the user's ratings for a given feature, as will be described in the next section.

Going back to our previous example presented in Figure 1, we can observe that the values of $c(u)$ match our intuition about which user is more coherent, since user in Figure 1a receives a higher value from the proposed measure.

Table 1. Possible functions $g(u, f)$ to be used in Equation 3, where $u(f)$ denotes the user's ratings associated with items linked to feature f, $u(\mathcal{F})$ is the same but for any feature in the feature space $\mathcal{F}$, and the probabilities $p(f|u)$ and $p(f)$ are computed normalising the rating values of a user or of the whole community for a given feature.

Function $g(u, f)$	Definition	Function $g(u, f)$	Definition
Entropy	$p(f|u) \log p(f|u)$	KLD	$p(f|u) \log \frac{p(f|u)}{p(f)}$
Mean	$\mu(u(f))$	Weighted Mean	$\mu(u(f)) \frac{\|u(f)\|}{\|u(\mathcal{F})\|}$
Std. dev.	$\sigma(u(f))$	Weighted Std. dev.	$\sigma(u(f)) \frac{\|u(f)\|}{\|u(\mathcal{F})\|}$
Size	$\|u(f)\|$		

3.3 A General Definition for User Coherence

Based on the simple formulation presented in Equation 2, we now introduce a more general definition for the coherence of a user. We now allow (see Equation 3) any arbitrary function defined upon the information known for a user u and a specific feature f to be used. This information will generally be the ratings given by u to the items associated with f, that is $u(f) = \{r : (u, i, r) \; \forall i \in \mathcal{F}^{-1}(f)\}$, where $\mathcal{F}(i)$ denotes the subset of features $f \in \mathcal{F}$ for item i.

$$c_g(u) = -\sum_{f \in \mathcal{F}} g(u, f) \tag{3}$$

Table 1 shows some possibilities for these functions applied over the vector of ratings $u(f)$. Entropy, Kullback-Leibler divergence (KLD), standard deviation, mean, and size are presented in the table, along with two weighted versions of the standard deviation and mean to account for the actual number of items rated by the user in each feature. We have to note that the basic coherence presented in the previous section corresponds to the one where standard deviation is used as the function $g(u, f)$.

We have to emphasise that any of these variations of coherence can be calculated using the same data available for training the recommender system, and that no information from the test set is required.

4   Experimental Setup

We now describe the two datasets used to test the predictive power of the proposed measures for user coherence introduced in Section 3. We also present the specific training and test splits we generate to properly assess the performance improvement by exploiting a user clustering into easy and difficult users once the proposed coherence measure is used.

Table 2. Statistics of the datasets used for the experiments, where *opinions* refers to those used to estimate the magic barrier as in [18]

Dataset	Users	Items	Ratings	Density	Range of ratings
Movielens	6,040	3,900	1,000,209	4.24%	[1-5]
Moviepilot	318,418	31,948	12,825,203	0.13%	[0-100]
Moviepilot opinions	306	2,309	6,299	0.89%	[0-100]

4.1 Datasets

We have used two datasets, whose statistics are presented in Table 2: Moviepilot and Movielens. The former is a snapshot of the commercial movie recommender system Moviepilot[2], having more than one million users, $55,000$ movies, and over 10 million ratings. Movies are rated on a 0 to 100 scale with a step size of 5. To estimate the magic barrier, in [18] a user study was performed to collect users *opinions* on movies that had been previously rated on Moviepilot. We refer the reader to the detailed description contained in that paper, the relevant part for the present work is that every user taking part in this study gave their opinion on at least 20 movies, which were collected and aggregated to calculate the magic barrier of the system as presented in Section 2.

The second dataset used in our experiments is one of the datasets provided by Movie-lens[3], containing one million ratings, more than $6,000$ users and almost $4,000$ items, as we can see in Table 2. Since the re-ratings or other opinions are not available for this dataset, the magic barrier cannot be estimated, but we can still use it (in Section 5.2) as a proof of concept that the proposed coherence functions are able to discriminate between difficult and easy users.

Table 3. Notation for the different training and test models considered

Name	Training	Test
All	$\text{Tr}_e \cup \text{Tr}_d$	$\text{Te}_e \cup \text{Te}_d$
All-Easy	$\text{Tr}_e \cup \text{Tr}_d$	Te_e
All-Diff	$\text{Tr}_e \cup \text{Tr}_d$	Te_d
Easy-Easy	Tr_e	Te_e
Diff-Diff	Tr_d	Te_d

4.2 Training and Test Splits

As stated in the research question **RQ2**, we aim to check if it is possible to cluster the users (into easy and difficult ones) such that the performance of the system is improved

---

[2] http://www.moviepilot.de/
[3] Available at http://www.grouplens.org/node/73

as a result of this user partition. To properly evaluate this, we propose the splits for the training and test sets summarised in Table 3. The training and test splits for the easy users are denoted as Tr_e and Te_e, whereas the splits corresponding to the difficult users are referred to as Tr_d and Te_d. Assuming that we have already classified the users as easy or difficult ones (e.g., using a percentage p of all the users labelled as easy users), we perform a 5-fold cross validation within the whole set of ratings relative to each of the easy and difficult users, in order to obtain a training and test split for each subset of the data. Other splitting conditions may be used (based on percentage or time conditions) instead of 5-fold, and will be considered in the future.

Once these splits are generated, we build the combinations for training and test models presented in Table 3. The rationale of these models goes as follows: the *All* model is a simple evaluation split where all the users are used to train and test a specific recommender system; the *Easy-Easy* and *Diff-Diff* evaluation models focus only on one type of user, by training and testing on the ratings associated with that corresponding type of user. The other two combinations use the same training information available as in *All*, but only evaluate one type of user, either those classified as easy users (*All-Easy*) or as difficult ones (*All-Diff*).

5   Results

In this section we present two experiments that aim to answer the research questions stated earlier, i.e. **RQ1)** is the rating coherence of a user a good predictor of the magic barrier?, and **RQ2)** is it possible to cluster the users into easy and difficult users so that the overall performance of the system is improved?

For these experiments, we have used the datasets described in Section 4.1. For the second experiment, we performed a standard 5-fold cross-validation evaluation, splitting the data according to the different strategies described in Section 4.2, where we assume that half of the users are easy and the other half are difficult (i.e., $p = 0.5$ from previous section), once they are sorted according to a particular coherence function. In each fold, the training and test splits contained 80% and 20% of the data respectively.

The recommendation algorithm tested is a standard user-based collaborative filtering method [21], using Pearson's correlation as the user similarity function and 50 neighbours.

Furthermore, for the features used to compute the coherence functions, we exploit, for the Movielens dataset, the genres provided in the original files. In the case of Moviepilot we use four of the available tagging features [17]: genres, plot keywords, emotion keywords, and intended audience.

The evaluation metric we use in our experiments is the Root Mean Squared Error (RMSE). We report this metric because it is related with the concept of magic barrier (indeed, the magic barrier is defined as *the RMSE of an optimal function* [18]), although in the future we plan to explore alternative evaluation metrics, e.g., precision, recall, nDCG, etc. RMSE is calculated for a test set T as:

$$\mathrm{RMSE} = \sqrt{\frac{1}{|T|} \sum_{(u,i)\in T} (r(u,i) - \tilde{r}(u,i))^2} \qquad (4)$$

Table 4. Spearman's correlation between coherence and user magic barrier. $\emptyset$ indicates that no feature space was used. Note that the desired correlation is negative as the more coherent a user is, the better performing she is (i.e. she has a lower magic barrier).

Coherence	Genres	Emotion keywords	Intended audience	Plot keywords	$\emptyset$
Entropy	0.050	0.016	0.048	0.000	NA
KLD	0.098	0.055	0.067	0.068	NA
Mean	0.114	0.113	0.097	0.106	0.104
Weighted Mean	0.010	0.068	0.072	-0.028	0.104
Std. dev.	-0.331	-0.438	-0.383	-0.279	-0.432
Weighted Std. dev.	-0.398	**-0.455**	-0.432	-0.394	-0.432
Size	0.077	0.074	0.066	0.088	0.072
Random			-0.015		
Number of ratings			-0.072		
Average rating			-0.104		

where $r(u,i)$ and $\tilde{r}(u,i)$ denote the real and predicted ratings for every pair of item i and user u contained in T.

5.1 User Coherence and Magic Barrier

In this experiment, we assess the validity of the proposed coherence functions as good predictors for the magic barrier to answer the research question **RQ1**. With this goal in mind, we show in Table 4 the Spearman's correlation values between the coherence and the magic barrier per user (Pearson's correlation was very similar). Note that Pearson's correlation coefficient is designed to capture linear relationships between the two variables whereas Spearman's captures non-linear dependencies. Both correlations provide scores in the range of -1 to 1, where 1 denotes a perfect correlation, -1 represents an inverse correlation, and the absolute value is the strength of the relationship.

We observe in Table 4 that the correlations for the weighted version of the coherence function (that is, where the importance of each feature in the user profile is ignored) show more predictive power only when the standard deviation is used. Besides, entropy and KLD do not perform very well. Additionally, *Emotion keywords* and *Intended Audience* seem to be the best feature spaces for most of the coherence formulations, and especially, for the cases where a strong correlation is obtained. We have to however note that these feature spaces offer a low coverage in terms of the items identified with these features [20], thus this aspect should also be taken into account when selecting the feature to use.

We have also analysed the behaviour of the proposed coherence functions when the feature space is reduced to having only one feature (which is shared among all the items). The results for this case (column $\emptyset$ in Table 4) evidence that the actual feature space may not be so important, and that the proposed coherence functions (except Entropy and KLD, which produce the same value – a zero – when computed for an event space of size 1) are able to predict a user's magic barrier using exclusively ratings.

Table 5. RMSE values using different features for the coherence and the training and test splits described in Section 4.2. ▲ and ▼ denote, respectively, the best and worst values obtained in each dataset (the lower the error, the better).

| Dataset | Training and Test Splits | | | | |
	All	All-Easy	All-Diff	Easy-Easy	Diff-Diff
Moviepilot	23.097	20.079	26.278	19.279▲	28.219▼
Movielens	1.090	0.974	1.195	0.933▲	1.226▼

This is especially true when standard deviation is used as function g. Note, however, that although the obtained correlations in this case are similar to those presented before, strongest relations are always found when a feature space is used.

In our analysis, we have also included a random magic barrier predictor to check its neutral correlations (around zero), along with two other baseline predictors based on the number of ratings each user has and her average rating. These results show that the proposed coherence function is not trivial, and that it is actually capturing something that other transformations based on the same information (ratings) are not able to provide.

This experiment hence confirms that the user coherence measured as proposed in Section 3 provides good predictions of the magic barrier; as a consequence, we should be able to exploit the ranking generated by sorting the users according to their coherence value to lower the magic barrier for the more coherent (or easy) users. In the next section, we show that this may be generalised when no information about the magic barrier is available, and only the final RMSE of the system can be measured.

5.2   User Coherence and Recommendation Performance

Now we aim to address research question **RQ2**, where we investigate if we can improve the recommendation performance by clustering the population of users according to their coherence.

Based on the results presented in the previous section, we are going to restrict our analysis on the weighted version of the standard deviation function for user coherence. Moreover, to ensure fair comparisons between Movielens and Moviepilot datasets, we use genres as feature space; recall that in this situation the correlation was not the strongest, but it was also significant (almost -0.4).

Table 5 shows the RMSE values for the different training and test splits presented in Table 3. We observe that the best result is always obtained when only easy users are included in the training set, that is, those classified as more coherent, and according to the correlation analysis, those having a lower magic barrier. Similarly, the difficult (less coherent) users produce the worst recommendation performance. This is an indicative that the magic barrier is a valid estimation of the final performance of the system.

Moreover, we also notice that the baseline performance (from the *All* split) is reduced when only easy (more coherent) users are evaluated. Besides, if we average the error found in *All-Easy* and *All-Diff* (since in each of these splits half of the users were evaluated) in Movielens, we obtain slightly better results than when we evaluate the complete dataset (specifically, we have an average RMSE of 1.0845). Note that in the three splits the recommendation model learnt from the training data is the same and the only difference is in the test set used to compute the RMSE.

These results evidence that the coherence function we have proposed in this paper is able to detect users that exhibit an inherent lower noise, even when no information about the magic barrier is available. On top of this, the user-based recommender we have tested takes advantage of this aspect and learns (and predicts) their preferences more accurately. On the other hand, the difficult users do not only receive bad recommendations, but they can improve their accuracy by training the recommendation model with more data; that is, whereas coherent users obtain decent performance by using only ratings from other coherent users, less coherent users need information from outside of their own cluster, showing their higher level of noise.

In summary, this experiment answers positively to the second research question, namely, that it is possible to exploit the coherence values to build different training and test models in such a way that the error decreases for the easy users, and in some cases (i.e., the Movielens dataset), even the average error obtained for the easy and difficult users is balanced out and outperform the overall error.

6   Related Work

Aiming to understand how recommenders fail for certain users, and attempting to characterise those users has been researched by some authors. Rashid et al. propose in [16] a measure of the effect of a user in the recommendations received by an algorithm, named as influence. Their original definition is very expensive, since it measures the effect a user has over the rest via the predictions they receive, for which they need to compute predictions for items using a training model where the target user has been removed.

In [6], Ekstrand & Riedl examine why some recommenders fail in the context of hybrid recommendation, with the goal of selecting better components to build more efficient ensembles. They found that recommenders fail on different users and items, and obtained specific user features – such as the user's rating count, the average rating, and their variance – that allow to predict the performance of an algorithm.

In [11], Kille & Albayrak assign a difficulty value reflecting the expected evaluation outcome of the user. The authors propose to measure this difficulty in terms of the diversity of the rating predictions and rankings when comparing the output of several recommender systems. Some diversity metrics from [13] are proposed, but they are not tested nor implemented in any real dataset.

By drawing from Information Retrieval related quantities, Bellogín et al. present in [3, 4] a family of performance predictors for users. Correlations found between ranking-based metrics and such predictors are strong, and the authors propose to exploit them in at least two applications: dynamic neighbourhood building and dynamic ensemble recommendation, where the weights for the neigbours or the recommenders would dynamically change depending on the predicted performance of each variable.

More recently, a similar approach was developed using a machine learning method based on decision trees. In [7], Griffith et al. aim to predict the user's performance in terms of the user's average error by extracting user's rating information (such as the number of ratings, average rating, standard deviation, number of neighbours, average similarity, etc.). The correlations obtained are very strong (around 0.8) but no actual applications are proposed in that paper.

In summary, the idea of predicting the performance of recommenders has attracted a lot of attention in the field so far, however, to the best of our knowledge, no other work has been able to predict an actual measure of user inconsistency – like the magic barrier – and successfully apply it to improve the performance of the whole (or even of a subset) of the system, as we have presented in this work.

7   Conclusions and Future Work

The research presented here aims to provide a deeper understanding of what user characteristics are related with the appropriateness and relevance of the recommender's suggestions for each user. We have observed that being statistically coherent – in terms of rating deviation – gives enough information to predict the user inconsistency as measured by her magic barrier, especially if such coherence is measured within an item's feature (e.g., genres). This opens up the possibility for a (production) recommender system to perform different actions on the users depending on their predicted inconsistencies, such as proactively asking some specific users (the ones predicted as most *difficult*) to rate more items or training separate models for the *easy* and *difficult* users. Our experiments show that by creating such separate training models improvements with respect to the global model can be achieved, specifically, around 14% for the subset of easier users. It should be feasible to improve these results if an ad-hoc tuning over the set of more difficult users is performed.

We have explored only one type of recommendation algorithm (i.e., collaborative filtering, and in particular, user-based methods), but it is an open question whether all recommenders may improve their performance in the same way with respect to the proposed coherence function. More importantly, apart from the error-based evaluation metrics used in this work, we are interested in evaluating with ranking-based metrics – like precision – to analyse if user inconsistencies are also reflected in terms of, or if they affect whatsoever, their ranking performance. We also plan to develop other coherence-related predictors proposed in the fields of Information Retrieval [8] and Machine Learning [14, 15], to capture additional insights about the user behaviour with respect to the recommender system.

Acknowledgments. This work was carried out during the tenure of an ERCIM "Alain Bensoussan" Fellowship Programme. The research leading to these results has received funding from the European Union Seventh Framework Programme (FP7/2007-2014) under grant agreements no. 246016 (ERCIM) and no. 610594 (CrowdRec).

References

1. Amatriain, X., Pujol, J.M., Oliver, N.: I like it... I like it not: Evaluating user ratings noise in recommender systems. In: UMAP, pp. 247–258 (2009)
2. Amatriain, X., Pujol, J.M., Tintarev, N., Oliver, N.: Rate it again: increasing recommendation accuracy by user re-rating. In: RecSys, pp. 173–180 (2009)
3. Bellogín, A.: Predicting performance in recommender systems. In: RecSys, pp. 371–374 (2011)
4. Bellogín, A., Castells, P., Cantador, I.: Predicting the performance of recommender systems: An information theoretic approach. In: Amati, G., Crestani, F. (eds.) ICTIR 2011. LNCS, vol. 6931, pp. 27–39. Springer, Heidelberg (2011)
5. Cosley, D., Lam, S.K., Albert, I., Konstan, J.A., Riedl, J.: Is seeing believing?: how recommender system interfaces affect users' opinions. In: CHI, pp. 585–592 (2003)
6. Ekstrand, M.D., Riedl, J.: When recommenders fail: predicting recommender failure for algorithm selection and combination. In: RecSys, pp. 233–236 (2012)
7. Griffith, J., O'Riordan, C., Sorensen, H.: Investigations into user rating information and predictive accuracy in a collaborative filtering domain. In: SAC, pp. 937–942 (2012)
8. He, J., Larson, M., de Rijke, M.: Using coherence-based measures to predict query difficulty. In: Macdonald, C., Ounis, I., Plachouras, V., Ruthven, I., White, R.W. (eds.) ECIR 2008. LNCS, vol. 4956, pp. 689–694. Springer, Heidelberg (2008)
9. Herlocker, J.L., Konstan, J.A., Terveen, L.G., Riedl, J.: Evaluating collaborative filtering recommender systems. ACM Trans. Inf. Syst. 22(1), 5–53 (2004)
10. Hill, W.C., Stead, L., Rosenstein, M., Furnas, G.W.: Recommending and evaluating choices in a virtual community of use. In: CHI, pp. 194–201 (1995)
11. Kille, B.: Modeling difficulty in recommender systems. In: RUE 2012. RecSys, pp. 30–32 (2012)
12. Kluver, D., Nguyen, T.T., Ekstrand, M.D., Sen, S., Riedl, J.: How many bits per rating? In: RecSys, pp. 99–106 (2012)
13. Kuncheva, L.I., Whitaker, C.J.: Measures of diversity in classifier ensembles and their relationship with the ensemble accuracy. Machine Learning 51(2), 181–207 (2003)
14. Misra, H., Cappé, O., Yvon, F.: Using lda to detect semantically incoherent documents. In: CoNLL, Stroudsburg, PA, USA, pp. 41–48 (2008)
15. Newman, D., Bonilla, E.V., Buntine, W.L.: Improving topic coherence with regularized topic models. In: NIPS, pp. 496–504 (2011)
16. Rashid, A.M., Karypis, G., Riedl, J.: Influence in ratings-based recommender systems: An algorithm-independent approach. In: SDM (2005)
17. Said, A., Berkovsky, S., Luca, E.W.D.: Movie recommendation in context. ACM TIST 4(1), 13 (2013)
18. Said, A., Jain, B.J., Narr, S., Plumbaum, T.: Users and noise: The magic barrier of recommender systems. In: Masthoff, J., Mobasher, B., Desmarais, M.C., Nkambou, R. (eds.) UMAP 2012. LNCS, vol. 7379, pp. 237–248. Springer, Heidelberg (2012)
19. Said, A., Jain, B.J., Narr, S., Plumbaum, T., Albayrak, S., Scheel, C.: Estimating the magic barrier of recommender systems: a user study. In: SIGIR, pp. 1061–1062 (2012)
20. Said, A., Kille, B., De Luca, E.W., Albayrak, S.: Personalizing tags: a folksonomy-like approach for recommending movies. In: HetRec 2011, New York, NY, USA. RecSys, pp. 53–56 (2011)
21. Shardanand, U., Maes, P.: Social information filtering: Algorithms for automating "word of mouth". In: Katz, I.R., Mack, R.L., Marks, L., Rosson, M.B., Nielsen, J. (eds.) CHI, pp. 210–217. ACM/Addison-Wesley (1995)

Toward Fully Automated Person-Independent Detection of Mind Wandering

Robert Bixler[1] and Sidney D'Mello[1,2]

[1] Departments of Computer Science, University of Notre Dame,
Notre Dame, IN 46556
[2] Departments of Psychology, University of Notre Dame,
Notre Dame, IN 46556
{rbixler,sdmello}@nd.edu

Abstract. Mind wandering is a ubiquitous phenomenon where attention involuntary shifts from task-related processing to task-unrelated thoughts. Mind wandering has negative effects on performance, hence, intelligent interfaces that detect mind wandering can intervene to restore attention to the current task. We investigated the use of eye gaze and contextual cues to automatically detect mind wandering during reading with a computer interface. Participants were pseudo-randomly probed to report mind wandering instances while an eye tracker recorded their gaze during a computerized reading task. Supervised machine learning techniques detected positive responses to mind wandering probes from gaze and context features in a user-independent fashion. Mind wandering was predicted with an accuracy of 72% (expected accuracy by chance was 62%) when probed at the end of a page and an accuracy of 59% (chance was 50%) when probed in the midst of reading a page. Possible improvements to the detectors and applications are discussed.

Keywords: gaze tracking, mind wandering, affect detection, user modeling.

1 Introduction

Most of us have had the experience of reading, listening to a lecture, or engaging in a personally-relevant task only to realize that our attention has gradually drifted away from the task at hand to off-task thoughts, such as dinner, childcare, or everyday worries and anxieties. It has been estimated that these automatic attentional shifts toward internal task-unrelated thoughts, referred to as *mind wandering* (MW, or zoning out), occur between 20-40% of the time depending on the task and the environmental context [12, 19, 24]. For example, one recent large-scale study tracked MW in 5,000 individuals with random prompts from an iPhone app and made the surprising discovery that people reported MW for 46.9% of the prompts [12].

MW is not merely incidental but also negatively effects performance for tasks requiring conscious control because an individual cannot simultaneously focus on both the task at hand and task-unrelated thoughts. Research has indicated that MW leads to performance failures during a number of tasks, such as increased error rates during

V. Dimitrova et al. (Eds.): UMAP 2014, LNCS 8538, pp. 37–48, 2014.
© Springer International Publishing Switzerland 2014

signal detection tasks [22], lower recall during memory tasks [20] and poor comprehension during reading tasks [9]. For computer-supported tasks, this suggests that there
is an opportunity for an intelligent interface to attempt to reorient attention to the task
at hand when MW occurs. This paper makes a first step towards this goal by automatically detecting MW in near real-time in a manner that generalizes to new users.

1.1   Related Work

User state estimation is a broad topic applicable to a variety of areas such as affective
computing, attention-aware computing, augmented cognition, and social signal
processing. MW detection is a unique instance of user state estimation, specifically the
detection of attentional states (or the lack thereof in the case of MW). Interest in modeling user attentional states has spurred research into how interface design decisions
affect attention. For example, Muir et al. [14] used eye movements to explore how
attention was affected by adaptive hints in an educational game. There have also been
efforts at attentional state estimation. Yonetani et al. [26] analyzed the relationship
between eye gaze and saliency dynamics of a video in order to determine if a user was
in a high level attention condition or a low level attention condition with an accuracy
of 80.6%. Additionally, Navalpakkam et al. [15] created hidden markov models that
accurately modeled attention while users chose to read one of eight articles displayed
on a computer screen. Although a growing number of studies have investigated attention, with the two exceptions noted below, none have considered MW behaviors.

MW is a distinct aspect of attentional state as it is defined by involuntary lapses in
attention. While numerous studies have investigated MW [9, 18, 23], research on
real-time *detection* of MW is in its infancy. Drummond and Litman [8] made one of
the first attempts to automatically detect MW (operationalized as zoning out) with
acoustic-prosodic (e.g., pitch) features. Their model attempted to discriminate "high"
versus "low" zoning out while users were engaged in a spoken dialogue with an intelligent tutoring system. Their accuracy of 64% reflects an important first step in MW
detection. However, their validation approach did not ensure independence of training
and testing sets, so generalization to new users is unknown. Furthermore, their MW
detector is limited to speech-enabled interfaces.

In this paper, we consider eye gaze as a possible modality for MW detection. Eye
movements are attractive since they are ubiquitous in most visual interfaces. There
has also been previous research linking eye movements and the occurrence of MW.
For example, research has found that individuals blink more often [24] and are less
likely to fixate, re-fixate, and look backward through previously read text [17] when
MW compared to normal reading. These studies, however, did not attempt to automatically detect MW from eye gaze and although eye gaze has been used for attentional state estimation (as cited above), there is no research directed at MW detection.

We recently took a step in this direction by making an initial attempt to use eye
gaze data to detect mind wandering during reading [6]. The best performing models
(supervised learners) yielded a detection accuracy of 60% on a down-sampled corpus
containing 50% "yes" and 50% "no" responses. Although these results are promising,
they are limited by the fact that classification accuracy was not very impressive.
Furthermore, the data set was downsampled prior to classification, thereby interfering
with the natural distribution of MW responses (35%).

1.2   Current Work

This study reports the development and validation of one of the first (aside from exceptions above) fully automated user-independent detector of MW during reading. We focus on a computerized reading task since reading is a critical component of many real-world tasks and is negatively affected by MW [9]. Our approach to MW detection entails collecting eye gaze data and self-reports of MW while users read texts on a computer screen (see Figure 1). We then extract features from the eye gaze signal and contextual cues (see below) and use supervised classification techniques to build models that discriminate instance of MW from normal reading. The models are constructed and validated in a user-independent fashion, so we will have some confidence that they generalize to new users.

Fig. 1. Gaze fixations (circles) and saccades (lines) of a sample page. Diameter of circle is proportional to fixation duration

The present research is novel in a number of respects. First, previous work on attentional state estimation has not considered MW, and other than the Drummond & Litman study [8] and our preliminary attempt [6], this work represents the first large-scale attempt at fully automated user-independent detection of MW. Second, it significantly expands upon our preliminary work with a much larger and more diverse data set. Third, we considered an enhanced set of gaze features in order to improve classification accuracy when compared to our preliminary attempt using an impoverished feature set. Fourth, eye gaze features were complemented with contextual cues, such as high-level text characteristics (e.g., difficulty) and reading behaviors (e.g., reading rate), as context might help disambiguate noisy gaze signals.

2   Data Collection

2.1   Participants

Participants were 178 undergraduate students from two U.S. universities that participated for course credit. 93 students were from a medium-sized private mid-western university while 85 were from a large public university in the mid-south. The average age of participants was 20 years (SD = 3.6). Demographics included 62.7% female, 49% Caucasian, 34% African American, 7% Asian, 6% Hispanic, and 4% "Other".

2.2   Texts and Experimental Manipulations

Participants read four different texts on research methods topics (i.e., experimenter bias, replication, causality, and dependent variables). On average the texts contained 1500 words (SD = 10) and were split into 30-36 pages with approximately 60 words per page. Texts were presented on a computer screen with size 36 Courier New font. There were two manipulations: difficulty and value. The difficulty manipulation consisted of presenting either an easy or a difficult version of each text. The value manipulation pertained to questions from "high-value" texts which counted three times more toward the test score than questions for the "low-value" texts. Participants were instructed they would be required to read additional material if they did not do well enough on the posttest, incentivizing them to do well on the posttest (and thus the "high-value" questions) to avoid an unappealing additional task. The difficulty and value manipulations were part of a larger research study and are less relevant here.

2.3   Mind Wandering Probes

Auditory probes were used to measure MW. Although misreports are possible, there is no clear alternative for tracking such a highly internal phenomena, and auditory probes are the standard and validated method for collecting online

Table 1. Incidence of mind wandering

Response Type	Yes	No	Total
End-of-page	209	651	860
Within-page	1278	2839	4117
Total	1487	3490	**4977**

MW reports [13, 23]. Nine pseudorandom pages in each text were identified as "probe pages." An auditory probe (i.e., a beep) was triggered on probe pages at a randomly chosen time interval 4 to 12 seconds from the time the page appeared. These probes were considered to be *within-page probes*. An *end-of-page probe* was triggered if the participant tried to advance to the next page before the within-page probe was triggered. Participants were instructed to indicate if they were MW or not by pressing keys marked "Yes" or "No," respectively. The instructions defined MW as consisting of having "no idea what you just read" and realizing that "you were thinking about something else altogether." Table 1 provides a summary of analyzed MW reports. The MW probabilities of 24% for end-of-page and 31% for within-page probes are similar to previous studies [19, 23].

2.4   Procedure

All procedures were approved by the ethics board of both Universities prior to any data collection. After signing an informed consent, participants were seated in front of either a Tobii TX 300 or Tobii T60 eye tracker depending on the university (both were in binocular mode). The Tobii eye trackers are remote eye trackers, so participants could read freely without any restrictions on head movement. Participants completed a brief 60-second standard calibration procedure. Participants were then instructed how to respond to the MW probes based on instructions from previous studies [9]. Next, they then read four texts for an average of 32.4 mins (SD = 9.09) on a page-by-page basis, using the space bar to navigate forward. They completed a posttest after reading all four texts and were fully debriefed.

3   Supervised Classification

3.1   Feature Engineering

Gaze fixations (points where gaze was maintained on the same location) were estimated from raw gaze data using a fixation filter from OGAMA, an open source gaze analyzer [25]. The series of gaze fixations and saccades (eye movements between fixations) were segmented into windows of varying length (4 secs, 8 secs, 12 secs), each ending with a MW probe. The windows ended immediately before the auditory probe was triggered in order to avoid confounds associated with motor activities in preparation for the key press in response to the probe. Windows that contained less than five fixations or windows that were shorter than four seconds were eliminated because these windows did not contain sufficient data to compute gaze features.

Three sets of gaze features were computed: 30 global features, 19 local features, and 12 context features, yielding 61 features overall. *Global features* were independent of the actual words being read and fell into three categories. *Fixation duration* was the length of time in milliseconds of a fixation. *Saccade duration* was the time in milliseconds between two subsequent fixations. *Saccade length* was the distance in pixels between two subsequent fixations. For each of these three categories, we computed the number of events (fixations, saccades, etc), min, max, mean, median, standard deviation, skew, kurtosis, and range, thereby yielding 27 features. Three additional global features were computed, totaling 30 global features overall. *Fixation dispersion* was the root mean square of the distances of each fixation from the average position of all fixations in the window. *Reading depth* was the ratio of the actual reading time to an expected reading time calculated by multiplying the number of words in the window by 200ms, an estimated average fixation length in milliseconds during reading [16]. The last global feature was the *fixation duration/saccade duration ratio*.

In contrast to global features, *local features* were sensitive to the words being read. The first set of local features consisted of different fixation types. *First pass fixations* were the first fixation on each word during the first pass through the text. *Regression fixations* were fixations on words that had already been passed. *Single fixations* were fixations on words that were only fixated on once. *Gaze fixations* were consecutive fixations on the same word. *Non word fixations* were fixations that were not on a word. Specific local features extracted from these different types of fixations included proportion of each fixation type compared to total number of fixations, and the mean and standard deviation of duration of each fixation type, totaling 15 local features.

Four additional local fixations pertained to the extent to which well-known relationships between characteristics of words (in each window) and gaze fixations were observed. These included correlations between fixation durations and: (a) word *length* (number of characters), (b) *hypernym depth*, which is the semantic specificity of a word (i.e. "crimson" is more specific than "red", which is more specific than "color"), (c) global *frequency* of a word, which is the overall frequency of the word in English as measured by the CELEX corpus [1], and (d) *Synset size* of a word, which was the number of synonyms of a word. The idea behind these features is that known relationships during normal reading, such as a negative correlation between word length and fixation duration, should break down during MW compared to normal reading. Taken together, this yielded 19 local features in all.

Context features captured the context of the reading task and included timing features and the difficulty and value of the text (see previous section). *Session time*, *text time*, and *page time* were the elapsed time between the MW probe and the beginning of the session, text, and page, respectively. *Session page number* and *text page number* were the number of pages read from the beginning of the session and text, respectively. *Average page time* was the average amount of time spent reading of all previous pages. *Previous page time* was the time spent reading the previous page. *Previous page time ratio* was the ratio of the previous page time to the average page time. *Current difficulty* and *current value* were the difficulty and value of the current text, respectively. *Previous difficulty* and *previous value* were the difficulty and value of the previous text, respectively. In all, there were 11 context features.

3.2   Model Building and Validation

Twenty supervised machine learning algorithms from WEKA [10] were used to build models discriminating MW (responding "Yes" to a MW probe) from normal reading (responding "No" to a MW probe). These included default WEKA implementations of: instance-based or lazy-learners (e.g., K-nearest neighbor), Bayesian probabilistic models, regression models, support vector machines, rule-based classifiers, decision trees, etc. We consider a large set of classifiers because we have no a priori prediction about the type of model that is best suited for this classification task.

Models were built from datasets with a number of varying parameters in order to identify the most accurate models as well as to explore how different factors affect classification accuracy. First, data sets included either *end-of-page or within-page* MW reports as defined above (see Data Collection section). These report types were analyzed separately because they occur at different moments during reading and might potentially be associated with different gaze characteristics.

Second, the *features* in each model were varied as each type of feature potentially captures a different aspect of gaze behaviors and we were interested in determining which feature set was most diagnostic of MW. Accordingly, models were built using global features, local features, context features, or a combination of the three.

Third, models were built either with or without *feature selection*. Feature selection was performed in order to remove the negative influence of features that convey the same information (i.e. number of fixations and number of saccades) and restrict the feature space in order to address the "curse of dimensionality" [7]. Features that were strongly correlated with other features but weakly correlated with MW reports were discarded using correlation-based feature selection (CFS) [11].

Fourth, we calculated features using four different *window lengths* to ascertain the amount of gaze data needed to predict MW. Windows that were either 4, 8, or 12 seconds before each MW probe were considered.

Fifth, we varied the *minimum number of fixations* that were required in each window before it was included in the data set. A lack of fixations could indicate gaze tracking problems, prolonged eye closure, off-screen gaze, etc. To account for this, each window was first required to have at least 5 fixations. In addition, windows were required to have a minimum of 1, 2, or 3 fixations per second.

Finally, the data was modified in five ways encompassing various combinations of *outlier treatment* and *downsampling*. The data was: unmodified (raw), trimmed, winsorized, trimmed and downsampled, or winsorized and downsampled. Outlier treatment was performed because outliers can cause model instability – especially for parametric models. Trimming consisted of removing values greater/lower than 3 standard deviations above/below the mean, while winsorization consisted of replacing those values with the corresponding value +3 or -3 standard deviations above/below the mean. Downsampling was also varied in data sets that were trimmed or winsorized as there was an uneven class distribution ("No" MW responses accounted for 70% of all responses), which can have adverse effects on classification accuracy. Instances from the most common MW response (i.e., "No" responses) were removed at random until there were an equal number of "Yes" and "No" responses in the training set. Importantly, downsampling was only applied to the training data.

A leave-several-participant-out validation method was used to ensure that data from each participant was exclusive to either the training or testing set. Data from a random 66% of the participants were placed in the training set, while data from the remaining 34% were placed in the testing set. Feature selection was done on the training set after this split, to ensure independence from the testing set. This process was repeated 20 times for each model and classification accuracy was averaged across these iterations. The kappa metric [5] was used to evaluate model performance as it corrects for random guessing when there are uneven class distributions as with the current data. The kappa metric is calculated using the formula K = (Observed Accuracy - Expected Accuracy) / (1 - Expected Accuracy), where Observed Accuracy is equivalent to recognition rate and Expected Accuracy is computed from the confusion matrix to account for the pattern of misclassifications. Kappas of 0, 1, > 0, and < 0 indicate chance, perfect, above chance, and below chance agreement, respectively.

4   Results

The parameters and results for the best (highest kappa) models for either end-of-page and within-page MW reports are listed in Table 2. Both were Bayesian models (Naive Bayes for end-of-page and Bayes Net for within-page), which suggests that these models might be suitable for this type of data and classification task.

Table 2. Results for best models. Standard deviations in parenthesis

Type of Probe	Features	Data	Win. Size(s)	Fix /S	Kappa	Acc.	Exp. Acc.
End-of-page	Global, Local, Context	Trimmed	8	0	.28 (.08)	72% (5%)	61% (5%)
Within-page	Global with CFS	Winsorized	12	3	.17 (.08)	59% (5%)	50% (3%)

Confusion matrices for each model are shown in Table 3. From this table, we note an approximately 50% chance of accurately classifying MW responses (hits) versus incorrectly classifying MW as normal reading (misses) for the end-of-page MW responses. The hits: misses ratio is higher for the within-page MW res-

Table 3. Confusion matrices for best models

Actual		Classified		Prior
		Yes	No	
End-of-page	Yes	.54 (hit)	.46 (miss)	.23
	No	.23 (FA)	.77 (CR)	.77
Within-page	Yes	.61 (hit)	.39 (miss)	.36
	No	.42 (FA)	.58 (CR)	.64

Note. Values are proportionalized and averaged over iterations.
FA = false alarm; CR = correct rejection

ponses (roughly 60% hits vs. misses). Note, however, that in both cases hit rates greatly exceed the prior probabilities of "Yes" MW responses. Correct rejections (correctly classifying normal reading or CRs) and false-alarms (incorrectly classifying normal reading as MW or FAs) for both models were in line with prior probabilities of "No" MW responses, but we note a higher proportion of CRs to FAs for end-of-page responses.

4.1 Parameter Comparison

As certain operations such as outlier treatment or downsampling increase complexity in real-time systems, we investigated the effect of each parameter on kappa values across the best performing classifier for each parameter configuration. The only parameter with a clear trend was feature type, which is shown in Figure 2. Models built with just global features outperformed models built with just local

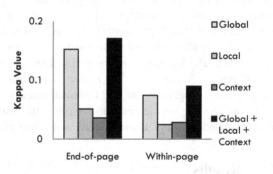

Fig. 2. Effect of feature type on kappa value

features or models built with just context features. However, models built with a combination of features resulted in a small improvement over global features alone.

4.2 Feature Selection

The 10 top ranked features for the best models are shown in Table 4. It is interesting to note that the top four features for the end-of-page model were context features. Furthermore, *maximum saccade length, mean saccade length, saccade length skew,* and *saccade length range* were among the top features for both models, indicating that saccade length is an important indicator of MW.

Table 4. Top 10 ranked features for each model

Rank	End-Of-Page	Within-Page
1	Previous Value	Maximum Saccade Length
2	Previous Difficulty	Median Saccade Length
3	Difficulty	Fixation Duration/Saccade Duration
4	Value	Saccade Length Range
5	Maximum Saccade Length	Mean Saccade Length
6	Saccade Length Range	Saccade Length Skew
7	Page Number	Median Fixation Duration
8	Saccade Length SD	Mean Fixation Duration
9	Mean Saccade Length	Mean Saccade Duration
10	Saccade Length Skew	Minimum Saccade Duration

5   General Discussion

Mind wandering (MW) is a highly frequent phenomenon that has a significant negative impact on performance. This suggests that systems that support critical tasks such as learning, vigilance, and decision making should have some mechanism for tracking and responding to wandering minds. As an initial step in this direction, the purpose of this paper was to build a system capable of automatically detecting MW using eye gaze in a manner that generalizes to new users.

Main Findings. A number of conclusions can be drawn from our results. First we have shown that it is possible to detect MW during reading by analyzing eye gaze features and aspects of the reading context. We were able to unobtrusively detect MW while reading both within a page and at the end of a page with accuracies of 59% and 72% respectively. Importantly, our user-independent validation method provides evidence that our models generalize to new users. Our work expanded on previous research by analyzing a richer eye gaze feature set that was complemented with an entire new set of context features which resulted in improved MW classification accuracy. Generalization was improved by obtaining participants from two universities with very different demographic characteristics.

Second, classification rates were much higher for end-of-page MW reports compared to within-page MW reports. One possibility is that gaze patterns are distinct within a page vs. at the end of a page, thereby resulting in different classification accuracies for the same features. Alternatively, MW itself could adopt different forms when occurring within vs. at the end of a page. Analyzing this temporal aspect could yield to a deeper scientific understanding of MW itself, which would then be leveraged towards improving MW classification accuracy.

Third, feature type had a profound effect on classification accuracy. Global features resulted in much higher classification accuracy when compared to local features, thereby suggesting that it might be more important to track overall gaze patterns (global features) rather than focusing on the specific words being read (local features). This is a significant finding because the global features are easier to compute and are more likely to generalize to different tasks beyond reading. Additionally, although context features were among the highest ranked features in the end-of-page model, context-only models performed poorly, indicating that alone they are not sufficient for proper classification. Future research is needed to understand how a global MW model built in one task context (e.g., reading) can generalize to closely related (e.g., text-diagram integration) or unrelated (e.g., watching a film) contexts.

Applications. The present findings are applicable to any user interface that contains a task involving reading comprehension of primarily textual information. MW reduces the ability to learn information from a text, so it has negative effects for any learning task involving text comprehension, which is the standard way to learn. In addition to reading, it is possible that gaze-based MW detection during a wider array of tasks and contexts could be attempted as well. Attentional state estimation has already been studied in a variety of areas, and any interface that would benefit from modeling attentional states would likely also benefit from modeling MW, which is an involuntary lapse in attention. Further research is needed to better understand the need and potential of automatic MW detection systems.

Limitations. It is important to discuss a number of limitations with our study. First, the cost of high quality eye trackers limits the scalability of eye gaze as a MW detection modality. That being said, it is possible that this will be resolved in the short term due to the steadily decreasing cost of eye tracking technology such as Eye Tribe ($99) and Tobii EyeX ($195) eye trackers, or web-cam based eye tracking [21]. Second, although the participants were more diverse than in the two previous attempts at MW detection, the sample was still restricted to data from undergraduate students collected in a lab setting. Hence, quantifying performance on a more diverse population and in more diverse settings would boost some of our claims of generalizability. Third, although self-reports of MW have been validated in a number of studies [22, 23], they rely on participants to respond accurately and honestly. However, at the current moment there is no clear alternative for tracking MW. One alternative that we are exploring involves experimentally inducing MW and tracking associated gaze-patterns. Finally, our highest accuracy of 72% can be considered to be moderate at best. However, this MW detection accuracy reflects a considerable improvement over chance, and is comparable with current user state detection systems when evaluated in a user-independent fashion [2–4]. Furthermore, MW is an internal, evasive, and noisy phenomenon, and generalizability was emphasized over accuracy by collecting naturalistic instances of MW and using a stringent validation method which guarantees independent training and testing sets. Accuracy would ostensibly be higher with models optimized for individual users.

Future Work. Future work could be focused in several areas. First, additional eye movement features could be considered. Possible features that were not included in the present study are eye blink features, pupillometry features, and temporal dynamics of gaze trajectories. Second, it is possible that easily collected individual differences such as a user's predisposition for MW or baseline measures of reading behavior could be used to improve detection rates. Third, instead of using the "probe-caught" method used in this study, a more naturalistic "self-caught" method could be employed where participants are instructed to self-monitor for MW and report whenever they do so. Finally, possible interventions to restore attention when MW is detected could be explored, including pausing the session, displaying the missed content in an alternate format, or even merely notifying the user that they were MW.

Concluding Remarks. In summary, the present study demonstrated that gaze data coupled with contextual cues can be effective in automatically detecting MW during reading. Importantly, our approach was relatively unobtrusive (remote gaze trackers are no-contact sensors), allowed for unrestricted head and body movement, involved an ecologically-valid reading activity, and used a supervised classification method that is likely to generalize to new individuals. Our results indicate that future attempts to detect MW using eye gaze data should at the very least include global features, which can be easily computed with low-cost eye tracking, though this is an empirical question that awaits further research.

Acknowledgment. This research was supported by the National Science Foundation (NSF) (ITR 0325428, HCC 0834847, DRL 1235958). Any opinions, findings and conclusions, or recommendations expressed in this paper are those of the authors and do not necessarily reflect the views of NSF.

References

1. Baayen, R.H., et al.: The CELEX Lexical Database, Release 2 [CD-ROM]. Linguistic Data Consortium, University of Pennsylvania, Philadelphia (1995)
2. Bednarik, R., et al.: What Do You Want to Do Next: A Novel Approach for Intent Prediction in Gaze-Based Interaction. In: Proceedings of the Symposium on Eye Tracking Research and Applications, pp. 83–90. ACM, New York (2012)
3. Biedert, R., et al.: A Robust Realtime Reading-Skimming Classifier. In: Proceedings of the Symposium on Eye Tracking Research and Applications, pp. 123–130. ACM, New York (2012)
4. Calvo, R.A., D'Mello, S.: Affect Detection: An Interdisciplinary Review of Models, Methods, and Their Applications. IEEE Transactions on Affective Computing 1(1), 18–37 (2010)
5. Cohen, J.: A Coefficient of Agreement for Nominal Scales. Educational and Psychological Measurement 20(1), 37–46 (1960)
6. D'Mello, S., et al.: Automatic Gaze-Based Detection of Mind Wandering During Reading. Educational Data Mining (2013)
7. Domingos, P.: A Few Useful Things to Know About Machine Learning. Communications of the ACM 55(10), 78–87 (2012)
8. Drummond, J., Litman, D.: In the Zone: Towards Detecting Student Zoning Out Using Supervised Machine Learning. In: Aleven, V., Kay, J., Mostow, J. (eds.) ITS 2010, Part II. LNCS, vol. 6095, pp. 306–308. Springer, Heidelberg (2010)
9. Feng, S., et al.: Mind Wandering While Reading Easy and Difficult Texts. Psychonomic Bulletin & Review, 1–7 (2013)
10. Hall, M., et al.: The WEKA Data Mining Software: an Update. ACM SIGKDD Explorations Newsletter 11(1), 10–18 (2009)

11. Hall, M.A.: Correlation-Based Feature Selection for Discrete and Numeric Class Machine Learning. In: Proceedings of the Seventeenth International Conference on Machine Learning, pp. 359–366 (2000)

12. Killingsworth, M.A., Gilbert, D.T.: A Wandering Mind is an Unhappy Mind. Science 330(6006), 932–932 (2010)

13. Mooneyham, B.W., Schooler, J.W.: The Costs and Benefits of Mind-Wandering: A Review. Canadian Journal of Experimental Psychology/Revue Canadienne de Psychologie Expérimentale 67(1), 11 (2013)

14. Muir, M., Conati, C.: An Analysis of Attention to Student – Adaptive Hints in an Educational Game. In: Cerri, S.A., Clancey, W.J., Papadourakis, G., Panourgia, K., et al. (eds.) ITS 2012. LNCS, vol. 7315, pp. 112–122. Springer, Heidelberg (2012)

15. Navalpakkam, V., Kumar, R., Li, L., Sivakumar, D.: Attention and Selection in Online Choice Tasks. In: Masthoff, J., Mobasher, B., Desmarais, M.C., Nkambou, R., et al. (eds.) UMAP 2012. LNCS, vol. 7379, pp. 200–211. Springer, Heidelberg (2012)

16. Rayner, K.: Eye Movements in Reading and Information Processing: 20 Years of Research. Psychological Bulletin 124(3), 372 (1998)

17. Reichle, E.D., et al.: Eye Movements During Mindless Reading. Psychological Science 21(9), 1300–1310 (2010)

18. Schooler, J.W., et al.: Meta-Awareness, Perceptual Decoupling and the Wandering Mind. Trends in Cognitive Sciences 15(7), 319–326 (2011)

19. Schooler, J.W., et al.: Zoning Out While Reading: Evidence for Dissociations Between Experience and Metaconsciousness. In: Thinking and Seeing: Visual Metacognition in Adults and Children, pp. 203–226 (2004)

20. Seibert, P.S., Ellis, H.C.: Irrelevant Thoughts, Emotional Mood States, and Cognitive Task Performance. Memory & Cognition 19(5), 507–513 (1991)

21. Sewell, W., Komogortsev, O.: Real-Time Eye Gaze Tracking with an Unmodified Commodity Webcam Employing a Neural Network. In: CHI 2010 Extended Abstracts on Human Factors in Computing Systems, pp. 3729–3744. ACM, Atlanta (2010)

22. Smallwood, J., et al.: Subjective Experience and the Attentional Lapse: Task Engagement and Disengagement During Sustained Attention. Consciousness and Cognition 13(4), 657–690 (2004)

23. Smallwood, J., et al.: When Attention Matters: The Curious Incident of the Wandering Mind. Memory & Cognition 36(6), 1144–1150 (2008)

24. Smilek, D., et al.: Out of Mind, Out of Sight Eye Blinking as Indicator and Embodiment of Mind Wandering. Psychological Science 21(6), 786–789 (2010)

25. Voßkühler, A., et al.: OGAMA (Open Gaze and Mouse Analyzer): Open-Source Software Designed to Analyze Eye and Mouse Movements in Slideshow Study Designs. Behavior Research Methods 40(4), 1150–1162 (2008)

26. Yonetani, R., et al.: Multi-mode Saliency Dynamics Model for Analyzing Gaze and Attention. In: Proceedings of the Symposium on Eye Tracking Research and Applications, pp. 115–122. ACM, New York (2012)

Hybrid Recommendation in Heterogeneous Networks

Robin Burke, Fatemeh Vahedian, and Bamshad Mobasher

Center for Web Intelligence, DePaul University, Chicago, IL 60604
{rburke,fvahedia,mobasher}@cs.depaul.edu

Abstract. The social web is characterized by a wide variety of connections between individuals and entities. A challenge for recommendation is to represent and synthesize all useful aspects of a user's profile. Typically, researchers focus on a limited set of relations (for example, person to person ties for user recommendation or annotations in social tagging recommendation).

In this paper, we present a general approach to recommendation in heterogeneous networks that can incorporate multiple relations in a weighted hybrid. A key feature of this approach is the use of the *metapath*, an abstraction of a class of paths in a network in which edges of different types are traversed in a particular order. A user profile is therefore a composite of multiple metapath relations. Compared to prior work with shorter metapaths, we show that a hybrid composed of components using longer metapaths yields improvements in recommendation diversity without loss of accuracy on social tagging datasets.

1 Introduction

The social web is characterized by a diversity of data types and relations. For example, the music-oriented website Last.fm contains information about artists, groups, songs, albums, playlists, and users, and connections can be drawn among any of these entities. There are also tags and other descriptive content. Diversity of information means that there are many kinds of recommendation that can be made to users: other users with whom to connect, artists to listen to, new songs for existing playlists, etc. At the same time, the complexity of the data means that there are many more types of information that can be integrated into user models for recommendation: should the system recommend songs from your friends' playlists or new music that your friends might not know yet? Often building recommenders for such sites involves devising individual ad-hoc user models for each recommendation problem.

To illustrate this type of recommendation, consider a user Alice who is a member of the Last.fm web site for music lovers, looking for a song to add to her current playlist:

Track	Song	Artist
1	Bad Girls	Blood Orange
2	Under the Gun	Supreme Beings of Leisure
3	The Sea	Morcheeba
4	Paris Train	Beth Orton

We might expect that a suitable song would also be mellow electronica featuring a female vocalist, but there will be a very large number of tracks with these characteristics. We might discriminate among these tracks using data from the Last.fm social network, as summarized in the schema in Figure 1.

V. Dimitrova et al. (Eds.): UMAP 2014, LNCS 8538, pp. 49–60, 2014.
© Springer International Publishing Switzerland 2014

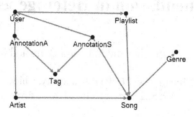

Fig. 1. Network schema for Last.fm

As the schema shows, a given song may have many possible associations. It may appear on multiple playlists; it may have been tagged by one or more users (AnnotationS); it may be associated with one or more artists (AnnotationA). We can select any of these data sources, and build a recommender system with that basis. For example, using a user-based collaborative approach we could look at similarities across playlists or across tagging histories. Any such choice inevitably excludes a great deal of possibly-relevant knowledge.

Ideally, we would like a recommendation method that is integrative – bringing all of the available data to bear. In this paper, we describe one such technique: the Weighted Hybrid of Low-Dimensional Recommenders (WHyLDR). The WHyLDR technique was originally developed for social tagging systems [14]; here we show how the concept can be extended to more complex networks.

The key insight of the WHyLDR design is that a complex network structure can be viewed as a set of two-dimensional projections from nodes of one type to nodes of another. Figure 2 illustrates this idea in the case of social tagging systems. The tagging system on the left has annotations consisting of users, tags and web resources the users have tagged. One projection (the UT projection) maps each user to the set of tags that user has applied. Another projection (UR) maps the user to the resources he or she has tagged. Other projections link resources to tags and to users: six such projections in total.

Given a two-dimensional representation, such as users represented by tags, it is quite straightforward to apply standard collaborative recommendation methodology:

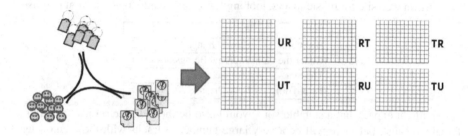

Fig. 2. Two-dimensional projections for a social tagging network

find neighborhoods of similar users and make recommendations on that basis. With a hybrid recommendation approach, it is not necessary to choose just one of these projections as the source of data: a recommendation can be made by combining the results of recommendation components built from these low-dimensional projections. Our previous work has shown that a linear weighted hybrid built of such components is more flexible and more accurate than integrative techniques such as matrix factorization that attempt to model all of the dimensions at once [14].

We extend this idea to more complex networks through the concept of the *metapath* [31]. A path in a network is a sequence of edges that can be traversed to move from one node to another. A metapath is an abstraction of a network path in a heterogeneous network into a sequence of edge types. Navigating a metapath from a node collects all destination nodes reachable by following edges of the appropriate type. For example, in the music recommendation scenario, we might have the SPU metapath $\langle song \rightarrow playlist \rightarrow user \rangle$. This path goes from a song to all playlists into which it is a part, and then to all users contributing those playlists. A different metapath would go from a song to all annotations in which it appears, to all users creating such annotations: $\langle song \rightarrow annotationS \rightarrow user \rangle$, denoted SAsU. Note that both the SPU and SAsU metapaths map songs to users, but they follow different routes through the network.

A metapath can be used to generate a two-dimension projection where each originating node is mapped to all of the terminating nodes reachable by following the path. For example, the SPU metapath can be used to generate an item-based matrix where each song is represented in terms of the users that have incorporated it into a playlist.

A metapath can be arbitrarily long, although we anticipate very long paths may not be very useful for recommendation. Metapaths may also contain multiple occurrences of the same object type. For example, the songs on the playlists of the user's friends of friends can be expressed via the UUPS metapath $\langle user \rightarrow user \rightarrow playlist \rightarrow song \rangle$. One of the key aims of this work is to investigate the value of using longer metapaths to build recommendation components.

2 Related Work

The integration of social network data into recommender systems has been studied extensively in recent years [11, 29, 30, 34]. Much of this work has been focused on system-specific solutions. For example, [20] shows a LastFM music recommender based on the combination of social data and annotations. A similar system incorporating social data and tags has been used to recommend publications in the Bibsonomy dataset [10]. In [26], Mihalkova et al. demonstrate a domain-specific approach for recommending collaborations on Wikipedia based on user-centered subgraphs. Hong et al. report on a domain-specific approach to recommending social streams in the social networking site LinkedIn [17]. In addition to click-through data, Hong's system uses features of users such as seniority of job title, as well as network-oriented features like PageRank. A more general technique is the multi-relational approach of [7] in which the heterogeneous network in Epinions is separated into multiple homogeneous networks and then an optimization approach is used to find the best combination of recommendations coming from the different networks. Kazienko and his colleagues [19] take a similar approach, treating the different kinds of relations in Flickr as "layers."

Recommendation in information networks is often equated with link prediction [3, 21]. Link prediction is the task of identifying missing, unobserved or yet-to-be-made connections in a network. For example, in our playlist example, if the system recommends a track and Alice adds it to her playlist, this will become a new $\langle playlist \rightarrow song \rangle$ link in the network. A variety of unsupervised techniques have been developed, including approaches based on graph metrics [1, 23], and random walks [18, 33]. Supervised methods for link prediction are gaining importance as well. See, for example, [24]. As discussed above, these approaches assume a homogenous network.

Our domain-independent approach for recommendation with social network data draws heavily on recent research in the area of complex heterogeneous information networks. According to Han [15], heterogeneous networks are "information systems which consist of a large number of interacting, multi-typed components". In particular, heterogeneous information networks involve multiple types of objects and multiple types of links denoting different relations [32]. Sun and Han [31] argue that information propagation across heterogeneous nodes and links can be very different from that across homogeneous nodes and links.

Some researchers have examined link prediction in heterogeneous networks. Cai et al. [6] examined link prediction in two-mode social networks with reciprocation – where a tie must to reciprocated in order to be created. Although this is a very special network type, their approach using multiple collaborative recommendation components has some similarity to the hybrid that we propose in general form here. In [8, 9], Davis et al. propose a method to predict the location and type of new edges in multi-relational networks. They build a set of homogenous projections of the network and then use supervised learning with feature extraction to build a set of individual predictors in a weighted combination. More recently, Yu and colleagues [35] have proposed a algorithm that predicts user associations with items using metapath-based user clustering.

Link prediction is obviously an important problem both for homogeneous and heterogeneous networks, with many valuable applications. However, there are a number of reasons why the conflation of link prediction with recommendation is problematic. First, link prediction is undertaken with a global view of the network. In typical link prediction experiments, links are deleted from the network (either randomly or based on time intervals) and the task is to see if these links can be predicted by an algorithm [22, 24]. Recommendation, on the other hand, is inherently personalized. A recommendation is made for a particular user, and must be generated with a user profile in mind, and judged by how well it satisfies that user's needs.

The accuracy of recommendations is certainly important, but there are other metrics that have been identified as useful for evaluating recommender systems. See [25] for a comprehensive discussion. It can be important to measure to what extent a recommender is capable of producing diverse and even surprising results [2, 36]. Also, in many applications, it is important that recommendations are transparent: that the recommendations can be explained in way that users find comprehensible [16]. These types of considerations have not yet found a place in link prediction research.

As discussed above, the work reported here is an extension of research applying linear weighted hybrids to recommendation problems in social tagging systems. Our prior work employed a collection of recommendation components including the two-dimensional projection components built as described above and used random-restart hill climbing to optimize the contribution of each component. Our results showed that it was at least as effective as other, more computationally-sophisticated techniques for the well-studied problem of tag recommendation, such as PITF [27], with the added advantages that it could be applied to a wider variety of recommendation problems and could be more easily updated. See [12–14] for more detail on this line of research.

3   Weighted Hybrid

A weighted hybrid recommender is a system comprised of multiple recommendation components, each of which returns a real-valued score for a combination of user and item. The scores from all the components are combined in a weighted sum [4]. The components needed for a hybrid recommender are a function of the recommendation task and the data available to support recommendation. In our work on social tagging systems, we identified a number of recommendation tasks appropriate to that context, including tag recommendation, resource recommendation, user recommendation, and others. Resource recommendation is the task of identifying items of interest for a user in social tagging system based on tagging behavior. Note that these items may or may not be items that the user "likes" – a user may tag disliked items with deprecatory tags, for example.

In the experiments reported in [14], the system (labeled H in our experiments) used the following recommendation components:

- Popular: A non-personalized recommender that scores resources based on their overall popularity.
- User-based kNN, user-tag matrix (kNN_{UT}): A user-based collaborative recommendation component in which users are compared by their usage of tags. The entries in this matrix are normalized counts – the fraction of annotations in which a user has employed a given tag. Pearson correlation is used to compare users and Resnick's algorithm is used to generate predictions.
- User-based kNN, user-resource matrix (kNN_{UR}): As above, but where users are compared on the basis of which resources they have tagged. The matrix is binary, reflecting whether or not the user tagged a particular resource. Predictions are computed as with kNN_{UT}.
- Item-based kNN, resource-tag matrix (kNN_{RT}): Item-based collaborative recommendation in which resources are compared on the basis of the tags that have been associated with them. This matrix is similar to kNN_{UT}, but instead of users, we are profiling resources. To make predictions, we use the adjusted cosine method from [28]. The predicted relevance of a resource is a function of the normalized tag counts of similar resources. Note that this component is not personalized: it will give the same predictions for all users.
- Item-based kNN, resource-user matrix (kNN_{RU}): Item-based collaborative recommendation in which resources are compared on the basis of the users who have tagged them. This matrix is the transpose of the UR matrix, and is also binary. Adjusted cosine is used here as well.

– Cosine: In this component, the user is represented as the vector of tags they have applied, normalized as in kNN_{UT} and each resource is represented as a vector of tags that have been applied to it as in kNN_{RT}. The scoring of a resource for a user is done by computing the cosine between the two vectors.

3.1   Metapath-Based Recommendation Components

Following Sun and Han [31], we define a heterogeneous information network as a directed graph $G = (v, \varepsilon)$ with an object type mapping function $\gamma : v \to A$ and a edge type mapping function $\phi : \varepsilon \to R$ where each object belongs to particular object type $a \in A$ and each edge belongs to a particular relation type $r \in R$. Two edges of the same type by definition share the same object types at their originating and terminating points.

A heterogeneous network is one where there are multiple object types and/or multiple edge types – typically both. For example, the music example above is clearly a hetereogeneous network. There are multiple types of nodes (artists, users, songs, etc.) and multiple types of relations (user-user, user-playlist, artist-song, etc.). A network schema, such as that shown in Figure 1, gives an overview of a heterogeneous network by indicating the different object types and the relations that exist between them. A metapath in a heterogeneous network is a path over the network schema, a sequenced composition of relations between two object types.

A social tagging system can be viewed as a heterogeneous network with four different types of nodes (users, tag, resources, and annotations). See Figure 3. With this in mind, consider the UR projection on which the kNN_{UR} component is built. This is a matrix in which the rows correspond to users and the columns correspond to resources, and the entries reflect the whether or not the user has tagged that particular resource. We can generate the same matrix using the schema shown in Figure 3 by following the metapath $\langle user \to annotation \to resource \rangle$. Since the schema has a simple star structure, we will omit the reference to the central annotation node (all navigation must go through it) and refer to this as the UR metapath.

Fig. 3. Network schema for Social Tagging Sytems

Adopting the metapath formalism allows us to express a much wider set of possible projections. We can expand the set of resources by which a user is represented by following an extended metapath: $\langle user \to annotation \to tag \to annotation \to resource \rangle$ or UTR for short. This path finds all tags a user has employed and then all annotations including those tags (even those not created by the user) and then the resources for that larger set of annotations. This can be seen as a kind of "query expansion" of the resource space by considering other users' annotations of the same resources.

Of course, this process can be extended indefinitely: UTTR, UTTTR, etc. We can envision in addition a wide variety of other metapaths: for example, UTUR would be all resources tagged by users who share tags with the target user. In our preliminary investigation found in [5], we opted to explore only a few possible components using short metapaths. These components together with the six from [14] make up the hybrid labeled H-M1 in the experiments that follow:

- User-based kNN with the user-tag matrix formed by following the URT metapath: kNN_{URT}.
- User-based kNN with the user-resource matrix formed by following the UTR metapath: kNN_{UTR}.
- A version of the Cosine metric above in which the vector of tags for a user is formed using the URT metapath: *Cosine-M*.

These components represent a one-step expansion of the UR and UT paths by incorporating the third link type. To investigate the value of using longer metapaths and of incorporating item-based approaches, we created four additional components for the hybrid H-M2. Two are additional expansions along the UR and UT dimensions, and two are item-based components analogous to kNN_{RU} and kNN_{RT} but with longer paths:

- User-based kNN with the user-tag matrix formed by following the URTRT metapath: kNN_{URTRT}.
- User-based kNN with the user-resource matrix formed by following the UTRTR metapath: kNN_{UTRTR}.
- Item-based kNN, with resource-tag matrix formed by following RUT metapath(kNN_{RUT}).
- Item-based kNN, resource-user matrix formed by following RTU metapath (kNN_{RTU}).

4   Experiments

For the experiments reported here, we used the **Bibsonomy** dataset, containing 357 users, 1.783 resources and 1,573 tags.[1] The data was filtered as described in [14] to eliminate rare and idiosyncratic tags and resources. We divided the data randomly into five partitions each having equal numbers of annotations. The first partition is used to learn the α weights for each component. The other partitions are used for cross validation: three partitions are used as training data and the fourth is used to test the system's predictions.

---

[1] We performed similar experiments on the MovieLens dataset but do not report the results here for reasons of space.

4.1 Methodology

The α values for the hybrid are learned empirically from the first data partition using random-restart hill climbing with the overall precision of the hybrid as the optimization measure. After 5,000 iterations, the weights leading to the highest recall at 10 items are then chosen for the rest of the experiment and that fold of the data is discarded.[2]

To measure the quality of recommendations, the remaining partitions are used for four-fold cross validation. For each user in the test partition, we calculate recommendation lists of size 1 through 10 and compare these results with the held-out resources tagged by that user, calculating precision and recall for each user and averaging across all users, averaging across the four folds. Then we perform weight learning with a different partition and compute another average result, continuing and averaging across all five possible choices of the first data partition.

We also evaluated the diversity of the recommendations returned. For this calculation, we perform a pairwise similarity comparison of the top 10 results. Since we are recommending resources, we can calculate similarity in two ways: using the set of users who have tagged the resource or using the set of tags that have been applied to it. In each case, we compare using cosine similarity. In the experiments below, we report results for both types of diversity. An average dissimilarity between all pairs of items recommended to a user can be calculated as: $K \sum_{i_k \in R, l < k} d(i_k, i_l)$, where $d(i_k, i_l)$ refers to distance or dissimilarity between two distinct items in a recommendation list and K is a normalization constant based on the list size. This metric is calculated for each recommendation list for each user and averaged across all users.

4.2 Results

Figure 4 shows precision versus recall curves for three weighted hybrids and their sub-components. The dashed line with square marks represents the original hybrid without extended meta-paths. The solid line with circular marks shows the results for the H-M1 hybrid; the H-M2 hybrid is also solid with asterisk marks. As we can see, the extended hybrid H-M2 has comparable or slightly poorer performance than the H-M1 version, and both improve on the original six component hybrid H, especially for shorter recommendation lists.

The figure also shows the performance of each component of the hybrids separately, omitting the non-personalized popularity-based component that has very poor performance on this data. The components of the original H hybrid also have dashed lines with square marks. The components of the H-M1 hybrid have circular marks; and the two extended components are far in the bottom left with asterisks. Each component is color-coded (and organized in the legend) by the two dimensions of the data that is associates. For example, kNN_{UR}, kNN_{UTR} and kNN_{UTRTR} are all user-based components that associate users with resources, using successively longer metapaths to do so.

Interestingly, if we rank the components by their dominance across the precision-recall space, we find that the extended components have exactly the opposite rank as the

---

[2] We are currently experimenting with particle swarm optimization algorithm as a more efficient optimization approach.

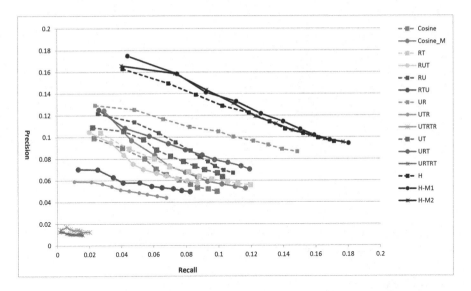

Fig. 4. Precision vs Recall for Bibsonomy Dataset

ones from the original hybrid. For example, kNN_{UR} is the best single step component for this task (not surprising because we are recommending resources to users), but kNN_{UTR} is the worst of the two-step components.

In the middle of the pack, there are the cosine and user-tag measures. Here the extended component actually has better precision-recall performance than the one based on shorter paths. We explain this phenomenon by considering the way that Bibsonomy data is generated. Users of the Bibsonomy system tend to tag articles with descriptive tags related to their reseach area. So, an article on population biology might be tagged by one user with labels having to do with its methodology and another user having to do with the specific species studied. In this scenario, it makes sense that a user's profile based on tags they have provided might not match a relevant article's tags because those tags might be have supplied by users with a different set of interests. However, the extended metapath creates a user profile based on all the tags that any user has given to the articles the user has tagged. There is a crowd-sourcing effect here so that the resources are better described by the union of all of their tags and personalization comes in the selection of resources rather than in the selection of tags. This pattern was also found in the MovieLens dataset, but we expect that other datasets with noisier tagging behavior might not exhibit it.

The diversity results are shown in Figure 5. These results are mixed and deserve greater exploration, but the key finding here is shown in the final set of results for tag-based diversity using the H-M2 hybrid. Tag diversity is probably what most users would understand as diversity: items that differ in terms of their content. So, the H-M2 hybrid is finding results of greater diversity with comparable precision and recall compared to the other hybrids. The user diversity measure provides some interesting clues about how this is achieved. User diversity goes down, suggesting that the H-M2 hybrid is

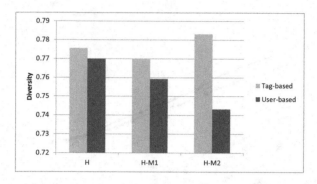

Fig. 5. Diversity Results for Bibsonomy Dataset

successful in finding the subgroup of peers whose research is of interest, even though they may not all describe that work using exactly the same tags.

5 Conclusions

One of the key challenges in social web recommendation is the effective integration of the many dimensions of the available data about users. In this paper, we describe a linear-weighted hybrid approach that generalizes our prior work on social tagging systems to a larger space of heterogeneous networks. In this paper, we have shown that our metapath-based approach to recommendation in heterogeneous networks yields improvements in both accuracy and diversity in these social tagging systems. We expand on the work reported in [5] to show that hybrids with extended components achieve greater diversity without sacrificing accuracy. We view this as a proof of concept suggesting that our technique will be effective in the more general class of heterogeneous information networks.

There are a number of intriguing results. First is that there are a number of non-obvious tradeoffs in creating larger hybrids from extended network metapaths. Greater diversity would be expected, but our results show that in the Bibsonomy dataset at least, tag-based diversity goes down and then up again as more extended paths are considered. Second is that, at least in some cases, components built from longer metapaths actually perform better than the corresponding component with a shorter path: the cosine component being the example in Bibsonomy. Predictive power is therefore not a simple decreasing function of the length of the path and there are domain- and data-specific factors at play.

One important question is whether the hybrid weights can be predicted or at least estimated from the characteristics of the data. This issue takes on greater urgency when we consider the fact that the set of metapath-based components is unbounded – it is always possible to consider more friends of friends, for example. We are experimenting with entropy-based measures of the contribution of each component, with the aim of finding a metric with which to discriminate between components and filter out those unlikely to be useful, prior to the weight learning step. Limiting the number of components is key to making weight learning efficient. In addition, a weight estimator might be useful for providing an initial seed for the hill-climbing step.

References

1. Adamic, L., Adar, E.: Friends and neighbors on the web. Social Networks 25(3), 211–230 (2003)
2. Adomavicius, G., Kwon, Y.: Improving aggregate recommendation diversity using ranking-based techniques. IEEE Transactions on Knowledge and Data Engineering 24(5), 896–911 (2012)
3. Benchettara, N., Kanawati, R., Rouveirol, C.: A supervised machine learning link prediction approach for academic collaboration recommendation. In: Proceedings of the fourth ACM Conference on Recommender Systems, pp. 253–256. ACM (2010)
4. Burke, R.: Hybrid recommender systems: Survey and experiments. User Modeling and User-Adapted Interaction 12(4), 331–370 (2002)
5. Burke, R., Vahedian, F.: Social web recommendation using metapaths. In: Proceedings of the Fifth ACM RecSys Workshop on Recommender Systems and the Social Web. ACM Press (2013)
6. Cai, X., Bain, M., Krzywicki, A., Wobcke, W., Kim, Y.S., Compton, P., Mahidadia, A.: Reciprocal and heterogeneous link prediction in social networks. In: Tan, P.-N., Chawla, S., Ho, C.K., Bailey, J. (eds.) PAKDD 2012, Part II. LNCS, vol. 7302, pp. 193–204. Springer, Heidelberg (2012)
7. Chen, J., Chen, G., Zhang, H.L., Huang, J., Zhao, G.: Social recommendation based on multi-relational analysis. In: International Conference on Web Intelligence and Intelligent Agent Technology, pp. 471–477 (2012)
8. Davis, D.A., Lichtenwalter, R., Chawla, N.V.: Multi-relational link prediction in heterogeneous information networks. In: ASONAM, pp. 281–288 (2011)
9. Davis, D.A., Lichtenwalter, R., Chawla, N.V.: Supervised methods for multi-relational link prediction. Social Netw. Analys. Mining 3(2), 127–141 (2013)
10. Doerfel, S., Jäschke, R., Hotho, A., Stumme, G.: Leveraging publication metadata and social data into folkrank for scientific publication recommendation. In: Proceedings of the 4th ACM RecSys Workshop on Recommender Systems and the Social Web, RSWeb 2012, pp. 9–16. ACM, New York (2012)
11. Durão, F.A., Dolog, P.: A personalized tag-based recommendation in social web systems. In: Proceedings of International Workshop on Adaptation and Personalization for Web 2.0 (2009)
12. Gemmell, J., Ramezani, M., Schimoler, T., Christiansen, L., Mobasher, B.: A fast effective multi-channeled tag recommender. In: European Conference on Machine Learning and Principles and Practice of Knowledge Discovery in Databases Discovery Challenge, Bled, Slovenia, pp. 59–63 (2009)
13. Gemmell, J., Schimoler, T., Mobasher, B., Burke, R.: Hybrid tag recommendation for social annotation systems. In: 19th ACM International Conference on Information and Knowledge Management, Toronto, Canada, pp. 829–838 (2010)
14. Gemmell, J., Schimoler, T., Mobasher, B., Burke, R.: Resource recommendation in social annotation systems: A linear-weighted hybrid approach. Journal of Computer and System Sciences 78(4), 1160–1174 (2012)
15. Han, J.: Mining heterogeneous information networks by exploring the power of links. In: Gama, J., Costa, V.S., Jorge, A.M., Brazdil, P.B. (eds.) DS 2009. LNCS, vol. 5808, pp. 13–30. Springer, Heidelberg (2009)
16. Herlocker, J., Konstan, J., Riedl, J.: Explaining collaborative filtering recommendations. In: Proceedings of the 2000 ACM Conference on Computer Supported Cooperative Work, pp. 241–250. ACM (2000)

17. Hong, L., Bekkerman, R., Adler, J., Davison, B.D.: Learning to rank social update streams. In: SIGIR, pp. 651–660 (2012)
18. Jeh, G., Widom, J.: Scaling personalized web search. In: WWW, pp. 271–279 (2003)
19. Kazienko, P., Musial, K., Kajdanowicz, T.: Multidimensional social network in the social recommender system. IEEE Transactions on Systems, Man and Cybernetics, Part A: Systems and Humans 41(4), 746–759 (2011)
20. Konstas, I., Stathopoulos, V., Jose, J.M.: On social networks and collaborative recommendation. In: Proceedings of the 32nd International ACM SIGIR Conference on Research and Development in Information Retrieval, SIGIR 2009, pp. 195–202. ACM, New York (2009)
21. Kunegis, J., Lommatzsch, A.: Learning spectral graph transformations for link prediction. In: Proceedings of the 26th Annual International Conference on Machine Learning, ICML 2009, pp. 561–568. ACM, New York (2009)
22. Liben-Nowell, D., Kleinberg, J.: The link-prediction problem for social networks. Journal of the American Society for Information Science and Technology 58(7), 1019–1031 (2007)
23. Liben-Nowell, D., Kleinberg, J.M.: The link prediction problem for social networks. In: 12th ACM International Conference on Information and Knowledge Management, pp. 556–559 (2003)
24. Lichtenwalter, R., Lussier, J.T., Chawla, N.V.: New perspectives and methods in link prediction. In: KDD, pp. 243–252 (2010)
25. McNee, S.: Meeting user information needs in recommender systems. PhD thesis, University of Minnesota (2006)
26. Mihalkova, L., Moustafa, W.E., Getoor, L.: Learning to predict web collaborations. In: WSDM Workshop on User Modeling for Web Applications (2011)
27. Rendle, S., Schmidt-Thieme, L.: Pairwise Interaction Tensor Factorization for Personalized Tag Recommendation. In: Proceedings of the Third ACM International Conference on Web Search and Data Mining, New York (2010)
28. Sarwar, B., Karypis, G., Konstan, J., Reidl, J.: Item-Based Collaborative Filtering Recommendation Algorithms. In: 10th International Conference on World Wide Web, Hong Kong, China (2001)
29. Siersdorfer, S., Sizov, S.: Social recommender systems for web 2.0 folksonomies. In: Hypertext, pp. 261–270 (2009)
30. Song, Y., Zhang, L., Giles, C.L.: Automatic tag recommendation algorithms for social recommender systems. ACM Transactions on the Web 5(1), 4 (2011)
31. Sun, Y., Han, J.: Mining Heterogeneous Information Networks: Principles and Methodologies. Synthesis Lectures on Data Mining and Knowledge Discovery. Morgan & Claypool Publishers (2012)
32. Sun, Y., Han, J., Yan, X., Yu, P.S., Wu, T.: Pathsim: Meta path-based top-k similarity search in heterogeneous information networks. In: Proceedings of the 37th International Conference on Very Large Databases, pp. 992–1003 (2011)
33. Tong, H., Faloutsos, C., Pan, J.-Y.: Fast random walk with restart and its applications. In: ICDM, pp. 613–622 (2006)
34. Yu, S.J.: The dynamic competitive recommendation algorithm in social network services. Inf. Sci. 187, 1–14 (2012)
35. Yu, X., Ren, X., Sun, Y., Gu, Q., Sturt, B., Khandelwal, U., Norick, B., Han, J.: Personalized entity recommendation: a heterogeneous information network approach. In: WSDM, pp. 283–292 (2014)
36. Zhang, M., Hurley, N.: Avoiding monotony: improving the diversity of recommendation lists. In: Proceedings of the 2008 ACM Conference on Recommender Systems, pp. 123–130. ACM (2008)

Recommendation Based on Contextual Opinions

Guanliang Chen and Li Chen

Department of Computer Science, Hong Kong Baptist University,
Hong Kong, China
{glchen,lichen}@comp.hkbu.edu.hk

Abstract. Context has been recognized as an important factor in constructing personalized recommender systems. However, most context-aware recommendation techniques mainly aim at exploiting item-level contextual information for modeling users' preferences, while few works attempt to detect more fine-grained aspect-level contextual preferences. Therefore, in this article, we propose a contextual recommendation algorithm based on user-generated reviews, from where users' context-dependent preferences are inferred through different contextual weighting strategies. The context-dependent preferences are further combined with users' context-independent preferences for performing recommendation. The empirical results on two real-life datasets demonstrate that our method is capable of capturing users' contextual preferences and achieving better recommendation accuracy than the related works.

Keywords: Context-aware recommender systems, user-generated reviews, aspect-level context, opinion mining, context-dependent preferences.

1 Introduction

It has been well recognized that context-aware recommender systems are able to outperform traditional recommenders because users' preferences can be depicted more accurately by capitalizing on contextual information [1]. Take one typical approach, *pre-filtering*[2], as an example, when estimating the rating of a user for an item, the recommender considers other users' data acquired in the same contextual situation of the target user given that they might be more valuable for capturing the user's contextual needs. However, the main limitation of existing context-aware techniques is that the preference modeling is purely at the item level. That is, the contextual preference is mainly related to the overall evaluation of an item, rather than to multiple aspects of the item (e.g., "food", "atmosphere", and "service" of the restaurant).

Although recent years some works have attempted to model users' preferences at the aspect level and employ multi-faceted preference profiles for product recommendation [3], movie recommendation [4, 5, 6], hotel recommendation [7], or restaurant recommendation [8], these works neglect the fact that such aspect-level preferences can be likely influenced by context. Consider a restaurant review from *Yelp* that is shown in Example 1.

V. Dimitrova et al. (Eds.): UMAP 2014, LNCS 8538, pp. 61–73, 2014.

Example 1. *I went to this place with my colleagues. The comfortable atmosphere here was perfect for business conversation. We ordered the salad and pizza, which were delicious. After I ate here, I decided to go back with my family because of the excellent food, even though the dining atmosphere here is not suitable for a family-gathering meal.*

In the above review, it can be seen that the aspect "atmosphere" is of more importance when the user is *having meals with colleagues*, while the aspect "food" is more of a concern when the user is *accompanied by family*. Thus, in our view, the aspect-level preferences can be context-sensitive. In other words, people may possess different aspect-level preferences in different contexts. We are hence interested in detecting such aspect-level contextual opinions particularly from user-generated reviews so as to more precisely model their preferences.

In our work, we emphasize two kinds of user preferences: *context-dependent* and *context-independent*. Specifically, the context-dependent preferences refer to the aspect-level contextual needs that are common to users who are under the same context; while the context-independent preferences are relatively less sensitive to contextual changes and reflect more stable requirements for an item's aspects over time. To derive the context-dependent preferences, we propose three variations of contextual weighting methods based on different text feature selection strategies: mutual information, information gain, and Chi-square statistic. They all focus on modeling the context-dependent preferences at the aspect level by analyzing the relation between the aspect frequency and context. The context-independent preferences, on the other hand, are also learned from reviews, but without considering the contextual influence. Our recommendation algorithm takes both kinds of preferences into account, which is empirically demonstrated superior to the state-of-the-art in terms of recommendation accuracy.

The following content is organized as follows. Section 2 briefly summarizes existing researches related to our work. Section 3 gives our research problem and methodology. Section 4 presents the experimental results on two real-life datasets. We draw the conclusion and indicate the future work in Section 5.

2   Related Work

Our work is mainly related to two branches of researches: context-aware recommenders and review-based recommenders.

Related Work on Context-Aware Recommenders. Existing context-aware techniques can be classified into three categories [1]: 1) *contextual pre-filtering*, by which data are first filtered according to contextual relationship before the classical recommendation approach (such as collaborative filtering) is applied [2, 9]; 2) *contextual post-filtering*, which adopts the contextual information to distill the recommendation results after the classical approach was applied [9]; 3) *contextual modeling*, which incorporates the context into the machine learning model (e.g., Tensor Factorization) for recommendation [10]. These works have been proven effective and successful in some applications like movie recommendation.

However, in reality, datasets that contain both ratings and the user-specified contexts rarely exist [11].

Compared to these works, the novelty of our work lies in that we utilize widely available reviews to establish the relation between aspect-level opinions and contextual factors for modeling users' preferences.

Related Work on Review-Based Recommenders. Review-based recommenders mainly rely on advanced opinion mining techniques to infer the reviewers' overall opinion (called virtual rating [12]) or even multi-aspect ratings, which are then leveraged into the standard recommenders [3, 5]. For instance, [8] developed a multi-label text classifier based on Support Vector Machine to reveal users' aspect-level evaluations of restaurants and generate recommendation through regression-based and clustering-based algorithms. In [3], the reviews are used to model users' multi-aspect preferences for computing user-user similarity during recommendation. Rather than using heuristic-based algorithms, some works turn to model-based approaches, such as Multi-Relational Matrix Factorization [5] or Tensor Factorization [4], for capitalizing on multi-aspect ratings as derived from reviews to augment recommendation. However, these works did not consider the contextual information that might also be extracted from reviews to derive the relation between aspects and contexts. To our knowledge, two works have endeavored to fill in this gap. [13] constructed the aspect-context relations via manual efforts and then combined them with user-specified preferences to generate recommendation, but it did not identify the contextual influences on users' aspect-level preferences. [14] created aspect-context relations by relating aspect-level opinions expressed in reviews with user-specified contexts, but it is still limited since the opinions on the same aspect in different contexts were not captured.

Compared to these works, our contribution rests in proposing an automatic review-based aspect-context relation detection method and carrying out in-depth research for revealing the impact of contextual factors on building users' aspect-level preferences.

3   Problem Statement and Methodology

As mentioned before, we mainly aim at addressing two problems: 1) *How to correlate aspect-level opinions with contextual factors and derive users' context-dependent preferences from their reviews?* 2) *How to leverage both context-dependent and context-independent preferences into computing the recommendation list?*

We summarize our solution in Figure 1. We first implement an automatic method to conduct contextual review analysis for mining contextual opinion tuples. Contextual opinion tuples refer to users' aspect-level evaluations of items under certain contexts, formally denoted as $\{\langle i, rev_{u,i}, a_k, Con_{i,k}\rangle \mid 1 \leq k \leq K\}$ (i.e., the user u's opinion a_k on the aspect k of item i under contexts $Con_{i,k}$ expressed in the review $rev_{u,i}$), where K denotes the number of aspects, and $Con_{i,k}$ is a vector whose element value equals 1 when the associated context

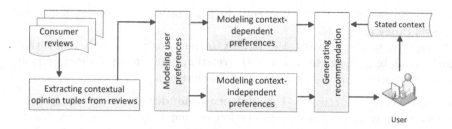

Fig. 1. Contextual preferences' detection and recommendation based on aspect-level review analysis

occurs and 0 otherwise. Then, we delve into detecting two types of user preferences. For context-independent preferences, we adopt the linear least-square regression method and the statistical t-test to attain users' weights (i.e., relative importance) laid on different aspects, and regard these weights as users' context-independent preferences. For context-dependent preferences, we propose three alternative contextual weighting methods to capture users' preference changes in different contexts. The three weighting methods are respectively based on three different text feature selection strategies: mutual information, information gain, and Chi-square statistic. Then, the context-independent and context-dependent preferences are combined via the multiplication approach for generating recommendation to the target user.

3.1 Extracting Contextual Opinion Tuples from Consumer Reviews

As described in Figure 1, the first step focuses on extracting contextual opinion tuples from reviews. Inspired by our previous work on aspect-level opinion mining [3] and related ones on context extraction [15, 11], we propose a synthetic method to perform contextual review analysis for extracting contextual opinion tuples. It mainly consists of four sub-steps:

1) **Aspect Identification.** In reviews, different terms are often used to refer to the same aspect of item. For example, terms "value", "price", "money" are all related to the aspect *Value* of restaurant. The task of aspect identification is thus to identify the relevant terms for each aspect. To this end, we adopt the bootstrapping method proposed in [16], by which each aspect is first equipped with a set of manually-selected keywords, and the other related terms are searched out through measuring the dependency between the aspect and the candidate terms based on Chi-square statistic [17]. Because the datasets collected for our experiments are about restaurants, we define five major aspects: *Value, Food, Atmosphere, Service,* and *Location*. Notice that only frequently occurring nouns and noun phrases, which are extracted by using a Part-of-Speech (POS) tagger[1], are considered as the prospective term candidates.

2) **Opinion Detection.** To determine users' opinions associated with each aspect-related term, we regard adjective words as opinion carriers. The adjectives

---

[1] http://nlp.stanford.edu/software/tagger.shtml

in the review are also extracted through the POS tagger and their sentiment polarity is determined with an opinion lexicon [18]. We summarize all of the opinions expressed in one sentence using a distance-based score: $score\,(s, f) = \sum_{op \in s} sent_{op} \, / \, d\,(op, f)$, where f denotes the aspect-related term that appears in sentence s, op denotes an opinion word in sentence s, $sent_{op}$ denotes its sentiment score (1 for positive and -1 for negative), and $d\,(f, op)$ denotes the distance from op to f.

3) Context Extraction. Before uncovering the aspect-context relation from reviews, we first employ a keyword matching method to extract contexts. Suppose that there are three contextual variables in restaurant reviews, including *Time*, *Occasion*, and *Companion*. Each contextual variable can be assigned with different values. For example, the values of *Companion* are "family", "friends", "colleague", "couple", and "solo". Moreover, each contextual value can be defined by a set of manually-selected keywords. For instance, the keywords related to contextual value "colleague" are {colleague, business, coworker, boss, etc.}. Therefore, once any of the keywords appear in a review sentence, the sentence will be tagged with the corresponding contextual value.

4) Aspect-Context Relation Construction. The next question is then how to relate the review's contextual values to its corresponding aspects, for which we propose to automatically construct the aspect-context relation based on the following rules: a) if both aspect-level opinion and context occur in the same sentence, they will be related; b) if a sentence only contains aspect-level opinion without mentioning context, the opinion will be related to contextual values that occur in the previous, nearest sentence. Notice that the user's opinion on the same aspect under different contexts could be different (such as the opinion on aspect "atmosphere" in Example 1). Thus, when constructing contextual opinion tuples, we sum up only the opinions pertinent to the aspect in the same context. In other words, the opinion a_k in tuple $\langle i, rev_{u,i}, a_k, Con_{i,k} \rangle$ is the aggregation of opinion scores of aspect-related terms that are under the same context $Con_{i,k}$. By applying our construction method, an aspect might be assigned with different opinion tuples in different contexts. For instance, the review presented in Example 1 can be extracted with tuples like $\langle i, rev_{u,i}, a_{\text{atmosphere}} = 1, Con_{i,\text{atmosphere}} = \text{"colleague"}\rangle$ and $\langle i, rev_{u,i}, a_{\text{atmosphere}} = -1, Con_{i,\text{atmosphere}} = \text{"family"}\rangle$ [2]. In this way, we expect that the user's preferences could be more precisely depicted.

3.2   Detecting Context-Independent Preferences

The context-independent preferences reflect the individual user's consistent aspect-level requirements for items. To detect such preferences, we adopt the linear least-square regression function with the statistical t-test to analyze the user's history data. To be specific, with aspect-level opinions obtained in Section 3.1, each review written by the user can be represented as a rating vector $\langle a_1, \ldots, a_K \rangle$ on the set of K aspects without considering their relations with

---

[2] To ease understanding, we use the context's value in the example, but it should be formally represented as a boolean vector.

contextual factors. All the rating vectors (corresponding to the set of reviews written by the user) can then be used to construct the linear least-square regression function, formally denoted as: $r_0 = \sum_{k=1}^{K} w_{u,k} \cdot a_k + \varepsilon$, in which the the overall rating r_0 is determined by the underlying interaction among multi-aspect ratings, ε denotes the error term, and $\langle w_{u,1}, \ldots, w_{u,K} \rangle$ denotes the user's weights laid on different aspects. Then, we apply the t-test to select weights that pass the significance level (e.g., $p < 0.1$) and regard these weights as the user's context-independent preferences.

3.3 Detecting Context-Dependent Preferences

The basic assumption behind our approach is that all the reviews written under the same context should be taken into account to capture the users' aspect-level context-dependent preferences. Therefore, we propose three variations of contextual weighting methods for assigning weights to aspects in different contexts and utilize these contextual weights to represent users' context-dependent preferences.

An intuitive method is to assign weights to aspects by analyzing the relation between the aspect's occurring frequency and the context. That is, the more frequently the aspect-related terms appear in the sentences of a specific context, the more important the aspect is to that context so it should receive higher weight. Hence, we first calculate the occurring frequency of aspect k under context c:

$$freq_{k,c} = \frac{\sum_{rev \in R} \sum_{s \in rev} \Delta_{s,c} \cdot \left(\sum_{f \in s} \Theta_{f,k} \right)}{\sum_{rev \in R} \sum_{s \in rev} \Delta_{s,c} \cdot \left(\sum_{f \in s} 1 \right)} \tag{1}$$

where f, s, and rev respectively represent an aspect-related term, a sentence, and a review, R denotes the set of all reviews, $\Delta_{s,c}$ denotes an indicator function whose value equals 1 if the sentence s is related to context c and 0 otherwise, and $\Theta_{f,k}$ denotes another indicator function whose value equals 1 if the term f is related to aspect k and 0 otherwise. In fact, Equation 1 computes the aspect frequency as the relative number of occurrences of its related terms in sentences related to context c. The aspect frequencies regarding different context values are used to compute the aspect's average frequency $avg_k = \sum_{c \in C} freq_{k,c} / |C|$ and standard deviation $stdv_k = \sqrt{\sum_{c \in C} \left(freq_{k,c} - avg_k \right)^2 / |C|}$ (where C denotes the set of context values), and we define $dev_{k,c} = freq_{k,c} - avg_k$. Then, we adopt the strategy proposed in [14] as our basis to compute the weight of aspect k regarding context value c:

$$w_{k,c} = \begin{cases} 1, & \text{if } |dev_{k,c}| < stdv_k \\ Max\left(0.1, 1/\left|\frac{dev_{k,c}}{stdv_k}\right|\right), & \text{if } \frac{dev_{k,c}}{stdv_k} <= -1 \\ Min\left(3, \frac{dev_{k,c}}{stdv_k}\right), & \text{else} \end{cases} \tag{2}$$

The above strategy mainly searches for important aspects based on the frequency identification. However, this method is limited in that it does not consider the importance of the aspect-related term in different contexts. For instance, the term *ambiance* may be important in both contexts: dining *as a couple* and *with colleagues*, but it might be more important to users in the first context than in the second one. To account for this, we propose to extend the above method by taking into account the term's weight. Particularly, as inspired by the research of Text Categorization in terms of how it selects representative features (i.e., words or terms) for categorizing documents, we propose three feature selection methods for identifying the context-dependent weights of aspect-related terms and compare their effectiveness in the experiment. The three methods include *Mutual Information, Information Gain,* and *Chi-Square Statistic,* which are detailed as follows.

Mutual Information. In information theory, mutual information is used to measure the mutual dependence between two random variables [17]. For our task, the two random variables can be *aspect-related term* and *context.* Given a term f and a context value c, the mutual information between them is defined as:

$$MI\left(f,c\right) = log\frac{p\left(f \wedge c\right)}{p\left(f\right) \cdot p\left(c\right)} \tag{3}$$

where $p\left(f\right)$ denotes the probability of f appearing in sentences, $p\left(c\right)$ denotes the probability of sentences that are associated with context c, and $p\left(f \wedge c\right)$ denotes the probability that f appears in sentences that are related to context c.

Information Gain. Information gain has been frequently employed in text categorization for measuring the number of bits of information obtained for categorizing documents by knowing the presence or absence of a word in a document [17]. We can hence apply this metric to measure the importance of an aspect-related term to a specific context. We concretely implement it as a binary classification model in which each sentence is classified into two categories, *related to* context c *or not:* $\mathcal{O} = \{c_{presence}, c_{absence}\}$. The information gain is then calculated as:

$$
\begin{aligned}
IG\left(f,c\right) = &- \sum_{c \in \mathcal{O}} p\left(c\right) \cdot log\, p\left(c\right) \\
&+ p\left(f\right) \sum_{c \in \mathcal{O}} p\left(c \mid f\right) log\, p\left(c \mid f\right) + p\left(\bar{f}\right) \sum_{c \in \mathcal{O}} p\left(c \mid \bar{f}\right) log\, p\left(c \mid \bar{f}\right)
\end{aligned}
\tag{4}
$$

where $\bar{f}$ denotes the absence of f in a sentence, and $p\left(c \mid f\right)$ denotes the probability that sentences containing f are related to context c.

Chi-Square Statistic. Based on Chi-square statistic, we can measure the lack of independence between an aspect-related term f and context c by computing the variance between the sample distribution and chi-square distribution [17]. The Chi-square statistic is formally defined as:

$$CHI\left(f,c\right) = \frac{D \times \left(D_1 D_4 - D_2 D_3\right)^2}{\left(D_1 + D_3\right) \times \left(D_2 + D_4\right) \times \left(D_1 + D_2\right) \times \left(D_3 + D_4\right)} \tag{5}$$

where D_1 is the number of times that f occurs in sentences related to context c, D_2 is the number of times that f occurs in sentences not related to c, D_3 is the number of sentences in context c that do not contain f, D_4 is the number of sentences that are neither related to context c nor containing f, and D is the number of times that all terms occur in sentences related to context c.

After obtaining the weights of the aspect-related terms via either of the three above-described methods, we further incorporate them into calculating the user's contextual weights placed on different aspects. Equation 1 is modified as follows:

$$freq_{k,c} = \frac{\sum_{rev \in R} \sum_{s \in rev} \Delta_{s,c} \cdot \left(\sum_{f \in s} \Theta_{f,k} \cdot MI\left(f,c\right) \right)}{\sum_{rev \in R} \sum_{s \in rev} \Delta_{s,c} \cdot \left(\sum_{f \in s} MI\left(f,c\right) \right)} \tag{6}$$

where $MI\left(f,c\right)$ is via Equation 3, which can be replaced with $IG\left(f,c\right)$ (Equation 4) or $CHI\left(f,c\right)$ (Equation 5). The results can then be applied in Equation 2 to determine the aspect's weight in a certain context.

3.4   Generating Recommendation

As stated before, users' behavior can be influenced by both context-independent preferences and context-dependent preferences. We hence combine both to compute a score of review $rev_{v,i}$ (wrote by user v for item i) for target user u:

$$score\left(u, rev_{v,i}, T\right) = \sum_{\langle i, rev_{v,i}, a_k, Con_{i,k} \rangle \in S(rev_{v,i})} \prod_{c \in T} \left(1 + \alpha \cdot w_{k,c}\right) \cdot w_{u,k} \cdot a_k \cdot g\left(Con_u, Con_{i,k}\right) \tag{7}$$

where $w_{k,c}$ is the context-dependent preference for aspect k under context c (derived via either of the three proposed variations of contextual weighting method in Section 3.3), $w_{u,k}$ is the target user's context-independent preference placed on aspect k (Section 3.2), α is a parameter used to control the relative contributions of context-independent and context-dependent preferences in computing the review's score, a_k is aspect k's score contained in contextual opinion tuple $\langle i, rev_{v,i}, a_k, Con_{i,k} \rangle$, $S\left(rev_{v,i}\right)$ is the set of contextual opinion tuples derived from $rev_{v,i}$, T is the set of contexts specified by the target user, Con_u denotes the vector form of T, and the function $g\left(Con_u, Con_{i,k}\right)$ is defined as:

$$g\left(Con_u, Con_{i,k}\right) = \begin{cases} 1, & \text{if } Con_u \cdot Con_{i,k} \neq 0 \\ 0, & \text{else} \end{cases} \tag{8}$$

Equation 8 ensures that only the aspect-level opinions pertinent to the target user's specified contexts are taken into account. The score of item i for user u is then finally calculated by averaging the scores of all of its reviews:

$$score\left(u, i\right) = avg_{rev_{v,i} \in R(i)} \left[score\left(u, rev_{v,i}, T\right)\right] \tag{9}$$

where $R\left(i\right)$ denotes the set of reviews for item i. The top-N items with highest scores are then retrieved and recommended to the target user. In the experiment, we set $N = 5, 10, 15$.

4   Experiment

4.1   Dataset and Evaluation Metrics

To conduct the experiment, we adopt two real-life restaurant datasets: one was crawled from TripAdvisor, and the other was from Yelp as published by the RecSys'13 challenge[3]. Table 1 shows their basic descriptions.

As for evaluation procedure, we adopt the per-user evaluation schema as commonly used in [19, 20]. That is, for each user, we randomly select three ratings which are above 4 (i.e., "like" the item), as well as the accompanying reviews (which are used to simulate the target user's contexts), that s/he provided to items as testing data while the others serve as training data. We then apply two metrics to measure the recommendation accuracy: 1) Hit ratio @ top-N recommendations (H@N), which measures the percentage of successes: H@N $= \sum_{t=1}^{T} \delta_{rank_t \leq N}/T$, where T is the number of testings, $rank_t$ is the ranking position of the user's choice (i.e., the item with high rating) in the t-th testing, and $\delta_{rank_t \leq N}$ is an indicator function that equals 1 if $rank_t \leq N$ (i.e., the recommendation list contains the choice), or 0 otherwise. 2) Mean reciprocal rank (MRR), which evaluates the ranking position of the target user's choice in the recommendation list: $MRR = \sum_{t=1}^{T} \frac{\delta_{rank_t \leq N}}{rank_t}/T$. Notice that, the target user's context for an item is simulated by performing the context extraction to the accompanying review in the testing data, and the parameter α is determined empirically through experimental trials. In addition, all of the reported results are the averages of per-user evaluations and the Student t-test is applied to compute the statistical significance of the difference between the compared methods.

Table 1. Dataset description

Dataset	#reviews	#users	#items	Sparsity	%reviews with contextual opinions
TripAdvisor	121932	6203	15315	99.87%	49.2%
Yelp	125286	3969	10581	99.70%	57.3%

4.2   Compared Methods

For the experiment, the following related methods were implemented to be compared with our proposed approaches MI/IG/CHI Connecter:

☐ **Context Freer.** This method adopts the regression-based method proposed in [6] to take into account the multi-aspect ratings derived from reviews. In fact, this method implements a simplified version of Equation 7, which does not consider the context-dependent preferences. We select this context-free method as our baseline and denote it as *Freer*.

---

[3] http://recsys.acm.org/recsys13/recsys-2013-challenge/

☐ **Context Pre-filter.** In accordance with [2], the extracted contextual information can be utilized at the item level, i.e., pre-filtering data according to contexts before applying the recommendation algorithm like *Freer*. That is, only the scores derived from reviews written under the target user's contexts are considered for calculating the item's score in Equation 9. We denote it as *Pre-filter*.

☐ **Default Connecter.** This method is similar to the one proposed in [14], which mines contexts from reviews and correlates them with users' opinions at the aspect level, but makes no distinction between users' opinions for the same aspect in different contexts. We denote it as *Default*.

☐ **Discriminative Connecter.** This method is also similar to the one proposed in [14], but relies on the results of contextual review analysis we obtained in Section 3.1 to assign context-dependent weights to aspects. Compared to our approaches, this method does not consider the weights of aspect-related terms. We denote it as *Discriminator*.

☐ **MI/IG/CHI Connecter.** The three methods proposed by us (see Section 3.3), which are different in terms of the feature selection metric used to calculate the aspect-related term's weight, respectively shorten to *MI* (mutual information), *IG* (information gain), and *CHI* (Chi-square statistic).

4.3   Results and Discussion

The experimental results on two datasets are shown in Table 2. We can have the following observations: 1) *Pre-filter* is better than *Freer*, which verifies that

Table 2. Experiment Results. Results marked with * are statistically significantly better than ($p < 0.001$) the method being compared. Here, the significance values are calculated between *Pre-filter* and *Freer*, *Default* and *Pre-filter*, *Discriminator* and *Default*, *MI/IG/CHI* and *Discriminator*.

Dataset	Method	H@5	H@10	H@15	MRR@5	MRR@10	MRR@15
Trip-Advisor	*Freer*	0.0145	0.0416	0.0760	0.0050	0.0085	0.0112
	Pre-filter	0.0296	0.0664*	0.1061*	0.0115*	0.0163*	0.0194*
	Default	0.0403*	0.0895*	0.1396*	0.0158*	0.0221*	0.0261*
	Discriminator	0.0464*	0.1008	0.1502*	0.0188*	0.0259	0.0297*
	MI	0.0565*	0.1173*	0.1707*	0.0237*	0.0317*	0.0359*
	IG	0.0680*	0.1369*	0.1938*	0.0301*	0.0391*	0.0436*
	CHI	**0.0915***	**0.1717***	**0.2310***	**0.0423***	**0.0528***	**0.0574***
Yelp	*Freer*	0.0205	0.0426	0.0598	0.0091	0.0119	0.0133
	Pre-filter	0.0267*	0.0521	0.0788*	0.0124*	0.0158*	0.0178*
	Default	0.0338*	0.0603*	0.0852*	0.0153*	0.0187*	0.0206*
	Discriminator	0.0487	0.0835*	0.1161*	0.0232	0.0277*	0.0303*
	MI	0.0543*	0.0951*	0.1261*	0.0266*	0.0320*	0.0345*
	IG	0.0729*	0.1195*	0.1608*	0.0361*	0.0422*	0.0454*
	CHI	**0.0985***	**0.1559***	**0.2075***	**0.0513***	**0.0588***	**0.0629***

it is meaningful to extract contexts from reviews and such contextual information does play an important part in enhancing recommendation; 2) *Default* defeats *Pre-filter*, which demonstrates that the contextual opinions can further be used to build more precise user profile, i.e., the aspect-level context-dependent preferences; 3) *Discriminator* is significantly superior to *Default* regarding most measures, which shows that it is meaningful to correlate users' aspect-level opinions with contexts based on review analysis. However, we also notice that the improvement achieved by *Discriminator* over *Default* is limited and some differences are not statistically significant. This is mainly owning to the limited amount of reviews that contain contextual opinions of the same aspect under different contexts (it is 23.01% in Yelp dataset and 17.6% in TripAdvisor dataset); 4) *MI/IG/CHI* are all significantly better than *Discriminator*, which suggests that the aspect-related term's relevance to context should also be considered when modeling the user's context-dependent preferences. Among the three variations, *CHI* achieves the best performance, followed by *IG*, and then *MI*. We believe that the differences can be explained by the way of how to compute the relevance of an aspect-related term to a specific context. The relevance weight computed by either *CHI* (i.e., Equation 5) or *IG* (i.e., Equation 4) takes all of the possible combinations of *presence* and *absence* statuses of the aspect-related term as well as the context into consideration. It hence can measure the weight more accurately over *MI* (i.e., Equation 3). In addition, *MI* tends to favor low-frequent terms, which might result in biases towards the calculation of the terms' relevance.

5 Conclusion and Future Work

In this paper, we presented a novel recommendation strategy that particularly performs contextual review analysis for detecting users' aspect-level context-dependent preferences and further combines them with users' context-independent preferences to generate recommendation. Through the experiment, we have successfully proved that: 1) it is meaningful to correlate users' aspect-level opinions (as expressed in their reviews) with the contextual factors; and 2) aspect-related terms are of important value to discriminate users' aspect-level preferences under different contexts. The experimental results on two datasets empirically show that our approaches significantly outperform the related context-aware recommendation techniques.

In the future, we plan to verify the performance of our method in other product domains, such as hotel recommendation. In addition, we will continue to explore different strategies for fusing together users' context-independent and context-dependent preferences. For instance, the parameter α in Equation 7 can be learned for each user by applying some machine learning techniques.

Acknowledgements. We thank grants ECS/HKBU211912 and NSFC/61272365.

References

[1] Adomavicius, G., Tuzhilin, A.: Context-aware recommender systems. In: Recommender Systems Handbook, pp. 217–253. Springer (2011)

[2] Adomavicius, G., Sankaranarayanan, R., Sen, S., Tuzhilin, A.: Incorporating contextual information in recommender systems using a multidimensional approach. ACM Transactions on Information Systems (TOIS) 23(1), 103–145 (2005)

[3] Chen, L., Wang, F.: Preference-based clustering reviews for augmenting e-commerce recommendation. Knowledge-Based Systems 50, 44–59 (2013)

[4] Wang, Y., Liu, Y., Yu, X.: Collaborative filtering with aspect-based opinion mining: A tensor factorization approach. In: 2012 IEEE 12th International Conference on Data Mining (ICDM), pp. 1152–1157. IEEE (2012)

[5] Jakob, N., Weber, S.H., Müller, M.C., Gurevych, I.: Beyond the stars: exploiting free-text user reviews to improve the accuracy of movie recommendations. In: Proceedings of the 1st International CIKM Workshop on Topic-Sentiment Analysis for Mass Opinion, pp. 57–64. ACM (2009)

[6] Adomavicius, G., Kwon, Y.: New recommendation techniques for multicriteria rating systems. IEEE Intelligent Systems 22(3), 48–55 (2007)

[7] Liu, L., Mehandjiev, N., Xu, D.L.: Multi-criteria service recommendation based on user criteria preferences. In: Proceedings of the Fifth ACM Conference on Recommender Systems, pp. 77–84. ACM (2011)

[8] Ganu, G., Kakodkar, Y.: Improving the quality of predictions using textual information in online user reviews. Information Systems 38(1), 1–15 (2013)

[9] Panniello, U., Tuzhilin, A., Gorgoglione, M., Palmisano, C., Pedone, A.: Experimental comparison of pre-vs. post-filtering approaches in context-aware recommender systems. In: Proceedings of the Third ACM Conference on Recommender Systems, pp. 265–268. ACM (2009)

[10] Karatzoglou, A., Amatriain, X.: Multiverse recommendation: N-dimensional tensor factorization for context-aware collaborative filtering. In: Proceedings of the Fourth ACM Conference on Recommender Systems, pp. 79–86. ACM (2010)

[11] Li, Y., Nie, J., Zhang, Y.: Contextual recommendation based on text mining. In: Proceedings of the 23rd International Conference on Computational Linguistics: Posters, pp. 692–700. Association for Computational Linguistics (2010)

[12] Zhang, W., Ding, G., Chen, L., Li, C., Zhang, C.: Generating virtual ratings from chinese reviews to augment online recommendations. ACM Transactions on Intelligent Systems and Technology (TIST) 4(1) (2013)

[13] Carter, S., Chen, F., Muralidharan, A.S., Pickens, J.: Dig: A task-based approach to product search. In: Proceedings of the 16th International Conference on Intelligent User Interfaces, pp. 303–306. ACM (2011)

[14] Levi, A., Mokryn, O., Diot, C., Taft, N.: Finding a needle in a haystack of reviews: Cold start context-based hotel recommender system. In: Proceedings of the Sixth ACM Conference on Recommender Systems, pp. 115–122. ACM (2012)

[15] Hariri, N., Mobasher, B., Burke, R., Zheng, Y.: Context-aware recommendation based on review mining. In: Proceedings of the 9th International Workshop on Intelligent Techniques for Web Personalization and Recommender Systems (ITWP), International Joint Conferences on Artificial Intelligence (IJCAI), pp. 30–36 (2011)

[16] Wang, H., Lu, Y., Zhai, C.: Latent aspect rating analysis on review text data: a rating regression approach. In: Proceedings of the 16th ACM SIGKDD International Conference on Knowledge Discovery and Data Mining, pp. 783–792. ACM (2010)

[17] Yang, Y., Pedersen, J.O.: A comparative study on feature selection in text categorization. In: Proceedings of the 14th International Conference on Machine Learning, vol. 97, pp. 412–420 (1997)

[18] Wilson, T., Wiebe, J., Hoffmann, P.: Recognizing contextual polarity in phrase-level sentiment analysis. In: Proceedings of the Conference on Human Language Technology and Empirical Methods in Natural Language Processing, pp. 347–354. Association for Computational Linguistics (2005)

[19] Shani, G., Gunawardana, A.: Evaluating recommendation systems. In: Recommender Systems Handbook, pp. 257–297. Springer (2011)

[20] Codina, V., Ricci, F., Ceccaroni, L.: Exploiting the semantic similarity of contextual situations for pre-filtering recommendation. In: Carberry, S., Weibelzahl, S., Micarelli, A., Semeraro, G. (eds.) UMAP 2013. LNCS, vol. 7899, pp. 165–177. Springer, Heidelberg (2013)

User Partitioning Hybrid for Tag Recommendation

Jonathan Gemmell, Bamshad Mobasher, and Robin Burke

Center for Web Intelligence
School of Computing, DePaul University
Chicago, Illinois, USA
{jgemmell,mobasher,rburke}@cdm.depaul.edu

Abstract. Tag recommendation is a fundamental service in today's social annotation systems, assisting users as they collect and annotate resources. Our previous work has demonstrated the strengths of a linear weighted hybrid, which weights and combines the results of simple components into a final recommendation. However, these previous efforts treated each user the same. In this work, we extend our approach by automatically discovering partitions of users. The user partitioning hybrid learns a different set of weights for these user partitions. Our rigorous experimental results show a marked improvement. Moreover, analysis of the partitions within a dataset offers interesting insights into how users interact with social annotations systems.

Keywords: User Partitioning, Personalization, Social Annotation Systems, Tag Recommendation, Hybrid Recommendation.

1 Introduction

Social annotation systems allow users to collect online resources such as music, videos, products or journal articles. The defining characteristic of these systems is the ability of users to assign tags to resources. The complex interaction of these users, resources and tags form a large multidimensional information space, often called a folksonomy. While these information spaces connect users to content in interesting and complex ways, they are also inherently difficult to navigate and benefit from recommender technologies.

Many forms of recommendation are possible in social annotation systems. Resources, tags or even users are all potential outputs for a recommender. In many cases, additional constraints can be applied. For example, a user may desire a resource recommendation based upon a tag they have clicked on or a resource they have recently consumed. In tag recommendation, the subject of this paper, the system recommends a set of tags to a user as she is annotating a resource. This recommendation reduces user effort, helps the user avoid misspellings or errors, and maintains a cleaner tag space.

Our previous work in tag recommendation for social annotation systems has focused on the use of linear weighted hybrids that relies on the combined efforts of several simple component recommenders. A key step is the generation of weights for each component, indicating how much influence a component will have in the recommendation. Experimental work has shown that different folksonomies require different sets of weights to produce optimal results.

V. Dimitrova et al. (Eds.): UMAP 2014, LNCS 8538, pp. 74–85, 2014.

This observation has led us to infer that users employ these systems in different ways. For example, in a social annotation system where users annotate journal articles, approaches that model users or resources as tags do well and get higher weights. It seems that scientists are careful about the tags they select and often draw tags from their domain of expertise. In contrast, models representing users as a vector of tags tend to do poorly in a system where users annotate music. These users appear more likely to use generic tags like "rock" and idiosyncratic tags such as "sawAtConcertWithSuzy." Yet, these inferences appear overly broad. Not every scientist is careful about the use of tags and not every music fan is careless.

In this work, we partition users and learn a separate set of weights for each partition. One approach may be to partition users based on some metric such as the size of the user profile or the variability of the user's resources. However, a preconceived metric may not produce optimal results. Instead, we attempt to automatically discover the partitions using an approach similar to the one in K-means clustering.

We first assign users to a random partition. Weights are trained for each partition, and users are then reassigned to the partition in which they best perform. This procedure is repeated until the system reaches equilibrium.

Our experimental findings show that a user partitioning hybrid outperforms previous approaches. The technique has the added benefits of being efficient, scalable and extensible. Finally, the partitions and their trained weights offer insights into how different segments of users interact with social annotation systems.

The rest of this paper is organized as follows. In Section 2 we discuss related work. Section 3 describes our data model and how we partition users for the user partitioning hybrid. Our experimental evaluation is presented in Section 4. Section 5 offers conclusions.

2 Related Work

A common thread found in research focusing on tag recommendation is the need for an integrative approach. FolkRank [9] is a variant of the well-known PageRank algorithm. The graph it induces from the folksonomy connects users, resources and tags. While known to be accurate, it suffers from the fact that it is computationally expensive to run.

Tucker decomposition has been used to factor the three dimensional tagging data into three feature spaces and a core residual tensor [18]. Once computed the matrices can be used to quickly recommend tags. However, the calculation of the matrices is prohibitive.

Pair-wise interaction tensor factorization [14, 15] formed the basis for the winning submission of the PKDD 2009 Tag Recommendation Challenge [12]. It is a model-based approach that generates factor matrices using a set of positive and negative examples. An iterative gradient-descent algorithm is used to optimize a ranking function that prefers positive examples over negative ones. We include $PITF$ in our experimental work as a means of comparison.

Our previous work in tag recommendation has demonstrated the benefits of hybrid recommenders [3–5]. In this paper, we extend those efforts.

3   Tag Recommendation Based on User Partitioning

This section first describes the data model used to represent social annotation systems. Our user partitioning hybrid is then presented. So too are the the component recommenders that make up the hybrid.

3.1   Data Model

A social annotation system can be modeled with four sets. The first set, U, includes the set of users that employ the system. The second set, R, includes the all resources that any of the users have collected. The third set, T, includes every tag any user has ever applied to a resource. The final set, A, is the set of annotations. An annotation includes a single user, a single resource, and all tags that user has applied to that resource.

This model can be translated to a three-dimensional matrix, which we call URT. An entry $URT(u,r,t)$ is 1 if u annotated r with t, and is otherwise 0. This three-dimensional matrix offers the convenience of generating aggregate projections. Aggregate projections reduce the dimensionality of the data making it easier to work with but sacrifices some information [6, 13].

One such projection is RT. In this projection, an entry $RT(r,t)$ is calculated as the number of users that have assigned t to r. Two other aggregate projections are possible, UR and UT. In these projections, an entry can be calculated as the number of times u has tagged a resource r or the number of times he has employed a tag t respectively. Given these projection we are able to model a user by drawing a row from either UR or UT. In the first case, the user is being modeled as a vector over the resource space, where the weight $w(r_i)$ in dimension i corresponds to the importance of resource, r_i:
$$\boldsymbol{u^r} = \langle w(r_1), w(r_2)...w(r_{|R|}) \rangle.$$

Likewise, a user could be modeled over the tag space to produce $\boldsymbol{u^t}$. Analogous models can be created for resources ($\boldsymbol{r^u}, \boldsymbol{r^t}$) and tags ($\boldsymbol{t^u}, \boldsymbol{t^r}$) by drawing either a row or a column from one the projections. Previous experimentation has shown that a binary version of UR yields better results and we continue to use the binary version in this work.

3.2   User Partitioning Hybrid

The motivation behind our approach to automatic user partitioning stems from the observation that users exhibit complex patterns in how they interact with social annotation systems. For example, some users may consistently employ popular tags, while others prefer idiosyncratic tags. If we could identify or predict a user's behavior, we might be able to select a recommendation strategy that best suits that behavior.

One possible approach would be to partition users based on some preconceived notion and then independently design a recommendation strategy for each partition. However, there is no guarantee that these partitions would be optimal or that the partitioning strategy would generalize across all social annotation systems. In this work, we instead opt to automatically identify optimal partitions through an iterative process similar to K-means clustering [7].

First, users are randomly placed into one of k partitions. A recommendation strategy is optimized for each partition of users. Then using a holdout set, each user is evaluated against the optimized strategies. User are reassigned to the partition in which they perform best. The recommenders are once again optimized against their new collection of users. This process iteratively repeats until the partitions stabilize.

While the approach is similar to K-means clustering, notice that users are not assigned to partitions based on a similarity metric between themselves or to a partition-mean. Users are instead assigned to a partition based on their performance in the partition. In this manner, users are partitioned based on their affinity to an optimized recommendation strategy.

More specifically, we begin by evaluating the function $\psi : U \times R \times T \rightarrow \mathbb{R}$ where a user $u \in U$, a resource $r \in R$ and a tag $t \in T$ results in a real-valued result p. This value represents the prediction of how well the tag is suited for that particular user-resource pair: $\psi(u, r, t) = p$. In order to generate a recommendation list, a ranked list of suggested tags for a particular user and resource is generated. Given a user u and resource r, we iterate over all tags and calculate their relevance. Finally, we sort the tag by this results and return the top n tags: $rec(u, r) = TOP_{t \in T}^n \psi(u, r, t)$.

Our user partitioning hybrid is built from simple components that focus on specific dimensions of the data [1]. The results are then aggregated to form the final recommendation. If each component is able to generate its own score for a user-resource-tag triple, then the hybrid can combine these scores.

More specifically, the hybrid takes a collection of tag recommenders C. When asked to make a recommendation for a user u and resource r, it will iterate over all tags querying each of its component recommenders, $c \in C$, for a tag, t, and combine the results in the linear model: $\psi_h(u, r, t) = \sum_{c \in C} \alpha_c \psi_c(u, r, t)$ where $\psi_h(u, r, t)$ is the linear weighted relevance score of the tag and α_c is the weight given to the component, c. Scores from the components are not guaranteed to be on the same scale. We therefore normalize the scores so that each $\psi_c(u, r, t)$ falls in the interval [0,1].

The linear weighted hybrid can include any number of components. In order to maximize its accuracy, we train their weights using a hill climbing technique. At first, the α vector is initialized with random positive numbers such that the sum of the vector is 1. A holdout set is used to evaluate the performance of the hybrid with those weights. We rely on recall (see Section 4.2).

The α vector is then randomly modified and tested against the holdout set again. If the performance is improved, we keep the change; otherwise, we reject it. Two small modifications ensure we are not trapped in a local maxima. First, we occasionally accept a change to the α vector even when it does not improve the performance. Second, we randomly restart, so that we may thoroughly examine the α space.

The α vectors in our previous work on linear weighted hybrids were trained against all users in the dataset. As a result, recommendations for users were drawn from the same combination of component recommenders. Our user partitioning hybrid segments the users and trains a unique α vector for each partition of users. After optimizing the α vectors for each partition, we reassign the users. Using the same holdout set, we calculate a user's recall for each partition and reassign the user to the partition in which he performs best. The optimization-reassignment procedure is repeated until the users no longer move from partition to partition.

3.3 Component Recommenders

Any number of components can be included in the user partitioning hybrid. We have purposely chosen simple components that exploit only a few dimensions of the data. Our goal is to create an integrative recommender by combining these components rather than building a single complex recommender. We now describe those components.

Popularity Models. Given the user-resource pair, the component may recommend the most popular tags for that particular resource. This strategy ignores the user and is strictly resource dependent. We define $\psi(u, r, t)$ for the resource based popularity recommender, pop_r, as $\psi(u, r, t) = \sum_{v \in U} \theta(v, r, t)$ where $\theta(v, r, t)$ is 1 if v tagged r with t and 0 otherwise. Likewise, a component may merely recommend the most popular tags for a particular user. This approach does not consider the resource and consequently may recommend some irrelevant tags. We define $\psi(u, r, t)$ for the user based popularity recommender, pop_u, as $\psi(u, r, t) = \sum_{s \in R} \theta(u, s, t)$.

User-Based Collaborative Modeling. Collaborative filtering works under the premise that patterns exist in how users interact with the system. User-based collaborative filtering [8, 11, 17] looks for similarities among users. For our work in tag recommendation, a neighborhood, N_r, of the k most similar users to u is identified through a similarity metric such that all the neighbors have tagged r. For any given resource the weighted sum can then be calculated as $\psi(u, r, t) = \sum_{v \in N_r} \sigma(u, v)\theta(v, r, t)$ where $\sigma(u, v)$ is the similarity between the users u and v.

Previous experiments have looked at many types of similarity metrics; we have found cosine similarity to most consistently produce the best results. When users are modeled as resources we call this approach KNN_{ur}. When users are modeled as tags we call this technique KNN_{ut}.

Item-Based Collaborative Modeling. Another form of collaborative filtering is item-based collaborative filtering [2, 16]. Rather than finding similarities among users, this approach creates a neighborhood of similar resources. As before, we notice that there are two ways in which we might model resources.

The model KNN_{ru} treats resources as a vector over the user space. The model KNN_{rt} treats resources as a vector over the tag space. We define N_u as the k nearest resources to r drawn from the user profile, u, and then define the relevance score of a tag for a user-resource pair as $\psi(u, r, t) = \sum_{s \in N_u} \sigma(r, s)\theta(u, s, t)$.

4   Experimental Evaluation

In this section, we provide information about our three real world datasets, including how we collected and preprocessed the data. We then describe our experimental methodology. We first limit our analysis to the individual datasets and then draw larger conclusions.

4.1 Datasets

Our exhaustive experimental analysis was conducted on three data sets: Citeulike, MovieLens and LastFM. After collecting the data, we generated p-cores [10]. A subset of the data was selected such that each remaining user, resource and tag is guaranteed to occur in at least p annotations, where an annotation represents a user, a resource and all tags applied by that user to that resource.

Extracting p-cores from the data discards information – it eliminates infrequent users, resources and tags – but it also yields some benefits. It reduces noise and enables algorithms than might otherwise be computationally expensive. Infrequent items are necessary when experimenting on the "long tail" or when investigating the cold start problem. This paper, however, is focused on the complex interactions between users, resources and tags. To this end, we are focused on the denser part of the graph.

Citeulike is used to manage and organize journal articles. It is mainly used by scientists and researchers. Data is available to download directly from the site. In this paper, we use a snapshot taken from 17 February 2009. While newer datasets are available, we opted to use the same dataset as in our previous work in order to maintain consistency. After we computed a 5-core, the dataset contained 2,051 users, 5,376 resources, 3,343 tags and a total of 105,873 annotations.

MovieLens is a movie recommendation website run by the GroupLens research lab at the University of Minnesota. They collect several datasets from their users and make these datasets available to researchers. In particular, one of those datasets contains tagging information. We created a 5-core from this data. The result was 35,366 annotations with 819 users, 2,445 resources and 2,309 tags.

LastFM provides many services for their users. User can upload playlists, share their tastes and connect to fans with similar interests. It also allows users to annotate songs, albums and artists. After selected 100 random users, and recursively crawling the "friend" network we were able to download user profiles for thousands of users. This data was denser than the previous datasets and permitted a p-core of 20. It contains 2,368 users, 2,350 resources, 1,141 tags and 172,177 annotations. These experiments focus on the album data, but parallel experiments show similar trends on the artist and song datasets.

4.2 Methodology

In order to train and evaluate our techniques we divide each of the user's annotations among five folds. We use four of these folds to build our recommenders. The fifth is used as training data. We use this fifth tune the model parameters; for example when selecting the number of neighbors for our collaborative filtering components. Moreover, we use this fifth fold during the training of the component weights and the reassignment of users to new partitions. We then discard the fifth folded, performing four fold cross validation on the remaining folds with the discovered parameters.

Given a testing annotation, we can submit the user u and resource r to a recommendation engine to produce set of recommended tags, T_r. Comparing these tags to the holdout set, T_h, we can evaluate our recommender with on recall and precision.

Recall is a common metric for evaluating the utility of recommendation algorithms. It measures the percentage of items in the holdout set that appear in the recommendation set. Recall is a measure of completeness and is defined as $recall = |T_h \cap T_r|/|T_h|$.

Precision is another common metric for measuring the usefulness of recommendation algorithms. It measures the percentage of items in the recommendation set that appear in the holdout set. Precision measures the exactness of the recommendation algorithm and is defined as $precision = |T_r \cap T_r|/|T_r|$.

The recall and precision will vary depending on the size on the recommendation set. In the following experiments we present the metrics with recommendation sets of size one through ten.

4.3   Experimental Results

Table 1 shows relative contribution of the component recommenders as learned through the hill climbing approach for Citeulike, MovieLens and LastFM. The first line, labeled "all", describes the contributions when all users are used to train the α vectors. In this approach, there are no partitions. For example, we see that the linear weighted hybrid has little use for Pop_u or Pop_r in Citeulike, but instead relies mostly on KNN_{rt} (50.9%). There are 2051 users in total.

The next five lines, labeled "1" through "5", describe the contribution of the component recommenders for five partitions. In this case, the α vectors were trained only on the users in the partitions. As described above, users were then reassigned to the partition in which they best performed. This process repeated until the partitions stabilized. We can see that partition 1 contains 264 users and that these users rely more strongly on Pop_u and Pop_r, 19.1% and 16.7% respectively.

Figures 1 through 3 present the performance of the algorithms. Recommendation sets were generated of size one through ten. These sets were then evaluated in terms of recall and precision. Each line in the graphs represents a particular recommendation technique. For example, we see that the worst performing approach in Citeulike is KNN_{ur}.

Citeulike. In Citeulike, we see that the three leading approaches are the interaction technique ($PITF$), the linear weighted hybrid ($Hybrid$) and the user partitioning hybrid (UPH). These results confirm our supposition that an integrative approach is needed which draws upon multiple dimensions of the data. When looking at their recall for ten tags, they all achieve nearly identical results.

In this dataset, it seems there is little advantage in partitioning users. The reason can be seen when inspecting the α vectors. Notice that when the hybrid is trained for all users, KNN_{rt} dominates the other components (50.9%). The next strongest contributor is KNN_{ut} (26.5%). In this domain, it seems that modeling resources and users in the tag space is to be preferred. This is not surprising since the users of Citeulike are researchers that are usually careful about how they apply their tags, often drawing on keywords from their area of expertise.

If we turn our attention to the user partitioning hybrid, we see that four of the five partitions have α vectors quite similar to that of the linear weighted hybrid. Partitions

Table 1. Contributions of the component recommenders to the the linear weighted hybrid and the user partitioning hybrid

Citeulike

	n	Pop_u	Pop_r	KNN_{ur}	KNN_{ut}	KNN_{ru}	KNN_{rt}
All	2051	0.007	0.034	0.066	0.265	0.109	0.509
1	264	0.191	0.167	0.049	0.208	0.253	0.133
2	591	0.017	0.043	0.058	0.173	0.110	0.600
3	304	0.099	0.036	0.143	0.081	0.206	0.435
4	541	0.026	0.101	0.044	0.366	0.029	0.433
5	351	0.098	0.061	0.009	0.098	0.155	0.602

MovieLens

	n	Pop_u	Pop_r	KNN_{ur}	KNN_{ut}	KNN_{ru}	KNN_{rt}
All	819	0.028	0.023	0.063	0.407	0.048	0.431
1	241	0.126	0.028	0.067	0.177	0.185	0.418
2	142	0.040	0.083	0.063	0.436	0.106	0.273
3	120	0.162	0.106	0.137	0.156	0.214	0.226
4	94	0.153	0.177	0.208	0.082	0.152	0.228
5	222	0.053	0.086	0.008	0.160	0.101	0.597

LastFM

	n	Pop_u	Pop_r	KNN_{ur}	KNN_{ut}	KNN_{ru}	KNN_{rt}
All	2368	0.017	0.032	0.011	0.471	0.430	0.038
1	347	0.187	0.083	0.383	0.304	0.216	0.173
2	465	0.036	0.035	0.125	0.039	0.403	0.362
3	401	0.179	0.205	0.019	0.340	0.162	0.094
4	750	0.011	0.047	0.024	0.425	0.383	0.110
5	405	0.061	0.158	0.060	0.340	0.335	0.047

2 through 4 all largely rely on KNN_{rt} and KNN_{ut}. It is only the first partition – and the smallest – that appears to require a uniquely different combination of components, relying more strongly on the popularity based techniques than any of the other partitions. These observations suggest not only that modeling users and resource as a vector of tags is preferred, but also that users are relatively uniform in how they interact with the system. The result is that a partitioning of users, offers little additional benefit.

MovieLens. Figure 2 show the performance of the recommendation techniques on the MovieLens dataset. Again, $PITF$, $Hybrid$ and UPH lead the pack. In this case, $Hybrid$ lags behind and UPH improves upon it enough to match $PITF$. Again, examination of the α vectors offer insights.

As in before, the linear weighted hybrid trained on all 819 MovieLens users is largely influenced by KNN_{rt} and KNN_{ut}. It seems that users are annotating movies with keywords drawn from the domain such as "drama" or using the names of actors. However,

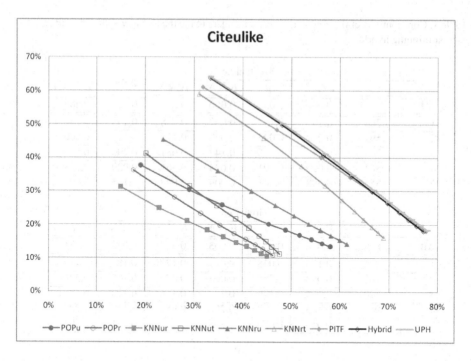

Fig. 1. Citeulike: recall versus precision

unlike Citeulike, when we inspect the α vectors for the user partitioning hybrid we see more variation.

Users in the first partition appear be influenced by KNN_{rt} and KNN_{ut}, but also tend reuse tags as evidenced by the weights in Pop_u and KNN_{ru}. Users in the third and fourth partitions rely on a combination of all the component recommenders. It is the second and fifth partitions that are most similar to the linear weighted hybrid. These two partitions account the plurality of the users but not to the degree we saw above. Consequently, there is a greater benefit for automatically partitioning users and training the component weights for each one. In short, it seems that there is more variance in how these users are interacting with the social annotation system.

LastFM. In our final dataset, we see that UPH outperforms $PITF$ and $Hybrid$. It would seem that users annotating resources in LastFM exhibit a greater variety of patterns than we observed above. The linear weighted hybrid is composed largely of KNN_{ut} and KNN_{ru}. The other components contribute very little.

It is the fourth partition of the user partitioning hybrid that most closely resembles the linear weighted hybrid. We see that 750 users were assigned to this partition, the largest allocation by far. This large crowd of users was likely influencing the linear weighted hybrid, which trains the model on all users.

However, when users are separated into partitions, these users consolidate around other combinations of component recommenders. We see users in the first partition

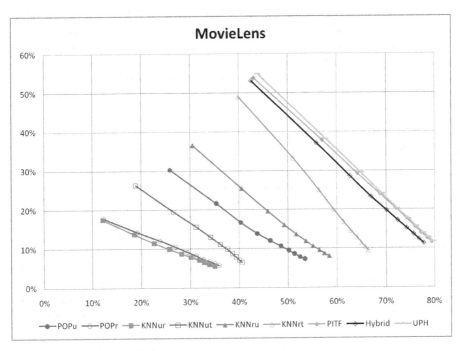

Fig. 2. MovieLens: recall versus precision

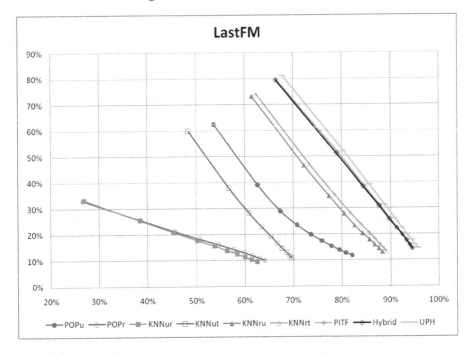

Fig. 3. LastFM: recall versus precision

taking advantage of KNN_{ur}, users in the second relying KNN_{rt}, users in the third partition benefiting from almost all the components except KNN_{ur}, and users in partition five putting more emphasis on Pop_r. This variation among the α vectors and the corresponding improvement of the user partitioning hybrid over the linear weighted hybrid support the notion that automatic user partitioning can improve recommenders by catering to the needs of groups of users rather than trying to build a single model to satisfy them all.

5   Conclusion

In this paper, we introduced a framework for tag recommendation based on automatically partitioning users. A user partitioning hybrid was constructed from several simple component recommenders. A vector of weights controlled the contribution of the components to the hybrid. When users are partitioned, a vector is trained for each partition. Users were then reassigned to the partition in which they performed best. The process repeated until the partitions stabilized. Our experimental evaluation on three real world datasets shows that automatic user partitioning can improve performance of a linear weighted hybrid. Moreover, examination of the components and their contribution can lead to valuable insights with regard to how users are interacting with different social annotation systems. Our future work aims to generalize this approach and apply it to other recommendation tasks in social annotation systems such as resource recommendation.

References

1. Burke, R.: Hybrid recommender systems: Survey and experiments. User Modeling and User-Adapted Interaction 12(4), 331–370 (2002)
2. Deshpande, M., Karypis, G.: Item-Based Top-N Recommendation Algorithms. ACM Transactions on Information Systems 22(1), 143–177 (2004)
3. Gemmell, J., Ramezani, M., Schimoler, T., Christiansen, L., Mobasher, B.: A fast effective multi-channeled tag recommender. In: European Conference on Machine Learning and Principles and Practice of Knowledge Discovery in Databases Discovery Challenge, Bled, Slovenia (2009)
4. Gemmell, J., Schimoler, T., Mobasher, B., Burke, R.: Improving folkrank with item-based collaborative filtering. In: Recommender Systems & the Social Web, New York (2009)
5. Gemmell, J., Schimoler, T., Mobasher, B., Burke, R.: Hybrid tag recommendation for social annotation systems. In: 19th ACM International Conference on Information and Knowledge Management, Toronto, Canada (2010)
6. Gemmell, J., Schimoler, T., Ramezani, M., Mobasher, B.: Adapting K-Nearest Neighbor for Tag Recommendation in Folksonomies. In: 7th Workshop on Intelligent Techniques for Web Personalization and Recommender Systems, Chicago, Illinois (2009)
7. Hartigan, J.A., Wong, M.A.: Algorithm as 136: A k-means clustering algorithm. Journal of the Royal Statistical Society. Series C (Applied Statistics) 28(1), 100–108 (1979)
8. Herlocker, J., Konstan, J., Borchers, A., Riedl, J.: An Algorithmic Framework for Performing Collaborative Filtering. In: 22nd Annual International ACM SIGIR Conference on Research and Development in Information Retrieval, Berkeley, California. ACM (1999)

9. Hotho, A., Jäschke, R., Schmitz, C., Stumme, G.: Information Retrieval in Folksonomies: Search and ranking. In: Sure, Y., Domingue, J. (eds.) ESWC 2006. LNCS, vol. 4011, pp. 411–426. Springer, Heidelberg (2006)

10. Jäschke, R., Marinho, L., Hotho, A., Schmidt-Thieme, L., Stumme, G.: Tag Recommendations in Folksonomies. In: Kok, J.N., Koronacki, J., Lopez de Mantaras, R., Matwin, S., Mladenič, D., Skowron, A. (eds.) PKDD 2007. LNCS (LNAI), vol. 4702, pp. 506–514. Springer, Heidelberg (2007)

11. Konstan, J., Miller, B., Maltz, D., Herlocker, J., Gordon, L., Riedl, J.: GroupLens: Applying Collaborative Filtering to Usenet News. Communications of the ACM 40(3), 87 (1997)

12. Marinho, L., Preisach, C., Schmidt-Thieme, L., Cantador, I., Vallet, D., Jose, J., Cao, H., Xie, M., Xue, L., Liu, C., et al.: ECML PKDD Discovery Challenge 2009-DC09 (2009)

13. Mika, P.: Ontologies are us: A unified model of social networks and semantics. Web Semantics: Science, Services and Agents on the World Wide Web 5(1), 5–15 (2007)

14. Rendle, S., Schmidt-Thieme, L.: Factor Models for Tag Recommendation in BibSonomy. In: ECML/PKDD 2008 Discovery Challenge Workshop, part of the European Conference on Machine Learning and Principles and Practice of Knowledge Discovery in Databases, Bled, Slovenia (2009)

15. Rendle, S., Schmidt-Thieme, L.: Pairwise Interaction Tensor Factorization for Personalized Tag Recommendation. In: Proceedings of the Third ACM International Conference on Web Search and Data Mining, New York (2010)

16. Sarwar, B., Karypis, G., Konstan, J., Reidl, J.: Item-Based Collaborative Filtering Recommendation Algorithms. In: 10th International Conference on World Wide Web, Hong Kong, China (2001)

17. Shardanand, U., Maes, P.: Social Information Filtering: Algorithms for Automating "Word of Mouth". In: SIGCHI Conference on Human Factors in Computing Systems, Denver, Colorado (1995)

18. Symeonidis, P., Nanopoulos, A., Manolopoulos, Y.: Tag recommendations based on tensor dimensionality reduction. In: Proceedings of the 2008 ACM Conference on Recommender Systems, Lausanne, Switzerland (2008)

Predicting User Locations and Trajectories

Eelco Herder, Patrick Siehndel and Ricardo Kawase

L3S Research Center, Leibniz University Hannover, Germany
{herder,siehndel,kawase}@L3S.de

Abstract. Location-based services usually recommend new locations based on the user's current location or a given destination. However, human mobility involves to a large extent routine behavior and visits to already visited locations. In this paper, we show how daily and weekly routines can be modeled with basic prediction techniques. We compare the methods based on their performance, entropy and correlation measures. Further, we discuss how location prediction for everyday activities can be used for personalization techniques, such as timely or delayed recommendations.

Keywords: GPS, Geolocation, Mobility Patterns, Personalization.

1 Introduction

Location-based services suggest new locations that match the user's inferred interests and preferences, making use of content-based or collaborative recommendation techniques. In most cases, distance is used as the main criterion for inclusion in the recommendations. As argued by Mokbel et al. [14], location-based services usually only take the current location into account. However, apart from visiting new locations, users often visit places that they visited before [13]. These revisited places include home and work locations, but also less frequently visited places, such as specialty stores, hiking areas, friends and relatives.

Several studies confirmed the intuition that human mobility is highly predictable [9,16], centered around a small number of base locations. This opens a wide range of opportunities for more intelligent recommendations and support of routine activities. Such recommendations may serve as reminders for activities or locations to be included in the user's schedule, and may be used to minimize traveling time between the destinations that a user is likely to visit.

In the literature, one can find only a few studies on common travel patterns, or on locations that are typically visited on certain hours during the week or during the weekend. Such insights are expected to be useful for selecting techniques for predicting a user's travel activity and likely destinations. In this paper, we analyze, visualize and discuss patterns found in a dataset of GPS trajectories. Further, we compare and analyze the performance of common prediction techniques that exploit the locations' popularity, recency, regularity, distance and connections with other locations.

The remainder of this paper is structured as follows. In the next section, we discuss background and related work. Then, we describe the dataset that we

V. Dimitrova et al. (Eds.): UMAP 2014, LNCS 8538, pp. 86–97, 2014.

used, the preprocessing steps for identifying travel sequences, visited locations, and the likely purpose of locations. Subsequently, we show regularities in user travel activities, discuss the nature of different locations visited during weekdays and weekends, followed by a comparison of the performance of various common prediction techniques. We conclude the paper with a discussion of implications and opportunities for personalization and recommendation.

2   Background and Related Work

In this section, we discuss four strands of related work. First, we summarize the main insights from several studies on general and individual mobility patterns, followed by a number of studies that aim to predict next locations. Then, we continue with a brief discussion on the role of locations in popular social media services. We conclude with an overview of location-based services.

2.1   Human Mobility Patterns

González et al. [9] studied people movements, based on a sample of 100,000 randomly selected individuals, covering a six-month time period. The results show that human mobility patterns have a high degree of spatial and temporal regularity. Further, individuals typically return to a few highly frequented locations and most travel trajectories are rather short in terms of distance and travel time.

Song et al. [16] found that 93% of human mobility is predictable; how predictable an individual's movements is, depends on the *entropy* of his patterns. However, for predictability it did not make a difference whether an individual's life was constrained to a 10-km neighborhood or whether he travels hundreds of kilometers on a regular basis.

Zheng et al. [19] used GPS data for mining interesting locations and 'classical sequences', based on the number of visits and the individual visitors' location interests. The outcomes are reported to be useful for tourists, who can easily discover landmarks and popular routes.

2.2   Predicting Next Locations

Ashbrook [2] calculated the probability of transitions between locations, which were extracted from raw GPS data, using various orders of Markov models. The authors discussed the models qualitatively, without mentioning overall accuracy measures.

Krumm and Brush [13] used probabilistic schedules to predict at what times people would be at home or away. The predictive performance of the algorithms was shown to be significantly better than the participants' self-reports. Etter et al. [8] won the Next-Place Prediction task of Nokia Mobile Data Challenge, making use of a wide range of predictors, including a Dynamic Bayesian Network that models the distributions of location transitions and popular locations on certain days and at certain times. Their models achieved a reasonable performance; still, the authors concluded with the open question whether 'unpredictability [is] mainly rooted in the users' personality' or 'a consequence of the data characteristics'.

The above-mentioned studies provide some insights on the predictability of individual mobility patterns. However, most of these studies did not investigate how this predictability depends on the temporal dynamics in human mobility. Biagioni and Krumm [4] provide some first insights, based on the assessment of the location traces of 30 volunteers. Making use of timeline visualizations, the volunteers indicated which days were most similar to each other. With edit-distance-based similarity measures, they managed to cluster similar days with up to 75% accuracy.

2.3 Location and Social Media

Apart from GPS data, a popular source for the analysis of human mobility is social media data. However, social media data is reported to be sparse: most Twitter users only mention a very generic home location and less than 1% of tweets contains metadata on the location where it stems from [6]. Similarly, data from Foursquare[1], a popular location-based social networking tool for mobile devices, is incomplete as well: Foursquare does not automatically track the locations of users and only registers the users' location when they 'check in' at some place. As argued by [11], Foursquare users typically do not 'check in' places that they consider uninteresting (e.g. home or work) or embarrassing (e.g. fast food restaurants).

2.4 Location-Based Services

Location-based information services are typically provided as recommendations [3] or as contextualized search results [18]. Several surveys show that restaurants and stores are the most popular locations that users search for, followed by local attractions and locations associated with leisure time [3,18]. As noted before, these services usually provide suggestions for new locations, based on the user's preferences and current location. In a recent study, Amini et al. [1] showed the benefits of trajectory-aware suggestions that are based on the distance to the user's predicted destination instead of the user's current location.

3 Dataset and Tools Used

As a basis for our analysis, we used the GeoLife GPS Trajectory Dataset [2] [19], which contains a total of 17,621 trajectories from 178 users, mainly located in Beijing. The dataset is complemented with the MSR GPS Privacy Dataset 2009 [3]

---

[1] http://foursquare.com/

[2] http://research.microsoft.com/en-us/downloads/b16d359d-d164-469e-9fd4-daa38f2b2e13/

[3] http://research.microsoft.com/en-us/um/people/jckrumm/gpsdata2009/index.html

[5], which contains 4,165 trajectories from 21 users, mainly located in and near Seattle, gathered in a 2-month period in 2009.

3.1   Preprocessing Steps

As we are interested in the start and end locations and the durations of the trajectories, we extracted the first and last entry of each trajectory in the dataset; this data was stored as a single entry in the database, representing a trajectory with a start point and an end point - the duration is the difference between the corresponding two time stamps.

Subsequently, the different longitudes and latitudes were merged into (numbered) locations, by comparing the distance of each new start point or end point with the person's previously stored locations. After experimentation with different thresholds (starting with 20 meter, which is reported to be the current precision of GPS [4]), we finally chose a fairly large threshold of 300 meter.

3.2   Estimation of Location Purposes

We estimated the likely purpose of the locations visited by the users by making use of the data provided by Foursquare, a location-based social networking website for mobile devices where users 'check in' at venues. The Foursquare API [5] provides access to all user-generated data, which allowed us to query for venues surrounding a given coordinate.

For each location, we identified venues up to 50 meters away from the location's coordinates. In total, we collected the name and categories from 21,167 venues, covering 4,487 unique locations in our dataset. Obviously, not all locations are associated with venues registered in Foursquare: particularly 'non-popular' sites, such as residential areas, have no nearby venues cataloged in Foursquare. For the GeoLife GPS Trajectory Dataset, we were able to find venues for 49% of the locations, while in the MSR GPS Privacy Dataset we found venues for more than 80% of the data.

4   Analysis of Patterns in Human Mobility

In this section, partially based on earlier work [10], we discuss patterns and regularities that we found in human mobility. First, we describe overall travel patterns on weekdays and during the weekend. Second, we exploit the category labels of the locations to identify their different purposes and to which ones users travel during different hours of the day.

---

[4] http://en.wikipedia.org/wiki/Global_Positioning_System
[5] http://developer.foursquare.com/docs

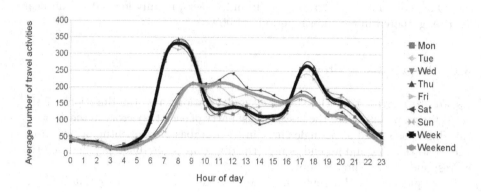

Fig. 1. Daily travel activity during the week and in weekends

4.1   Overall Travel Activity

Our data shows similar characteristics as reported in [9]: trajectories follow a power-law distribution, with only a few locations that account for the majority of visits and a small number of trajectories that users follow most of the time.

In Figure 1, we visualized the number of trips that started at a specific hour on a certain day or group of days (week, weekend). The thick black line is the average of the five weekdays (Monday till Friday) and the thick gray line averages the weekend days (Saturday and Sunday).

Some strong regularities can be observed. On weekdays, the morning rush hour has a strong peak at 8am; the evening rush hour is more spread between 5pm and 9pm. Between both rush hours, traffic is moderate, with a small peak during lunchtime. During weekends, traffic starts somewhat later and remains relatively stable throughout the day, with a slight increase of traffic just before dinnertime. These differences can obviously be explained by the fact that most people work during the week and use the weekend for spare-time activities.

A further insight of the study was how the different locations are related with one another. For individual users, we visualized the locations and the trajectories between them using the graph visualization toolkit Gephi [6], see Figure 2. The graph layout is force-directed. In the figure, four frequently visited locations can be seen, of which location 0 and 1 are presumably the user's office and home locations; location 2 could be a shopping mall, and location 13 might be a (sport) club (see [10] for more details). A particular observation is that the long tail of other locations is typically only connected to one of these main locations, or shared by two locations (the cluster of small dots between home and office probably represents places that are visited on the commute between home and office). We verified this pattern with various other users with sufficient travel data and found similar graphs.

---

[6] https://gephi.org/

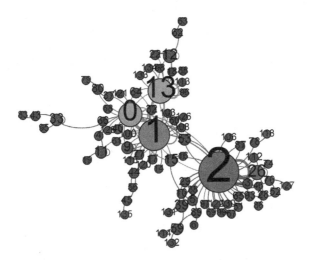

Fig. 2. Connections between locations of an exemplary user. The larger the node, the more often the user visited the corresponding location. The thicker the edge, the more often the user traveled between the two locations.

4.2   The Purposes of End Locations

Further information on typical activities that users engage in can be found by analyzing the purposes associated with typical locations on different times of the day. We extracted these purposes by manually aggregating Foursquare categories into 'purpose groups'. For example, the group 'Food' consists of different restaurant types, such as 'Japanese Restaurant' and 'Fast Food Restaurant'.

In Figure 3, the distribution of end-locations during the day is displayed, with separate graphs for weekdays and the weekend. The graphs are based on 6903 trajectories and corresponding end-locations on weekdays and 3199 end-locations during the weekend.

The distribution of the different category groups over the day shows some clear differences, which match common expectations and the observations from the previous subsection. On weekdays, locations related to transportation (e.g. train stations and bus stations) and work have peaks between 7am and 9am. During the remainder of the working day, travel activity remains low, with a slight peak during the lunch break. Shopping activities take place immediately after the lunch break or during the evening commute. At about 6pm, locations that are associated with food and sports are frequently visited; most people return home after having engaged in typical evening activities.

The distribution of peaks during the weekend is quite different from the weekday pattern. While weekday travel activities have peaks at the start and end of the day, weekend travel tends to be distributed throughout the day - we observed the same effect in Figure 1. Shopping activities show the same peaks as

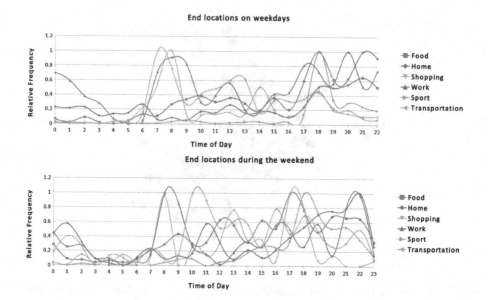

Fig. 3. Distribution over time for different groups of end-locations on weekdays and weekends

on working days, but with a larger emphasis on the end of the day. Similarly, sport activities mainly take place during the evening hours - as on weekdays -, but the spread is wider and includes afternoon hours. Particularly interesting is the distribution of the home category: people often return home at 11am after their morning activities; people who engage in evening activities such as sports often return home at 10pm; the peak at 1am seems to indicate people who return home from a pub or a party - a phenomenon that is not observed on weekdays.

5   Predicting Future Locations

In this section, we use the routine travel patterns, as discussed in the previous section, as a basis for comparing five basic methods for predicting when a person will revisit a particular location. This problem has several similarities with predicting page revisits on the Web, where users also typically revisit only a couple of pages on a frequent basis, and less frequently revisited pages are often revisited together with other pages [15]. In a previous study [12], we compared various combinations of methods for predicting Web revisitation. In the context of this paper, we only consider basic methods and do not attempt to find optimal combinations of these methods - as has been done, among others, by Etter et al [8]; our purpose is to verify the performance of each method and to what extent these prediction methods are correlated.

5.1   Prediction Methods

For predicting the next location a user will visit we applied five basic, commonly used methods. These methods are:

- *Top-N locations*: Take the top-N most popular locations and use this for predicting the next location (baseline).
- *Last-N locations*: This method uses the last N visited locations as a prediction for the next location - this approach is commonly applied for revisitation support in Web browsers.
- *Hour top-N locations*: Top-N endpoints that are most popular at a particular time of day (on a hourly basis).
- *Top-N closest locations*: The N locations that are closest to the user's current location. This approach is often used in location-based services.
- *Simple Markov Model*: This model calculates, based on previous travels, the probability that a user will travel to some location starting from the current location.

5.2   Evaluation Measures

As we are interested in predicting locations that people will revisit as part of their routine patterns, we apply the above-mentioned methods to each user individually. We only considered the 57 participants with more than 100 trajectories in their travel logs. We 'replayed' the users' travel activities and used each above-mentioned method for predicting the next location in the log.

As evaluation measures, we use the success rates $S@1$ and $S@5$, which indicate whether a next location is part of the set of predicted locations. For applications such as pro-active scheduling it is important that the next location achieves the first rank, but for many other applications it is sufficient if the next location is included in a small set of recommendations. The reported values are averages between users.

In order to verify to what extent the location predictions cover the whole set of frequently and less frequently visited locations, we also report the Shannon entropy for the location predictions and the actually visited locations.

5.3   Results

The prediction methods were applied to all end-locations for each individual user, covering both weekdays and the weekend. As weekend mobility follows different patterns than weekdays, we repeated the experiment with separate models for weekdays and weekends. The differences with the all-week models are discussed at the end of this section.

Success Rates. Table 1 shows the success rates for the prediction methods. As expected, the $S@1$ rates are relatively low, except for the Markov model, which performs in line with the results reported by Etter et al [8]. We focus on the

Table 1. Prediction results for all methods

	Top-N	Last-N	Hour	Distance	Markov
$S@1$	0.286	0.204	0.467	0.275	**0.626**
$S@5$	0.612	0.546	0.829	0.49	**0.931**

performance in terms of $S@5$, which - as discussed earlier - is often sufficient for recommendation purposes. The baseline method, Top-N, which always predicts the most frequently visited locations, has a moderate performance with $S@5$ of 61%. This confirms the importance to include the long tail of less frequently visited locations. The Last-N method, which predicts that the next location will be a recently visited location, has an even lower performance - which shows that recency plays only a moderate role in location revisitation.

The worst performing method is the distance-based approach, which predicts that users will revisit a location that is close to the current location. In less than 50% of the cases, this prediction is correct. This may come as a surprise, as most location-based services consider distance as an important factor for recommendations [14].

The hour-based method performs significantly better than the previous methods ($S@5$ about 83%). This indicates that location revisitation highly depends on the time of day, an effect that we have observed in the previous section. The simple Markov model achieves the best performance. If just one single location is predicted, the prediction is correct in 62% of the cases; a list of five locations contains the actual end-location in 93% of the cases.

Table 2. Entropy of locations for predictions and visited locations

	Top-N	Last-N	Hour	Distance	Markov	Actual
Top-1	0	4.142	1.803	4.165	2.852	4.139
Top-5	2.322	4.635	4.201	4.896	3.157	-

Entropy and Revisit Rate. Apart from the success rate of predicted locations, it is also important to take the variety and coverage of the predictions into account. For this, we employed the Shannon entropy measure [7]. Low entropy measures for a prediction method indicate that they often suggest the same (most popular or most visited) locations. As can be seen in Table 2, this is - not surprisingly - the case for the Top-N method. The hour-based method reaches a higher entropy and probably for this reason a higher success rate than Top-N. The Last-N and Distance-based methods reach the highest entropy values, but rather low success rates. Apparently, the variety in visited locations is not successfully captured by these methods. The Markov model has reasonable

---

[7] http://en.wikipedia.org/wiki/Entropy_(information_theory)

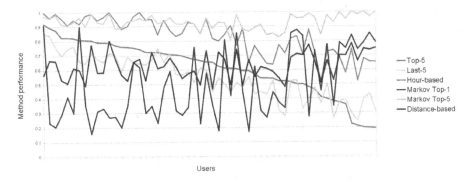

Fig. 4. Performance of the prediction methods for individual users, ordered by the top-5 performance

entropy values; the success rates indicate that the entropy within the Markov model represents actual user behavior.

There are no significant correlations between the method performance measures and the number of trips, or end locations, of a user. This indicates that the method performance does not depend on the data size.

Another measure on user mobility that may impact the method performance, is the extent to which a user revisits locations. Similar to [17] we define the *revisit rate* as the ratio between the number of end locations and the number of trips of a user. The average revisit rate for the participants in the analysis is 74% ($\sigma = .11$), with a minimum of 46% and a maximum of 91%. Indeed, there are significant correlations with $R > .5$ between the revisit rate and the Top-N, Last-N and hour-based methods. By contrast, the revisit rate corresponds negatively with the performance of the Markov and distance-based methods.

Correlations. Figure 4 shows a significant interaction between the Top-N, Last-N and hour-based prediction methods ($R > .84, P < .01$), which confirms that all three methods capture the most popular locations (as shown by [7], the last-n locations often contain top-n locations). Of the three, the hour-based method performs best in capturing the user's behavior. The Markov-based and distance-based methods are positively correlated ($R = .46, p < .01$), which indicates that there is a tendency to select next locations based on the distance, but that other factors (such as locations that are often visited together) play a role as well.

Given the differences in mobility patterns on weekdays and during the weekend - usually due to the absence of commuting on Saturday and Sunday - we repeated our experiments with separate models for weekdays and weekend. All prediction techniques performed more or less similar to the all-week versions. The $S@5$ values for Top-N and Last-N were about 7% higher during weekdays and about 7% lower during the weekend, which confirms our observation that weekend patterns are less stable than weekday patterns.

6 Discussion and Conclusions

In this paper, we analyzed human mobility patterns based on GPS data of 199 people. In line with [9], we observed that human mobility patterns contain strong regularities: people typically spend most of their time at and between a small number of locations. In addition, we found that these popular locations and most-followed trajectories (e.g. the daily commute) also serve as starting points for visits to several other locations that form the long tail of a person's whereabouts.

We also found that most people have a relatively regular schedule for traveling from one location to another (e.g. commuting on weekdays, fixed weekend activities). The purpose of the end-locations, as derived from keywords associated with the locations, also depends on the time of day.

The mobility patterns that we observed can be modeled with different basic methods for revisitation prediction. The comparison of several basic methods showed that a simple Markov model has the best performance, followed by the hour of the day. Note that the Markov model only needs location identifiers without geographic coordinates, which makes it a suitable technique for privacy-preserving location-based personalization. By contrast, distance between locations, even though widely used a main criterion for current location-based services, seems to be a less important factor. The entropy and correlation measures of these methods provide indications on how they can be combined in more complex models.

Most location-based services focus on the recommendation of new locations, usually based on the user's current location. Individual daily and weekly patterns provide a basis for supporting everyday activities involving already visited locations. Particularly the observation that most locations can be connected to one 'base location' or one trajectory - can be exploited in various ways, varying from recommendations to navigate to regular stops on the way back home to targeted advertisements at the moment that a user embarks on a Saturday-morning shopping trip.

References

1. Amini, S., Brush, A., Krumm, J., Teevan, J., Karlson, A.: Trajectory-aware mobile search. In: Proceedings of the 2012 ACM annual conference on Human Factors in Computing Systems, pp. 2561–2564. ACM (2012)
2. Ashbrook, D., Starner, T.: Using gps to learn significant locations and predict movement across multiple users. Personal and Ubiquitous Computing 7, 275–286 (2003)
3. Bellotti, V., Begole, B., Chi, E., Ducheneaut, N., Fang, J., Isaacs, E., King, T., Newman, M., Partridge, K., Price, B., et al.: Activity-based serendipitous recommendations with the magitti mobile leisure guide. In: Proceedings of the Twenty-Sixth Annual SIGCHI Conference on Human Factors in Computing Systems, pp. 1157–1166. ACM (2008)
4. Biagioni, J., Krumm, J.: Days of our lives: Assessing day similarity from location traces. In: Carberry, S., Weibelzahl, S., Micarelli, A., Semeraro, G. (eds.) UMAP 2013. LNCS, vol. 7899, pp. 89–101. Springer, Heidelberg (2013)

5. Brush, A.B., Krumm, J., Scott, J.: Exploring end user preferences for location obfuscation, location-based services, and the value of location. In: Proceedings of the 12th ACM International Conference on Ubiquitous Computing, Ubicomp 2010, pp. 95–104. ACM, New York (2010)

6. Cheng, Z., Caverlee, J., Lee, K.: You are where you tweet: a content-based approach to geo-locating twitter users. In: Proceedings of the 19th ACM International Conference on Information and Knowledge Management, CIKM 2010, pp. 759–768. ACM, New York (2010)

7. Cockburn, A., McKenzie, B.J.: What do web users do? an empirical analysis of web use. Int. J. Hum.-Comput. Stud. 54(6), 903–922 (2001)

8. Etter, V., Kafsi, M., Kazemi, E., Grossglauser, M., Thiran, P.: Where to go from here? mobility prediction from instantaneous information. Pervasive and Mobile Computing 9(6), 784–797 (2013)

9. Gonzalez, M.C., Hidalgo, C.A., Barabasi, A.L.: Understanding individual human mobility patterns. Nature 453(7196), 779–782 (2008)

10. Herder, E., Siehndel, P.: Daily and weekly patterns in human mobility. In: AUM 2012, Workshop on Augmented User Modeling. Extended Proceedings of UMAP 2012 (2012)

11. Joseph, K., Tan, C.H., Carley, K.M.: Beyond "local", "categories" and "friends": clustering foursquare users with latent "topics". In: Proceedings of the 2012 ACM Conference on Ubiquitous Computing, UbiComp 2012, pp. 919–926. ACM, New York (2012)

12. Kawase, R., Papadakis, G., Herder, E., Nejdl, W.: Beyond the usual suspects: context-aware revisitation support. In: Hypertext, pp. 27–36 (2011)

13. Krumm, J., Brush, A.J.B.: Learning time-based presence probabilities. In: Lyons, K., Hightower, J., Huang, E.M. (eds.) Pervasive 2011. LNCS, vol. 6696, pp. 79–96. Springer, Heidelberg (2011)

14. Mokbel, M.F., Bao, J., Eldawy, A., Levandoski, J.J., Sarwat, M.: Personalization, socialization, and recommendations in location-based services 2.0. In: Proceedings of the PersDB 2001 Workshop (2011)

15. Obendorf, H., Weinreich, H., Herder, E., Mayer, M.: Web page revisitation revisited: Implications of a long-term click-stream study of browser usage. In: CHI, pp. 597–606 (2007)

16. Song, C., Qu, Z., Blumm, N., Barabási, A.L.: Limits of predictability in human mobility. Science 327(5968), 1018–1021 (2010)

17. Tauscher, L., Greenberg, S.: How people revisit web pages: empirical findings and implications for the design of history systems. Int. J. Hum.-Comput. Stud. 47(1), 97–137 (1997)

18. Teevan, J., Karlson, A., Amini, S., Brush, A.J.B., Krumm, J.: Understanding the importance of location, time, and people in mobile local search behavior. In: Proceedings of the 13th International Conference on Human Computer Interaction with Mobile Devices and Services, MobileHCI 2011, pp. 77–80. ACM, New York (2011)

19. Zheng, Y., Zhang, L., Xie, X., Ma, W.Y.: Mining interesting locations and travel sequences from gps trajectories. In: Proceedings of the 18th International Conference on World Wide Web, WWW 2009, pp. 791–800. ACM, New York (2009)

A Two-Stage Item Recommendation Method Using Probabilistic Ranking with Reconstructed Tensor Model

Noor Ifada[*] and Richi Nayak

Queensland University of Technology, Brisbane, Queensland 4000, Australia
noor.ifada@if.trunojoyo.ac.id, {noor.ifada,r.nayak}@qut.edu.au

Abstract. In a tag-based recommender system, the multi-dimensional <user, item, tag> correlation should be modeled effectively for finding quality recommendations. Recently, few researchers have used tensor models in recommendation to represent and analyze latent relationships inherent in multi-dimensions data. A common approach is to build the tensor model, decompose it and, then, directly use the reconstructed tensor to generate the recommendation based on the maximum values of tensor elements. In order to improve the accuracy and scalability, we propose an implementation of the n-mode block-striped (matrix) product for scalable tensor reconstruction and probabilistically ranking the candidate items generated from the reconstructed tensor. With testing on real-world datasets, we demonstrate that the proposed method outperforms the benchmarking methods in terms of recommendation accuracy and scalability.

Keywords: tensor reconstruction, probabilistic ranking, item recommendation.

1 Introduction

Web personalization has become a solution to overcome the problem of abundant information on the internet [1]. The personalized systems gather information about users to build user profiles, and tailor them to recommend items interesting to users. With the growing user-generated information on the web, the Social Tagging Systems (STS) have gained great popularity as they allow users to annotate items like websites (delicious.com) or artists (www.last.fm). These reusable and sharable tags reveal user interests implicitly [2], and serve as an additional source of information to build user profiles for recommender systems [3, 4]. The performance of tag-based recommender systems heavily relies on how the tag assignments, representing the <user, item, tag> correlation, have been exploited. The user profiles model should expose the latent relationship between users, items, and tags. With using two-dimensional modeling approach [5], the total interaction between the three dimensions may be lost, and this will result in poor recommendation accuracy [4, 6]. Since the tag assignment data is a multi-dimensional data, it becomes obvious that user profiles should be modeled with higher-order data models rather than projecting them into lower dimension approach.

---

[*] Noor Ifada is currently on leave from University of Trunojoyo Madura, Indonesia.

V. Dimitrova et al. (Eds.): UMAP 2014, LNCS 8538, pp. 98–110, 2014.

Tensor modeling, a well-known approach to represent and analyze latent relationships inherent in multi-dimensions data [7], can be adapted in recommender systems. Researchers have used tensor models to recommend tags [4, 8-10] and items [4, 6, 11] to users. The nature of recommending item differs from the tag recommendation since item recommendation is generated based on the user information specified only while the later have more information about the subject to receive recommendation, i.e., the user-item combination [12]. There are two ways that a tensor model can be utilized in recommendation: (1) by decomposing the tensor model and inferring recommendations based on decomposition factors [8, 10]; and (2) by reconstructing the decomposed models and inferring recommendation from the reconstructed tensor [4, 6, 9, 11, 13]. As scalability is a common issue in the tensor model, existing studies propose to solve the problem within the decomposition process by implementing the memory efficient [14] and optimization criterion [10] methods.

The second type of approach, using reconstructed tensors, is a step further than the former. The model needs to be reconstructed, as an approximation of the initial tensor, to reveal the latent relationships between dimensions of the tensor model [6]. These latent relationships can form the basis of identifying new entries to be used as recommendations. Existing methods build the tensor model, decompose it using standard techniques and, then, directly use the reconstructed tensor to generate the recommendations based on the maximum values of tag assignments in each user-item combinations of tensor elements [4, 6, 11]. Those previous studies assume that tag assignment value in the reconstructed tensor represents the level of user preference for an item based on the tag value. However, they ignore the user's tagging history that has been found most influencive in forming user likelihood to the recommended items in recommendation research [5]. We conjecture that ranking of these items by utilizing the user's tagging history would improve the recommendation accuracy. Another problem with the existing approaches is scalability. Tensor reconstruction is an expensive process as all decomposed factors need to be multiplied to form an approximate tensor. We have not found the examples of reconstructing large size tensors (for instance, more than the size of $1000 \times 1000 \times 1000$ for a three-dimension tensor model) [4, 6, 8, 11, 13].

In this paper, we adopt tensor models for generating recommendation using the tensor reconstruction approach. Our focus is on improving scalability during the reconstruction step and improving recommendation accuracy after the model has been reconstructed. Approaching the complexity within the decomposition task is beyond the scope of this paper. We propose an item recommendation method that utilizes a memory efficient loop approach for scalable tensor reconstruction and a probabilistic ranking to improve the accuracy of recommendations generated from the reconstructed tensor. The memory efficient loop implements the n-mode block-striped (matrix) product to reconstruct the tensor by multiplying all decomposed elements. The probabilistic ranking calculates the probability of users to select candidate items generated from the reconstructed tensor using their tag preference list.

We evaluate the method with several variations implementing the two broad tensor decomposition technique families, Tucker (HOSVD, HOOI) and CP [7], on two real-world STS datasets. Extensive offline experiments have been conducted to find the effectiveness of the method with various sensitivity analysis over the benchmarking methods: conventional tensor-based method [4] and a state-of-the-art matrix-based method [5]. Empirical analysis shows that the proposed method is able to outperform the benchmarking methods in terms of recommendation accuracy and scalability.

2   A Two-Stage Tensor-Based Recommendation

2.1   The Tag Assignment Data

Let $U = \{u_1, u_2, u_3, ..., u_{|U|}\}$ be the set of all users, $I = \{i_1, i_2, i_3, ..., i_{|I|}\}$ be the set of all items and $T = \{t_1, t_2, t_3, ..., t_{|T|}\}$ be the set of all tags in the tag assignment data A. In STS, a vector of tag assignment, $a(u, i, t) \in A$ represents the tagging activity of user u for item i with tag t. For each tag assignment, possible value of v_A for $a(u, i, t)$ is $\{0, 1\}$ where 1 indicates that $a(u, i, t)$ exists and 0 indicates otherwise. The post O denotes the set of all distinct user-item combinations in A, $dom(O) \subset dom(A)$, as a user can tag an item with multiple values. For each post, the possible value of v_O for $o(u, i)$ is $\{0, 1\}$ where 1 indicates user u has tagged item i with a tag and 0 indicates user u has not tagged item i. The tag assignment data A is used in both generating the item recommendation candidates and ranking item recommendations, while the post data O is used for ranking item recommendations only.

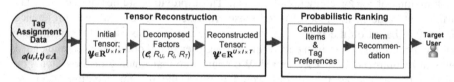

Fig. 1. High-level Definition of the Two-Stage Tensor-based Recommendation

2.2   High-Level Definition

Figure 1 illustrates the high-level definition of the proposed two-stage tensor-based recommendation method. The first stage is tensor reconstruction that generates candidate items which includes: initial third-order tensor constructed from the tag assignment data A, decomposed factors after factorization of the model, and the approximated tensor model generated with multiplications of the decomposed factors. The second stage is probabilistic ranking that generates the Top-N ranked list of item recommendations to users. This stage calculates the probability of a user to select a candidate item generated from the reconstructed tensor using his tag preference list and rank the items for a user according to their probability values.

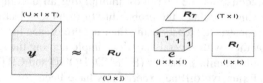

Fig. 2. The CP Decomposition Technique for Third-Order Tensor

2.3   Stage 1: Tensor Reconstruction

In this stage, we build an approximate tensor by using decomposed factors incorporating the latent relationships between the dimensions of users, items and tags. The reconstructed tensor will generate candidate items to be used in next stage for recommendation. From the tag assignment data A, an initial third order tensor $\mathcal{Y} \in \mathbb{R}^{U \times I \times T}$ is constructed where U, I, and T are the set of users, items and tags respectively. Each element of tensor is assigned with binary value v_A. The value will change to continuous value reflecting the significance of triplet after the decomposition process. Only the non-zero values are used in tensor construction to allow the creation of large tensor models as well as handling the sparsity problem in the tag assignment data. A decomposition technique is applied to tensor $\mathcal{Y}$ in order to derive the latent relationships inherent in the dimensions. Two broad family of decomposition techniques are Tucker (including the Higher-Order SVD (HOSVD) and Higher-Order Orthogonal Iteration (HOOI) methods) and Candecomp/Parafac (CP) [7]. CP can be considered as a special case of Tucker where the core tensor is diagonal [7]. In this section, we show the process of the third-order tensor decomposition using CP technique as illustrated in Figure 2. However, we also implemented the method with HOSVD and HOOI methods and empirically analyze the results as reported in the next section.

For the third-order tensor $\mathcal{Y} \in \mathbb{R}^{U \times I \times T}$, CP performs Singular Value Decomposition (SVD) on the matricized data [7] resulting three left singular matrices M_U, M_I, and M_T which correspond to each dimension of the tensor. By choosing size reduction of $j \in \{1, |U|\}, , k \in \{1, |I|\}$, and $l \in \{1, |T|\}$, the reduced factor matrices are obtained as $R_U \in \mathbb{R}^{U \times j}, R_I \in \mathbb{R}^{I \times k}, R_T \in \mathbb{R}^{T \times l}$. The diagonal core tensor $\mathcal{C}$ which defines the interaction between the users, items and tags [7] then can be calculated as:

$$\mathcal{C} = \mathcal{Y} \times_1 R_U{}' \times_2 R_I{}' \times_3 R_T{}' \tag{1}$$

where $\mathcal{C} \in \mathbb{R}^{j \times k \times l}$. The reconstructed tensor $\hat{\mathcal{Y}}$ is derived as:

$$\hat{\mathcal{Y}} = \mathcal{C} \times_1 R_U \times_2 R_I \times_3 R_T \tag{2}$$

The n-mode (matrix) product of a tensor $\mathcal{C} \in \mathbb{R}^{j \times k \times l}$ with a matrix $R \in \mathbb{R}^{D \times j}$ multiplies each n-mode tensor fiber by matrix R which denoted by $\mathcal{C} \times_n R$. It is equivalent to multiplying R by the appropriate transformation of tensor $\mathcal{C}$ into matrix C [7]:

$$\hat{\mathcal{Y}}_n = \mathcal{C} \times_n R \iff \hat{Y}_{(n)} = RC_{(n)} \tag{3}$$

Implementing the general n-mode matrix product for reconstructing tensor on a large dataset is expensive due to memory overflow. The problem becomes worse in the last step of multiplication where the effects of earlier decomposition factors have been included. We propose a memory-efficient loop approach to solve the problem of last iteration. We implement 1-mode and 2-mode (matrix) products to multiply the core tensor $\mathcal{C}$ with the reduced factor matrix R_U and R_I to obtain the intermediate tensor result $\hat{\mathcal{Y}}_1$ and $\hat{\mathcal{Y}}_2$ sequentially. To multiply $\hat{\mathcal{Y}}_2$ with the reduced factor matrix R_T, we implement a 3-mode block-striped (matrix) product. The multiplication task between matrix $\hat{Y}_2$ (the mode-3 matrix equivalent form of tensor $\hat{\mathcal{Y}}_2$) and R_T is split into N number of subtask, where $N = |T|$ div q and q is a user-given block-strip row size ($q \ll |T|$). At each subtask, a matrix W_N, where $/W_N| = q$, is obtained by R_T and multiplied with $\hat{Y}_2$. The complete reconstructed tensor $\hat{\mathcal{Y}}$ is achieved by combining all subtask results. The block-stripping of the matrix R_T and multiplication subtasks allow producing smaller manipulations that can fit in the allowed memory size.

The reconstructed tensor $\hat{\mathcal{Y}}$ identifies new entries that are inferred from the latent relationships hidden among the high-order ternary dimensions. It includes a set of triplets $\hat{a}(u, i, t) \in \hat{A}$ where $A \subset \hat{A}$. Tensor decomposition has recalculated v_A of each existing entry in $\mathcal{Y}$ as well as identified new entries as continues values $v_{\hat{A}}$ in $\hat{\mathcal{Y}}$ which represent the likeliness of user u to tag item i with tag t. Post $\hat{O}$ are assigned binary values $v_{\hat{O}}$ that represent the existence of user-item combinations. As we are generating item recommendation, new item for each user will be selected as new post $\hat{O} - O$ and new tags recommendation will be ignored. Figure 3 shows the process within tensor reconstruction approach used in our proposed method.

Algorithm: *Tensor Reconstruction*
Input: Tag assignment triplets (A) with $|U|$, $|I|$, and $|T|$ as the number of users, items and tags; Block-strip row size (q) where $q \ll |T|$, $|T|$ div $q = N$ and $|T|$ mod $q = b$.
Output: Reconstructed Tensor $(\hat{\mathcal{Y}})$
1. Construct initial tensor $\mathcal{Y} \in \mathbb{R}^{U \times I \times T}$ from A
2. Apply a decomposition technique to tensor $\mathcal{Y}$ to get:
    a. Left singular factor matrices: M_U, M_I, M_T
    b. Size reduction by choosing: $j \in \{1, |U|\}, k \in \{1, |I|\}, l \in \{1, |T|\}$
        The reduced matrices: $R_U \in \mathbb{R}^{U \times j}, R_I \in \mathbb{R}^{I \times k}, R_T \in \mathbb{R}^{T \times l}$
    c. Core tensor: $C \leftarrow \mathcal{Y} \times_1 R_U' \times_2 R_I' \times_3 R_T'$ where $C \in \mathbb{R}^{j \times k \times l}$
3. Reconstruct tensor:
    a. 1-mode (matrix) product: $\widehat{\mathcal{Y}_1} \leftarrow C \times_1 R_U, \widehat{\mathcal{Y}_1} \in \mathbb{R}^{U \times k \times l}$
    b. 2-mode (matrix) product: $\widehat{\mathcal{Y}_2} \leftarrow \widehat{\mathcal{Y}_1} \times_2 R_I, \widehat{\mathcal{Y}_2} \in \mathbb{R}^{U \times I \times l}$
    c. **For** $n \leftarrow 1$ to N
        $W_n \leftarrow R_T^{((n-1)q+1,l)}, W_n \in \mathbb{R}^{q \times l}$
        3-mode (matrix) product: $\widehat{\mathcal{Y}_{3n}} \leftarrow \widehat{\mathcal{Y}_2} \times_3 W_n, \widehat{\mathcal{Y}_{3n}} \in \mathbb{R}^{U \times I \times q}; \hat{\mathcal{Y}} \leftarrow \hat{\mathcal{Y}} + \widehat{\mathcal{Y}_{3n}}$
        End for
        If $b \neq 0$ **Then**
        $n \leftarrow n + 1; W_n \leftarrow R_T^{((n-1)q+1,l)}, W_n \in \mathbb{R}^{s \times l}$
        3-mode (matrix) product: $\widehat{\mathcal{Y}_{3n}} \leftarrow \widehat{\mathcal{Y}_2} \times_3 W_n, \widehat{\mathcal{Y}_{3n}} \in \mathbb{R}^{U \times I \times s}; \hat{\mathcal{Y}} \leftarrow \hat{\mathcal{Y}} + \widehat{\mathcal{Y}_{3n}}$
        End if /* $\hat{\mathcal{Y}} \in \mathbb{R}^{U \times I \times T}$ */
4. Use entries in $\hat{\mathcal{Y}}$, where $\hat{O} - O$, as candidate items for recommendation

Fig. 3. Tensor Reconstruction Algorithm

Example: Tensor Reconstruction. We explain the stage 1 process with a toy example. Figure 4(a) presents an initial third-order tensor $\mathcal{Y} \in \mathbb{R}^{3 \times 4 \times 4}$ showing 7 tagging and of 6 posting activities. Applying a decomposition technique with 2 as the reduction size results into three reduced-size factor matrices and one core tensor, $R_U \in \mathbb{R}^{3 \times 2}, R_I \in \mathbb{R}^{4 \times 2}, R_T \in \mathbb{R}^{4 \times 2}$, and $C \in \mathbb{R}^{2 \times 2 \times 2}$. Figure 4(b) shows the reconstructed tensor $\hat{\mathcal{Y}}$ derived by multiplying all decomposed elements. For ease of illustration, we are only showing the top 22 non-zero entries out of a total of 48 entries in $\hat{\mathcal{Y}}$ which grouped as 10 posts. It can be noted that tensor decomposition has recalculated v_A of each existing entry in $\mathcal{Y}$, and identified new entries, as $v_{\hat{A}}$. Since we are interested in recommending items, the process would identify new posts, finding new item for users (ignoring the new tags for existing <user-item> pairs). As highlighted in Figure 4(b), $\hat{\mathcal{Y}}$ generates four (new) items for two users, <2,1>, <2,3>,<3,1> and <3,2>, and utilize them as candidate items to be ranked on the second stage.

U	I	T	v_A	v_O
1	1	2	1	1
1	1	3	1	
1	2	1	1	1
1	3	3	1	1
1	4	4	1	1
2	2	2	1	1
3	4	4	1	1

(a) Initial Tensor $\mathcal{Y}$

U	I	T	$v_{\hat{A}}$	$v_{\hat{O}}$
1	1	1	0.0284	
1	1	2	1.1169	
1	1	3	1.1189	1
1	1	4	0.0001	
1	2	1	0.8796	
1	2	2	0.0001	
1	2	3	0.0001	
1	2	4	1.0000	1
1	3	1	0.9986	
1	3	2	0.0446	1
1	3	3	0.0065	
1	4	4	1.0301	1
2	1	1	0.0004	
2	1	2	0.0085	
2	1	3	0.0085	1
2	2	2	0.9980	1
2	3	1	0.0255	
2	3	3	0.4991	1
2	3	2	0.5002	
3	1	4	0.0001	1
3	2	4	1.0000	1
3	4	4	0.9988	1

(b) Reconstructed Tensor $\hat{\mathcal{Y}}$

Fig. 4. Example of Tensor Model from Toy Dataset with Only Non-zero Values Displayed

2.4   Stage 2: Probabilistic Ranking

This stage takes the new entries (or posts) generated from the reconstructed model and applies probabilistic ranking to rank them as Top-N list of item recommendations. Existing methods rank the candidate items based on the maximum value of $v_{\hat{A}} - v_A$ within every $\hat{O} - O$ [4, 6, 11, 13]. These approaches fail to consider the items and tags usage histories in the tag assignment A, and calculate the recommendations using the level of user preference for an item which based on a tag only. We propose to utilize Naïve Bayes [15] for generating a probabilistic model based on previously observed items and tags usage for ranking the candidate items. We approach the problem of item recommendation as a classification problem, making Naïve Bayes apt for finding an efficient solution [16].

For each user u, based on new posts $\hat{O} - O$ in $\hat{\mathcal{Y}}$, two sets are created. A set of candidate items, $Z_u = \{i_1, i_2, i_3, \ldots, i_r\}$ where $Z_u \subseteq I$ that the user u might be interested in, is generated. A tag preference set, $X_u = \{t_1, t_2, t_3, \ldots, t_t\}$ where $X_u \subseteq T$ and $|X_u| \leq |T|$ that user u has used to tag the candidate items, is generated. The tag preference set is generated based on the maximum values of $v_{\hat{A}} - v_A$ which are sorted in descending order. We use the Bayes' theorem for predicting the class candidate item Z_u that have the highest posterior probability given X_u, $p(Z_u|X_u)$. The posterior probability is utilized to calculate the preference probability of user u to select candidate items Z_u by observing the previous usage activities of tag preferences X_u in A. The conditional probability can be formulated as:

$$p(Z_u|X_u) = \frac{p(Z_u)p(X_u|Z_u)}{p(X_u)} \qquad (4)$$

where prior $p(Z_u)$ is the prior distributions of parameter set Z_u before X_u is observed; $p(X_u|Z_u)$ is the probability of observing tag preference set X_u given Z_u; and $p(X_u)$ is the probability of observing X_u. Using the assumption of multinomial event model distribution for the Naïve Bayes classifier, the posterior probability p_{u,i_r} of user u

with tag preference X_u for candidate item i_r, an instance of Z_u, is obtained by multiplying the prior probability of i_r, $p(Z_u = i_r)$, with the probability of tag preference t_c, an instance of X_u, given i_r, $p(t_c|Z_u = i_r)$:

$$p_{u,i_r} = p(i_r|X_u) = p(Z_u = i_r)\prod_{c=1}^{|X_u|} p(t_c|Z_u = i_r)^{\left(\left(\sum_{i=1}^{|I|} v_{a(u,i_*,t_c)}\right)+1\right)} \tag{5}$$

where $v_{a(u,i_*,t_c)}$ denotes the binary value of assignment A for user u who has used tag preference t_c to tag any item i. The $p(Z_u = i_r)$ and $p(t_c|Z_u = i_r)$ are calculated as:

$$p(Z_u = i_r) = \frac{\sum_{u=1}^{|U|} v_{O(u_*,i_r)}}{\sum_{i=1}^{|I|}\sum_{u=1}^{|U|} v_{O(u_*,i_*)}} \tag{6}$$

$$p(t_c|Z_u = i_r) = \frac{1+\sum_{u=1}^{|U|} v_{a(u_*,i_r,t_c)}}{|T|+\sum_{u=1}^{|U|}\sum_{t=1}^{|T|} v_{a(u_*,i_r,t_*)}} \tag{7}$$

where $v_{O(u_*,i_r)}$ and $v_{O(u_*,i_*)}$ denote the value of post O for any user u who has tagged candidate item i_r and any item i, respectively. The $v_{a(u_*,i_r,t_c)}$ and $v_{a(u_*,i_r,t_*)}$ denote the value of tag assignment A where candidate item i_r has been tagged by any user u using tag preference t_c and any tag t, respectively. To avoid zero values of Equation 5 and 7, we apply the Laplacean estimate [16] as a smoothing method by adding one to those equations.

For the target user u, the list of Top-N item recommendation is an ordered set of N items, $TopN_u$, obtained by sorting the p_{u,i_r} of user's candidate items in descending order. Figure 5 describes the probabilistic ranking algorithm for generating the Top-N list of item recommendation.

Algorithm: *Probabilistic Ranking*
Input: Initial tensor ($\mathcal{Y}$), Reconstructed tensor ($\hat{\mathcal{Y}}$), Tag preference size (s), Number of Recommendation (N)
Output: The list of N items $TopN_u$
1. Get the candidate item set $Z_u = \{i_1, i_2, i_3, ..., i_r\}$:
    $Z_u \leftarrow \hat{O} - O$ /*new items in $\hat{O}$ from $\hat{\mathcal{Y}}$ */
2. Get the tag preference set $X_u = \{t_1, t_2, t_3, ..., t_t\}$ such that ($|X_u| \leq s$):
    $X_u \leftarrow \max_{v_{\hat{A}} - v_A}(\hat{O} - O)$
3. Calculate posterior probability of each item in Z_u and use the value to generate Top-N item recommendation:
    For $r \leftarrow 1$ to N /* initialize the $ListP$ using the first N posterior values of Z_u */
    $p_{u,i_r} \leftarrow p(i_r|X_u)$; $ListP \leftarrow ListP \cup p_{u,i_r}$; $R \leftarrow R \cup r$
    End for
    For $r \leftarrow (N+1)$ to $|Z_u|$
    $p_{u,i_r} \leftarrow p(i_r|X_u)$
    If $p_{u,i_r} > (\min ListP)$ **then**
    $ListP \leftarrow ListP - (\min ListP)$; $R \leftarrow R - r_{min}$
    $ListP \leftarrow ListP \cup p_{u,i_r}$; $R \leftarrow R \cup r$
    End if
    End for
    $TopN_u \leftarrow \{i_r \in Z_u | r \in R\}$

Fig. 5. Probabilistic Ranking Algorithm

Example: Probabilistic Ranking. The reconstructed tensor as shown in Figure 4(b) generates four new items that correspond to u_2 and u_3. The set of candidate items and tag preferences of u_2 and u_3 are derived as $Z_{u_2} = \{i_1, i_3\}$, $X_{u_2} = \{t_1, t_2, t_3\}$ and $Z_{u_3} = \{i_1, i_2\}$, $X_{u_3} = \{t_4\}$, respectively. Using Equation 5, we calculate the posterior probabilities of u_2 to i_1 and i_3, and of u_3 to i_1 and i_2. Since p_{u_2,i_1}:0.0009 > p_{u_2,i_3}:0.0005, i_1 is more likely to interest u_2 than i_3. While p_{u_3,i_1}:0.0040 = p_{u_3,i_3}:0.0040, i_1 and i_3 are on the same level of interest for u_3. As a result, $TopN_{u_2}$ and $TopN_{u_3}$ are generated in the sequence order of $\{i_1, i_3\}$ and $\{i_1, i_2\}$, respectively. These results differ from the conventional tensor-based approaches which generate $TopN_{u_2}$ and $TopN_{u_3}$ as the sequence order of $\{i_3, i_1\}$ and $\{i_2, i_1\}$, respectively.

3   Empirical Analysis

Two real-world datasets from Delicious (http://delicious.com/) and LastFM (http://www.last.fm/) websites were used. The proposed method is benchmarked with the conventional tensor-based method ("Max") [4] and the state-of-the-art matrix-based method ("CTS") [5]. We demonstrated the variation of our method and the Max method with three commonly used tensor decomposition techniques (i.e. CP, HOOI, and HOSVD [7]) using the Matlab Tensor Toolbox [17]. The results are presented as TRPR-CP, TRPR-HOOI, TRPR-HOSVD, and Max-CP, Max-HOOI, Max-HOSVD for these variations. Adopting the standard practice of decreasing the data sparsity [4, 6, 11, 18], the datasets are refined by selecting users, items, and tags that have occurred in at least p number of posts using the p-core technique [19]. We implemented choices of p-core, as listed in Table 1, to avoid the non-stable results that tend to occur when only one choice of core size is used for the experiments [20].

Table 1. Dataset Statistic

Dataset	p-core	User	Item	Tag	Tag Assignment	Post
Delicious	15	1,609	719	1,761	32,839	17,077
	20	1,359	424	1,321	23,442	12,282
	25	1,198	282	1,053	17,682	9,402
LastFM	10	867	1,715	1,423	99,211	37,163
	20	601	681	838	61,739	22,407
	25	522	490	714	50,381	18,029

We divided the dataset randomly into a training set D_{train} (80%) and a test set D_{test} (20%) based on the number of posts. D_{train} and D_{test} do not overlap in posts, i.e., there exist no triplets for a user-item combination (u, i) in the training set if a triplet (u, i, t_*) is present in the test set. The Top-N items are predicted and ranked for the users present in D_{test}. The performance is measured using F1-Score, as the harmonic mean of overall precision and recall, and reported over the average values as the experiments were implemented using 5-fold cross-validation.

$$Precision(D_{test}, N) = avg_{(u,i) \in D_{test}} \frac{|Test_u \cap TopN_u|}{|TopN_u|} \qquad (8)$$

$$Recall(D_{test}, N) = avg_{(u,i) \in D_{test}} \frac{|Test_u \cap TopN_u|}{|Test_u|} \qquad (9)$$

$$F1(D_{test}, N) = \frac{2 \cdot Precision(D_{test}, N) \cdot Recall(D_{test}, N)}{Precision(D_{test}, N) + Recall(D_{test}, N)} \qquad (10)$$

Where $Test_u$ is the set of items tagged by target user in the D_{test} and $TopN_u$ is the Top-N list of items recommended to user from the reconstructed tensor $\hat{\mathcal{Y}}$ which do not exist in the initial tensor $\mathcal{Y}$.

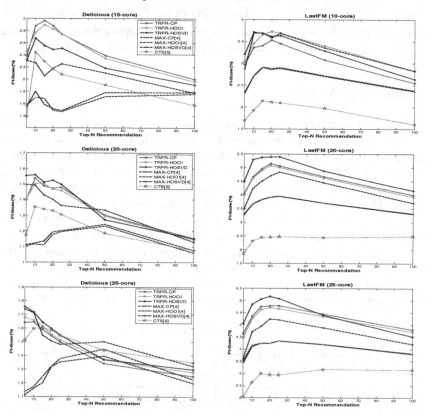

Fig. 6. F1-Score Comparison on Top-N lists for the Recommendation Accuracy

Accuracy: Using F1-score values, we compare the Top-N lists recommendation accuracy between the proposed method and the benchmarking methods. Figure 6 demonstrates that the proposed method outperforms the matrix-based method CTS and the conventional tensor-based method Max. Table 2 lists the average of TRPR recommendation accuracy improvement over the Max method to show the outperformance when implemented on different decomposition techniques used in this paper. The percentage scores are calculated by defining the F1-Scores of TRPR and Max as the current and the starting values, respectively. The scores are reported as an average improvement over all Top-N values. These results ascertain our claim that probabilistically ranking the candidate items, generated from the reconstructed tensor, with utilizing the user's past tagging activities can significantly improve the recommendation accuracy. These results also show the robustness of the proposed method with several decomposition methods. The method with HOOI and CP decomposition techniques achieve bigger improvement than the method with HOSVD. HOSVD optimizes each mode of tensor $\mathcal{Y}$ dimension separately and disregards the interaction among them [7]. Therefore the list of candidate items and tag preferences generated from the reconstructed tensor $\hat{\mathcal{Y}}$ could not reveal the user interest as much as it does for HOOI and CP which use the optimization approach to approximate tensor $\mathcal{Y}$ by taking all lateral interactions into consideration.

It is to be noted that, in general, F1-Scores achieved on offline experiments are low. Our experimental setting may be the reason behind this as the dataset were randomly divided into D_{train} and D_{test} based on the number of posts data. This does not guarantee that for each user in D_{train}, at least one of its post will be selected as D_{test}. Consequently, a target user in D_{test} may not possibly exist in D_{train} (the target user is actually a completely new user).

Table 2. Average TRPR Recommendation Accuracy Improvement over Max Method [4]

Delicious Dataset				LastFM Dataset			
Technique / p-core	CP	HOOI	HOSVD	Technique / p-core	CP	HOOI	HOSVD
15	58.70%	58.24%	11.31%	10	28.67%	26.49%	0.25%
20	21.70%	22.31%	4.43%	20	26.84%	25.43%	16.90%
25	20.35%	19.56%	1.15%	25	32.03%	29.76%	19.38%

Table 3. The Density of the Initial Tensor $\mathcal{Y}$ and Reconstructed Tensor $\hat{\mathcal{Y}}$

Dataset	p-core	$\mathcal{Y}$ constructed from D_{train}	Density $(A/(U \times I \times T))$		
			$\hat{\mathcal{Y}}$ where $\hat{O} - O$		
			CP	HOOI	HOSVD
Delicious	15	0.0014%	0.5239%	0.5110%	0.2753%
	20	0.0027%	1.1113%	1.1178%	0.6594%
	25	0.0043%	1.7970%	1.7916%	1.2622%
LastFM	10	0.0043%	2.1874%	2.2601%	3.2788%
	20	0.0163%	6.7643%	6.9043%	10.6287%
	25	0.0250%	9.4329%	9.3915%	14.3895%

Sensitivity: We examine the effect of choices of p-core to the recommendation accuracy improvement and to the tensor model density. As recorded in Table 2, the p-core size impacts recommendation accuracy. On the Delicious dataset, for all decomposition techniques, the bigger the size of p-core is, the less improvement is achieved. On the contrary, when the LastFM dataset is refined using bigger p-core, the accuracy improvement tend to increase. The characteristic of the datasets is the reason behind this. From Table 1, we can see that, the number of users is always greater than the number of items available on the Delicious dataset. The gap becomes larger as higher p-core is implemented. While on the LastFM dataset, there are sufficient number of items offered for the users resulted from various p-core. Table 3 displays the density of initial tensor $\mathcal{Y}$, built from D_{train}, and reconstructed tensor $\hat{\mathcal{Y}}$. We can examine that the density of $\hat{\mathcal{Y}}$, for all decomposition techniques, is much larger than the density of original $\mathcal{Y}$. Note that the posts in $\hat{\mathcal{Y}}$ which occurred in $\mathcal{Y}$ are excluded, $\hat{O} - O$, since we want to recommend items which have not been tagged by target users. As the purpose of implementing p-core technique is to decrease the dataset sparsity, the trends show that, for all datasets, the bigger the p-core is, the more dense the model.

Scalability: We use space consumption and CPU runtime as the performance metrics to evaluate the scalability of TRPR compared to the Max method [4]. Figure 7 shows the space and time required for tensor reconstruction process of different tensor dimensionalities by varying p-core on the Delicious dataset. Using 15, 50, 80, and 100 core sizes, we built four tensor models of different *user* × *item* × *tag* dimensionalities, $1,609 \times 719 \times 1,761$; $665 \times 52 \times 422$; $362 \times 13 \times 189$; and $250 \times 7 \times 125$, respectively. Accordingly, the bigger p-core size, the smaller the tensor dimensionality is achieved. Figure 7 demonstrates that, for the largest data ($1,609 \times 719 \times 1,761$), Max failed to run due to memory overflow. The trends show that TRPR is scalable for large tensor size on any decomposition techniques with nearly constant space consumption and a linear time computation to the tensor dimensionality. Consequently, for the purpose of accuracy benchmarking, we had to implement the n-mode block-striped (matrix) product to Max method for making it applicable for all datasets used.

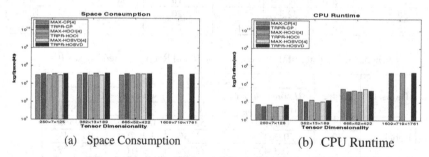

(a) Space Consumption   (b) CPU Runtime

Fig. 7. Scalability Comparison by Varying Tensor Dimensionality on Delicious Dataset

4   Conclusion and Future Work

In this paper, we proposed an item recommendation method using tensor reconstruction approach combined with probabilistic ranking. The method utilizes a memory efficient loop technique for scalable tensor reconstruction and probabilistic ranking to improve the recommendation accuracy of candidate items generated from the reconstructed tensor. Empirical analysis on real-world datasets, with the variations of p-core and decomposition techniques, shows that the proposed method outperforms the benchmarking methods in terms of accuracy and scalability. We have shown that recommendation accuracy can be improved with probabilistically ranking the candidate items, generated from the reconstructed tensor, with utilizing the user's past tagging activities. We also demonstrated that the implementation of n-mode block-striped (matrix) product makes the tensor reconstruction scalable for large datasets. In the future, we are planning to refine the quality of recommendation by implementing clustering approach to solve tag semantic problem.

References

1. Zhang, Z.-K., Zhou, T., Zhang, Y.-C.: Tag-Aware Recommender Systems: A State-of-the-Art Survey. Journal of Computer Science and Technology 26(5), 767–777 (2011)
2. Mezghani, M., Zayani, C.A., Amous, I., Gargouri, F.: A User Profile Modelling using Social Annotations: A Survey. In: The 21st International Conference Companion on World Wide Web, pp. 969–976. ACM, Lyon (2012)
3. Lü, L., Medo, M., Yeung, C.H., Zhang, Y.-C., Zhang, Z.-K., Zhou, T.: Recommender Systems. Physics Reports 519(1), 1–49 (2012)
4. Symeonidis, P., Nanopoulos, A., Manolopoulos, Y.: A Unified Framework for Providing Recommendations in Social Tagging Systems Based on Ternary Semantic Analysis. IEEE Transactions on Knowledge and Data Engineering 22(2), 179–192 (2010)
5. Kim, H.-N., Ji, A.-T., Ha, I., Jo, G.-S.: Collaborative Filtering based on Collaborative Tagging for Enhancing the Quality of Recommendation. Electronic Commerce Research and Applications 9(1), 73–83 (2010)
6. Rafailidis, D., Daras, P.: The TFC Model: Tensor Factorization and Tag Clustering for Item Recommendation in Social Tagging Systems. IEEE Transactions on Systems, Man and Cybernetics, Part A: Systems and Humans 43(3), 673–688 (2013)
7. Kolda, T., Bader, B.: Tensor Decompositions and Applications. SIAM Review 51(3), 455–500 (2009)
8. Leginus, M., Dolog, P., Žemaitis, V.: Improving Tensor Based Recommenders with Clustering. In: Masthoff, J., Mobasher, B., Desmarais, M.C., Nkambou, R., et al. (eds.) UMAP 2012. LNCS, vol. 7379, pp. 151–163. Springer, Heidelberg (2012)
9. Symeonidis, P., Nanopoulos, A., Manolopoulos, Y.: Tag Recommendations based on Tensor Dimensionality Reduction. In: The 2008 ACM Conference on Recommender Systems, pp. 43–50. ACM, Lausanne (2008)
10. Rendle, S., Schmidt-Thieme, L.: Pairwise Interaction Tensor Factorization for Personalized Tag Recommendation. In: The 3rd ACM International Conference on Web Search and Data Mining, pp. 81–90. ACM, New York (2010)
11. Nanopoulos, A.: Item Recommendation in Collaborative Tagging Systems. IEEE Transactions on Systems, Man and Cybernetics, Part A: Systems and Humans 41(4), 760–771 (2011)
12. Peng, J., Zeng, D.D., Zhao, H., Wang, F.-Y.: Collaborative Filtering in Social Tagging Systems based on Joint Item-Tag Recommendations. In: The 19th ACM International Conference on Information and Knowledge Management, pp. 809–818. ACM, Toronto (2010)
13. Kutty, S., Chen, L., Nayak, R.: A People-to-people Recommendation System using Tensor Space Models. In: The 27th Annual ACM Symposium on Applied Computing, pp. 187–192. ACM, Trento (2012)
14. Kolda, T.G., Sun, J.: Scalable Tensor Decompositions for Multi-aspect Data Mining. In: The 8th IEEE International Conference on Data Mining, pp. 363–372. IEEE, Pisa (2008)
15. Baker, L.D., McCallum, A.K.: Distributional Clustering of Words for Text Classification. In: The 21st Annual International ACM SIGIR Conference on Research and Development in Information Retrieval, pp. 96–103. ACM, Melbourne (1998)

16. Lops, P., Gemmis, M., Semeraro, G.: Content-based Recommender Systems: State of the Art and Trends. In: Recommender Systems Handbook, pp. 73–105. Springer US (2011)
17. Bader, B.W., Kolda, T.G., et al.: MATLAB Tensor Toolbox Version 2.5. (January 2012), http://www.sandia.gov/~tgkolda/TensorToolbox/
18. Jäschke, R., Marinho, L., Hotho, A., Schmidt-Thieme, L., Stumme, G.: Tag Recommendations in Folksonomies. In: Kok, J.N., Koronacki, J., Lopez de Mantaras, R., Matwin, S., Mladenič, D., Skowron, A. (eds.) PKDD 2007. LNCS (LNAI), vol. 4702, pp. 506–514. Springer, Heidelberg (2007)
19. Batagelj, V., Zaveršnik, M.: Generalized Cores. arXiv preprint cs/0202039 (2002)
20. Doerfel, S., Jäschke, R.: An Analysis of Tag-recommender Evaluation Procedures. In: The 7th ACM Conference on Recommender Systems, pp. 343–346. ACM (2013)

Time-Sensitive User Profile
for Optimizing Search Personlization

Ameni Kacem[1], Mohand Boughanem[2], and Rim Faiz[1]

[1] LARODEC, IHEC, Carthage Presidency, 2016 Tunis, Tunisia
`ameni.kacem@gmail.com, rim.faiz@ihec.rnu.tn`
[2] IRIT SIG, 118 Route de Narbonne, 31062, Toulouse CEDEX 9, France
`bougha@irit.fr`

Abstract. Thanks to social Web services, Web search engines have the opportunity to afford personalized search results that better fit the user's information needs and interests. To achieve this goal, many personalized search approaches explore user's social Web interactions to extract his preferences and interests, and use them to model his profile. In our approach, the user profile is implicitly represented as a vector of weighted terms which correspond to the user's interests extracted from his online social activities. As the user interests may change over time, we propose to weight profiles terms not only according to the content of these activities but also by considering the freshness. More precisely, the weights are adjusted with a temporal feature. In order to evaluate our approach, we model the user profile according to data collected from Twitter. Then, we rerank initial search results accurately to the user profile. Moreover, we proved the significance of adding a temporal feature by comparing our method with baselines models that does not consider the user profile dynamics.

Keywords: Personalized search, User profile, Freshness, Interests Dynamics, Kernel function.

1 Introduction

Personalization in information retrieval consists of providing search results that fit the individual user's information needs and match his/her interests instead of providing the same results to a query for all users [1]. To build the user profile, that is necessary to perform personalization, many works focused on leveraging user' activities for inferring interests.

To represent the user profile, the most common way is the vector space model (VSM) where interests are represented as a vector or vectors of keywords. The weight of the keywords, in most of the prior works, is assigned using the TF-IDF model or its variants [2] [3]. Other approaches extract taxonomies from the Open Directory Project (ODP) hierarchy to represent the user profile [4]. All these approaches assign more importance to the frequent terms no matter the moment of use. They did not explicitly integrate the time when the words

V. Dimitrova et al. (Eds.): UMAP 2014, LNCS 8538, pp. 111–121, 2014.

appeared in the user activities, but time is often used to discern short-term and long-term user profiles. Short-term profile considers current session while the long-term profile is built according to several search sessions. In fact, discerning the short- and long-term interests requires the use of a time interval that may include several interests [5], or session's boundaries mechanisms where a session is defined by a set of queries related to the same information need [6] [7].

However, the short-term profile integrates only interactions extracted from the current session but lays long-term interests aside. The long-term profile captures old interests without considering the actual user needs [8]. To overcome this shortcoming, we propose to consider both type of profile (short- and long-term) in the same framework and to assign a novel temporal weight to terms of the profile.

More precisely, we study how to leverage user's activities for user modeling and evaluate how do temporal dynamics affect the quality of user models in the context of personalized search. We propose a personalized search framework where the user profile is implicitly constructed from the user social Web activities and represented as a vector of weighted terms which correspond to the user's interests. We propose to weight the profiles terms according to both the freshness and the frequency in order to unify both the recent and persistent interests instead of using the delimitation of the session activities.

The remainder of this paper is organized as follows. In Section 2, we review related works focusing on personalized search systems and user profiling modeling and evolution. In Section 3, we propose a temporal-frequency user profile that adjusts the frequency notion by a temporal function. In particular, our model integrates a freshness feature in order to track changes implicitly without discerning explicitly the long-term and short-term user profiles. Section 4 describes the experimental methodology adapted to evaluate our proposed approach followed by the corresponding results and their discussion. The final Section presents a summary of our work and future dicrections.

2   Related Work

In this section, we first review some existing works on personalized search and social-based user profiling. Next, we examine and discuss the user profile evolution in terms of discerning the short-term and long-term user profiles.

2.1   Personalized Search

The user profiling strategies extract information about the user from different sources and model them into a profile using multiple representations. Current systems tend to collect information about the user by considering folksonomies as a primary source to define the user's profile. Many information sources have been used to model the user's profile such as users' personal information like users' manual input hobbies, search history [9], click-through records [10], Web browser history [11], folksonomies [2], annotations [12], Web communities [13] and groups [14].

User's interests are also sourced from the social Web. Users interact with each other by creating and sharing content and by expressing their interests on different social Websites [15]. Social-based users' profiles exploit those data in order to extract knowledge about the searcher's preferences and interests. Noll and Meinel [16] examined two types of profiles: the user's profile and the document's profile in order to define related tags that were used to rerank the non-personalized search results. Xu et al. [3] proposed a folksonomy-based personalized search using tags extracted from Delicious and Dogear. They applied the topic matching between the user's interests and the document's topic in order to rerank the web pages rather than using only the term matching between the query and the document's content. Carmel et al. [17] explored the user's connections in social networks. They re-ranked search results based on their connection strength with the user's related persons and topics. In fact, they used three types of profiles: with explicit familiarity connections, with connections obtained through common social activities and finally merging both of the previous types.

After collecting information about the user, his profile is often represented as a set of weighted keywords corresponding to the user interests [12] [11], as categories extracted from the Open Directory Project (ODP) hierarchy [4] [18] [7], or as semantic networks [19].

2.2   User-Profile Evolution

The evolution of the user profile is represented in prior works as either a short-term profile or a long-term profile. The short-term profile describes the interests and needs of users related to activities of the current search session. Some approaches [6] [22] [7] define the short-term user profile as all the interactions and interests related to a single information need. However, other studies [5] [20] define it as multiple interests emerged in a single time slot.

The second type of profile is the long-term profile, which refers to the use of specific information such as the users education level and general interests, user query history and past user clickthrough information. Teevan et al. [23] developed rich long-term user models based on desktop search activities to improve ranking. They altered the query term weights from the BM25 weighting scheme to incorporate user interests as captured by her desktop index. Similarly, Chirita, et al. [24] capture personalized query expansion terms for web search using three different desktop approaches: the entire desktop data, only the desktop documents relevant to each user query, and a natural language processing techniques to extract diffusing lexical compounds from relevant desktop resources. Besides, Tan et al. [9] studied long-term language model-based representations of users' interests based on queries, documents and clicks. They considered different amount of history and found that for fresh queries recent history was the most important, but for recurring queries long-term history was more significant.

Most of the existing approaches [8] exploit temporal factor after building the user profile in order to track its changing, rather than using it in the modeling step. For instance, [25] captured temporal dynamics of the individual profiles inferred from Twitter activities. They specify two types of users based on their interactions regarding a specific public topic. The first one is the continuously active users that interact during a long period. The second type is the sporadically active users that interact within a short period.

However, the fact of discerning the short-term and long-term user profiles does not necessarily reflect the user's needs. For users who are not very active on social services, the short-term profile can eliminate relevant results which are more related to their personal interests. This is because their social activities are few and separated over time. In addition, for users who are very active, the aggregation of recent activities without ignoring the ancient interests would be very interesting because this kind of profile is usually changing over time. Furthermore, in Sugiyama, et al. [11], the current interests are used in the active session while the persistent interests are stored for use in later search sessions. For all those reasons, we assume that a user profile can reflect both the recurrent (persistent) and the current (recent) interests but with different scales based on freshness.

In this paper, the user profile is represented as a vector of keywords terms corresponding to the user interests implicitly inferred from his activities on social Web systems. We will adjust the importance of each keyword according to the time of its use unlike non-time-sensitive approaches that do not consider the time but only the frequency [2] [3]. The specificity of the profile resides in weighting the terms by combining their frequency and their freshness. We assume that this way we naturally combine short-term profile and long-term profile into a single one in which we give importance to the recent interests without ignoring the continuous ones.

3   Time-Sensitive Personalization Approach

In the classical non-time sensitive approaches, the relevance of an interest in the user profile is assumed to be only decided by the counts of terms in the profile, but not by their position in time. As the user interests evolve, we propose to build a time-sensitive user profile under the assumption that older frequent terms should not outperform current and not frequent terms.

After collecting keywords from the user interactions in social Web, their weights are computed by combining both their frequency and their appearing moment. We consider the social Web but any other source does not affect our approach. More formally, given a document $D^{S_i} = (t_1, t_2...t_N)$ generated at moment S_i (day, hour or minute...) ,such as a tag or a microblog. By document, we mean any content generated by the user such as a tag or a microblog. We extract documents' terms and generate their normalized term frequency (nTF) described as:

$$nTF(t_i)^{Si} = \frac{freq^{S_i}(t_i)}{\sum_{\forall k \in D^{S_i}} freq^{S_i}(t_k)} \tag{1}$$

with: $freq^{S_i}(t_i)$ is the relative frequency of a term t_i in D^{S_i} and $\sum_{\forall k \in D^{S_i}} freq^{S_i}(t_k)$ represents the sum of the frequencies of all terms appeared in $D^{(}S_i)$.

To measure the freshness of a term, we review the notion of term frequency by adjusting it with a temporal-biased function. In fact, we assume the more the term is closer to the current date S^C, the more its temporal frequency would be significant. We use the Kernel Gaussian function as a temporal-biased function [26] [27]:

$$K(S^C, S_j) = \frac{1}{\sqrt{2.\varPi}.\sigma} \cdot \exp\left[\frac{-(S^C - S_j)^2}{2.\sigma^2}\right] \tag{2}$$

where σ is the interpolation coefficient, S^C is the current date and S_j is a prior date.

Figure 1 illustrates three terms distributions using first a simple cumulative term frequency of three terms (see Fig 1-a), compared with their revised cumulative frequency using Kernel (Fig1-b). We notice that term TF1 starting with high frequency (Fig1-a) its kernel version (CF1) increases slowly. However, term TF3 starting from low frequency (0 in this case), continue to increase until it reaches the same cumulative frequency than TF1. Its kernel version (CF3) overpasses CF1. Term TF2 which has a uniform distribution continue to increase uniformly. Thus, in each date S_j, we define the user profile as a vector U of terms and their corresponding global weights W:

$$\vec{U} = (t_1{}^{S_j} : W_1{}^{S_j}, t_2{}^{S_j} : W_2{}^{S_j}, ..., t_m{}^{S_j} : W_m{}^{S_j}) \tag{3}$$

where the temporal weight $W(t)^{S_c}$ of a term t in the profile is the sum of its time-biased relative frequency defined as follows:

$$W(t_k)^{S_c} = \sum nTF(t_k)^{S_j}.K(S^C, S_j) \tag{4}$$

The personalization strategy that we adopt consists of submitting a query to a standard search engine and measuring the similarity between the user profile and each returned Webpage-profile $\overrightarrow{WP} = (t_{wp1}, t_{wp2}, ..., t_{wpk})$ thanks to the cosine similarity measure. The time-sensitive based user profile can be further refined by smoothing it with the Webpage-query similarity obtained to personalize search results for all user's queries during the search session. Finally, the search results are re-ranked as follows:

$$Score(U, Q) = \alpha.Sim(\vec{U}, \overrightarrow{WP}) + (1 - \alpha).Sim(\overrightarrow{WP}, Q) \tag{5}$$

where $Sim(\overrightarrow{WP}, Q)$ is the score obtained from the original results reflecting the matching between the query and the Webpage, and $Sim(\vec{U}, \overrightarrow{WP})$ denotes the user-Webpage similarity. Both of the similarities are computed through the cosine function.

4   Experiments and Results

In this Section, we investigate the impact of the time-sensitive user profile strategy in the context of personalized search. More specifically, we examine the

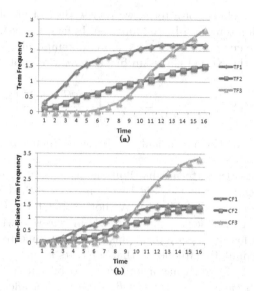

Fig. 1. Example of terms distribution using cumulative term frequency and a kernel version of the frequency

impact of our proposed temporal pattern in improving the accuracy of the Web search. Accordingly, our aim is to analyze and compare our approach with two different approaches. The first one is the ranked results returned by Google [1]. The second one is the non-time-sensitive metric nTF [16]. We particularly analyze how the proposed Time-Sensitive User Profile (TSUP), brought in Section 3, affects personalization and achieves better performances in comparison to non-time sensitive variants.

4.1   Data Set and Evaluation Methodology

Over a period of the first two weeks of December 2013, we crawled the microblogging system Twitter[2] posts (tweets) via the Twitter 4j API to randomly select 800 users and extract their 69000 tweets. For each tweet, we combine the relative frequencies with the temporal biased function that evaluates the distribution of the terms over time. The main details of our data set are presented in Table 1.

We select a unique query for each user profile related to his areas of interests defined on Twitter totaling 800 queries. Our queries are randomly selected from the online Twitter categories of interests (computer science, politics, chemistry, ...). Each query is submitted to a Web search engine (Google in our case). We select the top 100 documents per query. These documents are then proceeded to the stop words removal, stemming and tokenization of documents and users' extracted

---

[1] www.google.com
[2] www.twitter.com

terms thanks to Apache Lucene [3] classes including Porter Stemming Filter class before weighting the result keywords. Each Webpage is represented as vector of terms $\overrightarrow{WP} = (t_{wp1}, t_{wp2}, ..., t_{wpk})$. Each term in the Webpage profile is weighted using the TF-IDF model [3]. Finally, our personalizing approach consists of re-ranking the initial list of Webpages in accordance with each user profile.

Table 1. Data statistics

Number of Users	800
Period	01/12/2013 - 15/12/2013
Total Number of Tweets	69000
Average Number of Tweets per participant	86.25
Average Number of Tweets per participant per day	5.75

In order to measure the quality of the results, we use the Normalized Discounted Cumulative Gain (NDCG) at 10 (Jrvelin and Keklinen, 2000) for all the judged queries. Results are judged by 40 voluntary assessors with three levels of relevance, namely highly relevant (value equal to 2), relevant (value equal to 1) or irrelevant (value equal to 0). The assessors are graduate students in different fields, i.e., computer science, chemistry, tourism, electrical engineering, and medical. Each assessor evaluates 20 users' profiles. In addition, we used a second metric which is the Precision at top 10. We considered any positive judgment as relevant.

4.2   Results and Analysis

In this Section, we lay out the findings of our analysis. First, we present results obtained by comparing our model with the two baselines described in the beginning of this Section. Then, we try to specify the impact of growing information about the user's activities on the social Web.

Baselines Comparison Results. We compare our time-based user profile with the non-personalized results returned by Google and with the re-ranked list of documents returned by modeling the user profile according to the nTF scheme. From this comparison ($\alpha = 0.6, \sigma = 4$), we obtained the values summarized in Table 2 where we use two metrics namely the P@10 and the NDCG@10.

From the results presented in Table 2, we notice that the TSUP approach overcomes the results given by both of Google and the nTF approach for both of NDCG and P@10.

From our point of view, the reason of these promising values is the fact that the term frequency does not reflect the freshness of an interest but gives an overview of how often the user mentioned a term when interacting with the online social systems. However, standard search engines return relevant results to the user query's terms but they are indifferent to the users' interests especially when

---

[3] www.lucene.apache.org

Table 2. Comparison results

	P@10 (Average %)	NDCG (Average %)
Without Freshness		
Google	57.87	45.67
nTF	62.68	58.80
With Freshness		
TSUP personalization	74.72	78.15

the queries are short [28] or ambiguous [29]. Hence, the time-based user profile strategy defines current interests and needs of a user better than the non-time sensitive one. Furthermore, the standard search engine (e.g, Google) gives the same list of results without considering the user's individual needs because the ranking is based only on the matching of the docu-ment's terms to the query's keywords.

Consequently, merging both the freshness-feature and the term-frequency into our proposed weighting scheme has proved its effectiveness. The temporal-function al-lows considering the actual interests which are used to enhance the current search without overlooking the persistent interests and helps to person-alize recurrent infor-mation needs.

Impact of User's Profile Information Amount. In order to better evaluate the in-fluence of the temporal feature, we use the same personalization method-ology to compare the time-sensitive user profile (TSUP) with the nTF-based user profile in terms of three profiles' temporal aspects namely:

- Short-term profile: all tweets extracted during the current day,
- Long-term Profile: all previous tweets except for those in the current session (before current day),
- Single Profile: all the recent and old tweets as a single user profile.

As we can see in Figure 2, when we merge both of the interests into a single profile, we have a growing amount of profiling information that leads to better

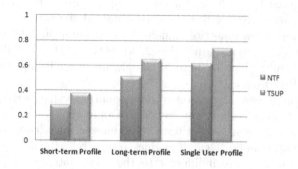

Fig. 2. Comparison of mean of P@10

improvements in retrieval relevance. A single user profile that exploits all user's interests give better results than using profiles based solely on short- or long-term interests. Indeed, our approach outperforms the nTF approach with the three temporal aspects.

5   Conclusion

In this paper, we explored the problem of personalized search and developed a user-modeling framework for Twitter microblogging system. In fact, the integration of the social data on the user model is accurate and efficient because people are likely to write a blog or bookmark a Webpage about something that interests them. Further-more, we investigate how the temporal-based user profile influences the accuracy of personalized search. We used a vector-based representation that takes into account the temporal-frequency measured by merging the term frequency and the freshness of each keyword using the Kernel function.

We find encouraging results when we compared our approach to two non-temporal sensitive approaches: the standard search engine Google and the user profiling using the Normalized Term Frequency scheme. In addition, we analyzed the aggregation of the current and recurrent interests. We found that increasing amount of profiling information yields to greater improvement in retrieval performance.

Future work will further research the temporal aspects when enriching the user pro-file by including diverse users' social behaviors by gathering data from multiple sources such as timelines from social networks namely Facebook[4] or bookmarks of interesting Webpages such as Delicious[5]. Moreover a comparison with other temporal models [17] [30] would be required to evaluate the effectiveness of our proposed measure.

References

1. Qiu, F., Cho, J.: Automatic identification of user interest for personalized search. In: 15th International Conference on World Wide Web, pp. 727–736. ACM, New York (2006)
2. Vallet, D., Cantador, I., Jose, J.M.: Personalizing Web Search with Folksonomy-based User and Document Profiles. In: Gurrin, C., He, Y., Kazai, G., Kruschwitz, U., Little, S., Roelleke, T., Rüger, S., van Rijsbergen, K. (eds.) ECIR 2010. LNCS, vol. 5993, pp. 420–431. Springer, Heidelberg (2010)
3. Xu, S., Bao, S., Fei, B., Su, Z., Yu, Y.: Exploring folksonomy for personalized search. In: 31st Annual International ACM SIGIR Conference on Research and Development in Information Retrieval, pp. 155–162. ACM, New York (2008)
4. Speretta, M., Gauch, S.: Personalizing search based on user search histories. In: 2005 IEEE/WIC/ACM International Conference on Web Intelligence, pp. 622–628. IEEE Press, New York (2005)

---

[4] www.facebbok

[5] www.delicious.com

5. Dumais, S., Cutrell, E., Cadiz, J., Jancke, G., Sarin, R., Robbins, D.: Stuff I've seen: a system for personal information retrieval and re-use. In: 26th Annual International ACM SIGIR Conference on Research and Development in Informaion Retrieval, pp. 72–79. ACM, New York (2003)

6. Shen, X., Zhai, C.: Exploiting query history for document ranking in interactive information retrieval. In: 26th Annual International ACM SIGIR Conference on Research and Development in Informaion Retrieval, pp. 377–378. ACM, New York (2003)

7. Daoud, M., Boughanem, M., Tamine-Lechani, L.: Detecting Session Boundaries to Personalize Search Using a Conceptual User Context. In: Ao, S.I., Gelman, L. (eds.) Springer 2009. Advances in Electrical Engineering and Computational Science, vol. 39, pp. 471–482. ACM, New York (2009)

8. Bennett, P.N., White, R.W., Dumais, S.T.: Modeling the Impact of Short- and Long-Term Behavior on Search Personalization. In: 35th International ACM SIGIR Conference on Research and Development in Information Retrieval, pp. 185–194. ACM, New York (2012)

9. Tan, B., Shen, X., Zhai, C.: Mining long-term search history to improve search accuracy. In: 12th ACM SIGKDD International Conference on Knowledge Discovery and Data Mining, pp. 718–723. ACM, New York (2006)

10. Dou, Z., Song, R., Wen, J.: A large-scale evaluation and analysis of personalized search strategies. In: 16th International Conference on World Wide Web, pp. 581–590. ACM, New York (2007)

11. Sugiyama, K., Hatano, K., Yoshikawa, M.: Adaptive Web search based on user profile constructed without any effort from user. In: 13th International Conference on World Wide Web, pp. 675–684. ACM, New York (2004)

12. Cai, Y., Li, Q.: Personalized search by tag-based user profile and resource profile in collaborative tagging systems. In: 19th ACM International Conference on Information and Knowledge Management, pp. 969–978. ACM, New York (2010)

13. Kritikopoulos, A., Sideri, M.: The compass filter: search engine result personalization using web communities. In: Mobasher, B., Anand, S.S. (eds.) ITWP 2003. LNCS (LNAI), vol. 3169, pp. 229–240. Springer, Heidelberg (2005)

14. Teevan, J., Morris, M., Bush, S.: Discovering and Using Groups to Improve Personalized Search. In: Second ACM International Conference on Web Search and Data Mining, pp. 15–24. ACM, New York (2009)

15. Orlandi, F., Breslin, J., Passant, A.: Aggregated, Interoperable and Multi-Domain User Profiles for the Social Web. In: 8th International Conference on Symantic Systems I-SEMANTICS, pp. 41–48. ACM, New York (2012)

16. Noll, M.G., Meinel, C.: Web Search Personalization via Social Bookmarking and Tagging. In: Aberer, K., Choi, K.-S., Noy, N., Allemang, D., Lee, K.-I., Nixon, L.J.B., Golbeck, J., Mika, P., Maynard, D., Mizoguchi, R., Schreiber, G., Cudré-Mauroux, P. (eds.) ASWC 2007 and ISWC 2007. LNCS, vol. 4825, pp. 367–380. Springer, Heidelberg (2007)

17. Carmel, D., Zwerdling, N., Guy, I., Ofek-Koifman, S., Har'el, N., Ronen, I., Uziel, E., Yogev, S., Chernov, S.: Personalized social search based on the user's social network. In: 18th ACM Conference on Information and Knowledge Management, pp. 1227–1236. ACM, New York (2009)

18. Liu, F., Yu, C., Meng, W.: Personalized Web Search For Improving Retrieval Effectiveness. IEEE Transactions on Knowledge and Data Engineering 16(1), 28–40 (2004)

19. Micarelli, A., Sciarrone, F.: Anatomy and Empirical Evaluation of an Adaptive Web- Based Information Filtering System. In: User Modeling and User-Adapted Interaction, vol. 14(2-3), pp. 159–200. Kluwer Academic Publishers Hingham, MA (2004)

20. Pretschner, A., Gauch, S.: Ontology Based Personalized Search. In: 11th IEEE International Conference on Tools with Articial Intelligence, pp. 391–398. IEEE Press, New York (1999)

21. Shen, X., Tan, B., Zhai, C.: Context-sensitive information retrieval using implicit feedback. In: 28th Annual International ACM SIGIR Conference on Research and Development in Information Retrieval, pp. 43–50. ACM, New York (2005)

22. Zemirli, W.: Modèle d'accès personnalisé à l'information basé sur les diagrammes d'influence intégrant un profil multidimensionnel. Paul Sabatier University, Toulouse (2008)

23. Teevan, J., Dumais, S.T., Horvitz, E.: Personalizing search via automated analysis of interests and activities. In: 28th Annual International ACM SIGIR Conference on Research and Development in Information Retrieval, pp. 449–456. ACM, New York (2005)

24. Chirita, P., Frian, C.S., Nejdl, W.: Summarizing local context to personalize global web search. In: 15th ACM International Conference on Information and Knowledge Management, pp. 287–296. ACM, New York (2006)

25. Abel, F., Gao, Q., Houben, G., Tao, K.: Analyzing temporal dynamics in Twitter Profiles for Personalized Recommendations in the Social Web. In: 3rd International Conference on Web Science, pp. 1–8. ACM, New York (2011)

26. Lv, Y., Zhai, C.: Positional language models for information retrieval. In: 32nd International ACM SIGIR Conference on Research and Development in Information Retrieval, pp. 299–306. ACM, New York (2009)

27. Gerani, S., Carma, M.J., Crestani, F.: Proximity Based Opinion Retrieval. In: 33rd International ACM SIGIR Conference on Research and Development in Information Retrieval, pp. 403–410. ACM, New York (2010)

28. Jansen, B.J., Spink, A., Saracevic, T.: Real life, real users, and real needs: a study and analysis of user queries on the web. Information Processing and Management 36(2), 207–227 (2000)

29. Cronen-Townsend, S., Croft, W.B.: Quantifying query ambiguity. In: Second International Conference on Human Language Technology Research, pp. 104–109. Morgan Kaufmann Publishers Inc., San Francisco (2002)

30. Billsus, D., Pazzani, M.J.: User Modeling for Adaptive News Access. In: Journal of User Modeling and User-Adapted Interaction, vol. 10, pp. 147–180. Kluwer Academic Publishers Hingham, MA (2000)

A Computational Model for Mood Recognition

Christina Katsimerou[1], Judith A. Redi[1], and Ingrid Heynderickx[2]

[1] Interactive Intelligence Group, Technical University Delft, The Netherlands
{C.Katsimerou,J.A.Redi}@tudelft.nl
[2] Human-Technology Interaction Group, Technical University Eindhoven, The Netherlands
I.E.J.Heynderickx@tue.nl

Abstract. In an ambience designed to adapt to the user's affective state, pervasive technology should be able to decipher unobtrusively his underlying mood. Great effort has been devoted to automatic punctual emotion recognition from visual input. Conversely, little has been done to recognize longer-lasting affective states, such as mood. Taking for granted the effectiveness of emotion recognition algorithms, we go one step further and propose a model for estimating the mood of an affective episode from a known sequence of punctual emotions. To validate our model experimentally, we rely on the human annotations of the well-established HUMAINE database. Our analysis indicates that we can approximate fairly accurately the human process of summarizing the emotional content of a video in a mood estimation. A moving average function with exponential discount of the past emotions achieves mood prediction accuracy above 60%.

Keywords: Emotion recognition, mood estimation, affective computing, pervasive technology.

1 Introduction

An indispensable feature for emotionally intelligent systems and affect-adaptive ambiences is recognizing (unobtrusively) the user's affect [1]. Technology endowed with this skill can, among others, drive or maintain the user to a positive affective state, for instance adapting the lighting system in a care centre room to comfort the inhabitants [2], or engage the user in natural interaction within virtual scenarios [3] [4].

Automatic affect recognition is often based on visual input (images and videos), due to the unobtrusiveness of visual sensors and the fact that people convey important affective information via their facial and bodily expressions [5]. A large body of work has been devoted to mapping visual representations of facial expressions [6], and body postures [7] into short-term affective states, commonly referred to as *emotions*. However, in certain applications based on affective monitoring, adapting the system behaviour to the dynamics of instantaneous emotions may be redundant, if not counterproductive. Take the case of a lighting system that adopts the optimal configuration to improve the occupant's affective state: it is neither necessary nor desirable that the light changes at the speed of instantaneous emotional fluctuations. A system that retains and summarizes the affective information over a certain time window, and adapts smoothly over time would be more appropriate.

V. Dimitrova et al. (Eds.): UMAP 2014, LNCS 8538, pp. 122–133, 2014.
© Springer International Publishing Switzerland 2014

It is useful, at this point, to make a distinction between two types of affective states: *emotion* and *mood*. In psychological literature these terms are typically distinguished based on the duration [8] and the intensity of their expression [9]. Unfortunately, these differences are hardly delineated in a quantifiable way, as little is known e.g. about the time spanned by either emotional or mood episodes. To cope with this vagueness and make as few assumptions as possible, in the rest of the paper we will use the term *emotion* to refer to a punctual (i.e. instantaneous) affective state and the term *mood* as an affective state attributed to the whole affective episode, regardless of the duration of this episode.

From an engineering perspective, mood is typically assumed to be synonym to emotion and the two terms are often used interchangeably. Very little research, indeed, has tried to perform explicitly automatic mood recognition from visual input, except for some remarkable yet preliminary attempts [10] [11], discussed in more detail in section 2. Nevertheless, psychological literature recognizes a relationship between underlying mood and expressed emotions [12] [13]. Thus, it may be possible to infer mood from a series of recognized emotion expressions. This would entail the existence of a model that maps, for a given lapse of time, punctual emotion expressions into an overall mood prediction (Fig. 1).

In this paper, we describe an experimental setup for gaining basic insights in how humans relate mood to recognized punctual emotions, when they annotate emotionally coloured video material. The research questions that we aim to answer are a) to what extent we can estimate (recognized) mood from punctual emotions and b) how a person accounts for the (recognized) displayed emotions when judging the overall mood of another person. Answering these questions will bring us closer to retrieving a model of human affective intelligence that can then be replicated for machine-based mood recognition.

As such, the main contributions of this work are: a) we formulate a model where the mood we want to unveil is a function with punctual emotions as arguments, b) we indicate an experimental setup for validating this model, c) we specify the best fitting mood function out of a number of possible ones, and d) we optimize its parameters in terms of accurate prediction and computational complexity.

2   Related Work

In psychology, emotion and mood are considered to be highly associated affective states, yet differing in terms of duration [8], intensity and stability [9], dynamics [14] and attribution (awareness of cause) [15]. Even though most literature agrees that there is a distinction between emotion and mood, in practice the terms are often used interchangeably and a one-to-one mapping between the two is typically assumed. Ekman [16], for example, claims that we infer mood from the signals of the emotions we associate with the mood, at least in part: we might deduce that someone is in a cheerful mood because we observe joy; likewise, stress as an emotion may imply an anxious mood. In the literature we find only one empirical study trying to identify the distinction between emotion and mood [12]. The authors conducted a so-called folk psychological study, in which they asked ordinary people to describe how they experience the difference between the two terms. A qualitative analysis on the responses indicated *cause* and *duration* as the two most significant distinctive features between the two concepts; nevertheless, their difference was not quantified.

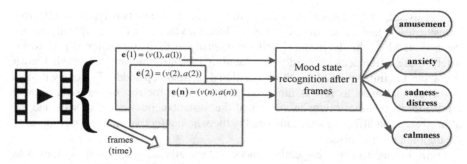

$$e(1) = (v(1), a(1))$$
$$e(2) = (v(2), a(2))$$
$$e(n) = (v(n), a(n))$$

Mood state recognition after n frames

amusement

anxiety

sadness-distress

calmness

frames (time)

Fig. 1. Framework of automatic mood recognition module from a sequence of emotions

Automating the process of mood recognition entails linking data collected from sensors monitoring the user (e.g. cameras, microphones, physiological sensors) to a quantifiable representation of the (felt) mood. In the case of visual input very scarce results are retrievable in literature. In fact, the latest studies in the field have been geared towards recognizing continuously the emotions along videos rich in emotions and emotional fluctuations, e.g. as requested by the AVEC challenge [17]. However, typically a decision on the affective state is made on frame-level, i.e., for punctual emotions, whereas no summarization into a mood prediction is attempted.

In [10] we find explicit reference to mood recognition from upper body posture. The authors induced mood with music in subjects in a lab, and recorded eight-minute videos focusing on their upper body after the induction. They analyzed the contribution of postural features in the mood expression and found that only the head position predicted (induced) mood with an accuracy of 81%. However, they considered only happy versus sad mood and the whole experiment was very controlled, in the sense that it took place in a lab and the subjects knew what they were intended to feel, making the genuine expression doubtful. Another reference to mood comes from [11], where the authors inferred again the bipolar happiness-sadness mood axis from data of 3D pose tracking and motion capturing. Finally, the authors of [18] were the first to briefly tap in the concept of summarizing punctual annotations of affective signals to an overall judgment. However, they only considered the mean or the percentiles of the values of valence and arousal as global predictors, without taking into account their temporal position.

In this study, we will extend significantly the latter work, by constructing systematically a complex mood model from simple functions, analyzing its temporal properties and proposing it as an intermediate module in automatic mood recognition from video, after the punctual (on frame level) emotion recognition module (Fig. 1).

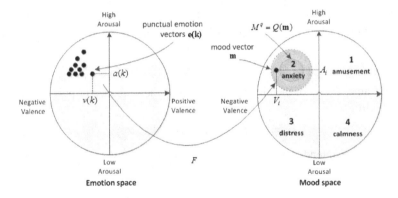

Fig. 2. Model of emotion and mood space. Each emotion is a point in the emotion space and the trajectory of points in the emotion space is mapped as a point in the mood space.

3   Problem Setup and Methodology

3.1   Domains of Emotion and Mood

To define a model that maps punctual emotion estimations into a single mood, it is necessary to first define the domains in which emotion and mood will be expressed. In affective computing there are two main trends for affect representation: the discrete [19] and the dimensional one [20] [21]. The latter most commonly identifies two dimensions, i.e., valence and arousal, accounting for most of the variance of affect. It allows continuous representation of emotion values, capturing in this way a wider set of emotions. This is why we resort to it in our work.

In this study we assume the valence and arousal dimensions to span a Euclidean space (hereafter referred to as the VA space), where emotions are represented as points-vectors. Analogously, mood can be represented in a Euclidean (mood) space as a tuple of valence and arousal values. We quantize the mood space in four partitions, corresponding to the four quadrants defined by the valence and arousal axes, namely (1) positive V- high A, (2) negative V- high A, (3) negative V- low A, and (4) positive V- low A[1] (shown in Fig.2). This 4-class mood discretization gives a trade-off between ambiguity and simplicity, being able to capture different possible moods expressed sufficiently, yet eliminating redundancies and diminishing the problem dimensionality.

3.2   Problem Formulation

Suppose we have a video clip i representing an affective episode of a user with a total number of frames n_i. Punctual emotions can be estimated from each video frame (static images) and the overall (quantized) mood M_i characterizes the whole clip i. In this study both emotions and mood refer to the affective state of the active person of the clip, as perceived by human annotators.

---

[1] The class numbering 1-4 serves for notation and not ranking.

For every independent clip i the punctual emotion vector $\mathbf{e}_i$ corresponding to the recognized emotion at frame k is expressed in the VA space as

$$\mathbf{e_i}(k) = \left(v_i(k), a_i(k)\right), k=1,2,..,n_i \,, \tag{1}$$

where $v_i(k)$ and $a_i(k)$ are recognized valence and arousal values of the emotion expressed at frame $k \leq n_i$ of the clip i. Assuming that the sequence of punctual emotion vectors for clip i

$$\mathbf{E_i} = \left(\mathbf{e_i}(1), \mathbf{e_i}(2),.., \mathbf{e_i}(n_i)\right), \tag{2}$$

is known, and we intend to estimate the overall mood, we want to express the mood vector $\mathbf{m}_i = \left(V_i, A_i\right)$ as

$$\mathbf{m_i} = F(\mathbf{E_i}), \tag{3}$$

where F is the function mapping the emotion sequence to the mood vector. We finally retrieve from the mood vector the quantized mood M_i through the function Q, defined as:

$$M_i = Q(\mathbf{m_i}) = Q(V_i, A_i) = \begin{cases} 2 - sgn(V_i) & if \quad sgn(V_i \cdot A_i) > 0 \\ 3 + sgn(V_i) & if \quad sgn(V_i \cdot A_i) < 0 \cdot \\ 0 & otherwise \end{cases} \tag{4}$$

In this study, we set M_i as the ultimate target of our discrete prediction model and F the function to be modeled.

3.3   Modeling Mood from a Sequence of Punctual Emotions

3.3.1 Basic Mapping Functions

We propose several possible formulations of the function F in eq. (3), which map punctual measurements of emotion into a representative value for the overall affective episode. This value is then used in eq. (4) to predict the mood class, unless stated otherwise.

Predictor 1: The mean emotion (mean). Probably the easiest assumption is that mood is formed by the equal contribution of all the emotions within a given timespan [18]. The average of the emotion points will then be the "station" mood point, which acts as a gravitational force on them [22]. More formally, the mean of an emotion sequence over a particular time window is predictor of the overall mood for this time window:

$$M_i = Q(F(\mathbf{E_i})) = Q\left(\sum_{k=1}^{n_i} \mathbf{e}_i(k)/n_i\right) = Q\left(\left(\sum_{k=1}^{n_i} v_i(k)/n_i, \sum_{k=1}^{n_i} a_i(k)/n_i\right)\right). \tag{5}$$

Predictor 2: The maximum emotion (max). Intuitively, the emotion with the highest intensity is expected to have a high impact on the overall mood within a given timespan. Thus, we may hypothesize it to be a predictor for the overall mood for the given time window. As a measure for the intensity of the emotion we use the Euclidean norm of the emotion vector, defined as

$$\|\mathbf{e_i}(k)\| = \sqrt{\left(v_i(k)\right)^2 + \left(a_i(k)\right)^2}, k = 1, 2,.., n_i \,. \tag{6}$$

Then the mood occurs from the emotion vector that maximizes the intensity over the sequence E_i, or

$$M_i = Q\left(F\left(E_i\right)\right) = Q\left(\underset{e_i(k)\in E_i}{\arg\max}\left(\|e_i(k)\|, k = 1, 2, .., n_i\right)\right) = Q\left(e_{\max}\right). \tag{7}$$

Predictor 3: The longest emotion (long). Another hypothesis is that the emotions that occur more within a given timespan will sustain the associated mood [23]. Thus, we may map individual emotion vectors into mood vectors directly and take the quadrant of the mood space containing the majority of them (see Fig.2); this quadrant may then be a predictor of the recognized mood. More formally, if we consider 4 disjoint subsets of Ei defined as

$$E_i^q = \left\{e_i(k) \mid Q\left(e(k)\right) = q, k = 1, 2, .., n_i\right\}, q = 1, 2, 3, 4, \tag{8}$$

each with cardinality $C(q) = \left|E_i^q\right|$, then the mood corresponding to the longest emotion is

$$M_i = F\left(E_i\right) = \underset{q\in\{1,2,3,4\}}{\arg\max}\left(C(q)\right). \tag{9}$$

Predictor 4: First emotion (FE). A reasonable property of the mood function is memory [24], in the sense that mood recognition involves the assessment of not only the current emotion, but also of the previously recognized ones. In the extreme case, the time span of the memory window may extend back to the beginning of the emotional episode, resonating the impact of the first points to the current moment. Therefore, we may hypothesize that the first of a sequence of emotions over a certain time window is a predictor for the overall mood for this time window, or

$$M_i = Q\left(e(1)\right). \tag{10}$$

Predictor 5: Last emotion (LE). Contrary to the previous hypothesis, we may assume that the significance of the previously recognized emotions in the mood estimation decreases as time lapses and only the latest recognized emotion defines the overall mood, that is:

$$M_i = Q\left(e(n_i)\right). \tag{11}$$

3.3.2   A More Complex Model of Mood Recognition from Emotions

The simple models proposed in section 3.3.1 may further be combined into a more complex one, occurring from a moving average of emotions over time, with memory retention expanding back to the preceding recognized emotions for a given portion of the timespan of the emotional episode. We can formulate this as

$$M_i = Q\left(F\left(E_i\right)\right) = Q\left(\sum_{k=n_i-w}^{n_i}\left(e_i(k)/w\right)\right), \tag{12}$$

where w is the size of the memory window. In fact, (12) is a moving average (*MA*) over w frames. In this formulation we consider a hard limit function to retain only the last w recognized emotions, disregarding the rest. In reality, a desirable property of mood assessment is smoothness over time [25], that is, it should gradually neglect the past, as it moves along the emotion sequence. This can be modeled through a discount function D_w of the previous frames, either linear *LD* (Eq. (13)), as seen in [23], or exponential *ED* (Eq. (14)).

$$D_w\left(k\right)=\frac{k-(n_i-w)}{n_i-w}\ ,k=n_i-w,..,n_i\ , \qquad (13)$$

$$D_w\left(k\right)=e^{\frac{k-(n_i-w)}{n_i-w}}\ ,k=n_i-w,..,n_i\ . \qquad (14)$$

Then the mood will be the weighted average of the last w emotions:

$$M_i=Q\left(F\left(E_i\right)\right)=Q\left(\sum_{k=n_i-w}^{n_i}e_i(k)\cdot\left(D_w\left(k\right)/\sum_{k=n_i-w}^{n_i}D_w\left(k\right)\right)\right). \qquad (15)$$

We expect these refined models to be able to properly capture the processes that regulate the relationship between recognized emotions and mood.

4   Experimental Validation

4.1   Data and Overview

To check whether any of the models proposed in section 3 properly captures the relationship between punctual emotions and mood, we searched the literature for an affective database which includes videos portraying affective episodes, and for which both punctual emotion annotations (over time) and global mood annotations (for the whole clip) were reported. The HUMAINE [26] audio-visual affective dataset proved appropriate for the purpose, including natural, induced and acted mood videos, portraying a wide range of expressions. It consisted of 46 relatively short video clips (5seconds-3 minutes), each annotated continuously by 6 experts in the VA domain, using ANVIL [27] as annotation tool. The continuous annotations were encoded into the emotion sequence of Eq. (2). Per video, also global mood annotations were given on a 7-point scale, for valence and arousal separately. From the latter, we determined the quantized mood we targeted by applying Eq.(4) to each VA mood annotation.

To overcome subjectivity issues in obtaining one ground truth per clip [18], we decided to focus on the mapping from emotions to mood *per coder* separately, which meant that the same video annotated by x coders would produce x different instances in our experimental set. This choice allowed us to study the interpersonal differences in the process of mood estimation. For simplicity, we excluded from our analysis the clips with multiple annotated moods, i.e. shifted (consecutive) moods or co-existing (simultaneous) moods. We consider that these cases require separate attention, and we demand their analysis to further work. As a result, in this experiment we analyzed 168 *single-mood* video-instances in total: 38 of class 1, 34 of class 2, 51 of class 3 and 46 of class 4.

In the following sections, we first test the simple models proposed in section 3.3.1. Then, we explore the temporal properties of the mood function. Based on the outcomes of this analysis, we set the parameter w of the more complex mood models proposed in section 3.3.2. All models are evaluated based on their accuracy, which is calculated as the ratio of the correct mood predictions over the number of instances.

4.2   Experimental Results

The prediction accuracy obtained by the basic mood functions of section 3.3.1 is presented in Fig.3, per coder and the "average" coder. The random benchmark marks the

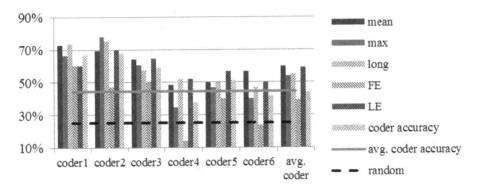

Fig. 3. Accuracy of mood prediction from emotions for the 5 simple models per coder and the average coder

lowest bound of randomly assigning moods to one of the 4 classes[2] (i.e., 25%). A second benchmark is the coder accuracy, namely how well human coders agree on the mood of a video (note that these annotations of mood use the full video and not a sequence of emotions - as our model does). We estimated the coder accuracy as the average rate of pairwise agreement in recognized mood per video between one coder and the rest. The average agreement across all possible pairs of coders results in the average coder accuracy (44%), marked with the solid line in Fig. 3.

For coders 1,3 and 6 the model predicting their mood annotations best is mean. For coders 4 and 5 the most accurate model is LE, being also a good predictor according to coder 3. For coder 2 max outperforms the other models. Overall mean predicts more accurately the mood (60%), similar accuracy with LE (59%), indicating an importance of previously recognized emotions as well as current emotions in mood recognition. The maximum emotion is in general a worse predictor than the longest emotion, which implies that duration is more important than intensity in mood prediction. FE is the significantly worst predictor (all pairwise t-tests between FE and each of the other predictors across all coders, df=5, resulted in $p<0.05$). Except for the FE, the predictors are significantly above the random choice ($p<0.01$). We also performed paired t-tests between the coder accuracy and the accuracy of each predictor. Only mean and LE could predict the mood annotations of a coder more accurately than the rest of the coders at the 5% significance level ($p<0.035$).

It is interesting at this point to check how properties of the video, i.e., its length, the density of the emotion sampling and the temporal position of the recognized emotions, influence the mood prediction. For this analysis, we investigate these effects on the *mean* mood model given by eq. (5) only, as this was the best predictor obtained from the previous test.

Length of the Affective Episode. We ran a Mann-Whitney U-test between the lengths of the videos for which the mood was correctly predicted and those of the misclassified videos. The test returned no significant difference between the median of the length of the correctly and misclassified videos ($p=0.31$, h=0, $z=1.01$),

---

[2] Our classifier handles each video independently, without prior knowledge of the number of videos in each class.

indicating that (at least for videos up to 3 minutes) the duration of the emotional episode does not influence the correctness of the mood prediction.

Sampling Rate. A typical emotion sequence produced by continuous annotations is
very rich in points, considering that they are sampled according to the video frame
rate (e.g. 25 frames/second). Hence, a sparser sampling may be sufficient, as well as
desirable in affect-adaptive applications, reducing computational requirements and
allowing the system to remain idle in cases of uncertainty. To determine the lowest
possible sampling rate, we sub-sampled the original E_i with sampling rate
$f_s = \lfloor (n_i -1)/(N-1) \rfloor$, with N the number of samples per sequence. Then we applied
F on the sub-sampled sequence E_i^{sub} with f_s as parameter. The hypothesis is that

$$F\left(E_i^{sub}\right) = F\left(\left\langle e_i(1), e_i(f_s+1), e_i(2 \cdot f_s+1)..,e_i\left((N-1)\cdot f_s+1\right)\right\rangle\right) = F(E_i), \quad (16)$$

where F is estimated from eq. (5). For $N=2$ only the first and last point of the
sequence are taken into account. In our experiments, we investigate the effect of subsampling the emotional sequence from 2 up to 11 points. Fig.4a illustrates the prediction accuracy of mood in relation to N. For $N>3$, namely sampling every temporal
third of the sequence, the accuracy stabilizes above 99% of its value when calculated
on the whole sequence, so eq. (16) is essentially satisfied. In real applications, where
the length of the affective episode is not known a priori, it would be useful to determine a bound for the sampling rate in seconds rather than number of samples. Thus,
we sampled the emotion sequences iteratively, increasing the sampling rate up to 1
minute with steps of 0.5 seconds. Based on the previous results, we excluded at each
iteration those clips with length lower than double the sampling rate, for which we

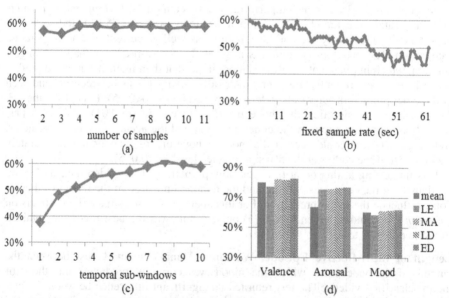

Fig. 4. Mood prediction accuracy of the mean predictor, as a function of a) number of samples
in the sequence, b) sampling rates expressed in seconds, c) temporal position of sub-windows
in the sequence. d) Overall valence, arousal and mood prediction accuracy of the average coder
with the two best basic (mean, LE) and the three complex models (MA,LD,ED).

would have sampled only the first and last points of the sequence. The accuracy of the mood prediction from the subsampled sequences obtained is illustrated in Fig. 4b. We can deduce that a safe sampling that still captures the global picture without discarding essential emotional information is every 3 seconds (98% of the accuracy achieved without subsampling). However, sampling up to every 20 seconds would still grant 90% of the accuracy of the original sequence.

Table 1. Confusion matrix of the predictor ED for mood, valence and arousal

Mood					Valence			Arousal		
Pred. Actual	1	2	3	4		Pos.	Neg.		High	Low
1	26	2	3	7	Pos.	62	23	High	40	20
2	1	23	10	0						
3	2	6	36	5	Neg.	8	75	Low	20	76
4	11	1	17	18						

Temporal Portions Contribution. We investigated to what extent the temporal position of an emotion point in the sequence contributes to the final mood decision. For this, we segmented each sequence in 10 equal non-overlapping temporal sub-windows, and predicted the mood as if we only had one of these portions of the sequence at our disposal. The average accuracy is depicted in Fig.4c. Mood is predicted from the last 30% of the sequence as accurately as if we used the whole sequence.

Based on the results above, we defined the length of the window w for the complex models MA (eq. 12), LD (eq. 13) and ED (eq. 14) as *30%* of the clip length n_i. The average accuracy of these models is summarized in Fig.4d, along with the accuracy for the mean and LE models as reference. The complex models perform in a similar way, although the ED scores the best, significantly better than LE (p=0.048), but not than the rest. Thus, a model where mood is influenced constantly by the past emotions, but the current state plays a more definitive role, may be a good template for further extensions of this work. Also, the performance of the discount factor seems to depend on the speed of the attenuation. The exponential discount is steeper than the linear, which seems to be beneficial to the model accuracy.

To gain more insights on the performance of the models, we also applied F on each of the sequences of punctual annotations of valence and arousal independently and computed how well they predict the global annotations of valence and arousal, respectively. As shown in Fig. 4d, overall valence is better predicted than overall arousal. Mean predicts valence with an accuracy higher than 80%, whereas the overall arousal is predicted better by the LE. ED predicts more accurately both the overall valence and arousal.

To go even more in detail, we report the confusion matrices of mood, valence and arousal prediction for the best performing ED model. The misclassifications occur in their vast majority between classes that share the valence or arousal axis, namely 1 vs.2, 2 vs.3, 3 vs.4 and 4 vs.1. Only in 6 cases misclassifications occur between opposite moods, i.e. between classes 1 and 3 (5 clips), and classes 2 and 4 (1 clip). This is rather intuitive, since the four mood classes occurred from a partition of the mood continuum, in which neighboring classes lie closer perceptually and, therefore, should be closer also computationally. It can also be noticed that low arousal moods (3 or 4) are more easily confused with the neighboring low arousal mood (4 or 3), rather than with the neighboring mood of the same valence (2 or 1). In fact, valence is predicted more accurately (82%) than arousal (77%), and in most cases the misclassification is due to an underestimation of valence. This is not true for arousal, for which the false negatives and false positives are in equal number. Finally, mood classes are not predicted equally well. Class 3 is the best predicted from punctual emotions, whereas class 4 is the least, which may imply that it is more complicated to judge moods of positive V – low A from an emotion sequence.

5   Conclusion and Outlook

We proposed a set of computational models that infer the long-term affective state of a person from a series of recognized emotion expressions. We showed that a model that has memory of the last recognized emotions, yet exponentially discounts their importance in the overall mood prediction, is able to recognize mood with 62% accuracy, which is well above random, as well as human agreement. In our experiments, we also found that a sequence of emotions recognized as sparsely as every 3 seconds predicts mood as well as a series of emotion recognized at video frame rate, which is relevant information for decreasing the computational complexity involved in designing empathic systems working in real time. Finally, we showed that valence and arousal values are predicted quite satisfactorily from our models, yet their combination into mood is less precise.

The latter could be due to the fact that we approached the mood prediction problem as classification, whereas in reality the mood space is continuous; our mood space partitioning was done arbitrarily, yet intuitively, and therefore may be suboptimal. Additionally, the short duration of the videos is not necessarily representative of the actual mood of people, which could last for an indeterminate lapse of time beyond the emotional episode represented in the video. Thus, the deployment and setup of the discount function may need to be optimized for longer videos.

A remark is that an emotional signal can reveal information about the mood, but presumably it is not the only factor people take into account. To fit the intricate mood estimation process we may need more complex models of emotion dynamics, also taking into account other factors (e.g., situational context, scene semantics, personal prejudices). Finally, the robustness of these models when applied on a series of machine-recognized rather than human-recognized emotions, still has to be proven.

References

1. Picard, R.W.: Affective computing. MIT Press (2000)
2. Kuijsters, A., Redi, J., de Ruyter, B., Heynderickx, I.: Improving the mood of elderly with coloured lighting. In: Wichert, R., Van Laerhoven, K., Gelissen, J. (eds.) AmI 2011. CCIS, vol. 277, pp. 49–56. Springer, Heidelberg (2012)
3. Porayska-Pomsta, K., Anderson, K., Damian, I., Baur, T., André, E., Bernardini, S., Rizzo, P.: Modelling Users' Affect in Job Interviews: Technological Demo. In: Carberry, S., Weibelzahl, S., Micarelli, A., Semeraro, G. (eds.) UMAP 2013. LNCS, vol. 7899, pp. 353–355. Springer, Heidelberg (2013)

4. Conati, C., Maclaren, H.: Empirically building and evaluating a probabilistic model of user affect. User Modeling and User-Adapted Interaction, 267–303 (2009)
5. Darwin, C.: The expression of the emotions in man and animals. Oxford University Press (1998)
6. De la Torre, F., Cohn, J.F.: Facial expression analysis. In: Visual Analysis of Humans, pp. 377–409 (2011)
7. Kleinsmith, A., Bianchi-Berthouze, N.: Affective Body Expression Perception and Recognition: A Survey. Transactions on Affective Computing, 15–33 (2013)
8. Jenkins, J., et al.: Human emotions: A reader. Blackwell, Malden (1998)
9. Lane, A.M., Terry, P.C.: The nature of mood: Development of a conceptual model with a focus on depression. Journal of Applied Sport Psychology 12(1), 16–33 (2000)
10. Thrasher, M., Van der Zwaag, M.D., Bianchi-Berthouze, N., Westerink, J.H.D.M.: Mood recognition based on upper body posture and movement features. In: D'Mello, S., Graesser, A., Schuller, B., Martin, J.-C., et al. (eds.) ACII 2011, Part I. LNCS, vol. 6974, pp. 377–386. Springer, Heidelberg (2011)
11. Sigal, L., Fleet, D.J., Troje, N.F., Livne, M.: Human attributes from 3D pose tracking. In: Daniilidis, K., Maragos, P., Paragios, N. (eds.) ECCV 2010, Part III. LNCS, vol. 6313, pp. 243–257. Springer, Heidelberg (2010)
12. Beedie, C., Terry, P., Lane, A.: Distinctions between emotion and mood. Cognition & Emotion 19(6), 847–878 (2005)
13. Mehrabian, A.: Pleasure-Arousal-Dominance: A General Framework for Describing and Measuring Individual Differences in Temperament. Current Psychology, 261–292 (1996)
14. Parkinson, B., et al.: Changing moods: The psychology of mood and mood regulation. Addison Wesley Longman (1996)
15. Russell, J.A.: Core affect and the psychological construction of emotion. Psychological Review 110(1), 145 (2003)
16. Ekman, P.: Basic emotions. In: Handbook of Cognition and Emotion, pp. 45–60 (1999)
17. Schuller, B., Valstar, M., Eyben, F., Cowie, R.: AVEC 2012-The Continuous Audio / Visual Emotion Challenge (2012)
18. Metallinou, A., Narayanan, S.: Annotation and Processing of Continuous Emotional Attributes: Challenges and Opportunities. In: EmoSPACE Workshop, Shangai (2013)
19. Ekman, P.: An argument for basic emotions. Cognition & Emotion 6(3-4), 169–200 (1992)
20. Rusell, J.: A circumplex model of affect. Personality and Social Psychology, 1161–1178 (1980)
21. Thayer, R.E.: The origin of everyday moods: Managing energy, tension, and stress. Oxford University Press (1996)
22. Dietz, R., Lang, A.: Affective agents: Effects of agent affect on arousal, attention, liking and learning. In: 3rd ICTC, San Francisco (1999)
23. Gebhard, P.: ALMA – A Layered Model of Affect. In: 4rth International Conference of AAMAS (2005)
24. Bradley, M.M.: Emotional Memory: A dimensional analysis. In: Emotions: Essays on Emotion Theory, pp. 97–134 (1994)
25. Hanjalic, A., Li-Qun, X.: Affective video content representation and modeling. IEEE Transactions on Multimedia, 143–154 (2005)
26. Douglas-Cowie, E., Cowie, R., Sneddon, I., Cox, C., Lowry, O., McRorie, M., Martin, J.-C., Devillers, L., Abrilian, S., Batliner, A., Amir, N., Karpouzis, K.: The HUMAINE database: addressing the collection and annotation of naturalistic and induced emotional data. In: Paiva, A.C.R., Prada, R., Picard, R.W. (eds.) ACII 2007. LNCS, vol. 4738, pp. 488–500. Springer, Heidelberg (2007)
27. Kipp, M.: Anvil: The video annotation research tool (2007)

Privacy and User Trust in Context-Aware Systems

Saskia Koldijk[1,2], Gijs Koot[1], Mark Neerincx[1,3], and Wessel Kraaij[1,2]

[1] TNO, The Netherlands
{name.surname}@tno.nl
[2] Radboud University Nijmegen, The Netherlands
[3] Technical University Delft, The Netherlands

Abstract. Context-aware systems (CAS) that collect personal information are a general trend. This leads to several privacy considerations, which we outline in this paper. We present as use-case the SWELL system, which collects information from various contextual sensors to provide support for well-being at work. We address privacy from two perspectives: 1) the development point of view, in which we describe how to apply 'privacy by design', and 2) a user study, in which we found that providing detailed information on data collection and privacy by design had a positive effect on trust in our CAS. We also found that the attitude towards using our CAS was related to personal motivation, and not related to perceived privacy and trust in our system. This may stress the importance of implementing privacy by design to protect the privacy of the user.

Keywords: Context-aware systems, privacy by design, user evaluation, trust.

1   Introduction

Advances in sensing, the rise of smartphones and mobile internet, together with trends such as personalization have led to both demand and possibilities in the area of context-aware systems (CAS) and such applications are now very common. Context-awareness for applications has been broadly defined as the use of environmental elements by applications to personalize their service for the user [1]. A simple example is given by a navigation application: you tell the application where you want to go, the explicit data, while the application obtains your current location from the mobile device, which is then the contextual data.

As the scale and application of data collection increase, privacy concerns are rising over the new worlds of possibilities that are revealed by data scientists. Privacy has been defined as the "boundary control process in which individuals regulate when, how, and to what extent information about them is communicated to others" (p. 21) [2]. There often seems to be a trade-off for users between using a service and their privacy: they can use a better personalized and contextualized service by providing more context information, often with the cost of losing control over their personal (context) data. [3] states that "Businesses inevitably collect and use more and more personal data, and while consumers realize many benefits in exchange, there is little doubt that businesses, not consumers, control the market in personal data with their

V. Dimitrova et al. (Eds.): UMAP 2014, LNCS 8538, pp. 134–145, 2014.

own interests in mind." (p.1). In [4] this problem is described as an 'asymmetry of information' in which the data collector knows much more about how the data will be used than the data owner, who has no control. This has led to debates about consumers' privacy and privacy legislation.

In this research we want to investigate how to address privacy in CAS and whether information on privacy has a positive impact on users' trust and attitude towards using the system. In [5] the authors found that in social networks, privacy and security had an effect on the user's trust in a system and the attitude towards the system, which in turn influenced the intention to use the system. An overview paper [6] outlines that firms can build trust by implementing fair information practices, communicating a privacy policy explicitly and/or using privacy notices and seals of approval.

We first analyze which privacy aspects are of particular interest in CAS by doing a Privacy Impact Assessment. We make use of a use-case called SWELL, in which work related behavior data is collected with sensors, to provide personalized feedback and support for well-being at work. As the collected data may include rather personal information (e.g. content worked on or facial expressions), interesting privacy aspects arise. This domain distinguishes our research from related research in which privacy is often investigated in context of social networks, user profiling, e-commerce, marketing or mobile location enhanced technologies [6]. We then outline how Privacy by Design [10] can be applied in CAS, resulting in some simple guidelines for developing privacy-friendly CAS. There are many papers on principles for privacy by design, but empirical studies are sparse. Therefore we performed a user study to investigate the effects of privacy by design on users. Our method is similar to the one used in a study on privacy concerns in location-based mobile services [7]: users were presented our envisioned system and were asked to give ratings. Our hypothesis is that when users have access to detailed information on data collection and privacy by design, the transparency of the system is higher and users have less privacy concerns and more trust in the system. As a consequence, we hypothesize, they have a more positive attitude towards using the CAS.

In the remainder of this paper we first introduce our use-case (Section 2). Then we present important privacy aspects (Section 3). In Section 4, we describe how privacy by design can be applied. We then present results of our user study (Section 5). We end with a Discussion (Section 6) and Conclusion (Section 7).

2   Context Aware System Use-Case: SWELL

In this section we present a use-case from the project SWELL[1] to apply our analyses regarding privacy to. The SWELL system makes use of a variety of contextual sensors, which makes it interesting for analyzing associated privacy issues. We first outline the CAS and then present a scenario.

---

[1] www.commit-nl.nl/projects/swell-smart-reasoning-systems-for-well-being-at-work-and-at-home

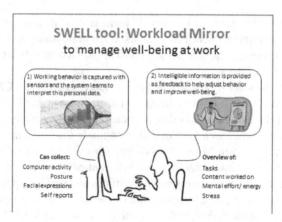

Fig. 1. Information about the SWELL system

SWELL Workload Mirror. The SWELL Workload Mirror is a CAS under current development that provides information about working behavior to help employees reach more well-being at work [8]. Knowledge workers often experience stress building up, which in the worst case results in burn-out. We think that helping knowledge workers to become more aware of what makes them feel stressed, can help them handle and avoid stress. The SWELL system senses data about an user's environment with unobtrusive sensors, combined with occasional self-reporting by the user. Smart reasoning algorithms extract the recent context and mental state from this data. The system is aimed at helping users to reach their well-being goals by providing information, feedback and support.

SWELL Scenario. Bob is 40 years old and works in an office from 9 to 5, where he performs knowledge work. Since some time now, Bob feels some tension and finds it hard to get work off his mind in the evenings. At the end of his working day he often notices that he has not completed all planned tasks and he feels stressed.

Bob decides to use the SWELL system (see Figure 1). At the end of his working day he opens the SWELL Workload Mirror to look back at his day. He sees an overview of the tasks he performed and content he worked on, combined with information on his subjective energy level. He notices that he worked very fragmented which probably caused his loss of overview and decline in energy. Bob decides that it would be better for him to stay focused on his planned work and determine a timeslot to do all ad-hoc tasks. He enables a functionality of the SWELL tool, which warns him when he makes too many task switches again. Bob also notices that, in fact, he has done a lot of useful things today and can go home satisfied.

3   Privacy Aspects

To analyse the potential privacy risks around collecting personal data with the SWELL system, we performed a Privacy Impact Assessment (PIA). As [9] describes it: "PIAs provide a way to detect potential privacy problems, take precautions and build tailored safeguards before, not after, the organisation makes heavy investments in the development of a new technology, service or product." (p. 54). We went through the PIA question catalogue[2] and in this section we present the resulting main privacy considerations and provide the most important PIA suggestions to build a privacy-friendly CAS.

- *Goal of data collection*: We found that it is very important to clearly describe the goal for which the data is collected. Only when users understand what the system does and why the collection of data is necessary, they will be able to take a well informed decision on how to use the system.
- *Type of data*: The PIA highlighted that the type of data should be suitable to fulfil the goal. Do not collect more data than necessary. Be aware that the combination of different sorts of data can be even more privacy sensitive. Store data as aggregated as possible, for example only store summaries of facial expressions instead of video. Time limit the storage of personal data. This prevents function creep, i.e. using the data for other purposes. In any case, identifiers such as full names and email-addresses should be avoided where possible.
- *Reactions to the system*: In the PIA it was pointed out that you should be aware that reactions to new innovative systems are hard to predict. The data that you want to collect can be sensitive, for example when you collect data on geo-location or work performance. Prevent reputational damage. The right story and suitable introduction will be essential to make the tool a success. There is a risk that people involved do not want to participate. For users who do not want to use e.g. a camera an alternative means to get the necessary information should be provided, e.g. let users input their mood themselves.
- *User control*: In the PIA it was recommended to let the user be in control of the system and the settings. You should tell the user which data is collected and (if applicable) who will have access to this data. Their permission should be given based on a free and well informed decision. Giving information on what is done with the data also contributes to transparency and evokes trust. Users have the right to see their own data and may request removal of data.
- *Quality of the data*: The PIA highlighted that it is important to pay attention to the quality of the data. The data should be up-to-date, correct and complete. Depending on the sensor, the data can be more accurate (e.g. computer logging) or less accurate (e.g. facial expressions from video analysis). You can reach better quality by for example letting the user check, correct or update the data. Be aware of consequences of using wrong data.
- *Security of the data*: Security of the data is a must. In the PIA it was recommended to set up a data security plan to establish which security actions are taken to guarantee suitable protection of the data. Prevent unwanted or unauthorized access of the data. Take the sensitivity of your specific data into account.

---

[2] Developed by Norea:
http://www.norea.nl/Norea/Actueel/Nieuws/Presentatie+PIA.aspx

- *Data responsibilities*: The PIA pointed out that the more parties are involved, the higher the risk of data getting lost, unclear responsibilities or use of data for other purposes. Take care that all parties handle the data carefully. Make a clear data description and a clear description of tasks and responsibilities. Make clear who has to take the measures necessary to prevent risks.
- *Data sharing*: We found that in case of data sharing, you should take care that the user gives consent and that the data is used in the intended way. Data can be shared in several ways. First of all data may be shared between users, when it is the wish of the specific user to share data for a personal goal or benefit. Second of all, data may be shared for improving the system, e.g. to train underlying models with all users' data. Thorough analysis should be done whether no personal information could leak in this way. Finally, it may be interesting to share collected datasets with the research community. When data is distributed you should describe the data well and take care that the distribution of data is in line with the expectations of the users involved. Make a clear data description document. Pay attention to purpose limitation and risks resulting from combining data from different sources.

Being aware of these points of interest at an early stage of design should enable developers to implement privacy into their context aware system.

4   Privacy by Design

In this section we present how the outlined privacy aspects for the SWELL use-case can be addressed from the developers perspective by using Privacy by Design [10]. We describe how 8 Privacy Design Strategies [11] can be applied to develop a context aware system that follows current privacy legislation. We also give some tips on specific Privacy Design Patterns that can be used to implement each strategy. For a more elaborate description and specific references refer to [12].

- First of all it is important to **INFORM** the user about the goal of the system and the data that will be collected for this aim. You should always use *Informed Consent*, which means that the you get permission from the user to collect data for a specified purpose. You can also provide the user a *Privacy Dashboard*, such that the user has an overview over his privacy settings.
- Moreover, it is important to give the user **CONTROL** over the data and what is done with it. There are different ways to let users feel in control. Information helps users to understand the system and power allows them to decide which data is collected, how it is used and with whom shared. Offering *Privacy Choices* helps to give them a feeling of control and a system that is easy to use also increases the perceived control.
- The task of the designer of the system is it to **MINIMIZE** the amount of data that the system stores. This can be accomplished by selecting only the most relevant features (e.g. storing facial expression features instead of raw video recordings). In any case it is a good idea to only use *Pseudonyms* as identifiers, instead of storing data together with the users' real names. Furthermore, take care of good

Anonymization. Even when you do not store the user's name, the unique combination of e.g. age and GPS location can make a user of the system identifiable. Prevent having identifiable entries and use *k-anonymity*. This means making at least k entries identical, for example by aggregating "age = 22" to "age = 20 to 30".

- By applying reasoning the data can often be **AGGREGATED** even further. Instead of detailed features, inferred information can be stored (e.g. whether someone experienced stress or not, instead of all facial expressions). You can for example *Aggregate Data over Time*, e.g. the main application of the last 5 minutes or the main facial expression. This also lessens the amount of data the system has to handle. Moreover you can also *Blur Personal Data*. This means you provide personal data only in a detail that is necessary and blur the rest, e.g. store location information not as a coordinates, but as a city name.

- The developer should take care to **HIDE** personal information, such that the data strictly belongs to the user and cannot be seen by others. When a user or application wants to access the data, *Authentication* should be used to ensure that no unauthorized access to the data takes place. To ensure the security of the data it is a good idea to *Store Data Encrypted*. You should encrypt the data locally on the users device and then send it over a secure connection to the cloud for storage. When the aim is to publish (parts of) the data one could apply *Sampling*. Instead of releasing all data a sample is drawn for releasing on the (public) cloud.

- Moreover it might be useful to **SEPARATE** different sorts of data. Storing data from different individuals at separate locations is called *Horizontal Data Separation*, while storing features in separated locations is called *Vertical Data Separation*. When handling privacy sensitive data it is also good to apply *Decentralization* and store (parts of the) data only locally, on the user's device.

- The system should be able to **ENFORCE** and **DEMONSTRATE** that it fulfils current legislation around privacy. You might want to use *Sticky Policies*, especially when sharing data. This means that you store alongside with your data its privacy policy for handling this data. In this way you prevent wrong use by 3rd parties.

By applying these 8 Privacy Design Strategies in the development of a CAS the resulting system will be privacy-friendly by design, adhering to current legislation.

5   User Perspective: Evaluation Study

Now we have seen how privacy can be addressed in the development of a CAS, we want to evaluate what effect giving information on privacy by design has on users. Our hypothesis is that when users are better informed about the data collection and privacy by design, the transparency of the system is higher and users have less privacy concerns and more trust in the system. As a consequence they have a more positive attitude towards using the system (see Figure 2 for our expected model). We also think personal characteristics play an important role. General privacy concerns might have an influence on perceived privacy and trust in a new system. Personal motivation might have an influence on attitudes towards use of the system. In the remainder of this section we outline how we tested our hypotheses in a user study with a mock-up of our SWELL tool.

5.1   Method

Participants. 124 people participated in our user study, 60% male, with an average age of 38 (SD = 10.6). Colleagues from other TNO departments (technical and behavioural sciences) were invited as participants, as they are knowledge workers and potential users of the SWELL tool to improve well-being at work. On a scale from 1-7 our participants scored on average slightly positive on well-being (4.7, SD = 1.2) and slightly positive on the item 'I want help to improve well-being' (*Motivation*) (4.9, SD = 1.7). Moreover, they scored on average neutral on *Privacy concerns* (4.1, SD = 1.5).

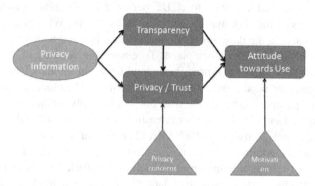

Fig. 2. Expected model. We manipulated whether participants had access to extra *Privacy Information*. Our 3 dependent variables are *Transparency* of the SWELL tool, attitudes regarding *Privacy and Trust*, and *Intention to Use* the SWELL tool. We expect that also personal characteristics (*Privacy concerns* and *Motivation*) play a role.

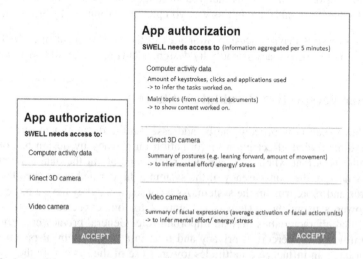

Fig. 3. Mock-up of the access rights dialogue. Left: Control condition, right: Privacy condition.

Design. We manipulated whether the participants did or did not get extra information on data collection and privacy by design. Our experiment had thus a between-subject design and our independent variable is 'privacy information' (no, yes).

Procedure. An email was sent out to various TNO departments. By clicking a link, the participant was randomly assigned to the condition with or without privacy information and shown a website. On this website, first a short presentation was shown, either with or without slides on privacy. Both groups were then asked to fill in the same questionnaire.

Materials. *Presentation.* The first 7 slides were the same for both groups and presented a scenario for the SWELL Workload Mirror (see Section 2). Both groups were told that the goal of the SWELL tool is to support self-management of stress and that the users could enable or disable functionalities as they wish, such that the SWELL tool optimally supports them with functionality that they desire (e.g. sharing information with others).

The privacy group got to see extended information on the data that the system would collect (see Figure 3). Moreover, an additional slide gave them the following information on privacy by design:

— *Purpose limitation*: The collected data is only used for giving yourself insights to enable self-management.
— *Control*: You can enable or disable the computer logging, camera or Kinect sensors.
— *Data minimization*: The tool only processes data that is necessary to provide the functionality that you desire, e.g. the tool will use document content only when you want an overview of topics worked on.
— *Data aggregation*: The sensor data is processed locally on your device. Only summary information, like topics, average posture or facial expression, is stored – no keystrokes or video.
— *Adequate protection*: Your data is hidden from unauthorized access.
— *Data subjects right*: You have full control over your data, can view or delete it.

Questionnaire. The questionnaire had items on the following main categories: transparency of the SWELL tool, perceived privacy and trust, and attitudes towards use of the SWELL tool (see Table 1, items partly adapted from [5]). Besides these main items of interest, we added some items on personal characteristics. We used 7-point Likert scales (1 = 'not' to 7 = 'very much').

Dependent Variables. To determine the main underlying concepts of the questionnaire items, we performed a factor analysis (PCA, see Table 1). We found 3 main underlying components, which represent: *'Transparency'*, *'Privacy/ Trust'*[3] and *'Attitude towards Use'*. To test the reliability of each scale, we calculated Cronbachs'

---

[3] Items on perceived privacy and trust (from Shin, 2010) seemed to all load on one component. Therefore they are not further distinguished in our analyses.

alpha (coefficient of internal consistency) for each set of items. As for all 3 scales alpha was high enough (> .6), we computed sum scores of the sets of items and averaged them to yield 3 main dependent variables.

Table 1. Questionnaire items (* *item adapted from [5]*), loadings on PCA components (with Varimax rotation), and Cronbachs' alpha for combining these items to one concept

Questionnaire item	C 1	C 2	C 3	Concept	α
I would trust SWELL to protect my privacy. *	**.862**	.176	.173		
I am confident that the information I provide will be secure. *	**.861**	.144	.105		
(reversed) I am concerned that the information I collect could be misused. *	**.832**	-.049	-.055	*Privacy/*	.884
(reversed) I believe inappropriate parties may view the information I provide. *	**.795**	-.022	-.048	*Trust*	
The SWELL tool is a trustworthy system.*	**.696**	.202	.236		
I feel in control of my personal data.	**.645**	-.027	.481		
The thought of using the SWELL tool is appealing to me. *	.071	**.923**	.053		
I think using a computer system like SWELL could help me improve my well-being at work.	.013	**.834**	-.020	*Attitude*	
I have positive feelings towards the SWELL tool in general.*	.231	**.802**	.127	*towards*	.890
I think benefits of using the SWELL tool outweigh potential costs (effort, time).	-.052	**.795**	.027	*Use*	
I want to use the SWELL tool.	.104	**.783**	.038		
I understand which information will be collected using the SWELL tool.	.146	.022	**.836**	*Transpar-*	.655
It is clear to me how the SWELL tool works.	.050	.102	**.830**	*ency*	
My current level of well-being at work (e.g. feeling in control, productive, energetic) is...					
I want help to improve my well-being.				Personal	
In general, I would say I am concerned about my privacy.				characteristics	

5.2   Results

Personal Characteristics. As we think personal characteristics may have an important influence on our dependent variables, we calculated Pearson correlations to check for these dependencies. We found a significant moderate correlation between *Privacy Concerns* in general and perceived *Privacy/ Trust* ($r = -.548$, $p < .001$). People who in general have many privacy concerns tend to score low on perceived privacy and trust regarding the SWELL tool. Furthermore, we found a significant weak correlation between the level of well-being and the desire to improve well-being ($r = -.337$, $p < .001$), as well as a significant moderate correlation between the desire to improve well-being and *Attitude towards Use* of the SWELL tool ($r = .457$, $p < .001$). This means that people with low well-being want to improve well-being more, and people who want to improve well-being more have a more positive attitudes towards using the SWELL tool. In the remaining analyses we will use these personal characteristics as covariates.

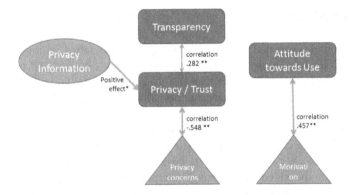

Fig. 4. Results. Influence of privacy information was analysed with ANOVA's. Relations among variables were analysed with Pearson correlations. (* *significant on the .05 level*, ** *significant at the 0.01 level*).

Effects of Privacy Information. We were interested in whether giving extra information on data collection and privacy by design would have a positive impact on *Transparency* of the SWELL tool, attitudes regarding *Privacy and Trust*, and finally on *Attitude towards Use* of the SWELL tool (see Figure 3 for our expected model). Therefore, we performed an ANOVA with privacy information (yes, no) as between-subject factor and *Privacy/Trust* as dependent variable, using the personal characteristic *Privacy Concerns* as covariate. We found a significant effect of privacy information on *Privacy/Trust* (p = .049). As expected, privacy information had a positive effect on attitudes regarding privacy and trust in the SWELL tool ($\mu_{control}$ = 3.85 vs. $\mu_{privacy}$ = 4.24, see Figure 4). Moreover, we performed an ANOVA with privacy information (yes, no) as between-subject factor and *Attitude towards Use* as dependent variable, using the personal characteristic *Motivation* as covariate. We did not find a significant effect of privacy information on *Attitude towards Use* (p = .616, $\mu_{control}$ = 4.03 vs. $\mu_{privacy}$ = 4.16). We also did not find a significant effect of privacy information on *Transparency* (p = .332, $\mu_{control}$ = 4.64 vs. $\mu_{privacy}$ = 4.86).

To further investigate the relationships between our 3 dependent variables we calculated Pearson correlations. We found a significant weak correlation between *Transparency* and *Privacy/ Trust* (r = .282, p = .001), meaning that a high score in transparency is slightly related to a high score in privacy and trust. We did neither find a meaningful correlation between *Transparency* and *Attitude towards Use* (r = .132, p = .143) nor between *Privacy/ Trust* and *Attitude towards Use* (r = .170, p = .059).

Summary. From our analyses we can conclude that attitudes regarding *Privacy and Trust* in the SWELL tool are moderately related to personal *Privacy Concerns*. Moreover, giving users privacy information seems to have a positive effect on perceived *Privacy and Trust* regarding the SWELL tool. We found that the *Attitude towards Use* of the SWELL tool is moderately related to personal *Motivation*, and contrary to our expectations, not related to attitudes on *Privacy and Trust*.

6   Discussion

Our first hypothesis was that when users have access to detailed information on data collection and privacy by design, they have less privacy concerns and more trust in the system. This hypothesis was confirmed in our user study. To build trust in your CAS it is a good idea to communicate information about data collection to the user and to address privacy.

Our second hypothesis was that users would have a more positive attitude towards using the CAS, as a consequence of trusting it more. This hypothesis was not supported by our data. We found that users base their attitude and intention to use the system mostly on the added value it has for them, and privacy and trust considerations might not be obvious or important enough to be taken into account. This has previously been found and termed the 'privacy paradox': people disclose personal information despite their privacy concerns [13]. We might see the consequences of this when users mindlessly accept all access rights in order to use a desired app. 'Privacy calculus' states that consumers weigh the risks against the benefits of disclosing information [6]. As far as users might be underestimating the risks, [3] suggests that responsibility for correct data usage should shift towards companies and away from users, who are often left in the dark after consenting to something they may not have read in full detail or understanding. Research has also shown that although people desire full control over their data, they favor technical and other supply-side solutions ('control paradox' [13]). Therefore we think it is important to implement privacy by design to adequately protect the privacy of the users.

We note that due to our methodology (using a presentation to outline the system and a questionnaire to assess the users' attitudes) only preliminary insights can be gained. Ideally, users should be asked to really install the CAS to do a more thorough analysis on the relation between perceived privacy and actual use of the system, which might deviate from stated attitudes and intentions, as pointed out by [6].

7   Conclusions

In this paper we addressed privacy and user trust in context aware systems (CAS), based on our SWELL use-case. As our SWELL system is a typical CAS in which context data is collected to provide the user with a service, the insights gained are also applicable to other CAS. In the first part of this paper, we found by means of a Privacy Impact Assessment the following important privacy aspects to address in CAS: *Goal of data collection, Type of data, Reactions to the system, User control, Quality of the data, Security of the data, Data responsibilities* and *Data sharing.*We outlined how these issues can be addressed from the developers side by presenting guidelines for Privacy by Design, which can be found in section 4.

In the second part of this paper we presented a user study, in which we found that privacy information had a positive effect on perceived privacy and trust in our system.

We also found that the attitude towards using our system was related to personal motivation, and not related to perceived privacy and trust. Therefore we think it is important to implement privacy by design to adequately protect the privacy of the users in context aware systems.

Acknowledgements. This publication was supported by the Dutch national program COMMIT (project P7 SWELL).

References

1. Abowd, G.D., Dey, A.K.: Towards a better understanding of context and context-awareness. In: Gellersen, H.-W. (ed.) HUC 1999. LNCS, vol. 1707, pp. 304–307. Springer, Heidelberg (1999)
2. Van De Garde-Perik, E., Markopoulos, P., De Ruyter, B., Eggen, B., Ijsselsteijn, W.: Investigating privacy attitudes and behavior in relation to personalization. Social Science Computer Review 26(1), 20–43 (2008)
3. Rubinstein, I.: Big Data: The End of Privacy or a New Beginning? NYU School of Law, Public Law Research Paper (12-56) (2012)
4. Jiang, X., Hong, J.I., Landay, J.A.: Approximate information flows: Socially-based modeling of privacy in ubiquitous computing. In: Borriello, G., Holmquist, L.E. (eds.) UbiComp 2002. LNCS, vol. 2498, pp. 176–193. Springer, Heidelberg (2002)
5. Shin, D.H.: The effects of trust, security and privacy in social networking: A security-based approach to understand the pattern of adoption. Interacting with Computers 22(5) (2010)
6. Smith, H.J., Dinev, T., Xu, H.: Information privacy research: an interdisciplinary review. . MIS Quarterly 35(4), 989–1016 (2011)
7. Barkhuus, L., Dey, A.K.: Location-Based Services for Mobile Telephony: a Study of Users' Privacy Concerns. In: INTERACT, vol. 3, pp. 702–712 (2003)
8. Koldijk, S.: Automatic recognition of context and stress to support knowledge workers. In: Proceedings of ECCE 2012, Edinburgh, Scotland, August 28-31 (2012)
9. Wright, D.: The state of the art in privacy impact assessment. . Computer Law & Security Review 28(1), 54–61 (2012)
10. Cavoukian, A.: Operationalizing Privacy by Design: A Guide to Implementing Strong Privacy Practices. Ontario: Information and Privacy Commissioner of Ontario (2012)
11. Hoepman, J.H.: Privacy Design Strategies. arXiv preprint arXiv:1210.6621 (2012)
12. Bodea, G., Huijboom, N., Kazemier, J., Koldijk, S., Koot, G., de Munck, S., Siljee, J.: Context-aware services: privacy concerns and strategies. TNO report (2013)
13. Compañó, R., Lusoli, W.: The Policy Maker's Anguish: Regulating Personal Data Behavior Between Paradoxes and Dilemmas. In: Economics of Information Security and Privacy, pp. 169–185. Springer US (2010)

Hoeffding-CF: Neighbourhood-Based Recommendations on Reliably Similar Users

Pawel Matuszyk and Myra Spiliopoulou

Otto-von-Guericke-University Magdeburg,
Universitätsplatz 2,
D-39106 Magdeburg, Germany
{pawel.matuszyk,myra}@iti.cs.uni-magdeburg.de

Abstract. Neighbourhood-based collaborative filtering recommenders exploit the common ratings among users to identify a user's most similar neighbours. It is known that decisions made on a naive computation of user similarity are unreliable, because the number of co-ratings varies strongly among users. In this paper, we formalize the notion of *reliable similarity* between two users and propose a method that constructs a user's neighbourhood by selecting only those users that are reliably similar to her. Our method combines a statistical test and the notion of a *baseline user*. We report our results on typical benchmark datasets.

Keywords: Reliable User Similarity, Reliable Recommendations, Reliability, Hoeffding Bound, Collaborative Filtering, Recommenders.

1 Introduction

Neighbourhood-based collaborative filtering (CF) engines return recommendations on the basis of user similarity. As shown in [4], similarity values computed from too few co-ratings cannot be trusted. In this study, we assert that even similarities between users with *many* ratings in common cannot always be trusted, and we introduce the concept of *reliable similarity* between users. We propose a mechanism that builds a user's neighbourhood by selecting only users, whose similarity is *reliably* useful for making recommendations to that user, no matter whether the common ratings are few or many.

User similarity on the basis of few co-ratings is unreliable [4]. Researchers have already proposed solutions to this problem, namely thresholds on the number of ratings two users should share to be considered similar, or assigning lower weights to users that have too few ratings in common [4,2,7]. Their inherent assumption is that similarity based on many co-ratings is informative. To see why this assumption does not always hold, assume a database with seven items $j_1, \ldots, j_7$ and assume that the average rating for j_1, j_2, j_6 is 4, the average rating for j_4 is 5, for j_4 is 2 and the average for j_3, j_7 is 3. Table 1 shows the ratings of four users for these items. Note that u_2, u_4 have given a rating of 1 to j_7 (lower than the average for the item), while u_3 gave the highest possible rating.

V. Dimitrova et al. (Eds.): UMAP 2014, LNCS 8538, pp. 146–157, 2014.
© Springer International Publishing Switzerland 2014

Given the similarity values between u_1 and each other user (last column of Table 1), should j_7 be recommended to u_1? The similarity of u_1 to u_2 and to u_4 is 1 but is based on too few ratings. If we set the threshold to 4 co-ratings, then u_2 and u_4 will be ignored or assigned very low weights, whereupon j_7 will be recommended, since the similarity of u_1 to u_3 is more than 0.99. However, u_3 assigns to each item the average rating for this item, while u_1 (similarly to u_2, u_4) rated j_2 higher than the average. What if people who love j_2 find j_7 intolerable, as *both* u_2 and u_4 do? Heuristics that assign higher weight to users with many ratings exacerbate this problem. Instead of a heuristic, we propose a significance-based solution, in which we decide whether a user (no matter how many co-ratings she has) is informative for a recommendation.

Table 1. Ratings of four users (best rating: 5, worst: 1), and their cosine similarity to user u_1, for whom recommendations must be computed

$Users \backslash Items$	j_1	j_2	j_3	j_4	j_5	j_6	j_7	cosine similarity to u_1
u_1	4	5	3	5	2	4	?	–
u_2	4	5	?	?	?	?	1	1
u_3	4	4	3	5	2	4	5	0.9957
u_4	?	5	3	?	?	?	1	1

In our approach, we first formalize the concept of *baseline user* – informally, the average user for the population under observation. Then, we introduce the concept of *reliable similarity*: we use the Hoeffding Bound (HB), derived from Hoeffding's Inequality [5], to test whether a given user is more similar to the active user than the baseline user is; we then consider as neighbours to the active user only those users whose similarity to her satisfies the bound. Hence, the recommender decides on statistical grounds whether it can make a recommendation on neighbourhood-based similarity, no matter how small this neighbourhood is.

The paper is organised as follows. The next section contains related work. In section 3 we present our method. In section 4, we evaluate our method on real datasets, focussing on the interplay among reliability, neighbourhood size and number of users with an empty neighbourhood. The last section summarizes the findings and discusses open issues.

2   Related Work

Neighbourhood-based collaborative filtering has been studied thoroughly in numerous publications. An overview and several studies on the most important aspects can be found in [9] (Chapters 1, 4, 5), where much emphasis is put on the predictive quality of a recommender's output. We, however, do not focus on further improvement of this criterion, but rather investigate how to improve the "reliability of recommendations". This should not be confused with the reliability of conclusions made about recommender systems, in the process of evaluation using hypothesis testing, as described in [10]. In contrast to statistical testing in the evaluation that aims to measure the significance of the error measures, we investigate the significance of the neighbourhood of a user.

Herlocker et al. introduce the term of significance weighting [4]. They recognize that similarity on only few co-ratings is not representative and the amount of trust in this value should be limited. To limit the influence of those unreliable similarity values they weight them with a term $n/50$, where n is the number of co-ratings. Ma et al. [7] change the weighting schema defined by Herlocker et al. Bell et al. also define a different weighting schema, which they call "shrinkage" [2]: they shrink the similarities towards a null-value to an extent that is inversely proportional to the number of co-ratings. The fewer co-ratings between users exist, the less influence does the particular similarity value have on the predicted rating value. However, none of these methods answers the question "how many co-ratings are enough?", nor addresses the more important underlying question "whose co-ratings are *useful* enough?". We formalize the latter question. Instead of using weights, we can decide whether a similarity between two users can be relied upon, independently of the exact number. We stress that our method is not a solution to the cold start problem, where no enough information about users is known. Our goal is to quantify the reliability of the known information.

3   Building Reliable Neighbourhoods of Users

Our approach consists of a formal model on *reliable similarity* of a user, an adjusted CF-based recommendation engine and a mechanism that builds a user's neighbourhood by only considering users that are truly similar to the peer user and ignoring all other users. We concentrate on user-user collaborative filtering, but our approach can be used for item-item CF as well.

3.1   Baseline Users

To compute the *neighborhood* of the active user u_A, for whom recommendations must be formulated, we first introduce the notion of a "baseline user" u_B – a default, fictive user. Informally, a user x is *reliably* similar to u_A, if u_A is more similar to x than to u_B; then, the neighbourhood of u_A consists of the users who are *reliably similar* to her. Formally, u_B is a vector:

$$u_B = [ir_1, ir_2, ..., ir_{n-1}, ir_n] \tag{1}$$

where ir_j is a rating of the item j and n is the total number of items. We consider three types of baseline users: the *average user*, the *random Gaussian user* and the *random uniform user*. For the computation of the baseline users, we use an initial sample of ratings R_{train} for training.

Average user: This baseline is computed by defining ir_j for an item j as the average rating on j in R_{train}:

$$ir_j = \frac{1}{|U(j)|} \sum_{x \in U(j)} r_{x,j} \tag{2}$$

where $r_{x,j} \in R_{train}$ is the rating of user x for item j and $U(j) = \{x | r_{x,j} \in R_{train}\}$ is the set of users who rated j.

Random Gaussian user: This baseline is computed by specifying that the ratings for each item j follow the normal distribution with parameters μ and σ approximated on R_{train}. The value of ir_j for any j is generated from this distribution:

$$ir_j \sim \mathcal{N}(\mu, \sigma^2) \tag{3}$$

Random uniform user: This baseline is computed by specifying that the ratings for each item j follow the discrete uniform distribution with r_{min} and r_{max} being the extreme rating values. Hence:

$$ir_j \sim \mathcal{U}\{r_{min}, ..., r_{max}\} \tag{4}$$

For example, if a rating can be one to 5 stars, then $r_{min} = 1$ and $r_{max} = 5$.

We use the term of a baseline user to define the concept of *reliable similarity*, which is based on a significance test.

3.2   Reliable Similarity between Users

To define *reliable similarity*, we begin with an arbitrary similarity function $sim()$. We will specify $sim()$ explicitly later.

Definition 1 (Reliable similarity). *Let $sim()$ be a similarity function, and let u_B be the baseline user learned on R_{train}. We define the "reliable similarity" sim_{rel} between a user u_A , for whom recommendations must be formulated, and an arbitrary other user x as*

$$sim_{rel}(u_A, u_B, x) = \begin{cases} sim(u_A, x) & , \text{ if } sim(u_A, x) \gg sim(u_A, u_B) \\ 0 & , \text{ otherwise} \end{cases} \tag{5}$$

where we use the symbol $\gg$ for "significantly greater than". User x is "reliably similar" to u_A if $sim_{rel}(u_A, u_B, x) > 0$.

Checking for Significance. We implement the "significantly greater than"-test of Def. 1 with help of the Hoeffding Inequality [5]:

$$Pr(\widehat{X} - \overline{X} \geq \varepsilon) \leq exp(\frac{-2n\varepsilon^2}{R^2}) \tag{6}$$

The Hoeffding Inequality quantifies the probability that the deviation of an observed average $\widehat{X}$ from the real average $\overline{X}$ of a random variable X is greater than or equal to ε. It takes as inputs the range R of the random variable and the number of observed instances n. The Hoeffding Inequality is independent of any probability distribution, however, it is thereby more conservative than other distribution-specific bounds [3]. The inequality can be transformed into the Hoeffding Bound that specifies the maximal allowed deviation ε given a confidence level of $1 - \delta$:

$$\widehat{X} - \overline{X} < \varepsilon \text{ , where } \varepsilon = \sqrt{\frac{R^2 \cdot \ln(1/\delta)}{2n}} \tag{7}$$

We apply the Hoeffding Bound to ensure that the true similarity between two users is inside the ε-vicinity of the observed similarity. In particular, let u_1, u_2 be two users. Then, $\widehat{X}$ stands for the observed difference in similarity between them and $\overline{X}$ stands for the difference of their true similarities, thereby demanding that the similarity function is an average, as dictated in [5].

Definition 2 (Similarity Function for Significance Testing). *Let u_1, u_2 be two users and let $I_{co\text{-}rated}(u_1, u_2)$ be the set of items that both have rated. Then, the similarity between u_1, u_2 is the following average (for a rating scale between 0 and 1, otherwise normalization is required):*

$$sim(u_1, u_2) = 1 - \frac{\sum\limits_{j \in I_{co\text{-}rated}(u_1, u_2)} |r_{u_1 j} - r_{u_2 j}|}{|I_{co\text{-}rated}(u_1, u_2)|} \tag{8}$$

On the basis of this similarity function, we state with confidence $1 - \delta$ that the non-observable true average similarity, denoted as $\overline{sim}(u_1, u_2)$, is within the ε-vicinity of the observed average similarity, denoted as $\widehat{sim}(u_1, u_2)$. The bound ε represents the uncertainty of the observed information. The fewer co-rated items we have for the two users, the larger is the possible deviation from the true unobserved values. This is captured by the number of observations n, which is here the cardinality of $I_{co\text{-}rated}(u_1, u_2)$. The smaller the value of n, the larger the bound ε (cf. Ineq.7) for a given confidence $1 - \delta$.

The use of the Hoeffding Bound in the significance test in Def. 1 means the following: when we observe that $\widehat{sim}(u_A, x) > \widehat{sim}(u_A, u_B)$, we want to state with confidence $1 - \delta$ that $\overline{sim}(u_A, x) > \overline{sim}(u_A, u_B)$, subject to a bound ε.

To this purpose, we first need to ensure that the same number of observations is used for both the observed similarity $\widehat{sim}(u_A, x)$ and for the observed similarity $\widehat{sim}(u_A, u_B)$. Evidently, the set of co-rated items between u_A, u_B is the set of items rated by u_A, since the baseline user u_B has a rating for every item. Therefore, for each user x, whom we consider as potential neighbor of u_A, we compute $sim(u_A, u_B)$ on $I_{co\text{-}rated}(u_A, x)$ rather than on $I_{co\text{-}rated}(u_A, u_B)$. Thus, the number of observations is fixed to $n = |I_{co\text{-}rated}(u_A, x)|$.

In the left part of Figure 1, we depict the relative positions of $\widehat{sim}(u_A, x)$, $\overline{sim}(u_A, x)$, $\widehat{sim}(u_A, u_B)$, $\overline{sim}(u_A, u_B)$ in a case where both the observed and the true average similarity between u_A, x is larger than the corresponding values for u_A, u_B. In the right part of Figure 1, we depict again the relative positions in a case where the observed average similarity between u_A, x is larger than the observed similarity between u_A, u_B, but the true similarity between u_A, x is smaller than the true similarity between u_A, u_B. Clearly, this is undesirable. Hence, we need a bound ϱ such that it holds:

$$\text{if } \widehat{sim}(u_A, x) - \widehat{sim}(u_A, u_B) > \varrho \text{ then } \overline{sim}(u_A, x) > \overline{sim}(u_A, u_B)$$

Fig. 1. Relative positions of the observed similarity between u_A, x and between u_A, u_B and true similarity within the ε-vicinity of the corresponding observed similarity; the observed similarities on the left allow the conclusion that the true similarity between u_A, x is larger than the true similarity between u_A, u_B; the observed similarities on the right lead to an erroneous conclusion, though.

To ensure with confidence $1 - \delta$ that $\overline{sim}(u_A, x) > \overline{sim}(u_A, u_B)$ for any values of $\widehat{sim}(u_A, x)$, $\widehat{sim}(u_A, u_B)$, we consider the extreme case, where $\widehat{sim}(u_A, x)$ is smallest and $\widehat{sim}(u_A, u_B)$ is largest, i.e. $\overline{sim}(u_A, x) = \widehat{sim}(u_A, x) - \varepsilon$ and $\overline{sim}(u_A, u_B) = \widehat{sim}(u_A, u_B) + \varepsilon$. Then, to ensure that $\overline{sim}(u_A, x) > \overline{sim}(u_A, u_B)$, following must hold:

$$\left(\widehat{sim}(u_A, x) - \varepsilon\right) - \left(\widehat{sim}(u_A, u_B) + \varepsilon\right) > 0 \text{ i.e. } \widehat{sim}(u_A, x) - \widehat{sim}(u_A, u_B) > 2\varepsilon$$

This means that $\varrho = 2\varepsilon$. Thus, we specify that:

$$sim(u_A, x) \gg sim(u_A, u_B) \Longleftrightarrow \widehat{sim}(u_A, x) - \widehat{sim}(u_A, u_B) > 2\varepsilon \qquad (9)$$

Definition 3 (Reliable Neighbourhood). *Let u_A be an active user. Subject to Def. 1, the similarity function of Eq. 8 and the two invocations of the Hoeffding Bound, we define her reliable neighbourhood as:*

$$relNeighbourhood(u_A, \theta) = \{x \in U | sim_{rel}(u_A, u_B, x) > \theta\} \qquad (10)$$

where U is a set of users and the similarity threshold θ is applied on reliable neighbours only. All unreliable neighbours are excluded, even if their similarity to u_A is larger than θ.

3.3   Algorithms

Algorithms 1 and 2 show a pseudocode of our extensions to collaborative filtering. Algorithm 1 computes a neighbourhood of an active user u_A using our method of checking the reliability of neighbours `isReliableNeighbour`, presented in Algorithm 2. This method requires two parameters: θ is a similarity threshold, also used in conventional CF, and δ controls the confidence of the Hoeffding Bound used for checking the reliability. Since the criterion of the reliable similarity is much stricter than the conventional similarity, it can happen that no neighbours for an active user can be found at all. For this case we also adjusted the conventional CF algorithm. Our method can either abstain from recommending any items until more information about the given user is collected, or it provides

Algorithm 1. Reliable CF	**Algorithm 2** isReliable(u_A, u_B, x)

reliableNeighbourhood(u_A) ← {}
 u_B ← $initializeBaseline(R_{train}, baseline\_type)$
 	
 for all $\{x \in U \vert x \neq u_A\}$ **do**
    x reliable ← isReliable(u_A, u_B, x)
    if x reliable **then**
      reliableNeighbourhood(u_A).add(x)
    end if
 end for
 if reliableNeighbourhood(u_A) == $\emptyset$ **then**
    abstain or recommend most popular items
 else
    for all item $i \in missingValues(u_A)$ **do**
      predict $\widehat{r}_{u_A,i}$(reliableNeighbourhood(u_A))
    end for
    return top-k ranked items
 end if
	x reliable ← true
	 if $sim(u_A, x) \leq \theta$ **then**
	    x reliable ← false
	 end if
	 ε ← computeHoeffdingBound(δ,
	 Range, numberCoRatings(u_A, x))
	 (cf. Ineq. 7 and Eq. 10)
	 if $\widehat{sim}(u_A, x) - \widehat{sim}(u_A, u_B) \leq 2\varepsilon$
	 then
	    x reliable ← false
	 end if
	 if x reliable **then**
	    return true
	 else
	    return false
	 end if

non-personal recommendations e.g. the most popular items from the trainings dataset. We state that it is beneficial to make fewer, but reliable recommendations, than to recommend items that will cause a negative attitude or a distrust of the user towards the recommender.

4   Experiments

We evaluate our method on the datasets MovieLens (100k), Flixter, Netflix and Epinions [8], comparing it to: a conventional user-based collaborative filtering recommender with cosine similarity, denoted as CF, to the method by Bell et al. called "shrinkage"[2] and to "significance weighting" by Herlocker et al.[4]. Since our goal is to compare different ways of building a neighbourhood, we implemented only the weighting schemas from the methods described in [2] and [4] and coupled them with the conventional CF algorithm. To ensure a fair comparison, all methods use the same core CF algorithm with no further extensions, so that only the way they build and weight their neighbourhoods differs.

We term our method "Hoeffding-CF", abbreviated hereafter as H-CF. We consider one variant of our method per type of baseline user, denoted as H-CF_Gauss (Gaussian user), H-CF_Uniform (uniform user) and H-CF_Avg (average user). To optimise the parameters of the methods we run multiple experiments using a grid search over the parameter space. Since the number of experiments in the grid search is high, we chose a sample of users per dataset, taking over all their ratings. The evaluation settings are detailed below. Further information regarding datasets and our samples is summarized in Table 2.

Table 2. Samples of users on four datasets

Dataset	total Ratings	sampled ratings
Flixter	572531	59560
MovieLens 100k	100k	100k (no sampling)
Netflix	100 M	216329
Epinions	550823	165578

4.1 Evaluation Settings

As basis for our evaluation we use (a) the RMSE of the predictions made by each method, and (b) the number of cases where the method encounters an empty neighbourhood and cannot make a neighbourhood-based prediction; this is denoted as *Missing Predictions*. However, a prediction is still provided using a fallback-strategy explained later. We further compute the *Average Neighbourhood Size*, the average size of non-empty neighbourhoods built by each method.

It is evident that the RMSE values for the three variants of our method are not directly comparable, because the value of *Missing Predictions* varies among the methods. Hence, we refine RMSE into following measures:

- *Neighbourhood-based RMSE*: the RMSE of the predictions made using the neighbourhoods of the users; limited to users with non-empty neighbourhoods (abbreviated hereafter as CF-RMSE)
- *Fallback-strategy RMSE*: the RMSE of the predictions made using the fallback strategy; limited to users with empty neighbourhoods
- *Global RMSE*: total RMSE by both *Neighbourhood-based RMSE* and *Fallback-strategy RMSE*

As fallback strategy we use the recommendation of the most popular items not rated by the active user. The impact of this strategy is encapsulated in *Fallback-strategy RMSE*.

For the variants of our method, we vary δ: the lower the value, the more restrictive is the confidence level of the Hoeffding Inequality and the less users are considered reliably similar to a given user. Hence, we expect that a decrease of δ will negatively affect the *Average Neighbourhood Size* and the *Missing Predictions*. For shrinkage and significance weighting we also optimize β and γ.

We further consider different similarity threshold values. As we have seen in section 1, setting the threshold to a high value is not adequate for prohibiting recommendations on the basis of unreliable neighbourhoods. It must be noted that the CF may also fail to build neighbourhoods for some users, if the threshold is set very restrictively. In total, we performed more than 250 experiments, all of which were evaluated using 5-fold cross validation.

4.2 Results

In Table 3, we present our results on each of the four datasets. For each of the methods we present only the best value found by the grid search in course of the optimization. The symbol "— " indicates that there are no applicable values for this position (e.g. delta is not applicable for the CF). The sizes of the neighbourhood in Table 3 is seemingly high, however, these are the values found as approximatively optimal by the grid search.

The best result on on the Movie Lens 100k dataset was achieved by our method (1st row in the Table) with a setting of $\delta = 0.999$, a uniform baseline user, and distance threshold of 0.25. The best value of global RMSE was 0.9864. The best result achieved by the conventional CF was 1.0207 (5th row in the table). This is a stable improvement verified using the 5-fold cross validation. Shrinkage and significance weighting yielded a result close to the conventional CF. When we compare our method with e.g. shrinkage with respect to the average neighbourhood size (row 1 and 3), then we notice an essential reduction from ca. 898 to 447 users. This means that our method reduced the neighbourhoods by 451 users on average and still performed better than the conventional CF.

Table 3. Results on four benchmark datasets sorted with respect to global RMSE (lower values are better) and grouped by the dataset

Row	Method	Distance Threshold	Setting	Missing Predictions	avgNeigh-borhoodSize	global RMSE	CF-RMSE	fallback-RMSE
			MovieLens 100k					
1	H-CF_Uniform	0.25	$\delta = 0.999$	2905	447	0.9864	0.9683	1.4929
2	H-CF_Gauss	0.25	$\delta = 0.95$	3229	259.55	0.9875	0.9684	1.4693
3	Shrinkage	0.2	$\beta = 500$	215	898.08	1.0192	1.0192	—
4	Sig. Weighting	0.2	$\gamma = 200$	215	898.08	1.0192	1.0192	—
5	CF	0.2	—	215	898.08	1.0207	1.0207	—
6	H-CF_Avg	0.4	$\delta = 0.999$	13079	132.38	1.0321	1.0390	0.9839
			Flixter (sample of 1000 users)					
7	H-CF_Gauss	0.8	$\delta = 0.95$	7047	78.14	1.0149	1.0133	1.0381
8	H-CF_Avg	0.8	$\delta = 0.95$	49918	5.84	1.0221	1.1355	0.9969
9	H-CF_Uniform	0.4	$\delta = 0.95$	4357	241.3580	1.0549	1.0532	1.1576
10	CF	0.7	—	3998	442.7564	1.0856	1.0856	—
11	Shrinkage	0.7	$\beta = 50$	3998	442.7564	1.0872	1.0872	—
12	Sig. Weighting	0.7	$\gamma = 50$	3998	442.7564	1.0889	1.0889	—
			Netflix (sample of 1000 users)					
13	H-CF_Gauss	0.2	$\delta = 0.95$	13601	199.66	0.9619	0.9511	1.1551
14	H-CF_Uniform	0.2	$\delta = 0.95$	11171	382.74	0.9622	0.9529	1.1849
15	H-CF_Avg	0.2	$\delta = 0.999$	60394	96.94	1.0075	1.0225	0.9669
16	Shrinkage	0.2	$\beta = 200$	4023	916.2519	1.0210	1.0210	—
17	Sig. Weighting	0.2	$\gamma = 100$	4023	916.2519	1.0214	1.0214	—
18	CF	0.2	—	4023	916.2519	1.0233	1.0233	—
			Epinions (sample of 10 000 users)					
19	H-CF_Avg	0.3	$\delta = 0.5$	165578	0	1.0074	—	1.0074
20	H-CF_Gauss	0.8	$\delta = 0.5$	164948	0.2770	1.01100	1.3964	1.0106
21	H-CF_Uniform	0.4	$\delta = 0.5$	159842	1.5113	1.0279	1.3215	1.0109
22	CF	0.7	—	113117	461.39	1.2843	1.2843	—
23	Shrinkage	0.7	$\beta = 50$	113117	461.39	1.2894	1.2894	—
24	Sig. Weighting	0.7	$\gamma = 100$	113117	461.39	1.2907	1.2907	—

Regarding the baseline users on the Movie Lens dataset, the best results were achieved by the uniform random baseline. The average user baseline led to small neighbourhoods. This can be explained by the fact that many users in the Movie-Lens dataset are similar to the average user. Using this baseline makes the differences between user vectors insignificant and, consequently, many of the users are not considered as reliable neighbours to the active user.

If no reliable neighbours of an active user can be found, then computing a rating prediction is not possible. We counted the occurrences of this case in our method (column "missing predictions"). In this situation a fallback-strategy (e.g. popular items) takes over the task of providing a recommendation (prediction error is included in global RMSE). We observed that those cases become more frequent when delta is low. This causes a more extensive pruning behaviour of our method, because more neighbourhoods are considered unreliable. If we allow our method to abstain from recommendation instead of using the fallback-strategy the improvement of RMSE is even higher (0.9683; row 1, column CF-RMSE). Also the conventional CF, shrinkage and significance weighting exhibit some missing predictions. They are caused by either new users or new items that are not known from the training dataset.

We performed similar experiments on a random sample of 1000 users on the Flixter dataset. Also on this dataset our method achieved the best *globalRMSE* value of 1.0149 this time using a Gaussian baseline. The conventional CF (row 10) yielded a value of 1.0856 using neighbourhoods bigger by 365 users on average. Shrinkage and significance weighting were not able to outperform CF.

Also on a random sample of 1000 users from the Netflix dataset our method outperformed other approaches with respect to global RMSE, reaching the level of 0.9619 using the Gaussian user baseline. When abstention was allowed the improvement was even more substantial and reached the level of 0.9511, compared to e.g. shrinkage with 1.0210 (row 16). Also here we observed an essential reduction of the neighbourhood cardinality from ca. 916 by the shrinkage method down to ca. 200 by our approach. This proves that our approach selects the reliable neighbours, who are more informative for the preferences of an active user than the competitive methods.

The last dataset we performed our experiments on is the (small) Epinions dataset (cf. Table 3). Here our method clearly dominated the conventional CF. Hoeffding-CF achieved an RMSE of 1.0074 compared to 1.2843 by the conventional CF. Significance weighting and shrinkage performed worse than CF. Our approach recognized unreliable neighbourhoods and switched from the neighbourhood-based recommendation to the fallback-strategy that performs better on this dataset (cf. the columns *CF-RMSE* and *fallback-RMSE*). The average number of neighbours in the first row shows that the neighbourhood was limited to the minimum and this yielded the best result. Differently than on the other datasets, here the average user baseline performed the best. The statement about its strictness in the significance testing still holds. This very strictness was beneficial on this dataset. In row 19 we see that the neighbourhood was reduced to 0 i.e. there was no neighbourhood-based recommendations.

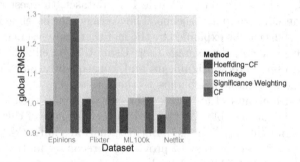

Fig. 2. Best results achieved by each method. Lower values of global RMSE are better. Our method, Hoeffding-CF, achieves best results on each dataset.

All recommendations were provided by the fallback-strategy that, in this case, performed better.

4.3   Summary of Findings

Our experiments show that Hoeffding-CF is capable of recognizing unreliable neighbourhoods and selecting neighbours that are informative for the preferences of an active user. It outperformed the conventional collaborative filtering, shrinkage and significance weighting on all datasets. When abstention from providing recommendations was allowed, the improvement in terms of RMSE was often even more substantial. All of the best results were achieved using a smaller neighbourhood than in case of conventional CF and remaining approaches. A summary of the best results by each method is presented in Figure 2.

We also observed that the parameter delta plays an important role in finding the optimal results. The lower its value, the stricter is the testing of the neighbourhood and the smaller is the average neighbourhood. Consequently, the number of predictions provided by the baseline method rises. The optimal value of delta varies across different dataset around 0.95. Cross-validation can be used for tuning on each dataset.

The choice of the baseline user has also an effect on the performance. We observed that the random-based user (Gaussian and uniform baseline) perform better than the average user baseline on most datasets. The reason for that is that many users are similar to the average user, so it is difficult to identify a user that is significantly more similar to a given user than the average. Hence, when the average user is the baseline, each user has only a few significant neighbours. On the Epinions dataset, however, this led to an improvement of accuracy.

5   Conclusions

We investigated the problem of neighbourhood-based recommendations when the similarity between users cannot be fully trusted. This problem does not emanate solely from data sparsity: even users with many ratings may be uninformative. We introduced the concepts of *baseline user* and of *reliable similarity*, and we use statistical testing to select, for a given user, those users who are informative, truly similar neighbours to her, ignoring users that do not contribute more information than the baseline user. To ensure efficient computation, we use the Hoeffding Inequality for statistical testing.

Experiments on real datasets show that the use of reliable similarity improves recommendation quality: our method is superior to the conventional CF, shrinkage and significance weighting on all datasets, while the superiority in the forth dataset is mainly owed to a good performance of the fallback-strategy rather than to neighbourhood-based recommendations. Our method outperforms other approaches, although it uses smaller neighbourhoods. This means that the reliability, rather than the size of a neighbourhood is decisive for good predictions.

Our next task is comparing our method to approaches presented in [6], [1] and also formulating reliable recommendations for matrix factorization, which is a popular method in recommenders, but relies on activities of heavy raters. Are heavy raters informative for a specific user, though? We intend to investigate this issue by extending our concepts of baseline user and reliable similarity towards reliable matrix-factorization-based recommenders.

References

1. Baltrunas, L., Ricci, F.: Locally Adaptive Neighborhood Selection for Collaborative Filtering Recommendations. In: Nejdl, W., Kay, J., Pu, P., Herder, E. (eds.) AH 2008. LNCS, vol. 5149, pp. 22–31. Springer, Heidelberg (2008)
2. Bell, R., Koren, Y., Volinsky, C.: Modeling relationships at multiple scales to improve accuracy of large recommender systems. In: 13th ACM SIGKDD (2007)
3. Domingos, P., Hulten, G.: Mining High Speed Data Streams. In: ACM SIGKDD Conference on Knowledge Discovery and Data Mining (2000)
4. Herlocker, J.L., Konstan, J.A., Borchers, A., Riedl, J.: An algorithmic framework for performing collaborative filtering. In: ACM SIGIR. ACM (1999)
5. Hoeffding, W.: Probability inequalities for sums of bounded random variables. J. Amer. Statist. Assoc. 58, 13–30 (1963)
6. Jin, R., Chai, J.Y., Si, L.: An automatic weighting scheme for collaborative filtering. In: SIGIR 2004, pp. 337–344. ACM Press, New York (2004)
7. Ma, H., King, I., Lyu, M.R.: Effective missing data prediction for collaborative filtering. In: ACM SIGIR, SIGIR 2007 (2007)
8. Massa, P., Avesani, P.: Trust-aware bootstrapping of recommender systems. In: Meersman, R. (ed.) OTM 2004. LNCS, vol. 3290, pp. 492–508. Springer, Heidelberg (2004)
9. Ricci, F., Rokach, L., Shapira, B., Kantor, P.B. (eds.): Recommender Systems Handbook. Springer (2011)
10. Shani, G., Gunawardana, A.: Evaluating Recommendation Systems. In: Ricci, F., Rokach, L., Shapira, B., Kantor, P.B. (eds.) Recommender Systems Handbook

Toward a Personalized Approach for Combining Document Relevance Estimates

Bilel Moulahi[1,2], Lynda Tamine[1], and Sadok Ben Yahia[2]

[1] IRIT Laboratory - 118 Route de Narbonne, 31062 Toulouse Cedex 9, France
{moulahi,tamine}@irit.fr
[2] Faculty of Science of Tunisia, LIPAH, 2092 Tunis, Tunisa
sadok.benyahia@fst.rnu.tn

Abstract. A large body of work in the information retrieval area has highlighted that relevance is a complex and a challenging concept. The underlying complexity appears mainly from the fact that relevance is estimated by considering multiple dimensions and that most of them are subjective since they are user-dependent. While the most used dimension is topicality, recent works risen particularly from personalized information retrieval have shown that personal preferences and contextual factors such as interests, location and task peculiarities have to be jointly considered in order to enhance the computation of document relevance. To answer this challenge, the commonly used approaches are based on linear combination schemes that rely basically on the non-realistic independency property of the relevance dimensions. In this paper, we propose a novel fuzzy-based document relevance aggregation operator able to capture the user's importance of relevance dimensions as well as information about their interaction. Our approach is empirically evaluated and relies on the standard TREC[1] contextual suggestion dataset involving 635 users and 50 contexts. The results highlight that accounting jointly for individual differences toward relevance dimension importance as well as their interaction introduces a significant improvement in the retrieval performance.

Keywords: Relevance, Aggregation, Personalization, Choquet Integral, Fuzzy Measure.

1 Introduction

Relevance has long been already a complex subject and a challenge which has received a steady attention in information retrieval (IR) studies over the last two decades [1][16]. In fact, an extensive body of works in IR have attempted to revisit this concept which yields to a shift from topical to multidimensional relevance, involving other document relevance criteria coming mostly from the user's perspective such as cognitive, situational and affective relevance. In practice, the key problem is how to design a document relevance scoring model able to involve individual relevance estimates linked to both user-dependent and user-independent

---

[1] Text REtrieval Conference.

V. Dimitrova et al. (Eds.): UMAP 2014, LNCS 8538, pp. 158–170, 2014.

relevance criteria and consider their overall interaction. This problem is faced in many IR settings including for instance personalized IR [17,6,5] mobile IR [10], social IR [15] and geographic IR [14]. For instance, in a social search activity involving Twitter, the task is driven by a variety of criteria such as *authority*, *topicality* and *recency* of *tweets* [15]. For the sake of addressing this challenge, previous approaches are mostly based on classical aggregation functions such as weighted means or linear combination schemes in the form of products and sums. However, these aggregation operators assume that relevance dimensions act independently [10] whereas other works have shown that they are not independent of each other and they interact in relevance judgments [18][2][16]. Although advanced aggregation operators were recently proposed [4][9][8], we are aware of only a few works that considered specifically the aggregation of relevance estimates in IR [8]. Most of state-of-the-art approaches tackle the IR problem without exploring the relevance dimension level within the IR task at hand and thus they do not consider the aggregation problem as a core in the ranking process. Aggregating methods proposed in previous work are generally built up considering the task relevance dimensions, ignoring the differences in the user's personal ratings of the different dimensions; For instance, in a Tweet search task, a user may prefer results that are relevant *w.r.t* both relevance criteria: recency and topicality or only authority and topicality. Thus, we need the aggregating operator to be able to offer insight to humans about why some relevance criteria were weighted more highly than other ones and to personalize the majority preference regarding the IR task specificity as well as the user preferences.

In this paper, we assume a more general scenario where different dependent or independent relevance dimensions are considered within a document retrieval task. More specifically, we address the following research questions:

RQ1. How to aggregate several interacting relevance criteria considering the user's IR task at hand?

RQ2. How to personalize relevance criteria importance regarding the user preferences in order to tailor the search results for each individual user?

Our specific contribution in this paper includes:

- A novel personalized multi-criteria aggregation approach for document relevance estimation: the core of the approach is based on the Choquet Integral [3][11], a fuzzy operator that allows (1) computing an aggregated document relevance score; (2) considering the interaction between relevance criteria; (3) personalizing the relevance score considering the user's importance rating of each relevance criterion.
- A large-scale experimental evaluation using a standard evaluation benchmark, namely the TREC contextual suggestion IR task that shows significant improvements in retrieval effectiveness from using our relevance aggregation operator.

The remainder of the paper is organized as follows. In Section 2, we briefly survey related work to put our contribution in context. Section 3 describes our multidimensional relevance aggregation operator. In Sections 4 and 5, we describe the experimental setup and then present the experiments and discuss the obtained results. Section 6 concludes the paper and outlines future work.

2   Related Work

The relevance concept has gathered a great attention in IR during the last decade [1][16]. The main outcome concerns the multidimensional nature of user relevance assessments that treats the IR process from a user-centered cognitive approach. Although there is no wide consensus, at a general level, this includes mainly content, object, validity, situational, affective and belief dimensions [16]. Each dimension refers to a group of criteria considered by the users to make relevance inferences. Besides, the main finding is that relevance dimensions are not independent of each other and generally those related to content, which include topical relevance, are rated as the highest ones in importance, but interact with other dimensions [16][8]. Considering this finding, several works in many recent IR tasks such as mobile IR [10], social IR [15] and personalized IR [6,17], attempt to go beyond the classical content dimension to cover as much as possible the dimensions related to user's context such as location and interests. However, the proposed approaches tackled the problem of relevance aggregation using simple linear combination strategies relying basically on the unrealistic assumption of both relevance dimension independency and additivity. Despite the fact that recent research has continued to exploit the relevance concept as a multi-faceted one, only a few have investigated how to accurately combine the individual document relevance estimates or scores related to the different relevance dimensions, regarding a given user and IR task [4][9][8]. Celia et al. [4] proposed a multidimensional representation of relevance and made use of 4 criteria: aboutness, coverage, appropriateness, and reliability through a general prioritized aggregation scheme involving two operators namely, "And" and "Scoring". These aggregation operators model a priority order over the set of relevance criteria which makes the weights associated to each criterion dependent upon the satisfaction of the higher preferred criterion. Gerani et al. [9] have proposed a multi-criteria aggregation model allowing to generate a global score that does not necessarily require the comparability of the combinable individual scores. The authors rely on the Alternating Conditional Expectation Algorithm and the BoxCox model to analyze the incomparability problem and perform a score transformation whenever necessary. More recently, Eickhoff et al. [8] introduced a statistical framework based on *copulas* to address the multidimensional relevance assessment and showed its performance in modeling complex dependencies between correlated relevance criteria.

From another side, learning to rank methods have been widely used in IR to combine multiple evidence with the goal of improving the overall search result quality [13]. Given a training set of queries and the associated ground truth containing document labels (relevant, irrelevant), the objective is to optimize a loss function that maps the document feature-based vector to the most accurate ranking score. However, these methods tend to offer only limited insight on how to consider importance and interaction between groups of features mapped to different relevance dimensions [8]. By contrast, we propose to investigate the combination of general level relevance dimensions using a fuzzy-based aggregation operator addressing: (1) the interaction between criteria through the Choquet integral, (2) the personalization of user's preferences regarding each relevance dimension.

3   Combining Relevance Estimates with the Choquet Integral

3.1   Viewing Relevance Aggregation by Means of the Choquet Integral

We address here the multidimensional relevance aggregation problem as a multi-criteria decision making (MCDM) problem. In fact, the difficulty in the aggregation problem is twofold: *(i) Criteria importance estimation*: correctly identifying which individual criterion and/or subset of criteria need to be enhanced *vs.* weakened regarding the IR task at hand and the user's preferences on the relevance criteria; *(ii) aggregation*: accurately combining the relevance criteria by taking into account their dependency.

Let $\mathcal{D} = \{d_1, d_2, \ldots, d_M\}$ be a set of documents, $\mathcal{C} = \{c_1, c_2, \ldots, c_N\}$ a set of relevance criteria and q a given query. The task of combining performance scores denoted by $RSV_{c_i}^u(q, d_j)$, of document $d_j \in \mathcal{D}$, obtained *w.r.t* each relevance criterion $c_i \in \mathcal{C}$, is called *aggregation*. The function $\mathcal{F}$ that computes the personalized relevance score of document d_j in response to query q, considering user u, has the following general form:

$$\mathcal{F} : \begin{cases} \mathbb{R}^N \longrightarrow \mathbb{R} \\ (RSV_{c_1}^u(q, d_j) \times \ldots \times RSV_{c_N}^u(q, d_j)) \longrightarrow \mathcal{F}(RSV_{c_1}^u(q, d_j), \ldots, RSV_{c_N}^u(q, d_j)) \end{cases}$$

Where $RSV_{c_i}^u(q, d_j)$ is the performance score of d_j *w.r.t* an individual criterion c_i, considering user u.

In the sequel, we rely on the Choquet operator as a multidimensional relevance aggregation. This mathematical function is built on a fuzzy measure (or *capacity*) μ, defined below.

Definition 1. *Let $I_{\mathcal{C}}$ be the set of all possible subsets of criteria from $\mathcal{C}$. A fuzzy measure is a normalized monotone function μ from $I_{\mathcal{C}}$ to $[0 \ldots 1]$ such that: $\forall I_{C_1}, I_{C_2} \in I_{\mathcal{C}}$, if $(I_{C_1} \subseteq I_{C_2})$ then $\mu(I_{C_1}) \leq \mu(I_{C_2})$, with $\mu(I_\varnothing) = 0$ and $\mu(I_{\mathcal{C}}) = 1$.*

For the sake of notational simplicity, $\mu(I_{C_i})$ will be denoted by μ_{C_i}. The value of μ_{C_1} can be interpreted as the importance degree of the interaction between the criteria involved in the subset C_1. The personalized Choquet integral based-relevance aggregation function is defined as follows:

Definition 2. $RSV_{\mathcal{C}}^u(q, d_j)$ *is the* d_j *document personalized relevance score for user* u *w.r.t the set of relevance criteria* $\mathcal{C} = \{c_1, c_2, \ldots, c_N\}$ *defined as follows:*

$$RSV_{\mathcal{C}}^u(q, d_j) = Ch_\mu(RSV_{c_1}^u(q, d_j), \ldots, RSV_{c_N}^u(q, d_j))$$

$$= \sum_{i=1}^{N} \mu_{\{c_i, \ldots, c_N\}}^u \cdot (rsv_{(i)j}^u - rsv_{(i-1)j}^u) \qquad (1)$$

Where Ch_μ is the Choquet aggregation function, $rsv_{(i)j}^u$ is the ith element of the permutation of $RSV(q, d_j)$ on criterion c_i, such that $(0 \leq rsv_{(1)j}^u \leq \ldots \leq rsv_{(N)j}^u)$, $\mu_{\{c_i, \ldots, c_N\}}^u$ is the importance degree of the set of criteria $\{c_i, \ldots, c_N\}$ for user u. In this way, we are able to automatically adjust the ranking model's parameters for each user and make results dependent on its preferences over the considered criteria. Note that if μ is an additive measure, the Choquet integral corresponds to the weighted mean. Otherwise, it requires fewer than 2^N capacity measures in the case where the fuzzy measure is $k-$order additive, *i.e.*, $\mu_A = 0$ for all criteria subsets $A \subseteq \mathcal{C}$ with $|A| > k$. From a theoretical perspective, the Choquet operator exhibits a number of properties that appear to be appealing from an IR point of view; since it is built on the concept of fuzzy measures, it allows modeling flexible interactions and considering complex dependencies among criteria [12]. To facilitate the task of interpreting the Choquet integral behavior, we exploit two parameters namely, the "importance indice" and the "interaction indice" [12] that offer readable interpretations and qualitative understanding of the resulting aggregation model. While the former assesses the average contribution that a criterion (c_i) brings to all possible combinations of criteria, the latter gives information on the phenomena of dependency existing among the criteria. Indeed, this is a key point of the Choquet operator, as it may give insight to humans about why some criteria were weighted highly (resp. low) for relevance or to see if the criteria are really correlated. For further details on the computation of these indices, the reader can refer to the original paper [12].

3.2   Training the Fuzzy Measures Within an IR Task

The objective of the training step is to optimize the fuzzy measures w.r.t a target IR measure (e.g. $P@X$) by identifying the values of the Choquet capacities allowing to personalize the search results toward a particular user considering his individual preferences over the relevance criteria.

Considering a user, the typical training data required for learning the Choquet fuzzy measures includes a set of training queries and for each query, a list of ranked documents represented by pre-computed vectors containing performance scores; each document is annotated with a rank label (*e.g.*, relevant or irrelevant). The adopted methodology for that purpose is detailed in Algorithm 1. Table 1 describes the notations used within the Algorithm. The latter runs in two main steps:

Table 1. A summary of notations used within Algorithm 1

Notation	Description
Q^u_{learn}	The set of queries used to train the capacity values belonging to user u
N	Number of relevance criteria
$\mathcal{D}$	The document collection
K	Number of top retrieved documents for each query used for learning
$\gamma^{i,r}$	List of ranked documents in response to query q_r $w.r.t$ a capacity combination $\mu^{(i)}$. Let $P@X(\gamma^{r,i})$ be the $P@X$ of $\gamma^{r,i}$ and $AVP@X(\gamma^i)$ be its $P@X$ average over all queries $\in Q_{learn}$ $w.r.t$ $\mu^{(i)}$
I_{Cr}	Subset of all possible criteria from Cr
$\mathcal{S}_\mu$	Set of the experimented capacity combinations values. Each combination $\mu^{(i)} \in \mathcal{S}_\mu$ contains the capacities values of all the set and subsets of criteria

1- Setting the initial values of the capacity combinations. For simplicity, we call capacity combination $\mu^{(\cdot)}$ the set of capacity values assigned to each criterion and subset of criteria. For instance, in the case of three relevance criteria, a possible capacity combination involves $(\{\mu_{c_1}; \mu_{c_2}; \mu_{c_3}; \mu_{c_1,c_2}; \mu_{c_1,c_3}; \mu_{c_2,c_3}\})$. In order to tune these values, we make use of a target IR measure such as $P@X$ over the training queries Q^u_{learn}. The tuning is conceivable since there is generally only a few relevance dimensions [16]. However, when the number of criteria is strictly higher than 3, we can avoid the tuning complexity by relying on sub-families of capacities namely 2-additive measures [12], requiring less coefficients to be defined and assuming that there is no interaction among subsets of more than 2 criteria. This assumption is made only in the initialization step.

2- Optimizing the capacity values. Starting from the initial capacity combination $\mu^{(*)}$ obtained in the previous step, we pull the top K documents returned by each training query $q \in Q^u_{learn}$. The scores of these documents, referred to as D^u_{learn}, are first interpolated to boil down the non relevant ones. After we obtain the desired overall relevance scores $RSV^{int}_C(q, d_j)$ for each document $d_j \in D^u_{learn}$, and since we are given the labels $RSV^u_{c_i}(q, d_j)$, we proceed to the application of the Least-squares based optimization, which is a generalization of classical multiple linear regression.

4 Experimental Design

Our experimental evaluation is based on TREC[2] 2013 Contextual Suggestion Track [7]. This IR track examines search techniques that aim to answer complex information needs that are highly dependent on context and user interests. Roughly speaking, given a user, the track focuses on travel suggestions (e.g., attraction places) based on two dependent relevance criteria: (1) users' interests

---

[2] http://trec.nist.gov

Algorithm 1. Training the Fuzzy Measures

Data: Q_{learn}^u, N, K.
Result: Optimal capacity combination $\mu^{(**)}$.
    Step 1: Initialize the capacity values
    $m \leftarrow (1 - N) \times N$;
1. **For** $i = 1$ to m {*Capacity combinations identification*} **do**
2. $\mu^{(i)} = (\bigcup\limits_{j:1..N} \{\mu_{c_j}\}) \cup (\bigcup\limits_{Cr \in C, |Cr| > 1} \{\mu_{I_{Cr}}\})$; $\mu_{I_{Cr}} = \sum\limits_{c_i \in Cr, |c_i| = 1} \mu_{c_i}$
3. **End for**
4. **If** $N \geq 4$ {*Assume 2-additivity*} **then**
5.   **For each** $I_{Cr} \in \mu^{(i)}$ such that $|Cr| > 2$ **do**
6. $\mu_{I_{Cr}} = 0$
7.   **End for**
8. **End if**
9. $S_\mu = \bigcup\limits_{i:1..m} \{\mu^{(i)}\}$
10. **For each** $\mu^{(i)} \in S_\mu$ {*Capacity tuning*} **do**
11.   Compute $AVP@X(\gamma^i)$
12. **End for**
13. $Cmax = \underset{1...|S_\mu|}{\text{Argmax}} (AVP@X(\gamma^i))$; $\mu^{(*)} = \mu^{(cmax)}$
    Step 2: Optimize the capacity values
14. $D_{learn}^u = \varnothing$
15. **For** $r = 1$ to $|Q_{learn}^u|$ {*Interpolate the global scores*} **do**
16. $D_{learn}^u = D_{learn}^u \cup \gamma^{*,r}$
17.   **For** $j = 1$ to K **do**
18. $RSV_C^{int}(q_r, d_j) = \underset{1...d_j' \in \gamma^{*,r}, d_j' >_C d_j}{\text{Max}} (RSV_C^u(q_r, d_j'))$; $\gamma^{*,r} = \gamma^{*,r} \setminus \{d_j\}$
19.   **End for**
20. **End for**
    {*Least-square based optimization*}
21. **Repeat**
    $\mathcal{F}_{LS}(\mu) = \sum\limits_{d_j \in D_{learn}^u} [Ch_\mu(RSV_{c_1}^u(d_j), \ldots, RSV_{c_N}^u(d_j)) - RSV_C^{int}(d_j)]^2$
22. **Until** convergence
23. **Return** the outcome $\mu^{(**)}$

---

which consist of his personal preferences and past history; (2) his geographical location. This section describes the used data sets and the evaluation protocol.

4.1 Datasets

We use the TREC 2013 Contextual suggestion data set [7] which includes the following characteristics:

- **Users:** The total number of users is 635. Each user is represented by a profile reflecting his preferences for places in a list of 50 example suggestions. An example suggestion is an attraction place expected to be interesting for the user. The preferences, given on a 5-point scale, are attributed for each place description including a title, a brief narrative description and a URL website. Positive preferences are those having a relevance judgment degree of about 3 or 4 *w.r.t* the above features. Ratings of 0 and 1 on example suggestions are viewed as non relevant and those of 2 are considered as neutral.

- **Contexts and queries:** A list of 50 contexts is provided, where each context corresponds to a particular city location, described with longitude and latitude parameters. Given a pair of user and context which represents a query, the aim of the task is to provide a list of 50 ranked suggestions satisfying as much as possible the considered relevance criteria.

- **Document collection:** To fetch for the candidate suggestion places, we crawl the open web through the Google Place API[3]. As for most of the TREC Contextual Suggestion track participants [7], we start by querying the Google Place API with the appropriate queries corresponding to every context based on the location. This API returns up to 60 suggestions, thus, we search again with different parameters, like place types that are relevant to the track. Approximately 157 resulting candidate suggestions are crawled on average per context and 3925 suggestions in total. To obtain the document scores *w.r.t* the geolocalisation criterion, we compute the distance between the retrieved places and the context, whereas we exploit the cosine similarity between the candidate suggestions description and the user profile to compute the user interest score. User profiles are represented by vectors of terms constructed from his personal preferences on the example suggestions. The description of a place is the result snippet returned by the search engine Google[4] when the URL of the place is issued as a query.

- **Relevance assessments:** Relevance assessments of this task are made by both users and NIST assessors [7]. The user corresponding to each profile, judged suggestions in the same way as examples, assigning a rating of $0-4$ for each title/description and URL, whereas NIST assessors judged suggestions in term of geographical appropriateness on a 3-point scale (2, 1 and 0). A suggestion is relevant if it has a relevance degree of about 3 or 4 *w.r.t* user interests (profile) and a rating of about 1 or 2 for geolocalisation criterion. Those relevance assessments will constitute our ground truth used for both training and testing, in the remainder.

4.2   Evaluation Protocol

Similar to a previous work [19], we adopt a fully-automated methodology through a 2-fold cross validation in order to train the users' capacity values and test the aggregation model effectiveness. For this purpose, we randomly split the 50 contexts into two equivalent sets, noted Q^u_{learn} and Q^u_{test} used respectively for training and testing. In addition, the set of contexts is randomly split into two different

---

[3] https://developers.google.com/places

[4] https://www.google.com

other training and testing sets in another round in order to avoid the learning overfitting. The objective of training is to learn the capacities ($\mu^u_{\{user\_interest\}}$, $\mu^u_{\{geolocalisation\}}$) viewed as the relevance criteria importance. We first start by an initial fuzzy measure giving the same importance weight for both relevance criteria and issued the $P@5$ measure for all contexts from Q^u_{learn}. Then, using the ground truth provided within the TREC 2013 Contextual suggestion track, and based on Algorithm 1, we learn for each user the personal preferences for both criteria: user interest and geographical location. We use the same data to train the best users' criteria priority scenarios for both prioritized aggregation operators baselines detailed in section 5.2. Finally, we use Q^u_{test} set to test the effectiveness of our approach based on the remaining queries, relying on the official measure of the track, namely the precision at rank 5 (P@5). This latter is a high precision measure computing the proportion of relevant suggestions ranked at the top 5 of the output list of suggestions.

5   Results and Discussion

5.1   Analyzing the Users' Relevance Criteria Importance

Here, we aim to analyze the learned capacity values issued from Algorithm 1, reflecting the users' relevance criteria importance degrees ($\mu^u_{\{user\_interest\}}$, $\mu^u_{\{geolocalisation\}}$). First we analyze the intrinsic importance of each criterion independently of each other. Figure 1 depicts the analysis of the variation of the capacity values on the relevance criteria over the learning set of contexts for each user. The x-axis represents each user (id's from 35 to 669) and the y-axis represents the capacity values of criterion user interest or geolocalisation for each user. Figure 1 shows that the user interest criterion is accorded a higher capacity than the location for all users. For instance, user 285 has a capacity value of about 0.23 for the first criteria and a measure of about 0.76 for the second one. This is natural given that users generally seek first for places that match their personal preferences even if they are not geographically relevant. However, we can see from Figure 1 that the capacity values distribution is far from being the same for all users and reveals values from 0.09 to 0.414 for geolocalisation and from 0.585 to 0.909 for user interest.

Second, we analyze the dependency between criteria through the computation of the interaction indice [12]. The obtained values are found to be positive and vary between 0.28 and 0.99. The average value for all users is 0.56 which implies a positive interaction between the considered relevance criteria when they are combined together. To get a better understanding of this phenomenon, we plot in Figure 2, the importance indice values [12] reflecting the overall relevance criteria importance degree for each user. Unlike Figure 1, Figure 2 highlights the average importance of each relevance criterion when it is mainly combined with the other one. One can observe from Figure 2 that users' preferences among the criteria are totally different. The smoothing of the obtained importance values $w.r.t$ both relevance criteria values gives the two linear curves with quite constant values

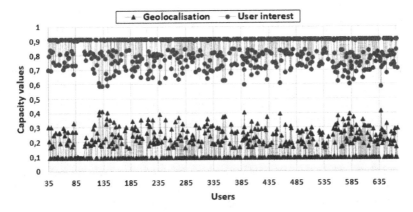

Fig. 1. Capacity values for TREC 2013 Contextual suggestion Track users

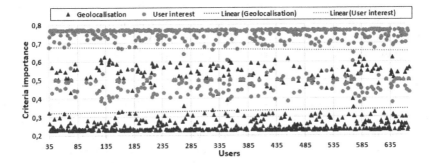

Fig. 2. Relevance criteria importance for Contextual suggestion Track users

which bear out the results obtained in Figure 1. The user interest relevance criterion is still given a quite high importance for the majority of users, but we can also see interestingly in the middle of the figure (values between 0.4 and 0.7), that some users have higher importance degree for the geolocalisation criterion and vice versa. We argue that this difference in preferring some criteria than others unveil the need to personalize the users' relevance importance degrees.

5.2   Evaluating the Retrieval Effectiveness

The objective here is to evaluate the effectiveness of our approach based on aggregation and personalization properties. For this aim, we compare the retrieval results using the testing set to the following baselines: the weighted arithmetic mean (WAM), the SCORING and AND aggregation operators [4] widely used in most approaches involving combination of relevance estimates. Note that we ran preliminary series of experiments through cross validation to find the best prioritized scenario for the SCORING and AND aggregation operators for each user, within the same learning set used to find the Choquet capacity values. Similar to the results obtained through the importance indice analysis, we also found that the best scenario is that giving a priority to the user interest relevance criterion, except that a prioritized operator is not able to quantify the importance degree of criteria. Furthermore, in order to show the personalization effectiveness, we compare our Choquet PERsonalised aggregation operator, denoted CHoPER with the classical non personalized aggregation Choquet operator. This latter is performed using Algorithm 1 once (not for each user), involving a learning method of criteria capacity values regardless of the users. This gives rise to a value of about 0.86 for the user interest criterion and a value of about 0.14 for the geolocalisation relevance criterion. Precision measures are averaged through the testing rounds, for all the different baselines over all the testing queries.

Table 2 shows the retrieval performances obtained using our operator, namely CHoPER, in comparison with the baselines described above. From Table 2, we can see that the performance of CHoPER is significantly higher than the overall baselines for the official measure P@5 but less important for the other measures. Interestingly, we also figure out that CHoPER performance is stable $w.r.t$ all the evaluated measures. Compared to the best baseline AND, the performance improvements for CHoPER reach 10.11% $w.r.t$ official measure P@5.

Those results are likely due to the fact that the AND aggregation operator is mainly based on the MIN operator, which could penalize places highly satisfied by the least important criterion. The obtained difference of performance, in favor of CHoPER, is explained by the consideration of the different preference levels toward the relevance criteria and the interaction that exist between both of them. In terms of personalization, the retrieval effectiveness results $w.r.t$ precisions at (5, 10, 20 and 30) between the classical Choquet operator and CHoPER show that the latter performs significantly for all the precision measures. The best improvement for Choquet is up to 9.29 for P@5 measure. These results confirm those obtained in the capacity training phase (Cf. Setion 5.1) where we show that the importance degree of criteria depends on the users' preferences and are not the same for all of them.

Table 2. Comparative evaluation of retrieval effectiveness. % change indicates the CHoPER improvements in terms of $P@5$. The last row shows the performance improvements against the best aggregation baseline, AND. The symbols § denotes the student test significance: "§": $t < 0.05$.

Operator	Precision				
	P@5	P@10	P@20	P@30	% change
WAM	0.1046	0.1255	0.1174	0.1093	+13.98% §
AND	0.1093	0.1267	0.1197	0.1104	+10.11% §
SCORING	0.1069	0.1267	0.1186	0.1108	+12.08% §
ChOQUET	0.1103	0.1269	0.1203	0.1116	+9.29% §
CHoPER	0.1216	0.1279§	0.1203	0.1131	—
	+10.11%§	+0.93%	+0.49%	+2.38%§	

6   Conclusion and Future Work

We presented a novel general multi-criteria framework for multidimensional relevance aggregation. Our approach relies on a fuzzy method based on the well studied and theoretically justified Choquet mathematical operator. The proposed operator supports the observation that relevance dimensions, measurable through criteria, may interact and have different weights (importance) according to the task at hand. The resulting model criteria behavior regarding the different user preferences is analyzed with readable interpretations through the importance and interaction indices. Empirical evaluation using a standard appropriate dataset shows that our approach is effective. In future, we plan to investigate how to extend the personalization toward groups of users rather than individual users. This would offer opportunities to learning relevance criteria importance from similar users and thus, tackling the lack of training user' examples of preferences.

References

1. Borlund, P.: The concept of relevance in IR. Journal of the American Society for Information Science and Technology 54(10), 913–925 (2003)
2. Carterette, B., Kumar, N., Rao, A., Zhu, D.: Simple rank-based filtering for microblog retrieval: Implications for evaluation and test collections. In: Proceedings of the 20th Text REtrieval Conference (2011)
3. Choquet, G.: Theory of capacities. Annales de l'Institut Fourier 5, 131–295 (1953)
4. da Costa Pereira, C., Dragoni, M., Pasi, G.: Multidimensional relevance: Prioritized aggregation in a personalized information retrieval setting. Inf. Process. Manage. 48(2), 340–357 (2012)
5. Daoud, M., Tamine, L., Boughanem, M.: A personalized graph-based document ranking model using a semantic user profile. In: De Bra, P., Kobsa, A., Chin, D. (eds.) UMAP 2010. LNCS, vol. 6075, pp. 171–182. Springer, Heidelberg (2010)
6. Daoud, M., Tamine, L., Boughanem, M., Chebaro, B.: Learning implicit user interests using ontology and search history for personalization. In: Weske, M., Hacid, M.-S., Godart, C. (eds.) WISE Workshops 2007. LNCS, vol. 4832, pp. 325–336. Springer, Heidelberg (2007)
7. Dean-Hall, A., Clarke, C., Kamps, J., Thomas, P., Simone, N., Voorhes, E.: Overview of the trec 2013 contextual suggestion track. In: Text REtrieval Conference (TREC), National Institute of Standards and Technology (NIST) (2013)
8. Eickhoff, C., de Vries, A.P., Collins-Thompson, K.: Copulas for information retrieval. In: Proceedings of the 36th Annual International ACM SIGIR Conference on Research and Development in Information Retrieval, Dublin, Ireland (2013)
9. Gerani, S., Zhai, C., Crestani, F.: Score transformation in linear combination for multi-criteria relevance ranking. In: Baeza-Yates, R., de Vries, A.P., Zaragoza, H., Cambazoglu, B.B., Murdock, V., Lempel, R., Silvestri, F. (eds.) ECIR 2012. LNCS, vol. 7224, pp. 256–267. Springer, Heidelberg (2012)
10. Göker, A., Myrhaug, H.: Evaluation of a mobile information system in context. Inf. Process. Manage. 44(1), 39–65 (2008)
11. Grabisch, M.: Fuzzy integral in multicriteria decision making. Fuzzy Sets and Systems 69(3), 279–298 (1995)

12. Grabisch, M., Murofushi, T., Sugeno, M., Kacprzyk, J.: Fuzzy Measures and Integrals. Theory and Applications. Physica Verlag, Berlin (2000)
13. Liu, T.-Y.: Learning to rank for information retrieval. Foundations and Trends in Information Retrieval 3(3), 225–331 (2009)
14. Mata, F., Claramunt, C.: Geost: geographic, thematic and temporal information retrieval from heterogeneous web data sources. In: Kim, K.-S. (ed.) W2GIS 2011. LNCS, vol. 6574, pp. 5–20. Springer, Heidelberg (2010)
15. Nagmoti, R., Teredesai, A., De Cock, M.: Ranking approaches for microblog search. In: Proceedings of the 2010 IEEE/WIC/ACM International Conference on Web Intelligence and Intelligent Agent Technology, WI-IAT 2010, vol. 1, pp. 153–157. IEEE Computer Society, Washington, DC (2010)
16. Saracevic, T.: Relevance: A review of the literature and a framework for thinking on the notion in information science. part iii: Behavior and effects of relevance. Journal of the American Society for Information Science 58(13), 2126–2144 (2007)
17. Sieg, A., Mobasher, B., Burke, R.: Web search personalization with ontological user profiles. In: Proceedings of the Sixteenth ACM Conference on Information and Knowledge Management, CIKM 2007, New York, NY, USA, pp. 525–534 (2007)
18. Wolfe, S.R., Zhang, Y.: Interaction and personalization of criteria in recommender systems. In: De Bra, P., Kobsa, A., Chin, D. (eds.) UMAP 2010. LNCS, vol. 6075, pp. 183–194. Springer, Heidelberg (2010)
19. Yang, P., Fang, H.: Opinion-based user profile modeling for contextual suggestions. In: Proceedings of the 2013 Conference on the Theory of Information Retrieval, ICTIR 2013, pp. 80–83. ACM (2013)

Adaptive Support versus Alternating Worked Examples and Tutored Problems: Which Leads to Better Learning?

Amir Shareghi Najar[1,*], Antonija Mitrovic[1], and Bruce M. McLaren[2]

[1] Intelligent Computer Tutoring Group, University of Canterbury, New Zealand
amir.shareghinajar@pg.canterbury.ac.nz,
tanja.mitrovic@canterbury.ac.nz
[2] Human-Computer Interaction Institute, Carnegie Mellon University, USA
bmclaren@cs.cmu.edu

Abstract. Learning from worked examples has been shown to be superior to unsupported problem solving when first learning in a new domain. Several studies have found that learning from examples results in faster learning in comparison to tutored problem solving in Intelligent Tutoring Systems. We present a study that compares a fixed sequence of alternating worked examples and tutored problem solving with a strategy that adaptively decides how much assistance the student needs. The adaptive strategy determines the type of task (a worked example, a faded example or a problem to be solved) based on how much assistance the student received in the previous problem. The results show that students in the adaptive condition learnt significantly more than their peers who were presented with a fixed sequence of worked examples and problems.

Keywords: Intelligent Tutoring System, adaptive worked examples, assistance, self-explanation.

1 Introduction

Learning from worked examples has been shown to be an effective learning strategy. Sweller and Cooper [1] suggested presenting worked examples to students in the initial stages of learning, followed by problem solving once students have acquired enough knowledge [2]. Examples are a suitable approach for novices, since examples reduce the cognitive load and increase initial learning. Sweller [3] explained the worked-example effect based on the Cognitive Load Theory. Novices often have incomplete knowledge which makes problem solving difficult due to the high cognitive load, but worked examples present step-by-step explanations of how problems are solved with associated knowledge.

Many studies have compared learning from examples to unsupported problem solving, and showed that learning from examples is more effective [4][5]. Intelligent Tutoring Systems (ITS) are different from unsupported problem solving as ITSs support problem solving by providing adaptive scaffolding in terms of feedback, guidance, problem selection and other types of help. Only recently several studies have compared learning from examples to learning with ITSs (e.g. [6][7][8]). However, little attention has been devoted so far to the difference between novices and

V. Dimitrova et al. (Eds.): UMAP 2014, LNCS 8538, pp. 171–182, 2014.
© Springer International Publishing Switzerland 2014

advanced students in learning from examples and learning from supported problem solving. Research shows that students need different levels of assistance [9] and therefore ITSs should provide it adaptively.

Salden et al. [10] compared fixed faded worked-out examples with adaptive ones. Fixed faded examples are the same for all students, but the solution steps in adaptive faded examples are removed in accordance to the student's prior knowledge. They conducted two studies, one in a lab (Germany), the other in a classroom (Pittsburgh). In the lab study, adaptive examples led to better learning and higher transfer compared to the other condition. In the classroom study, however, there was no significant difference in the immediate post-test, but in the delayed post-test students who used adaptive examples learned more.

Kalyuga and Sweller [11] proposed an adaptive model for using examples based on the Cognitive Efficiency (CE)[1], which is calculated form students' performance and self-reported cognitive load. They used a different formula from what was previously proposed [12][13] as it was necessary to calculate CE in real time during the experiment. Performance was based on the number of steps the student required to solve a problem. The method was tested using the Algebra cognitive tutor enriched with worked examples and faded examples. Students in the adaptive condition were allocated to one of the four stages of faded worked examples (stage 1 fully worked-out examples, stage 4 fully problem-solving tasks) based on their cognitive efficiency scores in the pre-test. All students had to proceed to the final stage of fading (stage 4) from the stage they started. In each stage, a diagnostic task decides if the student needs more information (in the forms of 2 worked examples or 4 shortened worked examples). The adaptive condition scored marginally significantly higher than the non-adaptive condition, and also showed significantly higher efficiency gains.

In our previous study, we compared learning from examples only (EO), alternating examples and tutored problems (AEP), and tutored problems only (PO) in the area of specifying database queries in SQL [8][14]. We scaffolded examples and problems with Self-Explanation (SE) prompts [15][16][17], requiring students to explain the worked examples provided or how they solved problems. The results showed that students benefitted the most from alternating examples and problems. In that study, we used a fixed sequence of examples and problems; therefore, it is possible that some students have received less or more information than they needed. This encouraged us to propose a new adaptive learning strategy that decides what type of task to present to the learner. The learning tasks are problem solving, 2-step faded examples, 1-step faded examples, and worked examples, with faded steps chosen based on the student's performance.

2   Study

The study was conducted in the context of SQL-Tutor, a constraint-based tutor [18][19] that teaches the Structured Query Language (SQL). Fig. 1 illustrates the problem-solving page in SQL-Tutor, which presents the problem text and the database schema. Students write queries by filling in the necessary boxes for the SELECT, FROM, WHERE, GROUP BY, HAVING, and ORDER BY clauses.

---

[1]   Cognitive efficiency = Performance / Cognitive Load.

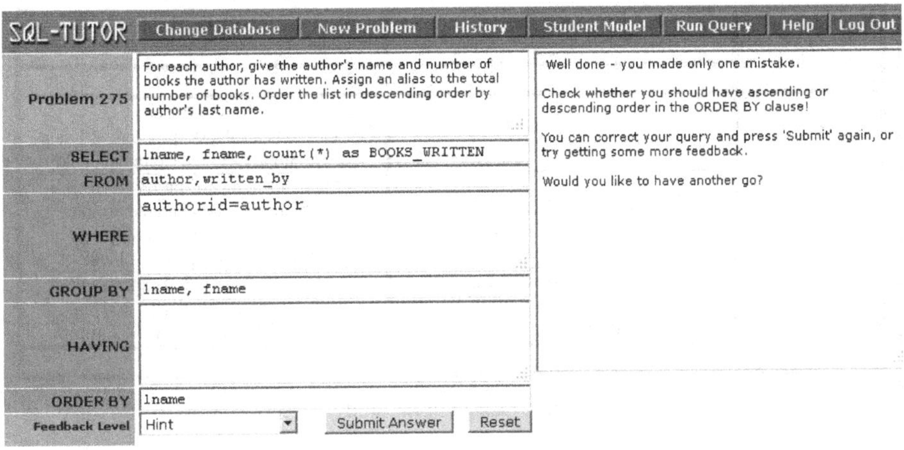

Fig. 1. Problem-solving environment in SQL-Tutor

Students can choose the level of feedback they want to receive in case their answer is incorrect. The level of feedback defines how much assistance is provided to the student. SQL-Tutor offers six levels of feedback: positive/negative feedback, error flag, hint, all errors, partial solution and complete solution. Positive/negative feedback has the lowest level of assistance, and it informs students whether their answer is correct or not. The message also shows how many errors students have in their solution. An error flag message identifies the clause in which the error happened. More information about the type of error will be provided when a hint-type feedback is requested (illustrated in Figure 1). The partial solution shows the correct content of the clause which the student got wrong. Feedback of type *all errors* displays hint-type messages for all errors the student has made. At the maximum level, the complete solution simply reveals the pre-specified ideal solution of the problem. When a student starts solving a new problem, the default feedback level is positive/negative. The student can attempt the same problem as many times as needed [19].

The version of SQL-Tutor used in this study had four modes: problem solving, 2-step or 1-step faded example, and worked example. The problem-solving mode is similar to the original SQL-Tutor. The 2-step / 1-step faded example modes differ in that the student needs to complete two or just one clause. The worked example mode presents the completed solution and an explanation.

The study was conducted in a single, 100-minute long session in which the participants (46 undergraduate students from the University of Canterbury) studied ten pairs of isomorphic tasks of increasing complexity. Fig. 2 shows the design of the study. The students took a pre-test for 10 minutes, consisting of eight multiple-choice and two problem-solving questions. The multiple-choice questions measured conceptual knowledge (one mark each). For the problem-solving questions, students had to write SQL queries (four marks each). Participants were randomly allocated to either the control (22 students) or experimental group (24).

	Control	Experimental
	n = 22	n = 24
	Pre-test	
Pair 1	1st task: problem 2nd task: example	1st task: problem 2nd task: rehearsal task (problem, 2/1 step faded example, worked example, or skip)
Pair 2 to 10	1st task in each pair: example 2nd task in each pair: problem	1st task in each pair: preparation task (problem, 2/1 step faded example, worked example, or skip) 2nd task in each pair: problem
	Each problem followed by a C-SE prompt and each example followed by a P-SE prompt	Each problem or faded example followed by a C-SE prompt, and each example followed by a P-SE prompt
	Post-test	

Fig. 2. Design of the study

The control condition worked with example-problem pairs: each pair consisted of an example followed by an isomorphic problem to solve. The only exception is the first pair, in which the control group received a problem followed by an example. Therefore, the control condition in this study is identical to the best condition (AEP - alternating examples/problems) from [8] with the exception of the first pair. The experimental group had pairs consisting of a preparation task followed by a problem, except for the first pair. The first pair consisted of a problem followed by a rehearsal task; this was necessary so that this problem can provide the necessary information for the adaptive strategy. Rehearsal tasks are the same as preparation tasks, but because they were provided after the isomorphic problem we called them rehearsal tasks. The adaptive strategy decided what type of preparation task to present.

Similar to [8], we presented participants with SE prompts after worked examples and problems. Conceptual-focused Self-Explanation prompts (C-SE) and Procedural-focused Self-Explanation prompts (P-SE) are meta-cognitive prompts requiring students to reflect on concepts required to solve problems or on procedural steps of worked examples. Students were given C-SE prompts after problems or faded examples, and P-SE prompts after examples. At the end of the session, students were given 10 minutes to complete the post-test. However, students could start the post-test during the learning session and finish the study earlier. The post-test was of similar complexity to the pre-test.

The fading strategy is based on the student's performance on the current task. Domain knowledge is represented in SQL-Tutor as constraints. Every time the student submits an attempt, the system analyses it and records information about the constraints that were satisfied or violated. It is therefore possible to find out how much the student learnt about a particular domain concept by comparing his/her knowledge before and after the current problem. Our fading strategy sorts the concepts that the student learnt in the current problem and selects the concept the student learnt the most (or the top two concepts, if two steps are to be faded). Then the system fades one or two steps of the next problem. If the next problem does not include the selected concept(s), the strategy fades the next concept (or two) from the sorted list. The idea is to help students rehearse what they have just learnt.

Our adaptive strategy is based on a measure of assistance the student received while solving a problem. Table 1 shows the score H_i we assigned to each level i of feedback in SQL-Tutor. Level 0 (H_0) presents minimum assistance (score = 1) and level 5 (H_5) shows the maximum assistance (score = 6).

Table 1. Assistance scores for different levels of help

Name	i	H_i
Positive/Negative	0	1
Error flag	1	2
Hint	2	3
Partial solution	3	4
All errors	4	5
Complete solution	5	6

The easiest way to calculate the assistance score is to sum up the assistance scores of all requested help, as in Equation 1. In SQL-Tutor, students can ask for the same level of feedback several times; therefore, the assistance scores of feedback messages are multiplied by the number of times they have been requested (n_i).

$$\text{Assistance score: T} = \sum_{i=0}^{5} H_i\, n_i \tag{1}$$

When a student has seen a particular feedback message, and then requests it again, the message does not contain the same amount of new information; therefore, the assistance score should be less than Equation 1. For instance, when a student requests a complete solution, the next time s/he asks for the complete solution, the same solution will be shown. Therefore, we multiplied the assistance score by the power two series of n, with n showing the number of requests for the level of feedback (Equation 2). Power two series converges to two, as shown in Equation 3.

$$\text{Power two series } (n): Po(n) = \sum_{j=1}^{n} \frac{1}{2^{(j-1)}} \tag{2}$$

$$\lim_{n \to \infty} Po(n) \approx 2 \tag{3}$$

In Equation 4, we rewrite Equation 1 using Equation 2:

$$T = \sum_{i=0}^{5} H_i Po(n_i) \tag{4}$$

While Equation 4 appears mathematically sound, it does not take into account the student's behaviour after receiving feedback. For instance, the current formula shows that Student A who solved a problem by receiving H_0 H_1 H_2 (without getting a partial or complete solution), received the same information as Student B who saw a complete solution (H_5) once. It is important to distinguish between students who complete problems with minimum assistance and students who request the complete solution in the first attempt. One way is to change the scoring system we presented in Table 1. However, changing the scoring system does not help to distinguish between students who saw a complete solution in the first attempt and students who saw a complete solution after several attempts to solve the problem. For instance, students who get a complete solution after several incorrect attempts may search for their mistakes when they see the complete solution. Moreover, seeing a complete solution in the first attempt encourages students to copy the solution, which leads to shallow learning [20].

In order to include the student behaviour in the assistance score formula, we introduced parameter B, which represents the average score of requested feedback levels (Equation 5). As an example, when a student requests H_1 three times followed by H_4, the value of B is 3.5. Parameter B indicates whether the student tends to use high or low levels of assistance; for instance, if B is 2.5, the student mostly uses low feedback levels, but when B is 4.5, the student uses high levels of feedback more than low-level feedback to solve the problem.

$$\text{Student Behaviour: } B = AVERAGE\ (H_m),$$
$$m \text{ is the list of requested feedback levels} \tag{5}$$

This information was not available in Equation 4. Having such information, we can design an appropriate coefficient, but would a linear coefficient be a suitable approach (Equation 6)? Equation 6 does not discriminate well between different levels of feedback. For instance, there is a small difference between B = 1, B = 2, B = 3 or B = 4. In fact, B = 4 shows that students used a partial or a complete solution to accomplish the task, while B = 3 shows that students definitely did not see a complete solution, but might use partial solution in conjunction with some other low assistance hints. Therefore, we should use different slopes for each behaviour. An appropriate function that accounts for this is shown in Equation 7.

$$T = B \sum_{i=0}^{5} H_i Po(n_i) \tag{6}$$

$$f(x) = \sin(\frac{\pi}{2}(\frac{x}{3} - 1)) + 1 \tag{7}$$

In order to make a bigger difference between low-level and high level assistance scores, in Equation 8 we use a power two of Equation 7. Since g(x) starts from zero, we incremented the formula to avoid a zero coefficient, and obtain Equation 9. We also changed the name of the function to Skewness slope.

$$g(x) = (\sin(\frac{\pi}{2}\frac{x}{3} - 1)) + 1)^2 \tag{8}$$

$$\text{Skewness slope: } K(x) = (\sin(\frac{\pi}{2}\frac{x}{3} - 1)) + 1)^2 + 1 \tag{9}$$

Overall, from Equation 6 and Equation 9, we rewrite the assistance score formula, and Equation 10 shows the final result.

$$T = K(B) \sum_{i=0}^{5} H_i Po(n_i) \tag{10}$$

We tested Equations 4 and 10 using the data from our previous study, in which 12 students solved problems in SQL-Tutor. The results show that Equation 10 leads to higher accuracy than Equations 1 and 4. Therefore, in this study we used Equation 10 to calculate the assistance score after each problem is solved.

Paas and Van Merrienboer [13] calculated cognitive efficiency as the difference between the z-scores of performance (P) and mental effort rating (R), $CE = z_P - z_R$. This way, CE can only be calculated after the experiment is completed. In order to determine CE in real time, Kalyuga and Sweller [11] used mental effort (R) and performance (P) to calculate Cognitive Efficiency as $CE = P \div R$. Mental effort was indicated by students, and performance was calculated from the number of steps the student required to solve a problem. Our adaptive strategy is also based on a measure of cognitive efficiency. The participants were asked to rate the mental effort (R) after solving each problem (*How much effort did you invest to complete this task?*) on a 9-point rating scale. We calculated the student's performance P from the assistance score T:

$$P = T_{High} - T \tag{11}$$

When a student asks for a partial solution several times, effectively the student modifies the problem into a worked example. Examples provide maximum assistance; the assistance score for the situation when the student has seen partial solution several times corresponds to a high level of assistance which we refer to as T_{High}. Thus, using Equation 10 we calculate T_{High} to be 26 ($H_3 = 4$; $K(4) = 3.25$). Therefore, performance P can be calculated as:

$$P = 26 - T \tag{12}$$

Please note that T can have a value greater than T_{High}. Because T_{High} represents turning problems into examples, we set all the assistance scores greater than T_{High} to 26. Therefore, P never becomes negative.

Performances are then scaled to the range [0, 9]. Like Kalyuga and Sweller (2005), we define the critical level of cognitive efficiency as $CE_{cr} = P_{max} \div R_{max}$, where $P_{max} = R_{max} = 9$. We consider $CE > CE_{cr}$ to be high cognitive efficiency; thus, students who solved a problem with $CE > 1$ were expected to be able to solve the next problem without needing a preparation task.

The first pair of tasks is different from the other pairs. In this pair, the participants worked with problem 1 followed by a rehearsal task. A rehearsal task is the same as a preparation task, but because this preparation task is provided after problem 1, we refer to it as a rehearsal task. If the student's CE is greater than 1 in problem 1, the system skipped the rehearsal task from the first pair and the preparation task of pair 2. As CE scores were updated after solving problems only, in the preparation task of the second pair the students received the same type of task as the rehearsal task from the first pair. The system behaviour for the second pair is the same as for all later pairs, as depicted in Fig. 3.

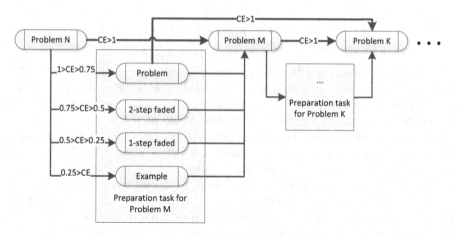

Fig. 3. Study flow

Our adaptive strategy uses cognitive efficiency CE to decide whether the student needs preparation before the next problem as shown in Table 2. A CE of below 1 and above 0.75 (6.75/9) shows relatively good performance on the current problem, but indicates the need to prepare for the next problem by solving an isomorphic problem first. Students with CE between 0.75 (6.75/9) and 0.25 (2.25/9) receive 2-step or 1-step faded examples as the preparation task. As we mentioned before, the steps are faded based on how much the student has learnt from the current task for each concept. Students who scored below 0.25 (2.25/9) get an isomorphic worked example before solving the next problem. When the student asked for a partial solution more than twice, or saw the complete solution, the strategy presents a worked example as a preparation task regardless of the student's CE. The system calculates the CE score only after problems. If a student performed well (CE>1) on a problem which is shown as a preparation task, the system skips the next problem and the preparation task for the subsequent problem.

Table 2. Decision table

Condition	CE>1	1>CE>0.75	0.75<CE<0.5	0.5<CE<0.25	CE<0.25
Preparation type	Skip preparation	Problem	2-step faded example	1-step faded example	Worked example

3   Results

The basic statistics about the two groups are presented in Table 3. There was no significant difference between the pre-test performances of the two groups. The t-test revealed a significant difference between the post-test results. The post-test performance of the control group was significantly lower than the experimental group. The students in both conditions improved significantly between the pre- and the post-test, as shown by the paired t-tests reported in the *Improvement* row of Table 3. Correlations between the pre- and post-test scores are also reported in Table 3, but only the control condition had a significant correlation ($p < .01$, $r = .55$). There was also a significant difference between the mean learning times of the two groups. The experimental group spent significantly less time in the intervention than the control group.

Table 3. Basic statistics for the two conditions (* denotes significance at the 0.05 level)

	Control (22)	Exper. (24)	p
Pre-test (%)	50.3 (13.7)	45.3 (18.9)	.31
Post-test (%)	77.8 (13.9)	85.7 (12.6)	*.05
Improvement	*p<.01, t=-9.9	*p<.01 , t=-10.5	
Pre/post-test correlation	p<.01, r=.55	p=.10, r=.34	
Learning time (min)	73.6 (16.3)	58.9 (19.0)	*<.01
Normalised learning gain	.56 (.25)	.73 (.20)	*.01
Conceptual knowledge gain	.76 (.30)	.88 (.18)	.13
Procedural knowledge gain	.30 (.38)	.62 (.37)	*<.01
Number of problems solved (incl. faded)	7.0 (2.5)	8.6 (3.0)	.06
Problems solved (excl. faded examples)	7.0 (2.5)	6.9 (2.4)	.95
2-step faded		.8 (1.2)	
1-step faded		.9 (1.2)	
Number of examples	7.9 (3.0)	1.8 (1.9)	*<.01
Number of attempts per problem	4.5 (2.0)	4.3 (1.7)	.72
Maximum complexity level	13.4 (5.2)	14.0 (5.3)	.71

The normalised learning gain[2] of the experimental group was significantly higher than the gain of the control group. When we analysed normalised learning gains on the conceptual knowledge questions (questions 1 to 8), we found no significant difference between the groups. On the other hand, the normalised learning gain on procedural knowledge (questions 9 and 10) of the experimental group was significantly higher than that of the control group ($p < .1$).

The experimental group participants solved marginally significantly more problems than the control group ($p = .06$), when faded examples are included. In order to solve faded examples, students had to fill in the faded steps. Therefore, we analysed the number of problems solved, excluding faded examples, and there was no significant difference between the two groups. The average number of 2-step faded examples solved by the experimental group is 0.8, and the average for 1-step faded examples is 0.9. The experimental group received significantly fewer examples than the control group ($p < .01$). There was no significant difference in the number of attempts per problem between the two conditions. The problem complexity gradually increased from pair 1 to pair 10. There was no significant difference between the average maximum complexity levels of problems the students in the two groups solved.

Students rated their mental effort after they solved problems (not after examples and faded examples, as we could not calculate performance in those cases), which the

---

[2] Normalised learning gain = (Post test - Pre test) / (Max score - Pre test).

adaptive strategy used to calculate CE. As mental effort rate is specified on a 9-point scale, we used non-parametric tests for this analysis. We used Spearman's rho test to analyse correlations, reported in Table 4. We found significant negative correlations between the pre-test scores and mental effort ratings, as well as between mental effort and CE, for both groups. There were significant positive correlations between the pre-test and CE for both groups. Next, we used the Mann-Whitney U test to compare the groups on CE and mental effort. There is no significant difference between the experimental and control groups ($p = .24$) on reported mental effort, but the experimental group had a marginally significantly higher CE scores than the control group ($p = .09$).

Table 4. Cognitive efficiency and mental effort analysis

	Control	Experimental	p
Correlation: pre-test and mental effort	p=.03, r = -.48	p=.02, r = -.48	
Correlation: pre-test and CE	p<.001, r = .69	p=.03, r = .44	
Correlation: mental effort and CE	p=.001, r = -.67	p<.001, r = -.73	
Cognitive Efficiency (CE)	2.28 (2.29)	2.70 (1.85)	.09
Mental effort	4.77 (1.71)	4.38 (1.20)	.24

As mentioned earlier, the participants received C-SE prompts after problems and P-SE after examples. We analysed the SE success rates for the two groups, which are reported in Table 5. There was neither significant difference between the groups in the overall SE success rate nor in the P-SE success rates, but there was a marginally significant difference in the C-SE success rate ($p = .08$). Students in the experimental condition performed better on C-SE than the control group.

Table 5. Analyses of SE prompts

	Control	Experimental	p
Overall SE success rate	82.6 (12.2)	88.0 (12.5)	.14
Procedural SE success rate	90.3 (12.9)	90. (11.5)	.97
Conceptual SE success rate	73.6 (15.9)	84.0 (20.1)	.08

Overall, the results show that the experimental group participants, who worked with the adaptive strategy, learnt more and faster than the control group. The results clearly show the effectiveness of our adaptive strategy in comparison with the non-adaptive sequence.

4   Conclusions

In this study, we compared a fixed sequence of alternating examples and problems with a strategy that adaptively decides how much assistance the student needs. The adaptive strategy determines the type of task (a worked example, a faded example or a problem to be solved) based on how much assistance the student received on the previous problem. We proposed a novel approach to measure the performance score.

Using performance and mental effort scores enable us to calculate the cognitive efficiency, which is then used to choose appropriate learning tasks for students. The fading strategy is also adaptive: the system fades the solution steps about the concepts that the student learnt the most in the previous task. The results show that the experimental group learnt more and faster than the control group.

Prior research has shown that adaptive faded examples are superior to non-adaptive faded examples [10], but their fading strategy was based on students' performance in answering self-explanation prompts. In our study, we used the student model to see how much students learnt about each concept, and then faded the steps about the concepts students learnt the most in the previous problem. Prior research also used cognitive efficiency to provide appropriate learning tasks [11], but they used students' performance which was based on how many steps students required to solve testing tasks. In our study, we measured cognitive efficiency based on how much assistance students received when solving problems.

Using our approach, an ITS can use assistance scores to identify novices and advanced students. If the system knows that a student is novice or advanced, then it is possible to provide proactive messages.

We have evaluated the adaptive strategy in the area of specifying SQL queries. One of the limitations of our study is the relatively small sample size. We plan to perform additional studies with a larger set of participants. It is also important to evaluate the adaptive strategy in other types of instructional tasks in order to test its generality. In future work, we plan to combine self-explanation scores and assistance scores to measure performance more accurately, which will result in improved cognitive efficiency scores. We also plan to evaluate such an improved performance measure and the adaptive strategy in other domains, including those with well-defined tasks.

References

1. Sweller, J., Cooper, G.A.: The Use of Worked Examples as a Substitute for Problem Solving in Learning Algebra. Cognition and Instruction 2, 59–89 (1985)
2. Kalyuga, S., Chandler, P., Tuovinen, J., Sweller, J.: When problem solving is superior to studying worked examples. Educational Psychology 93, 579–588 (2001)
3. Sweller, J.: The worked example effect and human cognition. Learning and Instruction 16, 165–169 (2006)
4. Atkinson, R.K., Derry, S.J., Renkl, A., Wortham, D.: Learning from Examples: Instructional Principles from the Worked Examples Research. Review of Educational Research 70, 181–214 (2000)
5. van Gog, T., Rummel, N.: Example-Based Learning: Integrating Cognitive and Social-Cognitive Research Perspectives. Educational Psychology Review 22, 155–174 (2010)
6. Schwonke, R., Renkl, A., Krieg, C., Wittwer, J., Aleven, V., Salden, R.: The worked-example effect: Not an artefact of lousy control conditions. Computers in Human Behavior 25, 258–266 (2009)
7. McLaren, B.M., Isotani, S.: When Is It Best to Learn with All Worked Examples? In: Biswas, G., Bull, S., Kay, J., Mitrovic, A. (eds.) AIED 2011. LNCS, vol. 6738, pp. 222–229. Springer, Heidelberg (2011)

8. Shareghi Najar, A., Mitrovic, A.: Examples and Tutored Problems: How can Self-Explanation Make a Difference to Learning? In: Lane, H.C., Yacef, K., Mostow, J., Pavlik, P., et al. (eds.) AIED 2013. LNCS, vol. 7926, pp. 339–348. Springer, Heidelberg (2013)

9. Koedinger, K., Aleven, V.: Exploring the Assistance Dilemma in Experiments with Cognitive Tutors. Educational Psychologist Review 19, 239–264 (2007)

10. Salden, R., Aleven, V., Renkl, A., Schwonke, R.: Worked Examples and Tutored Problem Solving: Redundant or Synergistic Forms of Support? Topics in Cognitive Science. Sci. 1, 203–213 (2009)

11. Kalyuga, S., Sweller, J.: Rapid dynamic assessment of expertise to improve the efficiency of adaptive e-learning. Educational Technology Research and Development 53, 83–93 (2005)

12. van Gog, T., Paas, F.: Instructional Efficiency: Revisiting the Original Construct in Educational Research. Educational Psychologist 43, 16–26 (2008)

13. Paas, F., Van Merrienboer, J.: The Efficiency of Instructional Conditions: An Approach to Combine Mental Effort and Performance Measures. Human Factors 35, 737–743 (1993)

14. Shareghi Najar, A., Mitrovic, A.: Do novices and advanced students benefit differently from worked examples and ITS? In: Wong, L.H., Liu, C.-C., Hirashima, T., Sumedi, P., Lukman, M. (eds.) Int. Conf. Computers in Education, Indonesia, Bali, pp. 20–29 (2013)

15. Chi, M.T.H., De Leeuw, N., Chiu, M.H., LaVancher, C.: Eliciting self-explanations improves understanding. Cognitive Science 18, 439–477 (1994)

16. Brown, A.L., Kane, M.J.: Preschool children can learn to transfer: Learning to learn and learning from example. Cognitive Psychology 20, 493–523 (1988)

17. Hattie, J.: Visible Learning: A Synthesis of Over 800 Meta-Analyses Relating to Achievement. Routledge, New York (2009)

18. Mitrović, A.: Experiences in implementing constraint-based modeling in SQL-Tutor. In: Goettl, B.P., Halff, H.M., Redfield, C.L., Shute, V.J. (eds.) ITS 1998. LNCS, vol. 1452, pp. 414–423. Springer, Heidelberg (1998)

19. Mitrovic, A.: An Intelligent SQL Tutor on the Web. Artificial Intelligence in Education 13, 173–197 (2003)

20. Deeks, A.: Web Based Assignments in Structural Analysis. Centre for Educational Development, Nanyang Technological University (2000)

Te,Te,Hi,Hi: Eye Gaze Sequence Analysis for Informing User-Adaptive Information Visualizations

Ben Steichen, Michael M.A. Wu, Dereck Toker,
Cristina Conati, and Giuseppe Carenini

Department of Computer Science, University of British Columbia
2366 Main Mall, Vancouver, BC, V6T1Z4, Canada
{steichen,mikewu,dtoker,conati,carenini}@cs.ubc.ca

Abstract. Information visualization systems have traditionally followed a one-size-fits-all paradigm with respect to their users, i.e., their design is seldom personalized to the specific characteristics of users (e.g. perceptual abilities) or their tasks (e.g. task difficulty). In view of creating information visualization systems that can *adapt* to each individual user and task, this paper provides an analysis of user eye gaze data aimed at identifying behavioral patterns that are specific to certain user and task groups. In particular, the paper leverages the sequential nature of user eye gaze patterns through *differential sequence mining*, and successfully identifies a number of pattern differences that could be leveraged by adaptive information visualization systems in order to automatically identify (and consequently adapt to) different user and task characteristics.

Keywords: Information Visualization, Eye Tracking, Pattern Analysis.

1 Introduction

Information visualization (Infovis) has long been established as a powerful tool to help humans understand and communicate information in a concise and effective manner. Many different types of Infovis techniques have been devised for a wide variety of applications, but they each typically follow a one-size-fits-all paradigm with respect to users, i.e., their design is seldom personalized to the specific characteristics of users (e.g. perceptual abilities) or their tasks (e.g. task difficulty). However, recent research has shown that user differences can significantly influence task performance and satisfaction with Infovis [1][2][3][4], suggesting that *user-adaptive* Infovis could be of significant benefit to individual users.

Such user-adaptive visualizations are the long-term goal of our research. In particular, we aim to design novel Infovis systems that can (i) identify relevant user and task characteristics in real-time (i.e., during interaction); and (ii) adapt to these characteristics in order to improve a user's visualization processing. This paper contributes to the first of these two challenges with an analysis of user gaze data, aiming to uncover specific gaze behaviors that are indicative of different user and task characteristics. These behaviors could then be used to drive a system that automatically identifies and dynamically adapts to new system users.

Previous work already indicates that different visualizations, tasks, and user characteristics impact a user's eye gaze behavior [5][6]. Furthermore, Steichen et al.

V. Dimitrova et al. (Eds.): UMAP 2014, LNCS 8538, pp. 183–194, 2014.
© Springer International Publishing Switzerland 2014

[7] have shown that gaze data can be leveraged to predict several user and task characteristics. However, the features used in this related work only include *summative* measures of gaze data (e.g. *total number of gaze fixations, mean of fixations durations, number of transitions between two areas,* etc.), as opposed to taking into account the *sequential* nature of eye movements. Furthermore, although the accuracies achieved using these summative gaze features were better than the baseline [7], they are arguably too low for reliable real-world application.

Our paper contributes to this line of research by leveraging the sequential nature of user eye gaze patterns through *differential sequence mining*, and our results show that several sequential gaze behaviors are indicative of specific user/task characteristics. Hence, our results complement prior work with valuable additional features that Infovis systems can leverage to more accurately identify and adapt to such characteristics.

In the rest of the paper, we first discuss related work on adaptive information visualization, pattern detection, and eye tracking. Next, we describe the user study that generated the gaze data used in the paper. We then present our method for analyzing gaze sequences, followed by the analysis results, discussion and future work.

2   Related Work

Information visualization research has traditionally maintained a one-size-fits-all approach, typically ignoring an individual user's needs, abilities and preferences. However, recent research has shown that, for example, cognitive measures such as perceptual speed and verbal working memory have an influence on a user's performance and satisfaction when working with visualizations (also depending on task difficulty) [1][2][8]. Likewise, Ziemkiewicz et al. [3], as well as Green and Fisher [9] have shown that the personality trait of locus of control can impact relative visualization performance for different visualizations. These results indicate that there is an opportunity to apply adaptation and personalization to improve usability.

One of the only attempts to adapt to individual user differences in visualization systems is presented in [10], where a user's visualization expertise and preferences are dynamically inferred through monitoring visualization selections (e.g. how long it takes a user to decide on which visualization to choose). Using this inferred level of user expertise and preferences, the system then attempts to recommend the most suitable visualizations for subsequent tasks. However, this work does not monitor a user's behavior *during* a task, and thus cannot adapt in real-time to help the user with the current task. By contrast, the system developed by Gotz and Wen [11] is, to the best of our knowledge, the only system that actively monitors real-time user behavior during visualization usage to infer needs for intervention. In their work, a user's interactions through mouse clicks are constantly tracked to detect *suboptimal usage patterns*, i.e., click activities that are of a repetitive (hence inefficient) nature. Each of these suboptimal patterns indicates that an alternative visualization may be more suitable to the current user activity. Once these patterns are detected, the system then triggers adaptation interventions similar to those in [10], namely they recommend alternative Infovis. However, there are a number of shortcomings of this work. First, their usage patterns are determined by experts *a priori*, rather than being based on empirical findings. Secondly, they only utilize explicit visualization interactions, therefore the approach is not suitable if a user is only "looking" at a visualization without manipulating its controls/data. Thirdly, they do not try to infer properties of the tasks (e.g. easy vs. difficult tasks), nor does their approach try to adapt to any user characteristics.

A solution to the first issue (i.e., requiring an expert's *a priori* identification of patterns) is presented in [12], albeit not applied to information visualization. Specifically, Kinnebrew and Biswas [12] present an approach to identify differences in activity patterns between two predefined groups (in their case 'effective learning' vs. 'noneffective learning') through *differential sequence mining*. By extracting all combinations of interaction sub-patterns for both groups, and then comparing the overall pattern occurrence differences between groups, they are able to identify patterns that are most discriminative. Thus, they propose to monitor these specific patterns in an adaptive system to be able to personalize to the inferred user characteristics. In this paper, we leverage this idea of differential sequence mining.

Regarding the second limitation of [11] (i.e. requiring explicit user interactions), we look at using *eye tracking* as an alternative/complementary source of real-time behavior information, since visual scanning and processing are fundamental components of working with any information visualization (and they are in fact the only components for non-interactive visualizations). Although such technology is currently confined to research environments, the rapid development of affordable, mainstream eye tracking solutions (e.g. using standard webcams) will soon enable the widespread application of such techniques [13]. In the fields of HCI and Infovis, research has already been conducted on identifying user gaze differences for alternative visualizations [6], task types (e.g. reading vs. mathematical reasoning) [14], or individual user differences [5]. Techniques used in these studies typically involve calculating *summative* measures (e.g. total number of gaze fixations, mean of gaze durations, number of transitions between two areas, etc.) [6][5] to identify differences between groups of users. By contrast, our work takes into account the *sequential* nature of gaze data. Related work on *sequential scan path analysis* typically involves comparing (using string distance functions) full gaze traces from a complete interaction [15][16]. Various tools have been developed for such analyses, such as eyePatterns [17], allowing the comparison/clustering of whole gaze path sequences. By contrast, our work consists of identifying individual (short) gaze patterns that could be tracked and leveraged *during* a user's interaction. In particular, we propose to apply the abovementioned idea of *differential sequence mining* [12] to *eye tracking* data, in order to uncover eye gaze patterns that are indicative of specific user and task characteristics. For this purpose, we leverage an additional functionality provided by eyePatterns [17], namely the counting of frequencies of shorter patterns within the full scan paths.

In terms of actually using eye tracking data for real-time prediction, most research has so far focused on identifying user intentions or activities, for example for predicting user intentions in playing simple puzzle games [18], for recognizing user activities within analytics and e-learning tasks [19], or for predicting user learning [20][21]. By contrast, our work is focused on predicting user and task characteristics during information visualization usage. In particular, in our previous work [7], we have proposed to classify users based on these features using machine learning techniques. While the experiment results in [7] have already shown promise for real-time user/task classification, the achieved accuracies were arguably too low for reliable real-world implementation. However, the features used in [7] only consisted of summative measures (similar to [18]), thereby leaving ample room for improvement through other features. In this paper, we provide additional features to potentially improve the results from previous work, by taking into account the sequential nature of users' gaze traces.

3   User Study

In order to investigate the effect of different task and user characteristics on a user's eye gaze behavior, we designed and ran a user eye tracking study with two basic visualization techniques, namely bar graphs and radar graphs. By choosing two different types of visualizations, we aimed to support the generalizability of our results. The study consisted of a set of tasks that required participants to evaluate student grades in eight different courses. The tasks were based on a set of low-level analysis tasks that Amar et al. [22] identified as largely capturing people's activities while employing Infovis. The tasks were chosen so that each of our two target visualizations would be suitable to support them. A first battery of tasks involved 5 questions comparing the grades of one student with the class average for 8 courses, e.g., *"In how many courses is Maria below the class average?"*. A second battery of tasks involved 4 questions comparing the performance of two different students along with the class average, e.g., "Find the courses in which Andrea is below the class average and Diana is above it?". Each user performed a total of 28 trials, which included 20 tasks from the first battery (10 per visualization) and 8 tasks from the second battery (4 per visualization).

The long-term user traits that we investigated in this study consisted of the following three cognitive abilities (which we found not to be correlated with each other): *perceptual speed* (a measure of speed when performing simple perceptual tasks), *verbal working memory* (a measure of storage and manipulation capacity of verbal information), *and visual working memory* (a measure of storage and manipulation capacity of visual and spatial information). Perceptual speed and visual working memory were selected because they were among the perceptual abilities explored by Velez et al. [2], as well as among the set that Conati and Maclaren [1] found to impact user performance with radar graphs and a Multiscale Dimension Visualizer (MDV). We also chose verbal working memory because we hypothesized that it may affect a user's performance with a visualization in terms of how the user processes its textual components such as labels. In the following sections, we describe our analysis and results regarding the effect that these *three user traits*, as well as *task difficulty* (defined in section 5.4) have on a user's gaze behavior.

4   Eye-Gaze Processing

An eye tracker captures gaze information through fixations (i.e., maintaining gaze at one point on the screen) and saccades (i.e., a quick movement of gaze from one fixation point to another), which can be analyzed to derive a viewer's attention patterns. In this paper, we analyze a user's attention with respect to so-called 'Areas of Interest' (AOI), which relate to specific parts of the Infovis used in the study.

4.1   Areas of Interest

A total of five AOIs were defined for each of our two visualizations, selected in order to capture their distinctive and typical uses. Figure 1 shows how the AOIs map onto bar and radar graph components respectively.

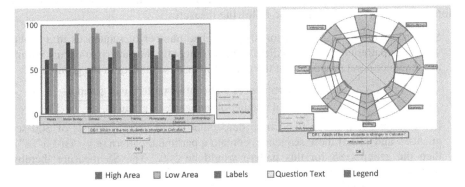

■ High Area   ■ Low Area   ■ Labels   □ Question Text   ■ Legend

Fig. 1. The five AOI regions defined over bar graph and radar graph

- *High Area (Hi):* covers the upper half of the data elements of each visualization. This area contains the relevant data values. For the bar graph, it corresponds to a rectangle over the top half of the vertical bars; for the radar graph, it corresponds to the combined area of the 8 trapezoidal regions covering the data points.
- *Low Area (Lo):* covers the lower half/the inner area of the bar/radar graph.
- *Labels (La):* covers all the data labels in each graph.
- *Question Text (Te):* covers the text describing the task to be performed.
- *Legend (Le):* covers the legend showing the mapping between each student and the color of the visualization elements that represent their performance.

4.2   Sequence Generation and Pattern Frequency Measures

Using the AOI definitions presented above, we converted users' raw eye gaze data into sequences of AOIs. Specifically, in this paper we define a *sequence* as *the sequence of AOIs for a complete user scan path of an entire trial*. To generate these sequences, for each trial we mapped each fixation onto one of the 5 AOIs. For example, '…Hi-La-Le…' represents one fixation at the 'High' AOI, followed by a fixation at the 'Label' AOI, followed by a fixation at the 'Legend' AOI. Similarly, '…Te-Te-Hi-Hi…' would represent two consecutive fixations at the 'Text' AOI, followed by two fixations at the 'High' AOI. In total, we converted the raw eye gaze data from 32 users (each having performed 28 trials), for a total of 725 complete corresponding sequences. Note, some user trials had to be removed due to issues with calibration or other user related matters (e.g., excessive user movements).

Using the eyePatterns tool [17], we then extracted frequencies of *patterns* within these complete sequences. In this paper, *patterns* are defined as *sub-sequences within a sequence*. We extracted patterns in both their "expanded" and "collapsed" form. An expanded pattern comprises all fixations, including consecutive fixations within the same AOI (i.e. *repetitions*). Collapsed patterns lump repetitions into a single AOI.

For each of the different user/task groups to be compared, e.g. high vs. low perceptual speed users (split via a median split, as was done for the other user characteristics), we extracted the occurrence frequencies of expanded and collapsed patterns of length 3 to 7[1]. Similar to Kinnebrew et al. [12], we then compared the frequencies of patterns (e.g. 'Hi-Hi-Hi', 'Hi-Hi-La', 'Hi-La-La' etc.) between different groups, in order to see whether some of these patterns are more common for particular groups. More specifically, we compared the following measures:

- *Sequence Support - SS* (s-support in [12]): The number of sequences in a group where the pattern occurs (regardless of how frequently the pattern re-occurs within the sequence) as a proportion of the total number of sequences in the group, i.e.,

$$SS_g(p) = \frac{\text{number of sequences that contain pattern } p \text{ in group } g}{\text{total number of sequences in group } g}$$

For example, if a group (e.g., high perceptual speed users) consists of 300 sequences, and 150 of these sequences contain a particular pattern (e.g. "Hi-La-Te"), then the group's SS for this pattern would be 50%. The SS measure thereby represents how 'common' it is for a pattern to appear for sequences of a particular group (i.e. if a pattern's SS is very high for a group, this means that most sequences from this group contain this pattern).

- *Average Pattern Frequency - APF* (instance support, or i-support, in [12]): Total number of occurrences of the pattern in all sequences of a group (including reoccurrences within a sequence), divided by the group's total number of sequences, i.e.,

$$APF_g(p) = \frac{\text{number of occurrences of pattern } p \text{ in group } g}{\text{total number of sequences in group } g}$$

For example, if a group consists of 300 sequences, and a particular pattern appears 600 times in total (including reoccurrences within a sequence), then the group's APF for this pattern would be 2. The APF thereby represents the 'reoccurrence frequency' of a pattern in a particular group (i.e. a pattern with a very high APF for a particular group means this pattern frequently reoccurs in this group).

- *Proportional Pattern Frequency – PPF*: Total number of occurrences of the pattern per group (including reoccurrences) as a proportion of the total number of patterns in the group, i.e.,

$$PPF_g(p) = \frac{\text{number of occurrences of pattern } p \text{ in group } g}{\text{total number of patterns in group } g}$$

For example, if the total number of patterns across all sequences (including reoccurrences) in a group is 10,000 and a particular pattern appears 600 times in total, then the group's PPF for this pattern would be 6%. The PPF thereby represents the 'relative frequency' of a pattern in a particular group, compared to all other patterns from the group (i.e. a pattern with a very high PPF for a particular group means that this pattern is, compared to other patterns, occurring more frequently).

---

[1] Patterns longer than 7 were very infrequent. Patterns of length 1 and 2 are typically included in simple summative analyses (as presented in Section 2).

While PPF was not included in [12], we believe that it allows an additional dimension of analysis, showing how patterns change in terms of *relative* frequency. In addition, while SS and APF are potentially influenced by overall task length (i.e. longer response times lead to more opportunities for sequences to emerge), this is less of a problem for PPF as it is proportional to the overall number of patterns.

4.3   Statistical Analysis

For our statistical analysis, we followed Kinnebrew et al.'s [12] approach of only considering patterns that are above a certain SS threshold in at least one of the groups to be compared (e.g., at least in either the high or low perceptual speed user group). This ensures that we do not analyze patterns that are too infrequent for any realistic application in an adaptive system. We used the threshold values of 40% for expanded patterns, and 30% for collapsed patterns[2]. To evaluate the statistical significance of SS and PPF differences, we conducted two sets of Pearson's chi-square tests for each user/task characteristic group (our independent measures), separately for expanded and collapsed sequences (with SS and PPF for each pattern being our dependent measures). Since we evaluated multiple patterns for differences within each set, we increased the likelihood of performing a type I error. Thus, we applied the Bonferroni correction to test individual comparisons at significance levels of α/n, where $\alpha = .05$ and n = the number of patterns analyzed in each set (with there being 8 sets in total, i.e. one expanded and one collapsed set per task/user characteristic).

In contrast to SS and PPF, calculating statistical significance for APF differences involves the comparison of means, hence requiring the variances of the pattern frequencies for individual sequences. However, this information is not available in the eyePatterns tool (only overall frequencies are available), and we were hence not able to calculate statistical significance for this measure. We will therefore not discuss APF in the results section below, except for cases where it may provide some complementary insight on intuitively contradictory results.

5   Results

With the goal of finding gaze patterns that may characterize users with specific cognitive characteristics, or are indicative of different task characteristics, we compared the SS and PPF across i) *low vs. user high perceptual speed users*, ii) *low vs. high user verbal working memory users*, iii) *low vs. high user visual working memory users*, and iv) *easy vs. difficult tasks*.

5.1   Perceptual Speed (PS) - Low vs. High

We found a number of patterns that statistically significantly differed in terms of SS and/or PPF between low and high PS users (see Table 1).

---

[2] Note that Kinnebrew et al. used 50% as a threshold, however, they allowed for 'gaps' in sequences, which is not supported by the pattern extraction feature in eyePatterns. We therefore slightly lowered the threshold of expanded sequences to 40%. Also, collapsed patterns are generally more infrequent, hence the slightly lowered threshold of 30%.

As shown in the first row of Table 1, patterns involving two fixations at the 'High' AOI (Hi-Hi), followed by a fixation at the 'Label' AOI (La) have a statistically significantly greater PPF for high PS users compared to low PS users. Similarly, the inverted pattern La-Hi-Hi (second row of Table 1) has a statistically significantly greater PPF for high PS users compared to their low PS counterparts. This means that high PS users comparatively make more use of the data labels after/before looking at multiple values displayed in the visualization (i.e. the 'High' AOI). The fact that we did not find a statistically significant difference for this pattern in terms of SS indicates that this pattern is still common for low PS users (i.e. it still occurs in a similar number of sequences), but it does not reoccur as often.

By contrast, 'High' AOI to 'Label' AOI transitions that are broken up by an intermediate fixation at the 'Low' AOI (i.e., Hi-Lo-La) occur more frequently for low PS users. This result was found for both SS and PPF, indicating a strong difference between groups. One possible interpretation for this finding might be that low PS users are less precise when trying to locate the small 'Label' AOIs after visiting one of the visualization values.

Table 1. Pattern differences that occurred between low and high perceptual speed users

Pattern	Sequence Support (SS) Stat. sig. greater for:	Proportional Pattern Frequency (PPF) Stat. sig. greater for:
Hi-Hi-La	-	High PS users
La-Hi-Hi	-	High PS users
Hi-Lo-La *	Low PS users	Low PS users
Te-Te-Lo	Low PS users	-
Te-Te-Te	Low PS users	-
Te (x4)	Low PS users	-
Te (x5)	Low PS users	-

* found for collapsed and expanded patterns

The final set of results in Table 1 shows that it is much more common for low PS users to have some repeated fixations within the 'Text' AOI. In particular, we found that the SS was greater for several 'Text'-related patterns (Te-Te-Te, Te (x4), etc.), suggesting that a single appearance of such a pattern in a user's sequence may indicate low PS. This finding may therefore signify that low PS users generally require more effort to process the larger textual components of visualizations.

None of these results were found using simple summative measures in previous work (e.g. [5]), hence showing that our sequential analysis can indeed reveal complementary features for inferring user characteristics.

5.2   Verbal Working Memory (Verbal WM) - Low vs. High

We found that it is much more common for low verbal working memory users to have *highly repeated fixations at the 'Text' AOI* (i.e., through patterns such as Te (x5, x6, x7)) compared to their high verbal working memory counterparts (see Table 2).

This is in line with previous results found in [5], where the overall proportion of time spent in the text AOI was found to be higher for low verbal working memory users. In fact, our findings further qualify these previous results, indicating that the increased time spent by low verbal working memory users stems from highly repeated transitions within the text AOI, rather than repeatedly coming back to the text AOI after visiting other AOIs. Another result we found was that it is more common for high verbal working memory users to have an increased frequency of the pattern La-Lo-Hi. The interpretation of this result is less intuitive, but nonetheless it may serve as an additional feature for detecting low/high verbal working memory users (as it represents another result not previously found using only summative measures).

Table 2. Pattern differences between low and high verbal working memory users

Pattern	Sequence Support (SS) *Stat. sig. greater for:*	Proportional Pattern Frequency (PPF) *Stat. sig. greater for:*
Te (x5)	Low Verbal WM users	-
Te (x6)	Low Verbal WM users	-
Te (x7)	Low Verbal WM users	-
La-Lo-Hi *	High Verbal WM users	-

* found for collapsed and expanded patterns

5.3   Visual Working Memory (Visual WM) - Low vs. High

While the study in [5] found no effect of visual working memory on gaze measures, our sequential analysis reveals that low visual working memory users had increased repetitions in the text AOI (however, only the Te (x6) pattern was statistically significant), as well as two increased patterns involving the 'High', 'Low', and 'Label' AOI (see Table 3). These results are similar to the above findings on perceptual speed and verbal working memory, and represent, to the best of our knowledge, the first results linking visual working memory to eye gaze behavior.

Table 3. Pattern differences for low vs. high visual working memory users

Pattern	Sequence Support (SS) *Stat. sig. greater for:*	Proportional Pattern Frequency (PPF) *Stat. sig. greater for:*
Te (x6)	-	Low Visual WM users
Hi-Lo-La *	-	Low Visual WM users
La-Lo-Hi *	-	Low Visual WM users

* found for collapsed and expanded patterns

5.4   Task Difficulty - Easy vs. Difficult

In addition to analyzing the effect of user characteristics, our work also aims to find the impact of characteristics related to a user's *task*. To this end, we also analyzed pattern differences with respect to the overall 'difficulty' of a task. For this measure, we generated, *a posteriori*, an aggregated difficulty value for each task through a principal component analysis (PCA) using *task completion time* and a user's reported *confidence* on the task (see [5] for a detailed description of this PCA analysis).

The results regarding the pattern frequency differences between *easy* and *difficult* tasks are shown in Table 4. As can be seen from this table, there were many differences regarding repeated fixations of the 'High' AOI (Hi-Hi-Hi, Hi x4, etc.). This difference occurred for both SS and PPF measures, showing that repeated fixations in the 'High' AOI are a strong indicator for a difficult task.

Table 4. Pattern differences for easy vs. difficult tasks

Pattern	Sequence Support (SS) *Stat. sig. greater for:*	Proportional Pattern Frequency (PPF) *Stat. sig. greater for:*
Hi-Hi-Hi	Difficult Tasks	-
Hi (x4)	Difficult Tasks	Difficult Tasks
Hi (x5)	Difficult Tasks	Difficult Tasks
Hi (x6)	Difficult Tasks	Difficult Tasks
Hi (x7)	Difficult Tasks	Difficult Tasks
Te-Te-Te	Difficult Tasks	Easy Tasks
Te (x4)	Difficult Tasks	Easy Tasks
Te (x5)	Difficult Tasks	-
Te (x6)	Difficult Tasks	-
Te (x7)	Difficult Tasks	Difficult Tasks
Te-Hi-Hi	Difficult Tasks	-
Te-Te-Hi	Difficult Tasks	-
Hi-Hi-Te	Difficult Tasks	-
Te-Hi-Hi-Hi	Difficult Tasks	-
Te-Te-Hi-Hi	Difficult Tasks	-
Te-Te-Te-Hi	Difficult Tasks	-
Te-Hi (x4)	Difficult Tasks	-

We also found that patterns involving repeated fixations in the 'Text' AOI had a larger SS for more difficult tasks. Interestingly, however, we found that PPF for two of these 'Text' AOI patterns was statistically significantly greater for easier tasks. In order to investigate this counterintuitive result, we also looked at the APF measure, which revealed that the average re-occurrence of repeated 'Text' AOI patterns actually increases for more difficult tasks. However, because the aforementioned 'High' AOI patterns had increased by a much greater extend (up to threefold), the *proportional* occurrence of 'Text' AOI patterns within the difficult task group (as measured by PPF) had actually decreased. While this analysis makes use of the APF measure that we could not check for statistical significance, these very high numbers for the 'High' AOI pattern increase therefore seem to be the most plausible explanation for this seemingly contradictory finding.

In addition to these patterns involving repeated fixations in either only the 'High' or 'Text' AOIs, we found that patterns involving the combination of the two (including intermediate fixations at the 'Low' AOI) also increased for difficult tasks.

None of these results have been found previously using summative measures, which confirms that our sequential pattern analysis was able to find many new discriminatory features.

6   Conclusion, Discussion, and Future Work

In conclusion, our analysis has found a number of gaze behavior differences between different user/task groups during Infovis usage. While some results confirm previous findings that were discovered using simple summative measures (e.g. increased fixations in the text AOI for high verbal working memory users), our novel application of *differential sequence mining* was able to uncover many additional results, including new results for perceptual speed, verbal working memory, visual working memory, and task difficulty. In particular, many results were found in terms of repeated transitions within a single AOI, such as frequent repetitions within the "high" or "text" AOIs being indicative of low values for certain user characteristics. Also, given that these results were found using rather simple tasks and visualizations, it is possible that more complex scenarios would lead to even stronger differences.

In view of building Infovis systems that can adapt to each individual user and task characteristics, these findings provide important indicators as to which particular patterns could be monitored for predicting and adapting to the various characteristics. For example, observing a user's frequent exhibition of a pattern that is common for a certain user/task group may indicate that the user belongs to this group, and that she may therefore benefit from a specific type of adaptive support. Carenini et al. [24] have already presented a number of possibilities for providing such support in Infovis systems, and have also highlighted that the effect of interventions indeed depends on various user/task characteristics (e.g., a user's subjective rating of different highlighting mechanisms is shown to be affected by visual WM).

While we found a number of patterns to be indicative for more than one user/task characteristic group (e.g. repeated patterns in the text AOI was found for all 4 characteristics), it is worth noting again that our pattern difference results can be complemented with features from i) other eye gaze features (e.g. non-sequential features, pupil dilation features), and/or ii) other interaction features (e.g. mouse clicks). To this end, the next steps of our research consist of complementing the results from this paper with previously reported summative features [5] to build a combined machine learning model for automatically inferring user/task characteristics.

References

1. Conati, C., Maclaren, H.: Exploring the role of individual differences in information visualization. In: Proc. of the Working Conf. on Advanced Visual Interfaces, pp. 199–206 (2008)
2. Velez, M.C., Silver, D., Tremaine, M.: Understanding visualization through spatial ability differences. In: IEEE Visualization, VIS 2005, pp. 511–518 (2005)
3. Ziemkiewicz, C., Crouser, R.J., Yauilla, A.R., Su, S.L., Ribarsky, W., Chang, R.: How locus of control influences compatibility with visualization style. In: 2011 IEEE Conference on Visual Analytics Science and Technology (VAST), pp. 81–90 (2011)
4. Dillon, A.: Spatial-semantics: How users derive shape from information space. J. Am. Soc. Inf. Sci. 51, 521–528 (2000)
5. Toker, D., Conati, C., Steichen, B., Carenini, G.: Individual user characteristics and information visualization: connecting the dots through eye tracking. In: Proceedings of the SIGCHI Conference on Human Factors in Computing Systems, pp. 295–304 (2013)

6. Goldberg, J., Helfman, J.: Eye tracking for visualization evaluation: reading values on linear versus radial graphs. Inf. Vis. 10, 182–195 (2011)

7. Steichen, B., Carenini, G., Conati, C.: User-adaptive information visualization: using eye gaze data to infer visualization tasks and user cognitive abilities. In: Proceedings of the 2013 International Conference on Intelligent User Interfaces, pp. 317–328 (2013)

8. Toker, D., Conati, C., Carenini, G., Haraty, M.: Towards adaptive information visualization: On the influence of user characteristics. In: Masthoff, J., Mobasher, B., Desmarais, M.C., Nkambou, R. (eds.) UMAP 2012. LNCS, vol. 7379, pp. 274–285. Springer, Heidelberg (2012)

9. Green, T.M., Fisher, B.: Towards the Personal Equation of Interaction: The impact of personality factors on visual analytics interface interaction. In: 2010 IEEE Symposium on Visual Analytics Science and Technology (VAST), pp. 203–210 (2010)

10. Grawemeyer, B.: Evaluation of ERST – an external representation selection tutor. In: Barker-Plummer, D., Cox, R., Swoboda, N. (eds.) Diagrams 2006. LNCS (LNAI), vol. 4045, pp. 154–167. Springer, Heidelberg (2006)

11. Gotz, D., Wen, Z.: Behavior-driven visualization recommendation. In: Proceedings of the 14th International Conference on Intelligent User Interfaces, pp. 315–324 (2009)

12. Kinnebrew, J.S., Biswas, G.: Identifying Learning Behaviors by Contextualizing Differential Sequence Mining with Action Features and Performance Evolution. In: Proc. of EDM, 5th Int. Conf. on Educational Data Mining, pp. 57–64 (2012)

13. Sesma, L., Villanueva, A., Cabeza, R.: Evaluation of pupil center-eye corner vector for gaze estimation using a web cam. In: Proceedings of the Symposium on Eye-Tracking Research & Applications, pp. 217–220 (2012)

14. Iqbal, S.T., Bailey, B.P.: Using eye gaze patterns to identify user tasks. Presented at the The Grace Hopper Celebration of Women in Computing (2004)

15. Duchowski, A.T., Driver, J., Jolaoso, S., Tan, W., Ramey, B.N., Robbins, A.: Scanpath Comparison Revisited. In: Proceedings of the 2010 Symposium on Eye-Tracking Research & Applications, pp. 219–226 (2010)

16. Madsen, A., Larson, A., Loschky, L., Rebello, N.S.: Using ScanMatch Scores to Understand Differences in Eye Movements Between Correct and Incorrect Solvers on Physics Problems. In: Proc. of Symp. on Eye Tracking Research & Applications, pp. 193–196 (2012)

17. West, J.M., Haake, A.R., Rozanski, E.P., Karn, K.S.: eyePatterns: software for identifying patterns and similarities across fixation sequences. In: Proceedings of the 2006 Symposium on Eye Tracking Research & Applications, pp. 149–154 (2006)

18. Eivazi, S., Bednarik, R.: Predicting Problem-Solving Behavior and Performance Levels from Visual Attention Data. In: 2nd Workshop on Eye Gaze in Intelligent Human Machine Interaction at IUI 2011 (2011)

19. Courtemanche, F., Aïmeur, E., Dufresne, A., Najjar, M., Mpondo, F.: Activity recognition using eye-gaze movements and traditional interactions. Interac. Comp. 23, 202–213 (2011)

20. Kardan, S., Conati, C.: Exploring gaze data for determining user learning with an interactive simulation. In: Masthoff, J., Mobasher, B., Desmarais, M.C., Nkambou, R. (eds.) UMAP 2012. LNCS, vol. 7379, pp. 126–138. Springer, Heidelberg (2012)

21. Bondareva, D., Conati, C., Feyzi-Behnagh, R., Harley, J.M., Azevedo, R., Bouchet, F.: Inferring Learning from Gaze Data during Interaction with an Environment to Support Self-Regulated Learning. In: Lane, H.C., Yacef, K., Mostow, J., Pavlik, P. (eds.) AIED 2013. LNCS, vol. 7926, pp. 229–238. Springer, Heidelberg (2013)

22. Amar, R., Eagan, J., Stasko, J.: Low-Level Components of Analytic Activity in Information Visualization. In: Proc. of 2005 Symp. on Information Visualization, pp. 15–21 (2005)

Text-Based User-kNN: Measuring User Similarity Based on Text Reviews

Maria Terzi, Matthew Rowe, Maria-Angela Ferrario, and Jon Whittle

School of Computing & Communications, InfoLab21,
Lancaster University
LA1 4WA Lancaster UK
{m.terzi,m.rowe,m.ferrario,j.n.whittle}@lancaster.ac.uk

Abstract. This article reports on a modification of the user-kNN algorithm that measures the similarity between users based on the similarity of text reviews, instead of ratings. We investigate the performance of text semantic similarity measures and we evaluate our text-based user-kNN approach by comparing it to a range of ratings-based approaches in a ratings prediction task. We do so by using datasets from two different domains: movies from RottenTomatoes and Audio CDs from Amazon Products. Our results show that the text-based user-kNN algorithm performs significantly better than the ratings-based approaches in terms of accuracy measured using RMSE.

Keywords: Recommender systems, Collaborative Filtering, Text reviews, Semantic similarity measures.

1 Introduction

Recommender systems work by predicting how users will rate items of potential interest. A common approach is Collaborative Filtering (CF); "k-Nearest Neighbors" (user-kNN), for example, predicts a user's rating according to how similar users rated the same item [1]. User-kNN matches similar users based on the similarity of their ratings on items. We argue that ratings alone are insufficient to fully reflect the similarity between users for two reasons: a) ratings do not capture the rationale behind a user's rating, and b) there is a high probability (p=0.8) that two ratings of the same value on the same item will be given for different reasons [2]. We identify this as a potential challenge for ratings-based approaches and define it as *a similarity reflection problem.*

Existing work [3, 4] reports that measuring the similarity of users using the sentiment of their text reviews, instead of ratings, improves the accuracy of user-kNN. However, we argue that a sentiment-based approach does not fully address the similarity reflection problem since *the reasons behind a sentiment of a review remain unexploited.* In other words, the sentiment, similar to a rating, says *how much* a person liked an item, but it misses the *reason why.* For example, in the case of a movie, did the reviewer like it because of the performance of a specific actor? Or because of the style of the director? We argue that text reviews potentially offer a substantiated opinion of a user for an item, making them an ideal source of knowledge for enhancing the recommendation process.

V. Dimitrova et al. (Eds.): UMAP 2014, LNCS 8538, pp. 195–206, 2014.

There is a growing body of research which aims to exploit the content of text reviews for various tasks. However, the analysis of text reviews to address the similarity reflection problem remains an under-explored area. Work in [5, 6] for example, uses text reviews to construct user preference profiles: sets of item features (such as plot or special effects in the movie domain) are extracted from the users' text reviews. These user preference profiles may then be used to measure user similarity in a user-kNN algorithm [5], or they are used to constrain CF by only using reviews similar to a user's profile when making recommendations [6]. These approaches assume that "the overall number of opinions regarding a certain item feature reveals how important that feature is to a user" [6]. An important aspect of this assumption, however, is that it generalizes the features a user finds interesting to all the items in a domain. For example, it assumes that if a user likes special effects in an action movie, s/he also likes to have special effects in a drama. Hence, such an approach does not *distinguish between user preferences across domains.*

Our previous investigation [2] indicated that users' similarity is not well reflected in rating-based approaches that only rely on users' ratings, and suggested the use of text reviews. In this paper, we present the text-based user-kNN, a modification of user-kNN algorithm,that uses text reviews to measure similarity between users, instead of using ratings.

Our text-based user-kNN applies text similarity measures directly on text reviews of co-reviewed items, instead of applying statistical similarity measures on ratings or constructing profiles of user preferences extracted from text reviews. In doing so, we attempt to form neighborhoods of users who have reviewed the same items with semantically similar reviews, while respecting the diversity of user feature preferences over items. We then identify a target user's nearest neighbor, and use their ratings to predict the target user's ratings. In an evaluation of the approach, we measure the accuracy of its predictions by comparing them to the target user's actual ratings.

This paper's two main contributions are:

1. A text-based user-kNN approach that measures the similarity of users by applying text similarity measures directly on users' text reviews for each co-reviewed item.
2. An extensive evaluation which includes:

a. An investigation of the performance of various text similarity measures in the text-based user-kNN approach. The investigation highlights a significant improvement of text semantic similarity measures over a simple lexical matching measure.

b. A comparison of text-based user-kNN with a range of ratings-based approaches in a ratings prediction task. Results show that the text-based user-kNN produces a small but significant improvement over ratings-based approaches in minimizing the RMSE between the actual and the predicted ratings. Our evaluation is performed using two different datasets – a RottenTomatoes dataset and an Audio CD dataset from AmazonProductReviews. The consistently higher accuracy of the text-based user-kNN approach verifies its better performance.

The novelty of our approach over previous work lies in the way we incorporate text reviews in user-kNN. We calculate the direct similarity of text reviews to measure the similarity between users and form neighborhoods of similar users. In addition, we provide evidence of the effectiveness of our approach in predicting ratings, over various state-of-art rating based approaches using two different datasets.

2   Related Work

The use of text reviews as implicit feedback to improve the recommendation process is an expansive topic. In matrix factorization CF approaches, text reviews have been used to define a 'regularizer' score for the factorization model. The regularizer is assigned one of three scores depending on the methodology used: the opinion score, calculated using feature extraction and sentiment analysis of text reviews [7]; the sentiment score, calculated using only sentiment analysis on text reviews [8]; or the review-quality score, calculated based on the occurrence of features in text reviews [9]. In addition, in [10], both ratings and features extracted from text reviews are used to define a regularizer. However, the above approaches are not focused on improving the performance of neighborhood based models, such as user-kNN.

In user-kNN approaches, similar to our work, research exploiting text reviews is limited to applying sentiment analysis on text reviews [3, 4], or building user profiles of feature preferences extracted from text reviews [5, 6]. Sentiment analysis has been applied on text reviews to either reflect a user's interest in an item in terms of a binary score (like/dislike) [3], or to refine a list of rating-based CF recommendations by removing items whose review is labeled with a negative sentiment [4]. However, in such approaches [3, 4], *the reasons behind a user's rating remain unexploited*. Chen and Wang [5] investigated regression models on user text reviews to infer weighted feature preferences. They then matched users with similar weighted feature preferences to produce the item recommendations. Musat et al. [6], proposed Topic Profile CF (TPCF), a technique which builds user profiles based on extracted 'topics' from the users' aggregated text reviews. They then use the item reviews that are most similar to the user's profile to predict the user's rating for the item.

In contrast to our work, TPCF does not form neighborhoods of similar users based on their text reviews. Chen and Wang [5], focused on producing item recommendations instead of predicting ratings. Furthermore, both approaches [5, 6] are based on building user profiles with features extracted from all text reviews thus assuming that what a user likes in one domain, s/he also likes in another domain.

User preference profiles have also been used by Content Based (CB) recommendation approaches. For example, Levi et al. [11], used text reviews to infer the 'traits' or preferences of contextually similar groups in a hotel recommender and then calculate the impression a user has for a hotel. The main difference our approach with Levi et al. [11], is that we form neighborhoods of users based on their text reviews rather than exploiting the preferences of predefined groups of users. Also, we measure the direct similarity of the users' text reviews, instead of building profiles of user preferences. In doing so, we distinguish user feature preferences across domains.

3   Text-Based User-kNN

In this section we present text-based user-kNN, a modification of user-kNN which incorporates text reviews in the measurement of similarity between users, shown in Figure 1. We are given a set of users $u \in U$, a set of items $i \in I$ and a set of

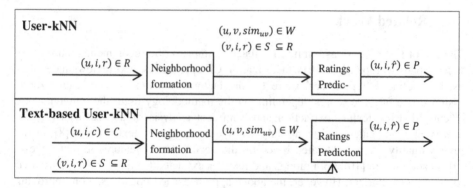

Fig. 1. User-kNN and Text-Based User-kNN

quadruples D, $(u, i, r, c) \in D$, with each quadruple corresponding to a review of user u on item i using the rating r and the content of text review c. We reserve special indexing letters for distinguishing users from items: for users u, v $(u, v \in U)$ and for items i $(i \in I)$. Our objective is to predict each unknown rating $\hat{r}$ of user u for item i in set P.

The first phase of user-kNN is the neighborhood formulation. During this phase the main goal is to measure the similarity between users and define a set of users $\in N$, who tend to review items similarly to u ("neighbors"). The similarity of two users is measured by applying similarity measures between their reviews on their co-reviewed items. User-kNN uses ratings to measure similarity between users. It accepts as input the set $R = \{(u, i, r): (u, i, r, c) \in D\}$, with each triple corresponding to a review of user u, on item i, using rating r. User-kNN calculates the similarity, sim_{uv}, between the users u and v, by applying statistical similarity measures such as Pearson, between the ratings of the two users. On the other hand, text-based user-kNN uses text reviews. In this phase text-based user-kNN accepts as input the set $C = \{(u, i, c): (u, i, r, c) \in D\}$. Each triple in C represents a review of the user u, on item i with content of the text review c. Text-based user-kNN measures similarity sim_{uv}, between the users u and v by applying a text similarity measure ψ over the content of the reviews of the two users' for each of their co-reviewed items (Equation 1). The measure ψ calculates the similarity between the content of two the text reviews to produce a numerical similarity score from 0 (no similarity) to +1 (strong similarity), $\psi: c \times c \rightarrow [0,1]$.

$$sim_{uv} = \frac{1}{|I_u \cap I_v|} \sum_{i \in I_u \cap I_v} \psi(c_{ui}, c_{vi}) \qquad (1)$$

where $I_u \cap I_v$ is the set of co-reviewed items of user u and user v, and $\psi(c_{ui}, c_{vi})$ the text similarity measure between the content c_{ui} of the text review of user u for item i and the content of text review c_{vi} of user v for item i.

The calculated similarity scores between the users are stored in set W, $(u, v, sim_{uv},) \in W$, and are used   a) to construct the set N using the k users who have the highest similarity score with user u and b) as a weight in the ratings prediction phase.

In order to estimate the unknown rating $\hat{r}_{ui}$ we resort to a set of users v, $N(v,k)$, who have the highest similarity with user u and actually rated item i (i.e., r_{vi} is known for each user $v \in N$). Both approaches use the set S, $(v, i, r) \in S \subseteq R$, in which each triple includes the rating r of the user v for an item i. The number of neighbors k is calculated during the training phase of the model. The estimated value of $\hat{r}_{ui}$ is taken as a weighted average of the neighbors' ratings:

$$\hat{r}_{ui} = \frac{\sum_{v \in N(v,k)} sim_{uv} \times (r_{vi})}{\sum_{v \in N(v,k)} |sim_{uv}|} \qquad (2)$$

where N is the set of k similar neighbors of user u; r_{vi} is the rating of the neighbor v for the item i; and sim_{uv} is the similarity between the users u and v stored in set W.

In cases where no formulation of neighborhood can be established, both user-kNN approaches use the average value of an item's ratings to predict a user's rating.

4   Short Text Similarity Measures

The core part of our text-based user-kNN uses a text similarity measure (ψ) that can identify 'similar reviews': reviews that use semantically similar wordings to review an item. A typical approach for finding the similarity between two text segments is to use a simple lexical matching method such as 'word overlap' to produce a similarity score based on the number of words that occur in both segments. While successful to a certain degree, such lexical methods cannot identify semantic similarity. For instance, there is an obvious similarity between the text segments "The movie has an amazing storyline" and "The plot of this film is good", but most of the text similarity measures will fail in identifying any kind of connection between these texts because of the lack of lexical overlap. The semantic similarity between two words can be measured using WordNet [12], an online lexical database of English terms structured based on synsets, that is, sets of synonymous words. Synsets are connected to one another through relations such as "is-a". For example, "plot" and "storyline" nouns are in the same synset, which is connected to the "noun communication" synset by an "is-a" relationship.

We employ six word similarity measures: a simple word overlap measure; two measures based on the path length two words in WordNet; and three that use the information content (IC) of a word. All the WordNet measures we employ are publicly provided by [13]. To derive the similarity score of two text reviews (ψ) we use the average of the similarity scores (s) between each of their words. All stop words have been removed from the datasets using the stop word lists provided by Lewis et al.[14].

Semantic Similarity Measures Based on Path Length
Two of the measures we use in our experiment, the measure provided by Leacock and Chodorow [15] and the measure provided by Wu and Palmer [16], are based on path length of a WordNet taxonomy. A path length is equal to the count of relation links of words in the taxonomy. The lower the distance between two words, the higher the similarity between them. For example, the path length of two synonymous words is 0. The measure by Leacock and Chodorow[15], denoted as s_{lch} , returns a similarity score based on the shortest path that connects two words and the maximum depth of the taxonomy:

$$s_{lch}(w_1, w_2) = -\log \frac{path(w_1, w_2)}{2 * D} \qquad (3)$$

where $path(w_1, w_2)$ is the shortest distance between the words w_1 and w_2, and D is a constant (e.g., the maximum depth in the WordNet taxonomy).

The similarity metric by Wu and Palmer [16], s_{wup}, is based on the depth of the two words in WordNet and that of their least common subsumer (LCS), that is, the word that is a shared ancestor of the two words. For example the LCS of the words 'car' and 'boat' would be 'vehicle'. The s_{wup} measure is determined by the equation below:

$$s_{wup}(w_1, w_2) = \frac{2*depth(\ LCS\ (w_1, w_2))}{depth(w_1) + depth(w_2)} \tag{4}$$

Where $LCS(w_1, w_2)$ is the LCS between the words w_1 and w_2 and $depth(w)$ is the length of the shortest path between the root and a word w.

Semantic Similarity Measures Based on Information Content
We employ three measures that are based on the IC: Resnik [17], Lin [18] and Jiang and Conrath [19]. IC is a measure of specificity of a word. High values of IC are associated with more specific concepts of words (e.g., mouse) and lower values are more general (e.g., animal). The IC is calculated from the observed frequency counts of a word in a sense-tagged corpus: a corpus annotated with WordNet senses. The IC value of a word w can be quantified as a negative log likelihood of the probability of that word:

$$IC(w) = -\log p(w) \tag{5}$$

The IC-based approaches operate by default using the SemCor [20] corpus, a sense-tagged portion of the Brown Corpus.

The measure by Resnik[17], denoted as s_{res}, only considers the IC of the LCS of the two compared words:

$$s_{res}(w_1, w_2) = IC\ (LCS\ (w_1, w_2)) \tag{6}$$

where $LCS(w_1, w_2)$ is the LCS between words w_1 and w_2.

The measure introduced by Lin [18] builds on Resnik's measure by adding a normalization factor consisting of the information content of the two input words:

$$s_{lin}(w_1, w_2) = \frac{2*IC\ (LCS\ (w_1, w_2))}{IC(w_1) + IC\ (w_2)} \tag{7}$$

Finally, we use the measure introduce by Jiang and Conrath[19], s_{jnc}, determined using the following equation:

$$s_{jnc}(w_1, w_2) = \frac{1}{IC(w_1) + IC(w_2) - 2*IC\ (LCS(w_1, w_2))} \tag{8}$$

where the IC of a word is defined by equation (4) and where $LCS(w_1, w_2)$ is the LCS between words w_1 and w_2.

5   Experimental Setup

To develop our text-based recommender system and run this evaluation we used the MyMediaLite 3.07 [21] C# library on Mono architecture. We evaluate the performance of the six text similarity measures from Section 4 on our approach compared to a range of representative ratings-based approaches using two datasets.

5.1   Datasets

RottenTomatoes Dataset

The Rotten Tomatoes movie review website allows two types of reviewers: critics and non-critics. Critics write movie reviews professionally. Non-critics or standard users are general members of the public. The API of the platform only offers the ability to collect reviews written from critics. To avoid any violations of the terms of the service of the platform, we only used the functionality offered by the API to construct this dataset. The RottenTomatoes dataset includes critics' reviews for the Top-100 movies for the years 2001 to 2010. Each entry in the dataset consists of a user id, a movie id, a timestamp, a rating and a short text passage. All reviews having a missing rating (30% of the reviews) or a missing text passage (0.09% of the reviews) have been removed from the dataset, resulting in a dataset of 62,365 reviews, 451 users and 1000 items.

Table 1. Properties of the two datasets used in our experiment

Dataset	Users	Items	Training	Validation	Test set (fold size)	Sparsity
RottenTomatoes	451	1000	40371	848	21200 (848)	86.17%
Audio CDs	53060	36381	66394	1397	34925 (1397)	99.99%

Since our goal is to improve the accuracy of ratings prediction for the standard users, rather than critics, we carried out an experiment to investigate the divergence between standard and critic's text reviews. Using 200 random standard and 200 critic reviews for the top five movies from 2010, we carried out a statistical analysis over the two sets. Results indicated that there is a Cosine similarity of 0.85 between the term frequencies of the two sets, thus indicating the high similarity of language used by critics and standard users. The similarity between two sets of 100 random reviews written by standard users is 0.96.

Audio CDs Dataset

The AmazonProductReviews dataset, by Jindal and Liu [24], contains user-item-rating-review quadruples on different categories of items. In this experimental evaluation, we used the category Audio CDs, since this has a reasonable number of users, items and reviews and has been used by related work [7][9].The dataset includes 102,714 reviews, 53,060 users and 36,381 items. In this dataset ratings are in a 1 to 5 scale.

5.2   Dataset Spitting Method

A common practice in the recommender systems domain is to split the dataset into three subsets: a training set, for learning the parameters of a model; a validation set, to evaluate the model over different parameter settings to derive optimum parameters; and a test set, to assess the predictive performance of the model on held-out data and thus judge over fitting of a learnt model.

For example, the dataset used in The Netflix Prize [25] consists of three splits: a training set of 95.9% of the ratings, a validation set of 1.36% of the ratings, while the remaining 2.77% of the ratings are used to form the two almost equal size test folds. Although popular, such a splitting method does not allow for statistical significance testing of the predictive performance of a model Testing the statistical significance of an evaluation is important due to the marginal increases in performance often observed in the literature, in assessing for the chance involvement in such increases and to be more confident in any improvement we find when assessing our own method.

The modified approach we apply in this experiment uses the 1.36% of the dataset for the validation [25]. However, instead of using only two test folds, we use 25 equal size test folds. Using a small number of test sets may lead to mislabeling of significant results as insignificant [28]. Our modified setup uses 64.64% of the reviews for training, 1.36% of the reviews for validation and 1.36% for each of the 25 testing folds.

Also, we preserve time ordering when splitting the dataset: the training set's reviews appeared before those in the validation set, and both training and validation contain reviews from before each of the 25 folds. A splitting method that preserves time ordering resembles, most closely, the situation of a recommender in a real system [23]. The system 'knows' only the previous reviews at recommendation time and knows nothing about the future. Cross Validation (CV) evaluation methods such as the 5-fold CV used by [7] or the 10-fold CV used by [9], on the Amazon ProductReviews dataset, introduce bias in a model by training on future results.

5.3   Ratings-Based Approaches

A common practice when evaluating the benefits of a modified ratings-based recommendation approach by incorporating text reviews is to compare the modified approach to the original ratings-based approach. For example, the TBCF approach [6] and the text reviews clustering approach to produce recommendations [5] were compared to a non-personalized baseline, and the Opinion-BMF [7] approach was compared to its ratings equivalent.

In this study, in addition to the ratings equivalent (user-kNN), we compare our approach to a range of ratings-based approaches organized into three categories:

a)   Baseline: approaches that make no use of personalized information such as UserItemAverage, which makes ratings predictions based on the average rating value of an item, plus a regularized user and item bias.

b)   Memory-based Neighborhood algorithms: We employ the rating equivalent of our approach user-kNN, and the Item-based k-Nearest Neighbors (item-kNN), which forms neighborhoods of similar items. We use both methods with Cosine and Pearson Correlation Coefficients similarity measures [1].

c) Matrix Factorization methods: approaches based on low-dimensional factor models. In this category we use SVD++ and BMF. SVD++ incorporates both the standard Singular Value Decomposition (SVD), representing users by their own factor representation, and the asymmetric SVD model, representing users as a bag of item vectors. We also use BMF – the standard MF method with explicit user and item biases [26].

5.4   Training the User-kNN Approaches

We trained all the approaches on the training set and then validated their performance on the validation set. During this procedure we observed that ratings-based user-kNN approaches required a different size of neighborhood (k) than the text-based user-kNN approaches to achieve their best performance. The user-kNN approaches on ratings tend to produce the lowest RMSE when using 100 or 200 neighbors (k=100, k=200), while the text-based user-kNN approaches performed better when using only the single most similar neighbor (k=1). In other words, the text-based approaches perform better when using the most proximate user in terms of sharing similar views about items, or when using a weighted average of the ratings of a large amount of users.

Intuitively, this is similar to how a person would ask for a recommendation in a real life scenario: a person interested in getting a recommendation for a restaurant will probably ask the one person whom s/he trusts most when choosing a restaurant, i.e., the one that s/he shares similar tastes and views on restaurants with. Otherwise, the person would crowdsource many opinions using social networking sites, reviewing websites, or asking people from the offline environment to get a large amount of opinions and make a final decision on which recommendation to follow. In the future, we aim to further explore this observation.

6   Results and Discussion

All results are reported on the test folds, which were excluded from the training process. For each of the test folds, we calculated the RMSE between the actual ratings and the predictions and averaged this over the 25 testing folds. All significant values reported were calculated using a Sign Test [22], as suggested by [23] due to its simplicity and lack of assumptions over the distribution of cases over the 25 testing folds.

The results of our evaluation, reported in Table 2, indicate that out text-based user-kNN approach performs consistently and significantly better than the ratings-based approaches over the two datasets. In the RottenTomatoes dataset, the best performing than the best of the rating based approaches item-kNN with cosine similarity which achieved a RMSE of 0.1466 between the actual and the predicted ratings.

In the Audio CDs dataset, the best performing text-based approaches were those using the Lin and Jiang & Conrath similarity measures. They achieved a RMSE of 1.1092, significantly better (p<0.0001) than the RMSE of 1.1190 of the user-kNN with Cosine similarity. In addition, it is significantly better (p<0.0001) than the best of the rating based approaches, SVD++, which achieved a RMSE of 1.1099. The better performance of the text-based user-kNN approach over the ratings-based user-kNN approaches and over the two datasets confirms our hypothesis that measuring similarity based on text reviews can help to overcome similarity reflection problems.

Table 2. Mean RMSE of text and rating-based approaches over the 25 test folds for the RottenTomatoes and Audio CDs datasets (lower is better)

Rating scale	RottenTomatoes 0.0 to 1.0	Audio CDs 1.0 to 5.0
Text–based user-kNN		
Leacock and Chodorow	0.1478	1.1094
Wu and Palmer	0.1472	1.1094
Resnik	**0.1461**	1.1093
Lin	0.1469	**1.1092**
Jiang and Conrath	0.1467	**1.1092**
Word Overlap	0.1462	1.1101
Rating-based approaches		
Pearson user-kNN	0.1485	**1.1190**
Cosine user-kNN	**0.1473**	1.1263
Pearson item-kNN	0.1473	1.1130
Cosine item-kNN	**0.1466**	1.1156
UserItemAverage	0.1483	1.1398
SVD ++	**0.1467**	**1.1099**
BMF	0.1476	1.1105

Moreover, text-based user-kNN with semantic similarity measures, particularly those using the IC, performed better than those using the simple lexical overlap. This provides some evidence of improvement when measuring text similarity using semantic similarity measures. This is also in agreement with the superior performance of IC measures in a paraphrase detection task [27] over the path based measures and other approaches including Latent Semantic Analysis (LSA).

Although the improvements of RMSE we obtain may seem small, they are significant. In addition, Koren [26] provides evidence that even a small improvement in a rating prediction error can affect the ordering of items and have significant impact on the quality of the top few presented recommendations and thus the overall performance of the recommender system.

7   Conclusion and Future Work

Related work has suggested using text reviews to overcome the similarity reflection problems of user-kNN by incorporating text reviews in the measurement of similarity. The suggested approaches use the sentiment of text reviews instead of ratings [3,4] or build user profiles of aggregated feature preferences extracted from text reviews [5, 6]. We argue that using the sentiment of a text review does not overcome completely similarity reflection problems since the reasons behind a rating remain unexploited. In addition, building user profiles by aggregating the feature preferences does not respect the diversity of the users' feature preferences across items.

To overcome the above limitations, we proposed text-based user-kNN: an approach that measures the direct semantic similarity of users' text reviews on co-reviewed items to form neighborhoods of similar users and minimize RMSE in a ratings prediction task. To measure the similarity between text reviews we investigate five semantic similarity measures based on WordNet, and a simple lexical word overlap measure, through their application in text-based user-kNN. We evaluate its performance by comparing it to BMF, SVD++, user-kNN and item-kNN with Cosine and Pearson correlation and UserItemAverage baseline, on the RottenTomatoes and Audio CDs datasets. Our results show that the text-based methods produce consistently and significantly lower RMSE than the rating-based approaches over the two datasets used in this experiment. In addition, we have shown that a text-based user-kNN that uses semantics similarity measures to calculate the similarity of text reviews performs better than when using a simple lexical word overlap measure.

In our future work, we will carry out an evaluation with other text-based approaches in an items prediction task to investigate how significant our approach is to users. In addition, in the future we will investigate other techniques to further enhance the measurement of similarity between text reviews such as sentiment analysis and evaluate different combinations of text, sentiment and ratings similarities. Furthermore, we would like to investigate the use of Linked Data to identify hidden similarity between entities found in text reviews to improve the similarity reflection between users.

References

1. Herlocker, J., Konstan, J., Borchers, J.A., Riedl, J.: An Algorithmic Framework for Performing Collaborative Filtering. In: Proceedings of the 1999 Conference on Research and Development in Information Retrieval (1999)
2. Terzi, M., Ferrario, M., Whittle, J.: Free Text In User Reviews: Their Role In Recommender Systems. In: Proceedings of the 3rd ACM RecSys 2010 Workshop on Recommender Systems and the Social Web, pp. 45–48. ACM, Chicago (2011)
3. Leung, C.W.K., Chan, S.C.F., Chung, F.: Integrating collaborative filtering and sentiment analysis: A rating inference approach. In: Proceedings of the ECAI 2006 Workshop on Recommender Systems, Riva del Garda, Italy, pp. 62–66 (2006)
4. Zhang, W., Ding, G., Chen, L., Li, C.: Augmenting Chinese Online Video Recommendations by Using Virtual Ratings Predicted by Review Sentiment Classification. In: Proc. of the IEEE ICDM Workshops. IEEE Computer Society, Washington, DC (2010)
5. Chen, L., Wang, F.: Preference-based Clustering Reviews for Augmenting e-Commerce Recommendation. In: Knowledge-Based Systems (2013)
6. Musat, C.C., Liang, Y., Faltings, B.: Recommendation using textual opinions. In: Proceedings of the 23rd IJCAI, pp. 2684–2690. AAAI Press (2013)
7. Pero, Š., Horváth, T.: Opinion-Driven Matrix Factorization for Rating Prediction. In: Carberry, S., Weibelzahl, S., Micarelli, A., Semeraro, G. (eds.) UMAP 2013. LNCS, vol. 7899, pp. 1–13. Springer, Heidelberg (2013)
8. Singh, V.K., Mukherjee, M., Mehta, G.K.: Combining collaborative filtering and sentiment classification for improved movie recommendations. In: Sombattheera, C., Agarwal, A., Udgata, S.K., Lavangnananda, K. (eds.) MIWAI 2011. LNCS, vol. 7080, pp. 38–50. Springer, Heidelberg (2011)

9. Raghavan, S., Gunasekar, S., Ghosh, J.: Review quality aware collaborative filtering. In: Proceedings of the 6th ACM Conference on RecSys, pp. 123–130. ACM, Chicago (2011)

10. McAuley, J., Leskovec, J.: Hidden factors and hidden topics: understanding rating dimensions with review text. In: Proceedings of the 7th ACM RecSys. ACM (2013)

11. Levi, A., Mokryn, O., Diot, C., Taft, N.: Finding a needle in a haystack of reviews: cold start context-based hotel recommender system. In: Proc. RecSys 2012, pp. 115–122. ACM, New York (2012)

12. Fellbaum, C.: WordNet: An Electronic Lexical Database. MIT Press, Cambridge (1998)

13. Pedersen, T., Patwardhan, S., Michelizzi, J.: WordNet: Similarity - Measuring the Relatedness of Concepts. In: Proc. of AAAI, pp. 1024–1025. AAAI, Menlo Park (2004)

14. Lewis, D.D., Yang, Y., Rose, T.G., Li, F.: Rcv1: A new benchmark collection for text categorization research. J. Mach. Learn. Res. 5, 361–397 (2004)

15. Leacock, C., Chodorow, M.: Combining local context and WordNet similarity for word sense identification. In: Fellbaum, C. (ed.), pp. 305–332. MIT Press (1998)

16. Wu, Z., Palmer, M.: Verb semantics and lexical selection. In: 32nd Annual Meeting of the Association for Computational Linguistics, pp. 133–138 (1994)

17. Resnik, P.: Using information content to evaluate semantic similarity in a taxonomy. In: Proceedings of IJCAI, pp. 448–453 (1995)

18. Lin, D.: An information theoretic definition of similarity. In: Proceedings of the 15th IICML. Morgan Kaufmann, San Francisco (1998)

19. Jiang, J.J., Conrath, D.W.: Semantic similarity based on corpus statistics and lexical taxonomy. In: ROCLING X. Academia Sinica, Tapei (1997)

20. Miller, G.A., Leacock, C., Tengi, R., Bunker, R.T.: A semantic concordance. In: Proceedings of the Workshop on HLT, Stroudsburg, PA, USA, pp. 303–308 (1993)

21. Gantner, Z., Rendle, S., Freudenthaler, C., Schmidt-Thieme, L.: Mymedialite: a free recommender system library. In: Proceedings of the 5th ACM Conference on Recommender Systems, pp. 305–308. ACM, New York (2011)

22. Demsar, J.: Statistical comparisons of classifiers over multiple data sets. Journal of Machine Learning Research 7, 1–30 (2006)

23. Shani, G., Gunawardana, A.: Evaluating recommendation systems. In: Ricci, F., Rokach, L., Shapira, B., Kantor, P.B. (eds.) Recommender Systems Handbook (2011)

24. Jindal, N., Liu, B.: Opinion spam and analysis. In: Proceedings of the Conference on Web Search and Web Data Mining (2008)

25. Bennet, J., Lanning, S.: The Netflix Prize. In: KDD Cup and Workshop (2007)

26. Koren, Y.: Factorization meets the neighborhood: a multifaceted collaborative filtering model. In: Proceedings of the 14th ACM SIGKDD, pp. 426–434. ACM, New York (2008)

27. Mohler, M., Mihalcea, R.: Text-to-Text Semantic Similarity for Automatic Short Answer Grading. In: EC-ACL 2009, Athens, Greece, pp. 567–575 (2009)

28. Gunawardana, A., Shani, G.: A survey of accuracy evaluation metrics of recommendation tasks. J. Mach. Learn. Res. 10, 2935–2962 (2009)

Using DBpedia as a Knowledge Source
for Culture-Related User Modelling Questionnaires

Dhavalkumar Thakker[1], Lydia Lau[1], Ronald Denaux[2], Vania Dimitrova[1],
Paul Brna[1], Christina Steiner[3]

[1] School of Computing, University of Leeds, United Kingdom
[2] iSOCO, Madrid, Spain
[3] Knowledge Technologies Institute, Graz University of Technology, Austria
{d.thakker,l.m.s.lau,v.g.dimitrova}@leeds.ac.uk,
rdenaux@gmail.com, paulbrna@mac.com, christina.steiner@tugraz.at

Abstract. In the culture domain, questionnaires are often used to obtain profiles of users for adaptation. Creating questionnaires requires subject matter experts and diverse content, and often does not scale to a variety of cultures and situations. This paper presents a novel approach that is inspired by crowdwisdom and takes advantage of freely available structured linked data. It presents a mechanism for extracting culturally-related facts from DBpedia, utilised as a knowledge source in an interactive user modelling system. A user study, which examines the system usability and the accuracy of the resulting user model, demonstrates the potential of using DBpedia for generating culture-related user modelling questionnaires and points at issues for further investigation.

Keywords: Culture-related user model, linked data, questionnaire generation.

1 Introduction

Today's globalising world requires a new set of skills and competences, among which culture takes a prominent role. Subsequently, a new breed of culturally-aware intelligent learning environments that address challenges when accommodating culture have emerged[1]. The application of the work presented here is set within the framework of the European project ImREAL[2] which considered user-adaptive situational simulations for interpersonal communication with cultural variations. Such simulation environments aim at developing intercultural competences and provide user-adaptive virtual learning experience by taking into account the learner's knowledge of other cultures. The example use cases range from medical interviews, business events (first meeting, business dinner) and the buddying of international students (meeting upon arrival, attending social events). Across the ImREAL use cases, dealing with cultural variations was an important common theme. Culture by nationality (country) was chosen as the prime focus, following findings in business and management indicating that nationality and countries are reliable indicators for tackling cultural diversity [1].

---

[1] http://cats-ws.org/previous-cats/
[2] http://www.imreal-project.eu/

V. Dimitrova et al. (Eds.): UMAP 2014, LNCS 8538, pp. 207–218, 2014.

The key challenge for user-adaptive cultural simulations is to derive a model of a user's knowledge of cultural dimensions relevant to the simulated situations; this is the well-known cold start problem. In the culture domain, questionnaires are often used to obtain profiles of users. This relies on availability of subject matter experts and creation of diverse content including cultural dimensions relevant to the application context [15]. A major challenge is scaling up questionnaire-based user modelling to address cultural diversity and to include engaging examples [2]. Furthermore, a flexible and extendable way of creating and utilising knowledge sources is needed.

To address this challenge a novel approach is proposed here inspired by crowdwisdom and taking advantage of freely available structured linked data. The paper presents an interactive way of deriving a model of a user's knowledge of selected cultural aspects by utilising semantic datasets from Linked Data[3] (in this case DBpedia [3]) to serve as the knowledge base for culture-related facts. The approach provides ontology-based knowledge probing, implemented as an interactive agent called Perico, which builds an overlay user model (UM) of knowledge on selected aspects related to culture by nationality. In the context of user-adaptive systems, Perico can provide an engaging way to derive an initial UM prior interacting with the system, or can be invoked within the system to extend/verify the existing user model.

Perico[4] was presented elsewhere [8], together with an initial validation in a CrowdFlower[5] study which indicated that the interaction was fairly intuitive, but did not give in-depth knowledge of the challenges faced while interacting with Percio (very little qualitative data was provided by the users). A study with two experts inspecting the performance of the system pointed at possible issues with the user model accuracy and utility of DBpedia facts. The findings lacked quantitative backing and were missing the perspective of a real user. In this paper, a controlled user study is reported involving representative users of Perico - adults who wish to extend their knowledge on certain cultural aspects that they may need in everyday intercultural encounters, e.g. visit to a country for business or tourism. Adding to [8], this paper specifically focuses on the DBpedia knowledge extraction mechanism, providing detail of its implementation and utilisation for knowledge probing in user modelling.

The key contribution to user-adaptive systems is a novel, flexible and extendable way to construct culture-related user modelling questionnaires from DBpedia which is validated in a user study. Section 2 outlines how DBpedia has been used as a knowledge source for user modeling. Section 3 presents the user study, and the results are discussed in Section 4. We conclude by positioning in relevant literature (Section 5) and drawing lessons learnt for culture-related UM (Section 6).

2   Using DBpedia as a Knowledge Pool for User Modelling

In order to probe a user's knowledge in a domain, a user modelling system requires access to a knowledge base with domain facts. In the case of culture, key requirements for selecting the knowledge source include diversity and intuitiveness. The knowledge base must contain facts about a wide variety of cultural groups to increase

---

[3] http://linkeddata.org/
[4] Perico is available online from http://imash.leeds.ac.uk:8080/perico/
[5] http://crowdflower.com/

the chance that it contains facts which are relevant to the user's own cultural group and to other cultural groups. Having a range of examples and authentic terms used in the specific cultural settings can increase the user's engagement with the question-like assessment format [2]. To meet these requirements, one of the largest multi-domain semantic dataset that currently exists, DBpedia [3], is chosen as the knowledge source. DBpedia is a community effort to extract structured information from Wikipedia and to make this information available on the Web. Over the last year, DBpedia has become a central interlinking hub for the emerging Web of Data [4]. DBpedia contains lots of instances, represents real community agreement and automatically evolves as Wikipedia changes [4].Extracting domain-related facts from DBpedia requires a set of seed topics and a strategy on how to extract relevant assertions as presented in next two sections.

Selection of Topics. The specific application domain in our case is cultural variations in interpersonal communication (the application focus of the ImREAL project). The relevant concepts in this domain were defined in an Activity Model Ontology (AMOn) underpinned by Activity Theory [5], including concepts like: Subject, Object, Tools, Motivation, Outcome, Community, etc. For example, interpersonal communication Tools are expanded to include Mental Tools (e.g. Verbal Communication, Nonverbal Communication and Body Language) and Physical Tools (e.g. Clothing). AMOn was further extended to AMOn+ by indicating the key interpersonal communication concepts that can possibly have cultural variations [6]. Both AMOn and AMOn+ are presented in earlier publications [5,6]. While these two ontologies provide structure for the important domain aspects (i.e. the abstract facts), the broad range of instantiations were missing (e.g. the variety of gestures, different clothing items or cuisine in different countries). DBpedia is used as a source for such instantiations. A set of seed concepts from AMOn+ is selected for extracting cultural-related facts from DBpedia (see Figure 1).

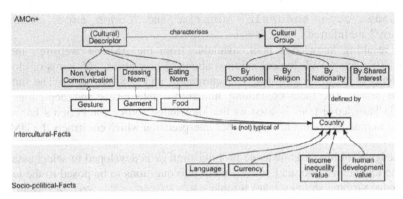

Fig. 1. Selected cultural-related topics following AMOn+. The top section shows a segment of AMOn+ that relates cultural descriptors relate to cultural groups. The middle section shows the types of intercultural facts extracted from DBpedia and their relation to AMOn+ concepts. The bottom section shows additional socio-political facts about countries.

Seven domain topics, grouped into two categories, were selected as entry points for extracting cultural-related facts. The first category includes three topics used to extract cultural facts related to the ImREAL use cases: gestures – a prominent element in non-verbal communication, clothing – a key element in dressing norms, linked to social and cultural conventions, and food - specifically related to interpersonal communication in informal settings. Socio-political facts about a country give useful knowledge in interpersonal communication situations; the following were selected: language, currency, human development index (HDI), and generalised inequality index (GNI).

DBpedia Facts Extraction Strategy. Knowledge pool of facts related to the selected topics is extracted from DBpedia by: (i) identifying DBPedia categories that relate to the selected concepts (for example, for the topic Clothing, the matching category is category:Clothing); (ii) traversing the DBpedia category network to find narrower pages (using skos:narrower) for the identified categories, i.e. searching for pages with a specific category as well as subcategories (for example, for the category:Clothing, dbpedia:Loden_cape is one of the narrower pages); (iii) traversing the DBpedia category network to find broader categories that are shared between the page to be extracted and the country linked to them; for example, traversing the category network for broader categories of dbpedia:Loden_cape, the categories German_Culture and Austrian_Culture and their respective super categories Germany and Austria, connected to dbpedia:Germany and dbpedia:Austria respectively, instances of a Country; (iv) inferring/adding new OWL axioms (basis statements an OWL ontology expresses)[6], such as: a class assertion axiom linking the DBpedia page with an OWL class that is (relevant to) a concept from the Cultural Variations module; an object property assertions linking the DBpedia page with one or more countries where this Cultural Variations concept occurs; and copying relevant literal data, such as labels and depictions. For example, from the extracted facts, assertions "Loden_cape is a Clothing" and "Loden_cape occursIn Austria" and "Loden_cape occursIn Germany" are inferred.

The resulting knowledge pool, available from the AMOn+ website[7], includes around 40K facts (OWL logical axioms) about 270 countries, 565 items of clothing, 4282 items of food, 88 gestures, 159 currencies and 288 languages. The ontology contains some 20K facts containing human-readable labels and depictions. The DBpedia knowledge pool is used as the knowledge source for Perico's knowledge probing, output generation and user input interpretation which constructs the UM.

Knowledge Probing. A knowledge probing strategy is developed to select assertions from the knowledge pool and convert them into questions to be posed to the learner. Knowledge probing strategy takes a tuple <P, Fi, G, T, Fo, A> as an input, and returns an OWL axiom. The input includes: P - a pool of facts represented as a set of OWL axioms; Fi - a set of focus items, i.e. OWL entities that the selected axioms must contain (in Perico, these are dbpedia:Country individuals); G - a

---

[6] http://www.w3.org/TR/2009/WD-owl2-primer-20090421/
[7] http://imash.leeds.ac.uk/ontologies/amon/

goal condition determining whether the strategy should keep selecting more axioms (in Perico, a goal is defined as a configurable number of facts that will be probed for each focus item); T - a function that assigns a topic to each OWL axiom in P using a selected set of topics, OWL entities, that specify the scope of the dialogue (in Perico, the topics include `gestures`, `food`, `clothing`, `language`, `currency`, `HDI`, and `GNI`); Fo - a function that assigns an axiom form to each axiom (currently, Perico includes two axiom forms - normal assertion, facts inferred from DBpedia, and negations, generated from inferred facts); A - a set of already probed axioms (Perico uses the list of probed axioms to avoid repetition of the facts the user is presented with).

The knowledge probing process ends either when the goal G has been met for all focus items, or when the fact pool does not provide enough axioms to meet the goal. When the knowledge probing mechanism returns a selected axiom, this is used as a basis for generating a *knowledge probing dialogue game*. Sentence openers are added to the informative assertions in order to indicate the communicative function of propositional-test-questions, in the form: `<Sentence opener> <axiom rendering> <?>`. Example sentence openers are: *"Is it true that"*, *"Do you think that"*, *"Is it likely that"*, *"Did you find that"* or *"Did you experience that"*.

User Profile Creation. The user's answers to the probing questions are used as evidence of his/her knowledge of the relevant cultural aspect about the country (focus item). Perico suggests pre-defined answers to the knowledge probing questions, such as: agreement, disagreement, inform-ignorance and inform-incorrect-question. Input interpretation includes recognising these pre-defined answers to the knowledge probing questions and annotating each answer with the appropriate discourse-related annotations. Once the answer is interpreted, the UM is changed accordingly. In particular, the UM contains: (i) scores for each of selected topics, plus an explanation containing the probed OWL axioms (e.g. *The user correctly disagreed with the assertion 'Moutza occurs in Spain'.*); (ii) an aggregated score for each of the focus items (countries which have been discussed), calculated as the average score for all the answers related to the country; and (iii) an overall score based on all probed countries. At the end of the dialogue, the aggregated scores and the overall score are presented to the user in a dialogue conclusion game.

3   User Study

A user study was conducted to address the following research questions:

RQ1: Is Perico usable and intuitive for the intended users; and what are the possible limitations of the interaction with Perico?

RQ2: Is the user model produced by Perico accurate against the user's perception of his/her knowledge in the selected cultural aspects?

Participants. The intended users of Perico are adults who can have everyday intercultural encounters, e.g. visit to a country for business or tourism; this relates to the ImREAL use cases - cultural encounters in interpersonal communication (Section 1). 22 participants (age 18-50, mean=28), living in the UK, were recruited on voluntary basis varying in their cultural exposure – British (11), Bulgarian(3), German(1), Greek(1), Indian(1),

Jordanian(1), Malaysian(1), Maltese(1), Nepalese(1) and Polish(1). The cultural exposure of the participants was examined based on the 10 country cultural clusters developed in the GLOBE project [1]. The participants were asked to state their familiarity with the countries in each cluster as (i) *none* (no encounter with the national culture); (ii) *low* (short visits to the country, limited contacts with people from this culture); (iii) *medium* (living in the country for a short period, sequence of regular short visits, relationships with people from this nationality); or (iv) *high* (living in the country for a while; strong relationships with people from this nationality). Based in the top country score for each GLOBE cluster and the number of clusters for which the top country score is *high* or *medium*, the participants were divided into two groups: *Group1 – Narrow Cultural Exposure* (the participants' exposure as high or medium was to one or two GLOBE clusters only – usually the UK and the country in which they were born); *Group 2 – Broad Cultural Exposure* (the participants had medium or high exposure to three or more clusters).

Method. The sessions were conducted individually via a given URL to access Perico[8] and to provide feedback before, during, and after the interaction, as follows:

Pre-study questionnaire included questions on basic demographic data and cultural exposure based on the GLOBE clusters (see above). This was followed by the Cultural Intelligence Scale[9] questionnaire (CQS): CQ-strategy, CQ-knowledge (extended with questions about gestures, food and clothes), CQ-motivation, and CQ-behaviour.

Interaction session with Perico (30-45 min) covered four countries selected by the user - one country for each level of familiarity: *none, low, medium* and *high*. A session included a total of 92 questions – for each country, five probing questions for each of the topics: gestures, food and clothing, and two for each of language, currency, HDI and GNI. At the end of the dialogue about a country, Perico showed the aggregated UM for each topic for that country: *not-good* (the user did not answer correctly any question related to the topic), *need-improvement* (less than 50% correct answers), ok (correct answers 50-70%), *very good* (more than 70% correct answers). The participant was then asked to rate the accuracy of their UM for the selected country and topic as: *accurate* (agrees with Perico's diagnosis), *underestimated* (Perico's assessment was lower than the user's personal judgement) or *overestimated* (Perico's assessement was higher than the user's personal judgement). Also, user comments on the UM scores and the session with Perico were collected. Overall, the dialogue sessions covered 36 different countries across all GLOBE Clusters. There were a total of 2024 questions – 440 for each of gestures, food and clothing, and 176 for each of language, currency, HDI,GNI.

Post-study questionnaire comprised of the CQ-knowledge part of the CQS questionnaire (see above), followed by the System Usability Scale (SUS)[10] questionnaire adapted for Perico - the first ten questions were unchanged; the last three questions were tailored to Perico's interaction: (SUS11) "The questions asked during the dialogue were easy to understand"; (SUS12) "The instructions provided during the dialogue were clear"; and (SUS13) "The assessment made by the dialogue was correct".

---

[8] The study URL is disabled; Perico can be accessed from
http://imash.leeds.ac.uk:8080/perico/
[9] http://www.linnvandyne.com/fourfac.html
[10] http://www.measuringusability.com/sus.php

4   Results

Usability Scores. The overall usability of Perico based on the SUS scores (see Table 1) was very good. SUS4 and SUS10 indicate that the system was easy to learn and did not require additional support. Given that the participants had to answer 92 questions in 30-45 minutes, the mean dialogue-score (Table 2) indicates good quality. The results on user model accuracy (see below) shed light on the scores for SUS13 (correctness of Perico's assessment). The score for SUS1 (frequent use) can be explained with the lack of usage context in the evaluation instructions.

Table 1. SUS scores for general usability (scale: 0-4, the higher the number, the better)

SUS1	SUS2	SUS3	SUS4	SUS5	SUS6	SUS7	SUS8	SUS9	SUS10
1.9	2.7	3.0	3.8	2.3	2.3	3.4	2.8	3.1	3.7

Table 2. SUS scores for the dialogue in Perico (scale: 0-4, the higher the number, the better)

SUS11	SUS12	SUS13	Mean dialogue-score
3.0	3.3	2.5	3.0

Interaction Feedback. The relatively low scores on SUS5 (integration) and SUS6 (consistency) relate to deficiencies of Perico's interaction, which were highlighted in the users' comments, as summarised below.

Inadequate assertions: The users pointed at errors based on the DBpedia knowledge pool, e.g. '*Spain has 132 human development*', '*People in Cyprus use a garment called Icknield High School*'. Some facts were seen as 'historic', e.g. referring to clothes not used any more, such as '*People in Germany use a Garment called Altdeutsche Tracht*', or making statements that are not true, such as '*Frank is currency used in Germany*'. A user noted that the knowledge pool did not take globalisation into account – food, clothing, gestures have become common in countries which they did not originate from. Inadequate assertions are hard to detect automatically. Allowing the users to indicate that something is wrong with the question enables further filtering or extending of the extracted DBpedia fact pool.

Limited content: Some users commented that the gesture questions they were asked were mainly for USA; or that for some countries, e.g. Jordan, the dialogue presented mainly facts related to other countries. These cases relate to the use of negation forms – while useful for generating questions, the negation forms are less indicative for cultural assessment, which should reflect the resultant UM. Most users had concerns about the HDI and GNI questions - finding them confusing or superficial. Additional aspects to include in the dialogue when discussing a country, such as capital, population, climate, religion, festivals, popular sports, points of interest, were suggested.

Lacking coherence: Some users felt that the interaction was jumping from question to question and lacked structure (which was due to the random selection from the pool of possible axioms). A way to add structure could be to follow the GLOBE clusters, including strategies for deepening, i.e. probing the knowledge on countries in the same cultural cluster, broadening, i.e. exploring countries from different clusters, or comparing, i.e. relating countries by cultural topic (e.g. a participant suggested questions like '*How does Italy's income inequality compare to the UK – higher/lower?*').

Misleading sentence openers: Several users commented that the sentence openers had influence on the answers - 'experience', 'think' or 'know' about something provokes different responses, e.g. 'think' is more likely to elicit a guess even if the user does not know. To deal with this, users suggested asking for an explanation or adding an option for indicating that the answer was given by guessing (in addition to 'I don't know' as at the moment).

Cultural Intelligence Scores. The earlier Crowdflower study [8] showed a statistically significant decrease in the user's CQ-knowledge scores as a result of the interaction with Perico. As crowdsourcing scores could be unreliable, in this study we also analysed the CQS changes comparing the pre- and post-test self-assessment scores. The average scores for all CQS questions did not change much (4.18 in the pre-test and 4.05 in the post-test; marks 1-7, where 7 is highest confidence). The average values for all users on the relevant CQ-knowledge scores were lower in the post-test (4.15 in the pre-test and 3.86 in the post-test) but this difference was not statistically significant (Man-Whitney, p=0.29). However, considering only the 12 participants who were quite confident (CQ-knowledge scores in pre-test >4; included users from both groups), there was statistically significant decrease in their post-test CQ-knowledge scores (5.13 in pre-test, 4.5 in post-test; Man-Whitney, p<0.0001). The study results confirm that the interaction with Perico has an effect on the user's confidence when self-assessing their CQ-knowledge on gestures, clothing and food, especially for users who have high confidence scores before the interaction. Participants who lowered their scores were further interviewed - the main reason for lowering the CQ-knowledge confidence was the exposure to a diversity of instances of the selected topics; this made them realise that their knowledge was not as high as they thought before interacting with Perico.

UM Accuracy Based on Topics and Cultural Exposure. The participants were asked to assess the accuracy of the user model for each country and selected topic. Zooming into the cultural exposure values per country sheds light into the reliability of the selected cultural topics, pointing at the usefulness of the questions generated from DBpedia on each topic. Based on all individual assessments, the percentage of accuracy perceived by users was 81%, 10% of all cases Perico overestimated the users and 9% of all cases were underestimates. When the users had *none* or *low* exposure to a country, they found Perico's UM overestimated in 17% of the cases and underestimated in 7% of the cases (76% were accurate). In contrast, when the users had *medium* or *high* exposure to a country, they felt their user model was accurate 86%, where 3% was overstimated and 12% was underestimated (Figure 2 gives details).

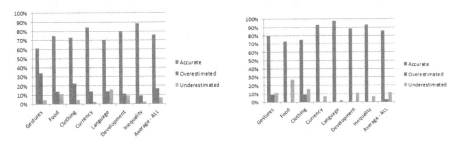

Fig. 2. User model accuracy based on selected cultural topics, compared against user exposure to the country – left (countries with none or low exposure) and right (medium or high)

Feedback on UM. The user comments in the cases when Perico overestimated or underestimated their UM provided useful feedback on the system's performance.

Answer indicated in the question: This feedback referred to cases when Perico overestimated the UM. The name of a country was given as part of the question and the correct answer was obvious. This happened mainly for currency, e.g. '*Indian Rupee*', '*Japanese Yen*', '*Bulgarian Lev*', '*Polish Zloty*', language, e.g. '*German is spoken in Germany.*' or gestures, e.g. '*Thai greeting*'. Such questions were seen as redundant, as they were not helpful for diagnosing the user's knowledge. Some possible strategies to avoid using the name directly could be: (i) identify countries which use the language, e.g. using `dbprop:regional` can be inferred that German is a regional language in Poland, and generate a question like '*Do Germany and Poland have a common language?*'; (ii) use `rdfs:label` to include a name without the country, e.g. use '*Z oty*' instead of '*Polish Zloty*', or `dbpprop:nickname` to include the nickname, e.g. use '*kint*' instead of '*Bulgarian lev*', or `dbpprop:subunitName` to use a subunit, e.g. '*Paisa*' instead of '*Indian rupee*'.

Answer given via knowledge elimination: Users felt that Perico evaluated their performance higher than what should be in the case when they had no knowledge of the countries they were evaluated for. They felt that they were able to answer the questions by knowing the facts (e.g. gesture or food facts) about other countries they knew rather than the focus item country for which they were diagnosed. For example, while evaluating a user on gestures from *Canada*, they knew the gesture in the question presented to them was a *Chinese gesture*, with which they had some exposure to. This enabled them to rule out the gesture's association with Canada and answer correctly. As commented above, a way to overcome the issue of user guessing is to (i) explicitly ask if the user knew or guessed the answer; and (ii) ask for additional justification or explanation. It should be noted that such questions are valuable for assessment of culture-related knowledge, as the correct answers require knowledge of cultural aspects for other countries. This should be taken into account in the UM update.

Answer given using a clue in the question. This refers to questions with pictures – users felt that their cultural knowledge was overestimated as they could answer based on the picture presented in the question. For example, one user reported that: "*I could often tell if gestures were used in Hong Kong by looking at the picture - Most of which were obviously not taken in Hong Kong. Without the pictures I would probably have made more mistakes.*" Although the pictures give clue, they also make the questions more engaging and authentic and should not be disregarded. As above, a way to address this is by asking for justification of the answer or checking for a user's guess.

Answers were assessed wrongly. A main reason for the participants' statements that Perico underestimated their knowledge was that they believed certain facts were incorrect, which was observed exclusively for `gestures` and `food`. For example, *"High five is definitely used in Poland. Sign of the cross is as well*", *"Gestures for UK and US are very similar - Hook 'em bears is definitely used here.*" Perico uses DBpedia as a closed world source, i.e. if a certain fact is not in Wikipedia, it is false.

Being a crowd-sourced knowledgebase, Wikipedia does not always contain all the possible countries where a particular gesture is practiced or a particular food is part of the cuisine. This is linked to the issue of globalisation and points at the need to include a way of collecting facts from the users while interacting with Perico to accommodate richer crowdsourced knowledge of cultural aspects.

5   Related Work

Linked Data in general, and DBpedia in particular (a community effort to extract structured information from Wikipedia and make it available for free use [3]), has been a productive and popular source in user modeling and personalisation approaches. Considerable work has been done on enriching and semantically annotating social web content using linked data to improve adaptation and recommendation for content retrieval [9]; or semantically enrich and classify social tags to profile users [10,11]. Our work contributes to this growing trend to utilise Linked Data to address user modelling challenges[19], in this case we use DBpedia as a source of common sense knowledge for interactive user modelling in a domain requiring diverse content.

Due to the time and effort necessary to create assessment items (test questions) in e-assessment, automatic or semi-automatic item generation has gained attention over the last few years [12]. Linked Data is seen as a useful source for the generation of assessment items, offering models of factual knowledge and structured datasets for the generation of item model variables [13]. Several question answering systems for RDF data have been proposed, which in an essence translate questions into triples that are matched against the RDF data to retrieve an answer [14]. We use DBpedia on a similar premise. Our contribution to existing work in question-answering is the adaptation of this approach for interactive user modelling in the domain of culture.

Nationality-based cultural dimensions have utilised for culturally-aware user interfaces, e.g. [17, 18]. The prominent work in [16] brought in the topic of culture-based UM and Adaptation, presenting a way of automated customisation of the user interface following a user's cultural model based on nationality. While the user's nationality is a useful source for adapting the interface, this is insufficient for user-adaptive learning environments when the focus is on developing cultural awareness skills. In such environments, the user's cultural exposure and awareness of cultural dimensions of other countries is crucial. To assess this, questionnaires are being used. However, questionnaires can become boring and user responses may get superficial [2]. While situational judgment tests, which assess a learner's recognition and understanding of cultural aspects by asking him/her to take decisions in carefully designed situations, can be effective, they require extensive design time by experienced subject matter experts [15]. Moreover, to be engaging, the test content has to include a range of examples, use images and other media [2]. Our approach paves a new avenue in culturally-aware user adaptive systems where freely available crowdsourced knowledge from Linked Data is utilised as a source of diversity for deriving culture-related UM.

6 Conclusions

Being an ill-defined domain, culture brings in an abundance of challenges for user modelling; given the rising importance of culture more attention will be paid at adding cultural dimensions in UM. The work presented here is an initial step in this direction. It extends conventional questionnaire approaches for deriving culture-related user profiles and addresses key limitations - dealing with diversity, enabling flexibility and extensibility. Cultural facts are derived from DBpedia and used for knowledge probing in an interactive user modelling system called Perico. It makes culture-related user modelling questionnaires more engaging by offering a diverse set of authentic examples and pictorial information in an intuitive and interactive way. In essence, Perico 'gamifies' questionnaires – a new strand of work which is seen as promising in a range of domains, including to deal with variations in cultural contexts [2].

The user study reported here shows that the approach has certain potential for user modelling. The users found Perico intuitive and, despite engaging in a 'questionnaire-like' interaction for more than 30 min, they gave positive usability scores. The users tend to agree with Perico's assessment in their UM. The systematic way to extract a portion of DBpedia facts, starting with seed concepts related to some aspects in interpersonal communication that have cultural variations, can be utilised to extend the knowledge pool with facts about country geography, religion, festivals, and tourism (suggested in the study). Having an underlying knowledge structure allows examining the UM accuracy based on categories; and hence the evaluation method can be repeated for an improved version of Perico with an extended knowledge pool.

Several remaining challenges require further investigation. Following a questionnaire style where examples are deliberately shown in a random-like way was seen as a lack of coherence in Perico's interaction. Ways for making Perico more conversational and open by allowing the user to provide justifications and suggest facts that are missing are worth investigating. The user modelling mechanism should be extended to take into account knowledge of other countries which is embedded in the questions. The utility of the questions can be further improved inferring more difficult facts (e.g. not making the answer obvious by giving the name of the country).

Acknowledgements. The research leading to these results has received funding from the European Union Seventh Framework Programme, grant ICT 257831 (ImREAL).

References

1. Gupta, V., Hanges, P.J., Dorfman, P.: Review Cultural clusters: methodology and findings. Journal of World Business 37(2), 11–15 (2002)
2. Puleston, J., Rintoul, D.: Can survey gaming techniques cross continents? Examining cross-cultural reactions to creative questioning techniques. In: ESOMAR Asia Pacific Conf. (2012)
3. Bizer, C., Lehmann, J., Kobilarov, G., Auer, S., Becker, C., Cyganiak, R., Helmann, S.: Dbpedia – a cristalization point for the Web of Data. Web Semantics: Science, Services and Agents on the World Wide Web,154–165 (2009)
4. Heath, T., Bizer, C.: Linked data: Evolving the web into a global data space. Synthesis lectures on the semantic web: theory and technology 1(1), 1–136 (2011)
5. Karanasios, S., Thakker, D., Lau, L., Allen, D., Dimitrova, V., Norman, A.: Making sense of digital traces: An activity theory driven ontological approach. Journal of the American Society for Information Science and Technology 64(12), 2452–2467 (2013)
6. Blanchard, E.G., Karanasios, S., Dimitrova, V.: A conceptual model of intercultural communication: Challenges, development method and achievements. In: Proc. of 4th Int. Workshop on Culturally-Aware Tutoring Systems CATS 2013 held at AIED 2013 (2013)
7. Denaux, R., Dolbear, C., Hart, G., Dimitrova, V., Cohn, A.G.: Supporting domain experts to construct conceptual ontologies: A holistic approach. Web Semantics: Science, Services and Agents on the World Wide Web 9(2), 113–127 (2011)
8. Denaux, R., Dimitrova, V., Lau, L., Brna, P., Thakker, D., Steiner, C.: Employing Linked Data and Dialogue for Modelling Cultural Awareness of a User. In: Proc. of IUI 2014 (2014)
9. Abel, F., Gao, Q., Houben, G.-J., Tao, K.: Analyzing user modeling on twitter for personalized news recommendations. In: Konstan, J.A., Conejo, R., Marzo, J.L., Oliver, N. (eds.) UMAP 2011. LNCS, vol. 6787, pp. 1–12. Springer, Heidelberg (2011)
10. Abel, F., Herder, E., Houben, G.-J., Henze, N., Krause, D.: Cross-system user modeling and personalization on the social web. Journal of UMUAI 23(2-3), 169–209 (2013)
11. Meo, P.D., Ferrara, E., Abel, F., Aroyo, L., Houben, G.-J.: Analyzing user behavior across social sharing environments. ACM TIST 5(1), 14 (2013)
12. Karpicke, J.D., Blunt, J.R.: Retrieval practice produces more learning than elaborative studying with concept mapping. Science 331(6018), 772–775 (2011)
13. Foulonneau, M.: Generating educational assessment items from linked open data: The case of dBpedia. In: García-Castro, R., Fensel, D., Antoniou, G. (eds.) ESWC 2011. LNCS, vol. 7117, pp. 16–27. Springer, Heidelberg (2012)
14. Unger, C., Bühmann, L., Lehmann, J., Ngonga Ngomo, A.C., Gerber, D., Cimiano, P.: Template-based question answering over RDF data. In: Proc. of the 21st International Conference on World Wide Web WWW 2012, pp. 639–648. ACM (2012)
15. Hays, M.J., Ogan, A., Lane, C.H.: The Evolution of Assessment: Learning about Culture from a Serious Game. In: Proc. of the Workshop on Intelligent Tutoring Technologies for Ill-Defined Problems and Ill-Defined Domains, held at ITS 2010, pp. 37–44 (2010)
16. Reinecke, K., Bernstein, A.: Tell me where you've lived, and i'll tell you what you like: Adapting interfaces to cultural preferences. In: Houben, G.-J., McCalla, G., Pianesi, F., Zancanaro, M. (eds.) UMAP 2009. LNCS, vol. 5535, pp. 185–196. Springer, Heidelberg (2009)
17. Marcus, A., Gould, E.W.: Crosscurrents: cultural dimensions and global Web user-interface design. Interactions 7(4), 32–46 (2000)
18. Dormann, C., Chisalita, C.: Cultural values in web site design. In: ECCE11 Proc. (2002)
19. Herder, E., Dietze, S., d'Aquin, M.: LinkedUp – Linking Web Data for Adaptive Education. In: UMAP 2013 Workshops (2013)

Eye Tracking to Understand User Differences in Visualization Processing with Highlighting Interventions

Dereck Toker and Cristina Conati

Department of Computer Science
University of British Columbia, Vancouver, Canada
{dtoker,conati}@cs.ubc.ca

Abstract. We present an analysis of user gaze data to understand if and how user characteristics impact visual processing of bar charts in the presence of different highlighting interventions designed to facilitate visualization usage. We then link these results to task performance in order to provide insights on how to design user-adaptive information visualization systems. Our results show how the least effective intervention manifests itself as a distractor based on gaze patterns. The results also identify specific visualization regions that cause   poor task performance in users with low values of certain cognitive measures, and should therefore be the target of personalized visualization support.

Keywords: User characteristics, Eye Tracking, User Evaluation, Adaptive Information Visualization.

1   Introduction

Information visualization (Infoviz) systems are widely used across many domains and applications in order to explore, manage, and better understand data. Despite their increasing frequency of use and the rise of big data, these systems have typically continued to follow a one-size-fits-all approach in terms of how they account for their users. An ever increasing body of research however, has shown that individual user differences can play a role in user performance or preference for a given infoviz system [1–5]. These findings suggest that visualization effectiveness may be improved by having Infoviz systems that can detect relevant user differences during visualization processing, and adapt accordingly. Researchers have already started looking at adaptation approaches that recommend *alternative visualizations* based on detected user needs (e.g., [6, 7]). By contrast, in this paper we focus on exploring the potential of adaptive interventions aimed at improving the effectiveness of the *visualization currently used*. In particular, we use eye-tracking to evaluate the impact on visualization processing of four *highlighting interventions* which could eventually be used to provide adaptive support by dynamically redirecting the user's attention to different subsets of the visualized data as needed (e.g., when the visualization is used together with a verbal description that discusses different aspects of a dataset [1]). Previous work has already looked at the impact of these interventions on user task performance [1]. In this paper however, we analyze user gaze behavior based on eye tracking data

V. Dimitrova et al. (Eds.): UMAP 2014, LNCS 8538, pp. 219–230, 2014.

collected during the study in [1], in order to gain a more fine-grained understanding of how the study factors (e.g., interventions, user differences, task complexity) impact visualization processing. For gaze data analysis, we employ the same methodology proposed in [8], consisting of several stages of data preprocessing and statistical modeling. The work in [8] looked at a simple gaze data set to understand how a set of individual differences affect visualization processing while performing a variety of tasks with two different visualizations (bar graphs and radar graphs). In this paper, we focus on bar graphs only, and extend the work in [8] by looking at (i) a larger set of individual differences; (ii) more complex data sets, and (iii)   if/how the related visual processing is impacted by different highlighting interventions. We also include a new region of visualization processing (*answer input* area of interest), to track gaze behaviors within the region where users input their answers to the study tasks. The research questions we investigate here in this paper are as follows:

Q1. How do the tested sets of user characteristics, highlighting interventions, and task complexity impact gaze behavior during bar graph visualization processing?

Q2. How do results in Q1 relate to results on the impact of these factors on task performance reported in [1], and what are the implications for adaptive visualizations?

In answering these research questions, our objective is to inform the next stages of design for a real-time user-adaptive information visualization system. Our results do in fact show significant impacts of user characteristics, task type, and interventions on gaze behaviors. These results are then used to shed light on why significant performance differences occurred during visualization processing as reported in [1]. Based on these outcomes, we offer design recommendations for providing adaptive visualization support for bar graph processing using highlighting interventions.

2   Related Work

Recent work has begun to evaluate the benefits of user-adaptation for information visualization systems. Both Grawemeyer [7], and Gotz & Wen [6] found positive results when evaluating systems that provide recommendations on a set of available visualizations based on a user's tasks, prior knowledge, and performance. While these systems adapt only to user features such as domain knowledge or performance tracked via interface-related behaviors, several studies have shown that other user characteristics can impact visualization performance. Various cognitive abilities such as perceptual speed, verbal working memory, and visual working memory have been shown to impact user performance and/or user subjective experience with Infoviz tasks [1, 2, 4, 5]. Researchers have also shown that personality traits (e.g., locus of control) can have similar impacts on performance [3]. Given this increasing evidence on the impact of user differences in visualization performance, researchers have been investigating ways to capture the relevant user traits in real-time so as to inform adaptive information visualization systems, with substantial attention being devoted to approaches leveraging gaze data. For example, Gridinger et al. [9] used group-wise similarity of gaze patterns to predict domain expertise in processing visualizations of weather patterns. Steichen et al. [10] and Toker et al. [11] predict, respectively, user characteristics and skill acquisition based solely on tracking a large set of aggregate gaze features collected during infoviz tasks. Eye-tracking has also been investigated as a promising source of information for understanding how to adapt to specific user traits for supporting effective visualization processing. For instance, several studies have shown significant differences in gaze patterns of experts and novices during visualization tasks in a variety of domains, including chemistry (e.g., [12, 13]) and general information search [14]. It should be noted however, that little work has been done to formally connect differences in gaze behaviors due to user characteristics, to objective measures of task performance. Building this connection is key in order to understand how to improve visualization performance by tailoring support to specific user traits. Toker et al. [8] have begun to address this gap by running a formal analysis of eye gaze behaviors with bar and radar graph visualizations. In a previous study with these visualizations, users with low values for perceptual speed had been found to perform poorly compared to users with high perceptual speed [4]. By then analyzing the gaze data, [8] explains this performance difference in terms of the higher processing time that low perceptual speed users need to devote to the visualization's legend. Based on these findings, [8] recommended that low perceptual speed users ought to be supported by designing interventions that target the legend region. In this paper, we apply the same methodology as [8] towards the performance results from the study reported in [1] in order to gain a better understanding of how user differences impact visualization processing when highlighting interventions are available.

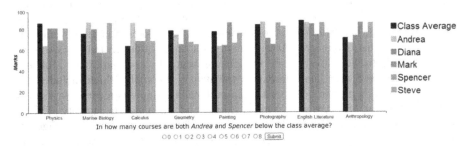

Fig. 1. Sample bar graph visualization and task administered in the study

3   User Study

The study that generated the data used in this paper investigated the effectiveness of four highlighting interventions designed to help the processing of bar graphs, as well as how this effectiveness is impacted by both task complexity and different user traits. The study was a single session, within-subjects design, lasting at most 90 minutes. 62 participants performed tasks using bar graphs (Fig.1) with a fully-automated interface. Gaze was tracked using a Tobii T120 eye-tracker and calibration was taken twice: once at the start and once at the mid-point of the study. Bars graph were chosen because they are a common visualization for which there is already evidence of the impact of individual differences and the need for adaptive support [4].

Task complexity was varied by having subjects perform 2 different types of tasks, chosen from a standard set of primitive data analysis tasks in Amar et al. [15]. The first task type was Retrieve Value (RV), one of the simplest task types in [15], which in the study consisted of retrieving the value for a specific individual in the dataset and comparing it against the group average (e.g., "Is Michael's grade in *Chemistry*

above the class average?"). The second, more complex task type, was Compute Derived Value (CDV) which in the study required users to first perform a set of comparisons, and then compute an aggregate of the comparison outcomes (e.g., "In how
many cities is the movie *Vampire Attack* above the average revenue and the movie
How to Date Your Friends below it?"). All tasks involved the same number of data
points (6), and series elements (8). It should be noted that these datasets were more
complex than those used in a previous study on the impact of individual differences
on bar graph processing [8], which involved at most three data points per series.

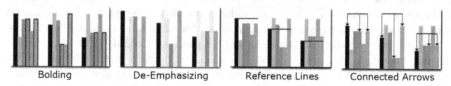

| Bolding | De-Emphasizing | Reference Lines | Connected Arrows |

Fig. 2. The four highlighting interventions evaluated in the study

Each intervention evaluated in the study (shown in Fig. 2) was designed to highlight graph bars that were relevant to answer the current question, to guide a user's
focus to a specific subset of the visualized data while still retaining the overall context
of the data as a whole [16]. The *Bolding* intervention draws a thickened box around
the relevant bars; *De-Emphasis* fades all non-relevant bars; *Average Reference Lines*
draws a horizontal line from the top of the left-most bar (representing the average) to
the last relevant bar; *Connected Arrows* involves a series of connected arrows pointing downwards to the relevant bars. Participants began by completing a set of tests
that measured the 5 user characteristics evaluated in the study which included: (1)
Perceptual speed, a measure of speed when performing simple perceptual tasks [17];
(2) *Visual Working Memory*, a measure of storage and manipulation capacity of visual
and spatial information [18]; (3) *Verbal Working Memory*, a measure of storage and
manipulation capacity of verbal information [19]; (4) *Bar Graph Expertise*, a self-
reported measure of a user's experience with using bar graphs; (5) *Locus of Control*, a
personality trait measuring whether individuals tend to take responsibility for their
circumstances or blame them on external factors. These measures were selected because they had been previously shown to influence user performance or satisfaction in
bar graph studies [1, 2, 4, 5] or other visualizations [3]. Next, each participant performed each of the two task types (RV & CDV) with each of the 4 interventions as
well as *No Intervention* as a baseline for comparison, in a fully randomized manner,
yielding a total of 80 trials per participant.

4   Eye Tracking Pre-processing and Analysis

Following the same approach in [8], the eye tracking data is processed in three stages.
First, we generate a set of gaze features from the raw data. Next, principal component
analysis (PCA) is performed on these features to obtain a set of factors which will act
as the dependent measures for statistical analysis. Lastly, linear mixed-effect models
(mixed models) are used to evaluate the impact of the study factors and user characteristics on the eye tracking components.

4.1   Generate Low-Level Eye Tracking Features

Eye tracking data consists of fixations (i.e., gaze points on the screen), and saccades (i.e., paths between fixations). We processed the raw gaze data from the study using EMDAT, an open-source toolkit[1] which computes gaze features including sums, averages, and standard deviations of a variety of gaze measures, such as fixation rate and duration, saccade length, and absolute/relative saccade angles. These features can be computed with respect to the overall screen, using no information on the displayed content (e.g., mean fixation duration, sum lengths of saccades, average angles of saccades), and there are 14 such features, called *High-level* features, from now on. Features can also be computed for specific areas of interest (AOI) in the interface (*AOI-level* features). These include both proportionate measures indicating relative attention to each AOI (e.g., proportion of time/fixations spent looking at an AOI), as well as transition measures indicating how a user's attention shifts between two AOIs (e.g., transition from AOI *x* to AOI *y*). This ensemble of features constitute the building blocks for comprehensive gaze processing [20]. The set of AOIs for the bar graph used in the study consists of: (1) 'High' AOI, a rectangular area that covers the top half of the vertical bars; (2) 'Low' AOI covers the lower half of the vertical bars, (3) 'Labels' AOI: covers the series elements labels, (4) 'Legend' AOI: covers the legend, (5) 'Question' AOI: covers the text describing the task to be performed, and (6) 'Input' AOI: covers the radio buttons and submit button, (refer to Fig. 1).

4.2   Generate Components Using Dimensional Reduction

The goal of this step is to use principal component analysis (PCA) in order to identify and combine groups of inter-related gaze features into components more suitable for data analysis [21]. We first group the gaze features into three non-overlapping families according to how the measures are intuitively related: *High-level family*, *AOI-proportionate family*, and *AOI-transitions family*. We then conduct a separate PCA on each family, of which the results are described next. In the subsequent tables, '**' indicates features that are negatively correlated to the component they are member to. Since [8] used the same families of gaze features for their PCAs, we will comment on the similarities and differences with our results to show where the consistencies exist across different visualization contexts.

Performing PCA on the 14 high-level gaze features generated five components (x^2 = 22035.01, df = 91, $p < .001$, explained variance 88.31%), shown in Table 1. The names for the components are based on commonalities among their features. These 5 components are identical to those found in [8], even though the underlying gaze features were generated from two different studies (one using radar graphs and bar graphs, and one using only bar graphs and interventions). This is initial yet strong evidence that the relationships between the 14 High-level gaze features may be consistent regardless of the visualization context.

Performing PCA on the 12 features in the *AOI-proportionate* family produced five components (x^2= 15271.10, df = 66, $p < .001$, explained variance 93.71%), shown in Table 2. Although the 'Input' AOI was not examined in [8], there are still strong similarities between their PCA results and ours. In both PCAs, proportionate

[1] Eye Movement Data Analysis Toolkit, available at:
http://www.cs.ubc.ca/~skardan/EMDAT/

Table 1. PCA results for high-level family.

Component Name	High-level family gaze features
Sum-Measures	*Total-num-fixations, Sum-rel.-saccade-angles, Sum-abs-saccade-angles, Sum-saccade-length, Sum-fixation-durations*
Fixation-Measures	*Mean-fixation-durations, Std-dev-fixation-durations, Fixation-rate***
Saccade-Length	*Mean-saccade-length, Std-dev-saccade-length*
Saccade-Angles	*Mean-rel.-saccade-angles, Std-dev-rel.-saccade-angles, Std-dev-abs-saccade-angles*
Mean-Abs-Saccade-Angles	*Mean-abs-saccade-angles*

measures of total-duration and total-fixations for any AOI always appear together in some component, indicating that these features are strongly correlated. Furthermore, the components related to proportionate attention to 'Label', 'Low', and 'Legend' AOI are identical to those in [8]. One obvious difference with [8] is that here we included an additional AOI, whose proportionate features were grouped by PCA in the same component (prop-Input in Table 2). A second difference is that in [8] the 'Question' and 'High' AOI-proportionate gaze features produced separate components, whereas here they were combined into one component (prop-Question/High in Table 2). This is an indication that unlike High-level gaze features, certain AOI related gaze behaviors are likely dependent on interaction contexts (e.g., visualization type, task complexity).

Table 2. PCA results for AOI-proportionate family

Component Name	AOI-proportionate family gaze features
prop-Question/High	*Question-prop-total-duration, Question-prop-total-fixations, High-prop-total-duration**, High-prop-total-fixations***
prop-Low	*Low-prop-total-duration, Low-prop-total-fixations*
prop-Labels	*Labels-prop-total-duration, Labels-prop-total-fixations*
prop-Input	*Input-prop-total-duration, Input-prop-total-fixations*
prop-Legend	*Legend-prop-total-duration, Legend-prop-total-fixations*

Table 3. PCA resutls for AOI transitions faimly

Component Name	AOI-transitions family gaze features
trans-Label/Low	*Low→label, Label→low, Label→labels, Question→label, Label→question, Label→legend, Legend→label, Legend→low, Low→low, Low→legend, Question→low, Question→question, Low→question*
trans-High/ Legend/Question	*High→legend, Legend→high, Legend→question, Question→legend, High→ question, High→high, Question→question, Question→high, Legend→legend*
trans-Input	*Legend →input, Input→legend, Input→input, Question→input, Input→question, Input→low, Low→input*
trans-Low	*Low→high, High→low, Low→low, Question→low, Low→question*
trans-Label/Question	*Input→label, Label→high, Label→input, High→high, Label→question, Question→label, Input→question*

Performing PCA on the 36 gaze features in the AOI-transition family generated five components ($x^2 = 22755.8$, df = 630, $p < .001$, explained variance 48.2%), shown in Table 3. Unlike [8], where each transition component included features related mostly to one specific AOI, here the transition components are a lot more noisy, meaning that there is more overlap between which AOI(s) primarily comprise a given component. These findings indicate that of the 3 families of gaze features examined, transitions features are the least similar across interaction contexts, which is likely due to the finer granularity of interaction with the visualization that they capture.

4.3   Mixed Model Analysis

The final step of our analysis involves running a formal statistical model (mixed-model) to evaluate the impact of our study parameters (task complexity, interventions) and user characteristics on gaze components. For each of the three families of gaze features described in the previous section, we run a set of mixed models on each component (for a total of 15 sets of mixed models). Each mixed model is a 2 (task type) by 5 (intervention) with the respective component as the dependent measure. Additionally, as was done in [1], each of the five covariates (perceptual speed, verbalWM, visualWM, expertise, locus of control) are separately analyzed by running an additional mixed model for each covariate and the experimental factors. Given the high number of covariates, this approach ensures that we do not over-fit the models. To account for multiple comparisons within each family of gaze features, each mixed model is adjusted using a Bonferroni correction with value equal to the number of components in each family (i.e., 5), resulting in an overall total of 15 corrections. Statistical significance is thus reported post-correction at the .05 level.

5   Results

In this section, we report a selection of results from the gaze analysis, organized into three parts: results on effects relating to user characteristics; results relating to highlighting interventions; and results relating to task type (i.e., *Compute Derived Value & Retrieve Value*) that that do not directly involve user characteristics. All reported results are statistically significant ($p < .05$), however due to space limitations only the effect sizes (R^2) are shown.

5.1   Impact of User Characteristics on Gaze Patterns

The user differences for which we found significant effects on gaze data are perceptual speed (PS), visual working memory (VisualWM), and verbal working memory (VerbalWM). These are also the user characteristics that were found to significantly impact user performance in [1]. In particular, users with low measures of PS and VisualWM were significantly slower when completing harder tasks (CDV) than users with high VerbalWM. Users with low VerbalWM were significantly slower than high VerbalWM users regardless of task type. In the following sections, we link differences in task performance (previous results presented in [1]) to gaze behaviors (new results in this paper), which together offer explanations as to where/how poor performance is occurring within a task, as well as how this knowledge can inform the design of user-adaptive support. Results for user characteristics are presented based on a median split of users along these measures (e.g., low vs. high perceptual speed).

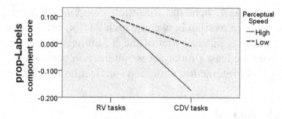

Fig. 3. Interaction effect between PS and TaskType on *prop_Labels*

Interaction Effect - PerceptualSpeed * TaskType. We found an interaction effect between PS and TaskType on *prop-Labels* (R^2 = .009), shown in Fig 3. This effect indicates that, for harder tasks (CDV), users with low PS are spending more of their time looking at the labels of the bar graph. Similar results were also reported in [8], where they found that users with low PS transitioned more often to the labels when working on harder tasks. Given that low PS users showed poorer performance in harder tasks [1], these results reinforce the need to consider offering adaptive interventions that can help low PS users to process graph labels. For instance, we may want to extend our set of highlighting interventions to apply to labels.

Interaction Effect - VisualWM * TaskType. We found interaction effects for visualWM*TaskType on features in both the AOI-proportionate and AOI-transitions families: *prop-Input* (R^2 = .014)   and   *trans-Input* (R = .016), shown in Fig. 4.

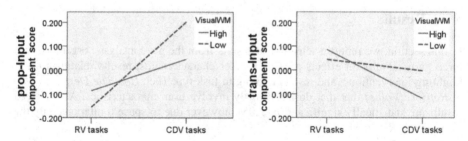

Fig. 4. Interaction between visualWM and TaskType for two 'Input' AOI related components

These effects indicate that for harder tasks, users with low visualWM spend more of their time looking at the 'Input' AOI and are also transitioning more frequently to it, compared to users with high visualWM. The latter finding on transition frequency specifically suggests that low visualWM users likely have difficulty connecting the answer options in the input area with the information in the graph, which causes them to go back and forth between the input and the other graph areas more often than high visualWM users do. This behavior can explain why in [1] low visualWM users were found to be slower at solving the tasks than their high visualWM counterparts. This combination of findings suggest that we may want to experiment with designing adaptive support for low visualWM users that focuses on facilitating processing of the input options in relation to the task (e.g., experiment with different input methods or visual representations of radio buttons).

We also found an interaction effect between visualWM and TaskType on the *Saccade-Length* component (R^2 = .008) indicating that, for harder tasks, users with low visualWM had longer saccades and a greater standard deviation of saccade lengths. This is akin to these users taking 'broader strokes' as they look about the screen, as well as having less consistently sized saccades. This finding may be an additional manifestation of the difficulty these users experience with harder tasks, further explaining why they were slower at completing them. Interestingly, no links between visualWM and gaze behaviors were found in [8]. One explanation is that the more complex datasets used for the visualizations targeted in this paper provided an increase in visual complexity which drew out the impact of visualWM capacity.

Main Effect - VerbalWM. We found a main effect of verbalWM on the AOI-transitions family, specifically on the *trans-High/Legend/Question* component (R^2 = .005). This effect indicates that users with low verbalWM transitioned over the 'High', 'Legend', and 'Question' AOIs more often than users with high verbalWM. Both legend and question are textual elements, thus this finding is consistent with the fact that users with lower verbal capacity may need to review these textual elements more often. Similarly, [8] reported a main effect of verbalWM on the proportion of time users spent looking at the main textual elements of the visualization. They were, however, unable to establish whether these behaviors affected performance and may warrant adaptive interventions. In contrast, we can link the main effect discussed here to the increase in task completion time for low VisualWM reported in [1], indicating that it is worthwhile to investigate adaptive interventions that aid the processing of a visualization's textual component for these users.

5.2   Impact of Interventions on Visualization Processing

Previous results in [1] show that three of the four highlighting interventions described in Section 3 led to better task performance compared to having no interventions, whereas the Avg.Ref.Line intervention did not. The eye tracking results in this subsection may help shed some light on this finding.

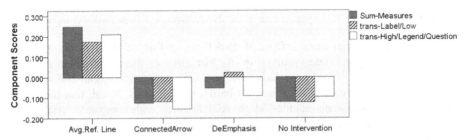

Fig. 5. Main effect of intervention on three different gaze components

We found main effects of intervention type on three different gaze components: *Sum-Measures* (a component of the High-level family consisting of sums over measures for overall fixations and saccade angles, R^2 = .102), as well as two components of the AOI-transitions family: *trans-Label/Low* (R^2 = .056) and *trans-High/Legend/Question* (R^2 = .049). Pairwise comparisons of the interventions indicated that for all three gaze components, Avg.Ref.Line has significantly higher values than ConnectedArrow and DeEmphasis (see Fig. 5). In [1], Avg.Ref.Line was suggested to be a visual *distractor* that interferes with visualization processing because to its poor performance. Our results seem to confirm this suggestion, by showing that this intervention generated significant additional visual work (i.e., increased sum measures and gaze transitions). It is interesting to note that, even though in [1] Avg.Ref.Line is comparable to No Intervention in terms of task performance, pairwise comparisons also indicated that the three gaze components values for No Intervention are significantly lower than Avg.Ref.Line, and are in fact more comparable to the other 3 interventions. Thus, it appears that for No Interventions, users still perform poorly, but not because of visual distraction. Since no other significant results were found based on the interventions, this eye-gaze analysis cannot account for why [1] found that three of the interventions were better than No Intervention.

5.3   Impact of TaskType on AOI Processing

In this subsection, we report the most compelling results relating exclusively to main effects of TaskType. These results are interesting because under some conditions, an adaptive system may not have reliable information on its user's cognitive abilities. Our results show that gaze behavior may help an adaptive system ascertain the complexity of the task at hand (e.g., easier vs. harder task), which by itself can be a valuable basis for providing adaptive support.

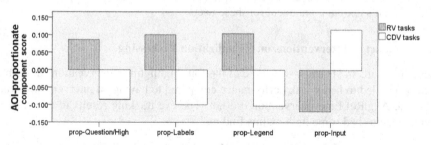

Fig. 6. Main effect of TaskType on four of the five AOI-proportionate family components

There are significant main effects of TaskType on four of the five components from the AOI-proportionate family (Fig. 6). For three of these components: *prop-Question/High* ($R^2 = .133$), *prop-Labels* ($R^2 = .305$), and *prop-Legend* ($R^2 = .149$); values are higher for easier (RV) than for harder (CDV) tasks. Recall that the *prop-Question/High* component includes 'High' AOI features with a negative correlation (see Table 2) implying that the less time a users spends in the 'Question' AOI, the more time they spent in the 'High' AOI. Thus in terms of attention to the corresponding AOIs, these effects indicate that when performing harder tasks, users spend less time (in proportion) in the 'Legend', 'Label', and 'Question' AOIs, and more time in the 'High' AOI. This result is quite intuitive considering that this is the region were the actual data values are displayed, and thus users may need more time to process this information for more complex tasks. Adaptive interventions like the ones targeted in these papers may help alleviate this problem. For the fourth component: *prop-Input*

(R^2 = .114), values increase during harder tasks, indicating that for these tasks users also devote a higher proportion of their attention to the 'Input' AOI, as they do for the 'High' AOI. These findings offer further evidence that the response input region may play an important role in supporting optimal user performance, thus making it worthwhile to investigate forms of adaptations that target not only user differences (as discussed in a previous section), but also task complexity.

6   Conclusions and Future Work

We presented an analysis of user gaze data to understand if and how user characteristics impact visual processing of bar charts in the presence of different highlighting interventions designed to facilitate visualization usage. We then linked these results to task performance, obtained from a previous study, in order to provide insights on how to design user-adaptive information visualization systems.

Our first research question (Q1) asked if and how our tested sets of user differences, highlighting interventions, and task complexity impact gaze behavior during bar graph visualization processing. We found several positive answers. For instance, with harder tasks, users with low perceptual speed (PS) spent more time processing the 'Label' AOI, whereas users with low visualWM spent more time looking at the 'Input' AOI and transitioning between that AOI and other parts of the screen. Similarly, users with low verbalWM spend more time processing some of the textual elements of the graph. Similar results for PS were obtained in [8], however, the findings related to verbalWM and visualWM are unique of our work. All users, regardless of cognitive abilities, spent more time processing the 'High' AOI as well as the 'Input' AOI when dealing with harder tasks. As for the highlighting interventions, Avg.Ref.Line caused significantly more transitions as well as an increase in fixations and saccades.

Our second research question (Q2) asked how the above findings can be related to user performance results reported in [1], and the implications for adaptive visualizations. We found that most of our significant effects on gaze behaviors mirrored effects found on task performance in [1], allowing us to explain poor performance in terms of both specific gaze patterns, as well as the user differences that caused them. These connections indicate several new avenues of investigation for adaptive interventions, in addition to those discussed, for instance, in [8]. In particular, adaptive support may benefit users with low visualWM on harder tasks by targeting the input regions of bar graphs. Low verbalWM users may benefit from interventions that facilitate processing the textual information related to the task questions and legend. We also discussed evidence as to why the Avg.Ref.Line intervention was distracting and did not improve performance, which provides preliminary abstract guidelines on what constitutes a distraction (e.g., increased Sum-Measures and AOI-transitions).

In future work, we will evaluate pupil dilation data from the same study to understand how the study factors and user differences affect cognitive load. We will also design and evaluate adaptive interventions based on the results in this paper (e.g., various types of support for the input AOI and labels AOI).

References

1. Carenini, G., et al.: Highlighting Interventions and User Differences: Informing Adaptive Information Visualization Support. In: CHI 2014 (2014)
2. Conati, C., Maclaren, H.: Exploring the role of individual differences in information visualization. In: AVI 2008, pp. 199–206 (2008)
3. Green, T.M., Fisher, B.: Impact of personality factors on interface interaction and the development of user profiles. Information Visualization (2012)
4. Toker, D., Conati, C., Carenini, G., Haraty, M.: Towards adaptive information visualization: On the influence of user characteristics. In: Masthoff, J., Mobasher, B., Desmarais, M.C., Nkambou, R. (eds.) UMAP 2012. LNCS, vol. 7379, pp. 274–285. Springer, Heidelberg (2012)
5. Velez, M.C., Silver, D., Tremaine, M.: Understanding visualization through spatial ability differences. In: IEEE Visualization, VIS 2005, pp. 511–518 (2005)
6. Gotz, D., Wen, Z.: Behavior-driven visualization recommendation. In: IUI 2009 (2009)
7. Grawemeyer, B.: Evaluation of ERST – an external representation selection tutor. In: Barker-Plummer, D., Cox, R., Swoboda, N. (eds.) Diagrams 2006. LNCS (LNAI), vol. 4045, pp. 154–167. Springer, Heidelberg (2006)
8. Toker, D., et al.: Individual user characteristics and information visualization: connecting the dots through eye tracking. In: CHI 2013, pp. 295–304 (2013)
9. Grindinger, T., Duchowski, A.T., Sawyer, M.: Group-wise similarity and classification of aggregate scanpaths. In: ETRA 2010, pp. 101–104 (2010)
10. Steichen, B., et al.: Inferring Visualization Task Properties, User Performance, and User Cognitive Abilities from Gaze Data. Trans. on Intelligent Interactive Systems IIS (2014)
11. Toker, D., et al.: Towards facilitating user skill acquisition - Identifying untrained visualization users through eye tracking. In: IUI 2014 (2014)
12. Tai, R.H., et al.: An exploration of the use of eye-gaze tracking to study problem-solving on standardized science assessments. Int. J. of Research & Method in Education (2006)
13. Tang, H., et al.: Permutation test for groups of scanpaths using normalized Levenshtein distances and application in NMR questions. In: ETRA 2012, pp. 169–172 (2012)
14. Kules, B., Capra, R.: Influence of training and stage of search on gaze behavior in a library catalog faceted search interface. J. of the Amer. Soc. for Inf. Sci. and Tech. (2012)
15. Amar, R., et al.: Low-Level Components of Analytic Activity in Information Visualization. In: IEEE Symposium on Information Visualization, pp. 15–21 (2005)
16. Few, S.: Now you see it: simple visualization techniques for quantitative analysis. Analytics Press, Oakland (2009)
17. Ekstrom, R.B., Research, U.S.O. of N.: Manual for Kit of Factor Referenced Cognitive Tests. Educational Testing Service (1976)
18. Fukuda, K., Vogel, E.K.: Human Variation in Overriding Attentional Capture. J. Neurosci. 29, 8726–8733 (2009)
19. Turner, M.L., Engle, R.W.: Is working memory capacity task dependent? Journal of Memory and Language 28, 127–154 (1989)
20. Goldberg, J.H., Helfman, J.I.: Comparing information graphics: a critical look at eye tracking. In: BELIV 2010 Workshop, pp. 71–78 (2010)
21. Field, A.P.: Discovering statistics using SPSS. SAGE (2009)

Evil Twins: Modeling Power Users in Attacks on Recommender Systems

David C. Wilson and Carlos E. Seminario

University of North Carolina at Charlotte
Charlotte, North Carolina, USA
{davils@uncc.edu, cseminar@uncc.edu}

Abstract. Attacks on Collaborative Filtering Recommender Systems (RS) can bias recommendations, potentially causing users to distrust results and the overall system. Attackers constantly innovate, and understanding the implications of novel attack vectors on system robustness is important for designers and operators. Foundational research on attacks in RSs studied attack user profiles based on straightforward models such as random or average ratings data. We are studying a novel category of attack based explicitly on measures of influence, in particular the potential impact of high-influence *power users*. This paper describes our approach to generate synthetic attack profiles that emulate influence characteristics of real power users, and it studies the impact of attack vectors that use synthetic power user profiles. We evaluate both the quality of synthetic power user profiles and the effectiveness of the attack, on both user-based and matrix-factorization-based recommender systems. Results show that synthetic user profiles that model real power users are an effective way of attacking collaborative recommender systems.

Keywords: Recommender Systems, Power User, Attacks, Evaluation.

1 Introduction

Recommender systems help to support users in finding information or items, typically by aligning the active user's preference information with preference information from the community of system users. And these systems are subject to attack by unscrupulous users who enter false information in order to "game the system" for their own ends — promoting their own items ("push"), demoting competitors ("nuke"), or simply disrupting the system itself. As is common with enterprise security breaches, recommender system operators tend not to discuss or disclose successful attacks on their systems. But we know that attacks do occur and take on a variety of forms including fake reviews and opinion spam.[1] Attacks on ratings-based Collaborative Filtering (CF) Recommender Systems (RS) bias predictions and recommendations, potentially corrupting the system dataset and causing users to distrust the results and the system. Most RS attack

---

[1] For example see, http://www.reuters.com/article/2013/09/23/us-fake-reviewers-idUSBRE98M0YU20130923

V. Dimitrova et al. (Eds.): UMAP 2014, LNCS 8538, pp. 231–242, 2014.
© Springer International Publishing Switzerland 2014

research has examined similarity-focused statistical models of user ratings, such as random and average hypothetical users; and attack detection techniques have been developed based on these models of rating behavior[1–3]. However, because attackers constantly find new ways to attack, understanding the implications of novel attack vectors on system robustness is important for designers and operators. Our main research question asks: what happens when malicious users shift to influence-based attacks modeled after real, influential *power users*?

We are studying a novel category of RS attack based explicitly on measures of influence, in particular the potential impact of high-influence, or power users. Power users in the RS context are those that are able to influence the largest group of RS users; influence is indicated by the ability of power user i to change (positively or negatively) the RS prediction for another user j, or for power user i's target item to appear in user j's top-N list. Measures of influence have been studied extensively in Social Network Analysis, demonstrating that being central in a network indicates person(s) of high prestige and visibility that are influential in the spread of ideas and opinions [4]. Viral Marketing finds that users who are well connected to other users are better able to exert influence on them, especially for new items [5, 6]; e.g., Amazon Vine^{TM}invites trusted reviewers to post opinions about new and pre-release items.[2] As a foundation for understanding influence based attacks, we adapt established network measures of influence to the context of RSs, in order to identify power users in the underlying dataset. In our previous work [7, 8], we identified *real power users* (RPUs) using selection methods based on network centrality, user-user similarity, and, rating behavior. We then used those RPUs to mount a Power User Attack (PUA) and found that accuracy and robustness metrics were negatively impacted for commonly used RS approaches. *For clarity, the power user attack envisioned in this research is not about having hundreds or thousands of actual power users colluding to mount an attack, rather, it is about an attacker being able to generate a set of power user profiles that, when stealthily injected into a RS, can effectively bias the recommendations.*

Knowing that a Power User Attack with RPUs can be effective, the natural next question is whether RPUs can be modeled to enable / automate the generation of completely *synthetic power user* (SPU) profiles with the same degree of impact as attack vectors. In effect, the "evil twins" of the real power users. This paper describes our approach to generate synthetic attack profiles to emulate and exploit the influence characteristics of real power users, and it studies the impact of attack vectors that employ synthetic power user profiles. Specifically, we investigate the Research Questions: (RQ1) Can SPU profiles be generated that effectively model RPUs? (RQ2) Can SPU profiles be effective in attacking RSs? The paper begins with a discussion of related work in RS attacks and measures of influence, and Section 3 provides a summary of our previous work as a foundation for the current analysis. Section 4 presents our new research for RQ1, developing and evaluating a model for synthetic power user profile generation. Section 5 goes on to examine RQ2, evaluating the effectiveness of SPU attacks

---

[2] http://www.amazon.com/gp/vine/help

on both User-based weighted [9] and Matrix-factorization-based (Singular Value Decomposition or SVD) [10–12] recommender systems. Results show that synthetic user profiles that model real power users are an effective way of attacking collaborative RSs.

2   Related Work

Attacks on RSs by providing false ratings are generally known as *profile injection attacks* [1, 3] or *shilling attacks* [2]. A recent summary [13] provides an overview of RS attack models, attack detection, and algorithm robustness. Previous work in this area has targeted the use of similarity-focused attack models that inject attack user profiles generated with: (1) random item ratings selected from a normal distribution around the mean rating of the dataset (not very effective as an attack), (2) item ratings selected from a normal distribution around the mean rating for each item (a more effective attack against neighborhood-based collaborative filtering algorithms), or (3) a variant of these [2, 3]. These approaches focus on attack coverage by broad similarity to all users or to a segment of users in the RS, but do not employ explicit measures of influence for coverage.

Power users are of particular interest to RS operators and their client companies when launching a new item, because a positive endorsement (high rating) can result in making item recommendations to many other users. This "market-based" use of RS has been previously promoted as a solution to the "cold-start" or "new item" problem [6, 14, 5]. Power users in the RS context have been referred to as users with a large number of ratings [15] as well as those that are able to influence the largest number of other users [5, 14, 6, 16].

Finding a set of power users whose product endorsement maximizes the number of other users to whom the product is recommended is an NP-hard problem to solve optimally as well as NP-hard to approximate [16, 17]. Several heuristics were analyzed by [16] in order to select groups of influential users including Most Central (those with highest aggregate similarity to other users), Most Positive (those with the highest positive average rating), Most Active (those who have rated the highest number of items), and Random (a control group comprised of randomly selected users). Their results show that the Most Central, Most Positive, and Random heuristics are comparable and provide the best set of influential power users. But power user identification work has not been examined in the context of RS attacks.

Previous research on attacks has revealed that knowledge of the underlying RS algorithms and dataset characteristics can enhance the effectiveness of an attack even though this knowledge may be difficult to obtain. But the characteristics of real, and more influential "power" users have largely been ignored. Thus influence-based vectors of attack remain an open question in RS robustness research that we continue to explore in this study.

3 Overview of Foundational Power User Attack Research

In order to study RS attacks based explicitly on measures of influence, we pre-viously defined a *Power User Attack* model as a set of power user profiles with biased ratings that influence the results presented to other users [8]. Like other attack models, PUA profiles contain the set of ratings a power user has made using the recommender system. The intent of an attack is to either promote ("push") a target item by setting the rating to the maximum value or demote ("nuke") a target item by setting the rating to the minimum value. The PUA consists of one or more user profiles containing item ratings (called attack user profiles) that push or nuke a specific item. In that work, the PUA was evaluated using user-based and item-based CF recommender algorithms.

The PUA relies critically on the method of power user identification/selection, so we also developed and evaluated a novel use of degree centrality concepts from social network analysis for identifying influential RS power users for attack pur-poses [8]. In addition, we chose to use the Most Central and Most Active heuris-tics from [16] because this would provide us with their best-case and worst-case scenarios that we could then use to compare with our degree centrality approach. The power user selection methods that we have used previously are as follows:

1. **InDegree:** Our approach based on in-degree centrality — power users par-ticipate in the highest number of neighborhoods. For each user i compute similarity with every other user j applying significance weighting $n_{cij}/50$, where n_{cij} is the number of co-rated items and 50 items was determined empirically by [18] to optimize RS accuracy; then discard all but the top-N neighbors for each user i. Count the number of similarity scores for each user j (# neighborhoods user j is in), and select the top-N user j's.
2. Aggregated Similarity (**AggSim:**) The Most Central heuristic from [16]. Top-N users with the highest aggregate similarity scores become the selected set of power users. This method requires at least 5 co-rated items between user i and user j and does not use significance weighting.[3]
3. Number of Ratings (**NumRatings:**) This method is based on [15] where "power user" refers to users with the highest number of ratings; it also is called the Most Active heuristic in [16]. We selected the top-N users based on the total number of ratings they have in their user profile.

To evaluate power user selection methods, we use an ablation approach [19, 8], where accuracy of the RS is measured as power users are removed from the dataset. If accuracy gets worse when power users are removed, the implication is that power users are impacting the RS recommendations. The intuition is that the power user selection method that is able to identify the set of users with the greatest negative impact on system accuracy is the better method. We previously reported an ablation analysis for RPUs using the MovieLens 100K, 1M, and 10M datasets for user-based, item-based, and SVD-based recommenders [8, 20, 7]. The results indicated that all three power user selection methods described above

---

[3] Based on personal communication with the authors.

show an increase in Mean Absolute Error (MAE), i.e., accuracy gets worse, as power users are removed and that this effect is stronger with the InDegree and NumRatings methods than with AggSim.

4   Power User Model

Our first research question (RQ1) is how to effectively generate synthetic power user profiles, which has two main aspects. First, we must be able to effectively identify real power users. For this study we employ the methods we have used previously (§ 3). Second, with a mechanism in place to identify real power users, the next step is to develop a generative model for synthetic power users based on the identified RPUs. This section describes our proposed new model.

Unlike classic attack models (e.g., random, average, bandwagon) that employ straightforward statistical templates (e.g., average item rating, popularity, and likability) to generate synthetic attack profile filler items [3], very little is known about the characteristics of power users. And without this knowledge, it is difficult to generate synthetic power user profiles. Therefore, we have developed a Power User Model (PUM) that can be used to generate synthetic power users (SPU) for attack purposes. We base our PUM on the primary factors considered in order to build effective RS attacks [2, 3], which include:

1. Attack size: the number of attack user profiles to be injected. A larger attack size is more effective, however, it is more easily detectable.
2. Filler size: the number of item ratings in the attack user profile, excluding the target item. A larger filler size is more effective, however, it is also more easily detectable.
3. Filler item selection: items that are likely to correlate with many other users in the system will be more effective.
4. Filler item rating: ratings that are likely to correlate with many other users in the system will be more effective.
5. Target item selection: items with few ratings are more vulnerable to attack.
6. Target item rating: on a 1-5 rating scale, use 5 for "push" attacks and 1 for "nuke" attacks

With these dimensions as guidelines, we generate synthetic user profiles in the following manner by collecting targeted statistics of identified real power users. For this initial evaluation of the PUM, we use the MovieLens 100K dataset[4] to identify/select RPU's. We then collect user, item, and neighborhood characteristics from the dataset and begin to build the power user model to generate SPU profiles:

1. Attack size: The attack size or number of profiles is an experimental design parameter and is usually expressed as a percentage of the total number of user profiles in the dataset. Previous work [3] has shown that a 5-10% attack size should be sufficient to have an impact on recommendation robustness; therefore, we use a conservative 5% attack size or 50 SPU's for this analysis.

---

[4] 100,000 ratings, 1,682 movies, 943 users, 93.7% sparsity.

2. Filler size or the number of items in each profile is an experimental design parameter and is usually expressed as a percentage of the total number of items in the dataset. Previous work [3] has shown that a 5-10% filler size should be sufficient to have an impact on recommendation robustness. However, in this study, the filler size for each profile is selected randomly from a normal distribution around the mean and standard deviation (σ) of the number of ratings in the dataset for the RPUs identified/selected by each selection method. This approach was used so that it would closely mimic the behavior of real power users. For this study, the filler size distributions varied by selection method: InDegree (μ=317.78 and σ=124.981), NumRatings (μ=395.32 and σ=93.031), and AggSim (μ=35.64 and σ=21.886).

3. Item selection is based on the average number of user ratings by item category for the RPU's identified in the dataset; for this study, the item category is popularity or the number of ratings for the item. We selected popularity as an initial approach with the intent of using other characteristics, such as likability and genre, in the future. For each power user selection method, we determined the distribution of items rated for the RPU's in five item popularity "buckets" and required each SPU profile to contain a similar distribution, as shown in Table 1. The buckets were defined taking into account that the "number of ratings" characteristic usually follows a power law wherein a large number of items have a relatively small number of ratings (i.e., the least popular movies) and a small number of items have a large number of ratings (i.e., the most popular movies):
   - Low: items with an average number of ratings
   - Medium Low: items with an average number of ratings + 1σ
   - Medium: items with an average number of ratings + 2σ
   - Medium High: items with an average number of ratings + 3σ
   - High: items with greater than average number of ratings + 3σ

Table 1. Distribution of items by popularity bucket

% items/bucket	Low	MedLow	Medium	MedHigh	High
InDegree	25.79%	32.20%	21.65%	12.52%	7.83%
NumRatings	29.86%	32.75%	19.83%	11.08%	6.48%
AggSim	14.42%	23.79%	23.63%	16.44%	21.72%

4. Item rating value for each item in the profile is selected randomly from a normal distribution around the mean and standard deviation of the average item's rating in the dataset for the RPU's identified/selected by each selection method. Our intent was for SPU's to have a rating profile similar to RPU's rather than just randomly assigning rating values. We used a normal distribution because this has been typical in RS attack research [2, 3] and because it may be the best fit given the overall average item rating for ML100K of μ=3.077 and σ=0.780 on a 1-5 scale.

4.1   Evaluating the Power User Model: Results and Discussion

For RQ1, we want to know whether SPU profiles can be generated that effectively model RPUs. For this experiment, we consider the following hypotheses:

- (1) A majority of the SPU profiles injected into a given dataset will be successfully identified by the same power user selection method used to identify the respective RPU profiles, i.e., precision and recall scores will be > 50%.
- (2) Datasets, with SPU profiles for each power user selection method, evaluated using an ablation approach will indicate a statistically significant increase in MAE as SPU profiles are removed from the dataset.
- (3) The MAE differences achieved for the power user selection methods will be comparable to what was observed when RPUs were removed from those same datasets.
- (4) Statistical characteristics of RPUs and PUM-generated SPUs will be measured and no statistically significant differences will be found between them for average number of ratings per user, average user rating, and average item rating.

To evaluate the SPU profiles (before the attack), we remove the top 50 RPU's from the original ML100K dataset using each of the three selection methods (InDegree, NumRatings, AggSim) and replace them with 50 SPU profiles to create modified ML100K datasets.[5] We remove the RPU's to see how well the 50 SPU's would replace them. Then, we identify/select the top 50 power users from the modified datasets using each of the three selection methods.

First, we use precision and recall metrics to determine the extent to which the 50 SPU's are actually selected by each method. The PUM generated SPU profiles with varying degree of success based on the power user selection method used. For InDegree, 70% of the SPU's were identified and NumRatings achieved 83% precision and recall scores, while AggSim was only able to achieve a 32% precision and recall score. Although there is no precedent for determining whether these scores are adequate or inadequate, the next two evaluation methods will also need to be considered. Hypothesis (1) is accepted for InDegree and NumRatings, rejected for AggSim, meaning that the PUM generated an acceptable number of SPU's that were successfully identified/selected by the InDegree and NumRatings methods and not the AggSim method.

Next, we look at the ablation results in Figures 1 and 2 comparing RPU (left graphs) and SPU (right graphs) behavior. We observe that as InDegree-selected SPU's are removed, MAE increases ($p < .01$ for SVD-based and $p < .05$ for User-based); for NumRatings and AggSim, MAE is either flat or decreases ($p < .02$ for decrease in SVD-based NumRatings). Hypothesis (2) is accepted for InDegree and rejected for NumRatings and AggSim, and this would indicate that InDegree-generated SPU's are more effective in influencing recommendations than the other two methods.

---

[5] NB: The desired attack size (5% of users in the dataset) is equivalent to 50 SPU's; the same number of SPU profiles are evaluated before and after the attack.

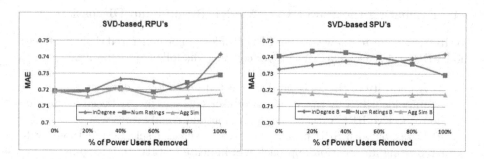

Fig. 1. MAE impacts after removing Power Users using ML100K

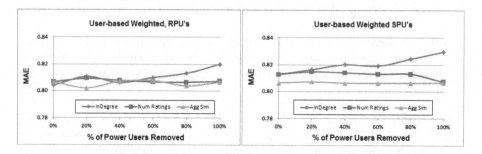

Fig. 2. MAE impacts after removing Power Users using ML100K

For SVD RPU's, MAE differences for all three methods are only significantly different from each other at 100% removal ($p < .02$). For SVD SPU's, with the exception of NumRatings at 100% removal, both InDegree and NumRatings are significantly different from AggSim ($p < .01$) at all removal levels; and there is no significant difference between InDegree and NumRatings at any level of removal. For User-based RPU's, MAE differences for all three methods are only significantly different from each other at 100% removal as follows: InDegree-NumRatings ($p < .05$), InDegree-AggSim ($p < .02$). For User-based SPU's, InDegree-AggSim are significantly different at all removal levels and InDegree-NumRatings are significantly different only at 100% removal ($p < .01$). Hypothesis (3) is rejected for SVD-based and accepted for User-based analyses. This would indicate that, in general for SPU's, InDegree and NumRatings tend to have better ablation performance than AggSim; furthermore, InDegree SPU's achieve an equal or higher MAE at 100% removal than RPU's indicating a strong level of influence for these SPU's.

Finally, when comparing statistical characteristics between SPU's and the RPU's upon which they are based, we found significant differences in user and item rating entropy as well as global rating values for SPU's across all three power user selection methods ($p < .01$). Notably, the NumRatings method was able to significantly impact the global average rating value (downward from 3.302 to 3.190) between the RPU's and SPU's groupings as well as for the full

ML100K dataset ($p < .01$ in both cases); this may help to explain the performance of the NumRatings method in the ablation study as well as in the PUA results. Hypothesis (4) is accepted for InDegree, NumRatings, and AggSim, i.e., no statistically significant differences were found between RPU's and SPU's for the key measures of average number of ratings per user, average user rating, and average item rating. This indicates that the PUM is generating SPU's that match the key statistical measures, however, work is needed to improve the user and item rating entropy measures.

5 Synthetic Power User Attack

For RQ2, we want to understand whether generated SPU profiles can be effective in attacking RSs. For this experiment, we consider the following hypotheses:

- (5) SPU profiles identified using the InDegree power user selection method will have a higher level of impact, compared to SPU profiles identified using NumRatings or AggSim, on RS predictions and top-N recommendation lists as measured with Average Hit Ratio and Average Rank robustness metrics.
- (6) A relatively small number of power users ($<=5\%$ of all users) can have significant effects on RS predictions and top-N lists of recommendations, measured with an Average Hit Ratio $> 50\%$ and Average Rank < 10.

To mount the PUA, synthetic power user profiles were generated as described in § 4 and converted to attack profiles by setting target items to the max rating. Target items were selected to simulate a 'new' item attack because this is a typical scenario in which power users are asked to provide ratings. Evaluations were performed before and after the attack using the Apache Mahout 0.8 platform[6].

Evaluation Metrics: To evaluate the PUA, we use Mean Absolute Error (MAE) and prediction coverage [15, 21] using a random holdout-partitioned 70/30 train/test dataset. We also use Hit Ratio, Prediction Shift, and Rank robustness measures [3, 13] where a high Hit Ratio and a low Rank indicates that the attack was successful (from the attacker's standpoint). Since the PUA being evaluated here is for new items (i.e., not very many ratings in the dataset), the Prediction Shift is expected to be close to the max rating defined by the RS.

Datasets and Algorithms: We used MovieLens 100K (ML100K) where each user has 20 or more ratings to avoid the 'new' user problem. The algorithms used were provided in Apache Mahout. For SVD, we used RatingStochastic-GradientDescent (RSGD); run-time parameter settings were number of features ($=100$) and number of training steps or iterations ($=50$) and were determined empirically to optimize recommender accuracy. The user-based weighted CF algorithm was used for comparative purposes.

---

[6] http://mahout.apache.org/

Power User Selection: Methods are described in § 3.

Target Item Selection: Given our objective to attack 'new' items, 50 target items with only one rating were selected randomly from the dataset.

Attack Parameter Selection: The Attack Intent is Push, i.e., target item rating is set to max (= 5). The Attack Size or number of power users in each attack was varied in this experiment: 50, 30, 10, 5, 2, and 1, where 50 power user profiles equate to a 5% attack for ML100K. The Attack profiles used were SPU profiles described in § 4 and we injected the target item rating at run time. The Filler size for each profile varied for each SPU and is described in § 4.

Test Variations: The test variations consisted of 2 prediction algorithms, one dataset, 3 power user selection methods, and 6 attack sizes. Each test variation was executed 50 times (once for each of the 50 target items) and data results were averaged over the 50 target items.

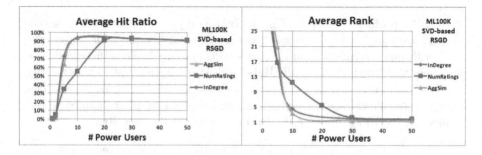

Fig. 3. ML100K – SVD-based Results

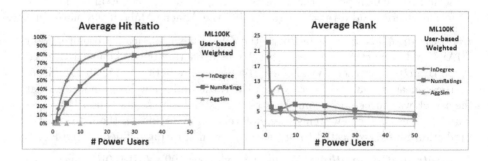

Fig. 4. ML100K – User-based Results

5.1 Evaluating the Power User Attack: Results and Discussion

The PUA on SVD in Figure 3 shows significant impacts to recommendations between 5 and 50 SPU's for InDegree, NumRatings, and AggSim. NumRatings SPU influence on Avg Hit Ratio begins to break down below 30 power users and is also evident in the Avg Rank; the difference between NumRatings and both InDegree and AggSim is significant between 5 and 30 power users ($p < .01$). The results for InDegree and AggSim, as well as the trend for NumRatings, are consistent with our previous work with attacks on SVD recommenders using RPU's [7]. Previous work on RS attacks has indicated that SVD is robust to attack [22]. However, this is the case only when attackers have been detected and removed from the recommendations; our experimentation does not remove attackers prior to generating recommendations. The PUA on User-based in Figure 4 shows significant impacts to recommendations between 10 and 50 power users for InDegree and NumRatings while AggSim is never a factor($p < .01$). These findings are consistent with our previous PUA research [8]. The InDegree-generated SPU's produces a strong set of power users, both before and after the attack; InDegree results are significantly different from NumRatings in the range of 2 to 30 power users ($p < .01$). Hypothesis (5) is rejected for SVD-based and partially accepted for User-based analyses (no difference at 50 SPU's). The interpretation of this result is that InDegree may be a more superior power user selection method than NumRatings and AggSim for User-based recommenders and that there is no clear superior power user selection method for SVD-based recommenders. Hypothesis (6) is accepted for both SVD-based and User-based analyses, meaning that a relatively small number of power users (5% or less of the user base on a given dataset) can have significant effects on RS predictions and top-N lists of recommendations regardless of power user selection method.

6 Conclusion

Power users are important to recommender systems and contribute to their improved prediction accuracy; however, we have found power user attacks that are effective against popular recommender systems. In this study we have developed a power user model that is able to generate synthetic power user profiles that, in specific configurations, can be used to mount effective power user attacks against SVD-based and User-based recommenders measured by Hit Ratio and Rank robustness metrics. We have shown that our power user model generates effective synthetic (vs. actual) power user profiles as measured with accuracy, precision, and recall metrics. We have also shown that a relatively small number of synthetic power users can have significant effects on RS predictions and top-N recommendation lists for new items. Future work includes cluster analysis of power users identified in the dataset, extending the power user model to optimize synthetic power user attack profile performance, iterating on other power user selection methods, item rating characteristics (popularity, likability, genre, etc.), and methods for estimating item ratings. We also plan to scale our analysis to other recommender algorithms, larger datasets, and additional domains.

References

1. O'Mahony, M.P., Hurley, N., Silvestre, G.C.M.: Recommender systems: Attack types and strategies. In: Proceedings of the 20th National Conference on Artificial Intelligence, AAAI 2005 (2005)

2. Lam, S.K., Riedl, J.: Shilling recommender systems for fun and profit. In: Proceedings of the 13th International Conference on World Wide Web. ACM (2004)
3. Mobasher, B., Burke, R., Bhaumik, R., Williams, C.: Toward trustworthy recommender systems: An analysis of attack models and algorithm robustness. ACM Trans. Internet Technol. (2007)
4. Wasserman, S., Faust, K.: Social Network Analysis: Methods and Applications. Cambridge University Press, New York (1994)
5. Domingos, P., Richardson, M.: Mining the network value of customers. In: Proceedings of KDD 2001. ACM (2001)
6. Anand, S.S., Griffiths, N.: A market-based approach to address the new item problem. In: Proceedings of the ACM Recommender Systems Conference (2011)
7. Seminario, C.E., Wilson, D.C.: Assessing impacts of a power user attack on a matrix factorization collaborative recommender system. In: Proceedings of the 27th Florida Artificial Intelligence Research Society Conference (to appear, 2014)
8. Wilson, D.C., Seminario, C.E.: When power users attack: assessing impacts in collaborative recommender systems. In: Proceedings of the 7th ACM Conference on Recommender Systems, RecSys 2013. ACM (2013)
9. Desrosiers, C., Karypis, G.: A comprehensive survey of neighborhood-based recommendations methods. In: Ricci, F., Rokach, L., Shapira, B., Kantor, P.B. (eds.) Recommender Systems Handbook. Springer (2011)
10. Sarwar, B.M., Karypis, G., Konstan, J.A., Riedl, J.T.: Application of dimensionality reduction in recommender system – a case study. In: ACM WEBKDD Workshop (2000)
11. Koren, Y., Bell, R., Volinsky, C.: Matrix factorization techniques for recommender systems. Computer (2009)
12. Amatriain, X., Jaimes, A., Oliver, N., Pujol, J.M.: Data mining methods for recommender systems. In: Ricci, F., et al. (eds.) Recommender Systems Handbook. Springer (2011)
13. Burke, R., O'Mahony, M.P., Hurley, N.J.: Robust collaborative recommendation. In: Ricci, F., et al. (eds.) Recommender Systems Handbook. Springer (2011)
14. Rashid, A., Karypis, G., Riedl, J.: Influence in ratings-based recommender systems: An algorithm-independent approach. In: Proceedings of the SIAM International Conference on Data Mining (2005)
15. Herlocker, J.L., Konstan, J.A., Terveen, L.G., Riedl, J.: Evaluating collaborative filtering recommender systems. ACM Transactions on Information Systems (2004)
16. Goyal, A., Lakshmanan, L.V.S.: Recmax: Exploiting recommender systems for fun and profit. In: Proceedings of KDD 2012 (2012)
17. Kempe, D., Kleinberg, J., Tardos, E.: Maximizing the spread of influence through a social network. In: Proceedings of KDD 2003 (2003)
18. Herlocker, J.L., Konstan, J.A., Borchers, A., Riedl, J.: An algorithmic framework for performing collaborative filtering. In: Proc of the ACM SIGIR Conf. (1999)
19. Lathia, N., Hailes, S., Capra, L.: knn cf: A temporal social network. In: Proceedings of the 2nd ACM Recommender Systems Conference, RecSys 2008 (2008)
20. Seminario, C.E.: Accuracy and robustness impacts of power user attacks on collaborative recommender systems. In: Proceedings of the 7th ACM Conference on Recommender systems, RecSys 2013. ACM Press, New York (2013)
21. Shani, G., Gunawardana, A.: Evaluating recommendation systems. In: Ricci, F., et al. (eds.) Recommender Systems Handbook. Springer (2011)
22. Mehta, B., Nejdl, W.: Attack resistant collaborative filtering. In: SIGIR 2008: Proceedings of the 31st Annual International ACM SIGIR Conference on Research and Development in Information Retrieval. ACM (2008)

Personality Profiling from Text:
Introducing Part-of-Speech N-Grams

William R. Wright and David N. Chin

University of Hawai'i at Mānoa
Department of Information and Computer Sciences
1680 East-West Road, POST 317, Honolulu, HI 96822 USA
{wrightwr,chin}@hawaii.edu

Abstract. A support vector machine is trained to classify the Five Factor personality of writers of free text. Writers are classified for each of the five personality dimensions as high/low with the mean personality score for each dimension used for the dividing point. Writers are also separately classified as high/medium/low with division points at one standard deviation above and below mean. The two-class average accuracy using 5-fold cross validation of 80.6% is much better than the baseline (pick most likely class) accuracy of 50%, but the 3-class accuracy is only slightly better (7.4%) than baseline because most writers fall into the medium class due to the normal distribution of personality values. Features include bag of words, essay length, word sentiment, negation count and part-of-speech n-grams. The consistently positive contribution of POS n-grams (averaging 4.8% and 5.8% for the 2/3 class cases) is analyzed in detail. The information gain for the most predictive features for each of the five personality dimensions are presented and discussed.

Keywords: personality, classifier, part-of-speech n-grams, information gain, support vector machine.

The ability to profile user personality, particularly by inferring stable personality traits given an author's available writings promises a variety of useful applications, such as in organizational management, marketing, education, and social media (e.g. dating websites). Some successful demonstrations have already been conducted [18,13]. Since personality consists of stable differences in individual behavior, accurate predictions about someone's personality can be can be used to predict their preferences and future behavior with sufficient accuracy to be very useful. It is well known that users attribute personalities to computer systems. Given knowledge of a user's personality, a natural language generation system could project a personality adapted to that of the user, such that the interactions are more effective. Language samples gathered during a dialogue between a user and such a system may offer an increasingly accurate representation of a user's personality, allowing the system to adapt with increasing accuracy.

The personality predictions are performed by training models using various machine learning algorithms, such as Naive Bayes and support vector machines

V. Dimitrova et al. (Eds.): UMAP 2014, LNCS 8538, pp. 243–253, 2014.
© Springer International Publishing Switzerland 2014

(SVMs), with features extracted from text written by a subject. Besides bag-of-words features, which are highly predictive throughout a homogenous sample but not very generalizable between populations, researchers have identified some additional features that are useful for personality inference. Word sentiment is strongly correlated to the personality of a writer [11,5], as are quantity of words and punctuation.

Despite the strength of the correlations, they are neither of sufficient magnitude to explain significant differences between individuals' behavior along the various personality dimensions, nor to predict personality with as much accuracy as could be desired. Thus the search for additional features continues. Although the field acknowledges that features with linguistic basis hold promise, little has been done to identify additional features of that nature. Meanwhile a rich set of natural language processing techniques are available for this purpose.

The search must focus on features that actually improve the accuracy of classifiers. Blindly exploring huge feature sets has its limitations: feature selection is a computationally intractable problem whose solutions become more difficult to approximate as one considers larger feature sets. Some theory to guide the search may illuminate appropriate features amongst the sea of features, and even suggest entirely new, untapped feature classes.

One appealing avenue to explore is that of part-of-speech (POS) n-grams: they describe deeply embedded grammatical structures that seem unlikely to vary for a given author [1]. One study [8] employed Dutch language part-of-speech n-grams to predict Myers-Briggs Type Indicator (MBTI) types. They were able to get improvements in accuracy beyond guessing the majority class of 1.3% (Judging vs. Perceiving), 1.4% (Feeling vs. Thinking), 8.3% (iNtuitive vs. Sensing) and 10.3% (Introversion vs. Extroversion). Unlike the Five Factor model, MBTI does have absolute divisions in its 4 dimensions, so choosing the majority class is not equivalent to choosing a random class. This study did not use bag-of-words or other features beyond lexical and POS (both fine-grained and course-grained) n-grams, so could not compare the improvements of adding POS n-grams features to other common features.

To take the effort forward, we train SVM classifiers on some texts to predict the personalities of authors. As much as possible, we replicate the features used in [15], part of a project to identify human threats within corporate networks. We offer the following contributions: we describe how to build a successful personality classifier, including feature extraction and selection. We introduce the use of POS n-grams to predict authors' Five Factor personality and quantify its contribution to improving accuracy. Finally we report our results to inform others attempting to build a personality predictor.

1   Personality and Text

Personality traits are consistent patterns in a person's behavior over time— behavior that is significant and varies between individuals. Below is a list of the five personality traits enumerated by the prevailing model of human personality (the Five Factor Model). The seminal work [6] established the generality of these dimensions. Factors I and II are considered mainly interpersonal dimensions; they describe modes of interaction with others. The factors are in approximate ascending order of the degree to which they account for individual differences. (Descriptions below adapted from [4,7].)

Factor I: *Extraversion*. The Extravert approaches the world with energy, enthusiasm, lack of inhibition and a sense of adventure, especially when it comes to social engagement.

Factor II: *Agreeableness*. The second interpersonal dimension, Agreeableness is what it sounds like, and a person can be high on Extraversion yet low on Agreeableness or any of the other dimensions.

Factor III: *Conscientiousness*. This factor describes effectiveness in performing prescribed rote, repeated activities. Also assiduous following of rules. However assessments on this trait do not generally ask questions about a person's ethics [2].

Factor IV: *Neuroticism*. Also called Emotional Stability, reversing the measure. Neurotic individuals tend to perceive events negatively, and to be very sensitive to such events, to lack confidence, and apt to cease action in the face of difficulty or to refuse action in anticipation of obstacles.

Factor V: *Openness*. This dimension is related to qualities that nurture the mind, i.e. openness to considering unfamiliar ideas and participating in new experiences.

Clearly a very telling aspect of a person's behavior is verbal. The advent of computer technology, particularly digital storage and retrieval of text allows us to examine this aspect of behavior. Simple word frequency (bag-of-words counts) along with overall stem and word counts comprise some of the most intuitive and common features extracted from text. When relevant, such as in e-mail exchanges, speech acts may predict personality (e.g. the disagreeable person is apt to repeat demands without offering a variety of other speech acts) [15], and punctuation and word sentiment certainly do [18].

2   Method

To create a predictor of personality from author text, one extracts predictive features from texts written by authors of known personalities. The known personality scores (as determined by self-report personality assessment questionnaires or human observer reports) then function as labels for supervised learning. For our data feature selection matters—skipping that step leads to failed or inferior models, notwithstanding occasional reports to the contrary from others working with different data sets.

When training for the binary classification task, one divides participants into two or more sets (discretization) for each personality dimension. Although regression of personality score is possible, perhaps even more useful for many applications, researchers tend to report their accuracy on the binary or 3-class classification task. In sequence, the typical steps, as also observed in this study, are:

- Collect text corpora from participants.
- Collect personality questionnaire scores.
- Extract predictive features from each author text.
- Perform feature selection.
- Train and test a binary classifier: Binary classification, low/high classes on each personality dimension. Techniques include SVM, Naive Bayes classifier, NN, decision tree, etc. Training and testing of the classifier is performed with stratified (meaning that so far as possible, folds contain the same proportions of instances of each class) n-fold cross validation.

A wide variety of text features have been shown to be predictive of writer personality, falling in the following categories:

- Word sentiment
- Speech acts (such as, negotiate, greet, deliver, remind)
- Punctuation (repetition, smileys)
- Bag of words
- Part of speech (POS) n-grams

We extracted all of the above, excluding speech acts, which are more relevant for e-mail messages or other text intended as direct communication between participants in an activity.

3   Experimental Details

Our participants are 2,588 university students in North America who each wrote freely, on topics of their own selection for 20 minutes in English. If a writer stopped writing, the computer would stop the clock until typing resumed. The essays span 2005 through 2008, and the average of the essay word counts is 787. Each student also took the Five Factor Inventory, a personality questionnaire [9]. To preserve anonymity, the essays and personality scores are assigned ID numbers in place of participants' names.

3.1   Features Extracted

We extracted features commonly used for personality prediction, and as well as POS n-grams. We tokenize each participant essay and extract the features of interest; some features are extracted using pre-existing tools, while others involve tools that we implemented for use in these experiments. Finally a script outputs the feature data into a format readable by WEKA [19], a suite of implemented machine learning algorithms.

Bag of words. After tokenizing each essay, we extracted the bag-of-words features, counting the frequency of words appearing in a list of the 20,000 most common words from TV and movie scripts, while excluding common names per the latest available U.S. Census data. These measures help us preserve the general usefulness of the features by denying inappropriate emphasis to unusual words or to particular people mentioned in the essays.

Essay and vocabulary size. We counted tokens and stems. For our stemmer we chose the Porter stemming algorithm, which is well specified, fast, and thoroughly tested. We implemented Martin Porter's latest revision of his specifications, which he has constantly updated on his website [12], and tested our code on the list of 30,000 test words offered there. Then we counted the stems present in each essay (disregarding duplicate appearance of words with a common stem such as "run" and "running"). This count of unique stems reflects the variety of vocabulary the author employed in an essay.

Word sentiment. We employed the sentiment polarity lexicon from UPitt [17] [10], counting positive/negative words, and word subjectivity (high/low).

Negations. We implemented our own count of negations including contractions (not, never, can't, won't, etc.)

Part of speech (POS) n-grams. Used a POS tagger, an implementation of that discussed in [16]. Among the POS features is the count of pronouns that the previous study employed (pronouns are positively correlated with the neuroticism score). We also computed the POS n-grams for n from 1 to 3.

3.2 Results of Classification and Discussion

Although Big Five personality assessments do not label people into binary classes (e.g. "Extraverted" vs. "Introverted"), binary classification of participants falling in high or low ranges on each dimension is useful in decision making applications. We arbitrarily selected the median value for each personality dimension among the our participants as the dividing point for high versus low for each personality dimension so that an equal number of participants are labeled as high versus low. The additional 3-class partitioning follows the method of [15], dividing participants into three sets (high, medium and low) whose bounds are the scores falling one standard deviation above or below the mean personality score for each personality dimension. Given the features we extracted and the known personality classes, we trained SVM classifiers to distinguish between authors falling in the high/low (2-class) and in the high/medium/low (3-class) ranges on each personality dimension. To determine whether POS n-grams improve prediction accuracy, we trained with and without POS n-grams. Training with 5-fold cross validation was conducted with LibLINEAR (an SVM with no kernel popular for text mining) linked with the Weka platform. Cross validation was performed with stratification, meaning that we selected instances for each fold in proportion to their classes: in the binary classification case this was performed with the aid of a random number generator to create a random ordering of the instances, then, as closely as possible, selecting equal numbers of instances from each class for each fold. Random sampling was used for the 3-class case, yielding folds whose instance membership reflected the sizes of the classes.

As is evident in Fig. 1 the presence of POS n-grams indeed improved the accuracy of personality prediction (Table 1 provides accuracy, precision, recall averages over 5 replications). Following [14], the significances of the improvements were calculated for a single 5-fold cross validation with the Binomial test. [14] argues that a t-test is simply the wrong test for comparing classifiers because the t-test assumes that the test sets for each "treatment" (each algorithm) are *independent* and when two algorithms are compared on the same data set, the test sets are obviously not independent. Instead [14] recommends using the Binomial test to compare the number of examples that algorithm A (in our case, the classifier without POS n-grams) got right and algorithm B (in our case, the classifier with POS n-grams) got wrong versus the number of examples that algorithm A got wrong and algorithm B got right, ignoring examples that both got right or both got wrong. All improvements of the classifier with POS n-grams over the classifier without POS n-grams were statistically significant at $p < 0.0001$ except for the 2-class Extraversion ($p = 0.186$) and the 3-class Agreeableness ($p = 0.767$). Since one study [3] suggests that erroneous conclusions can result from significance tests depending on only a single partitioning into n-folds, we also ran 50 replications of 5-fold cross validation with each repetition consisting of different partitions of the space into 5 folds, then applied the paired Student t-test separately to each 5-fold cross validation, averaged the t-values and converted this to a significance value. These significance values agree with the previous Binomial test. Table 2 summarizes all the significance scores.

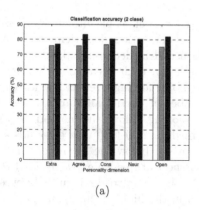 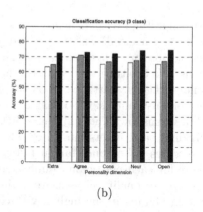

(a)   (b)

Fig. 1. Classification accuracy: 2 class and 3 class.

Baseline
Without POS n–grams
With POS n–grams

Table 1. Classification results by class (percentages)

Class Personality Dimension	Baseline	Without POS *n*-grams							With POS *n*-grams								
		Avg. accuracy avg. ±stdev	Low Precision avg. ±stdev	Low Recall avg. ±stdev	Medium Precision avg. ±stdev	Medium Recall avg. ±stdev	High Precision avg. ±stdev	High Recall avg. ±stdev	Avg. accuracy avg. ±stdev	Low Precision avg. ±stdev	Low Recall avg. ±stdev	Medium Precision avg. ±stdev	Medium Recall avg. ±stdev	High Precision avg. ±stdev	High Recall avg. ±stdev	Accuracy improvement over baseline	Accuracy improvement due to POS *n*-grams
2 Classes																	
Neuroticism	50	75.69 / 0.59	72.86 / 0.472	81.86 / 0.820	n/a	n/a	79.30 / 0.825	69.50 / 0.485	80.28 / 0.71	79.18 / 1.795	82.28 / 1.869	n/a	n/a	81.58 / 1.085	78.26 / 2.793	30.28	4.59
Extraversion	50	75.81 / 0.37	72.62 / 0.327	83.00 / 0.636	n/a	n/a	80.06 / 0.568	68.64 / 0.573	76.82 / 1.94	81.36 / 1.997	79.08 / 4.420	n/a	n/a	79.34 / 3.372	72.80 / 5.545	26.82	1.01
Conscientiousness	50	76.60 / 0.36	75.96 / 0.434	77.80 / 0.628	n/a	n/a	77.26 / 0.451	75.42 / 0.630	80.41 / 0.86	81.36 / 1.997	79.08 / 4.420	n/a	n/a	79.78 / 2.782	81.74 / 3.440	30.41	3.81
Openness	50	75.20 / 0.21	72.26 / 4.119	86.82 / 0.646	n/a	n/a	82.82 / 0.536	63.58 / 0.867	81.99 / 0.39	80.92 / 0.311	83.76 / 1.026	n/a	n/a	83.18 / 0.804	80.24 / 0.503	31.99	6.79
Agreeableness	50	75.83 / 0.41	78.98 / 0.630	70.42 / 0.383	n/a	n/a	73.30 / 0.316	81.26 / 0.702	83.36 / 0.65	84.44 / 0.654	81.78 / 1.178	n/a	n/a	82.36 / 0.913	84.92 / 0.729	33.36	7.53
3 Classes																	
Neuroticism	66.31	67.71 / 0.08	93.76 / 2.094	4.42 / 0.409	67.28 / 0.084	99.86 / 0.055	94.70 / 0.367	4.48 / 0.286	74.28 / 0.24	79.22 / 2.243	25.70 / 1.070	73.34 / 0.152	97.50 / 0.158	83.58 / 1.911	31.96 / 0.666	7.98	6.57
Extraversion	63.29	64.83 / 0.17	86.60 / 9.580	3.46 / 0.297	64.38 / 0.084	99.64 / 0.134	89.54 / 0.844	6.38 / 0.363	72.47 / 0.39	73.04 / 2.620	26.30 / 2.036	71.22 / 0.239	96.88 / 0.110	81.48 / 0.978	32.06 / 0.865	9.18	7.64
Conscientiousness	65.15	66.82 / 0.12	77.56 / 5.915	4.00 / 0.628	66.32 / 0.084	99.76 / 0.055	100.00 / 0.000	6.12 / 0.179	72.20 / 0.41	74.54 / 2.032	28.52 / 0.572	72.00 / 0.245	96.42 / 0.363	72.92 / 2.295	39.64 / 31.547	7.06	5.39
Openness	65.30	67.18 / 0.17	97.10 / 4.422	5.72 / 0.610	66.66 / 0.114	98.88 / 1.890	84.04 / 3.014	6.36 / 0.594	74.66 / 0.29	86.12 / 0.893	28.94 / 1.218	73.40 / 0.265	97.80 / 0.308	80.66 / 0.844	33.32 / 1.574	9.36	7.48
Agreeableness	69.55	71.07 / 0.14	95.66 / 0.422	6.36 / 0.650	70.74 / 0.089	99.60 / 0.122	79.54 / 5.315	5.56 / 0.559	73.04 / 1.47	56.76 / 0.090	26.20 / 0.032	76.18 / 0.008	92.82 / 0.039	60.32 / 0.123	29.26 / 0.062	3.49	1.98

Table 2. Probability of significant improvement in classifier accuracies

Personality Dimension	With vs. without POS n-grams				Without POS n-grams vs. baseline*			
	2-class		3-class		2-class		3-class	
	Binomial test	Bradford-Brodley†	Binomial test	Bradford-Brodley†	Binomial test	Bradford-Brodley†	Binomial test	Bradford-Brodley†
Extraversion	0.1860	0.4356	<0.0001	0.0001	<0.0001	<0.0001	<0.0001	<0.0001
Agreeableness	<0.0001	0.0003	0.7670	0.2762	<0.0001	<0.0001	<0.0001	<0.0001
Conscienciousness	<0.0001	0.0052	<0.0001	0.0005	<0.0001	<0.0001	<0.0001	<0.0001
Neuroticism	<0.0001	0.0044	<0.0001	0.0004	<0.0001	<0.0001	<0.0001	<0.0001
Openness	<0.0001	0.0006	<0.0001	0.0019	<0.0001	<0.0001	<0.0001	<0.0001

*The "With POS n-grams vs. baseline" case is not shown here; all probabilities are $p < 0.0001$.
†Following [14].

We repeat the use of these two tests to assess the utility of our classifiers over the baseline. Baseline predictions consist of assuming all participants fall in the majority class, which is arbitrary in the 2-class cases (the classes are of equal size) and is the medium class in the 3-class cases. In both 2-class and 3-class cases for all five personality traits, the improvement over the baseline in terms of accuracy of the SVM classifiers both with and without n-gram features were statistically significant to $p < 0.0001$ in all cases as calculated for a single 5-fold cross validation.

Given this way of dividing participants into 3 classes, the low and high classes represent participants falling at the extremes of the personality dimensions. In the case of Agreeableness, the available n-gram features are useful for predicting in which of the dichotomous 2-classes (high vs. low, i.e. Extravert vs. Introvert) participants fall. However, the features available to us do not help much in predicting which participants fall in the outer extremes: the 3-class results show no significant improvement in classifier accuracy when we conduct training with POS n-gram features included. The opposite was true with Extraversion. POS n-gram features were significantly helpful in the 3-class case, but not in the 2-class case. A plot of the errors vs. personality scores shows that the Extraversion error distribution did not change much when POS n-gram features were added. On the other hand, the Agreeableness error distribution showed much higher error rates in the medium Agreeableness region when POS n-grams were used. These errors negated the gains in the high and low regions, which collectively are smaller than the medium region.

An important goal of this project was to find new predictive features that may be generalizable to other populations. Among the features of highest predictive power (shown in Table A.1), several are already well known to indicate personality, for example the use of "me" and words with negative sentiment are positively correlated with higher neuroticism scores. The remaining features will ultimately fall in two categories: those that generalize to other populations, and those that do not. Some features, such as homework, hurricane, Arkansas and evacuate for Conscientiousness, are predictive for our participants due to their unique circumstances in time and geography. Our participants were students living near Hurricane Katrina during and soon after the event. Such features seem unlikely to generalize to populations spanning more varied geography and chronology. Others seem promising, such as "fascinating" and "lesbian", both of which bear positive correlations with Openness scores.

Among POS n-gram features, of interest is the (ADV ADJ to) collocation, wherein adverbs modify adjectives. Table 3, examples 4, 5 and 6 show "so" and "extremely" employed as intensifiers. One explanation may be that gregarious extraverts are apt to pile on words to drive their point home, rather than to deliberate about the choice of perhaps a stronger verb—or simply to speak in less emphatic terms. Features such as these may persist across time and other circumstances, rendering them useful for personality prediction among various populations.

Table 3. POS n-gram examples

Ex.													
(1) that's	a	bad	habit N	I PRO	need	to	work	on	,	procrastination	.		
(2) SAE's are	so	damn	arrogant	and	have	nothing	to	be	arrogant ADJ	about PREP	. PERIOD		
(3) two	faces	that	can	be	perceived	as	kissing	or	just	looking 	at	you	dead on . ADJ PREP PERIOD
(4) I	am	so ADV	excited ADJ	to to	be	done	with	school!					
(5) It's	so ADV	funny ADJ	to to	me	.								
(6) After	a	busy	and	funfilled	weekend	it	is	extremely ADV	boring ADJ	to to	sit	in front of a computer

4 Conclusion

Since their presence during training significantly improved classification test results, indeed for this population grammatical structures as represented by POS n-grams are indicative of writer personality. Their consistency over the lifetime of a writer should render them useful for personality prediction among a variety of populations. In addition to the grammatical features, a few bag-of-words features emerge as possibly generalizable.

5 Future Work

It may be possible to extend this work by including coarse-grained parts of speech (e.g. noun phrases) extracted by chunking tools. Adjustments in the feature selection methodology may improve the general usefulness of the resulting classifiers, reducing the nuisance of features that are only predictive of the current population or sample. Further testing of promising features may establish their generalizability to a variety of populations. Lastly, compelling explanations of why particular POS n-grams are indicative of personality would be of great interest in directing the exploration of new text features useful for personality prediction.

Acknowledgment. We extend grateful thanks to James W. Pennebaker for making this research possible by sharing the essays and personality scores.

References

1. Argamon., S., et al.: Stylistic text classification using functional lexical features. Journal of the American Society for Information Science and Technology 58(6), 802–822 (2007)
2. Block, J.: The five-factor framing of personality and beyond: Some ruminations. Psychological Inquiry 21(1), 2–25 (2010)
3. Bradford, J.P., Brodley, C.E.: The effect of instance-space partition on significance. Machine Learning 42(3), 269–286 (2001)
4. Costa, P.T., McCrae, R.R.: Neo PI-R professional manual. Psychological Assessment Resources 396, 653–665 (1992)
5. Golbeck, J., et al.: Predicting personality from twitter. In: 3rd International Conference on Social Computing, pp. 149–156. IEEE (2011)
6. Goldberg, L.R.: An alternative description of personality: the big-five factor structure. Journal of Personality and Social Psychology 59(6), 1216 (1990)
7. John, O.P., et al.: Handbook of personality: theory and research. The Guilford Press (2008)
8. Luyckx, K., Daelemans, W.: Using syntactic features to predict author personality from text. In: Proceedings of Digital Humanities 2008 (DH 2008), pp. 146–149 (2008)
9. McCrae, R.R., et al.: The NEO–PI–3: A more readable revised NEO personality inventory. Journal of Personality Assessment 84(3), 261–270 (2005)
10. http://mpqa.cs.pitt.edu/ (retrieved October 2013)
11. Pennebaker, J.W., King, L.A.: Linguistic styles: language use as an individual difference. Journal of Personality and Social Psychology 77(6), 1296 (1999)
12. Porter, M.: The English (Porter2) stemming algorithm (2006), http://snowball.tartarus.org/algorithms/english/stemmer.html (Online; accessed March 2, 2013)
13. Roshchina, A., et al.: User Profile Construction in the TWIN Personalitybased Recommender System. In: Sentiment Analysis where AI meets Psychology (SAAIP), p. 73 (2011)
14. Salzberg, S.L., Fayyad, U.: On Comparing Classifiers: Pitfalls to Avoid and a Recommended Approach. Data Mining and Knowledge Discovery, 317–328 (1997)
15. Shen, J., Brdiczka, O., Liu, J.: Understanding Email Writers: Personality Prediction from Email Messages. In: Carberry, S., Weibelzahl, S., Micarelli, A., Semeraro, G. (eds.) UMAP 2013. LNCS, vol. 7899, pp. 318–330. Springer, Heidelberg (2013)
16. Toutanova, K., et al.: Feature-rich part-of-speech tagging with a cyclic dependency network. In: Proceedings, Conference on Human Language Technology, pp. 173–180. Association for Computational Linguistics (2003)
17. Wilson, T., et al.: Recognizing contextual polarity in phrase-level sentiment analysis. In: Proceedings of the Conference on Human Language Technology and Empirical Methods in Natural Language Processing, pp. 347–354. Association for Computational Linguistics (2005)
18. Wright, W.: Literature Review, http://www2.hawaii.edu/~wrightwr/WilliamWright/_literature/_review.pdf (Online; accessed March 2, 2013)
19. http://www.cs.waikato.ac.nz/ml/weka/ (retrieved October 2013)

A   Appendix Tables

Table A.1. The 15 most predictive features for each personality dimension. *IG* is Information Gain.

	$IG \cdot 10^2$	Category	Feature		$IG \cdot 10^2$	Category	Feature
Extraversion	0.834	POS *n*-gram	N PRO	**Conscientiousness (cont.)**	0.582	Word sentiment	weaksubj
	0.670	Bag-of-words	tonight		0.570	Bag-of-words	excited
	0.596	Bag-of-words	we		0.509	Bag-of-words	homework
	0.595	Bag-of-words	yay		0.491	Bag-of-words	arkansas
	0.575	POS *n*-gram	MOD ADV N		0.489	Bag-of-words	nice
	0.572	Bag-of-words	out		0.483	Bag-of-words	evacuate
	0.552	Bag-of-words	have		0.466	POS *n*-gram	ADJ to VB
	0.551	Bag-of-words	all	**Neuroticism**	0.658	Word sentiment	negative
	0.551	POS *n*-gram	ADV ADJ to		0.582	POS *n*-gram	N CC WADV
	0.526	POS *n*-gram	PREP PRO		0.544	Bag-of-words	and
	0.525	POS *n*-gram	WADV PROP		0.523	POS *n*-gram	VBP ADJ
	0.511	POS *n*-gram	VBZ PRO N		0.508	POS *n*-gram	COMMA NS VBP
	0.504	Bag-of-words	am		0.485	Bag-of-words	feel
	0.494	POS *n*-gram	VBG to		0.484	Bag-of-words	things
	0.482	POS *n*-gram	N PRO VBP		0.468	Bag-of-words	game
Agreeableness	0.669	POS	NS		0.465	POS *n*-gram	PARENS PREP ADJ
	0.601	POS *n*-gram	ADJ PREP PERIOD		0.464	Bag-of-words	im
	0.591	Bag-of-words	family		0.464	POS *n*-gram	PRO VBP COMMA
	0.585	Bag-of-words	mom		0.463	POS *n*-gram	PRO VBP ADJ
	0.567	POS *n*-gram	PREP PRO CC		0.455	Bag-of-words	saturday
	0.563	POS *n*-gram	VBP ADV ADJ		0.454	Bag-of-words	me
	0.525	Bag-of-words	me		0.450	Bag-of-words	everything
	0.437	POS *n*-gram	WDT VBZ WADV	**Openness**	0.486	POS *n*-gram	ADV VB NS
	0.428	POS *n*-gram	ADJ PERIOD PRO		0.465	POS *n*-gram	CC PREP ADV
	0.428	POS *n*-gram	PREP NP WADV		0.465	Bag-of-words	lesbian
	0.426	Bag-of-words	billions		0.443	POS *n*-gram	VBN PROP NS
	0.426	POS *n*-gram	VBD ADJR PRO		0.438	Bag-of-words	please
	0.426	Bag-of-words	italian		0.435	POS *n*-gram	PERIOD CC VBP
	0.412	POS *n*-gram	PROP NS		0.435	POS *n*-gram	VBP COMMA WADV
	0.410	Bag-of-words	patient		0.427	POS *n*-gram	to N
Conscientiousness	1.014	Bag-of-words	hurricane		0.426	POS *n*-gram	PROP ADJS CC
	0.744	POS *n*-gram	PROP N		0.426	POS *n*-gram	N VBD PREP
	0.693	Bag-of-words	mom		0.412	POS *n*-gram	VB COMMA WADV
	0.625	Bag-of-words	go		0.408	Bag-of-words	fascinating
	0.617	POS *n*-gram	ADJ to		0.398	POS *n*-gram	VBD CD NS
	0.602	Bag-of-words	goodness		0.387	Bag-of-words	determine
	0.601	Bag-of-words	week		0.387	Bag-of-words	cursed
	0.582	POS *n*-gram	RP ADV PRO				

Note: An index defining each POS tag is available online: http://www.williamwright.info/downloads/pos_tags.pdf

Collaborative Compound Critiquing

Haoran Xie, Li Chen, and Feng Wang

Department of Computer Science, Hong Kong Baptist University
hrxie2@gmail.com, {lichen,fwang}@comp.hkbu.edu.hk

Abstract. Critiquing-based recommender systems offer users a conversational paradigm to provide their feedback, named *critiques*, during the process of viewing the current recommendation. In this way, the system is able to learn and adapt to the users' preferences more precisely so that better recommendation could be returned in the subsequent iteration. Moreover, recent works on experience-based critiquing have suggested the power of improving the recommendation efficiency by making use of relevant sessions from other users' histories so as to save the active user's interaction effort. In this paper, we present a novel approach to processing the history data and apply it to the compound critiquing system. Specifically, we develop a history-aware collaborative compound critiquing method based on preference-based compound critique generation and graph-based similar session identification. Through experiments on two data sets, we validate the outperforming efficiency of our proposed method in comparison to the other experience-based methods. In addition, we verify that incorporating user histories into compound critiquing system can be significantly more effective than the corresponding unit critiquing system.

Keywords: Conversational recommender systems, history-aware compound critiquing.

1 Introduction

Product recommender systems (RS) have become critical part of many online e-commerce systems as they can assist users in effectively navigating through the large product space for making accurate choices. Specifically, critiquing-based recommender systems offer users a conversational paradigm to provide their feedback to the current recommendation, named *critiques* (e.g., "slower CPU" or "cheaper price" to a laptop), so as for the system to be able to refine its understanding of users' needs and return better recommendation to them in the next cycle [6]. Particularly, it has been found that such kind of system is highly competent to support users in revising and completing preferences in the high-risk product domains (such as cars, laptops, houses) given that users are often unable to fully state their preferences at the start due to the unfamiliarity with the products [1]. Prior works showed that a certain amount of conversational cycles is often required till the user locates her/his target choice [15,16]. The most critical question is then how to minimize users' interaction effort, without

V. Dimitrova et al. (Eds.): UMAP 2014, LNCS 8538, pp. 254–265, 2014.

compromising the decision accuracy that they can obtain by using the critiquing-based RS.

Recently, some researchers have attempted to utilize other users' critiquing histories to serve the current user. For example, in [13], the relevant historical sessions between other users and the current user are identified according to the number of their overlapping critiques, and then the accepted items in similar sessions will be considered for recommending to the current user. Later, this *experience-based* approach has been improved by incorporating the compatibility score [13] and item similarity [17]. However, there are two main limitations of these related works: 1) they neglect the sequence of items/critiques in identifying similar sessions; 2) they are applied to unit critiquing system only. Indeed, from the aspect of critiquing unit, there are two major types of critiquing-based RS: *unit critiquing* and *compound critiquing* [6]. In the former system (e.g., FindMe [3]), users are allowed to critique a single attribute at a time, like "faster processor" or "cheaper" to an example laptop, while in the compound critiquing system, each critique can be a combination of multiple unit critiques which operates over multiple attributes simultaneously (e.g., "different manufacture, lower processor speed and cheaper") [15]. The experiment done in [16,12] showed that the total number of recommendation cycles can significantly decrease when users selected the compound critiques. It is hence meaningful to study how to incorporate other users' critiquing histories into the standard compound critiquing system, so as to further save the current user's interaction effort.

Therefore, in this paper, we present a novel approach, named *collaborative compound critiquing*, to achieve the above-mentioned goal. From the perspective of method improvement, rather than simply counting the overlapping critiques among users' sessions, we develop a graph-based similarity measure to identify similar sessions based on other users' critiquing history data. Moreover, a new product ranking function is proposed by taking sub-session similarity into consideration. In the experiments, we compared our method with related approaches in both compound and unit critiquing systems. The results show that our method can significantly outperform the existing approaches.

The remainder of this paper is structured as follows. In Section 2, we review the related researches about critiquing-based recommender systems. Our proposed methodology is introduced in Section 3, which is divided into subsections including *compound critique generation, similar session identification,* and *item recommendation*. The experiment setup and results analysis are given in Section 4. We finally summarize this research and indicate its future research directions in Section 5.

2   Related Work

In this section, we review the related work from two aspects: critiquing unit and critiquing history-awareness. Note that the mentioned works all aim to suggest a set of critiques to the currently recommended item during each interaction cycle for users to select. The user-selected critique is then taken as feedback for the system to recommend a new item in the next cycle.

As mentioned before, there are two major kinds of **critiquing unit** in current critiquing-based recommender systems: *unit critiquing* and *compound critiquing*. The unit critiquing refers to a simple quantity or quality based feedback on a single attribute. According to [10], some users are willing to make unit critiques due to the simplicity and low cognitive load that they consume. FindMe system was the first well-known unit critiquing system [3]. It uses knowledge about the product domain to help users navigate through the multi-dimensional space, by proposing several pre-designed unit critiques (e.g., "cheaper", "bigger", and "nicer") which are called "tweaks" in their system, for users to select [3]. When a user finds the current recommendation short of her/his expectation and responds to a tweak, the remaining candidates will be filtered to leave only those candidates satisfying this tweak. In another related system ATA (Automated Travel Assistant), two *extrema*, i.e., the cheapest trip and the best non-stop trip, are suggested to the user [8].

However, considering that the unit critiques might mislead users that individual features are independent and hence make them be engaged in unnecessary cycles when searching for their desired product [4], Dynamic Critiquing proposed to generate a set of compound critiques, each of which operates over multiple attributes simultaneously (e.g., "different Manufacture, lower processor speed and cheaper") [15,11]. With such compound critique, users can see which attributes are highly dependent between each other. The compound critiques are concretely computed by discovering the recurring sets of unit differences between the currently recommended item and the remaining products through association rule mining [15]. Zhang and Pu [18] further improved this approach by adapting the generation and selection of compound critiques to users' preferences which are modeled based on Multi-Attribute Utility Theory (MAUT) [7]. In comparison, Preference-based Organization technique [5] can be considered as a combination of the advantages of Dynamic Critiquing [15] and MAUT-based compound critiques [18]. It can not only dynamically generate critiques adaptive to users' MAUT-based preference model, but also apply the association rule mining tool to discover compound critiques being representative of the remaining dataset. In addition, the critiques and their contained products are diversified so as to assist users in refining and accumulating their preferences more effectively.

From the aspect of **critiquing history-awareness**, some researchers have recently attempted to reuse past users' critiquing histories to serve the current user, so as to save her/his interaction effort. For example, in [13], considering that the critiquing histories might carry valuable information about other users' attribute preferences, they proposed the *experience-based critiquing* to harness these histories to guide the critiquing process for the current user. [9] further improved this work when selecting items as recommendation candidates, which include not only ones finally accepted by like-minded users who have critiquing sessions relevant to the current user, but also the items recommended during these sessions. More lately, [17] incorporated the item similarity between two sessions into discovering similar sessions, which gained better performance than the other approaches in terms of cycle reduction. However, these approaches mainly focus on improving unit critiquing system. Their methods are also limited in taking into account the sequential relationship between items/critiques in one session when identifying similar sessions.

3   Methodology

Research Problem Formulation. We focus on the research problem of how to realize *collaborative compound critiquing*. Formally, it can be modeled as a mapping function θ:

$$\theta : I \times Q \times S \to R \tag{1}$$

where I is the set of all items in the system, Q is the current critiquing session, S is the set of critiquing sessions from other users, and R is the set of ranking scores over all items. In each interaction cycle, the system will recommend the item with the highest ranking score. The process continues until the user accepts one item as the final choice. Specifically, the procedure of computing recommendation contains three sub-processes (see Figure 1): *compound critique generation*, *similar session identification*, and *item recommendation*. In the following, we will in detail describe how each sub-process is conducted in our system.

Compound Critique Generation. Because the Preference-based Organization technique [5] was demonstrated achieving the highest critique prediction accuracy and recommendation accuracy relative to the other compound critique generation approaches, in this work, we aim to enhance this compound critiquing system by incorporating other users' critiquing histories. The definition of compound critique in such system is as follows.

Definition 1. *(Compound Critique). The compound critique, denoted as C_i, is an element in the power set of all elemental (unit) critiques, i.e., $C_i \in \mathcal{P}(\mathbb{C})$, where $c_n \in \mathbb{C}$ is a triplet in the form of attribute, operator, and value:*

$$c_n = (attribute_n, operator_n, value_n)$$

where $attribute_n$ is the attribute (category) for critiquing, $operator_n$ is an element in the operator set $\{=, \neq, >, <\}^1$, and $value_n$ is the value for the operator. Note that each element c_n in a compound critique C_i is a unit critique. An example of compound critique for the laptop is "CPU speed $> 2.30GHz$; price $< HK\$6000$", which is formed of two unit critiques.

The preference-based organization technique [5] is composed of two main steps. Firstly, a set of frequently occurring attribute sets ($attribute_n$, $operator_n$, $value_n$) (where the *value* is of the current recommendation) among items in the remaining dataset are discovered by the association rule mining Aprior algorithm, which are then taken as the critique candidates. Next, each candidate is computed with a score via the function ϕ:

$$\phi(C_i) = U(C_i) \times D(C_i, SC) \tag{2}$$

---

[1] $=, >, <$ are used for numerical attributes, and $=, \neq$ are for categorical ones.

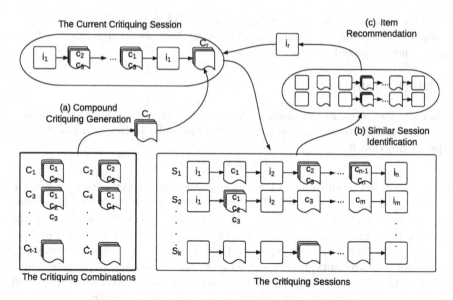

Fig. 1. The framework of our proposed *collaborative compound critiquing* system.

which takes into account both tradeoff utility $U(C_i)$ of the currently considered critique candidate C_i and its diversity with the critiques selected so far $D(C_i, SC)$. Specifically, the utility function U is defined as:

$$U(C_i) = \sum_{n=1}^{|C_i|} (\alpha_n * w(attribute_n)) \times \frac{1}{SR(C_i)} \sum_{i \in SR(C_i)}^{|SR(C_i)|} u(i) \qquad (3)$$

where each unit critique in C_i is associated with a trade-off parameter α_n set as default value 0.75 if better than the current recommendation's attribute value, or 0.25 if worse, and w is the attribute's relative importance. $\frac{1}{SR(C_i)} \sum_{i \in SR(C_i)}^{|SR(C_i)|} u(i)$ is the average utility of all items $SR(C_i)$ that satisfy C_i. The utility of each item $u(i)$ is calculated based on the Multi-Attribute Utility Theory [7]. Due to space limit, more details can be referred to our earlier work [5].

The critique candidates with the highest ϕ scores are presented to the user, as the critique suggestions. Once the user selects a critique, the user's preferences (i.e., the weights and value functions placed on critiqued attributes) are accordingly refined. The system will then recommend a new item to the user in the next cycle. In the original preference-based organization system, the product that is with the highest utility as well as satisfying the user selected critique is recommended. However, it did not consider other users' history data, which motivates us to propose the following history-aware approach.

Similar Session Identification. Similar to related history-aware (also called experience-based) approaches [9,13,17], we also aim to incorporate *experiences* from past users, but the difference lies in the measurement of similar sessions. In our approach, each critiquing session is defined as a *sequence* of critiques (along with the critiqued items) made by a user during her/his interaction with the system.

Definition 2. *(Critiquing Session). The critiquing session, denoted as s_k, is a sequential vector with the recommended item $i_{x,k}$ and the compound critique $C_{x,k}$ of each cycle:*

$$s_k =< i_{1,k}, C_{1,k}; i_{2,k}, C_{2,k}; ...; i_{n,k}, C_{n,k} >$$

where $C_{x,k}$ is the compound critique made on item $i_{x,k}$, $C_{n,k} = \emptyset$ since the item $i_{n,k}$ is the final choice made by the user in that session, and n is the total number of critiquing cycles that the user consumes.

The purpose of similar session identification is then to identify whether two critiquing sessions are similar, for which the definition of proper similarity measure is crucial. In [9,13], $OverlapScore$, which gives the number of overlapping critiques between two sessions, was used to measure their similarity. [17] improved this metric by taking into account items' similarity as well:

$$Sim(s_i, s_j) = \beta \times ItemSim(s_i, s_j) + (1 - \beta) \times OverlapScore(s_i, s_j) \quad (4)$$

where $ItemSim(s_i, s_j)$ is the average similarity between all items in two sessions s_i and s_j (i.e., $\frac{\sum_{i' \in s_i} \sum_{i^* \in s_j} Sim(i', i^*)}{|I'||I^*|})^2$, $OverlapScore(s_i, s_j)$ is the square of the number of overlapping critiques[3], and β was tuned as 0.75 in [17].

However, those similarity metrics do not consider the sequence of items/critiques that is embodied in the session. To illustrate this problem, we can take a look at the following example:

Example 1. Suppose the current critiquing session s_a is

$$s_a =< i_1, C_1; i_2, C_2 >$$

where $C_1 = \{c_1, c_2, c_3\}$ and $C_2 = \{c_4, c_5\}$. s_a can also be represented as:

$$s_a =< i_1, \{c_1, c_2, c_3\}; i_2, \{c_4, c_5\} >$$

We have two critiquing sessions S_b and S_c from other users' history data:

$$s_b =< i_1, \{c_1, c_2, c_3\}; i_2, \{c_4, c_5\}; i_3, \emptyset >$$

$$s_c =< i_1, \{c_1, c_2\}; i_2, \{c_3, c_4, c_5\}; i_4, \emptyset >$$

---

[2] $|I'|$ and $|I^*|$ are the numbers of items in s_i and s_j respectively (the finally accepted item is excluded).

[3] $OverlapScore(s_i, s_j) = [\sum_{c' \in s_i} \sum_{c^* \in s_j} match(c', c^*)]^2$; if $c' = c^*$, $match() = 1$, otherwise, $match() = 0$.

Obviously, the session s_b is more similar to session s_a than s_c (so we should recommend item i_3 for the current session), in that it contains the same critiques and items regarding the first two cycles, which are also with the same sequence, as in session s_a. However, if we adopt similarity metric Equation 4, the same similarity value will be obtained for sessions s_b and s_c, which is $\beta \times ItemSim(\{i_1, i_2\}, \{i_1, i_2\}) + (1 - \beta) \times 25$ (since there are 5 overlapping critiques: c_1, c_2, c_3, c_4 and c_5, so the square is 25). This problem is mainly caused by the fact that it neglects the sequential relationship between items/critiques. To address this problem, we propose a graph-based similarity measure. Specifically, a directed graph can be built for each critiquing session:

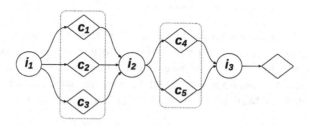

Fig. 2. The session graph built for $s_b =< i_1, \{c_1, c_2, c_3\}; i_2, \{c_4, c_5\}; i_3, \emptyset >$

Definition 3. *(Session Graph). The session graph for a critiquing session s_k, denoted as G_k, is in the form of two-tuple:*

$$G_k =< V_k, E_k > (V_k = I_k \cup C_k; E_k = E_k^{i \to c} \cup E_k^{i \leftarrow c})$$

where the vertex set $I_k = \cup_{j=1}^n i_{j,k}$ denoting all items in s_k, $C_k = \cup_{j=1}^n C_{j,k}$ which is the vertex set of all critiques contained in the session (note that each compound critique $C_{j,k}$ is composed of a set of unit critiques), and the edge set E_k includes two kinds of edge: $E_k^{i \to c}$ from an item vertex to a critique vertex (e.g., the edge from i_1 to c_1 in Figure 2), and $E_k^{i \leftarrow c}$ from a critique vertex to an item vertex (e.g., the edge from c_1 to i_2 in Figure 2).

Thus, it can be seen that the similarity metric Equation 4 takes only the graph's vertices into consideration while ignoring edges, that is why it can not distinguish sessions which are with the same vertices but different edges. The new similarity metric that we propose is given in Equation 5:

$$RSim(G_x, G_y) = \frac{|I_x \cap I_y|}{|I_x \cup I_y|} \cdot \frac{|C_x \cap C_y|}{|C_x \cup C_y|} \cdot \frac{|E_x^{i \to c} \cap E_y^{i \to c}|}{|E_x^{i \to c} \cup E_y^{i \to c}|} \cdot \frac{|E_x^{i \leftarrow c} \cap E_y^{i \leftarrow c}|}{|E_x^{i \leftarrow c} \cup E_y^{i \leftarrow c}|} \quad (5)$$

where G_x and G_y are two session graphs for critiquing sessions s_x and s_y respectively. The four considered factors are respectively item vertices, critique vertices, edges from critique to item, and edges from item to critique. To avoid zero result, we adopt $e^{RSim(G_x, G_y)}$ as the final similarity score. If we revisit Example 1 using Equation 5, $RSim(G_a, G_b) = 1$ and $RSim(G_a, G_c) = \frac{4}{9}$, which is consistent with our observation (i.e., session s_b is more similar to session s_a than s_c).

Item Recommendation. The next step is then to determine the item to be recommended for the current session. Similar to the idea suggested in [9], we consider all items contained in the most similar sessions as candidates for recommendation. However, instead of using $Compatibility(i_t, q)$ [4] as the ranking score [9], we define a R function to calculate an item's relevance to the current session:

$$R(i_t, q, S) = \underset{\forall s_k \in S}{\text{argmax}}\, e^{RSim(G(q), G(s_k^{(i_t)}))} \qquad (6)$$

where q is the current critiquing session, S is the set of similar critiquing sessions from other users, $G(s_k^{(i_t)})$ is the session graph that starts from the start till the item i_t in session s_k (i.e., $s_k^{(i_t)} = s_k - \{i_t, C_t; ...; i_{n,k}, C_{n,k}\}$), and the maximal value $e^{RSim(G(q), G(s_k^{(i_t)}))}$ is taken as item i_t's ranking score. The item with the highest ranking score will hence be recommended to the user. At this point, either the user finds her/his target choice and thus terminates her/his interaction with the system, or s/he makes further critique in order to obtain more accurate recommendation in the subsequent cycle.

4   Experiment

Data Sets and Evaluation Metrics. Two public data sets were used for evaluating our proposed method. The first one is the car data set including 406 cars each characterized by 10 attributes (3 categorical and 7 numerical attributes) [14]. Another is the laptop data set which contains 836 laptop items each with 20 attributes (12 categorical and 8 numerical attributes) [2]. To measure the efficiency of our proposed method, we use the session length (i.e., the critiquing cycles consumed for reaching the target choice) as the metric, so as to identify whether it could reduce users' interaction cycles in the pre-condition that users do not need to compromise their decision accuracy (i.e., they are still able to find their target choice at the end). To perform simulation, we adopt the leave-one-out strategy that has been commonly used in related works [13,17]. To be specific, at one time, one item was randomly withdrawn from the dataset that is called "test item", and the item most similar to it is taken as the "target choice". A subset of attribute values of the test item are treated as the simulated user's initial preferences based on which the system will return the first recommendation (which is best matching to the user's initial preferences), and generate a set of compound critiques (by the method described in Section 3 "*Compound Critique Generation*"). The critique that is most compatible with the target choice is assumed being selected by the simulated user. Then, the critiquing sessions most similar to the current session will be determined (Section 3 "*Similar Session Identification*"), and the recommendation can then be decided for the next

---

[4] $Compatibility(i_t, q)$ is the number of satisfied critiques in the current session q for the item i_t (i.e., $Compatibility(i_t, q) = |\{c_i | satisfies(i_t, c_i), c_i \in q\}|$).

cycle (Section 3 *"Item Recommendation"*). The user's preferences will also be accordingly updated for generating new critiques in the next cycle. The process continues until the target choice is reached.

Compared Methods. We compared our method (shorted as *graph-based*) to the three most related ones (as mentioned in Section 2). See Table 1 for the summary of their main differences. We applied each method in both types of critiquing systems: *unit critiquing* and *compound critiquing*. The baseline unit critiquing approach is the standard one without considering other users' history data [3], and the baseline compound critiquing approach is the original preference-based organization method [5].

Table 1. Methods for experimental comparison

Method	Short description
Experience-based [13]	*OverlapScore* for similar session identification (Footnote 3)
NN-based[a] [9]	*Compatibility* for item recommendation (Footnote 4)
History-aware [17]	*Sim*() for similar session identification (Equation 4)
Graph-based (our proposed method)	*RSim*() for similar session identification (Equation 5) and *R*() for item recommendation (Equation 6)

[a] NN is the abbreviation of 'nearest-neighbor'.

Results Analysis. The overall comparison between our proposed method and related ones can be found in Figure 3 (car dataset) and Figure 4 (laptop dataset). Note that we set $Size_{initial-pref} = 3$ (the initial preferences' size), $Size_{critiques} = 3$ (the number of unit critiques contained in each compound critique), and $Size_{base} = 406$ (the base size denoting the number of critiquing sessions from other users) for the overall comparison.

It can be seen that the results from both data sets show the similar trends: 1) all compound critiquing based methods take shorter session length than the corresponding unit critiquing based systems. The differences reach at significant level according to Student's t-test analysis ($p < 0.01$). 2) All history-aware methods are more effective than the baseline methods that do not consider other users' critiquing histories, which is valid in both unit critiquing ($p < 0.05$) and compound critiquing systems ($p < 0.01$). 3) Our proposed *graph-based* method achieves the best performance among all the compared methods for compound critiquing (e.g., with average 16.01% length reduction in car dataset and 14.25% length reduction in laptop dataset ($p < 0.05$)), which phenomenon is also valid in unit critiquing system. The results hence verify our hypothesis that considering sequential relationship between items/critiques in the critiquing session (as implemented in our *graph-based* method) can help identify similar sessions more accurately.

In Figure 5, we further show the methods' comparison in terms of recommendation accuracy on per cycle basis in an accumulated way (in the compound critiquing system with car dataset[5]). It shows that the *graph-based* method is more accurate than the others during each cycle. In addition, we can see all curves become convergent when the session length increases to 25.

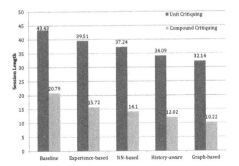

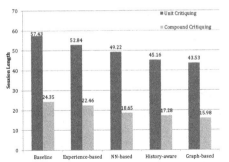

Fig. 3. Overall comparison among all methods (car dataset)

Fig. 4. Overall comparison among all methods (laptop dataset)

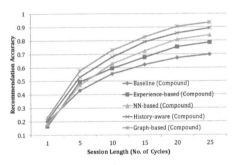

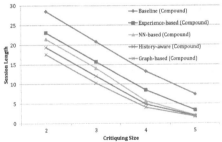

Fig. 5. Comparison w.r.t. recommendation accuracy on per cycle basis (car dataset)

Fig. 6. Comparison w.r.t. critiquing size (car dataset)

Parameter Influence. As mentioned before, there are three main parameters: $Size_{critiques}$, $Size_{initial-pref}$, and $Size_{base}$. In Figure 6, we vary $Size_{critiques}$ from 2 to 5 (since according to [5], the maximal number of attributes contained in each compound critique should be no more than 5, in order to reduce information overload to users), with $Size_{initial-pref}$ and $Size_{base}$ respectively set as 3 and 406[6]. We can find that the session length decreases when $Size_{critiques}$ is increased, as the larger critiquing size will narrow down the product space. Furthermore, to see the effect of varying the initial preferences' size $Size_{initial-pref}$,

---

[5] The results in unit critiquing system and laptop data set show the similar trends, so the figures are not shown due to space limit.

[6] This is base size set in car dataset. In laptop dataset, it is set as 836.

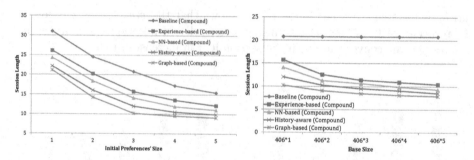

Fig. 7. Comparison w.r.t. initial preferences' size (car dataset)

Fig. 8. Comparison w.r.t. base size (car dataset)

we set it's range from 1 to 5 (which covers all sizes used in [10,13]) and the other parameters with fixed values ($Size_{critiques} = 3$ and $Size_{base} = 406$). Similarly, it can be seen in Figure 7 that the session length decreases when $Size_{initial-pref}$ increases. Moreover, as shown in Figure 8, shorter session lengths for all methods are obtained when base size $Size_{base}$ is increased from 406 to 2436 in car dataset (when $Size_{critiques} = 3$ and $Size_{initial-pref} = 3$). This is mainly because the larger base size can provide more critiquing sessions for identifying similar ones to the current session. The chance of locating the target choice from these sessions would be higher. Besides, all of the figures show that the performance of *graph-based* method can always obtain the best result relative to the other approaches no matter which parameter is varied.

5   Conclusion

In this paper, we present a *collaborative compound critiquing* approach that not only generates compound critiques based on user preferences, but also locates recommended items from other users' critiquing histories. It models the critiquing session as a directed graph, and proposes a novel *graph-based* similarity measure to identify similar sessions. To understand the new approach's efficiency in saving users' interaction efforts, we conducted experiment on two data sets to compare it with three related history-aware (also called experience-based) critiquing approaches [9,13,17]. The experimental results show that our method achieves significantly higher efficiency than all of the compared methods. Moreover, it was found that the history-aware compound critiquing systems can take shorter session length than the corresponding unit critiquing systems, and they are also more effective than the baseline systems that do not involve other users' history data.

Thus, we believe that our collaborative compound critiquing approach can well improve the efficiency of existing critiquing based recommender systems in terms of reducing users' efforts, while still allowing them to reach target choice. In the future, we will validate these results through user evaluations. We will also investigate the algorithm's efficiency and scalability in larger-scale data sets.

Acknowledgements. We thank grants ECS/HKBU211912 and NSFC/ 61272365.

References

1. Adomavicius, G., Tuzhilin, A.: Toward the next generation of recommender systems: A survey of the state-of-the-art and possible extensions. IEEE Transactions on Knowledge and Data Engineering 17(6), 734–749 (2005)
2. Becerra, C., Gonzalez, F., Gelbukh, A.: Visualizable and explicable recommendations obtained from price estimation functions. In: Proc. ACM RecSys 2011, pp. 27–34 (2011)
3. Burke, R.D., Hammond, K.J., Yound, B.: The findme approach to assisted browsing. IEEE Expert 12(4), 32–40 (1997)
4. Chen, L.: User Decision Improvement and Trust Building in Product Recommender Systems. PhD thesis, Ecole Polytechnique Federale De Lausanne (EPFL), Lausanne, Switzerland (August 2008)
5. Chen, L., Pu, P.: Preference-based organization interfaces: Aiding user critiques in recommender systems. In: Conati, C., McCoy, K., Paliouras, G. (eds.) UM 2007. LNCS (LNAI), vol. 4511, pp. 77–86. Springer, Heidelberg (2007)
6. Chen, L., Pu, P.: Critiquing-based recommenders: survey and emerging trends. User Modeling and User-Adapted Interaction 22(1-2), 125–150 (2012)
7. Keeney, R.L.: Decisions with Multiple Objectives: Preferences and Value Trade-offs. Cambridge University Press (1993)
8. Linden, G., Hanks, S., Lesh, N.: Interactive assessment of user preference models: The automated travel assistant. In: Proc. UM 1997, pp. 67–68 (1997)
9. Mandl, M., Felfernig, A.: Improving the performance of unit critiquing. In: Masthoff, J., Mobasher, B., Desmarais, M.C., Nkambou, R. (eds.) UMAP 2012. LNCS, vol. 7379, pp. 176–187. Springer, Heidelberg (2012)
10. McCarthy, K., McGinty, L., Smyth, B.: Dynamic critiquing: An analysis of cognitive load. In: Proc. ICAICS 2005, pp. 19–28 (2005)
11. McCarthy, K., Reilly, J., McGinty, L., Smyth, B.: On the dynamic generation of compound critiques in conversational recommender systems. In: De Bra, P.M.E., Nejdl, W. (eds.) AH 2004. LNCS, vol. 3137, pp. 176–184. Springer, Heidelberg (2004)
12. Mccarthy, K., Reilly, J., Smyth, B., Mcginty, L.: Generating diverse compound critiques. Artificial Intelligence Review 24(3-4), 339–357 (2005)
13. McCarthy, K., Salem, Y., Smyth, B.: Experience-based critiquing: Reusing critiquing experiences to improve conversational recommendation. In: Bichindaritz, I., Montani, S. (eds.) ICCBR 2010. LNCS, vol. 6176, pp. 480–494. Springer, Heidelberg (2010)
14. Quinlan, J.R.: Combining instance-based and model-based learning. In: Proc. ICML 1993, pp. 236–243 (1993)
15. Reilly, J., McCarthy, K., McGinty, L., Smyth, B.: Dynamic critiquing. In: Funk, P., González Calero, P.A. (eds.) ECCBR 2004. LNCS (LNAI), vol. 3155, pp. 763–777. Springer, Heidelberg (2004)
16. Reilly, J., McCarthy, K., McGinty, L., Smyth, B.: Incremental critiquing. Knowledge-Based Systems 18(4), 143–151 (2005)
17. Salem, Y., Hong, J.: History-aware critiquing-based conversational recommendation. In: Proc. WWW 2013, pp. 63–64 (2013)
18. Zhang, J., Pu, P.: A comparative study of compound critique generation in conversational recommender systems. In: Wade, V.P., Ashman, H., Smyth, B. (eds.) AH 2006. LNCS, vol. 4018, pp. 234–243. Springer, Heidelberg (2006)

Sparrows and Owls: Characterisation of Expert Behaviour in StackOverflow

Jie Yang, Ke Tao, Alessandro Bozzon, and Geert-Jan Houben

Delft University of Technology, Mekelweg 4, 2628 CD Delft, The Netherlands
{j.yang-3,k.tao,a.bozzon,g.j.p.m.houben}@tudelft.nl

Abstract. Question Answering platforms are becoming an important repository of crowd-generated knowledge. In these systems a relatively small subset of users is responsible for the majority of the contributions, and ultimately, for the success of the Q/A system itself. However, due to built-in incentivization mechanisms, standard expert identification methods often misclassify very active users for knowledgable ones, and misjudge activeness for expertise. This paper contributes a novel metric for expert identification, which provides a better characterisation of users' expertise by focusing on the quality of their contributions. We identify two classes of relevant users, namely *sparrows* and *owls*, and we describe several behavioural properties in the context of the StackOverflow Q/A system. Our results contribute new insights to the study of expert behaviour in Q/A platforms, that are relevant to a variety of contexts and applications.

Keywords: Question answering systems, Expert modelling, Expert behaviour.

1 Introduction

Question Answering (Q/A) platforms like Yahoo! Answers or StackExchange are an important class of social Web applications. Users access such platforms: 1) to look for existing solutions to their issues; 2) to post a new question to the platform community; 3) to contribute by providing new answers; or 4) to comment or vote existing questions and answers. As a result, users jointly contribute to the creation of evolving, crowdsourced, and peer-assessed knowledge bases.

To foster participation, Q/A platforms employ effective gamification mechanisms [1] that motivate users by showing a public *reputation score* (calculated by summing the number of preferences obtained by all the posted questions and answers), and by assigning *badges* after achieving pre-defined goals (e.g. complete at least one review task, achieve a score of 100 or more for an answer).

As shown in several studies, Q/A platforms are fuelled by a set of highly active users that, alone, contributes to the vast majority of the produced content. Such users, that we call *sparrows*, are clearly an important component of a Q/A ecosystem: as their name suggests, they are numerous, highly active, and highly "social" users. However, *sparrows* are not necessarily functional to knowledge

V. Dimitrova et al. (Eds.): UMAP 2014, LNCS 8538, pp. 266–277, 2014.

creation. Being driven by the gamification incentives, their goal might not be to provide a thorough answer to a question, but simply to "add up" reputation score. To this end, their answers, while quantitatively relevant, might be of low quality and/or low utility (i.e. having low scores from other users and/or ranked low among all the answers in a question); also, to minimise their effort, they might target simple or non-relevant questions.

Sparrows can guarantee responsive and constant feedback, thus playing an important role in keeping the community alive. However, we claim that there exists another category of users having comparable, if not greater importance. Such a category, that we call *owls*, contains users that, while being active members of the community, are driven by another motivation: to increase the overall knowledge contained in the platform. *Owls* are **experts** in the discussed topic, and they prove their expertise by providing useful answers, possibly to questions that are perceived as important or difficult by the community.

Previous studies focused on the characterisation of experts in Q/A platforms [6,10,11]. However, existing methods for expert identification mainly targeted *sparrows*, as they focused on quantitative properties of users' activities (e.g. reputation score, number of answers) while ignoring the inflationary effect that gamification incentives could trigger.

This paper targets `StackOverflow`, a question answering system specialised in software-related issues, and provides two main contributions: 1) a novel expertise assessment metric, called `MEC` (Mean Expertise Contribution), which helps in better discriminating *owls* from *sparrows* and normal users in Q/A platforms; and 2) a comparative study of the behaviour of *owls* and *sparrows* in `StackOverflow`. With respect to the second contribution, we address the following research questions:

- **RQ1:** How do *owls* and *sparrows* differ in terms of knowledge creation and community participation behaviours?
- **RQ2:** How do the overall activities of *owls* and *sparrows* evolve over time?

Understanding the nature of experts, their activity behaviour, and their role is of fundamental importance to drive the economy and prosperity of this class of social Web systems. Although the study specifically focused on `StackOverflow`, we believe that our results are of general interest. A better characterisation of the quality of users' contributions can also help in improving the performance of user modelling, expert retrieval, and question recommendation systems. Moreover, Q/A platforms can develop targeted motivation, engagement, and retention policies specifically addressed to different type of contributors, thus maximising their effectiveness. Finally, companies can better elicit the actual expertise of a potential employee, by exploiting a more accurate characterisation of their social reputation.

The remainder of the paper is organised as follows: Section 2 briefly introduces the dataset used in our study. Section 3 describes and evaluates the new `MEC` metric. Section 4 compares the behaviour of *owls* and *sparrows*. Section 5 describes related work, before Section 6 presents our conclusions.

2 Dataset Description

Launched in 2008, `StackOverflow` is one of the dominant domain-specific Q/A systems on the Web: with 2.3M users, 5.6M active questions, 10.3M answers, and 22.7M comments, `StackOverflow`[1] aims at becoming a very broad knowledge base for software developers, and it adopts a peer-reviewed moderation policy to close or remove duplicate and off-topic questions. Questions are topically classified by their submitters using one or more *tags*.

Definitions. Given a topic t, we define: 1) Q_t as the set of all t-related questions. 2) A_t as the set of all t-related answers; 3) U_t as all the users that participate in discussions about t; 4) A_t^u as the set of answers provided by a user $u \in U_t$ for topic t; 5) Q_t^u as the set of questions answered by user $u \in U_t$ for topic t; 6) $A_{q,t}$ as the set of answers provided for the question $q \in Q_t$ for topic t.

A question $q \in Q_t$ is associated with an owner $u_q \in U_t$, the content c_q, the timestamp of creation ts_q, and the number of views v_q. Similarly, an answer $a \in A_t$ is described by its creator $u_a \in U_t$, content c_a, the timestamp of creation ts_a, and the number of votes it received v_a.

Table 1 reports some descriptive statistics related to the topic C#, the most discussed topic in `StackOverflow`. It clearly emerges a strongly biased distribution in the number of answers provided by each user. Fig. 1 plots on a `log-log` scale the distribution of number of answers per question, and number of answers per users in the C# topics. Both quantities resemble a power-law distribution. Fig. 2 clearly shows that there are a few users giving many answers.

Table 1. Descriptive statistics about users activity for the C# topic

Description	Characteristic
Number of questions	472,860
Number of answers	1,071,750
Number of answerers	117,113
Average voting scores $a_t \in A_t$	2.18±7.35
Average number of answers to question $q_t \in Q_t$	2.27±1.74
Average number of answers given by user $u_t \in U_t$	9.15±76.66

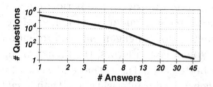 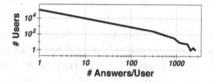

Fig. 1. C# topic: distribution of number of answers per question

Fig. 2. C# topic: distribution of number of answers per user

---

[1] The dataset can be accessed at https://archive.org/details/stackexchange. Our study is based on data created up until September 2013.

This is a property that is exhibited by the whole `StackOverflow` platform, where the most 13% active users, which provided at least ≥ 10 answers, are responsible for 87% of all the answers. We refer to such users as **Sparrows**, i.e. users that, for a given topic, have $|A_{u,t}| \geq 10$.

3   Expertise Metric

An expert can be defined as someone who is recognised to be skilful and/or knowledgable in some specific field [4], according to the judgment of the public or his or her peers; expertise then refers to the characteristics, skills, and knowledge that distinguish experts from novices and less experienced people.

In the context of a Q/A system, social judgement is critical for expert identification. A question is usually answered by a set of users, whose answers are voted up or down by other members of the platform. On the one hand, answering questions reflects a user's capability of applying knowledge to solve problems. On the other hand, the *voting* from other users can be viewed as a cyber simulation of *social judgement* for the answerers' expertise level.

Note that asking a question and posting a comment may also provide evidence of a user's expertise. However since answering a question can *directly* reflect the knowledge of a user in solving real problems – i.e., actionable knowledge – we limit our discussion of expertise judgement within the scope of answerers. Such choice is also aligned with previous studies of expert identification on Q/A systems [3,10,11,14].

3.1   Characterisation of Expertise

Previous works related expertise to the overall activeness of users in the platform. A classical and often used metric of expertise is the $Z_{Score} = \frac{a-q}{\sqrt{a+q}}$ [14], which measures users according to the number of posted questions q and answers a. Alternatively, one can look at the *reputation* of the user as calculated by the platform [6,10], a metric that is highly correlated with the number of provided answers.[2]

These two measures suffer from a common problem: they are heavily biased towards user activeness, thus favouring highly engaged users – the *sparrows* – over the ones that provide high level contributions – the *owls*. To support our claim, we performed an analysis of the distribution of the quality of users contribution for *C#*. We considered two dimensions:

1. The **debatableness** of a question, measured according to the *number of answers* it generated;
2. The **utility** of an answer, measured according to its relative *rank* in the list of answers.

---

[2] For instance, the Spearman correlation between user reputation and total number of answers given by users in topic C# is 0.68.

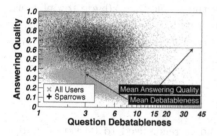
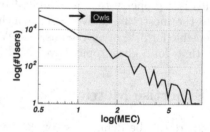

Fig. 3. Distribution of users according to the avg. debatableness of questions they answer, and the avg. answer quality. *Sparrows*: users with $|A_{u,t}| \geq 10$.

Fig. 4. Distribution of MEC (Mean Expertise Contribution) values in the considered user population. *Owls*: users with MEC ≥ 1.

Intuitively, difficult questions generate a lot of discussions, and several answers; also, the higher in the rank an answer has been voted, the more potentially useful it is to solve the related question, and the more it provides evidences about the expertise of the answerer in the topic. Table 2 contains a representative example[3] of debatable StackOverflow question. 13 out of 14 answers were provided by very active users, but the best answer was given by a user with only 2 questions answered.

Table 2. An example question to which all answers were provided by sparrows except the best answer

	Question: *C# to C++ 'Gotchas'.*	
Rank	**Content**	**#Answered questions**[*]
1st	*C++ has so many gotchas...*	2 answered questions
2nd	*Garbage collection!*	26 answered questions
3rd	*There are a lot of differences...*	175 answered questions
...	...	...
14th	*The following isn't meant*	24 answered questions

[*]This column shows the number of historical answers to C# questions by the corresponding answerer.

Such phenomenon is not rare, as shown in Fig. 3, which visualizes the entire C# dataset. Each dot represents one of the $\sim$ 117K users that provided at least one answer for the C# topics. A user is described by the average **utility** of his/her answers (a value in the $[0,1]$, where 1 represents maximum utility), and by the average **debatableness** of the questions he/she contributed to. The $\sim$ 15K *Sparrows* are highlighted with black crosses. An evident phenomenon can be observed: the vast majority of users answers less debated questions, while only a few (approximately 10%) are able to consistently provide relevant contributions to highly debated questions. Only a fraction ($\sim$30%) of the *sparrows* belongs to the latter group, clearly showing how activeness does not suffice as a measure of expertise.

---

[3] This question can be accessed at http://stackoverflow.com/questions/21475723

3.2   Identifying Owls

To better identify expert users, we devise a novel strategy for expertise judgement called MEC (Mean Expertise Contribution). Differently from existing measures, MEC values three expertise factors, namely: answering quality, question debatableness, and user activeness. MEC relates to a given topic t, and it is defined as:

$$MEC_{u,t} = \frac{1}{|Q_t^u|} \sum_{\forall q_i \in Q_{u,t}} \mathcal{AU}(u, q_i) * \frac{\mathcal{D}(q_i)}{\mathcal{D}_t^{avg}}$$

where:

- $\mathcal{AU}(u, q_i)$ is the **utility** of the answer provided by user u to question q_i; in our study, $\mathcal{AU}(u, q_i) = \frac{1}{Rank(a_{q_i})}$, that is the inverse of the rank of the answer provided by u for question q. The larger $\mathcal{AU}$, the higher the expertise level shown by the user in question q_i;
- $\mathcal{D}$ is the **debatableness** of the question q_i, calculated as the number of answers $|A_{q_i,t}|$ provided for question q_i;
- $\mathcal{D}_t^{avg}$ is the **average debatableness** of all the questions related to the topic t, calculated as $\frac{1}{|Q_t|} * \sum_{\forall q_j \in Q_t} |A_{q_j,t}|$.

The use of the inverse rank of a question allows to capture the quality of an answer regardless of the judgment expressed by the question provider: indeed, a requester can accept an answer as the right one, although the community, in the long run, might have a different opinion. The sum-up value of the **utility** of the provided answers acts as an indication of the expertise level of a user in a topic. By weighting in the relative debatableness questions, MEC accounts for the average difficulty of questions about a given topic. Note that $\mathcal{AU}(u, q_i)*\mathcal{D}(q_i)$ can be interpreted as the inversed *relative ranking* of u's answer among all answers to question q_i. To factor out user activeness, the resulting value is normalised over the total number of answers a user gave.

A value of $MEC_{u,t} = 1$ indicates that the user u, on average, provides the best answer to averagely debated questions, while $MEC_{u,t} = 0.5$ indicates that u ranks second in answering averagely debated questions, or ranks first in answering less debatable questions.

Fig. 4 depicts the log-log scale distribution of MEC w.r.t. the population of users involved in the C# topic. Only 11,910 users (approximately 10%) possess a MEC ≥ 1: we refer to such users as *Owls*, and observe that for the considered topic their number is significantly lower than the number of *sparrows*.

Fig. 5 shows the characterisation in terms of number of answers, reputation, and Z_{Score} of *sparrows*, *owls*, and the overall population: *sparrows* consistently obtain higher values, thus erroneously taken as experts. By conservatively considering only the *sparrows* classifying in the top 10% according to number of answers, reputation, and Z_{Score}, we observe that, respectively, only the 9.9%, 21.9% and 10.2% of them also belong to the set of *owls* (i.e. MEC ≥ 1).

In the following sections we will delve into more details about the different nature of *owls* and *sparrows*, highlighting their divergent behaviours and roles in StackOverflow.

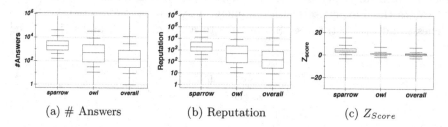

(a) # Answers	(b) Reputation	(c) Z_{Score}

Fig. 5. Comparison of expertise metrics

4   Comparison of Sparrows and Owls

RQ1: How do *sparrows* and *owls* differ in terms of participation and quality of contribution? To answer this question we first compared the mean numbers of questions and answers posted by the two groups of users. As depicted in Fig. 6a, the ratio between answered and submitted questions is significantly higher for *sparrows*. *Owls*, on the other hand, show a behaviour more similar to average users, thus further highlighting the distinctive "hunger" for answers of *sparrows*.

Such a distinction is evident not only in absolute terms, but also with respect to the type of questions and overall utility of answers.

Fig. 6b shows the distribution of questions answered by *sparrows* and *owls* with respect to the their debatableness: *sparrows* are more focused on questions in a smaller range (and value) of debatableness, while *owls* exhibit a broader range of participation, and a distribution very similar to the one of average users.

Fig. 6c compares the quality of the answers provided by *sparrows* and *owls* with respect to the debatableness of the answered question. To provide a fair comparison, we just consider questions answered by at least one user in each group. Vertical axis depicts the value of $1-$ *relative ranking* (i.e., $1 - 1/(\mathcal{AU}(u, q_i) * \mathcal{D}(q_i))$). As question debatableness is same for *owls* and *sparrows*, the answering quaity is only determined by utility: a higher value in this figure indicates higher answering quality. We observe that *Owls* consistently provide answers with higher utility, thus showing their grater value for the platform in terms of knowledge creation. The results shown in Fig. 6c indicate the ability of MEC to identify highly valuable users that, even if not driven by the need for higher reputation in the platform, are able to provide relevant and useful answers.

4.1   Preferences in Knowledge Creation

This section describes the different behaviours of *sparrow* and *owls* in terms of knowledge creation. We focus on the properties of the questions answered and posted by the two group of users.

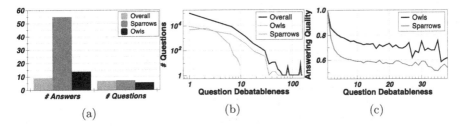

Fig. 6. Comparison of activity profiles of *sparrows* and *owls*: a) distribution of number of questions and answers; b) distribution of preferences for question debatableness; c) distribution of quality of contribution for question debatableness

Finding 1: *Owls* answer questions that are more difficult, and more popular. We consider two dimensions: **question popularity**, measured in terms of the number of times a question has been viewed in StackOverflow; and **time to solution** [6], measured in terms of the number of hours needed for the question creator to accept an answer as satisfactory. Time to solution can also be an indicator of the difficulty of a question: intuitively, the longer the time to accept an answer, the more difficult is the question.

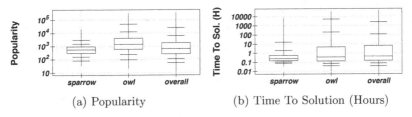

Fig. 7. Comparison of question preferences of *sparrows* and *owls*

Fig. 7a shows that questions answered by *sparrows* are, on average, significantly less popular than the ones picked by *owls*. Such difference is even more evident when considering the time required to close a questions – Fig. 7b.

These results might be interpreted as a clear indication of the different motivation and expertise level of the two group of users. *Sparrows* appear focused in building their reputation, which they increase by consistently answering to a lot of easy and non-interesting questions. Their behaviour is however providing important contribution to the community, as they can guarantee fast answers to many questions. On the other hand, *owls* intervene when their expertise is needed the most, i.e. in difficult question. Notice that such questions are not necessarily the most debated ones, as shown in Fig. 6b.

Finding 2: *Owls* post questions that are more difficult, and more popular. An analysis performed on the popularity of question posted by *sparrows* and *owls* show another difference between the two groups: questions submitted by *sparrows* are less popular than those posted by the *owls*. On the other hand, the time to completion for such questions is comparable. These results also suggest a difference in the expertise level of the two groups of users, as more popular questions might be a sign of the better understanding that *owls* possess on the subject. However, the higher (on average) difficulty and popularity of *sparrows*'s answers w.r.t. the average of users, also suggests that *sparrows* are good contributors in terms of new problems to be addressed by the community.

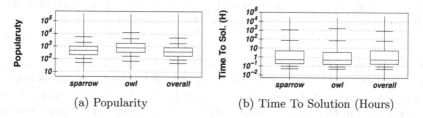

(a) Popularity   (b) Time To Solution (Hours)

Fig. 8. Comparison of question posted by *sparrows* and *owls*

4.2 Temporal Evolution of Activities

RQ2: How do the overall activities of *sparrows* and *owls* evolve over time?

Fig. 9a shows, cumulatively, the number of *sparrows* and *owls* active with the C# topic that registered in StackOverflow. Interestingly, only half of the users in those two categories registered in the first half of StackOverflow's lifetime. A decline can be observed in the number of new registration starting from 2012.

Fig. 9b and Fig. 9c describe the temporal evolution of the activities of *sparrows* and *owls*. For each type of users, we extract the number of actions including posting questions, answers and comments, which we refer to as the *activity counts*, together with the corresponding timestamp. For each action and for each user group, we averaged the overall amount of activities in the reference timeframe with respect to the number of *sparrows* and *owls* registered up to that time, plotting the resulting value over the time axis.

Finding 3: gamification incentives can more effectively retain *sparrows* than *owls*. Despite the increasing number of *sparrows* and *owls* over time, the average number of questions per user remains roughly the same, as shown by the black curve in Fig. 9b and Fig. 9c. This result indicates a relatively stable question posting behaviour, which can be explained in two ways: on one hand, posting questions is not as rewarding (in terms of increased reputation) as providing answers; therefore, what we observe is the result of a genuine questions for new information. On the other hand, one can argue that such stable behaviour can be due to a turnover in the number of active users for the topic.

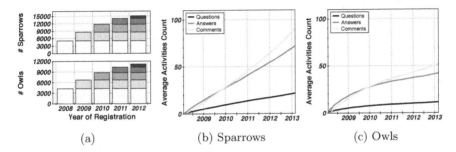

(a)   (b) Sparrows   (c) Owls

Fig. 9. Activity evolution of the *sparrows* and *owls*: a) registration date distribution; b) and c) answers, questions and comments.

A different behaviours can be observed with answers and comments. The average activity level of *sparrows* increases over time: this is expected, given the important role that reputation incentives play for these users. *Owls*, however, are, on average, less and less active, especially with respect to the number of answers. This result calls for a more detailed analysis of the evolution of *sparrows* and *owls* activities over time.

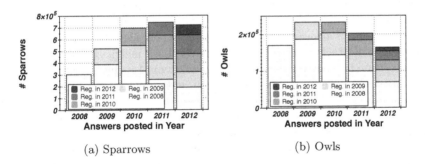

(a) Sparrows   (b) Owls

Fig. 10. Distribution of answers for according to registration date.

Fig. 10 depicts the temporal distribution of answers given by *sparrows* and *owls* (Figure 10b) partitioned by the registration date of the answerer. Fig. 10b shows how "older" *owls* always contribute for the larger portions of the provided answers. However, *owls* consistently tend to decrease their activity in time, especially for more recently registered users. On the other hand, new *sparrows* significantly contribute to a share of answers produced by their group and, although in the long term a decrease in the overall activities of the older member can be seen, the effect is less important. These results suggest that the gamification incentives put in place by StackOverflow are really effective to retain the activity of sparrows.

5   Related Work

Collectively edited Q/A systems have been emerging as important collective intelligence platforms. A specialised Q/A system such as StackOverflow is reforming the way people are communicating and accessing opinions and knowledge [13]. Given such background, matching expertise to the right answerer in Q/A system has recently been a relevant research stream [11,14,15]. We introduce the related work by focusing on two aspects: 1) expert finding, and ii) expert modelling in Q/A systems.

Expert finding, a classic problem in information retrieval, has been recently re-investigated in the case of Q/A systems. An early work [14] focused on the Java developer platform, where it emerged that such expertise network shows a few different characteristics with traditional social networks. In particular, it was found that a simple expertise metric called Z_{Score} (introduced in Section 3) outperforms graph-based metric such as the expertise propagation method (adapted from PageRank). Graph-based methods were then explored for Yahoo! Answers, a much larger Q/A platform [7]. A similar topic was also studied in [3], where the author proposed to use the number of best answerers for user expertise estimation. They employed Bayesian Information Criterion and Expectation-Maximization to automatically select the right number of users as experts.

A more recent work [11] adapted Z_{Score} for expert finding in StackOverflow, by using the number of answers a user posted as the ground truth for expertise identification. A similar expertise metric *reputation*, which is highly correlated with the number of answers, was also used for expert identification in the most recent studies of StackOverflow [6,10]. However, both metrics are biased to user activeness, therefore partially suitable for StackOverflow due to its gamification design, given that users activities are largely influenced by the reputation and badge rewarding [1]. An important difference between our method for expertise judgement and existing methods is that we take into account the user activeness and eliminate its effect on expertise judgement.

From the point of view of expert modelling, previous works were mostly investigated in the area of software engineering, through analyzing source code [9], version history [8], and developers' interaction history with development environment [5]. Specific to Q/A systems, expert modelling focused on modelling the property of questions and answers. In Yahoo! Answers [2], it was found that considering the mutual reinforcing effect between Q/A quality and user reputation can improve the effectiveness of expert modelling. Question selection preferences of active users were studied in StackOverflow [11,12]. While these studies are biased to active user, we target modeling user expertise directly. Our study address the difference between active users and the experts, although the application of our findings is left to future work.

6   Conclusions

As Q/A systems grow in popularity and adoption, identifying and motivating the users that effectively contribute to their success is becoming more and more crucial. This paper contributes a novel metric for the characterisation of experts in Q/A systems, showing its resilience to bias introduced by gamification incentives. Using `StackOverflow` as reference platform, we investigated differences in the behaviour of most active users (the *sparrows*) and most savvy users (the *owls*), showing how the two groups exhibit very distinct fingerprints in terms of knowledge creation, community participation, and temporal evolution of activities. Although targeted at a single topic, investigations show that similar results can be observed for other topics of similar overall amount of participation.

Acknowledgements. This publication was supported by the Dutch national program COMMIT. This work was carried out on the Dutch national e-infrastructure with the support of SURF Foundation.

References

1. Anderson, A., Huttenlocher, D., Kleinberg, J., Leskovec, J.: Kleinberg J., and Leskovec J.: Steering user behavior with badges. In: WWW 2013, pp. 95–106. ACM (2013)
2. Bian, J., Liu, Y., Zhou, D., Agichtein, E., Zha, H.: Learning to recognize reliable users and content in social media with coupled mutual reinforcement. In: WWW 2009, pp. 51–60. ACM (2009)
3. Bouguessa, M., Dumoulin, B., Wang, S.: Identifying authoritative actors in question-answering forums: The case of yahoo! answers. In: KDD 2008, pp. 866–874. ACM (2008)
4. Ericsson, K.A.: The Cambridge handbook of expertise and expert performance. Cambridge University Press (2006)
5. Fritz, T., Ou, J., Murphy, G.C., Murphy-Hill, E.: A degree-of-knowledge model to capture source code familiarity. In: ICSE 2010, pp. 385–394. ACM (2010)
6. Hanrahan, B.V., Convertino, G., Nelson, L.: Modeling problem difficulty and expertise in stackoverflow. In: CSCW 2012, pp. 91–94. ACM (2012)
7. Jurczyk, P., Agichtein, E.: Discovering authorities in question answer communities by using link analysis. In: CIKM 2007, pp. 919–922. ACM (2007)
8. Kagdi, H., Hammad, M., Maletic, J.I.: Who can help me with this source code change? In: ICSM 2008, pp. 157–166. IEEE (2008)
9. Ma, D., Schuler, D., Zimmermann, T., Sillito, J.: Expert recommendation with usage expertise. In: ICSM 2009, pp. 535–538. IEEE (2009)
10. Pal, A., Chang, S., Konstan, J.A.: Evolution of experts in question answering communities. In: ICWSM 2012. AAAI (2012)
11. Pal, A., Harper, F.M., Konstan, J.A.: Exploring question selection bias to identify experts and potential experts in community question answering. ACM Trans. Inf. Syst. 30(2), 10 (2012)
12. Pal, A., Konstan, J.A.: Expert identification in community question answering: exploring question selection bias. In: CIKM 2010, pp. 1505–1508. ACM (2010)
13. Vasilescu, B., Serebrenik, A., Devanbu, P., Filkov, V.: How social q&a sites are changing knowledge sharing in open source software communities. In: CSCW 2014, ACM (2014)
14. Zhang, J., Ackerman, M.S., Adamic, L.: Expertise networks in online communities: structure and algorithms. In: WWW 2007, pp. 221–230. ACM (2007)
15. Zhou, Y., Cong, G., Cui, B., Jensen, C.S., Yao, J.: Routing questions to the right users in online communities. In: ICDE 2009, pp. 700–711. IEEE (2009)

Generalizability of Goal Recognition Models in Narrative-Centered Learning Environments

Alok Baikadi, Jonathan Rowe, Bradford Mott, and James Lester

North Carolina State University, Raleigh, North Carolina, USA
{abaikad,jprowe,bwmott,lester}@ncsu.edu

Abstract. Recent years have seen growing interest in automated goal recognition. In user-adaptive systems, goal recognition is the problem of recognizing a user's goals by observing the actions the user performs. Models of goal recognition can support student learning in intelligent tutoring systems, enhance communication efficiency in dialogue systems, or dynamically adapt software to users' interests. In this paper, we describe an approach to goal recognition that leverages Markov Logic Networks (MLNs)—a machine learning framework that combines probabilistic inference with first-order logical reasoning—to encode relations between problem-solving goals and *discovery events,* domain-specific representations of user progress in narrative-centered learning environments. We investigate the impact of discovery event representations on goal recognition accuracy and efficiency. We also investigate the generalizability of discovery event-based goal recognition models across two corpora from students interacting with two distinct narrative-centered learning environments. Empirical results indicate that discovery event-based models outperform previous state-of-the-art approaches on both corpora.

Keywords: Goal recognition, narrative-centered learning environments, intent recognition.

1 Introduction

A key challenge in user-adaptive systems is recognizing users' intentions and plans. *Goal recognition*, also known as intent recognition, is the process of identifying the high-level objective that a user is pursuing based on an observed sequence of actions performed by the user. It is a restricted form of plan recognition, which involves identifying both the user's goal and the action sequence that will achieve the goal. The capacity to reason about users' plans, activities, and intentions enables user-adaptive systems to predict actions that will be performed by the user. Computational models of goal recognition have been investigated across a range of applications, including intelligent tutoring systems [1], dialogue systems [2], and digital games [3, 4].

One type of user-adaptive system that particularly stands to benefit from goal recognition models is narrative-centered learning environments. Narrative-centered learning environments combine the personalized educational support of intelligent tutoring systems with the engaging, interactive storylines of digital games [5, 6]. In narrative-centered learning environments, goal recognition models can be used to

V. Dimitrova et al. (Eds.): UMAP 2014, LNCS 8538, pp. 278–289, 2014.

support struggling students by detecting erroneous problem-solving approaches or misconceived strategies that require remediation. Models for goal recognition can also be used to pre-emptively adapt learning environments' interactive narratives, dynamically adjusting difficulty or providing personalized scaffolding and guidance.

In this work, we investigate the generalizability of goal recognition models that leverage Markov logic networks (MLNs) [7] to encode relations between students' goals and problem-solving progress in narrative-centered learning environments. Markov logic is a statistical relational learning framework that combines probabilistic inference with first-order logical reasoning. In our work, we examine the impact of a domain-specific representation of problem-solving progress, called *discovery events,* on MLN-based goal recognition models' accuracy and efficiency. Discovery events encode major plot milestones that convey key problem-solving information to students during narrative-centered learning. We examine the impact of incorporating logical representations of discovery events into MLN-based goal recognition models, comparing discovery event-based models to a MLN-based baseline approach.

To investigate the generalizability of the models, we train and evaluate them using corpora from two distinct narrative-centered learning environments: a narrative-centered learning environment for middle school microbiology that centers on diagnostic problem solving and another narrative-centered learning environment for elementary science education that emphasizes exploration-focused quests on maps, models, and landforms. Empirical results from the evaluation indicate that discovery event-based goal recognition models outperform prior state-of-the-art MLN approaches. Furthermore, the findings generalize across both learning environments, indicating that discovery event-based MLN models for goal recognition are an effective approach for predicting students' goals during narrative-centered learning.

2   Related Work

Goal recognition, along with the related tasks of activity recognition and plan recognition, has been the subject of considerable interest in the AI community for decades. A wide variety of computational frameworks, including symbolic representations [8–10], probabilistic representations [11, 12], grammar-based models [12, 13], and hybrid models [2, 14, 15] have been investigated extensively, both from theoretical and empirical perspectives. Goal recognition models have also been examined across a range of applications, including dialogue management [16], learning environments [1], cybersecurity [10], story understanding [11], and games [3, 4, 15, 17, 18].

Over the past few years, Markov logic networks have received growing attention for their promise in plan, activity, and goal recognition [15, 19, 20]. Sadilek and Kautz [15] used Markov logic to investigate activity recognition in a multi-agent Capture the Flag game using GPS data. In their model, a Markov logic network combines hard and soft constraints derived from Capture the Flag rules to de-noise and label GPS data in terms of "capture" events. Experiments demonstrated that the MLN model significantly outperformed alternate probabilistic and nonprobabilistic approaches, correctly identifying 90% of capture events. Singla and Mooney [19] devised a method for constructing MLN-based plan recognition models using abductive reasoning over planning domains. Experiments found that Singla and Mooney's approach improved predictive accuracy over competing techniques. However, by framing the problem in terms of abductive inference, their approach requires a formal description of the planning domain be available.

We extend prior work on goal recognition in narrative-centered learning environments by examining the impact of logical representations of discovery events on the accuracy and efficiency of goal recognition [20, 21]. Further, we investigate discovery event-based models' capacity to generalize across multiple narrative-centered learning environments.

3   MLN-Based Goal Recognition with Discovery Events

We formalize goal recognition as a classification task: given a sequence of actions performed in a narrative-centered learning environment, determine the goal that is most likely associated with the actions. We use Markov logic networks [7], a statistical relational learning framework, to perform classification. *Markov logic networks* (MLNs) unify logical and probabilistic representations for reasoning over a knowledge base. A MLN is a set of first-order logical formulae with associated weights. Each weight denotes the formula's strength as a constraint on the set of possible worlds described by the knowledge base. During inference, the formulae and weights are transformed into a Markov network, a graphical model with each node representing a random variable, and each undirected edge representing conditional dependencies. The joint probability distribution is defined as $P(X = x) = \frac{1}{Z}\prod_k \phi_k(x_{\{k\}})$, where ϕ_k is a potential function over a clique in the graph. The potential function is derived from the weight of a formula and the groundings of the individual predicates in the training corpus.

For this work, weights are learned using Markov: The Beast, an open source implementation of Cutting Plane Inference for the MLN learning framework [22]. Cutting Plane Inference uses Weighted MAX-SAT [7] inference by incrementally adding violated formulae to a knowledge base and solving the remaining Markov network.

Classification within MLNs is similar to other probabilistic graphical models. A random variable, or predicate in MLNs, is created for the class to be predicted. During inference, probabilities for different groundings of the hidden predicate are computed for each time step in the student interaction data.

In order to prepare our goal recognition corpora for training, validating, and evaluating classification models, we make several assumptions about our domains. First, we assume students only pursue a single goal at a time. Second, we assume that the distribution between observations and goals is fixed across players. Third, we assume that the student is not aware that the system is monitoring their goals, and therefore the system does not influence students' goal-directed behavior.

Based upon these assumptions, we annotate each student action in a goal recognition corpus using the following process. First, the students' interaction traces are scanned for points in which goals are achieved. These observations are annotated with the goal. Because we assume there are no interleaved goals, every remaining action is annotated with the next goal observed. Afterward, the original goal-achieving actions are removed, because it would be trivial to recognize a goal from a goal-achieving action.

Table 1. Predicates for goal recognition

Predicate	Semantics
`action(t,a)`	Observed player performing action a at time t
`argument(t,a)`	Object a was involved in the player's action at time t
`location(t,l)`	Observed player at location l at time t
`state(t,s)`	Player has passed the milestones for state s before time t
`goal(t,g)`	Player is attempting goal g at time t

Table 1 shows the four predicates used to describe each observation in a narrative-centered learning environment. To represent location symbolically, the virtual environment is discretized, and each region is assigned a unique identifier. These discrete regions are specified as arguments to location predicates. Logical formulae were developed to connect these observed predicates to a hidden predicate representing the student's goal associated with that action. Formulae were included to ensure that only one goal was associated for any given time step.

In addition to formulae connecting the observed predicates to the goal predicates, we introduce new formulae to capture significant milestones in the interaction history: discovery events. Within a narrative-centered learning environment, the overall task can be conceptualized in terms of resolving a central driving question about the plot. Central questions often revolve around the nature of the setting (e.g., Where are we?), what characters will do or have done (e.g., Who committed the crime?), or the consequences of a major event (e.g., What is going to happen now?).

Discovery events represent the user's narrative progress by encoding partial answers to the plot's central driving question. For example, in the context of a mystery plot, discovery events represent clues that the player obtains. To illustrate, consider the following medical mystery scenario. The protagonist, a medical detective, is investigating a disease afflicting a group of sick patients. In order to learn more about the illness, the protagonist asks a sick patient about his symptoms and recent medical history. The resulting conversation is a discovery event; the protagonist gains valuable information to diagnose the illness and resolve the story's central question: "What is making the patients sick?" Later in the investigation, the protagonist runs a laboratory test on some eggs that the sick patient recently consumed. The eggs test positive for salmonella. This is another discovery event that reveals the likely transmission source for the disease. In addition to plot revelations, discovery events can include first-time demonstrations of game mechanics that are required to advance the interactive narrative's plot. For example, when the protagonist demonstrates that she can successfully use the laboratory's testing equipment for the first time, the action is considered a discovery event. In this manner, discovery events encompass a broad range of events that transpire in interactive narratives.

4   Testbed Narrative-Centered Learning Environments

In order to investigate the effectiveness and generalizability of discovery event-based models of goal recognition, we train and evaluate the models on goal recognition corpora from two distinct narrative-centered learning environments. The first environment, CRYSTAL ISLAND: OUTBREAK, is an educational interactive narrative for middle school science that focuses on diagnostic problem solving. The second environment, CRYSTAL ISLAND: UNCHARTED DISCOVERY, is an educational interactive narrative for upper elementary science that emphasizes quests about maps, models, and landforms. In this section, we describe each of the learning environments.

4.1   Crystal Island: Outbreak

CRYSTAL ISLAND: OUTBREAK is a narrative-centered learning environment for middle school microbiology. The environment features a science mystery where students attempt to discover the identity and source of an infectious disease that is plaguing a research team stationed on a remote island. Students explore the research camp from a first-person viewpoint and manipulate virtual objects, converse with characters, and use lab equipment and other resources to solve the mystery.

In order to represent students' problem-solving progress in OUTBREAK's interactive narrative, we identified seven narrative sub-goals that are central to the solving the science mystery. These goals are never directly presented to the student; rather, they are discovered by the student during the course of gameplay. Five of the goals involve interviewing virtual characters. One goal involves successfully running a laboratory test on the disease's transmission source. The final goal involves submitting a correct diagnosis to a virtual character, thereby solving the mystery.

There are nineteen different types of actions in the OUTBREAK environment. These actions include interactions with virtual objects, talking with virtual characters, gathering and recording information in a diagnosis worksheet, and interacting with the testing equipment in a virtual laboratory. There are seven major regions of the island. Each of these locations is further divided into several sub-areas in a rough grid. In total, there are 39 distinct, non-overlapping locations that are recorded throughout interactions with the narrative-centered learning environment. Narrative state is conceptualized in terms of three phases of the plot: an introductory phase, a laboratory testing phase, and a diagnosis worksheet phase. After the introduction, the latter two phases can be attempted in either order. Narrative state is encoded as a binary vector indicating which of the phases have been completed.

In addition to the narrative state, six discovery events were identified in the plot. The discovery events represent moments in the interaction where critical plot-related information is communicated to the student. Three of the discovery events occur during dialogue with virtual characters, two occur during interactions with in-game books and posters, and two occur during interactions with a diagnosis worksheet tool that students' use in the environment.

4.2   Crystal Island: Uncharted Discovery

CRYSTAL ISLAND: UNCHARTED DISCOVERY takes place on a fictional island in the Oceania region of the Pacific Ocean. Students take on the role of a child who has been shipwrecked on an island after a tropical storm along with a crew of explorers. After an introductory cinematic, the student joins a cast of virtual characters on the island in establishing a new life. From there, the student explores a rich 3D environment as she performs tasks for the various island inhabitants. As students learn about landforms, navigation and modeling, they are asked to perform several quests that assess their skills. Following a brief tutorial segment to familiarize students with the interface and gameplay, students have access to a virtual tablet device that provides access to several in-game applications to support problem solving.

In the dataset used in this work, students completed four quests. Two of the quests focused on understanding landforms, such as plateaus, deltas and waterfalls. Two of the quests involved understanding navigation, both through reading a map and following a heading for a specified amount of distance. Each quest was associated with three goals. These goals were used as the targets for goal recognition. Once a quest was begun, its three goals could be pursued in any order. Quests could also be repeated, since faster times were given in-game rewards in the form of trophies.

There were thirty-seven distinct actions that the student could perform in UNCHARTED DISCOVERY. These range from general actions (e.g., moving between areas, managing items), to quest management (e.g., accepting quests, quitting quests), to quest-specific actions (e.g., taking photographs, collecting flags). There are sixty outdoor locations on the island, as well as three buildings that may be entered. The phases of the narrative state are partitioned in terms of the quests; the completion of a quest marks the transition from one phase to another. Because the plot of UNCHARTED DISCOVERY is organized in terms of quests, discovery events are also defined in terms of quests. Two of the discovery events involve quest management, accepting a quest and quitting a quest. Another three occur during interactions with the table. The students are able to view a map of the island, access a virtual encyclopedia, and take freeform notes to organize their thoughts. Finally, three discovery events are quest-specific actions, such as placing signs at specific locations, taking photographs, and picking up colored flags.

5   Goal Recognition Corpora

The OUTBREAK corpus was gathered from 153 8th grade students, aged 12-15 (M=13.3) in a North Carolina public school. Sixteen players were removed due to incomplete data or prior experience with the narrative-centered learning environment. Of the remaining 137 players, 77 were male and 60 were female. A minority, 41.6% of students, completed the mystery in the allotted time. Twenty of the 137 players experienced a game crash, and were instructed to restart the game. In these cases, both sets of observations will be used for this work [5].

The students were first presented with an overview of OUTBREAK, which introduced the backstory and task description and the game controls. They were also given handouts, which contained that information, as well as a map of the island and a description of the characters in the virtual environment. The students were then given a pre-survey, which assessed their science content knowledge, in addition to various psychological instruments. The students interacted with the system for a maximum of 60 minutes. At the end of 60 minutes, or when they completed the mystery, the students were given a post-survey. The whole interaction lasted about 120 minutes.

The UNCHARTED DISCOVERY corpus was collected from eight North Carolina public elementary schools. Each fifth-grade classroom interacted with the software over a 4-week period. A total of 831 students participated in the data collection, of which 49% were male. The schools represented urban (40%), suburban (20%), and rural settings (40%) [23].

$$\forall t : |\forall g : goal(t, g)| = 1 \tag{1}$$

$$\forall t, g : goal(t, g) * w_2(g) \tag{2}$$

$$\forall t, a, g : action(t, a) \Rightarrow goal(t, g) * w_3(a, g) \tag{3}$$

$$\forall t, l, g : location(t, l) \Rightarrow goal(t, g) * w_4(l, g) \tag{4}$$

$$\forall t, s, g : state(t, s) \Rightarrow goal(t, g) * w_5(s, g) \tag{5}$$

$$\forall t, a, s, g : action(t, a) \wedge state(t, s) \Rightarrow goal(t, g) * w_6(a, s, g) \tag{6}$$

$$\forall t, a, g : action(t - 1, a) \Rightarrow goal(t, g) * w_7(a, g) \tag{7}$$

$$\forall t, l, g : location(t - 1, l) \Rightarrow goal(t, g) * w_8(l, g) \tag{8}$$

$$\forall t, s, g : state(t - 1, s) \Rightarrow goal(t, g) * w_9(s, g) \tag{9}$$

$$\forall t, a, s, g : action(t - 1, a) \wedge state(t - 1, s) \Rightarrow goal(t, g) * w_{10}(a, s, g) \tag{10}$$

$$\forall t, a_1, a_2, g : action(t - 1, a_1) \wedge action(t - 1, a_2) \Rightarrow goal(t, g) * w_{11}(a_1, a_2, g) \tag{11}$$

$$\forall t, a_1, a_2, g_1, g_2 : \left(\begin{array}{c} action(t - 1, a_1) \wedge action(t - 1, a_2) \\ \Rightarrow [goal(t - 1, g_1) \Rightarrow goal(t, g_2)] \end{array} \right) * w_{12}(a_1, a_2, g_1, g_2) \tag{12}$$

Fig. 1. Baseline formulae

The students interacted with the software six times over the 4-week period, supplemented with six teacher-led lessons. Each interaction with UNCHARTED DISCOVERY was 50 minutes long. For this work, only sessions from the first two weeks were considered. During the first two weeks, four quests were available to the students. During the remaining two weeks, the students had access to two quests that were entirely contained within a single set of actions. From a goal recognition standpoint, these quests would necessitate special consideration, since the student is effectively prevented from performing many of the available actions while attempting the quest. The data from the tutorial level were also removed. Observations from all sessions were concatenated to produce one observation sequence for each student.

6   Results

The evaluation of our goal recognition model focused on three principal metrics: F1, convergence rate, and convergence point. F1 measures the predictive accuracy of the models. The F1 measure is defined as the harmonic mean between precision and recall. However, since our MLN formulae enforce that only one prediction is made for each time step, the multi-class precision and recall are equivalent to the F1 measure. Convergence rate is the percentage of sequences that are eventually classified to the correct goal. Any sequence whose final action is predicted as belonging to the correct goal is said to have converged on the goal. Convergence point measures the percentage of a converged sequence that was observed before the correct goal was consistently predicted. For this measure, a lower number indicates improved performance.

Two models were trained and evaluated on each of the corpora. The baseline model was a previously published model for goal recognition on the OUTBREAK corpus [20]. It was comprised of 13 logical formulae (Fig. 1) with weights learned using Markov: The Beast [22].

$$\forall t, g : |\forall t_2 < t : action(t_2, \text{"Worksheet"})| \geq 1 \Rightarrow goal(t, g) * w_{13}(g) \tag{1}$$

$$\forall t, g : |\forall t_2 < t : action(t_2, \text{"Test"})| \geq 1 \Rightarrow goal(t, g) * w_{14}(g) \tag{2}$$

$$\forall t, g : |\forall t_2 < t : argument(t_2, \text{"Eating Habits"})| \geq 1 \Rightarrow goal(t, g) * w_{15}(g) \tag{3}$$

$$\forall t, g : \left|\forall t_2 < t : \begin{matrix} action(t_2, \text{"Read"}) \wedge \\ argument(t_2, \text{"Salmonellosis"}) \end{matrix}\right| \geq 1 \Rightarrow goal(t, g) * w_{16}(g) \tag{4}$$

$$\forall t, g : |\forall t_2 < t : argument(t_2, \text{"Symptoms"})| \geq 1 \Rightarrow goal(t, g) * w_{17}(g) \tag{5}$$

$$\forall t, g : |\forall t_2 < t : argument(t_2, \text{"Bacteria"})| \geq 1 \Rightarrow goal(t, g) * w_{18}(g) \tag{6}$$

Fig. 2. Discovery event formulae for CRYSTAL ISLAND: OUTBREAK

$$\forall t, g : |\forall t_2 < t : action(t_2, \text{"Pickup Flag"})| \geq 1 \Rightarrow goal(t, g) * w_{19}(g) \tag{1}$$

$$\forall t, g : |\forall t_2 < t : action(t_2, \text{"Drop Flag"})| \geq 1 \Rightarrow goal(t, g) * w_{20}(g) \tag{2}$$

$$\forall t, g : |\forall t_2 < t : action(t_2, \text{"Take Notes"})| \geq 1 \Rightarrow goal(t, g) * w_{21}(g) \tag{3}$$

$$\forall t, g : |\forall t_2 < t : action(t_2, \text{"Take Photo"})| \geq 1 \Rightarrow goal(t, g) * w_{22}(g) \tag{4}$$

$$\forall t, g : |\forall t_2 < t : action(t_2, \text{"Use IslandPedia"})| \geq 1 \Rightarrow goal(t, g) * w_{23}(g) \tag{5}$$

$$\forall t, g : |\forall t_2 < t : action(t_2, \text{"Begin Quest"})| \geq 1 \Rightarrow goal(t, g) * w_{24}(g) \tag{6}$$

$$\forall t, g : |\forall t_2 < t : action(t_2, \text{"Quit Quest"})| \geq 1 \Rightarrow goal(t, g) * w_{25}(g) \tag{7}$$

$$\forall t, g : |\forall t_2 < t : action(t_2, \text{"Check Map"})| \geq 1 \Rightarrow goal(t, g) * w_{26}(g) \tag{8}$$

Fig. 3. Discovery event formulae for CRYSTAL ISLAND: UNCHARTED DISCOVERY

The *discovery events* models extended the baseline model in two ways. First, the model was simplified by removing formulae that referenced previous time steps (i.e., formulae 7-12 in Fig. 1); only formulae that included references to the current time step were maintained. These formulae formed the cores of the models for both the OUTBREAK and UNCHARTED DISCOVERY corpora.

In addition, new sets of formulae were added to encode discovery events in each of the new models. The discovery events allowed the models to reference key events students had completed in the narratives. For each discovery event, a new formula was created. Each discovery event was expressed in terms of the predicates described in Section 3. For example, the *Testing* discovery event for the OUTBREAK corpus was defined as `action(t,"Test")`. The *Eating Habits* dis covery event is defined as `argument(t,"Eating Habits")` because it can be triggered by multiple different types of actions. The encoded discovery events were placed within the milestone formulae, which served as indicator nodes to determine if the discovery event had happened in the interaction history.

The formulae in Fig. 2 capture the discovery events for CRYSTAL ISLAND: OUTBREAK. The formulae in Fig. 3 capture the discovery events for CRYSTAL ISLAND: UNCHARTED DISCOVERY.

The models were trained using 10-fold cross validation. The folds were formed using the number of students, rather than the number of goal sequences, to ensure independence between folds. The three evaluation metrics (F1, convergence rate, convergence point) were computed across each of the ten evaluations. The four models were compared statistically using one-way analysis of variance. The results of cross validation on the CRYSTAL ISLAND: OUTBREAK corpus can be found in Table 2, and the results for the CRYSTAL ISLAND: UNCHARTED DISCOVERY corpus can be found in Table 3.

Table 2. Goal recognition model comparison for CRYSTAL ISLAND: OUTBREAK

Model	F1		Convergence Rate		Convergence Point	
Baseline	0.488	F(1,18)=7.661	30.906	F(1,18)=133.7	50.865	F(1,18)=27.98
Discovery Event	0.546	p<0.05	50.056	P<0.001	35.862	p<0.001

Table 3. Goal recognition model comparison for CRYSTAL ISLAND: UNCHARTED DISCOVERY

Model	F1		Convergence Rate		Convergence Point	
Baseline	0.226	F(1,18)=14.58	11.915	F(1,18)=709.1	87.786	F(1,18)=61.66
Discovery Event	0.244	p<0.01	29.973	p<0.001	79.350	p<0.001

7   Discussion

The empirical results suggest that logical encodings of domain-specific discovery events improve performance of goal recognition models. The discovery event models outperformed the previous state-of-the-art baselines on all three metrics for both corpora. In both cases, the discovery event models were significantly more accurate than the baseline models, as demonstrated by analyses of variance on F1 scores. In addition, the discovery event models consistently generated accurate predictions earlier in the observation sequences. Early prediction is particularly important for goal recognition in narrative-centered learning environments, as it provides time for computing and executing interventions to dynamically shape interactive narratives. In the future, it may be useful to consider alternate measures of early prediction. One example would be to define a sequence as converged if there is high probability that a large proprotion of the observations are consistent.

It is important to note that there are several limitations to the work. First, there are some restrictions on the types of interactive environments in which this approach can be used. The approach is most compatible with environments that are explicitly goal-oriented. Automatically encoding user progress is a necessary part of defining discovery events. Identifying meaningful progress measures for an environment without well-defined goals is likely to be problematic. It is conceivable that navigating physical landmarks could serve as progress milestones for purely exploration-focused environments, and this type of investigation is left for future work.

A second limitation is the assumption that there are no concurrent goals. Relaxing this assumption would likely require a resource-intensive manual annotation effort to determine how various actions contribute to the goals to be recognized. Alternatively, asking students to periodically self-report their goals—either through the software or think aloud protocol—could also be explored.

Lastly, there is the question of appropriate grain size for discovery events representations. On the one hand, it is possible that a coarse-grained representation that solely denotes which goals have been completed would provide sufficient context for effective goal recognition. On the other hand, every individual action performed by a student provides context for inferring the goal she is trying to accomplish. The discovery events presented in this work were chosen because they provide salient pieces of plot-related information to the student; a retelling of the story would be incoherent without including the information conveyed by the discovery events. It is unclear whether this is necessarily the optimal grain size for encoding discovery events, but ultimately it is an empirical question. In the future, additional studies should be conducted to determine the appropriate representational characteristics for encoding discovery events to drive goal recognition in narrative-centered learning environments.

8   Conclusions and Future Work

Goal recognition has a long history of study in artificial intelligence. In narrative-centered learning environments, goal recognition models enable interactive narrative planners to personalize events to individual students and their problem-solving behaviors. In this paper, we have presented a goal recognition framework that leverages Markov logic networks to encode relations between users' goals and discovery events, key milestones denoting user progress in a narrative-centered learning environment. Discovery event-based models were compared to a previous state-of-the-art MLN model across two narrative-centered learning environments. Empirical analyses demonstrated that the discovery event-based models consistently outperformed the baseline model on all considered goal recognition metrics: F1 score, convergence rate, and convergence point.

There are several promising directions for future work. First, it will be important to investigate ways to relax the simplifying assumptions used in the work, such as the assumption that whenever a student achieves a goal, it is the same goal that she had been seeking to achieve. Another assumption it will be important to relax is the assumption that goals are pursued serially. In open-ended narrative-centered learning environments, such as both editions of CRYSTAL ISLAND, it is possible for students to pursue multiple goals concurrently, and in some cases synergistically. Finally, it will be important to incorporate discovery event-based goal recognition models into run-time narrative-centered learning environments to investigate their capacity to drive user-adaptive systems.

Acknowledgments. The authors wish to thank members of the IntelliMedia Group for their assistance, as well as Valve Software for access to the Source^{TM} engine and SDK. We would also like to thank Eunyoung Ha, for providing the baseline model. This research was supported by the National Science Foundation under Grant DRL-0822200. Any opinions, findings, and conclusions or recommendations expressed in this material are those of the authors and do not necessarily reflect the views of the National Science Foundation. Additional support was provided by the Bill and Melinda Gates Foundation, the William and Flora Hewlett Foundation, and EDUCAUSE.

References

1. Gal, Y., Reddy, S., Shieber, S.M., Rubin, A., Grosz, B.J.: Plan Recognition in Exploratory Domains. Artif. Intell. 176, 2270–2290 (2012)
2. Blaylock, N., Allen, J.: Hierarchical Instantiated Goal Recognition. In: Kaminka, G., Pynadath, D.V., Geib, C.W. (eds.) Proceedings of the Workshop on Modeling Others from Observations, pp. 8–15. AAAI Press, Menlo Park (2006)
3. Gold, K.: Training Goal Recognition Online from Low-Level Inputs in an Action-Adventure Game. In: Youngblood, G.M., Bulitko, V. (eds.) Proceedings of the Sixth Conference on Artificial Intelligence in Interactive Digital Entertainment, pp. 21–26. AAAI Press, Menlo Park (2010)
4. Kabanza, F., Bellefeuille, P., Bisson, F., Benaskeur, A.R., Irandoust, H.: Opponent Behaviour Recognition for Real-Time Strategy Games. In: Sukthankar, G., Geib, C.W., Pynadath, D.V., Bui, H.H. (eds.) Proceedings of the Workshop on Plan, Activity, and Intent Recognition, pp. 29–36. AAAI Press, Menlo Park (2010)
5. Rowe, J.P., Shores, L.R., Mott, B.W., Lester, J.C.: Integrating Learning, Problem Solving, and Engagement in Narrative-Centered Learning Environments. Int. J. Artif. Intell. Educ. 21, 115–133 (2011)
6. Thomas, J.M., Young, R.M.: Annie: Automated Generation of Adaptive Learner Guidance for Fun Serious Games. IEEE Trans. Learn. Technol. 3, 329–343 (2010)
7. Domingos, P., Kok, S., Poon, H., Richardson, M., Singla, P.: Unifying Logical and Statistical AI. In: Gil, Y., Mooney, R.J. (eds.) Proceedings of the Twenty-First National Conference on Artificial Intelligence, pp. 2–7. AAAI Press, Menlo Park (2006)
8. Kautz, H.A., Allen, J.F.: Generalized Plan Recognition. In: Kehler, T. (ed.) Proceedings of the Fifth National Conference on Artificial Intelligence, pp. 32–37. Morgan Kaufmann, San Francisco (1986)
9. Ng, H.T., Mooney, R.J.: Abductive Plan Recognition and Diagnosis: A Comprehensive Empirical Evaluation. In: Third International Conference on Principles of Knowledge Representation and Reasoning, Cambridge, MA, pp. 499–508 (1992)
10. Geib, C.W., Goldman, R.P.: A Probabilistic Plan Recognition Algorithm Based on Plan Tree Grammars. Artif. Intell. 173, 1101–1132 (2009)
11. Charniak, E., Goldman, R.P.: A Bayesian Model of Plan Recognition (1993)
12. Pynadath, D.V., Wellman, M.P.: Probabilistic State-Dependent Grammars for Plan Recognition. In: Boutilier, C., Goldszmidt, M. (eds.) Proceedings of the Sixteenth Conference on Uncertainty in Artificial Intelligence, pp. 507–514. IUAI Press, Corvallis (2000)
13. Geib, C.W.: Delaying Commitment in Plan Recognition Using Combinatory Categorial Grammars. In: Boutilier, C. (ed.) Proceedings of the Twenty-First International Joint Conference on Artificial Intelligence, pp. 1702–1707. AAAI Press, Menlo Park (2009)
14. Wu, T., Lian, C., Hsu, J.Y.: Joint Recognition of Multiple Concurrent Activities using Factorial Conditional Random Fields. In: Pynadath, D.V., Geib, C.W. (eds.) Proceedings of the Workshop on Plan, Activity, and Intent Recognition, pp. 82–88. AAAI Press, Menlo Park (2007)
15. Sadilek, A., Kautz, H.: Location-Based Reasoning about Complex Multi-Agent Behavior. J. Artif. Intell. Res. 43, 87–133 (2012)
16. Carberry, S.: Techniques for Plan Recognition. User Model. User-adapt. Interact. 11, 31–48 (2001)

17. Albrecht, D.W., Zukerman, I., Nicholson, A.E., Bud, A.: Towards a Bayesian Model for Keyhole Plan Recognition in Large Domains. In: Jameson, A., Paris, C., Tasso, C. (eds.) Proceedings of the Sixth International Conference on User Modeling, pp. 365–376. Springer, New York (1997)

18. Laviers, K., Sukthankar, G.: A Real-Time Opponent Modeling System for Rush Football. In: Walsh, T. (ed.) Proceedings of the Twenty-Second International Joint Conference on Artificial Intelligence, pp. 2476–2481. AAAI Press, Menlo Park (2011)

19. Singla, P., Mooney, R.J.: Abductive Markov Logic for Plan Recognition. In: Burgard, W., Roth, D. (eds.) Twenty-Fifth National Conference on Artificial Intelligence, pp. 1069–1075. AAAI Press, Menlo Park (2011)

20. Ha, E.Y., Rowe, J.P., Mott, B.W., Lester, J.C.: Goal Recognition with Markov Logic Networks for Player-Adaptive Games. In: Bulitko, V., Riedl, M.O. (eds.) Proceedings of the Seventh Conference on Artificial Intelligence in Interactive Digital Entertainment, pp. 32–39. AAAI Press, Menlo Park (2011)

21. Baikadi, A., Rowe, J.P., Mott, B.W., Lester, J.C.: Improving Goal Recognition in Interactive Narratives with Models of Narrative Discovery Events. In: Si, M., Cavazza, M., Zook, A. (eds.) Proceedings of the Sixth Workshop on Intelligent Narrative Technologies, AAAI Press, Menlo Park (2013)

22. Riedel, S.: Improving the Accuracy and Efficiency of MAP Inference for Markov Logic. In: McAllester, D.A., Myllymäki, P. (eds.) Proceedings of the Twenty-Fourth Annual Conference on Uncertainty in Artificial Intelligence, pp. 468–475. IUAI Press, Corvallis (2008)

23. Lester, J.C., Spires, H.A., Nietfeld, J.L., Minogue, J., Mott, B.W., Lobene, E.V.: Designing Game-Based Learning Environments for Elementary Science Education: A Narrative-Centered Learning Perspective. Information Sciences 264, 4–18 (2014)

Extending Log-Based Affect Detection to a Multi-User Virtual Environment for Science

Ryan S. Baker[1], Jaclyn Ocumpaugh[1], Sujith M. Gowda[2],
Amy M. Kamarainen[3], and Shari J. Metcalf[4]

[1] Teachers College Columbia University, New York
[2] Arizona State Unversity, Tempe, Arizona
[3] NY Hall of Science, New York
[4] Harvard University, Massachusetts
baker2@exchange.tc.columbia.edu, jo2424@columbia.edu,
mgsujith@gmail.com, akamarainen@nyscience.org,
shari_metcalf@gse.harvard.edu

Abstract. The application of educational data mining (EDM) techniques to interactive learning software is increasingly being used to broaden the range of constructs typically incorporated in student models, moving from traditional assessment of student knowledge to the assessment of engagement, affect, strategy, and metacognition. Researchers are also broadening the range of environments within which these constructs are assessed. In this study, we develop sensor-free affect detection for EcoMUVE, an immersive multi-user virtual environment that teaches middle-school students about casualty in ecosystems. In this study, models were constructed for five different educationally-relevant affective states (boredom, confusion, delight, engaged concentration, and frustration). Such models allow us to examine the behaviors most closely associated with particular affective states, paving the way for the design of adaptive personalization to improve engagement and learning.

Keywords: student modeling, educational data mining, intelligent tutoring system, science inquiry, MUVEs, affect detection.

1 Introduction

Researchers are increasingly interested in automated affect detection within educational software [cf. 8], which can be used both to drive automated intervention [3,16] and to conduct basic research on affect and learning [13,18]. One popular approach in affect detection within educational software is to leverage physical sensors of various sorts, including visual images obtained through webcams posture sensors, and electroencephalograms [1, 21, 29, 30]. Detectors built using physical sensors have typically been successful at identifying student affect in laboratory settings [12], but in classrooms as well [2]. One limitation of physical sensors in education research, however, is that they can be both costly and fragile. Combined with bandwidth restrictions, these issues can reduce the practicality of real-time sensor-based detection, especially in school environments.

V. Dimitrova et al. (Eds.): UMAP 2014, LNCS 8538, pp. 290–300, 2014.

Consequently, many researchers are now working towards sensor-free affect detection [see 6, 11, 17, 22, 26]. The quality of detectors developed in this fashion has now reached a point where detector agreement with expert field coders is about half as good as inter-rater agreement between human experts [cf. 6, 22]. Furthermore, sensor-free detectors of student affect have been able to predict standardized measures of student learning [22] and even which students will choose to attend college several years later [27]. Many of the sensor-free affect detectors developed have been developed for intelligent tutoring systems [6, 12, 17, 22].

In this paper, we build detectors that can infer a range of student affective states within the context of a multi-user virtual environments (MUVE), a computer-based learning program where each student controls an avatar who moves through a virtual world in a more autonomous fashion, interacting with non-player characters and objects in order to solve puzzles and learn educational content [15]. Affect detection has been developed previously for one MUVE, Crystal Island [26]. Their model was developed from a combination of baseline data obtained from a series of questionnaires and data from student interactions with the MUVE. The present study builds on this pioneering work, developing a sensor-free affect detector for EcoMUVE without using baseline questionnaires.

2 Data

The data analyzed were collected from 153 students studying with two teachers at a suburban middle school in the Northeastern United States. Students were predominantly White and Asian-American, with small numbers of Latino and African-American students. Only 1% was eligible for the free/reduced-price lunch program, considerably below the national average.

Students in this study were using EcoMUVE, a computer-based curriculum designed to teach about ecosystems. This 3D virtual world simulates real-life ecological environments, allowing students to develop an understanding of the complex interrelationships characteristic of ecosystems by maneuvering avatars throughout pond (module 1) and forest (module 2) ecosystems like that shown in Figure 1 [19]. Each 2-week module allows students to explore the simulated ecosystem over a number of virtual days, providing opportunities to observe interactions among ecological components (e.g., water, algae, fish) and the impact of human development on these multifaceted relationships. One module, for example, introduces a pond environment negatively affected by the nearby development of human infrastructure. Through investigation of the ecosystem (e.g., measuring bacterial composition of the pond, interviewing residents), students uncover causes of observed changes—in this instance, fertilizer runoff from an adjacent golf course and housing development is producing an algal bloom [19].

Fig. 1. Screenshots of the EcoMUVE virtual environment and tools

3   Method

3.1   Obtaining Ground Truth Labels through BROMP

Student affect and behavior was observed *in situ* during EcoMUVE use. Both were coded simultaneously by an expert field observer, the second author, using the Baker-Rodrigo Observation Method Protocol (BROMP), [20]. BROMP has been used for several years to study behavior and affect in educational settings [5, 7, 25, 29] and has been used as the basis for successful automated detectors of affect [6, 22]. At present, 59 individuals have been certified, achieving inter-rater reliability (Cohen's Kappa > 0.6) with one or more other BROMP-certified coders. The coder in this study has successfully certified six other BROMP coders and has experience coding for a variety of different educational systems in populations that represent a wide range of regional, ethnic, and socioeconomic differences.

BROMP is implemented using the HART field observation synchronization software [6] developed for the Android platform. This software enforces a pre-determined order that prevents observers from being biased towards coding only the most interesting classroom events. HART also synchronizes observations to internet time so that they can be matched with the corresponding log files of the educational software being observed. In line with previous research on optimizing affect identification [23], BROMP-trained coders make holistic judgments based on contextualized observations of the student's actions, utterances, facial expressions, posture, and interactions with teachers or peers [7, 20]. Coders use side-glances to minimize observer effects, ignoring the affect and behavior of any students other than the one currently being observed. They record the first affective state they observe but have up to 20 seconds to make their observation.

In this study, seven affective states were recorded: boredom, engaged concentration (the affective state associated with flow – cf. [7]), confusion, delight, disgust, frustration, and sorrow. The categories were selected based on several criteria, including evidence about prevalent categories from previous learning research [7, 10], evidence about the prevalence of delight in games [24], qualitative reports from teachers and EcoMUVE developers, and discoveries made during a pilot study. Affective states which did not fit these categories and observations which occurred when a student could not otherwise be coded (e.g. if the student left the room or the teacher paused EcoMUVE activity for lecture), were coded with a "?".

Students were observed over the course of up to three class days (one class period per day). Observations for which a "?" was recorded or that occurred when the student was logged out of EcoMUVE were excluded, resulting in 2187 observations across all students and an average of 14.29 observations per student (SD = 5.35).

Within the field observations, the most common affective state was engaged concentration (67%). The remaining affective states were far less frequent. Delight was observed 7.1% of the time (much higher than typically seen in intelligent tutors), and confusion was recorded in 3.1% of the observations. Frustration (0.9%), boredom (0.5%), disgust (0.4%) and sorrow (0.1%) accounted for less than 2% of the data combined. The remaining 20.9% of the observations were labeled with the "?" that BROMP coders use when another affective state is being presented, when a student's affective state is ambiguous, or when the student otherwise cannot be observed. In this study, many of these cases involved the teachers pausing EcoMUVE activity for lecture or asking students to get out of their seats for group activities.

3.2 Creation of Affect Models

Log file data was synchronized with BROMP data, so that each 20-second period preceding the entry of an observation (termed a clip) was tagged with the corresponding affect and behavior labels. Models were constructed at the clip level for the five most common affective states (boredom, confusion, delight, engaged concentration, and frustration).

Features were distilled from available information within EcoMUVE's log files. As in previous research of affect and other educationally relevant constructs, features included specific descriptions of individual actions (e.g. picking up a particular object), classification of different actions by types (e.g. picking up similar objects), information about whether or not an action was novel or repetitive, and temporal information. As with previous investigations of virtual environments, they also included information about EcoMUVE's virtual locations (e.g. whether an action was completed in the submarine or near the pond) and interactions between students.

Attempts were made to fit each detector using six common classification algorithms (i.e., K*, JRip, J48, REPTree, Bayesian Logistic Regression, and Linear Regression), which are representative of a variety of different patterns but are less susceptible to over-fitting than many other algorithms.

Features for machine learning algorithms were chosen using forward selection, an iterative process in which features are added individually. At each iteration, the feature that most improves model goodness is added; this process continues until model performance no longer improves. In this study, cross-validated Cohen's (1960)

Kappa, which scales from -1 to 1, was used as the goodness metric during feature selection. Features that performed below chance in single-feature models (Kappa ≤ 0) were excluded prior to this process in order to reduce the chance of over-fitting.

Detectors were evaluated at the student level using 5-fold cross-validation (e.g. detectors were trained on data from four student groups and tested on data from a fifth). In addition, students were stratified into fold assignments based on their training labels, guaranteeing a representative number of majority and minority class observations in each fold. After the creation of each fold, an alternate version of each training fold was created through resampling so that an equal number of examples where the construct was present or absent occurred in each fold. In this process, clips that contain the construct being detected were duplicated in order to artificially increase that construct's frequency within the training set. However, in order to ensure validity, model performance was always tested on data that had not been resampled.

In addition to Cohen's Kappa, which was also applied during the forward selection process, A' was used to assess final detector performance and select the optimum algorithm for each detector. A' scales from 0 to 1 (chance = 0.5) and assesses the probability that the detector will correctly identify whether a specific affective state is present or absent in a specific clip. A' is equivalent to W, the Wilcoxon statistic, and closely approximates the area under the Receiver-Operating Curve [14]. Because current implementations of AUC ROC available in data mining and statistics packages over-estimate goodness for the special case where multiple data points have the same confidence, A' was calculated using software available at http://www.columbia.edu/~rsb2162/computeAPrime.zip.

4   Results

Each of the five detectors constructed for EcoMUVE performed better than chance under cross-validation. In particular, Kappa values for these models were generally comparable to values seen for sensor-free affect detection in recent papers [e.g. 6, 22, 26], but A' was somewhat lower than the values seen in [22].

The best detector of Boredom used JRip, and achieved a Kappa of 0.31 and an A' of 0.65. It relied upon five features: (1) a normalized metric of student speed based on a calculation called TimeSDtype (see below), (2) the largest amount of time between two actions in a clip, (3) the number of zoom changes within the submarine, (4) the number of times the student has viewed the data he or she has collected, and (5) and the number of player actions in the clip.

The best detector of Confusion used J48 and achieved a Kappa of 0.23 and an A' of 0.60. It relied upon five features: (1) the ratio between the number of times the student has viewed his or her data and taken measurements, (2) the number of times the student has repeated the same measurement in the current zone, (3) the total number of measures that the student has taken so far, (4) the average number of characters in each text chat, and (5) the number of player actions in the clip.

Table 1. Features used in boredom detector

Boredom	
B1	Across the last 5 actions, the sum of TimeSDType. For each student action, TimeSDType is the degree to which the current student action is faster or slower than the average action by all students involving the same type of action (e.g. air temperature measurements or entering the submarine), in standard deviations faster (-) or slower (+) than the average.
B2	The largest amount of time between two actions during the clip (not considering whether or not the student logged out between actions).
B3	The total number of *zoom* changes within the submarine so far.
B4	The total number of times the student used the *view data* application so far.
B5	The number of student actions in the clip.

Table 2. Features used in confusion detector

Confusion	
C1	The ratio between the number of times the student *viewed data* up until the current action, and the number of times the student took measurements up until the current action.
C2	The number of times the student has repeated the same measurement in the current zone so far.
C3	The total number of measures that the student has taken so far.
C4	The average number of characters in each text chat the player engaged in during the clip. (Actions other than chats are counted as 0 characters).
C5	The number of student actions in the clip.

The best detector of Delight used Bayesian Logistic Regression, achieving a Kappa of 0.19 and an A' of 0.62. It relied upon six features: (1) the number of student actions involving plants, (2) the percentage of photos not followed by accessing the relevant species page, (3) a largest number of measures that the student has taken per trip to each zone, (4) the ratio between the amount of time spent in the submarine and the number of measures taken in it, and (5) the largest value of the second feature in this model, and (5) the number of student actions in the clip.

The best detector of Engaged Concentration used J48, achieving a Kappa of 0.24 and an A' of 0.56. It relied upon seven features: (1) a normalized measure of how fast or slow student actions are based on their peers' typical response time for the same kind of action, (2) the amount of time the student has spent using EcoMUVE during the real-world day, (3) the amount of time the student has spent interacting with NPCs, (4) the amount of time the student has interacted with plants, (5) another normalized measure of how fast or slow student actions are, (6) the number of photos taken in the real-world day, and (7) the number of student actions per clip.

Table 3. Features used in delight detector

Delight	
D1	The total number of student actions involving plants so far.
D2	The percentage of photographs a student takes without immediately accessing the relevant species page.
D3	The number of measurements taken per student trip to each zones so far. Then the largest value of this feature at any point in the clip is taken.
D4	The ratio between the amount of time spent in the submarine and the number of measurements taken in the submarine
D5	The percentage of photographs a student takes without immediately accessing the relevant species page. Then the largest value of this feature at any point in the clip is taken.
D6	The number of student actions in the clip.

Table 4. Features used in engaged concentration detector

Engaged Concentration	
E1	Across the last 3 actions, the sum of TimeSDType. (See definition of TimeSDType in boredom detector features, Table 1.)
E2	The total time the student spent using EcoMUVE so far in the real world day, as calculated from the beginning of the clip.
E3	The total time spent by the player interacting with NPCs so far.
E4	The total amount of time spent by the player interacting with plants.
E5	Across the last 5 actions, the sum of TimeSDObjectType. For each student action, TimeSDObjectType is the degree to which the current player action is faster or slower than the average action by allstudent involving the same type of action, but only for actions involving interaction with an object/animal/plant (e.g. taking a photo of an animal), in standard deviations faster (-) or slower (+) than the average. Then, the largest value of this feature at any point in the clip is taken.
E6	The total photographs taken in the current, real-world day so far.
E7	The number of student actions in the clip.

The best detector of Frustration used K*, achieving a Kappa of 0.27 and an A' of 0.65. It relied upon seven features: (1) the average amount of time the student has taken to read a species page, (2) the average time per measure in the submarine, (3) the smallest values of the second feature, (4) the ratio between the time spent reading (for the first time) and rereading a species page, (5) the number of player actions in the clip, (6) the time spent in the submarine divided by the number of measurements taken during that time, and (7) the time per field guide access divided by the number of times a student has accessed a species page for the first time.

Table 5. Features used in frustration detector

Frustration	
F1	The average amount of time a student takes to read a species page.
F2	The average time per measurement taken in the submarine.
F3	The average time per measurement taken in the submarine. Then the smallest value of this feature at any point in the clip is taken.
F4	The ratio between the total time a student spent reading species pages and the number of times he or she re-reads a species page for the second or subsequent time.
F5	The number of student actions in the clip.
F6	Time spent in submarine (*from enter submarine* to next *enter zone*), divided by number of measurements taken from within submarine.
F7	Time per field guide access (from opened to closed), divided by total number of species page accesses—but *only* for cases where student is accessing a species page for the first time.

As can be seen, there were some key commonalities between the features utilized by the different models. Most notably, the number of actions that a student made within the 20-second clip being examined was included in the detector of every single construct. This feature gives some information about the speed with which students are working within the system. Temporal features were generally important, forming part of the model even beyond this feature for engaged concentration, frustration, and boredom. Student measurements played a prominent role for confusion and frustration – and also, somewhat surprisingly, for delight. In particular, repeating the same measurement was an indicator of confusion. Students who access the data without regard to the measurements they are taking are more likely to be bored, while those who are doing so frequently, though with more purpose, are more likely to be confused. Similarly, actions within the submarine were indicators of both positive and negative emotions (delight, frustration, and boredom). Students who took many photos, but who did not follow them up by reading the species page, were more likely to be delighted. Text chat with other students was an indicator of confusion, while interaction with the game's non-player characters was an indicator of engaged concentration.

5   Discussion and Conclusions

In this paper, we present five sensor-free models of educationally-relevant affective states for the virtual environment, EcoMUVE, a multi-user virtual environment (MUVE) for learning about ecosystems. In recent years, it has been demonstrated that affective models can be developed for a range of online learning environments. To our knowledge, this is the first paper demonstrating that sensor-free affect detectors can be developed for a MUVE without changing the student experience in any way. In the prior work on affect detection in MUVEs [26], questionnaire data was incorporated into the models, and the student experience was changed in order to develop models, with students completing pop-up surveys on their affect. We extend this pioneering work by developing models using non-intrusive BROMP field observations, and develop models that can make decisions using no data other than the unmodified interactions between the student and the learning system.

In particular, we believe that our model of delight makes an important contribution to the nascent area of sensor-free, automated affect detection in online learning systems, since, to the best of our knowledge, this is the first time that a cross-validated sensor-free model of this construct has performed above chance for the original data distribution. While delight is less common in the intelligent tutoring systems within which much of the work on sensor-free affect has taken place, it is prominent within game-like environments, as shown by its relatively high frequency in the EcoMUVE data. As this area of research advances and suites of sensor-free affect detectors become available for more systems, delight will likely prove to be an important indicator of engagement.

The resultant models presented here achieve an average performance of Kappa = 0.25 and A' = 0.61, an average Kappa higher than that seen in [26] and not far below the values seen for sensor-free affect detectors developed for intelligent tutoring systems [cf. 6, 22]. While considerable room for improvement remains, it is worth noting that detectors of comparable goodness were recently developed for ASSISTments using BROMP observations and similar data mining techniques [22]. ASSISTments' affect detectors have since been successful at predicting long-term learning outcomes for middle-school students, including success on state standardized exams [22] and even which students will attend college several years after using a learning system [27].

Even without further refinement, these detectors should be sufficient for the development of fail-soft interventions that can be implemented without interrupting the learning process and for discovery with models research, such as the approach used to make long-term predictions in ASSISTments. Further study of EcoMUVE log files using these detectors is also likely to provide insight into what aspects of the learning system are most boring, frustrating, or confusing, supporting the development of design changes to make EcoMUVE more engaging and effective.

Acknowledgements. Portions of this material are based upon work supported by the Institute of Education Sciences, U.S. Department of Education, through Grant R305A080514. This research was also supported by grant (#OPP1048577) from the Bill & Melinda Gates Foundation. Thanks also to Belinda Yew for help in editing and to the teachers and students who made this study possible.

References

1. AlZoubi, O., Calvo, R.A., Stevens, R.H.: Classification of EEG for affect recognition: An adaptive approach. In: Nicholson, A., Li, X. (eds.) AI 2009. LNCS, vol. 5866, pp. 52–61. Springer, Heidelberg (2009)
2. Arroyo, I., Cooper, D.G., Burleson, W., Woolf, B.P., Muldner, K., Christopherson, R.: Emotion Sensors Go To School. AIED, vol. 200 (2009)

3. Ivon, A., Woolf, B.P., Cooper, D.G., Burleson, W., Muldner, K.: The impact of animated pedagogical agents on girls' and boys' emotions, attitudes, behaviors and learning. In: 2011 11th IEEE International Conference on Advanced Learning Technologies, ICALT, pp. 506–510. IEEE (2011)

4. Baker, R.S.J.D., Gowda, S.M., Corbett, A.T., Ocumpaugh, J.: Towards automatically detecting whether student learning is shallow. In: Cerri, S.A., Clancey, W.J., Papadourakis, G., Panourgia, K. (eds.) ITS 2012. LNCS, vol. 7315, pp. 444–453. Springer, Heidelberg (2012)

5. Baker, R.S.J.d., Mitrović, A., Mathews, M.: Detecting gaming the system in constraint-based tutors. In: De Bra, P., Kobsa, A., Chin, D. (eds.) UMAP 2010. LNCS, vol. 6075, pp. 267–278. Springer, Heidelberg (2010)

6. Baker, R.S.J.D., Gowda, S.M., Wixon, M., Kalka, J., Wagner, A.Z., Salvi, A., Aleven, V., Kusbit, G., Ocumpaugh, J., Rossi, L.: Towards Sensor-free Affect Detection in Cognitive Tutor Algebra. In: Proceedings of the 5th International Conference on Educational Data Mining, pp. 126–133 (2012)

7. Baker, R.S., D'Mello, S.K., Rodrigo, M.M.T., Graesser, A.C.: Better to be frustrated than bored: The incidence, persistence, and impact of learners' cognitive–affective states during interactions with three different computer-based learning environments. International Journal of Human-Computer Studies 68(4), 223–241 (2010)

8. Calvo, R.A., D'Mello, S.: Affect detection: An interdisciplinary review of models, methods, and their applications. IEEE Transactions on Affective Computing 1(1), 18–37 (2010)

9. Cohen, J.: A coefficient of agreement for nominal scales. Educational and Psychological Measurement 20(1), 37–46 (1960)

10. Craig, S., Graesser, A., Sullins, J., Gholson, B.: Affect and learning: an exploratory look into the role of affect in learning with AutoTutor. Journal of Educational Media 29(3), 241–250 (2004)

11. Conati, C., Maclaren, H.: Empirically building and evaluating a probabilistic model of user affect. User Modeling and User-Adapted Interaction 19(3), 267–303 (2009)

12. D'Mello, S.K., Craig, S.D., Witherspoon, A.W., McDaniel, B.T., Graesser, A.C.: Automatic Detection of Learner's Affect from Conversational Cues. User Modeling and User- Adapted Interaction 18(1-2), 45–80 (2008)

13. D'Mello, S., Graesser, A.: The half-life of cognitive-affective states during complex learning. Cognition & Emotion 25(7), 1299–1308 (2011)

14. Hanley, J., McNeil, B.: The Meaning and Use of the Area under a Receiver Operating Characteristic (ROC) Curve. Radiology 143, 29–36 (1982)

15. Ketelhut, D.J., et al.: A multi-user virtual environment for building and assessing higher order inquiry skills in science. British Journal of Educational Technology 41(1), 56–68 (2010)

16. Lehman, B.A., D'Mello, S.K., Strain, A., Millis, C., Gross, M., Dobbins, A., Wallace, P., Millis, K., Graesser, A.C.: Inducing and tracking confusion with contradictions during complex learning. International Journal of Artificial Intelligence in Education 22(2), 85–105 (2013)

17. Litman, D.J.: Recognizing student emotions and attitudes on the basis of utterances in spoken tutoring dialogues with both human and computer tutors. Speech Communication 48(5), 559–590 (2006)

18. Liu, Z., Pataranutaporn, V., Ocumpaugh, J., Baker, R.S.: Sequences of Frustration and Confusion, and Learning. In: Proceedings of the 6th International Conference on Educational Data Mining, pp. 114–120 (2013)

19. Metcalf, S.J., Kamarainen, A., Grotzer, T., Dede, C.: Ecosystem science learning via multi-user virtual environments. International Journal of Gaming and Computer-Mediated Simulations 3(1), 86 (2011)
20. Ocumpaugh, J., Baker, R.S.J.D., Rodrigo, M.A.: Quantitative Field Observation (QFOs) Baker-Rodrigo Observation Method Protocol (BROMP) 1.0 Training Manual version 1.0 (October 17, 2012)
21. Pantic, M., Leon, J.M.: Rothkrantz. Toward an affect-sensitive multimodal human-computer interaction. Proceedings of the IEEE 91(9), 1370–1390 (2003)
22. Pardos, Z.A., Baker, R.S., San Pedro, M.O., Gowda, S.M., Gowda, S.M.: Affective states and state tests: Investigating how affect throughout the school year predicts end of year learning outcomes. In: Proceedings of the Third International Conference on Learning Analytics and Knowledge, pp. 117–124. ACM (2013)
23. Planalp, S., DeFrancisco, V.L., Rutherford, D.: Varieties of Cues to Emotion in Naturally Occurring Settings. Cognition and Emotion 10(2), 137–153 (1996)
24. Rodrigo, M.M.T., Baker, R.S.J.D.: Comparing Learners' Affect While Using an Intelligent Tutor and an Educational Game. Research and Practice in Technology Enhanced Learning 6(1), 43–66 (2011)
25. Rodrigo, M.M.T., Baker, R.S.J.D.: Coarse-Grained Detection of Student Frustration in an Introductory Programming Course. In: Proceedings of ICER 2009: the International Computing Education Workshop (2009)
26. Sabourin, J., Mott, B., Lester, J.C.: Modeling learner affect with theoretically grounded dynamic bayesian networks. In: D'Mello, S., Graesser, A., Schuller, B., Martin, J.-C. (eds.) ACII 2011, Part I. LNCS, vol. 6974, pp. 286–295. Springer, Heidelberg (2011)
27. San Pedro, M.O.Z., Baker, R.S.J.D., Bowers, A.J., Heffernan, N.T.: Predicting College Enrollment from Student Interaction with an Intelligent Tutoring System in Middle School. In: Proceedings of the 6th International Conference on Educational Data Mining, pp. 177–184 (2013)
28. San Pedro, M.O.Z., Baker, R.S.J.d., Gowda, S.M., Heffernan, N.T.: Towards an understanding of affect and knowledge from student interaction with an intelligent tutoring system. In: Lane, H.C., Yacef, K., Mostow, J., Pavlik, P. (eds.) AIED 2013. LNCS, vol. 7926, pp. 41–50. Springer, Heidelberg (2013)
29. Sebe, N., Cohen, I., Gevers, T., Huang, T.S.: Multimodal approaches for emotion recognition: a survey. In: International Society for Optics and Photonics Electronic Imaging 2005, pp. 56–67 (2005)
30. Zeng, Z., Pantic, M., Roisman, G.I., Huang, T.S.: A survey of affect recognition methods: Audio, visual, and spontaneous expressions. IEEE Transactions on Pattern Analysis and Machine Intelligence 31(1), 39–58 (2009)

Utilizing Mind-Maps for Information Retrieval and User Modelling

Joeran Beel[1,2], Stefan Langer[1,2], Marcel Genzmehr[1], and Bela Gipp[1,2]

[1] Docear, Magdeburg, Germany
[2] Otto-von-Guericke University, Magdeburg, Germany
[3] University of California, Berkeley, USA
{beel,langer,genzmehr,gipp}@docear.org

Abstract. Mind-maps have been widely neglected by the information retrieval (IR) community. However, there are an estimated two million active mind-map users, who create 5 million mind-maps every year, of which a total of 300,000 is publicly available. We believe this to be a rich source for information retrieval applications, and present eight ideas on how mind-maps could be utilized by them. For instance, mind-maps could be utilized to generate user models for recommender systems or expert search, or to calculate relatedness of web-pages that are linked in mind-maps. We evaluated the feasibility of the eight ideas, based on estimates of the number of available mind-maps, an analysis of the content of mind-maps, and an evaluation of the users' acceptance of the ideas. We concluded that user modelling is the most promising application with respect to mind-maps. A user modelling prototype – a recommender system for the users of our mind-mapping software *Docear* – was implemented, and evaluated. Depending on the applied user modelling approaches, the effectiveness, i.e. click-through rate on recommendations, varied between 0.28% and 6.24%. This indicates that mind-map based user modelling is promising, but not trivial, and that further research is required to increase effectiveness.

Keywords: mind-maps, content analysis, user modelling, information retrieval.

1   Introduction

Information retrieval (IR) applications utilize many items beyond the items' original purpose. For instance, emails are intended as a means of communication, but Google utilizes them for generating user profiles and displaying personalized advertisement [1]; social tags can help to organize private web-page collections, but search engines utilize them for indexing websites [2]; research articles are meant to publish research results, but they, or more precisely their references, are utilized to analyze the impact of researchers and institutions [3].

We propose that mind-maps are an equally valuable source for information retrieval as are social tags, emails, research articles, etc. Consequently, our research objective was to identify, how mind-maps could be used to empower IR applications. To achieve our objective, we 1) analyzed the extent to which mind-mapping is used, to decide if mind-map based IR is a field worth researching, 2) brainstormed how mind-maps might be utilized by IR applications, 3) analyzed the feasibility of the ideas, and

V. Dimitrova et al. (Eds.): UMAP 2014, LNCS 8538, pp. 301–313, 2014.
© Springer International Publishing Switzerland 2014

Fig. 1. Mind-map example (draft of this paper)

4) implemented a prototype of the most promising idea, which – to anticipate the result – is a recommender system that creates user models based on mind-maps. All estimates in this paper are based on data collected from our own mind-mapping software *Docear* [4, 5], *Google Trends* and the mind-mapping tools' websites.

We hope to stimulate a discussion with this paper that encourages IR and user modelling researchers to further analyze the potential of mind-maps. We believe that researchers will find this new research field rewarding, and the results will enable developers of mind-mapping tools to devise novel services for their millions of users.

2   Related Work

Mind-maps are typically used to develop ideas and organize information. As such they are often used for tasks including brainstorming, project management and document drafting. Figure 1 shows an example of a mind-map, created with our mind-mapping software *Docear (http://docear.org)* [5]. We created the mind-map to represent a draft of this paper. The root node represents the title of this paper. From the root node, child nodes branch to represent each chapter, additional child nodes branch off for each paragraph, sentence and reference. We also added a list of relevant conferences, to which we planned to submit the paper. Red arrows indicate a link to a website. A PDF icon indicates a link to a PDF file on the hard drive. A "circle" on a node indicates that the node has child nodes that are currently hidden.

There has been plenty of research showing the effectiveness of mind-mapping as a learning tool [6]; creating mind-maps automatically from full-text streams [7]; and evaluating whether paper-based or electronic mind-mapping is more effective [8]. To the best of our knowledge, mind-maps have not been researched with regard to information retrieval or user modelling. However, there are two types of information retrieval applications, which utilized mind-maps in practice.

The first type of application is a search engine for mind-maps. Several mind-mapping tools, for instance *XMind* and *MindMeister*, allow their users to publish their mind-maps in so called "mind-map galleries". These galleries are similar to photo galleries. They show thumbnails of mind-maps that users uploaded to the gallery. Visitors of the galleries may search for mind-maps containing certain keywords, and download the corresponding mind-maps. According to *MindMeister*, around 10% of mind-maps being created by their users are published in the galleries[1]. The other mind-maps remain private.

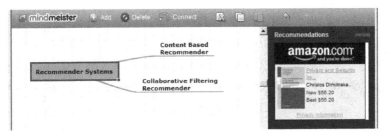

Fig. 2. Personalized advertisement in MindMeister

The second type of application is a user modelling system. Only two companies – *MindMeister* and *Mindomo* – implemented such a system to generate user models and display personalized advertisement. *MindMeister* extracted the terms of the node that a user last edited or created – typically, a node contains two or three terms [9]. These terms were sent to Amazon's Web Service as search query. Amazon returned book recommendations matching the search query, which *MindMeister* displayed in a window besides the mind-map (Figure 2). *Mindomo* had a similar concept, only that Google AdSense instead of Amazon was used. Meanwhile, both companies abandoned personalized advertisement, though they still offer and actively maintain their mind-mapping tools. In an email, *Mindomo* said that "people were not really interested" in the advertisement[2].

3   Popularity of Mind-Mapping and Mind-Mapping Tools

Some reviewers of previous papers were skeptical whether there is enough interest in mind-mapping to justify the effort for researching the potential of IR applications utilizing mind-maps. We believe this skepticism to be unfounded, because, as shown in the next paragraphs, there is a significant number of mind-mapping tools and users who could benefit from the research.

The popularity of *mind-mapping*, based on search volume, is similar to the popularity of e.g. *note taking, file management*, or *crowdsourcing*, and significantly higher than for *reference management, user modelling, recommender systems*, or *information retrieval* (Figure 3). The website *Mind-Mapping.org* lists 142 mind-mapping tools being actively maintained, although some tools offer mind-mapping only as secondary feature in addition to other visualization techniques, such as concept maps or Gantt charts. When discontinued tools are included in the count, there are 207 tools. Of the 'pure' mind-mapping tools, i.e. those that focus on mind-mapping functionality, *XMind* is the most

---

[1] Email from MindMeister's CEO Michael Hollauf, June 28, 2011. Permission for publication was granted.
[2] Email by Daniel Sima of the Mindomo team, October 3, 2011. Permission for publication was granted.

popular tool, based on search volume (25%) (Figure 4)[3]. Other popular tools are *Free-Mind* (23%), *MindManager* (13%), and *MindMeister* (8%). The search volume for *XMind* is in the same league as search volume for the *Dropbox* alternative *ownCloud*, the reference manager *Zotero*, or the Blog *TechCrunch*, and the volume is significantly higher than for academic conferences such as *UMAP*, *SIGIR*, or *RecSys* (Figure 5).

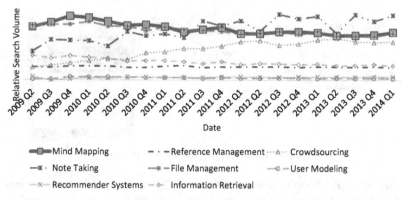

Fig. 3. Search volume for "Mind-Mapping" and other selected search terms

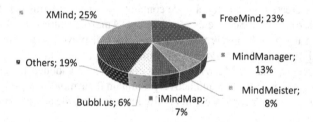

Fig. 4. Search volume for mind-mapping tools

According to the tools' websites, *XMind* has more than 1 million users, *Bubbl.us* more than 1.5 million, *MindManager* more than 2 million, and *MindMeister* more than 2.5 million users. In sum, this makes 7 Million users for four tools that accumulate 52% of the search volume (Figure 4). Interpolating from the search volume, we can estimate that the remaining tools (48% of the search volume) must have around 6.5 million users. This results in a total of around 13.5 million mind-map users. To us, it seems likely that these numbers also include inactive users. For our own mind-mapping software *Docear*, 10 to 20% of the users who registered in the past years, are active, i.e. they started Docear in the past month. Based on this information, we may estimate the numbers of active mind-map users to be between 1.35 and 2.7 million.

The claimed user counts do not always correlate with the search volume. For instance, MindMeister accumulates less than 8% of the search volume, and claims 2.5

---

million users. In contrast, XMind accumulates 25% of the search volume, but reports only around 1 million users. We assume that these differences result from different registration and usage concepts. MindMeister is a web-based tool that requires everyone to register. XMind is a desktop software that can also be used without registration. As such, our estimate remains a rough guess. However, another estimate leads to a similar result. The open source mind-mapping software *FreeMind* was downloaded 1.4 million times in the past 12 month (we considered only downloads of the latest stable release)[4]. Assuming, that the number of active users is around 1/3 of users who downloaded the software in the past year, leads to the estimate that FreeMind has around 450,000 active users. Interpolating from the search volume (22.58%), leads to an estimate of 2 million active mind-map users.

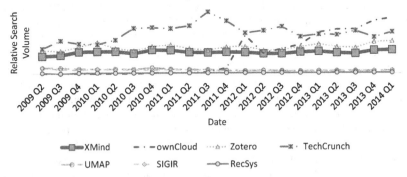

Fig. 5. Search volume for "XMind" and other selected search terms

We believe that these numbers indicate a substantial interest in the topic of mind-mapping, and the active user base justifies the effort to research the potential of utilizing mind-maps for IR applications.

4   Ideas for Mind-Map Based IR Applications

To develop ideas, how IR applications could utilize mind-maps, we conducted a brainstorming session with a group of five experts from the fields of mind-mapping (two experts) and information retrieval (three experts). Before the session was conducted, the information retrieval experts were given an introduction to mind-mapping and the mind-mapping experts were given an introduction on how information retrieval is applied to emails, social tags, etc. The following eight ideas evolved from the brainstorming (for more details, refer to [10]).

Search Engines for Mind-Maps: Mind-maps contain information that probably is not only relevant for the given authors of a mind-map, but also for others. Therefore, a search engine for mind-maps might be an interesting application. As described in the "Related Work" section, such systems already exist.

User Modelling: Analog to analyzing users' authored research papers, emails, etc., user modelling systems could analyze mind-maps to identify users' information needs

---

[4] http://sourceforge.net/projects/freemind/files/stats/timeline

and expertise. User models could be used, for instance, for personalized advertisements, or by recommender systems, or expert search systems. For instance, when employees create mind-maps, we would assume that the mind-maps would be suitable to infer the employees' expertise. This information could be used by an expert search system. As described in the "Related Work" section, *Mindomo* and *MindMeister* implemented user modelling systems, but Mindomo reported that users were not interested in the results. Hence, they removed the system from their mind-mapping application. Apparently, user modelling based on mind-maps is not trivial and does not always lead to satisfying results.

Document Indexing / Anchor Text Analysis: Mind-maps could be seen as neighboring documents to those documents being linked in the mind-maps, and anchor text analysis could be applied to index the linked documents with the terms occurring in the mind-maps. Such information could be valuable, e.g., for classic search engines.

Document Relatedness: When mind-maps contain links to web pages or other documents, these links could be used to determine relatedness of the linked web pages or documents. For instance, with citation proximity analysis [11], documents would be assumed to be related that are linked in close proximity, e.g. in the same sentence. Such calculations could be relevant for search engines and recommender systems.

Document Summarization: Mind-maps could be utilized to complement document summarization. If a mind-map contains a link to a web-page, the node's text, and maybe the text of parent nodes, could be interpreted as a summary for the linked web page. Such summaries could be displayed by search engines on their result pages.

Impact Analysis: Mind-maps could be utilized to analyze the impact of the documents linked within the mind-map, similar to PageRank or citation based similarity metrics. This information could be used by search engines to rank, e.g., web pages, or by institutions to evaluate the impact of researchers and journals.

Trend Analysis: Trend analysis is important for marketing and customer relationship management, but also in other disciplines [12]. Such analyses could be done based on mind-maps. For instance, analyzing mind-maps that stand for drafts of academic papers would allow estimating citation counts for the referenced papers. It would also predict in which field new papers can be expected.

Semantic Analysis: A mind-map is a tree and nodes are in hierarchical order. As such, the nodes and their terms are in direct relationship to each other. These relationships could be used, for instance, by search engines to identify synonyms, or by recommender systems to recommend alternative search terms or social tags.

5   Feasibility

We evaluated the ideas' feasibility in three steps. First, we estimated whether there are enough mind-maps and mind-map users available to realize the ideas. Second, we analyzed whether the content of mind-maps is suitable for realizing the ideas. Finally, we gauged whether users are accepting the ideas.

5.1   Number of Mind-Map Users and (Public) Mind-Maps

Most of the ideas hinge on the availability of a large number of mind-maps. It is also important to distinguish between public and private mind-maps. If many mind-maps were available publicly, the ideas could be realized by anyone. If mind-maps were private, i.e. only available to the developers of the mind-mapping tools, only these developers could realize the ideas.

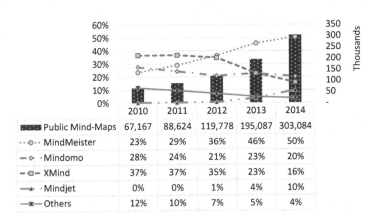

	2010	2011	2012	2013	2014
Public Mind-Maps	67,167	88,624	119,778	195,087	303,084
MindMeister	23%	29%	36%	46%	50%
Mindomo	28%	24%	21%	23%	20%
XMind	37%	37%	35%	23%	16%
Mindjet	0%	0%	1%	4%	10%
Others	12%	10%	7%	5%	4%

Fig. 6. Public mind-maps

There are more than 300,000 mind-maps in public galleries, 50% of them in the gallery of MindMeister, 20% in the gallery of Mindomo, and 16% in the gallery of XMind (Figure 6)[5]. Over the years, the number of public mind-maps increased from 67,167 in 2010 to 303,084 in 2014. Given, that MindMeister's users published around 62,000 mind-maps between 2013 and 2014, we estimate that MindMeister's users created approximately 620,000 mind-maps during that period, since around 10% of mind-maps being created are also published[1]. Interpolating these numbers with the search volume (Figure 4), we can estimate that overall 4.6 million mind-maps were created between 2013 and 2014. Another estimate confirms this number: Mind-map users create between 2 and 3 mind-maps per year on average [9]. A calculation with 2.5 mind-maps per year, and 2 million mind-map users, leads to an estimate of 5 million mind-maps created per year. Considering that mind-mapping tools have been used for many years, a few dozens of millions mind-maps must exist on the computers of mind-map users.

5.2   Content of Mind-Maps

We recently analyzed the content of 19,379 mind-maps, created by 11,179 *Mind-Meister* and *Docear* users [9]. On average, mind-maps contained a few dozens of nodes, each with two to three words on average. Some mind-maps even contained a

---

[5] Over the past four years, we retrieved the numbers of mind-maps each year directly from the web-pages of the galleries.

few thousand nodes, with some nodes containing more than a hundred words. This amount of nodes, and words, is comparable to the number of words in emails or web pages. Since emails and web pages are successfully utilized by information retrieval applications, the content of mind-maps might be suitable for those ideas that depend on the existence of terms. However, the number of links in mind-maps is low. Almost two thirds of the mind-maps did not contain any links to files, such as academic articles or other documents (63.88%), and most of the mind-maps that did contain links, contained only few of them. Links to web-pages were not available in 92.37% of Docear's mind-maps and 75.27% of MindMeister's mind-maps. Consequently, those ideas based on link-analysis seem less attractive.

5.3   User Acceptance

We evaluated the user acceptance of the eight ideas with our mind-mapping software *SciPlore MindMapping* [13]. 4,332 users were shown at first start a settings dialog. In this dialog, users could (un)select four options relating to the different ideas we proposed (Figure 7). It was randomly chosen whether options were pre-selected.

When all options were pre-selected, 61% of the users accepted user modelling to receive recommendations based on their mind-maps (Figure 7). 38% of the users accepted that the content of their mind-maps could be utilized e.g. for anchor text analysis. 32% of users agreed that SPLMM could also analyze the content of the documents they linked in their mind-maps. Usage mining, i.e. the general analysis of how users are making use of a software, was accepted by 48% of the users.

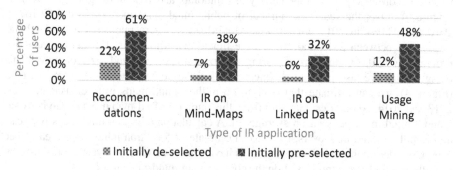

Fig. 7. User acceptance of IR on their mind-maps

If options were not pre-selected, fewer users allowed the analysis of their data. 22% activated recommendations, 7% activated information retrieval on mind-maps, 6% activated IR on the linked documents, and 12% activated usage mining.

5.4   Discussion of the Feasibility

Due to the generally few links available in mind-maps, anchor text analysis, calculating document relatedness, document summarization, and impact analysis seem less feasible for the majority of mind-mapping tools (Table 1). However, there might be exceptions, for instance in the case of Docear. Docear's mind-maps contain comparatively many links to PDF files, because most users are researchers who manage their academic papers with Docear. Assuming that Docear's users create enough mind-maps, the link-based ideas might be interesting to pursue.

Those ideas that depend on the availability of terms seem more feasible, considering the content of mind-maps. However, only a small number of mind-maps are publicly available (around 300,000). This makes the ideas less interesting for third parties who do not offer their own mind-mapping software. The same is true for developers of mind-mapping software with only a few users. A mind-map search engine or trend analysis using for example only 50,000 mind-maps, cannot attract many people. For the major players, such as XMind, FreeMind, or MindMeister, this might be different. They potentially have access to millions of mind-maps, which should be sufficient to achieve reasonable results. One idea is also relevant for the less popular mind-mapping tools, namely user modelling. User modelling, more precisely recommender system, personalized advertisement, or expert search, should be well applicable even with few users. User modelling has also the highest acceptance rate among the users. User Modelling for a recommender system was accepted by 61% or the users. User acceptance of the other ideas was lower. Around 10% of mind-maps are published, and around 30-40% of users accept IR to enhance external applications.

Table 1. Feasibility of the ideas

	Mind Map Availability		Content Suitability	Users' Acceptance	Overall
	For 3rd parties	For MM tool developers			
Search Engine	Low	Depends	Good	Low	Low
Document Indexing	Low	Depends	Low	Medium	Low
Document Relatedness	Low	Depends	Low	Medium	Low
Document Summarization	Low	Depends	Low	Medium	Low
Impact Analysis	Low	Depends	Low	Medium	Low
Trend Analysis	Low	Depends	Medium	Medium	Medium
Semantic Analysis	Low	Depends	Good	Medium	Medium
User Modeling	---	Good	Good	Good	Good

Overall, user modelling seems to be the most promising idea: The content of mind-maps is suitable, user acceptance is rather high, and user modelling is relevant for all developers of mind-mapping software, and companies whose employees use mind-maps. In addition, user modelling *directly* benefits the mind-mapping tools and may be fundamentally important for a company. For instance, Google is generating almost its entire profit from personalized advertisements [14], and Amazon is also making a significant amount of revenue through its recommender system [15]. In contrast, applications such as semantic analysis are usually not fundamental to a company's business.

However, user modelling based on mind-maps already had been implemented, but results indicate that it is not as promising as our analysis suggests. MindMeister and Mindomo created user models for displaying personalized advertisement but both abandoned this after a while. This leads to the question, whether mind-maps actually can successfully be utilized by user modelling systems.

6   Prototype

To analyze whether user modelling based on mind-maps can be done effectively, we integrated a recommender system into our mind-mapping tools *SciPlore MindMapping* (SPLMM) [13], and its successor *Docear* [5]. Both tools are primarily used by researchers. Therefore, the recommender system recommends research papers. We implemented different recommendation approaches that we evaluated using click-through rate (CTR), i.e. the ratio of clicked recommendations against the number of displayed recommendations. Please note that due to space restriction we may only provide superficial information on the recommender system and its evaluation. We are about to publish a paper that will present the architecture of Docear's recommender system in more detail, as well as a discussion on the suitability of CTR as an evaluation metric for recommender systems. These papers will be available soon at http://www.docear.org/publications/.

For SPLMM, we implemented an approach similar to MindMeister's approach. Each time, a user modified, i.e. edited or created, a node, the terms of that node were send as search query to Google Scholar. Google Scholar's Top 3 results were shown in a separate window above the currently opened mind-map. Between July and December 2011, 78,698 recommendations were displayed, of which 221 were clicked, i.e. an overall CTR of 0.28% was achieved (Figure 8). A CTR of 0.28% is low. If MindMeister and Mindomo should have achieved similarly CTRs, it is no surprise that they abandoned the personalized advertisement.

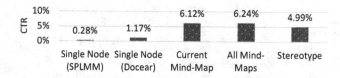

Fig. 8. CTR of different approaches

In Docear, we integrated a new recommender system [4]. The new system showed recommendations only when users explicitly requested them, or automatically every five days on start-up of Docear. Recommendations were based on Docear's own document corpus, consisting of around 1.8 million full-text articles. The recommender system used four different approaches and displayed 21,445 recommendations between July 2012 and February 2013. The first approach made use of the terms of the last modified node, similar to the approach of SPLMM. This led to a CTR of 1.17% (Figure 8). The reasons why CTR was around four times higher than CTR in SPLMM, may be manifold. Maybe, the lower frequency of displaying recommendations (every five days instead of continuously) or the source (Docear's corpus vs Google Scholar), influenced CTR. However, 1.17% is still a rather low CTR. The second approach utilized the most frequent words of the user's current mind-map. This increased CTR to 6.12%. When the most frequent words of *all* mind-maps were utilized, CTR was also above 6%. For the fourth approach, we manually compiled a list of ten research articles relating to academic writing. Most of Docear's users are researchers and therefore we assumed that these articles would be relevant to most of

Docear's users. When recommendations were given based on this approach – the stereotype approach [16] – CTR was 4.99%.

The results show that a single node, typically containing two to three words, does not express a user's information needs thoroughly. Instead, entire mind-maps are needed for analysis. To analyze this factor in more detail, we modified the recommender system, so it randomly chose the number of nodes to analyze. The results show that there is a strong correlation between the number of nodes analyzed and the CTR (Figure 9). When the recommender system utilized only the last 1 – 9 modified nodes, CTR was 3.16% on average. When 10 to 49 nodes were utilized, CTR increased to 4% on average. Utilizing between 500 and 999 nodes resulted in the highest CTR (7.47%). When more than 1,000 nodes were utilized, CTR began to decrease (though, the difference is not statistically significant).

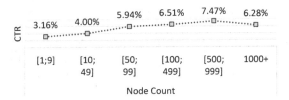

Fig. 9. CTR by number of analyzed nodes

7   Summary

Mind-maps have thus far been widely neglected by the information retrieval community. We found that there are more than 100 mind-mapping tools and that, based on search volume, the popularity of mind-mapping is comparable to the popularity of note taking, file management, or crowdsourcing. Popular mind-mapping tools, such as XMind, are as popular as popular reference management software (e.g. Zotero), or Tech Blogs (e.g. TechCrunch). Overall, we estimated, there are around 2 million people who actively create mind-maps using a mind-mapping software. Based on these numbers, we conclude that it is worth to research whether the developers of mind-mapping tools, and their users, might benefit from new applications, which utilize mind-maps.

We presented eight ideas of how mind-maps could be utilized to enhance information retrieval applications: search engines for mind-maps could help to find interesting information; user modelling based on mind-maps could enable the implementation of recommender systems, personalized advertisement, and expert search; anchor text analysis applied to mind-maps could enhance the indexing of web-pages and other documents; similarly, anchor-text analysis could enhance the summarization of web-pages and documents being linked in mind-maps; citation and link analysis could help to calculate document relatedness, which might be useful to enhance search engines or recommender systems; similarly, citation and link analysis in mind-maps could be used for impact and trend analysis; finally, semantic analyses could be applied to mind-maps to identify synonyms and other relationships of words,

Not all ideas are equally feasible. We analyzed the content of mind-maps and learned that mind-maps often do not contain any citations or links. In addition, there are only around 300,000 mind-maps publicly available, although around 5 million mind-maps are created each year. The user's acceptance to utilize their mind-maps was mediocre. 38% of the users allowed the use of their mind-maps for e.g. anchor text analysis, 61% accepted recommendations based on their mind-maps. We concluded that, out of the eight ideas, user modelling is the most feasible use case. The content of mind-maps is suitable for user modelling, the users' acceptance seems reasonably high, and user modelling is relevant for all developers of mind-mapping software, not only the major players.

We implemented a prototype of a user modelling system, namely a research paper recommender system, and, overall, results are promising. While the most simple user modelling approach – utilizing terms of the currently edited or created node – performed poorly (CTRs around 1% and lower), utilizing terms of users' entire mind-maps achieved click-through rates above 6%. This shows that user modelling based on mind-maps is not trivial, and strongly depends on the applied approaches. Further research is required to identify the unique characteristics of mind-maps, and to use these characteristics successfully in user modelling systems such as expert search, and recommender systems.

References

1. Google: Ads in Gmail and your personal data (2012),
   https://support.google.com/mail/answer/6603
2. Zubiaga, A., Martinez, R., Fresno, V.: Getting the most out of social annotations for web page classification. In: Proceedings of the 9th ACM Symposium on Document Engineering, pp. 74–83 (2009)
3. Jacso, P.: Testing the calculation of a realistic h-index in Google Scholar, Scopus, and Web of Science for FW Lancaster. Library Trends 56, 784–815 (2008)
4. Beel, J., Langer, S., Genzmehr, M., Nürnberger, A.: Introducing Docear's Research Paper Recommender System. In: Proceedings of the 13th ACM/IEEE-CS Joint Conference on Digital Libraries, JCDL 2013, pp. 459–460. ACM (2013)
5. Beel, J., Gipp, B., Langer, S., Genzmehr, M.: Docear: An Academic Literature Suite for Searching, Organizing and Creating Academic Literature. In: Proceedings of the 11th International ACM/IEEE Conference on Digital Libraries, pp. 465–466. ACM (2011)
6. Nesbit, J.C., Adesope, O.O.: Learning with concept and knowledge maps: A meta-analysis. Review of Educational Research 76, 413 (2006)
7. Brucks, C., Schommer, C.: Assembling Actor-based Mind-Maps from Text Stream. arXiv preprint (abs/0810.4616) (2008).
8. Mahler, T., Weber, M.: Dimian-Direct Manipulation and Interaction in Pen Based Mind Mapping. In: Proceedings of the 17th World Congress on Ergonomics, IEA 2009 (2009)
9. Beel, J., Langer, S.: An Exploratory Analysis of Mind Maps. In: Proceedings of the 11th ACM Symposium on Document Engineering, DocEng 2011, pp. 81–84. ACM (2011)
10. Beel, J., Gipp, B., Stiller, J.-O.: Information Retrieval on Mind Maps - What could it be good for? In: Proceedings of the 5th International Conference on Collaborative Computing: Networking, Applications and Worksharing, CollaborateCom 2009, pp. 1–4 (2009)

11. Gipp, B., Beel, J.: Citation Proximity Analysis (CPA) - A new approach for identifying related work based on Co-Citation Analysis. In: Proceedings of the 12th International Conference on Scientometrics and Informetrics ISSI 2009, pp. 571–575. International Society for Scientometrics and Informetrics, Rio de Janeiro (2009)
12. Chi, Y., Tseng, B.L., Tatemura, J.: Eigen-trend: trend analysis in the blogosphere based on singular value decompositions. In: Proceedings of the 15th ACM International Conference on Information and Knowledge Management, pp. 68–77. ACM (2006)
13. Beel, J., Gipp, B., Mueller, C.: SciPlore MindMapping' - A Tool for Creating Mind Maps Combined with PDF and Reference Management. D-Lib Magazine 15 (2009)
14. Google: Annual Report (2010),
    `http://investor.google.com/pdf/2010_google_annual_report.pdf`
15. Kiwitobes: Lessons on recommendation systems. Blog (2011),
    `http://blog.kiwitobes.com/?p=58`
16. Rich, E.: User modeling via stereotypes. Cognitive science 3, 329–354 (1979)

iSCUR: Interest and Sentiment-Based Community Detection for User Recommendation on Twitter

Davide Feltoni Gurini, Fabio Gasparetti,
Alessandro Micarelli, and Giuseppe Sansonetti

Department of Engineering,
Artificial Intelligence Laboratory, Roma Tre University,
Via della Vasca Navale, 79, 00146 Rome, Italy
http://ai-lab-03.dia.uniroma3.it/people/

Abstract. The increasing popularity of social networks has encouraged a large number of significant research works on community detection and user recommendation. The idea behind this work is that taking into account peculiar users' attitudes (i.e., sentiments, opinions or ways of thinking) toward their own interests can bring benefits in performing such tasks. In this paper we describe (i) a novel method to infer sentiment-based communities without the requirement of obtaining the whole social structure, and (ii) a community-based approach to user recommendation. We take advantage of the *SVO (sentiment-volume-objectivity)* user profiling and the Tanimoto similarity to evaluate user similarity for each topic. Afterwards we employ a clustering algorithm based on modularity optimization to find densely connected users and the Adamic-Adar tie strength to finally suggest the most relevant users to follow. Preliminary experimental results on Twitter reveal the benefits of our approach compared to some state-of-the-art user recommendation techniques.

1 Introduction

Recently user recommendation on Twitter[1] has gained a lot of importance as a result of the stunning success of this micro-blogging service. There has been also extensive work on detecting social network communities on it, especially by characterizing contents and tags extracted from tweets [6]. Apart from a few notable exceptions, state-of-the-art approaches for user recommendation that rely merely on tweet contents have low precision as tweets are typically short and noisy, while collaborative filtering approaches that leverage users' social graphs lead to higher precision but data sparsity remains a challenge. The rationale of this work is that users might have similar interests but different opinions or feelings on them. Therefore, considering the contribution of user sentiments may yield useful insights into community detection and user recommendation. In this paper, we propose a novel approach - named iSCUR - that enables us

---

[1] twitter.com

V. Dimitrova et al. (Eds.): UMAP 2014, LNCS 8538, pp. 314–319, 2014.

to focus on sentiments and extract them from tweets, to exploit such knowledge for inferring communities, one for each topic, and to suggest similar users that belong to the same communities. Forming communities allows us to mitigate the data sparsity problem and focus on discovering the latent characteristics of communities instead of individual users. The proposed approach proves effective in improving the recommendation precision (by as much as 5%) as demonstrated by results of online and offline preliminary experiments.

2   Community Detection

The idea behind this work is that taking into account user attitudes towards his own interests can yield benefits in recommending friends to follow. Specifically, we consider (i) which is the sentiment expressed by the user for a given concept, (ii) how much he is interested in that concept, and (iii) how much he expresses objective comments on it. For *concept* we mean any entity (e.g., hashtag) or topic extracted from a tweet that can somehow characterize it. In our model the first contribution is the *sentiment* $S(u, c)$, which represents a feeling or opinion about a concept c expressed by the user u, and is obtained as follows:

$$S(u, c) = norm \left(\frac{Pos(u, c) - Neg(u, c)}{Pos(u, c) + Neg(u, c)} \right) \tag{1}$$

where $Pos(u, c)$ and $Neg(u, c)$ are the sums of the positive and negative tweets written by the user u regarding the concept c, respectively. Such values are calculated by means of a supervised Machine Learning algorithm based on a Naïve Bayes classifier [8]. The *norm* function is used to normalize the output value within the $[0, 1]$ range and its expression is the following:

$$norm(x) = \frac{1}{1 + (k^{-x})} \tag{2}$$

where $k = 10$. The second contribution is the *volume* $V(u, c)$, that is, how much a user u wrote about a specific concept c and is defined as follows:

$$V(u, c) = \frac{tweets(u, c)}{\sum_{i=1}^{C} tweets(u, c_i)} \tag{3}$$

where $tweets(u, c)$ is the number of tweets written by the user u about a specific concept c, and C is the total number of concepts dealt with by u. The third contribution is the *objectivity* $O(u, c)$, which expresses how many tweets about a concept c do not contain sentiments. $O(u, c)$ is defined as follows:

$$O(u, c) = \frac{Neutral(u, c)}{Pos(u, c) + Neg(u, c) + Neutral(u, c)} \tag{4}$$

where $Pos(u, c)$, $Neg(u, c)$ and $Neutral(u, c)$ are the sums of the positive, negative and neutral tweets written by the user u relative to the concept c, respectively. Based on such contributions, we define a *sentiment-volume-objectivity*

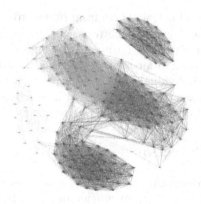

Fig. 1. Graph layout with the communities detected for a given concept c

(SVO) vector, which takes into account all of them. If we consider a user u and a concept c, it is defined as follows:

$$SVO(u,c) = [\alpha S(u,c), \beta V(u,c), \gamma O(u,c)] \tag{5}$$

where α, β, and γ are three constants in the $[0,1]$ interval, such that $\alpha + \beta + \gamma = 1$. In order to determine the optimal values of those parameters, we implemented a *mini-batch gradient descent* algorithm, so obtaining the configuration $\alpha = 0.3, \beta = 0.6, \gamma = 0.1$. Hence, these weights appear to favor the contribution of the *volume* and *sentiment* in comparison with the *objectivity*. For each concept c we compute the Tanimoto similarity between users u_i and u_j as follows:

$$sim(u_i, u_j, c) = \frac{SVO(u_i, c) \cdot SVO(u_j, c)}{\parallel SVO(u_i, c) \parallel^2 + \parallel SVO(u_j, c) \parallel^2 - SVO(u_i, c) \cdot SVO(u_j, c)} \tag{6}$$

The similarity value lies in between $[0,1]$. Once the similarities between users are computed, we build a graph for each concept as follows. If the similarity value between users exceeds a threshold value, we consider an edge between them. Also the optimal threshold value was determined through a gradient descent algorithm that maximizes the recommender precision. Such value was 0.8. Afterwards a clustering algorithm based on modularity optimization [7] allows us to detect the user communities for the considered concept c (see Fig. 1).

3   User Recommendation

In our recommender system, a generic user u is profiled as follows:

$$P(u) = \{(c, SVO(u,c)) | c \in C_u, u \in U\} \tag{7}$$

where the vector $SVO(u,c)$ gives the relevance of the concept c for the user u, C_u is the set of concepts cited by the user u, and U is the set of users. The user profile representation is generated by monitoring the user activity, that is, all the tweets included in the observation period. Once identified the communities for all the concepts expressed by the target user u_i, the user recommender system works as follows. For every user u_j in the dataset, for each mentioned concept c we verify if it was also mentioned by the user u_i. In the negative case we analyze the next concept, otherwise we consider the related graph. If the users u_i and u_j are connected by an edge, we consider its weight, which is equal to their Tanimoto similarity $sim(u_i, u_j, c)$. If there is no edge between them, we calculate the measure of tie strength according to the metric proposed by Adamic and Adar [2]:

$$TieStrength(u_i, u_j, c) = \sum_{N \in \Gamma(u_i) \cap \Gamma(u_j)} \frac{1}{log|N|} \qquad (8)$$

where $\Gamma(u_i)$ and $\Gamma(u_j)$ are the neighborhoods of the users u_i and u_j respectively, and N is the number of nodes belonging to both of them. To calculate the total score between the two users, we consider the sum of all the previous contributions:

$$Score(u_i, u_j) = \sum_{c \in C_{u_i} \cap C_{u_j}} s(u_i, u_j, c) \qquad (9)$$

with

$$s(u_i, u_j, c) = \begin{cases} sim(u_i, u_j, c), & \text{if } \exists \, edge(u_i, u_j) \\ TieStrength(u_i, u_j, c), & \text{otherwise} \end{cases} \qquad (10)$$

We evaluate the total score between the target user u_i and all the users u_j in the dataset, and suggest to him a ranked list of relevant users based on such value.

4   Experimental Evaluation

In order to evaluate the recommendation performance, we considered the 2013 Italian political elections. Using the Twitter API [2] we selected 31 hashtags and keywords for retrieving the Twitter streams about politician leaders and parties from Jan 25th to Feb 27th. The final dataset counted 1085000 tweets. We randomly selected 1000 users that (i) posted at least 10 tweets in the observed period, and (ii) had more than 15 friends and followers. To compare different profiling approaches and recommendation strategies, we need to determine when a user u_i is indeed relevant to another user u_j. We suppose that u_i is relevant to u_j if a *following relationship* exists between them. This assumption has already been proposed in literature [1,9,3] and is supported by the phenomenon of *homophily*, that is, the tendency of individuals with similar characteristics to associate with each other. We performed a preliminary evaluation in order to assess the effectiveness of the proposed approach. For the sake of brevity, in Figure 2 we report the results of a comparative analysis of our system (denoted as *SVO-Community*) with (i) an approach *(SVO)* we proposed in a previous work [8], which relies on the

---

[2] dev.twitter.com

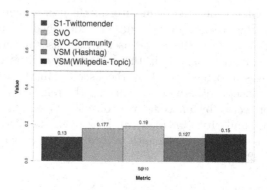

Fig. 2. Comparative analysis among our approach (SVO-Community), a SVO-based system (SVO) [8], and two traditional methods that do not consider any attitude

SVO user profiling but without community detection, and two traditional techniques that do not consider any attitude: (ii) cosine similarity in a vector space model where vectors are weighted hashtags *(VSM(Hashtag))* or topics extracted through the WikipediaMiner [3] tool *(VSM(Wikipedia-Topic))*, and (iii) the function $S1$ proposed by Hannon et al. [9] *(S1-Twittomender)*. We used the *Success at Rank K (S@K)* metric, which provides the mean probability that a relevant user is located in the top K positions of the list of suggested users. As can be seen, our approach outperforms the other ones. These findings confirm the potential of sentiment as a valuable feature for improving user recommender systems. Interestingly, our experimental tests enabled us to notice strong correlations among communities related to some concepts (see Fig. 1). We plan to further investigate this issue in order to fully understand the real nature of those interactions and exploit such knowledge in the recommendation process, thus improving the performance compared to those obtained by approaches of different nature [4,5]. Arguably, for certain concepts (e.g., politics) recommending users belonging to the same communities seems to be effective, while for other ones (e.g., technology) recommending users of different communities might be more useful.

5   Related Work

In spite of the growing body of research on exploiting user-generated contents in recommendation engines, there are few attempts to consider user attitudes in micro-posts for community detection or user recommendation. In [11] the authors formulate the problem of sentiment community discovery as a semidefinite programming (SDP) problem and as an optimization problem, and solve both of them using a SDP-based rounding method. Nguyen et al. [10] address the problem of clustering blog communities into groups, called *hyper-communities*, based on user sentiments, and propose a non-parametric clustering algorithm

---

[3] wikipedia-miner.cms.waikato.ac.nz

for its solution. To the best of our knowledge, the impact of sentiment on user recommendation performance has not been researched yet.

6 Conclusion

In this paper we have described an approach to community detection for people recommendation. Our work emphasizes the use of implicit sentiment analysis in improving recommendation performance. We have defined a novel weighting function that takes into account sentiment, volume, and objectivity related to the user interests. This technique allowed us to build more complete user profiles than traditional content-based approaches. Preliminary results reveal the benefits of our model compared with some state-of-the-art methods.

As future work, we plan to consider other elements (e.g., named-entities, persons, products) and attitudes. A future study will also explore the use of the implicit sentiment analysis within the collaborative filtering in social media.

References

1. Abel, F., Gao, Q., Houben, G.-J., Tao, K.: Analyzing user modeling on twitter for personalized news recommendations. In: Konstan, J.A., Conejo, R., Marzo, J.L., Oliver, N. (eds.) UMAP 2011. LNCS, vol. 6787, pp. 1–12. Springer, Heidelberg (2011)
2. Adamic, L.A., Adar, E.: Friends and neighbors on the web. Social Networks 25(3), 211–230 (2003)
3. Arru, G., Feltoni Gurini, D., Gasparetti, F., Micarelli, A., Sansonetti, G.: Signal-based user recommendation on twitter. In: Proc. of the 22nd International Conference on World Wide Web Companion, pp. 941–944 (2013)
4. Biancalana, C., Flamini, A., Gasparetti, F., Micarelli, A., Millevolte, S., Sansonetti, G.: Enhancing traditional local search recommendations with context-awareness. In: Konstan, J.A., Conejo, R., Marzo, J.L., Oliver, N. (eds.) UMAP 2011. LNCS, vol. 6787, pp. 335–340. Springer, Heidelberg (2011)
5. Biancalana, C., Gasparetti, F., Micarelli, A., Sansonetti, G.: An approach to social recommendation for context-aware mobile services. ACM Trans. Intell. Syst. Technol. 4(1), 10:1–10:31 (2013)
6. Biancalana, C., Gasparetti, F., Micarelli, A., Sansonetti, G.: Social semantic query expansion. ACM Trans. Intell. Syst. Technol. 4(4), 60:1–60:43 (2013)
7. Blondel, V., Guillaume, J., Lambiotte, R., Mech, E.: Fast unfolding of communities in large networks. J. Stat. Mech., P10008 (2008)
8. Gurini, D.F., Gasparetti, F., Micarelli, A., Sansonetti, G.: A sentiment-based approach to twitter user recommendation. In: Proc. of the 5th ACM RecSys Workshop on Recommender Systems and the Social Web (RSWeb 2013) co-located with the 7th ACM Conference on Recommender Systems (RecSys 2013) (2013)
9. Hannon, J., Bennett, M., Smyth, B.: Recommending twitter users to follow using content and collaborative filtering approaches. In: Proc. of the 4th ACM Conference on Recommender Systems, pp. 199–206. ACM, New York (2010)
10. Nguyen, T., Phung, D.Q., Adams, B., Venkatesh, S.: A sentiment-aware approach to community formation in social media. In: ICWSM. The AAAI Press (2012)
11. Xu, K., Li, J., Liao, S.S.: Sentiment community detection in social networks. In: Proc. of the 2011 iConference, pp. 804–805. ACM, New York (2011)

Towards Identifying Contextual Factors
on Parking Lot Decisions

Klaus Goffart[1], Michael Schermann[2], Christopher Kohl[2],
Jörg Preißinger[1], and Helmut Krcmar[2]

[1] BMW Group Research and Technology, Munich, Germany
[2] Technische Universität München, Munich, Germany

Abstract. The relevance of contextual factors that adapt in-car recommendations to the driver's current situation is not yet fully understood. This paper
presents a field study that has been conducted in order to identify relevant contextual factors of in-car parking lot recommender systems. Surprisingly, most
contextual factors examined, i.e., weather, luggage, and traffic conditions, did
not have a significant effect on the parking lot decision in the conducted field
study. Only the urgency of the trip and the willingness to walk have significant
effects on the decision outcome. Therefore, automobile manufacturers should
focus on understanding the relevance of different contextual factors when developing user models for in-car recommender systems.

Keywords: in-car recommendations, contextual factors, decision making.

1 Introduction

The usage of location-based services on smart phones and handheld devices is a
common phenomenon these days. Surprisingly, the usage of location-based services
in cars is still in its infancies but automobile manufacturers are working on in-car
recommender systems suggesting suitable parking lots to the driver.

Mobile recommendations are strongly influenced by contextual factors [1,2]. Recommendation quality relies on a user model that captures the important contextual
factors affecting decisions. The relevance of various contextual factors that adapt in-
car recommendations to the driver's current situation, however, is not yet fully understood.

In this paper, we present the results of a field study conducted in close cooperation
with a German premium automobile manufacturer. We used a prototype of an in-car
recommender system suggesting parking lots while driving to study parking lot choices of employees commuting between company facilities. During this field study we
observed six contextual factors possibly influencing the participant decision. The
generated data allows us to identify two contextual factors, which seem to be especially important for parking lot decisions and should be utilized in user models.

In the following, section 2 summarizes the state of the art on contextual factors of
parking lot decisions and develops our hypotheses. Section 3 describes the design and
execution of the field study, followed by the results presented in section 4. Finally,
section 5 summarizes the findings and limitations and shows areas of future work.

V. Dimitrova et al. (Eds.): UMAP 2014, LNCS 8538, pp. 320–325, 2014.
© Springer International Publishing Switzerland 2014

2   Literature and Hypothesis Development

Recommender systems used for location-based services are personalized to tailor the recommendations to the personal preferences of the user [3]. The recent research stream of context-aware recommender systems aims at improving recommendation quality by incorporating contextual factors that describe the dynamic preferences and requirements of users [4]: "[c]ontext is the set of environmental states and settings that either determines an application's behavior or in which an application event occurs and is interesting to the user" [5]. For instance, contextual information such as environmental states are found to be crucial for the acceptance of mobile services [1]. Furthermore, Xu et al. [2] show that location, weather, time, mobility and urgency have a significant influence on the acceptance of a recommendation system for dispatching taxis.

In a pre study, we identified price and distance to destination as the main influence factors for parking lot decisions, followed by the following contextual factors: weather, urgency, willingness to walk, luggage, and traffic. From the results, we extracted a value function that maps price and distance to user value. In order to measure the effect of the contextual factors, we used parking lots with the same user value in terms of price and distance in the field study. Therefore, the prices of the parking lots offered in the field study increased proportionally to the decreasing distance according to the determined value function, leaving the participants indifferent and reluctant on contextual factors.

We measure weather in terms of rainfall and outside temperature and hypothesize:

H1   *Rainfall promotes the spending on parking lots compared to non-raining conditions.*

H2   *Extreme temperatures promote the spending on parking lots compared to temperatures considered to be normal at the time and location of the study.*

Urgency was measured as the time left to get to the appointment when arriving at the parking lot.

H3   *The urgency of the current trip promotes the spending on parking lots compared to non-urgent trips.*

We hypothesize that the current willingness to walk, i.e., does the participant consciously choose to walk, directly effects the parking lot decision:

H4   *A greater willingness to walk suppresses the spending on parking lots compared to participants with less willingness to walk.*

Similarly, the carried luggage might affect the parking lot decision:

H5   *Carried luggage promotes the spending on parking lots compared to participants with no luggage.*

The traffic level experienced on the trip might affect parking lot decisions:

H6   *High traffic promotes the spending on parking lots compared to trips with low traffic.*

3   Field Study Design

By conducting a field study [6,7], we were able to monitor contextual influence factors on parking lot decisions in the real world, eliminating the hypothetical bias possibly present in other available methods [8].

The parking lot recommender system was implemented in a standard vehicle modified for testing purposes. Based on the location, the in-vehicle information system shows a pop-up presenting three possible parking lots with prices and walking distances between parking lot and final destination. The driver uses the standard jog dial controller to select the preferred parking lot. Upon selection, the navigation target of the onboard navigation system is set to the selected parking lot location.

The field study was conducted with employees of an automobile manufacturer that used the vehicle to commute between distant (across town) business meetings. Thus, we ensured that all trips were embedded in similar daily business activities. We used a supervised design to collect observational data, i.e., the participants drove the car with a supervisor on the passenger seat. Before each trip, the supervisor briefed the participants that they had to make a parking lot decision during the trip and the distance from the selected parking lot to the destination had to be walked by the participants. Since all trips were used to commute to work facilities, it can be assumed that the areas were well known to the participants. We simulated the payment by subtracting the price of the selected parking lot from the compensation, which the participants received for participating in the study. Before starting the trip, the participants were guided through the parking lot recommender system.

During the trip, the instructor triggered the parking lot pop-up for 3 possible parking lot options: a budget parking lot costing only 2.50€ but requiring the participant to walk 400m / 6:50 minutes, a medium option costing 3.50€ and 200m / 3:20 minutes of walk and an expensive option for 4.50€ with no walking required. These price points have been determined in a pre study.

We used car sensors to detect rainfall and to get the current temperature. Additionally, the supervisor noted the average amount of traffic during the trip and if the participant was carrying any luggage. After arriving at the selected parking lot, the participants were asked when their appointment starts, in order to calculate the time left, and we coded if they were willing to walk at that time, based on the reasons for their decision. Finally, the participants received their compensation minus the price of the selected parking lot and walked the respective distance to their final destination.

4   Results

The field study was conducted with 34 participants (5 female and 29 male) with an average age of 31.85 years. About 29% of the participants were PhD students, about 68% were employees, and about 3% held a supervising position.

The most frequently selected parking lot option was the medium option (50%) followed by the budget option (44%) and the expensive option (6%). On average, the participants spent 3.12€ for the parking lot, representing 69.3% of their available compensation payment.

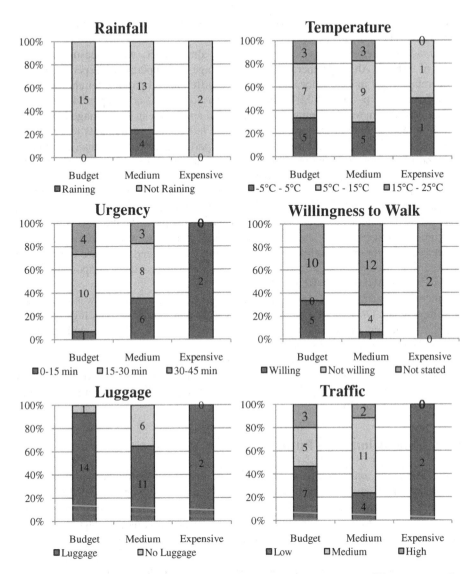

Fig. 1. Participant decisions in regard to rainfall, temperature, urgency, willingness to walk, luggage, and traffic

Fig. 1 shows a bar plot for each of the six evaluated contextual factors. The horizontal axis indicates the chosen parking lot option mapped to the distribution of the observed contextual factor's values on the vertical axis.

Only 4 of the 34 trips experienced rainfall, representing 12% of all participants. All of those 4 participants chose the medium parking lot option. A significance test showed a p-value of 0.180 (N=34, U=86)[1], indicating that rainfall is not a significant

---

[1] Wilcoxon–Mann–Whitney test with a significance level of p<0.05 [9].

influence on the parking lot decision outcome. Therefore, we did not find support for hypothesis H1.

Average trip temperatures between 0°C and almost 23°C were measured, with a mean of 9.09°C. Although there was a wide range of temperatures experienced, the temperature chart in Fig. 1 does not indicate a difference in parking lot choices. This is confirmed by a p-value of 0.913 $(N=34)^2$. Therefore, H2 is not supported.

The urgency, in terms of minutes left until the appointment, had a range between 3 and 45 minutes, with an average of 22 minutes left for the participants to get to the meeting. A trend can be identified in Fig. 1 that participants with less than 15 minutes left tend to choose the medium and expensive options. A p-value of 0.022 $(N=34)^2$ indicates strong support for hypothesis H3.

After the trip, participants indicated if their decision was influenced by their current willingness to walk. 18% of the participants indicated that they were willing to walk while 12% indicated that they did not want to walk, 71% did not express any walking preferences. Fig. 1 shows that participants willing to walk tend to choose the budget parking lot option, while those not willing to walk tend to choose the medium or expensive options. A significance test shows that there is strong support for hypothesis H4 with p=0.038 $(N=10, U=2)^1$.

Since participants were commuting, the carried luggage commonly was just a standard laptop bag. Only 21% of the participants were commuting without luggage, most of them choosing the medium option as shown in Fig. 1. Though, with p=0.222 $(N=34, U=65)^1$ we did not find support for H5.

The traffic experienced during the trip was noted by the field study supervisor. 38% of the participants experienced low, 47% medium, and 15% high traffic trips. A significant influence could not be measured with p=0.564 $(N=34)^2$. Therefore, we did not find support for H6.

5   Conclusions and Future Work

In the field study, only the urgency of a trip and the current willingness to walk had a significant effect on the parking lot choice and therefore the money spent. In contrast, rainfall, temperature, luggage, and traffic were not found to have a significant effect on the decision. This leads to the conclusion that sophisticated user models might be overkill for parking lot choice prediction and a restricted model of contextual factors could be sufficient.

Limitations of the research conducted are the relatively low sample size of 34 and the sample distribution of employees of the automobile manufacturer. Additionally, the fact that all trips commuted to business meetings could limit the influence of contextual factors like luggage, limiting the explanatory power for other kind of trips. The low share of trips experiencing rain could limit the measurable influence of this contextual factor. Though, the high range of experienced temperatures might indicate that the influence of the weather is limited.

Future research should repeat similar field studies with a higher number of participants to verify the findings. Additionally, it would be interesting to compare the

---

[2] Kruskal–Wallis test with a significance level of p<0.05 [9].

influence of contextual factors in different situations to the results of this study. Finally, the acceptance of recommender systems using the identified contextual factors should be researched to verify that users appreciate the recommender system.

For the automobile manufacturers the findings imply that a restricted user model might be sufficient to integrate contextual influences in the in-car recommendation process. Additionally, it should be researched how the urgency of a trip and the current willingness to walk can effectively be captured. Possibilities to estimate the urgency might include the integration of the driver's calendar into the recommender system, learning regularities, or analyzing the current driving style. In order to estimate the willingness to walk, activity trackers or running apps could be used. Moreover, integrated heart rate or blood pressure sensors could be used to learn the willingness to walk in a certain physiological state.

References

1. Mallat, N., Rossi, M., Tuunainen, V.K., Öörni, A.: The Impact of Use Situation and Mobility on the Acceptance of Mobile Ticketing Services. In: Proceedings of the 39th Annual Hawaii International Conference on Service Sciences, pp. 1–10. IEEE, Washington, DC (2006)
2. Xu, Z., Zhang, C., Ling, H.: A Contextual Acceptance Model of Mobile Commerce Based on TAM. In: The Third International Multi-Conference on Computing in the Global Information Technology, pp. 75–79. IEEE, Los Alamitos (2008)
3. Ricci, F., Rokach, L., Shapira, B.: Introduction to Recommender Systems Handbook. In: Ricci, F., Rokach, L., Shapira, B., Kantor, P.B. (eds.) Recommender Systems Handbook, pp. 1–35. Springer, Boston (2011)
4. Adomavicius, G., Tuzhilin, A.: Context-Aware Recommender Systems. In: Ricci, F., Rokach, L., Shapira, B., Kantor, P.B. (eds.) Recommender Systems Handbook, pp. 217–253. Springer, Boston (2011)
5. Chen, G., Kotz, D.: A survey of context-aware mobile computing research. In: Tech. Rep. TR2000-381, Dept. Comput. Sci. Dartmouth Coll. 1 (2000)
6. Bohnert, F., Zukerman, I., Laures, J.: GECKOmmender: Personalised Theme and Tour Recommendations for Museums. In: Masthoff, J., Mobasher, B., Desmarais, M.C., Nkambou, R. (eds.) UMAP 2012. LNCS, vol. 7379, pp. 26–37. Springer, Heidelberg (2012)
7. Tullio, J., Dey, A.K., Chalecki, J., Fogarty, J.: How it works: a field study of non-technical users interacting with an intelligent system. In: Proceedings of the SIGCHI Conference on Human Factors in Computing Systems, pp. 31–40. ACM, New York (2007)
8. Hensher, D.A.: Hypothetical bias, choice experiments and willingness to pay. Transp. Res. Part B 44, 735–752 (2010)
9. Hollander, M., Wolfe, D.A.: Nonparametric statistical methods. Wiley, New York

Trust-Based Decision-Making for Energy-Aware Device Management

Stephan Hammer, Michael Wißner, and Elisabeth André

Human Centered Multimedia, Augsburg University
Universitaetsstr. 6a, 86159 Augsburg, Germany
{hammer,wissner,andre}@hcm-lab.de
http://www.hcm-lab.de

Abstract. Smart energy systems are able to support users in saving energy by controlling devices, such as lights or displays, depending on context information, such as the brightness in a room or the presence of users. However, proactive decisions should also match the users' preferences to maintain users' trust in the system. Wrong decisions could negatively influence users' acceptance of a system and at worst could make them abandon the system. In this paper, a trust-based model, called User Trust Model (UTM), for automatic decision-making is proposed, which is based on Bayesian Networks. The UTM's construction, the initialization with empirical data gathered in an online survey, and its integration in an office setting are described. Furthermore, the results of a user study investigating users' experience and acceptance are presented.

Keywords: Energy-Saving, Trust, Bayesian Networks, Proactive Systems, Context Awareness.

1 Introduction

Reducing energy consumption has been a major concern for more than four decades, and many approaches that were aimed to support sustainability were developed during this time [1,2]. Some tried to improve people's environmental awareness by providing detailed feedback on their energy usage [3]. Others tried to persuade people to reduce their energy demand by exploiting social factors and utilizing, for example, cooperative pervasive games [4].

A number of energy management systems allow users to control devices, such as displays or lights, remotely or by setting up time tables. Furthermore, attempts have been made to adjust the energy consumption implicitly based on various context information that describes the users' and the system's surroundings [5]. For example, displays or lights, can be switched off if they are not needed. On the one hand, a system that autonomously performs energy saving actions contributes to the users' convenience. On the other hand, proactive system actions are not always understood by users and limit their control over the system. As a consequence, users might loose trust in such a system and give up using it.

V. Dimitrova et al. (Eds.): UMAP 2014, LNCS 8538, pp. 326–337, 2014.

For illustration, let us assume a lamp is burning in the user's office even though daylight suffices for performing the work. How should an energy management system react in such a situation? Should it trust the users are aware of their energy consumption and will take necessary actions themselves? Should it switch off the light autonomously? Or should it ask the user for permission via messages presented on the user's display or mobile phone?

In the first case, the system would leave the responsibility for energy reduction with the users, and there would be the risk that users do not see any benefit in the energy management system. The second approach bears the danger that the users do not understand the rationale behind the system's behavior and perceive it as not sufficiently self-explanatory or even randomly acting. In the last case, the system's behavior might appear transparent. However, users might nevertheless be upset because permanent and obtrusive messages interrupt their workflow. The example illustrates that a system needs to carefully balance the benefits and drawbacks of possible actions so as not to risk the users losing trust in its workings.

In this paper, a decision-theoretic approach to a trust management system for smart and proactive environments based on Bayesian Networks, the User Trust Model (UTM), is presented. It assesses users' trust in a system, monitors it over time, and applies appropriate system reactions to maintain users' trust in critical situations [6]. Section 2 discusses prior work in modelling trust considering work done in the area of agent-based modeling, social media and adaptive and personalized systems. After that, the UTM's construction, its integration in an office setting, and the initialization with empirical data are described. Section 5 presents a user study investigating the users' experience with and acceptance of the system.

2   Related Work

Since trust is a social phenomenon, it seems to be a promising to exploit models that have been developed to characterize trust in human societies as a basis for computational models of trust. Especially in the area of multi-agent systems, computational models for trust-based decision support have been researched thoroughly. Pioneering work in this area has been conducted by Marsh [7] who modeled trust between distributed software agents as a basis for the agents' cooperation behavior. Computational mechanisms that have been proposed for trust management in agent-based societies include Bayesian Networks [8], Dempster-Shafer Theory [9], Hidden-Markov Models [10], Belief Models [11], Fuzzy models [12], game-theoretic approaches [13] or decision trees [14]. There is empirical evidence that the performance of agent-based societies may be improved by incorporating trust models.

In contrast to the approaches above, work in the area of social media aims to model trust between human users, see [15] or [16] for a survey investigating trust in social networks. Using algorithmic approaches or machine learning techniques, trust between users is derived from objective observations, such as behavior patterns in social networks. For example, Adali et al. [17] assess trust between two users based on the amount of conversation and the propagation of messages within Twitter. Other approaches derive trust that is given to users from community-based reputation or social feedback (e.g. [18]).

Our research focuses on trust which users experience when interacting with a software system. A system may be robust and secure, but nevertheless be perceived as little trustworthy, for example, because its behavior appears little transparent or hard to control. Following the terminology by Castelfranchi and Falcone [12], our work focuses on the affective forms of trust that are based on the user's appraisal mechanisms. That is we aim at the development of computational trust models that capture how a system - in this paper a smart environment for energy saving - is perceived by a user who is confronted with it.

Computational models that assess trust felt by a user while interacting with a system are rare. There is a large amount of work that aims to identify factors that impact user trust. For example, Glass and colleagues [19] research trust-enhancing factors for adaptive and personalized applications. However, they do not implement a model of the user's trust into an adaptive and personalized system based on these factors. Yan and colleagues' [6] model captures trust users experience when interacting with mobile applications. In order to present users with recommendations that help increase users' trust, they identified various behaviors that can be monitored by a mobile device in addition to external factors, such as brand impact. The benefits of this approach have been shown by means of simulations. However, the approach has not been embedded in an adaptive and personalized mobile application to control the selection of system actions during an interaction with the user.

3   Modelling User Trust

We have chosen to model the users' feelings of trust by means of Bayesian Networks. A Bayesian Network (BN) is a directed, acyclic graph in which the nodes represent random variables while the links connecting nodes describe the direct influence in terms of conditional probabilities [20]. The basic idea is to derive user trust from so-called trust dimensions, such as *Comfort of Use*, *Transparency*, *Controllability*, *Privacy*, *Reliability*, *Security*, *Credibility*, and *Seriousness*. The trust dimensions are based on earlier user studies [21] which showed significant positive correlations between these trust dimensions and user trust. BNs were chosen because they meet requirements that should be accounted by models that are aimed to assess users' trust towards computer systems very well:

Trust as a Subjective Concept: Users respond individually to one and the same event. While some might find it critical if a system acts autonomously, others might not care. In a BN the system's uncertain belief about user's trust can be represented by a probability distribution over different levels of trust.

Trust as a Non-Deterministic Concept: The connection between events and trust is inherently non-deterministic. For example, we cannot always be sure that the user notices a critical event at all. Users may also consider a critical event as rather harmless. BNs allow us to make predictions based on conditional probabilities that model how likely the value of a child variable is given the value of the parent variables. For example, we may model how likely it is that the user has a moderate level of trust if the system's behavior is moderately transparent.

Trust as a Multifaceted Concept: Computational models should be able to represent the relative contribution of different trust dimensions to the assessment of trust and should help predict user's trust based on dimensions, such as the perceived transparency of a system. With BNs the modelling of relationships between trust and its dimensions is rather intuitive. For example, it is rather straightforward to model that reduced transparency leads to a decrease of trust. In the BN in Fig. 1 each trust dimension is represented by a specific node. Since exact probabilities are difficult to determine, the conditional probabilities were derived from empirical data collected in an online survey, see Section 4.1.

Trust as a Dynamic Concept: Trust depends on experience and changes over time. According to Lumsden [22], *User Trust* is affected by *Initial Trust* and *Interaction-Based Trust*. Initial trust dimensions, such as seriousness, come into effect as soon as a user gets in touch with a software system while interaction-based trust dimensions, such as transparency of system behavior, influence the users' experience of trust during an interaction.

In Fig. 1, a BN for modeling trust in the smart energy system is shown. To describe the determinants of *Initial Trust*, we introduce nodes for *Security*, *Seriousness* and *Credibility*. *Security*, for example, could be conveyed by the use of certificates. A system's *Seriousness* is reflected, for example, by its look-and-feel. *Credibility* could be supported by additional information, such as a company profile. Furthermore, we introduce a node for *Interaction-Based Trust*, which depends on *Quality of Interaction* and *Reliability*. The *Quality of Interaction* is characterized by *Transparency*, *Controllability* and *Comfort of Use*. Both the establishment of *Initial Trust* and *Interaction-Based Trust* are influenced by the users' *Trust Disposition* which is characterized by their *Competence* and general *Confidence* towards technical systems. The trust dimensions cannot be observed directly, but may be inferred from observable context variables that depend on the specific system. For example, the BN that decides on the reactions related to the light in an office considers the current *User* state, the *Social Context*, and the *Luminance Outside*, see Fig. 1. Knowing the contextual situation, the BN can estimate the impact of certain system reactions on the trust dimensions and thus on the user's trust. *Controllability*, for example, could be negatively affected if the system switches the light on and off autonomously.

In order to use the BN for decision-making, it was extended to an influence diagram by adding the decision node *System Action*, representing all actions the system could do to react on context changes, such as "Switch the light on automatically" if the "User is arriving", and a *Utility* node that computes the utility of all possible actions and their consequences and returns the action with the highest utility. Since the goal of our work is to maintain and maximize user

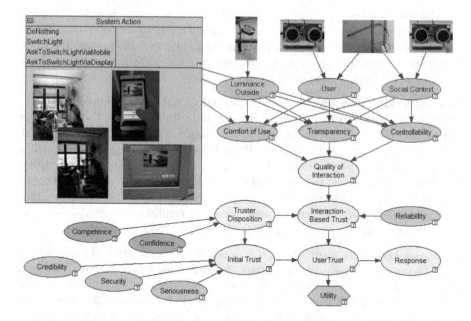

Fig. 1. User Trust Model (Light): green: Context Information (Sensors: Light, Ultrasonic, Flex-Sensor); red: User Traits; blue: Trust Dimensions; orange: Decision Nodes (System-Actions and Utility-Node)

trust, the *Utility* node is attached to a node representing the *User Trust* and measures the utility of each single decision in terms of the resulting user trust.

4   Building a Smart Office

In the following, we demonstrate how the User Trust Model (UTM) guides decision-making in an energy-aware device management system that controls the displays and the light in an office occupied by several people. For each type of device, a Bayesian Network (BN) was constructed and integrated using the GeNIe modeling environment and the SMILE reasoning engine[1]. Fig. 1 presented the BN for operating the light. Whether and which action the system takes to control the light basically depends on environmental information, the user's presence and the social context. In case the system recognizes a situation in which the light might be adjusted, it may perform the corresponding action autonomously or ask the user for permission via the mobile phone or via the display of the user's PC. In order not to risk disturbing the user, the UTM might even decide not to do anything even if there was an action that could save energy. The BN for the display has a similar structure. However, it relies on a more fine-grained representation of the user's current activity to distinguish, for example, whether

---

[1] http://genie.sis.pitt.edu/

Table 1. Possible system reactions in different contextual combinations

Device	Situation			System Reaction
	User	Social Context	Luminance Outside	
Display	1) WorkingAtPC	-	-	a) Switch on Display
	2) IdleAtDesk	-	-	b) Ask To Switch on Display
	3) AwayFromDesk	-	-	Via Mobile Phone
	4) OutOfRoom	-	-	c) Do Nothing
Light	1) Arriving	1) Coworker	1) Dark	a) Switch off Light
	2) Present	Present	2) Bright	b) Ask Via Mobile Phone
	3) Leaving	2) Coworker		c) Ask Via Display
		Away		d) Do Nothing

the user is sitting in front of a computer and working with it or engaged in other activities, such as reading a book. An overview on possible system actions and the utilized context information in both BNs is given in Table 1.

The data needed to recognize the context information for both BNs was gathered by Arduino-Sensors[2] that were distributed in the office. For example, we utilized light sensors to measure the outdoor luminance and ultrasonic sensors attached to the displays to detect the presence of persons. The control of the devices was conducted via a HomeMatic[3] system and remote controlled plugs.

4.1 Gathering Empirical Data (Online Survey)

In order to be able to generate decisions, the BNs had to be initialized with data. Both for the light and the display, we collected data in a web-based survey. In both surveys, participants were confronted with textual descriptions of typical situations during daily office routines. For each situation, possible system actions were proposed for the respective device that were supposed to improve the energy consumption of the users. Table 1 summarizes the situations represented by different settings of contextual variables and the possible system reactions.

The purpose of the survey was to discover for each situation which of the system reactions succeeded in maintaining user trust and which did not. To this end, the participants had to rate the system reaction in terms of transparency, controllability, comfort of use, and trust using a 5-point Likert scale:

- Q1: I understood why the system was reacting in this way.
- Q2: I had control over the system.
- Q3: I found the system comfortable to use.
- Q4: I found the system to be trustworthy.

All in all, 16 participants (7 female, 9 male) evaluated the situations for the light; and 22 participants (9 female, 12 male) rated the situations for the display. The participants were aged between 24 and 51 years (mean: 28).

---

[2] http://arduino.cc/
[3] http://www.homematic.com/

4.2   Initializating the Bayesian Network

The quantitative data obtained in the online survey enabled us to derive and model probability distributions for each trust dimension for all combinations of context and system reaction. The probability distributions for other node combinations, that were not part of the data inquired in the survey (e.g. how *Confidence* and *Competence* influence *Trust Disposition*) were modeled after the results from a previous study [23]. However, data for other user groups can be easily integrated into the BN by replacing the corresponding distributions in the BN. An interesting resource to explore is the work by Westin who conducted a large number of studies to determine the percentage of people with certain levels of distrust or privacy concerns, see [24] for a survey of these studies.

5   User Study

Web-based data are relatively easy to obtain. However, they might not completely reflect the experience of users interacting with the actual system. To investigate to what extent the BN is able to predict user trust and user preferences in a live setting, we conducted a study with the developed smart office environment. The purpose of this study was to evaluate the decisions taken by the UTM focusing on two criteria: (1) Would the chosen system reactions affect the users' feelings of trust and the related trust dimensions in a positive way? (2) Would the system reactions match the actions favored by the users? Apart from evaluating the BN approach, we investigated the users' experience and acceptance of our smart office environment.

5.1   Experimental Setting

During the study the participants had to run through different tasks and situations that in total simulated the daily routine in an office occupied by several people. Changes of the participant's and the colleague's state (social context) were triggered by the participants themselves and by one of the experimenters that played the role of the participant's colleague. To ensure that all participants conducted the study under the same conditions and with a most realistic experience the room was darkened and changes of the outdoor luminance were simulated by a lamp and by covering and uncovering the light sensor.

5.2   Conducting the Study

At first the participants had to provide general demographic information and information about their experience with home automation systems and their trust towards computer systems in general. Furthermore, the participants were asked whether they considered themselves confiding.

After a short introduction to the setting and the scenario, the participants had to conduct the first task, and the system showed the reactions that were selected for both devices according to the UTM. After that, the participants had to fill in a short questionnaire for each of the reactions. Each questionnaire included the questions Q1-Q4 that were also asked in the online survey. Furthermore, the users were asked to choose their preferred system action. For instance, the statement concerning the display and the first task was: "When I enter my office and sit at my desk, I prefer...

- P1: ...no reaction from the display."
- P2: ...to switch the display on automatically."
- P3: ...to be asked via smartphone for permission to switch on the device."

After that, the procedure continued with the next task and the respective questionnaire. All tasks, the corresponding situations and the selected system reactions triggered by context changes are summarized in Table 2. To make the experiment more realistic, the tasks were embedded in a coherent story.

Table 2. Tasks, changed context variables and system reactions of the user study

Task	Situation			System Reaction	
	User State	Social Context	Outside Luminance	Light	Display
1. Enter the room	Arriving	Coworker Away	Dark	Confirm Via Mobile	
2. Sit down at PC and	WorkingAtPC				Switch On
It is getting light.					
3. Check slides for mistakes.			Bright	Confirm Via Display	
The participant's colleague enters the room and sits down at the desk.					
4. Take book X out of the shelf.	AwayFromDesk	Coworker Present			Do Nothing
5. Come back and read chapter Y.	IdleAtPC				Switch Off
6. Add a slide about Z.	WorkingAtPC				Switch On
It is getting dark.					
			Dark	Confirm Via Mobile	
The participant's colleague leaves the room.					
7. Finish work and leave.	Leaving	Coworker Away		Confirm Via Mobile	
8. Don't forget to close the door.	OutOfRoom				Switch Off

After rating the last task, the participants had to state what they liked and disliked about the system and to rate statements related to their experience during the usage and their attitude towards the system on a 5-point Likert scale.

5.3   Results

Overall six women and 18 men aged between 23 and 33 (mean: 26) took part in the study. They studied and worked in all kind of professions related (88%) and not related (12%) to computer science. All statements in the questionnaires could be rated on a 5-point Likert scale. Ratings lower than 3 were interpreted as disagreement, ratings higher than 3 as agreement with a statement. Only, five persons reported a significant amount of experience with technology for controlling parts of their home environment, such as automatic timers or blind control systems. Half of the participants never used such a technology.

The participants also had to reflect on their confidence. They had to answer on two general statements and one statement related to computer systems. Concerning the statement: *I act based on the saying "Trust, but verify"*, 63% of all participants agreed. Only one participant disagreed. Concerning the statements *I am overly trusting* and *On most systems, you can be assured that they will do what they should*, one third agreed, disagreed, or rated neutrally.

The participants gave consistently high ratings for the criteria "Transparency", "Controllability", "Comfort of Use", and "Trust" when evaluating the reactions the system had chosen for the adjustment of the light. The lowest average rating was achieved for the trustworthiness of "asking to switch the light off via the user's mobile phone" when the participants left the room and closed the door (Mean (M): 3.92, Standard Deviation (SD): .86). Two participants, for example, missed feedback that the light was switched off successfully. All other average scores were between 4 and 5. Despite these high ratings, in situations in which the system sent a message to the participants' phone, other system reactions were preferred. When they (a) entered or (b) left the room, the participants preferred the system to automatically switch on or off the lamp (a: 75%; b: 67%). When it was getting dark and they sat at the desk, they preferred to be asked for confirmation via their display (58%). Correspondingly, the system' decision to ask users for confirmation via their display when it was getting bright, matched the preference of 79% of the participants. These findings were in line with several statements of the participants. For example, one participant stated that he would prefer a message on the device he is currently using. Several users mentioned that using a phone is uncomfortable in many situations - either because it is not within reach or because they have to interrupt their work to read the message on the phone. Accordingly, some users preferred autonomous system actions instead of repeated messages on their phones because this would make the system less obtrusive. Apparently, the users were not aware of these issues in the online study.

In contrast, the automatically generated reactions for the display matched the participants preferences in all situations. Most of the participants wanted the system to decide autonomously whether the display should be switched on or off (Entering the room: 54%; Idle-State: 71%; Leaving the room: 79%) as opposed to asking the user for confirmation first or to not showing any reaction. However, they did not wish any adjustment when they left their desk only for a short time (88%). The participants clearly favored autonomous reactions for the display (as in the online condition), but at the expense of "Controllability" and

"Trust". While the average trust ratings still were above 3.0 for the idle state (M: 3.63; SD: 0.95) and for "leaving the room" (M: 3.88, SD: 0.88) the average ratings for "Controllability", except for "leaving the room" (M: 3.46; SD: 1.44), were lower than 3 with the lowest average rating for automatic control in the idle-state (M: 2.50, SD: 1.29). The ratings for the trustworthiness of autonomous reactions were affected, among other things, by a lack of feedback when leaving the room and by a missing authentification mechanism when entering the room. The low ratings for "Controllability" could be explained by requests for functionality to set or disable the automatic control of the display in the idle state.

The concluding questions also showed promising results. Most participants were satisfied (83%; M:3.96; SD: .68) and agreed that the system supported them to improve their energy consumption (96%; M: 4.71; SD: .54), that it behaved adequately (88%; M: 4.38; SD: .70), and that it was transparent (100%; M: 4.96; SD: .20). The lower, but still acceptable results for unobtrusiveness (58%; M: 3.71; SD: 1.10) could be mainly explained by the fact that the users had to operate the mobile phone. Further results showed that most of the participants did not feel distracted (75%; M: 2.00; SD: 1.00), restricted (88%; M: 1.83; SD: 1.07), or observed (63%, M: 2.33; SD: 1.18).

6   Conclusion

We presented an approach for trust-based decision-making for smart and proactive environments based on Bayesian Networks, the User Trust Model (UTM). It assesses users' trust experienced while interacting with a system and applies appropriate system reactions to maintain users' trust in critical situations. We described the UTM's construction, its integration in an office setting, and its initialization with empirical data. The results of a user study revealed that the system succeeded in maintaing the users' trust in the investigated situations. Even though the approach has been developed and evaluated for an energy management system, the basic mechanism is applicable to other applications of adaptation and personalization as well. While the basic structure of the BN representing the dependencies between trust and its dimensions could be reused, the nodes representing the context and possible system actions would have to be adapted to the corresponding applications.

Future work should investigate which factors in addition to trust impact the user's ultimate choice of a system action. Although, the participants provided high ratings for the chosen system actions, their preferences were not always in line with the system's decisions. Furthermore, we will investigate how to improve the accuracy of the UTM by incorporating knowledge about user-specific attitudes. Depending on their trust disposition, users might favor different system reactions. For example, users that tend to distrust technical systems might give more importance to a high level of control than to a high level of comfort. A promising approach might be to distinguish between different categories of users based on multiple dimensions [25]. Another important aspect is the decision making for more than one user. For example, some participants wondered whether they were the only person in control of the light. Therefore, the UTM should be extended to be able to consider the trust of all affected users. Finally, we intend to extend the Bayesian Network to a Dynamic Bayesian Network in order to consider how user trust felt at a particular point in time depends on user trust experienced at an earlier point in time.

Acknowledgments. This research is co-funded by OC-Trust (FOR 1085) of the DFG and IT4SE of BMBF.

References

1. Hazas, M., Friday, A., Scott, J.: Look back before leaping forward: Four decades of domestic energy inquiry. IEEE Pervasive Computing 10(1), 13–19 (2011)
2. DiSalvo, C., Sengers, P., Brynjarsdóttir, H.: Mapping the landscape of sustainable hci. In: Proc. of the SIGCHI Conf. on Human Factors in Computing Systems, CHI 2010, pp. 1975–1984. ACM, New York (2010)
3. Gamberini, L., Spagnolli, A., Corradi, N., Jacucci, G., Tusa, G., Mikkola, T., Zamboni, L., Hoggan, E.: Tailoring feedback to users' actions in a persuasive game for household electricity conservation. In: Bang, M., Ragnemalm, E.L. (eds.) PERSUASIVE 2012. LNCS, vol. 7284, pp. 100–111. Springer, Heidelberg (2012)
4. Simon, J., Jahn, M., Al-Akkad, A.: Saving energy at work: the design of a pervasive game for office spaces. In: Proc. of the 11th Int. Conf. on Mobile and Ubiquitous Multimedia, MUM 2012, pp. 9:1–9:4. ACM, New York (2012)
5. Cheverst, K., Byun, H., Fitton, D., Sas, C., Kray, C., Villar, N.: Exploring issues of user model transparency and proactive behaviour in an office environment control system. User Modeling and User-Adapted Interaction 15(3-4), 235–273 (2005)
6. Yan, Z., Holtmanns, S.: Trust Modeling and Management: From Social Trust to Digital Trust. IGI Global (2008)
7. Marsh, S.: Trust in distributed artificial intelligence. In: Castelfranchi, C., Werner, E. (eds.) MAAMAW 1992. LNCS, vol. 830, pp. 94–112. Springer, Heidelberg (1994)
8. Wang, Y., Vassileva, J.: Bayesian network trust model in peer-to-peer networks. In: Moro, G., Sartori, C., Singh, M.P. (eds.) AP2PC 2003. LNCS (LNAI), vol. 2872, pp. 23–34. Springer, Heidelberg (2004)
9. Yu, B., Singh, M.P.: An evidential model of distributed reputation management. In: Proc. of the 1st Int. Joint Conf. on Autonomous Agents and Multiagent Systems: Part 1, AAMAS 2002, pp. 294–301. ACM, New York (2002)
10. Vogiatzis, G., MacGillivray, I., Chli, M.: A probabilistic model for trust and reputation. In: van der Hoek, W., Kaminka, G.A., Lespérance, Y., Luck, M., Sen, S. (eds.) 9th Int. Conf. on Autonomous Agents and Multiagent Systems (AAMAS 2010), Toronto, Canada, May 10-14, vol. 1-3, pp. 225–232. IFAAMAS, Richland (2010)
11. Jøsang, A., Hayward, R., Pope, S.: Trust network analysis with subjective logic. In: Estivill-Castro, V., Dobbie, G. (eds.) 29th Australasian Computer Science Conf (ACSC2006), January 16-19. CRPIT, vol. 48, pp. 85–94. Australian Computer Society, Darlinghurst (2006)
12. Castelfranchi, C., Falcone, R.: Trust Theory: A Socio-Cognitive and Computational Model. Wiley (2010)

13. Sankaranarayanan, V., Chandrasekaran, M., Upadhyaya, S.: Towards modeling trust based decisions: A game theoretic approach. In: Biskup, J., López, J. (eds.) ESORICS 2007. LNCS, vol. 4734, pp. 485–500. Springer, Heidelberg (2007)
14. Burnett, C., Norman, T.J., Sycara, K.P.: Trust decision-making in multi-agent systems. In: Walsh, T. (ed.) IJCAI 2011, Proc. of the 22nd Int. Joint Conf. on Artificial Intelligence, IJCAI/AAAI, pp. 115–120 (2011)
15. Sherchan, W., Nepal, S., Paris, C.: A survey of trust in social networks. ACM Comput. Surv. 45(4), 47:1–47:33 (2013)
16. Bhuiyan, T., Xu, Y., Jøsang, A.: A review of trust in online social networks to explore new research agenda. In: Arabnia, H.R., Clincy, V.A., Lu, J., Marsh, A., Solo, A.M.G. (eds.) Proc. of the 2010 Int. Conf. on Internet Computing, ICOMP 2010, July 12-15, pp. 123–128. CSREA Press, Las Vegas (2010)
17. Adali, S., Escriva, R., Goldberg, M.K., Hayvanovych, M., Magdon-Ismail, M., Szymanski, B.K., Wallace, W.A., Williams, G.T.: Measuring behavioral trust in social networks. In: Yang, C.C., Zeng, D., Wang, K., Sanfilippo, A., Tsang, H.H., Day, M.Y., Glässer, U., Brantingham, P.L., Chen, H. (eds.) IEEE Int. Conf. on Intelligence and Security Informatics, ISI 2010, Proc., pp. 150–152. IEEE, Vancouver (2010)
18. Ivanov, I., Vajda, P., Korshunov, P., Ebrahimi, T.: Comparative study of trust modeling for automatic landmark tagging. IEEE Transactions on Information Forensics and Security 8(6), 911–923 (2013)
19. Glass, A., McGuinness, D.L., Wolverton, M.: Toward establishing trust in adaptive agents. In: Proc. of the 13th Int. Conf. on Intelligent User Interfaces (IUI 2008), pp. 227–236. ACM (2008)
20. Russell, S.J., Norvig, P.: Artificial Intelligence: A modern approach, 2nd edn. Prentice Hall, Upper Saddle River (2003)
21. Kurdyukova, E., André, E., Leichtenstern, K.: Trust management of ubiquitous multi-display environments. In: Krueger, A., Kuflik, T. (eds.) Ubiquitous Display Environments, pp. 177–193. Springer (2012)
22. Lumsden, J.: Triggering trust: To what extent does the question influence the answer when evaluating the perceived importance of trust triggers? In: Proc. of the 2009 British Computer Society Conf. on Human-Computer Interaction (BCS HCI 2009), pp. 214–223. British Computer Society (2009)
23. Bee, K., Hammer, S., Pratsch, C., Andre, E.: The Automatic Trust Management of Self-Adaptive Multi-Display Environments. In: Trustworthy Ubiquitous Computing. Atlantis Ambient and Pervasive Intelligence, vol. 6, pp. 3–20. Atlantis Press (2012)
24. Kumaraguru, P., Cranor, L.F.: Privacy indexes: A survey of westin's studies. Technical Report CMU-ISRI-5-138, Technical Report, Institute for Software Research Int (ISRI), Carnegie Mellon University (2005)
25. Knijnenburg, B.P., Kobsa, A., Jin, H.: Dimensionality of information disclosure behavior. Int. J. Hum.-Comput. Stud. 71(12), 1144–1162 (2013)

Doing More with Less:
Student Modeling and Performance Prediction with Reduced Content Models

Yun Huang[1], Yanbo Xu[2], and Peter Brusilovsky[1]

[1] Intelligent Systems Program, University of Pittsburgh, Pittsburgh, PA 15260, USA
{yuh43,peterb}@pitt.edu
[2] RI-NSH 4105, Carnegie Mellon University, Pittsburgh, PA 15213-3890, USA
yanbox@cs.cmu.edu

Abstract. When modeling student knowledge and predicting student performance, adaptive educational systems frequently rely on content models that connect learning content (i.e., problems) with its underlying domain knowledge (i.e., knowledge components, KCs) required to complete it. In some domains, such as programming, the number of KCs associated with advanced learning contents is quite large. It complicates modeling due to increasing noise and decreases efficiency. We argue that the efficiency of modeling and prediction in such domains could be improved without the loss of quality by reducing problems content models to a subset of most important KCs. To prove this hypothesis, we evaluate several KC reduction methods varying reduction size by assessing the prediction performance of Knowledge Tracing and Performance Factor Analysis. The results show that the predictive performance using reduced content models can be significantly better than using original one, with extra benefits of reducing time and space.

Keywords: adaptive educational systems, student modeling, performance prediction, Knowledge Tracing, Performance Factor Analysis.

1 Introduction

When modeling student knowledge and predicting student performance, adaptive educational systems rely on connections between learning content (i.e., items, problems, problem steps) and elements of domain knowledge required to complete it. Frequently these connections are provided by content authors in the form of content models that list knowledge components (KC) associated with each problem. In some domains, such as programming, the number of KCs associated with advanced learning contents can be very large. It complicates modeling due to increasing noise and decreases efficiency, especially in cases when there is only a relatively small size of training data and(or) time and space are more restricted. This paper argues that the efficiency of modeling and prediction in domains with large content models could be improved without the loss of quality by reducing problems content models to a subset of the most important KCs.

V. Dimitrova et al. (Eds.): UMAP 2014, LNCS 8538, pp. 338–349, 2014.

To prove this hypothesis, we explore several promising KC reduction methods based on item contents and student responses, assess the effect of reduction size and the value of reduction using the most popular student modeling and prediction approaches, Knowledge Tracing (KT) and Performance Factor Analysis (PFA).

KT [4] has been the de-facto standard for inferring students' hidden knowledge from their observed performance data, by using Hidden Markov Models. The original KT, however, lacks the ability to fit items that require multiple KCs, thus many researchers have extended it to address the problem [3,6,7,12,14]. PFA [13] uses logistic regression to predict student performance, which by design is able to model items with multiple KCs. It predicts students' current response based on their previous responses, and estimates each KC's initial easiness and learning rates from correct and incorrect practices.

So far, no prior work has explored the effect of reducing KCs and varying reduction sizes for PFA and KT. We advocate the idea, propose several ways of reduction, and demonstrate that the essential content of an advanced learning item related to many KCs can be estimated very well from only a few KCs.

2   Content Model Reduction

The focus of our study is the Java programming domain, more specifically, a class of programming problems from a personalized learning system, JavaGuide [11], where each problem provides a complete program and asks students to mentally execute it and to enter the output of the code or the value of a variable. Each problem is indexed by a set of Java *programming concepts*, i.e., KCs (ranging from 9 to 55) by experts aided by a Java programming language ontology and a Java concept parser [10]. (We refer to this mapping relation from an item to a set of KCs as the *content model*, while the knowledge ontology, which is a structured set of all KCs is referred to as the domain model.)

The large number of KCs per JavaGuide problem makes it quite hard to use regular approaches for student modeling and performance prediction in this system. It is not clear whether all KCs that form the content model are important for knowledge assessment and performance prediction. In our paper we propose the idea of *content model reduction* trying to assess the hypothesis that a small subset of the most important KCs per item might be sufficient to maintain a good quality of modeling. Due to the nature of the programming domain (where each concept might be critical for some set of problems) we determine importance on the item level, not domain level, i.e., we propose to select important KCs for each item rather than removing "less important" concepts from the domain model. This is an important aspect of our reduction approach since traditional *feature selection* focuses on selecting a subset of features for all datapoints (a domain) and thus cannot be readily used in our context of study. We propose a framework where we select most important KCs for each item based on the *item-level ranking* of KC importance scores within each item, and we propose to determine the importance score by three types of methods from different information sources: (1) the characteristic of the item's original content model, (2) students' responses (performance) on the item, and (3) experts' judgment. The first two ways are automatic while the third requires more manual effort. These proposed reduction methods are described below.

2.1   Reduction Methods

Content-Based Methods (IDF and TFIDF): We argue that the relative specificity of an item's KC should reflect the importance of the KC in the current item, and that we can capture the speciality by examining frequencies (appearances) of the KC. Inspired by information retrieval content indexing approaches, we treat an item as a document and the KCs mapped to the item as its words, and approach selecting important KCs of an item as selecting important keywords of a document. We hypothesize that the less a KC appears in other items, the more specific and important it is in the current item, which could be measured by the popular *IDF* (Inverse Document Frequency) approach. In addition, we also hypothesize that the more a KC appears in the current item, the more important it can be in the current item. This corresponds to *TFIDF* (Term Frequency - Inverse Document Frequency) keyword weighting approach. We are able to extract the frequency information by the indexing method mentioned before. These two methods have different advantage since IDF can be more generalizable to other contexts when TF information is not available, while TFIDF should be able to make use of more information. We define a *SCORE* function assigning the importance score of KC k in item i with a higher value corresponding to higher importance. For the IDF method,

$$SCORE(k,i) = log(\frac{|I|}{|\{i\,|\,i \in I, k \in i\}|}) \tag{1}$$

and for the TFIDF method,

$$SCORE(k,i) = freq(k,i) \times log(\frac{|I|}{|\{i\,|\,i \in I, k \in i\}|}) \tag{2}$$

where I is the complete set of items, $|\{i\,|\,i \in I, k \in i\}|$ is the number of distinct items in I that KC k appears, and *freq(k,i)* is the raw frequency of KC k in item i. Based on the importance score, we can further conduct item-level ranking and select KCs with highest score values within each item.

Response-Based Method (EASINESS-COEF): We believe that when a student encounters an item, the most difficult KCs are the ones that determine the response (correct or incorrect) of the student and are the main ones that the student is learning. We should be able to infer the difficulty of KCs by using student response information. We propose that one way to use this information is to use the coefficients from performance prediction models, and particularly, Performance Factor Analysis (PFA) which has been shown to be effective in predicting student performance and have interpretable coefficients. As mentioned before, PFA is a logistic regression model predicting the probability of a correct response of student j on item i (p_{ji}) based on every KC k related to the item:

$$log(\frac{p_{ji}}{1 - p_{ji}}) = \sum_{k \in \{k | k \in i\}} (\beta_k + \gamma_k s_{jk} + \rho_k f_{jk}) \tag{3}$$

where s_{jk}, f_{jk} are the counts of student j's previous correct and incorrect practices on KC k, and β_k, γ_k, ρ_k are coefficients interpreted as initial easiness, learning rates from previous correct and incorrect practices of KC k. We hypothesize that the initial easiness coefficient of a KC (β_k) is a proper measure to determine the importance of a KC, and define the $SCORE$ function assigning the importance score of KC k in item i using this coefficient directly as follows:

$$SCORE(k, i) = -\beta_k \tag{4}$$

Here, although $SCORE(k, i)$ remains constant for the same KC across all relevant items since it reflects a KC's intrinsic initial difficulty, we conduct item-level ranking so that an KC's importance in different items can be differentiated by its different ranking positions.

Expert-Based Method (OUTCOME): In many practical courses, learning contents (items, problems) are assigned to course topics that are arranged by the expert (instructor) in a specific order (mostly from easy to hard). When working on problems, the students are expected to follow the order of topics. Taking into account the expert judgment on the order of topics and content arrangement within topics, KCs can be separated into prerequisite and outcome KCs. Prerequisite KCs are the ones students are supposed to know before starting the current item. They are the most basic KCs or appear many times in previous topics (items) that students should have already mastered. Outcome KCs are the ones students are supposed to learn while practicing the current item. Most of them are new KCs that students haven't practiced (enough). So we propose OUTCOME method where for each item we only use KCs that are labeled as *outcome* for current item by experts (here experts labeled each KC in an item as either prerequisite or outcome deterministically without giving scores). We believe that prerequisite-outcome separation is a generic approach that could be used in many tutoring systems where the content is organized by experts (authors) and thus it is worthwhile to be explored.

2.2   Reduction Sizes

Given the proposed reduction methods, it is still unclear how many KCs each method should retain. We explore two ways to change reduction size and examine the corresponding model performance in order to determine the proper reduction size (we cannot vary reduction size for OUTCOME method in this study since experts didn't provide scores for KCs in items).

Reducing Non-Adaptively to Items (*TopX*) : We select x KCs per item with the highest importance scores (if there are less than x KCs in an item, we keep all of them). For items that originally have many KCs and those that have few, we use the same x assuming that the number of KCs responsible to students' real learning keeps the same for each item.

Reducing Adaptively to Items (*TopX%*): We select $x\%$ KCs per item with the highest importance scores. For items that originally have many KCs and those that have few, the selected number of KCs of the former is still larger than the latter so that the relative content complexity of items can be reserved.

2.3   Evaluating Reduction on PFA and KT

We evaluate different reduction methods and the effect of reduction size by examining the predictive power of PFA and KT using different content models PFA by design is able to handle multiple KCs items while the original KT lacks this ability. We explored several KT variants summarized in the thorough survey [14] and found out many of them have similar performance on our dataset, and some of them are not suitable for our context of study. For example, the variant of KT [6] that multiplies each KC's predicted probability together is not suitable, because in our context each item is associated with a large number of KCs, and the product of these probabilities is prone to result in a very small one even when each KC predicts a high probability of correct response (e.g., nine KCs each of which predicts 0.9 probability of correct response yield a final prediction of $0.9^9 = 0.39$). Our experiments actually indicated that this variant of KT using original content model almost predicts an incorrect response for all instances while the majority is correct response in the real labels. Then reduction on this variant would naturally raise the predicted probability of correct response and we will be prone to overstate the effectiveness of reduction and any reduction methods. We chose one of the suitable variants which we think wouldn't lead to overstated benefits [14]: during parameter fitting, we split a multiple KCs item into multiple single KC items by assigning full responsibility of the performance to each one of the KC; during predicting, we take the minimum probability of the predicted correct response performance of all associated KCs assuming that the likelihood of a student getting a correct answer is dominated by his (her) knowledge of the weakest KC; during updating, we update all KCs with the same evidence observing a correct response evidence, but we only update the weakest KC by incorrect evidence and update others by correct evidence when observing an incorrect response (we refer to this variant as KT in following sections). In future work we would explore more other suitable KT variants [7,12,14].

3   Experiments and Results

We conducted our study on the the dataset collected from an online self-assessment Java programming learning system, JavaGuide [11]. As mentioned before, each problem provides a program asking students the output or the value of a variable. The codes are generated from a template, in which different parameters are filled for each attempt so that students can have multiple attempts on slightly different version until they master the skills or give up. A problem is indexed by experts aided by a Java ontology and parser into $9 \sim 55$ KCs, resulting in a total number of 124 KCs. The dataset was collected from 2009 Spring to 2012 Spring (7 semesters), including $19,809$ records from 132 students working on 94 questions with about 69.3% of them being correct responses.

We used logistic regression in WEKA [9] to run PFA, and implemented the variant of KT based on tool [15] which uses EM algorithm for parameter learning. We conducted two runs of 5-fold user-stratified cross-validation where in each run we trained on 80% of the users, and tested on the remaining 20%. We ensured that each question in the test set appears at least once in the training set so that we predict unseen students on seen questions which suits most practical cases.

We computed IDF and TFIDF from the entire data, while E-COEF only from the training set in each run. OUTCOME is provided by the original dataset, which reduces the number of KCs per item from the range of $9 \sim 55$ to $1 \sim 8$. For *TopX* reduction, we set X=35, 25, 15, ..., 1 as our experiments showed that models' performance changes dramatically when $X < 16$ while slightly when $X > 35$. For *TopX%* reduction, we set $X\% = 90\%, 80\%, ..., 10\%$. We report the Area Under the Curve (AUC) of the Receiver Operating Characteristic (ROC) curve, a suitable metric for binary classifiers on unbalanced data. AUC equals 0.5 when the ROC curve corresponds to random chance and 1.0 for perfect accuracy. We list the mean AUC on test sets across the 10 runs, and use Wilcoxon Signed Ranks Test ($\alpha = 0.05$) to test the significance of difference.

3.1   The Effect of Reduction Methods and Reduction Sizes

In this section, we explore the effect of different reduced content models with varying reduction sizes on PFA and KT. Firstly, we conduct experiments on PFA. According to Fig. 1(a) and Table 1(a), the curves of *TopX* are roughly in bell shapes with fluctuations. As for IDF and TFIDF, PFA has significant improvement over ORIGINAL when X is between $5 \sim 15$, and starts to decrease yet maintains similar ability as ORIGINAL otherwise (except at $X = 1$ where TFIDF is significantly worse than ORIGINAL). As for E-COEF, PFA beats ORIGINAL at some points ($X = 13, 12, 5$), and similarly starts to decrease when $X < 5$. Surprisingly, RANDOM performs similarly as E-COEF with fluctuating performance. Fig. 1(b) and Table 1(b) show much flatter curves for *TopX%* with fluctuation. IDF works significantly better than ORIGINAL at X%=70%, 60%, 40%, while all other methods (including OUTCOME which is not listed) maintain comparable performance as ORIGINAL. Considering the above results, we claim that reduction on PFA to a moderate size can provide comparable or even better prediction than using original content models. We observe that it could hurt if the reduction size goes too small (e.g. < 5 in our data), possibly because PFA was designed for fitting items with multiple KCs and the item contents require a certain number of KCs to be retained. Overall, IDF seems to be the best for PFA since it can outperform ORIGINAL more steadily within a wide range in terms of both *TopX* and *TopX%*; TFIDF's performance is similar to IDF with slightly worse performance in *TopX%*. E-COEF is not as effective as the others, possibly because PFA re-using itself cannot provide much extra useful information. RANDOM seems to have an acceptable performance here, but we will clarify this in Section 3.2.

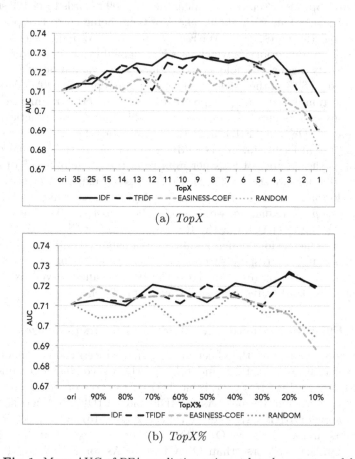

(a) *TopX*

(b) *TopX%*

Fig. 1. Mean AUC of PFA prediction using reduced content models

Now we conduct experiments on KT. According to Fig. 2 and Table 2, we see both curves of *TopX* and *TopX%* from KT are more homogeneous than PFA, where reduction provides significant prediction gain ranging a much bigger span and scale. In contrast, KT achieves the best performance when the reduction size is small (e.g. $X < 7$ or $X\% < 30\%$), which illustrates KT may be more sensitive to the size of content models (KCs) and tend to have better performance using less KCs. It also indicates our reduction methods have selected promising KCs that are the important (or the "hardest") ones for KT making predictions. IDF reaches its optimal AUC at $X = 2$ and $X\% = 10\%$. TFIDF is similar as

Table 1. Significant tests for AUC comparison between reduced content models and ORIGINAL on PFA (+/−: significantly better/worse than ORIGINAL)

	(a) *TopX*												(b) *TopX%*					
	35	25	15-14	13	12	11-10	9	8-7	6	5	4-2	1	≥80%	70%	60%	50%	40%	≤30%
IDF			+	+	+		+	+	+	+	+		+	+			+	
TFIDF	+		+	+			+	+	+	+	+	−						
E-COEF			+	+						+		−						
RANDOM				+				+	+									−

IDF, or even better, since it beats ORIGINAL more consistently. E-COEF on KT, unlike on PFA, shows steadily significantly better results than ORIGINAL, suggesting PFA coefficients can provide useful extra information for reducing the KT content models. RANDOM can still outperform ORIGINAL with a large number of KCs but performance drops significantly with a small number of KCs ($X < 6$ or $X\% < 30\%$) which will be explained in Section 3.2. OUTCOME which reduces KCs by experts also significantly outperforms ORIGINAL.

Table 2. Significant tests for AUC comparison between reduced content models and ORIGINAL on KT (+/−: significantly better/worse than ORIGINAL)

	(a) *TopX*													(b) *TopX%*								
	35	25	15	14	13	12-11	10	9	8	7	6-3	2	1	90%	80%	70%	60%	50%	40%	30%	20%	10%
IDF			+	+		+	+	+		+	+	+			+		+			+	+	+
TFIDF	+	+	+	+	+	+	+	+	+	+	+			+				+		+	+	+
E-COEF	+	+	+	+	+	+	+	+	+	+	+	+		+		+	+	+	+	+	+	+
RANDOM	+		+	+			+		+		+		−	+	+		+	+	+	+		−

Overall, reducing content models on PFA and KT provides a significant gain. Reducing them to some certain size(s) can lead to significantly better predictions, where the best trade-off between model complexity and model fit is achieved.

3.2 Further Study of Reduction Methods

Now we further examine the automatic reduction methods by comparing with expert-based method OUTCOME and RANDOM within the range where proposed methods start to increase performance over ORIGINAL (note that OUTCOME method always has the same reduction size as explained before).

Table 3 shows, for both PFA and KT, IDF and TFIDF are comparable to OUTCOME, and can perform significantly better than it with several reduction sizes. For E-COEF, it doesn't show any significant advantage over OUTCOME on PFA, but can outperform it significantly on KT with $X = 6, 5, 4$. We conclude that our proposed automatic reduction methods are not only comparable to the expert-based method but even outperform it given proper reduction sizes.

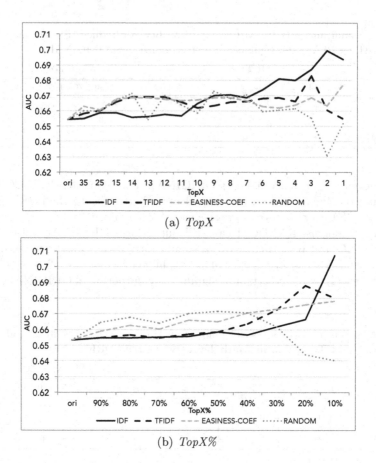

(a) *TopX*

(b) *TopX%*

Fig. 2. Mean AUC of KT prediction using reduced content models

Table 4 shows unclear patterns on PFA of proposed methods against RANDOM, yet previous Fig 1(a) and Table 1(a) show that using IDF and TFIDF still provide much higher probability than RANDOM to outperform ORIGINAL if the 5 ~ 13 important KCs are selected per item (we explained before that E-COEF is not suitable for reduction on PFA). Meanwhile, Table 4 shows that KT steadily outperforms RANDOM when reduction size is small (except at X=1 for TFIDF), which is consistent with previous Fig 2 and Table 2. We hypothesize the reason why RANDOM are occasionally good when the remaining size is large is that RANDOM can have a high probability to target one or a subset of the important KCs when allowed to select a large set of KCs, and then on PFA, it takes advantage of PFA's logistic regression to adjust the weights (coefficients) of other non-important KCs it selects to fit the data, while on KT, RANDOM can take advantage of KT to pick out the most important one in the set by computing the "weakest" KC. When remaining size of KCs is relatively small, all reduction methods start to decrease performance (on KT this decrease

Table 3. AUC comparison between proposed methods and OUTCOME on PFA and KT (+/–: significantly better/worse than OUTCOME, •: the optimal AUC)

	PFA								KT							
	13-12	11	10	9	8	7-5	60%-30%	20%	6	5	4	3	2	1	20%	10%
IDF		+•	+	+			+		+				+•		+	+•
TFIDF		+				+•					+	+				
E-COEF									+	+	+					

Table 4. AUC comparison between proposed methods and RANDOM on PFA and KT (+/–: significantly better/worse than RANDOM, •: the optimal AUC)

	PFA											KT							
	13	12	11	10	9-7	6	5	60%	50%	40-30%	20%	6	5	4	3	2	1	20%	10%
IDF	+		+•		+	+			+			+	+	+	+•	+	+		+•
TFIDF		+		+	+				+	+•				+	+			+	+
E-COEF			+		+										+	+	+	+	

appears when reaching much smaller remaining size comparing with PFA), while RANDOM drops more dramatically. This indicates that a certain number of KCs should still be maintained particularly for PFA no matter which reduction method is used. Overall, we think that for PFA proposed reduction methods can still be better than RANDOM though not substantially owning to PFA model formulation's nature being less sensitive to reduction, while for KT proposed reduction methods outperforms RANDOM substantially showing that they are able to select really important KCs rather than selecting randomly.

Why does fluctuation exist for our proposed methods in terms of AUC values? We admit that all our proposed methods have cases (which are not major) where they assign low scores to important KCs. For example, IDF could assign a low score to an important and hard KC if the KC requires a lot of practices through many items; TFIDF could assign a low score to a KC which is important but appears few times within the item; E-COEF could assign a low score to a KC which is initially easy but when combined with other KCs it easily causes confusion or slips. But still we have shown a clear gain from reduction through the proposed methods.

4   Conclusions and Future Work

This paper argued student modeling and performance prediction in adaptive educational systems with complex multi-KC problems might benefit from a reduced content model. In other words, instead of modeling a problem that requires the application of many knowledge components (KCs), it might be useful to represent it using a small subset of the most important KCs. This paper presented the first attempt to perform an extensive exploration of the content reduction idea in the domain of Java programming. We suggested and explored several content reduction methods based on different sources of information (such as item content and student response) and examined the effect of reduction at varying sizes.

We assessed the impact of reduction on the performance of popular modeling and prediction approaches - PFA and KT. While our original intention was to demonstrate that the more computationally efficient reduced model can maintain comparable performance with the original models, our study shows that reduction, in fact, can help PFA and KT to achieve significantly higher predictive performance given the proper scale of reduction compared with the original content model. Our study also shows that KT is more sensitive to reduction and has larger gain from it than PFA. We observe that PFA's best performance is achieved with a moderate range of reduction while KT achieves that with just a small number of KCs. These different best reduction ranges might indicate different zones where each model can get the best balance between model complexity and model fit. We also demonstrate that, given proper reduction sizes, our proposed reduction methods can beat an expert-based method. Interestingly, the reduction methods using PFA's coefficients provide significant gain for KT that may encourage more ideas of combining these two models.

Our work is related to a broader ongoing research topic, cognitive model discovery or refinement in psychometrics and educational data mining. There has been many works addressing this topic including LFA [2], Q-Matrix Method [1], Matrix Factorization [5], Topical Hidden Markov Model [8]. However, all these approaches focus on domains (tutoring systems) where items are designed to have relatively low content complexity (most of the datasets are from the mathematics domain), i.e., only a small number of KCs is related to each item. We are the first to advocate the need of reduction for complex learning content through several promising ways of reduction.

In our study we attempted to stay as much domain-independent as we could. While the nature of KCs and the approach for KC extraction might be different in other domains, as long as a content item is mapped into a considerable number of KCs (e.g. > 5), our proposed methods can be applied without losing generality. Admittedly, our conclusions drawn so far are from a specific domain, a specific set of reduction approaches, and the selected PFA and KT variants. We need to explore whether the observed magnitude of the reduction effect can be maintained, and whether a clear relationship among best reduction size, datapoints, and characteristics of items exist when exploring other domains (datasets, etc.).

The study opens several interesting questions to explore. Firstly, it would be interesting to see how learning systems using reduced sizes of KCs compare to systems using the original KCs. Secondly, we can improve reduction methods by combining content and response information altogether, considering the nature or type of response, etc. Finally, it would be valuable to automate the choice of proper reduction size and reduction method by using the insights of this study and integrate it with other model refinement (discovery) approaches.

Acknowledgement. This research is partially supported by the Advanced Distributed Learning Initiative (http://www.adlnet.gov/). We thank Dr. José P. González-Brenes, Dr. Zachary A. Pardos, and Dr. Kenneth R. Koedinger for advising and initiating the project at the 9th Annual 2013 LearnLab Summer School at CMU.

References

1. Barnes, T., Bitzer, D.L., Vouk, M.A.: Experimental Analysis of the Q-Matrix Method in Knowledge Discovery. In: Hacid, M.-S., Murray, N.V., Raś, Z.W., Tsumoto, S. (eds.) ISMIS 2005. LNCS (LNAI), vol. 3488, pp. 603–611. Springer, Heidelberg (2005)
2. Cen, H., Koedinger, K.R., Junker, B.: Learning factors analysis – a general method for cognitive model evaluation and improvement. In: Ikeda, M., Ashley, K.D., Chan, T.-W. (eds.) ITS 2006. LNCS, vol. 4053, pp. 164–175. Springer, Heidelberg (2006)
3. Cen, H., Koedinger, K.R., Junker, B.: Comparing Two IRT Models for Conjunctive Skills. In: Woolf, B.P., Aïmeur, E., Nkambou, R., Lajoie, S. (eds.) ITS 2008. LNCS, vol. 5091, pp. 796–798. Springer, Heidelberg (2008)
4. Corbett, A.T., Anderson, J.R.: Knowledge tracing: Modeling the acquisition of procedural knowledge. User Modeling and User-Adapted Interaction 4(4), 253–278 (1994)
5. Desmarais, M.C., Naceur, R.: A Matrix Factorization Method for Mapping Items to Skills and for Enhancing Expert-Based Q-Matrices. In: Lane, H.C., Yacef, K., Mostow, J., Pavlik, P. (eds.) AIED 2013. LNCS, vol. 7926, pp. 441–450. Springer, Heidelberg (2013)
6. Gong, Y., Beck, J.E., Heffernan, N.T.: Comparing Knowledge Tracing and Performance Factor Analysis by Using Multiple Model Fitting Procedures. In: Aleven, V., Kay, J., Mostow, J. (eds.) ITS 2010, Part I. LNCS, vol. 6094, pp. 35–44. Springer, Heidelberg (2010)
7. González-Brenes, J.P., Huang, Y., Brusilovsky, P.: General Features in Knowledge Tracing: Applications to Multiple Subskills, Temporal Item Response Theory, and Expert Knowledge. In: Proceedings of the 7th International Conference on Educational Data Mining (accepted, 2014)
8. González-Brenes, J.P., Mostow, J.: What and When do Students Learn? Fully Data-Driven Joint Estimation of Cognitive and Student Models. In: The 6th International Conference on Educational Data Mining, Memphis, TN (2013)
9. Hall, M., Frank, E., Holmes, G., Pfahringer, B., Reutemann, P., Witten, I.H.: The WEKA data mining software: an update. ACM SIGKDD Explorations Newsletter 11(1), 10–18 (2009)
10. Hosseini, R., Brusilovsky, P.: JavaParser: A Fine-Grain Concept Indexing Tool for Java Problems. In: The First Workshop on AI-supported Education for Computer Science (2013)
11. Hsiao, I.-H., Sosnovsky, S., Brusilovsky, P.: Guiding students to the right questions: adaptive navigation support in an E-Learning system for Java programming. Journal of Computer Assisted Learning 26(4) (2010)
12. Koedinger, K.R., Pavlik Jr., P.I., Stamper, J.C., Nixon, T., Ritter, S.: Avoiding Problem Selection Thrashing with Conjunctive Knowledge Tracing. In: Proceedings of the 4th International Conference on Educational Data Mining, Eindhoven, NL, pp. 91–100 (2011)
13. Pavlik, P.I., Cen, H., Koedinger, K.R.: Performance Factors Analysis – A New Alternative to Knowledge Tracing. In: Proceedings of the 14th International Conference on Artificial Intelligence in Education, pp. 531–538 (2009)
14. Xu, Y., Mostow, J.: Comparison of methods to trace multiple subskills: Is LR-DBN best? In: Proceedings of the Fifth International Conference on Educational Data Mining, Chania, Crete, Greece, pp. 41–48 (2012)
15. Yudelson, M.V., Koedinger, K.R., Gordon, G.J.: Individualized Bayesian Knowledge Tracing Models. In: Lane, H.C., Yacef, K., Mostow, J., Pavlik, P. (eds.) AIED 2013. LNCS, vol. 7926, pp. 171–180. Springer, Heidelberg (2013)

The Role of Adaptive Elements in Web-Based Surveillance System User Interfaces

Ricardo Lage, Peter Dolog, and Martin Leginus

IWIS, Department of Computer Science, Aalborg University,
Selma Lagerloef Vej 300, Aalborg East, Denmark
http://iwis.cs.aau.dk

Abstract. In this paper we present an analysis of improvements to a web-based Graphical User Interface (GUI) for health surveillance systems. Such systems are designed to provide means to detect and suggest outbreaks and corresponding information about them from both formal (e.g., hospital reports) and informal (e.g., news sites) sources. However, despite the availability of different such systems, few studies have been carried out to discuss the elements of the system's GUI and how it can support users in their tasks. To this end, we investigate techniques for adapting, structuring and browsing information in an intuitive and friendly way to the user, focusing on a transition from a static to a dynamic adapted web experience. We conduct a case study with health surveillance experts where we present a case for recommendations matching the user's preferences within a system and discuss improvements to the presented GUI. We discuss improvements in the light of the feedback provided by these users, proposing how adapted elements of a GUI can be used to improve the user experience in a surveillance task.

1 Introduction

One of the main tasks of medical surveillance personnel is to identify whether there is a risk of an epidemic outbreak and, if this risk has high significance, act upon it. Surveillance systems work towards the goal of supporting this task by providing means to detect and suggest those outbreaks and their related documents. Previously, traditional Event-Based Surveillance systems continuously monitored documents (e.g., hospital reports, news sites, scientific articles) for health threats detection and reporting, following an user-defined set of rules. They followed a structured representation of diseases or symptoms which are extracted from the raw text and, when relevant to the user rules, marked as an event to this particular user. These events can be aggregated to produce signals, aimed at representing an indication or sign of early warnings against potential public health threats. However, public health officials may assess not only information from official sources but also from informal ones (e.g., social media such as blog posts or messages from a service like Twitter). This can potentially lead to a one-size-fits-all list of signals, making them impractical for risk assessment.

This problem can be aggravated when the system's Graphical User Interface (GUI) does not provide enough elements to assist the user in finding the desired information or in giving feedback to the system in order for it to improve its detections. In fact,

V. Dimitrova et al. (Eds.): UMAP 2014, LNCS 8538, pp. 350–362, 2014.

the GUI is one aspect of a surveillance system which is often neglected from analysis. There are only a few studies which specifically look into the elements of a GUI and its design choices in the context of healthcare [10] and specifically surveillance system. Such studies or reports do present such systems and their GUIs or provide general guidelines for designing them. These tend to limit themselves to descriptions of what was developed or general guidelines of what should be, without addressing for example the direct feedback of users.

In a previous work [11], we started to look at the problem of dealing with a large number of signals from both formal and informal sources. We did not, however, looked into details of the GUI provided to the users. In this work, therefore, we propose an analysis of presentation options aimed at investigating techniques for adapting, structuring and browsing information in an intuitive and friendly way to the end user of a health surveillance system. This analysis is carried out in the context of two focus group discussions that took place with health surveillance experts, users of surveillance systems. Initially, we proposed a simple, static web-based GUI where users interacted with recommendation of signals received from their predefined rules. This was followed by the first focus group discussion and its input was used to change this initial GUI. We incorporated dynamic elements with the intent of reducing the clutter from the GUI and to provide more efficient means for the users to provide feedback on the recommendations received. We then conducted a similar experiment with the modified GUI in order to assess the users' opinions about it and compare it with the original GUI proposed.

We argue that the adapted elements such as dynamic pagination, tabbed browsing and asynchronous requests help reduce the clutter while improving the user experience. It also facilitates the feedback by users when it does not interfere with the current state of a web page. In addition, we discuss how to give the user more information related to the task at hand: Tag clouds can help improve the navigation in the system and providing an explanation to recommendations gives more input to the user to provide an informed feedback about their quality.

In the next section we discuss related works and GUI elements that we take into account for building our initial GUI prototype. Section 4 presents the initial GUI and describes how it was evaluated by users. Section 5 discusses the feedback given by the users and presents the changes made to the GUI reflecting this feedback. We end this work in Section 6 with conclusions and directions for future works.

2 Related Work

Previous works discussing user interfaces for surveillance systems typically provide only descriptive information about them. [5] describes the software behind HealthMap, a platform on the web that provides means to visualize unstructured reports on disease outbreaks. The evaluation conducted focus on the accuracy of the reports shown. Similarly, [16] only describes a Real-time Outbreak and Disease Surveillance (RODS) system. Interface elements such as graphs and maps are explained but not justified. The same approach of describing a system in general are conducted in [12]. Specially lacking is a feedback that could be provided by the users of such systems.

News recommendations systems such as the ones discussed in [1,2] are also related to our work. The main difference is the way the information is aggregated and how urgent it is. The task of a person for traditional news recommendations is to update his knowledge or awareness while the task of a person who is using our system is to correlate information from the social media with official reports for decision making.

We also acknowledge the findings from the area of notification and awareness such as [6,8]. As reported there, we also follow a strategy, where users are drivers of the explorations to not disturb them in their task. We provide rather visualization help in the system in the form of maps, aggregations, and annotated lists to support their awareness.

As for the visualization, our work is related to [13] where a topicflow interface is shown for trending topics on twitter. We contribute to that stream of work by analyzing and designing the map and list based visualizations with adapted annotations. Our design is different due to the different objective of users. We need to provide aggregates (signals) which are significant for the surveilance task. We need to position the signals within geographical area in question. We can find similarities between list of topics and their summaries and our tag cloud, although we use more visual attributes and focus not only on frequencies in generation of tag clouds. We also contribute to the line of work similar to [17] as we support explorative surveilence task. Our contribution lies in the application of visualization techniques in the recommendation systems area which suit the best the survailence users and perform study with real users although only with limited numeber of experts.

As for the evaluation, [10] utilizes the think aloud method in combination with video recording to design a user interface for a pediatric oncologists computerized patient record. According to [9], however, although this method can provide deep insight into problems encountered by end users, it requres extensive data analyses and requires a high level of expertise by those carrying the evaluation. The author compares this method with two others, the heuristic evaluation and the cognitive walkthrough, having similar drawbacks. He then concludes that none of them alone have been proven effective in all circumstances.

For this reason, we opted in this work for a simpler method, a focus group discussion. A focus group is defined in [15] as a moderated discussion on a specific set of topics where 6-12 people participate. The small group allows for a shared understanding of specific topics while allowing individual differences to be voiced. Questions are open-ended but an initial set of them are pre-defined. A moderator ensures that the discussions stay within the proposed topics. Advantages of focus groups include flexibility, due to its open format. It also benefits from the opportunity of a direct interaction with the participants, allowing for clarifications and further exploration of specific topics. In that sense, other participants can build on each other's comments, enriching the discussion [15].

We conducted two rounds of discussions in order to evaluate an initial GUI and then to follow-up on the changes resulted from the first round. To build the initial GUI, we consider a number of information retrieval interfaces [7] discussed below:

- Graph-based query refinement tools - users can retrieve a subset of documents by exploring a graph where a node represents a concept and an edge indicates a relation between two concepts. The drawback of these methods is that concepts are given by the referenced terminology. The Cat-a-Cone interface supports an exploration of large hierarchies of pre-defined terms with corresponding sets of documents.

TileBars is a visualization tool which represents retrieved documents with horizontal bars where rows represent an occurrence of the searched terms within the document. This approach indicates relative length of documents, frequency (distribution) of search terms in the document but also with respect to all retrieved documents.

- Clustering - documents are grouped based on some similarity measure and each cluster represents a subset of documents that share some common properties. The labeling of obtained clusters is the main limitation of this approach.
- Faceted search tools - documents are divided into pre-defined categories (each category represents a particular facet). It allows an exploration of specific subsets of documents. The problem is that facets have to be pre-defined in advance and it can limit the discovery of unexpected subsets of documents. Aduna Autofocus enterprise search system provides a standard textual faceted navigation interface where on the left side of the page are displayed different facets.
- Tag cloud - a subset of documents is retrieved by a clicking on the term available in the interface. Terms called tags displayed in the tag cloud are defined by users or automatic annotation tools. Therefore, various combinations of tags result in different subsets of retrieved documents and all emerging trends and relationships in the available set of documents can be explored.

In addition to the interface itself, we look into potential elements to include in the GUI to allow the user to give the system feedback about the content he or she received. This feedback is then used by the system to tune future recommendation of contents. We describe below the items we consider in our prototype:

- *Rating Scale* is a means of assessment in terms of quality, quantity, or some mix of both. Rating scales are commonly used in questionnaires with ratings measuring specific constructs/factors. Important aspects of such questionnaires are their validity and reliability. An example of such questionnaires that are used in Computer Science is the System Usability Scale (SUS) a usability scale that can be used for global assessments of systems usability [3].
- *Thumbs-up or thumbs-down* is a hand gesture with the thumb extended upward or downward in approval or disapproval, respectively. This approach can be thought of as a simplified, binary version of a rating scale. The advantage of this approach is that it simplifies the rating of an item, facilitating its integration to systems. At the same time, the disadvantage is that a user may be ambivalent and none of the options will actually represent his feeling. Another advantage, however, is that it helps reduce the rating bias effect. According to [14] and [4], users tend to rate heavily items they like with the highest score and to some extent items they hate with the lowest. But the three other points in a 5-point rating scale are often neglected.
- *Bookmarking* is a direct indicator of a user's preferences once the user explicitly determines what his preferences are. This premise is more reliable when the bookmarks can be labeled as "Favorite" or related meaning, indicating a measure of preference or a "thumbs-up".

– *Comments* is a means of users to describe their impression about the system itself textually. The advantage of this method is that they are not constrained by a set of alternatives. The contents of comments can also be used with information retrieval techniques. The drawback is that only a few users voluntarily provide comments.

In the next section, we describe the first prototype we built taking into account the elements described above.

3   Initial GUI Prototype

Our first prototype was designed to provide minimum functionality for the users to interact with the signals recommended to them, related to the criteria they specified. The main objective for the prototypy was to provide a toll which will signal epidemics related activities from social networks to the user. Signal is an aggregated set of messages and documents which match criteria given by a user such as symptoms, location, disease, and source. Figure 1 shows the second and main step of setting up such criteria which our users also called rules. The user can specify the diseases and/or symptoms (i.e., medical conditions), locations and information sources he or she is interested in receiving information about health threats. The content of the selection boxes have been defined by users from their vocabularies and dictionaries.

These criteria are then used by system to generate the recommendation of signals and documents listed in Figure 2. Signals are listed to the left and the documents corresponding to the selected signal are listed to the right. As can be seen, the signal is annotated with the criteria selected by a user and a time interval when the documents aggregated by the signal have been observed. When the mouse is over a signal, a rating scale is shown so that the user can rate from 1 to 5 the selected signal. By ratings, the user is expressing a relevance and validity of the signal for his survailance task expressed as criteria for signal.

Our prototype aggregates documents from different sources with different natures. Therefore, a process of pre-defining concepts or facets as described in Section 2 is not feasible. Because of that, a tag cloud interface is chosen for summarization and query refinement tasks. A tag cloud supports a retrieval of specific subsets of documents so that the exploitation of vast amount of documents is improved. Figure 2 shows also an example of such a tag cloud for an outbreak of E. coli in Berlin. It provides a general

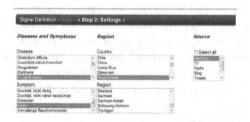

Fig. 1. A screenshot for setting up criteria for signals of interests

Fig. 2. A screenshot of signal recommendations (on the left), document recommendation (on the right), and tag cloud (on the bottom)

picture of the documents related to a signal selected by the user, highlighting terms believed by the system to be relevant in them.

4 Evaluation

4.1 Methodology

To evaluate the initial GUI described in Section 3, we proposed a scenario using real data produced from the M-Eco health surveillance system [1]. The main goal of this system is to perform early detection of health threats to reduce the impact of epidemics. The project complements traditional sources of health related events with Social Media as unofficial information sources for Epidemic Intelligence. This information is then combined with the preferences of the user to generate personalized recommendations of health threats.

We opted for a small number of participants in order to restrict it only to health surveillance experts. They were representatives of the World Health Organization (WHO), the French Institut de veille sanitaire (Sanitary Surveillance Institute - INVS), the European Centre for Disease Prevention and Control (ECDC) and the Mekong Basin Disease Surveillance (MBDS) consortium. 8 participants joined the evaluation as users of a prototype of the M-Eco.

Once logged in the system, the users were asked to create rules according to their interest, choosing from a set of medical conditions and locations, and providing a description of their intent with the rule. The system then produced the recommendations

---

[1] http://www.meco-project.eu/

of existing signals and documents to the users based on these rules. After they browsed through these signals, we conducted a focus group discussion as discussed in Section 2 where the participants provided feedback on their experience with the prototype. In this evaluation, the initial questions posed in the discussion were:

1. How would recommendations help you deal with the excess of information you might receive?
2. How would you like to evaluate the recommendations you receive?
3. How should the recommendations be placed in the system?

Discussions took approximately one hour and a half. We did not seek exact answers to these questions from the participants. Rather, we opted to use them as triggers to topics that could help us understand how health surveillance experts perceive the benefits of recommendations and how they are presented. Our goal was to learn from them how to present recommendations in surveillance systems and how to offer them alternatives of giving feedback to improve recommendations over time.

More specifically, question 1 aimed at assessing whether recommendations can indeed help users of surveillance system and whether they find it necessary/important. Question 2, at the other end, has the objective of identifying how the users would like to evaluate recommendations received. For instance, more feedback can help to improve future recommendations but, at the same time, to prevent more users to do so due to time constraints. Finally, question 3 focuses on stimulating discussions on the GUI, in order to assess how recommendations should be provided in a surveillance system.

5   Discussion

The participants agreed only with specific properties of the GUI they analyzed. For example, they considered the tag cloud useful and agreed that rating of signals and documents is a necessary tool for giving feedback. On the other hand, the process of searching for signals, the information they provide, and the way content is organized were all points that should be further improved, according to the users.

All participants agreed that the current listing of signals is not enough to search for signals. There should be some explicit functionality for that purpose. In general, there was some disagreement on the GUI's ability to communicate information. They disagreed, for example, that the initial M-Eco page provides a complete overview of what should be relevant to the user. This seems to be mainly because the signals were presented in a long textual list. Most participants agreed that this presentation could be improved. Similarly, some of them showed concern with regard to understanding the summary found in each signal.

They also found that a tag cloud model is an useful information retrieval interface. According to them, it facilitates an exploration, browsing and validation process of a large number of documents. Despite, these benefits, they raised the following suggestions and issues:

– Users should be able to assign new tags and also to remove the pregenerated taggings from the documents and in doing such, change the structure of the tag cloud.

– Terms marked as (ir)relevant should be exposed to other users so they can dynamically adjust the retrieval process of documents.

When looking specifically into the answers given to the questions raised in the previous section, in the first question, participants were asked whether recommendations can indeed help users of surveillance system and whether they find them necessary/important. In general, all participants agreed that the system advises users about something that they are missing or have not considered to define in the rules. That is, recommendations should help them discover topics related but not an exact match to their current preferences. In that regard, they mention that the system should also be flexible enough in order to learn from the user feedback but also to "forget", as one of them said, so that the users' changing preferences are updated in the system. In addition, the participants also agreed that recommendations should assist users in overcoming the overload of signals they might receive. However, the system should avoid turning the recommendations into a problem themselves, by overloading the users with them. According to one of them, *"it is normal that similar alerts are set up by different users"* so recommendations should avoid focusing too much on many similar signals.

The second question asked how the participants would like to evaluate the recommendations. Most participants agreed with the evaluation options provided currently in the GUI but one in particular suggested that the same options should be available also for the documents of a particular signal, not only the signals. In addition, another participant suggested that users should be allowed to tell their preferred recommendations by re-ranking the list provided. According to him, this could be complemented by a *"I don't want to see this anymore"* option. This option is similar to a "dislike" or "irrelevant" button as others pointed out. The "dislike" button could also help to avoid the problem of recommending very similar topics as pointed out by one of the participants.

Fig. 3. Tabbed view of the front page highlighting signals in Germany

These ratings could then be complemented by an explanation given by the user. The idea discussed is that relevance is relative and a "yes/no" evaluation may not represent the proper interests of the user. A free-text explanation then could be used as a complementary evaluation tool. Similarly, the relevance is also relative in terms of time. As mentioned before, the system should be able to learn and also forget previously defined user preferences, so that it can adapt to changing behavior. To the participants, a rating given to a recommendation can never be considered as an absolute and definitive statement of user's preferences.

The third and last question focused on the elements of the GUI related to the recommendations. First, they considered that the term "recommendation" or "recommended signal" (as it was displayed in the GUI) is not very appropriate. Instead, separated areas could be provided with proper designations of what are the recommendations about. The examples given were "Related signals" and "Other signals that might interest you". In fact, one of the participants' main suggestions was that an explanation should be given to the user about the origin of a recommendation. That is, they would like to know the reason why each recommendation was generated in order to give an accurate feedback to it. For instance, by knowing that a particular recommendation came from a specific set of rules, a user could mark it as irrelevant because he is not interested in more information about that particular topic.

We address the points raised by the participants developing a new GUI. We wanted to keep the simplicity of the first version but at the same time provide more information in a organized fashion. To achieve this goal, we opted for an adaptive dynamic GUI using the Django framework [2]. It is a high-level web framework based on Python which focus on simple and clean designs using the Don't Repeat Yourself (DRY) principle [3]. It also facilitates the use of dynamic adaptive elements and asynchronous requests, in line with our goals. On top of the Django framework, we also used elements from the YUI open-source library provided by Yahoo [4] and the Google Maps API [5].

In the second focus group discussion, participants commented on the changes. The changes have been positivelly received by all participants. In fact, it prompted one of them to suggest more, specifically, a timeline view where the signals in a particular location could be seen over time. According to him, more tabs could be added to the GUI in order to offer the user more visualization options without adding clutter to the GUI. Specifically to the tag clouds, participants considered it beneficial. They argued that, compared with a table listing, it provides additional context about considered signals and simplifies the browsing process as it is easier to retrieve a specific subset of relevant documents related to the specific signal. In the next subsections we detail the changes carried out in the new GUI.

5.1   Changes to the Frontpage

Figure 3 shows the tabbed view of the front page highlighting signals in Germany. The user can click on the red marks to see more details about a particular signal and browse through its documents. Selecting the first tab, "Signal Listing", gives the user a table listing of the signals as shown in Figure 4. The first noticeable change is that the list of signals is now dynamically paginated. In the initial GUI presented in Section 3, the

---

[2] https://www.djangoproject.com/

[3] http://c2.com/cgi/wiki?DontRepeatYourself

[4] http://yuilibrary.com/

[5] https://developers.google.com/maps/documentation/javascript/controls

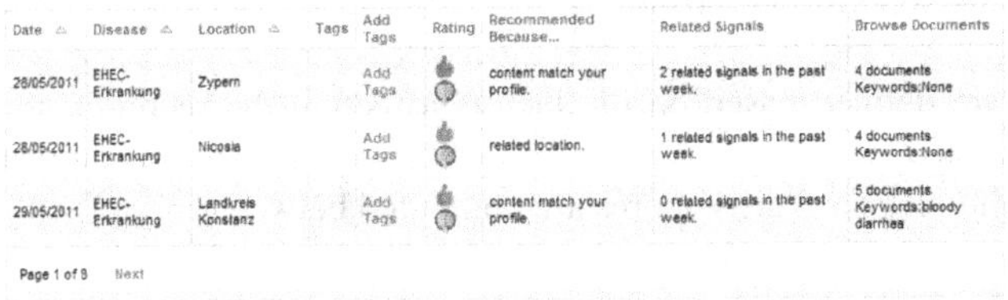

Fig. 4. Redesigned table to navigate through the signals

full list of signals for the logged user was fetched, slowing down the response time and at the same time the quality of the user experience. Pagination, then, allows the user, if he or she wants, to browse through all the signals relevant to him or her, without the overload of one big list.

In each page of the table listing the signals, we tried to make the ability to tag or rate the signal more explicit. These two forms of feedback are now explicitly listed as columns in the table. The rating is simplified from a scale to a 'thumbs up' or 'down' option. It is adapted so that when the 'thumbs up' or 'down' is selected, it is immediately greyed and saved. We also added the total number of documents available for this signal in the last column. This information is a link to list those documents through the tag cloud. The addition of such link makes the access to the documents more explicit to the user, facilitating the navigation.

In addition, we raise a new hypothesis for storing the order of the rated signal. For instance, if the user rates positively the first signal in the table list, we believe that this signal should have a lower importance than, say, the signal in position ten which was also rated positively. The intuition behind this approach is that positive ratings in the first positions should be expected whereas positive ratings in lower positions need to be weighted up. Conversely, negative ratings rated in the first positions should receive a higher negative weight than negative ratings down the list. We also give a higher weight to the 'thumbs down' than 'thumbs down'. Since the majority of users tend to only rate what they like, we wanted to emphasize the cases where a negative rating is actually given [4].

More sorting options are now available, not only by date, but by disease or location as well. Notice the small arrow next to these headers. Once the user clicks one of those, the table is sorted by the elements of the corresponding column. We also added two new columns: 'Recommended Because...' and 'Related Signals'. The first provides an explanation for why the signal is being listed to the user. The second shows the number of signals that are related to the current signal in the last 7 days. Related here is considered to be signals that contain the same disease or symptom in the same or similar locations within the specified period of time. Finally, in the column 'Browse Documents', we add a list of keywords. These are words extracted from the documents of the signal, that we believe can also represent the signal and give additional context to the user.

5.2   Explaining Recommendations

Explanations are defined based on the factors affecting the recommendations, based on the signals rated by the user. Currently, depending on the user interaction with the system, the following similarity scores are computed between:

1. the user rules and the contents of each signal's documents;
2. the user rules and the properties (i.e., disease and location values) of each signal;
3. the user's specific rules for locations, similar locations and each signal's documents;
4. the user's specific rules for locations, similar locations and the locations together with similar locations of each signal;
5. the tag set of the user and the contents of each signal's documents;
6. the tag set of the user and the properties of each signal;
7. the date of the signal and the date when the recommendation is being computed.

Each of these items (we call them 'factors') have a similarity score which is fed to a multi-factor model to compute their respective weights. We then aggregate these weights in four categories: content, location, tag, and date. Items 1 and 2 above refer to the first category, items 3 and 4 to the second, items 5 and 6 to the third, and item 7 to the fourth category. We sum their respective scores and show a message to the user according to the category that received the highest score. Figure 4 shows an example with three of these messages.

5.3   Changes to the Tag Clouds

Finally, Figure 5 shows the modified tag cloud interface. It has a cleaner look with a reduced number, more selective, number of tags. It also allows tags detected automatically by the system to be removed, which is then used as implicit feedback for improvements in future tag detections. At the same time, it allow users to add or remove his own desired tags. It provides benefits when more users view the same tag cloud and users want to point out relevant documents to each other.

Fig. 5. The tag cloud after removal of the irrelevant tag **Euro fever** (see original tag cloud in the Motivation section). The improved model also allows to add user tags to a selected document.

6   Conclusion and Future Works

This paper presented changes to a GUI for a health surveillance system and discussed them with health surveillance experts in focus group discussions. It showed the preferences of users for more information without adding clutter to the GUI. Participants overall approved the changes made, encouraging more additions that could improve the way they interact with the information given by the system. In future works we plan to look into more ways to evaluate changes in a GUI. Specifically, we want to obtain more quantitative information about the use of a GUI in order to complement the information given by the participants in the focus groups conducted in this work.

References

1. Ardissono, L., Console, L., Torre, I.: An adaptive system for the personalized access to news. AI Commun. 14(3), 129–147 (2001)
2. Billsus, D., Pazzani, M.J.: User modeling for adaptive news access. User Modeling and User-Adapted Interaction 10(2-3), 147–180 (2000)
3. Brooke, J.: Sus-a quick and dirty usability scale. Usability Evaluation in Industry 189, 194 (1996)
4. Farmer, R.: Ratings bias effects (2009), http://buildingreputation.com/writings/2009/08/ratings_bias_effects.html (accessed on February 20, 2013)
5. Freifeld, C.C., Mandl, K.D., Reis, B.Y., Brownstein, J.S.: HealthMap: global infectious disease monitoring through automated classification and visualization of internet media reports. Journal of the American Medical Informatics Association 15(2), 150–157 (2008)
6. Gross, T., Wirsam, W., Gräther, W.: Awarenessmaps: visualizing awareness in shared workspaces. In: Cockton, G., Korhonen, P. (eds.) Extended abstracts of the 2003 Conference on Human Factors in Computing Systems, CHI 2003, pp. 784–785 (April 2003)
7. Hearst, M.: Search user interfaces. Cambridge Univ. Pr. (2009)
8. Iqbal, S.T., Horvitz, E.: Notifications and awareness: A field study of alert usage and preferences. In: Proceedings of the 2010 ACM Conference on Computer Supported Cooperative Work, CSCW 2010, pp. 27–30. ACM, New York (2010)
9. Jaspers, M.W.: A comparison of usability methods for testing interactive health technologies: Methodological aspects and empirical evidence. International Journal of Medical Informatics 78(5), 340–353 (2009)
10. Jaspers, M.W., Steen, T., van den Bos, C., Geenen, M.: The think aloud method: a guide to user interface design. Intl. Journal of Medical Informatics 73(11-12), 781–795 (2004)
11. Lage, R.G., Durao, F., Dolog, P., Stewart, A.: Applicability of recommender systems to medical surveillance systems. In: Proc. of the 2nd Intl. Workshop on Web Science and Inform. Exchg. in the Medical Web, MedEx 2011, pp. 1–6. ACM, New York (2011)
12. Lopes, L.F., Silva, F.A.B., Couto, F., Zamite, J., Ferreira, H., Sousa, C., Silva, M.J.: Epidemic marketplace: An information management system for epidemiological data. In: Khuri, S., Lhotská, L., Pisanti, N. (eds.) ITBAM 2010. LNCS, vol. 6266, pp. 31–44. Springer, Heidelberg (2010)
13. Malik, S., Smith, A., Hawes, T., Papadatos, P., Li, J., Dunne, C., Shneiderman, B.: Topicflow: Visualizing topic alignment of twitter data over time. In: Proceedings of the 2013 IEEE/ACM International Conference on Advances in Social Networks Analysis and Mining, ASONAM 2013, pp. 720–726. ACM, New York (2013)

14. Rajaraman, S.: Five stars dominate ratings (2009), http://youtube-global.blogspot.fr/2009/09/five-stars-dominate-ratings.html (accessed on February 20, 2013)

15. Stewart, D.W., Shamdasani, P.N., Rook, D.W.: Focus groups: theory and practice. SAGE (2007)

16. Tsui, F.-C., Espino, J.U., Dato, V.M., Gesteland, P.H., Hutman, J., Wagner, M.M.: Technical description of RODS: a real-time public health surveillance system. Journal of the American Medical Informatics Association 10(5), 399–408 (2003)

17. Wilson, M.L., Kules, B., Schraefel, M.C., Shneiderman, B.: From keyword search to exploration: Designing future search interfaces for the web. Foundations and Trends in Web Science 2(1), 1–97 (2010)

Uncovering Latent Knowledge: A Comparison of Two Algorithms

Danny J. Lynch and Colm P. Howlin

Research and Development Laboratory,
CCKF Limited, Greenhills Road, Dublin, Ireland
{danny.lynch,colm.howlin}@cckf-it.com

Abstract. At the beginning of every course, it can be expected that several students have some syllabus knowledge. For efficiency in learning systems, and to combat student frustration and boredom, it is important to quickly uncover this latent knowledge. This enables students to begin new learning immediately. In this paper we compare two algorithms used to achieve this goal, both based on the theory of Knowledge Spaces. Simulated students were created with appropriate answering patterns based on predefined latent knowledge from a subsection of a real course. For each student, both algorithms were applied to compare their efficiency and their accuracy. We examine the trade-off between both sets of outcomes, and conclude with the merits and constraints of each algorithm.

Keywords: Latent Knowledge, Knowledge Spaces, Technology Enhanced Learning, Intelligent Tutoring Systems, Learner Models.

1 Introduction

There are now many intelligent learning environments that guide students through the learning material within a curriculum [1]. When students are first introduced to such environments, it is reasonable to expect they might have some prior knowledge of those materials. We say that each student has *latent knowledge*. A goal of these learning environments is to uncover this knowledge, so that each student may begin learning new material and not be forced to cover knowledge items already known. One naïve approach is to test the student on each item in the curriculum. This is obviously impractical due to time constraints and the cognitive burden on the student. More intelligent methods of selecting knowledge items and interpreting the results are needed. This is akin to Computerized Adaptive Testing where a pool of items or questions is optimally searched. However, in this case, additional structure can be added to the item pool by taking advantage of the prerequisite nature of knowledge. Mastery of certain items is necessary in order to begin others. This forms the set-theoretical basis of Knowledge Spaces introduced by Doigon and Falmagne in 1985 [2,3]. In this framework, a curriculum is treated as a graph structure where each node represents an item or a question, and a directed edge between two nodes represents a prerequisite connection. A *knowledge state* is defined as a

V. Dimitrova et al. (Eds.): UMAP 2014, LNCS 8538, pp. 363–368, 2014.

feasible subset of nodes that a person could be capable of answering. The *knowledge space* is then the collection of all these knowledge states. Once this graph structure is defined for a curriculum, the list of possible knowledge states can be combinatorially calculated. While trivial for small networks, this is a computationally difficult problem for larger networks, as we detail in Section 2.2. The goal of intelligent learning environments is to uncover the *latent knowledge state* of every student. In this paper, we investigate two algorithms that achieve this. One of the fundamental differences between the algorithms is the requirement of pre-computing all knowledge states prior to run-time. In any case, intelligent learning environments should strive to efficiently achieve this goal by using as few knowledge items as possible and in the shortest possible time.

2   Uncovering the Latent State

For the purposes of this paper, we compare two algorithms that can be used to uncover the latent state of a student. To emulate real world behavior we test these algorithms on the knowledge space of a real network used for Grade 6 Probability in the Realize[it] learning environment. This particular network is a subset of a much larger network and, as shown in Fig. 1(a), has 23 nodes and 27 prerequisites links. This produces a total of 6932 feasible knowledge states that a student may have in this curriculum network. The distribution of these states by size, which represents the number of items a student could know, is shown in Fig. 1(b). For example, we find there are only three knowledge states with one item while there are 850 states with thirteen items.

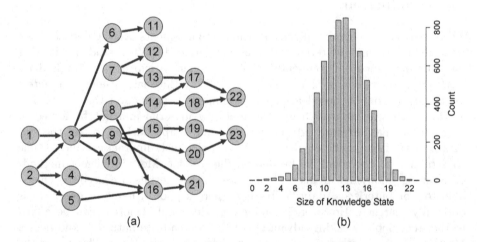

(a)   (b)

Fig. 1. (a) The 23 node network knowledge domain with a total of 6932 knowledge states and (b) the distribution of the knowledge states according to their size

2.1   Simulation

Simulated students are used to evaluate the algorithms in this paper, which is a common technique found in education research [4]. For each possible knowledge state, a simulated student was created with that state defining their latent knowledge. When probed on items from the domain, these students would respond appropriately based on their latent state. However, to emulate more realistic behavior, a probabilistic response rate was introduced to create cases whereby the simulated student does not respond appropriately.[1] For instance, a response rate of 0.9 signifies the student responds accurately every 9 out of 10 questions. Moreover rather than generating these students' responses on the fly, they were well-defined prior to the algorithm simulation. In this manner, both algorithms obtained the same response when probing the simulated students on the same item, allowing for a fairer comparison of results. The two algorithms were then applied to each simulated student with the objective of uncovering the latent knowledge state. Both of these algorithms select the item which they deem *best* and test the student with it. Based on the student response, the algorithm can then narrow down the feasible knowledge states and select the next *best* item. This process is repeated until a unique state remains or a stopping condition is reached. A number of data points were recorded at the end of each simulation. These include the total number of questions asked (to measure algorithm efficiency) and the count of differences between the defined and the uncovered latent knowledge state (to measure algorithm error rate). Further, due to the non-deterministic nature of these algorithms, each simulation was run five times to produce a mean value for all the collected data points.

2.2   The Algorithms

The first algorithm was developed by Doigon and Falmagne through their work on Knowledge Spaces. Although not formally titled, we refer to this algorithm as *Knowledge Space Theory* (KST) in this paper. The process assigns a probability of being latent to every knowledge state [2,3]. These probabilities are then updated as students are tested on items. This is repeated until a stopping condition is reached. The second algorithm is a component of the Realize[it] learning environment developed by CCKF Limited. Referred to as *Determine Knowledge* (DK), this process begins with all items having the potential to be part of the latent state. When students are tested on these items, their response dictates which should be included or excluded. This is repeated until no items are left.

One requirement of the KST algorithm is that all knowledge states are known by the system. This is indeed a trivial process for small networks. For instance, it took under ten seconds to calculate the knowledge states for the 23 node network in Fig. 1(a). To prevent loading times and delays, this computation should not be done on the fly and must instead be completed prior to any student

---

[1] In the literature this is commonly referred to as the probability of a lucky guess or careless error. For simplicity, these are treated as identical in this paper.

interaction. Further, it would need to be recomputed with every change to the network as this can result in dramatically altered knowledge states. Although this in itself is quite manageable, the required computation time explodes as these networks get larger. In fact, we can show that this computation is equivalent to finding all maximal cliques of an associated network of the same size. This is NP-complete and one of Karp's NP-complete problems [5]. The enumerative algorithms for computing these cliques run in exponential time. A modified version of the Bron-Kerbosch algorithm is documented to be of time complexity of order $O(3^{n/3})$ where n is the size of the network. Indeed, we have found that this computation quickly becomes impractical for larger networks, requiring long computation times and large memory footprints. It was avoidance of these issues that prompted the creation of the DK algorithm.

In comparing the two algorithms, we find that KST lends itself to being flexible whereas DK is more rigid. This is clear from the scenario where a student makes a careless error on an item. This error made during the DK process will eliminate the true latent state, whereas the error in KST just diminishes the probability. On the flip side, this means that the KST process can repeatedly ask the same questions whereas DK only asks each at most once. The impact of this rigidity will be investigated though the simulations and discussed in Section 3.

Algorithm 1: Knowledge Space Theory

There are many variations of the KST algorithm. In particular, there are multiple methods for selecting items (known as Questioning Rules), and multiple methods for updating the probabilities after response (known as Updating Rules). For the purposes of this paper, the following algorithm was used to represent KST.[2]

1. Start with all states having equal probability.
2. Choose the item to be tested using the *Half Split* questioning rule.
3. Update the probabilities based on student response using the *Multiplicative with Parameters* updating rule.
4. Repeat steps 2 and 3 until a unique state has the highest probability, or earlier if other stopping criteria have been met (see [3] 17.2).

Algorithm 2: Determine Knowledge

1. Start with an empty knowledge state and an item pool containing all items.
2. Calculate the information content for each item in the pool.[3]
3. Choose the item to be tested with the maximum information content.
4. Based on the student response, remove appropriate items from the pool and update the knowledge state accordingly.
5. Repeat steps 2 through 4 until the item pool is empty.

---

[2] Detailed documentation can be found in [3], sections 13.4.4 and 13.4.7, with an overview of the process in section 17.2.

[3] This is based on the structure of the network and defined using Shannon Entropy.

3   Results

For each simulated student and algorithm, the number of questions asked and the calculated accuracy were recorded. These values were classified according to two simulation parameters: the size of the latent knowledge state and the student response rate. For all parameter pairings, the data for each algorithm was averaged and compared to determine if the results were significantly different (at a 95% confidence level). The performance output can be visualized by the two heat maps shown in Fig. 2. In general we find that the DK algorithm asks students fewer questions. The main exception occurs in a region shown at the top of Fig. 2(a). In Fig. 2(b) we find that the KST algorithm is more accurate, but that this accuracy only starts to dominate for knowledge states above size 7. However the most striking feature of this heat map is the yellow bar across the top. This shows that in the absence of student errors, both algorithms achieve the same accuracy for all knowledge states, and in fact determine the correct state. Nevertheless they do use differing numbers of questions to achieve this.

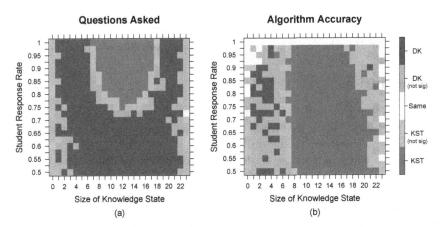

Fig. 2. Heat maps showing which algorithms performed better for (a) questions asked and (b) algorithm accuracy, across all simulation parameters

For a more detailed analysis, the recorded values for each simulation were also subtracted from each other (KST − DK). These were then averaged according to each simulation parameter to produce the four graphs of Fig. 3. In terms of knowledge state size, graph (a) shows that DK tends to ask fewer questions. However graph (b) indicates that KST is often more accurate in these simulations, being on average one item closer to the true latent state for sizes over 7 items. Secondly, in terms of student response rate, graph (c) exhibits a linear relationship where initially DK outperforms with fewer questions but inverts at a response rate of 0.75. Finally graph (d) shows us that KST has greater accuracy across all student response rates, but that the difference diminishes for higher rates. The lack of DK in this graph can be accounted for by the dominance of KST in Figure 2(b) between states of size 8 and 19 in each horizontal slice.

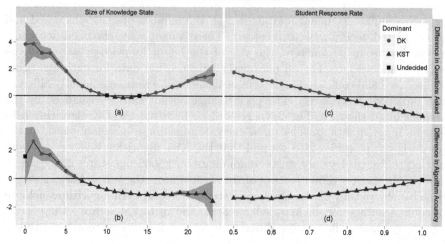

Fig. 3. Summary of simulation differences. The mean value and 95% confidence interval are shown for the *Differences in Questions Asked* and *Difference in Algorithm Accuracy*, outlined according to the size of latent state and student response rate of the simulation.

4   Conclusions

There is a clear trade-off between the number of questions asked and the algorithm accuracy. While DK tends to ask fewer questions, KST makes up for it in accuracy. However, as these differences are often not large, the question remains as to which side of the trade-off is more beneficial. Similar results have been found for simulations run on other networks of various sizes and densities. For those where the knowledge states are computable in a reasonable amount of time, KST makes the overall preferable choice while DK remains a practical alternative. However as the networks evolve and grow, the required computation times become excessive and unmanageable, and DK becomes the better algorithmic choice. Part of our future work aims to introduce more flexibility into the DK algorithm in order to capture student errors.

References

1. Desmarais, M.C., de Baker, R.S.J.: A Review of Recent Advances in Learner and Skill Modeling in Intelligent Learning Environments. UMUAI 22, 9–38 (2012)
2. Falmagne, J.C., Cosyn, E., Doignon, J.P., Thiéry, N.: The Assessment of Knowledge, in Theory and in Practice. In: Missaoui, R., Schmidt, J. (eds.) Formal Concept Analysis. LNCS (LNAI), vol. 3874, pp. 61–79. Springer, Heidelberg (2006)
3. Falmagne, J.C., Doignon, J.P.: Learning Spaces. Springer, Berlin (2011)
4. Abdullah, S.C., Cooley, R.E.: Using Simulated Students to Evaluate an Adaptive Testing System. In: ICCE, pp. 614–618. IEEE Computer Society (2002)
5. Bomze, I.M., Budinich, M., Pardalos, P.M., Pelillo, M.: The Maximum Clique Problem. In: Handbook of Combinatorial Optimization, pp. 1–74. Springer (1999)

Client-Side Hybrid Rating Prediction
for Recommendation

Andrés Moreno[1,2], Harold Castro[1], and Michel Riveill[2]

[1] School of Engineering, Universidad de los Andes, Bogotá, Colombia
[2] I3S, Université de Nice Sophia Antipolis, France
{dar-more,hcastro}@uniandes.edu.co, riveill@unice.fr

Abstract. The centralized gathering and processing of user information made by traditional recommender systems can lead to user information exposure, violating her privacy. Client-side personalization methods have been created as a mean for avoiding privacy risks. Motivated by limiting the exposure of user private information, we explore the use of a client-side hybrid recommender system placed on the online learning setting. We propose a prediction model based on an ensemble blender of an online matrix factorization CF model and a logistic regression model trained on item metadata with a probabilistic feature inclusion strategy. The final prediction is a blend of the two models on a weighted regret approach. We validate our approach with the Movielens 10M dataset.

Keywords: recommender systems, privacy, online learning, regret.

1 Introduction

Organizations that offer personalization services gather and store as much information as possible about users and items supported by the current availability of cheap storage, apply computational intensive algorithms to train models that scale up to the size of the collected data and use the trained models to adequately answer to a large amount of personalization requests made on behalf of the users of the system.

Recommender systems are personalization systems that automatically calculate the relevance of a large collection of data items for a user. The relevance mapping between users and items is used to select, screen out or rank items based on how relevant the user will perceive them based on her preferences and situation. As any other personalization system, recommender systems gather as much information as possible about the user in order to learn an accurate user profile useful for recommendation purposes.

Figure 1 gives an overview of the components of a traditional recommendation system: The *interaction log component* is in charge of gathering feedback information about the interaction between the users and items in the system; The *recommendation component* is in charge of two tasks delegated onto two components: (1) The *training component* learns the parameters of a predictive model by going through the user-item historic interaction kept in the system logs, and

V. Dimitrova et al. (Eds.): UMAP 2014, LNCS 8538, pp. 369–380, 2014.
© Springer International Publishing Switzerland 2014

(2) the *prediction component* that actively searches among the database of available items the most relevant ones for the user based on the learned parameters (user and item profiles). Both user-item feedback information and the profiles of users and items in the system are kept under the direct administration of the organization.

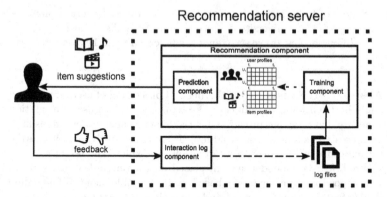

Fig. 1. Traditional recommender systems

A traditional model for the rating prediction task [19] can be described as follows: Let $U=\{u_1, u_2 \ldots ,u_m\}$ be the set of m users available in the system and let $I=\{i_1, i_2 \ldots ,i_n\}$ be the set of n possible data items that are available for the users. A matrix R is used to register the ratings that users give to items. Taking μ as the average of the known ratings, b_u and b_i as the *bias* or deviation from the mean that are observed for each user and item respectively, matrix factorization models build up two matrices representing the user $(X_{m \times k})$ and the item $(Y_{n \times k})$ under a lower dimensionality such that $R \approx \mu + b_* + XY^T$. The relevance prediction of this model is given by the following equation:

$$\hat{r}_{ui} = \mu + b_i + b_u + \left(x_u^T y_i\right) \tag{1}$$

In order to learn the parameters of the bias and the X and Y matrices, a least squares optimization is done to minimize the error over the entries of the matrix R that are known:

$$\min_{b_*, x_*, y_*} \sum_{R_{ui} \neq null} \left(R_{ui} - \mu - b_i - b_u - x_u^T y_i\right)^2 + \lambda \left(\|x_u\|^2 + \|y_i\|^2\right) \tag{2}$$

These parameters can be learned using an alternating least squares strategy where one matrix (X or Y) is fixed and the parameters of the other one are adjusted [4], or by a stochastic gradient descent technique popularized by [13].

1.1 Privacy Risks in Personalization Systems

As explained by Foner. [12], the storage of private user information under the direct management of an organization raises privacy threats. User's trust that the information gathered by the organization will be used for personalization, however this trust can be transgressed and information of the user can be *exposed*. Foner gives five examples of the exposure risk present in traditional personalization systems:

- *Deception by the recipient:* The system can lie about its privacy policies and trick users to reveal personal information, using it later for a different purpose from the original. For example selling user information or sharing it with other organizations.
- *Mission creep:* Initially the policy of usage of personal information is defined clearly by the system, but later the system expands its goals in a previously unforeseen manner, changing the use of personal information for other purposes related to the new goals of the organization.
- *Accidental disclosure:* Information about users can be made available accidentally, for example leaving private information on a server that can be accessed by a search engine over the Internet.
- *Disclosure by malicious intent:* Storage servers' security can be breached and users' personal information can be stolen.
- *Forced disclosure:* Systems must disclose the information for legal reasons (Subpoenas).

Motivated by the fact that the exposure risks are a consequence of a centralized entity managing the information about users, client-based personalization systems move the information gathering, processing and storage from a centralized entity to each user's device. In this paper we propose a client-side profiling agent placed under the online learning model. Predictions will be based on a blending of a Collaborative Filtering (CF) technique based on matrix decomposition and a Content Based (CB) based on logistic regression.

The paper is organized as follows: In section 2 we will present the proposed architecture of the system. On section 3 we will present the learning model proposed. In section 4 we will present how the system behaves on a online recommendation setting using the Movielens-10M dataset from GroupLens research group [1]. Finally on section 5 we will present the related work and on section 6 the conclusions and future work.

2   System Architecture

In order to keep the organization from gathering the information of the user, a client-side agent is introduced to safeguard the user information. The client-side agent is in charge of keeping up to date the user profile, as well as giving the necessary information to the recommendation server to keep the item profiles up to date without revealing the opinions the user has expressed on the items.

In Figure 2 an overview of the proposed architecture is presented: The *user interaction component* is in charge of receiving feedback information about the

---

[1] http://www.grouplens.org

interaction between the user and the items. In our system, when a user u interacts with an item i, she will assign a rating $r_{ui} \in \mathcal{O}$. The set $\mathcal{O}$ is the set of possible ratings the user can assign to an item. (e.g $\mathcal{O} = \{1, 2, 3, 4, 5\}$ or $\mathcal{O} = \{+, -\}$). When a user interacts with an item, this information is given to the *user training component*. This component updates the user profile based on the item's profile and the rating given to the item by the user. After updating the user profile, this component sends back to the *item training component* on the recommendation server information from the user profile that is used to keep an up to date version of the item profile, without disclosing the action the user made on the item.

In order to bring relevant items to the user, the *user-item integration component* is in charge of actively going through the item database to offer the user items she might be interested in. This component can be installed either on the server or the client side. Finally, the *prediction component* on the client side filters out or ranks the items sent to it by the user-item integration by calculating the relevance prediction function with the local user profile and the item profile. In the next section the prediction models and algorithms will be reviewed.

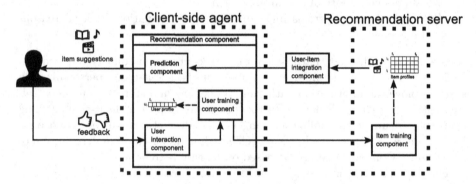

Fig. 2. Proposed architecture for recommender system

3   Model

According to [1], recommender systems can be divided into three general categories according to how the systems employ the user information to calculate the relevance of an item: Content based filtering (CB) which uses the features or characteristics of the items to find out the relevance for the user, collaborative filtering (CF) which uses only the opinions of the users on the items, and hybrid systems (HS) that use an ensemble of different systems. Other authors such as [7] identify other categories such as knowledge based recommender systems and demographic based recommender systems but since they rely heavily on user and item features we classify them under the CB approach.

Single paradigms for recommendation have their own problems: CB approaches are known to be vulnerable to the overspecialization problem since they only can detect the relevance of items that are similar to the ones the user has seen before, on the other hand CF approaches are known to be vulnerable to sparsity and cold-start problems. In order to avoid the problems of single techniques, we propose a *weighted* [7] hybridization technique that operates a CB agent (Section 3.1) and a CF agent (Section 3.2) at the client-side. The weighted approach generates a relevance prediction for each model and applies a weighting of both predictions based on the historical regret of the models (Section 3.3).

3.1 Content Based Model

For the content based model, each item i is described by a set of concepts C_i. A user u has a profile with a list of non duplicate concepts C_u and a set of $|\mathcal{O}|$ vectors $w^o \in \mathbb{R}^{|C_u|}, o \in \mathcal{O}$. As each user interacts with the items present in the system, each of the concepts that are related to the item (C_i) are considered for addition into her list C_u. We use an inclusion policy using a sliding window min-count sketch structure [11] based on the work developed in [21]: All concepts seen by the user at least N times during the window duration of the sketch are present in the user's list, and the size of the vectors w^o is updated.

After modifying the list and the w^o vectors' length, the weights of the vector are adjusted using an online logistic regression strategy. Let $r_{ui} \in \mathcal{O}$ be the rating user u gives to item i, t_u be the number of items the user has rated and $m_{ui}(C_i \times C_u) \to \mathbb{R}^{|C_u|}$ a function that takes the concept set of an item and converts it into a binary vector where each coordinate is 1 if the user's concept belong to the items list $(m_{ui}[f] = \mathbb{1}_{C_u[f] \in C_i})$. For each vector w^o, we predict $\sigma(\langle w^o, m_{ui} \rangle)$ and update each of the vectors as follows:

$$w_u^o \leftarrow w_u^o - \gamma(t_u)(\sigma(\langle w^o, m_{ui} \rangle) - \mathbb{1}_{r_{ui}=o})m_{ui} \tag{3}$$

Where $\langle w^o, m_{ui} \rangle$ is the dot product between vectors w^o and m_{ui}, $\sigma(c) = 1/(1 + \exp(-c))$ is the sigmoid function and $\gamma(t)$ is a function of the learning rate that decreases as the number of trainings of the user increases, e.g $\gamma_t = \gamma_0(1 + \alpha\gamma_0 t)^{-c}$ [26].

The rating prediction under this model is calculated as follows:

$$\hat{r}_{ui} = \frac{\sum_{o \in \mathcal{O}} \sigma(\langle w^o, m_{ui} \rangle) \times o}{\sum_{o \in \mathcal{O}} \sigma(\langle w^o, m_{ui} \rangle)} \tag{4}$$

3.2 Collaborative Filtering Model

Following the work of Isaacman et al. [15], we will define the problem of predicting a user rating for an item as an estimation of a probability distribution of the item ratings over the user's information using a matrix factorization technique.

Our system will predict the rating a user might have given to an item by estimating the rating probability distribution of items. Let $\tilde{\pi}_{ui}^o$ be the probability that user u will give a rating $o \in \mathcal{O}$ to item i, the goal of our system is to estimate each of the coordinates of each of the matrices $\tilde{\Pi}^o = [\tilde{\pi}_{ui}^o]$. Assuming these matrices are low-rank, they can be reconstructed from the multiplication of two lower rank matrices of rank F: $\tilde{Q}^o$ of size $m \times F$ and $\tilde{P}$ of size $n \times F$.

In order to approximate the ideal matrices $\tilde{Q}^o$ and $\tilde{P}$, we define for each item a vector p_i that approximates the i-th row of matrix $\tilde{P}$. This vector is subjected to represent a probability distribution of items across the latent factors, therefore is restricted to $p_{i,f} \geq 0$ and $\sum_{f \in F} p_{i,f} = 1$. Analogously, we define for each user a vector q^o that approximates the u-th row of each matrix $\tilde{Q}^o$ for $o \in \mathcal{O}$. Each of the $|\mathcal{O}|$ vectors of the user represent a probability distribution of the preferences of the user across the latent factors, and is as well restricted to $q_{u,f} \geq 0$ and $\sum_{f \in F} q_{u,f}^o = 1$.

Given these definitions , the estimation of the probability that user u has given rating o to item i is:

$$\pi_{ui}^o = \sum_{f \in F} q_{u,f}^o \times p_{i,f} = \langle p_i, q_u^o \rangle \tag{5}$$

In order to maintain user privacy, the matrix of item profiles P is kept by the recommendation server and the matrix Q is distributed among the users since each user has her own user profile. When a user assigns a rating for an item r_{ui}, the item profile of the item is available to her and adjusts the weights of the q^o profile vectors as follows:

$$\begin{aligned} q_u^o &\leftarrow q_u^o + \gamma(t_u)(\mathbb{1}_{r_{ui}=o} - (\langle p_i, q_u^o \rangle))p_i \\ q_u &\leftarrow \textstyle\prod_{D_{user}}(q_u) \end{aligned} \tag{6}$$

Where t_u is the number of items the user has rated, $\gamma(t)$ is a function of the learning rate that decreases as the number of trainings of the user increases as in the previous section , and $\prod_{D_{user}}$ projects the rows of q_u into a probability distribution after the update.

Differing from [15], in order to update the item profile p_i, we don't send the q_u profile and the reported rating r_{ui} to the agent that updates the item profile since this would violate the purpose of decentralization to keep the user privacy. Instead we only send to the recommendation server the vector q_u^o where $r_{ui} = o$ without disclosing r_{ui} to the recommendation server, the update is as follows:

$$\begin{aligned} p_i &\leftarrow p_i + \gamma(t_i)(1 - (\langle p_i, q_u^o \rangle))q_u^o \\ p_i &\leftarrow \textstyle\prod_{D_{item}}(p_i) \end{aligned} \tag{7}$$

Where t_i is the number of times the item has been rated, $\gamma(t)$ is a function of the learning rate that decreases as the number of trainings of the item increases as in the previous section , and $\prod_{D_{item}}$ projects p_i into a probability distribution after the update.

The rating prediction under this model is calculated as follows:

$$\hat{r}_{ui} = \sum_{o \in \mathcal{O}} \langle p_i, q_u^o \rangle \times o \tag{8}$$

3.3   Hybrid Blending of Predictions

We place our system under the framework of prediction with expert advice [6]. Under this framework the final relevance prediction of the client-side recommendation agent is calculated as a *exponentially weighted average forecaster* of two experts: The CB model and the CF model.

In this section we drop the u from the notation purposes for clarity. Let $\hat{p}_{i,t}$ be the final prediction of the forecaster for item i at turn t after taking into account the predictions of the experts, $\mathcal{E} = \{1,2\}$ is set of expert indexes, $\hat{r}_{i,t}^{E}$ is the prediction of expert E at time t for item i and $\ell(\mathbb{R} \times \mathcal{O}) \to \mathbb{R}$ is a non-negative loss function that scores a prediction (either from the final forecaster or from an expert) against the true rating that the user gave to the item.

In the prediction with expert advice model, when a user rates an item i at time t, the item profile of i is presented to the experts and they make a prediction $\hat{r}_{i,t}^{E}$. The final forecaster accesses these predictions and makes a final prediction $\hat{p}_{i,t}$, the real rating of the item $r_{i,t}$ is revealed to the experts and each one incurs on a loss $\ell(\hat{r}_{i,t}^{E}, r_{i,t})$. The forecaster incurs on a loss $\ell(\hat{p}_{i,t}, r_{i,t})$.

The *cumulative regret* is defined as the difference between the cumulative losses of the final predictor and an expert. The regret of the forecaster with respect with expert E after n trains is defined as:

$$R_{E,n} = \sum_{t=1}^{n} \left(\ell(\hat{p}_{i,t}, r_{i,t}) - \ell(\hat{r}_{i,t}^{E}, r_{i,t}) \right) \tag{9}$$

Each expert prediction has a weight that is used by the forecaster to compute its prediction, the expert's weight is computed as follows:

$$W_{E,t-1} = \frac{\exp\left(\eta_t R_{E,t-1}\right)}{\sum_{e \in \mathcal{E}} \exp\left(\eta_t R_{e,t-1}\right)} \tag{10}$$

The forecaster prediction after turn t is:

$$\hat{p}_{i,t} = \frac{\sum_{E \in \mathcal{E}} W_{E,t-1} \hat{r}_{i,t}^{E}}{\sum_{E \in \mathcal{E}} W_{E,t-1}} \tag{11}$$

4   Model Validation

We test our model on the Movielens 10M dataset. This dataset contains 10000054 ratings of 10681 movies by 71567 users. We restrict the possible ratings that a user can assign to an item to the set $\mathcal{O} = \{1, 2, 3, 4, 5\}$. The ratings file has 4 fields per line: an user id, an item id, the rating she gave to the item and a timestamp.

In order to create the train set and validation set, we used the split_ratings utility distributed with the dataset. This utility splits the ratings file and splits it into two files: r.train with 9301274 ratings and r.test with 698780 ratings. The test file contains exactly 10 ratings per user, while the rest of the ratings of each user goes to the train file. Since we need to adjust some parameters such as the dimension of the CF profiles F and the initial gamma of the learning rate schedule, we further divide the test file in two equal parts randomly: `r.test.cv` and `r.test.test`. The `r.train` dataset is sorted by the timestamp field in order to simulate what would happen in an online setting.

In order to define the set of concepts C_i that describe each item we use the mapping information released in the 2001 HetRec workshop [9] which uses the datasets information from the IMDb website[1] and the Rotten Tomatoes website[2] for the Movielens dataset. We use the following concepts to describe a movie: actors, directors, writers and genres. The feature space size is 131407 concepts.

The measure we choose to evaluate the predictive performance of the system is the RMSE of the system. Let T be the rating set of a hold-out set (cv or the test set) and T_{ui}, the rating that the user u gave to item i, the RMSE is defined as follows:

$$\text{RMSE} := \sqrt{\frac{1}{|T|} \sum_{T_{ui} \in T} (\hat{p}_{ui} - T_{ui})^2} \tag{12}$$

The first experiment we made was to set the dimensions F and the initial gamma for the learning rate scheduling $\gamma_t = \gamma_0 (1 + \alpha \gamma_0 t)^{-c}$ for the CF model since there is a tradeoff versus the number of dimensions the model has and the weight of the learning rate scheduling. By choosing $c = 1$ and $\alpha = 1e - 06$ We ran the model for different γ_0 and F. The results are in figure 3a. As it can be seen, the RMSE of the system is lower at small dimensions. Taking these results into account, we fix the dimensionality of the CF model to $F = 5$.

The next experiment compares our implementation of the CF model on which we based the one presented in this paper. In [15] the item update is performed as follows:

$$\begin{aligned} p_i &\leftarrow p_i + \gamma(t_i) \sum_{o \in \mathcal{O}} (\mathbb{1}_{r_{ui}=o} - (\langle p_i, q_u^o \rangle)) q_u^o \\ p_i &\leftarrow \prod_{D_{item}} (p_i) \end{aligned} \tag{13}$$

As seen in figure 3b no significant difference between the observed cross validation error between the proposed model and the model implemented in [15] that shares the full profile and rating with the item producer. Finally, a search was followed to find an adequate learning rate for the CB approach. Keeping the min-sketch count at $N = 5$ for feature inclusion, we vary the γ_0 and we obtained the results seen in figure 3c.

Once each individual model is adjusted, we report the RMSE on the test set for the hybrid model. For ℓ we use the quadratic loss function used to calculate the cumulative regret of each expert, and since the loss function is convex we use $\eta_t = \sqrt{8 \ln(2)/t}$ in order to maintain an uniform bound over time with respect to the best performing expert. In figure 3d the result show that the hybrid predictor outperforms the predictive performance of the individual models.

---

[1] http://www.imdb.com
[2] http://www.rottentomatoes.com

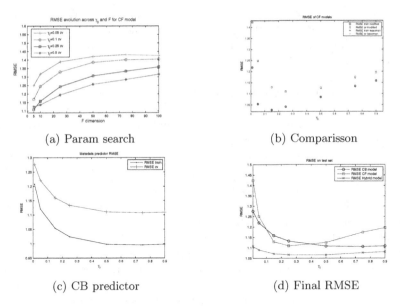

(a) Param search   (b) Comparisson

(c) CB predictor   (d) Final RMSE

Fig. 3. (a) shows RMSE across different dimensions F and γ_0 on the proposed CF model, (b) shows the RMSE difference between our CF model and the model proposed in [15], (c) shows the RMSE of the CB model for different γ_0 (d) RMSE on test set, γ_0 varies for CF model, γ_0 for CB model = 0.75

5   Related Work

Client-side agents for personalization are a *privacy by architecture* solution to the personalization vs privacy paradigm. CB strategies don't have to change in order to operate on a client-side agent architecture, however changes to the traditional recommendation architecture must be induced in order to apply a CF strategy [18]. One popular solution is the adoption of p2p networks in order to distribute useful information of users without the intervention of the recommendation server, either by broadcasting their profile on the network and gathering information to operate a local based CF approach [25] or by actively searching for peers that have the information they need [17] [16] over the p2p network, where a random peer search was found a reasonable strategy [3].

Client-side agents can collaborate to calculate matrix factorization models. In [24] a lower dimensional representation of each user profile is calculated using a gossip protocol on a p2p network. Isaacman et al. work [15] exchanges profiles between producers and consumers as described in section 3.2 . Since these proposals expose their profile to other peers, some configurations add random perturbation of the profile before sharing it to other peers to protect the user privacy [5].

Client-side agents have been also proposed for pervasive environments where the communication between agents or a peer service are limited or very occasional. In these works when two users meet they exchange profile information: In [23] [10] they exchange their local profile when meeting. In [22] an internal item to item similarity matrix is updated based on the item to item correlations present on the peer's profile.

Client-side agents can also use public information posted in a public server to avoid disclosing private information . In [20] a set of random profiles is made public. Each agent keeps a local version of her profile and calculates the concordance of the user with each profile in the public dataset. This information can be used to calculate a similarity measure between users. Expert-CF [2] is similar: Some user-profiles are published on a server and the local client applies a CF algorithm using only the public profiles. The public profiles are mined from already public trustable information such as public critics.

Finally, public servers can be used as a blackboard where users collaborate without disclosing private information by using public key cryptology and homomorphic encryption. In [8] users calculate a matrix that represents the items on a lower dimensional CF profile. The approximation to this matrix can be calculated as a gradient descent problem where the gradient function can be expressed as a sum of the contributions of each of the peers information. The peers collaborate using a multi-party calculation based on a Pedersen scheme. At each iteration, users transmit to an aggregation server their encrypted part of the calculation of the gradient. The server adds up the encrypted contributions of the users and they collaborate to decrypt the new final aggregate. The incremental model of [22] also considers a homomorphic encryption scheme to obtain the correlations between items.

6   Conclusions

We have presented a client-based approach for recommendation using a model based hybrid approach that outperforms the single models that compose it. The online model mixes two low computational complexity models at both training and prediction phase, scaling up to the number of items present in the system and the number of predictions the agent must make over time; avoiding the need to find peers with useful profiles for recommendation [25] [17] [16] or the public information needed to calculate client-side recommendations [2]. This comes with the price of a significant lower predictive performance when compared to other client-based systems that spend more time at prediction phase or the model based ones that incur in heavy synchronized tasks to calculate a prediction model [24] [8].

On the privacy concern, although the decentralized model presented here doesn't share the whole profile of the user with the recommendation server, under a curious but honest behavior, the proposed system still lets know the recommendation server which items the user has interacted. Anonymization networks [14] could be used to hide the identity of the user, with the cost of having a negative impact in the scalability of the system.

References

1. Adomavicius, G., Tuzhilin, A.: Toward the next generation of recommender systems: a survey of the state-of-the-art and possible extensions. IEEE Trans. on Knowl. and Data Eng. 17(6), 734–749 (2005), http://dx.doi.org/10.1109/tkde.2005.99
2. Amatriain, X., Lathia, N., Pujol, J.M., Kwak, H., Oliver, N.: The wisdom of the few: a collaborative filtering approach based on expert opinions from the web. In: Proceedings of the 32nd International ACM SIGIR Conference on Research and Development in Information Retrieval, SIGIR 2009, pp. 532–539. ACM, New York (2009), http://dx.doi.org/10.1145/1571941.1572033
3. Bakker, A., Ogston, E., van Steen, M.: Collaborative filtering using random neighbours in peer-to-peer networks. In: CNIKM 2009: Proceeding of the 1st ACM International Workshop on Complex Networks Meet Information & Knowledge Management, pp. 67–75. ACM, New York (2009), http://dx.doi.org/10.1145/1651274.1651288
4. Bell, R.M., Koren, Y.: Scalable collaborative filtering with jointly derived neighborhood interpolation weights. In: Proceedings of the 2007 Seventh IEEE International Conference on Data Mining, ICDM 2007, pp. 43–52. IEEE Computer Society, Washington, DC (2007), http://dx.doi.org/10.1109/icdm.2007.90
5. Berkovsky, S., Eytani, Y., Kuflik, T., Ricci, F.: Enhancing privacy and preserving accuracy of a distributed collaborative filtering. In: Proceedings of the 2007 ACM Conference on Recommender Systems, RecSys 2007, pp. 9–16. ACM, New York (2007), http://dx.doi.org/10.1145/1297231.1297234
6. Bianchi, N.C., Lugosi, G.: Prediction, Learning, and Games. Cambridge University Press, New York (2006)
7. Burke, R.: Hybrid recommender systems: Survey and experiments. User Modeling and User-Adapted Interaction 12(4), 331–370 (2002), http://dx.doi.org/10.1023/A:1021240730564
8. Canny, J.: Collaborative filtering with privacy. In: Proceedings of the 2002 IEEE Symposium on Security and Privacy, pp. 45–57 (2002), http://dx.doi.org/10.1109/secpri.2002.1004361
9. Cantador, I., Brusilovsky, P., Kuflik, T.: 2nd workshop on information heterogeneity and fusion in recommender systems (hetrec 2011). In: Proceedings of the 5th ACM Conference on Recommender Systems, RecSys 2011. ACM, New York (2011)
10. Del Prete, L., Capra, L.: diffeRS: A mobile recommender service. In: 2010 Eleventh International Conference on Mobile Data Management (MDM), pp. 21–26. IEEE (May 2010), http://dx.doi.org/10.1109/mdm.2010.22
11. Dimitropoulos, X., Stoecklin, M., Hurley, P., Kind, A.: The eternal sunshine of the sketch data structure. Comput. Netw. 52(17), 3248–3257 (2008), http://dx.doi.org/10.1016/j.comnet.2008.08.014
12. Foner, L.N.: Political Artifacts and Personal Privacy: The Yenta Multi-Agent Distributed Matchmaking System. Ph.D. thesis, Program in Media Arts and Sciences, School of Architecture and Planning, Massachusetts Institute of Technology (June 1999)
13. Funk, S.: Netflix update: Try this at home (2006) http://sifter.org/~simon/journal/20061211.html (accesed online January 2014)
14. Haddadi, H., Hui, P., Brown, I.: MobiAd: private and scalable mobile advertising. In: Proceedings of the Fifth ACM International Workshop on Mobility in the Evolving Internet Architecture, MobiArch 2010, pp. 33–38. ACM, New York (2010), http://dx.doi.org/10.1145/1859983.1859993

15. Isaacman, S., Ioannidis, S., Chaintreau, A., Martonosi, M.: Distributed rating prediction in user generated content streams. In: Proceedings of the Fifth ACM Conference on Recommender Systems, RecSys 2011, pp. 69–76. ACM, New York (2011), http://dx.doi.org/10.1145/2043932.2043948

16. Kermarrec, A.M., Leroy, V., Moin, A., Thraves, C.: Application of random walks to decentralized recommender systems. In: Lu, C., Masuzawa, T., Mosbah, M. (eds.) OPODIS 2010. LNCS, vol. 6490, pp. 48–63. Springer, Heidelberg (2010), http://dx.doi.org/10.1007/978-3-642-17653-1_4

17. Kim, J.K., Kim, H.K., Cho, Y.H.: A user-oriented contents recommendation system in peer-to-peer architecture. Expert Systems with Applications 34(1), 300–312 (2008), http://dx.doi.org/10.1016/j.eswa.2006.09.034

18. Kobsa, A.: Privacy-enhanced personalization. Commun. ACM 50(8), 24–33 (2007), http://dx.doi.org/10.1145/1278201.1278202

19. Koren, Y.: Factorization meets the neighborhood: a multifaceted collaborative filtering model. In: Proceedings of the 14th ACM SIGKDD International Conference on Knowledge Discovery and Data Mining, KDD 2008, pp. 426–434. ACM, New York (2008), http://dx.doi.org/10.1145/1401890.1401944

20. Lathia, N., Hailes, S., Capra, L.: Private distributed collaborative filtering using estimated concordance measures. In: Proceedings of the 2007 ACM Conference on Recommender Systems, RecSys 2007, pp. 1–8. ACM, New York (2007), http://dx.doi.org/10.1145/1297231.1297233

21. McMahan, H.B., Holt, G., Sculley, D., Young, M., Ebner, D., Grady, J., Nie, L., Phillips, T., Davydov, E., Golovin, D., Chikkerur, S., Liu, D., Wattenberg, M., Hrafnkelsson, A.M., Boulos, T., Kubica, J.: Ad click prediction: A view from the trenches. In: Proceedings of the 19th ACM SIGKDD International Conference on Knowledge Discovery and Data Mining, KDD 2013, pp. 1222–1230. ACM, New York (2013), http://dx.doi.org/10.1145/2487575.2488200

22. Miller, B.N., Konstan, J.A., Riedl, J.: PocketLens: Toward a personal recommender system. ACM Transactions on Information Systems 22(3), 437–476 (2004), http://dx.doi.org/10.1145/1010614.1010618

23. Schifanella, R., Panisson, A., Gena, C., Ruffo, G.: MobHinter: epidemic collaborative filtering and self-organization in mobile ad-hoc networks. In: RecSys 2008: Proceedings of the 2008 ACM Conference on Recommender Systems, pp. 27–34. ACM, New York (2008), http://dx.doi.org/10.1145/1454008.1454014

24. Tomozei, D.C., Massoulié, L.: Distributed user profiling via spectral methods (September 2011), http://arxiv.org/abs/1109.3318

25. Tveit, A.: Peer-to-peer based recommendations for mobile commerce. In: WMC 2001: Proceedings of the 1st International Workshop on Mobile Commerce, pp. 26–29. ACM, New York (2001), http://dx.doi.org/10.1145/381461.381466

26. Xu, W.: Towards optimal one pass large scale learning with averaged stochastic gradient descent (December 2011), http://arxiv.org/abs/1107.2490

Combining Distributional Semantics and Entity Linking for Context-Aware Content-Based Recommendation

Cataldo Musto, Giovanni Semeraro, Pasquale Lops, and Marco de Gemmis

Department of Computer Science
University of Bari Aldo Moro, Italy
{cataldo.musto,giovanni.semeraro,pasquale.lops,marco.degemmis}@uniba.it

Abstract. The effectiveness of content-based recommendation strategies tremendously depends on the representation formalism adopted to model both items and user profiles. As a consequence, techniques for semantic content representation emerged thanks to their ability to filter out the noise and to face with the issues typical of keyword-based representations. This article presents Contextual eVSM (C-eVSM), a content-based context-aware recommendation framework that adopts a novel semantic representation based on distributional models and entity linking techniques. Our strategy is based on two insights: first, entity linking can identify the most relevant concepts mentioned in the text and can easily map them with structured information sources, easily triggering some inference and reasoning on user preferences, while distributional models can provide a lightweight semantics representation based on term co-occurrences that can bring out latent relationships between concepts by just analying their usage patterns in large corpora of data.

The resulting framework is fully domain-independent and shows better performance than state-of-the-art algorithms in several experimental settings, confirming the validity of content-based approaches and paving the way for several future research directions.

1 Introduction

Recommender Systems (RS) can support users in (real-time) decision-making by providing them with personalized access to digital content and services. However, classical personalization strategies may not be enough for some scenarios, since it is clear that people choices are also influenced by the *context* in which they have to be made. For example, the mood and the company could direct the choice of the movie to be watched. Thus, it is acknowledged that an effective recommendation algorithm can't ignore contextual information sources such as location, mood, task, company and so on, since all these factors clearly influence the perceived usefulness of a recommendation.

As a consequence, several techniques for generating context-aware recommendations recently came into play. State of the art approaches [1] are split in three

V. Dimitrova et al. (Eds.): UMAP 2014, LNCS 8538, pp. 381–392, 2014.

main categories: *Pre-filtering* assumes that contextual information is used to filter out irrelevant ratings *before* they are used for computing recommendations with standard methods. *Post-filtering* assumes that contextual information is used *after* the standard non-contextual recommendation methods are applied to the recommendation data. Finally, *contextual modeling* assumes that contextual information is used *inside* the recommendation algorithm together with the user and item data.

Regardless of the contextualization strategy, most of the current literature investigated context-aware collaborative filtering algorithms, especially those based on matrix factorization techniques [9]. On the other side, context-aware content-based strategies [10] did not receive the same attention, even if content-based approaches may be helpful to overcome the *new item* problem and to avoid scalability issues. Furthermore, differently from matrix factorization techniques which make the recommendation process similar to a *black box*, content-based profiles are typically more transparent and human-readable [15], thus a content-based algorithm can easily *explain* its recommendations. Finally, content-based strategies can also accelerate serendipitous encounters by triggering some reasoning and inference on the features stored in the user profile in order to introduce novel and unexpected concepts [15].

In this paper we present an extension of CONTEXTUAL eVSM [14], a content-based recommendation framework that adopts a *post-filtering* strategy to provide users with context-aware suggestions. The main contribution of this paper is the adoption of a novel representation based on both distributional semantics models [18] and entity linking techniques. The use of distributional models can provide items (and profiles) with a lightweight semantics representation based on term usages and concept co-occurrences in large corpus of data, while entity linking can be helpful to extract and identify the most relevant concepts in textual descriptions, in order to give them more emphasis when user preferences have to be modeled. Furthermore, entity linking algorithms may act as a bridge to connect free text with structured information sources, such as those coming from the Linked Open Data (LOD) cloud, thus making simpler to enable reasoning and inferences about user preferences.

The paper is organized as follows. Section 2 presents an overview of the most relevant work in the area of context-aware recommender systems. In Section 3 we focus the attention on CONTEXTUAL eVSM, by describing the novel semantic representation as well as the profiling strategies and recommendation step. Section 4 describes the experimental protocol and discusses the outcomes of the evaluation of the framework. Finally, Section 5 contains conclusions and sketches future directions of this research.

2   Related Work

The area of context-aware RSs (CARS) is quite recent, and has been fostered by the recent series of CARS[1] and CAMRa[2] workshops. The first proposal of a context-aware recommendation algorithm dates back to the work by Herlocker and Konstan [8], who proposed to adapt the recommendation list to the specific task of the user. The most recent trends in the area of CARS were discussed in a recent survey [1]. The aforementioned classification in *pre-filtering*, *post-filtering* and *contextual-modeling* was introduced by Adomavicius and Tuzhilin [3].

Typically, the approaches for providing context-aware recommendations are based on the manipulation of the user × item matrix: in [2], the authors propose a *multi-dimensional model* able to enrich that matrix with contextual information. In order to compare the results of our approach, in the experimental evaluation we used the same dataset and settings proposed in that paper. Similarly, Karatzoglou et al. [9], followed this research line by proposing a framework, called *multiverse recommendation*, in which different types of context are considered as additional dimensions in the representation of the data as a tensor. The factorization of this tensor leads to a compact model of the data which can be used to provide context-aware recommendations.

Our main contribution is the definition of a context-aware content-based recommendation framework. A similar attempt is described in [4], in which contextual information is used to improve the performance of a content-based news recommender system. The approach to context-aware recommendation proposed in this paper is inspired to the *weighted post-filtering* introduced in [16], since we used the vector space representation of the context as a weighting factor, that is combined with a vector space representation of user preferences. With respect to the current literature, the novelty of our approach lies in the fact that we exploit distributional models to build a semantic vector space representation of the context. The main insight behind distributional models [18] is that the semantics of a term can be inferred in a totally unsupervised way by just analyzing its usage patterns in a large corpus of textual data. According to this insight, our proposal is centered around the construction of a semantic vector space representation of the context, which leverages the usage of the terms adopted to label the items that are relevant under specific contextual constraints. Even if the effectiveness of these models has been acknowledged for several tasks [6], there is only a little evidence about their performance in content-based RSs [13]. Similarly to our work, Codina et al. [5] proposed a pre-filtering approach based on the intuition that ratings acquired in contextual situations similar to the target one may be used to predict missing ratings in that target contextual situation. The main differences of our approach compared to [5] are the use of the distributional semantics as a *weighting factor* to influence the final recommendation score, and the use of a content-based strategy for representing contexts.

---

[1] http://cars-workshop.org/
[2] http://camrachallenge.com/

3   Contextual eVSM

Contextual eVSM (C-eVSM) is a context-aware content-based recommendation
framework. It extends the enhanced Vector Space Model (eVSM) [12] by taking
into account contextual information as well. The recommendation process follows
the workflow depicted in Figure 1. The only prerequisite of the algorithm is that
each item to be recommended is provided with some textual content (the plot
of a movie or the the content of a news, generic metadata, etc.).

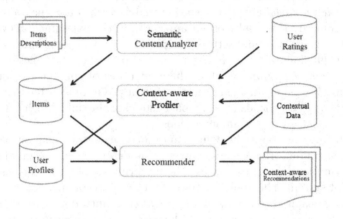

Fig. 1. Contextual eVSM workflow

The first step is performed by a SEMANTIC CONTENT ANALYZER, which processes textual descriptions through a pipeline of natural language processing
(NLP) and entity linking algorithms, in order to identify the most relevant concepts found in the text. Next, by exploiting distributional semantic models, each
item is represented as a (semantic) vector of co-occurrences of the concepts and
their (latent) connections learned from the text. Afterwards, a CONTEXT-AWARE
PROFILER builds a model of user preferences by collecting the semantic features
describing the items liked in the past and combines them with contextual data.
For example, if a user usually watches romantic movies on Friday night, the
contextual profiler will store her preferences along with the information about
the specific context the preference has been expressed. Finally, given a specific
contextual setting (e.g., movie for the weekend), a RECOMMENDER module computes the relevance of an unseen item for a target user by matching the features
stored in the contextual user profile with those describing the available items,
with the assumption that a larger feature overlap corresponds to a greater degree of interest. In the following sections the whole pipeline will be thoroughly
described.

3.1   Content Representation

The effectiveness of content-based recommendation strategies tremendously depends on the ability of the algorithm to filter out the noise from textual descriptions. As a consequence, in C-eVSM we paid attention to define a pipeline of state-of-the-art NLP and representation techniques able to produce a richer and fine-grained semantic content representation. In our approach, each textual description has been processed through a sequence of *entity linking* algorithms. Specifically, we chose DBpedia Spotlight[3], Wikipedia Miner[4] and Tag.me[5]. The goal of these algorithms is to analyze the content and to idenfify and extract the most relevant concepts mentioned in the text. As an example, the resulting representation obtained for the movie Matrix is provided in Figure 2. The text processed by the algorithms is the plot of the movie gathered from Wikipedia.

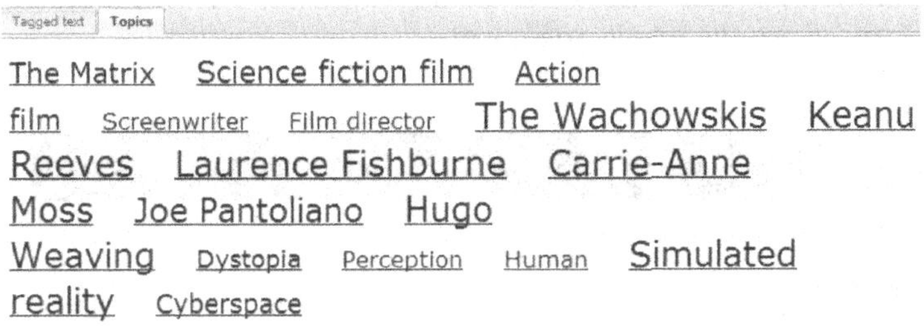

The Matrix   Science fiction film   Action
film   Screenwriter   Film director   The Wachowskis   Keanu
Reeves   Laurence Fishburne   Carrie-Anne
Moss   Joe Pantoliano   Hugo
Weaving   Dystopia   Perception   Human   Simulated
reality   Cyberspace

Fig. 2. Entity-based Representation for the movie Matrix

It immediately emerges that such a representation, beyond being more transparent and human-readable, automatically incorporates stopwords removal, bigrams recognition as well as entities recognition and word sense disambiguation. Furthermore, it is worth to note that each concept extracted from the text is mapped to a univocal reference (in our case, a Wikipedia page). Given that each concept is mapped to a Wikipedia page, we decided to enrich the representation by performing a simple browsing on the Wikipedia categories tree. Specifically, for each concept extracted from the text the ancestor categories were included. In our case, given the concept *The Wachowskis*, the representation was enriched by adding as extra features concepts such as *Writers from Chicago* and *American Directors*, thus extending the representation with other relevant features that may be of interest for the target user.

However, even a fine-grained representation based on Wikipedia concepts does not take into account any information about the *semantics* of the terms. In order to tackle this issue, we adopted DISTRIBUTIONAL MODELS (DMs) to provide each item with a semantic vector space representation. DMs are based

---

[3] http://dbpedia-spotlight.github.io/demo/
[4] http://wikipedia-miner.cms.waikato.ac.nz/
[5] http://tagme.di.unipi.it/

on a simple insight: as humans infer the meaning of a word by understanding the contexts in which that word is typically used, distributional models get information about the meaning of a word by analyzing its usage in large corpora of textual documents. This means that it is possible to infer the semantics of a term (e.g. *beer*) by analyzing the meaning of the other terms it typically co-occurs with (*wine, glass*, etc.) [17]. In the same way, the correlation between different terms (e.g., *beer* and *party*) can be inferred by analyzing the similarity between the contexts in which they are used. These approaches rely on the distributional hypotesis [7], according to which *Words that occur in the same contexts tend to have similar meanings*. This means that words are semantically similar to the extent that they share contexts. DMs represent information about terms usage in a term-context matrix (Figure 3). The advantage is that the context is very flexible, and can be adapted to the specific granularity level of the representation required by the application: for example, given a word, its context could be either a single word it co-occurs with, or a sliding window of terms that surrounds it, or a sentence, or yet the whole document.

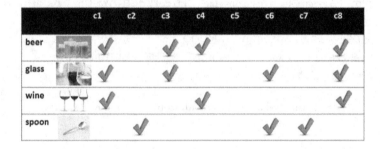

Fig. 3. An example of term-context matrix

In our setting, we exploited distributional models to build a semantic representation of each item. First, each Wikipedia concept found in the text is represented as a vector according to the co-occurrences with the other Wikipedia concepts. Next, we easily represented each item as a (semantic) vector by combining the vector space representation of all the Wikipedia concepts that describe it. The combination is obtained as a simple sum of the vectors, weighted through the relevance of each Wikipedia concept in the description. In this way, we combined the advantages of a fine-grained representation based on entity linking algorithms with the lightweight semantics provided by the adoption of distributional models, thus encoding semantic information without the need of implementing a complex word-sense disambiguation strategy.

3.2   Contextual Profiling and Recommendation

In C-eVSM we defined the *context* as a set of variables $C = \{c_1, c_2 \ldots c_n\}$. Each contextual variable c_k has its own domain $dom(c_k)$, which is typically categorical.

Formally, $dom(c_k) = \{v_1, v_2 \ldots v_m\}$, where v_j is one of the m values allowed for the variable c_k. For example, if we consider as contextual variable the *task* to be accomplished, $dom(task) = \{studying, running, dancing \ldots\}$.

According to this definition, we defined two different contextual profiling models, which extend those already introduced in [12]. Both models are based on a simple insight: as DMs learn a vector-space representation of the items according to the co-occurences between the terms that describe them, a semantic vector space representation of the *context* can be built according to the co-occurences between the concepts that more frequently describe the items labeled as relevant in that specific contextual settings. In other terms, our assumption is that there exists a set of terms that is likely to be more descriptive of items relevant in a certain context. For example, if a user is looking for a restaurant for a romantic night, it is likely that restaurant descriptions containing terms such as *candlelight* or *sea view*, are more suitable and thus relevant in that specific context. Hence, we decided to deeply analyze the usage patterns of terms describing items relevant in different contextual situations, in order to learn a representation of the context based on those terms more relevant in that contextual setting. Up to our knowledge this is a novel contribution in the area of context-aware content-based recommender systems.

Formally, given a user u and contextual variable c_k which assumes values v_j (e.g. $task = running$), the contextual user profile can be defined as a linear combination, tuned by a parameter α, of $WRI(u)$ and $context(u, c_k, v_j)$:

$$C - WRI(u, c_k, v_j) = \alpha * WRI(u) + \tag{1}$$
$$(1 - \alpha) * context(u, c_k, v_j) \tag{2}$$

$WRI(u)$ is an uncontextual representation of user preferences, defined as the sum over the vector space representation of the items the user liked in the past, labeled as I^+, weighted with the normalized rating $r(u, i)$:

$$WRI(u) = \sum_{i=1}^{|I^+|} d_i * \frac{r(u, i)}{MAX} \tag{3}$$

and $context(u, c_k, v_j)$ is the vector space representation of the context, defined as the weighted sum over the items labeled as relevant under that specific contextual setting:

$$context(u, c_k, v_j) = \sum_{i=1}^{|I_u^+(c_k, v_j)|} d_i * \frac{r(u, d_i, c_k, v_j)}{MAX} \tag{4}$$

Next, we defined a second contextual profiling model, called C-WQN, which encodes the information coming from the items the user disliked and adopts a QUANTUM NEGATION operator to combine positive and negative profile vectors in a single uniform representation. The discussion about the negation operator is out of the scope of this paper. For further reading refer to [13], which contains a discussion about the application of the operator in content-based recommender systems, or refer to the original Widdows' paper [19]. Finally, given a contextual setting and a semantic vector space representation of both items and user profiles, C-eVSM generates the suggestions by calculating the *cosine similarity* between the vector representing user preferences in that specific context and the vector representing the item. The recommended items may be the top-N or those whose similarity overcomes a certain threshold.

4   Experimental Evaluation

In order to validate the performance of our framework, we carried out an extensive experimental session. The experiments had a twofold goal:

1. Evaluation of the predictive accuracy of the contextual eVSM model with respect to both a non-contextual baseline and a contextual baseline based on a simple keyword-based representation;
2. Comparison of the predictive accuracy of the contextual eVSM model with respect to state of the art algorithms.

In order to compare the accuracy of our framework with respect to state of the art algorithms, we adopted the same dataset and experimental design proposed by Adomavicius et al. [2]. In that paper, the authors evaluated their context-aware recommender system in a movie recommendation scenario. They used a dataset crawled from IMDB[6], containing 1,755 ratings expressed by 117 users under different contextual situations. Specifically, four different categorical contextual variables were defined: TIME (weekday, weekend), PLACE (theater, home), COMPANION (alone, friends, boy/girlfriend, family) and MOVIE-RELATED (release week, non release week). The complete dataset has been further processed, as in [2], to filter all the ratings coming from users that did not rate at least 10 movies. The final dataset contained 1,457 ratings coming from 62 users on 202 movies. Given that our framework needs some textual content to feed the recommendation algorithm, we gathered textual information from Wikipedia. For each movie we crawled the plot, the abstract, the genre, the title, the director and the actors. Textual content was preprocessed by just filtering out stopwords according to a common stopwords list for English language.

As in the experimental protocol proposed in [2], we split the dataset into several overlapping subsets, called *contextual segments*. Each contextual segment modeled the ratings provided by the users under a specific context, in order to evaluate the ability of the approach to provide users with accurate suggestions in specific contextual settings. The contextual segments containing less than 145 ratings (10% of the dataset) were filtered out. To sum up, our algorithm was evaluated against nine different contextual segments: HOME (727 ratings), FRIENDS (565 ratings), NON-RELEASE (551 ratings), WEEKEND (538 ratings), WEEKDAY (340 ratings), GBFRIEND (319 ratings), THEATER-WEEKEND (301 ratings), THEATER-FRIENDS (274 ratings). In all the experiments, we adopted the

---

[6] http://www.imdb.com/

bootstrapping method [11] as experimental protocol: for each contextual segment, 500 random re-samples were performed. In each sample 29/30th of data were used as training and 1/30th as test. Each movie was rated on a 13-point discrete scale. All the ratings above 9 were considered as positive.

4.1   Discussion of the Results

In the first experiment we investigated the effectiveness of our novel representation based on distributional semantics and entity linking against both a non-contextual baseline and a contextual variant of C-eVSM based on just distributional semantics (without entity linking). We considered WRI and WQN as non-contextual baselines, and we compared them with contextual eVSM profiles (C-WRI and C-WQN) configurations. In this preliminary evaluation we set α to 0.2, 0.5 and 0.8, without implementing a specific optimization strategy. We labeled as *recommended* all the items whose cosine similarity overcame 0.6. To sum up, for each contextual segment 8 different configurations were evaluated. Results were validated using a paired t-test ($p \ll 0.05$). Results reporting F1 measure are provided in Table 1.

The main outcome is that our novel representation based on both distributional semantics and entity linking improves the predictive with respect to both baselines. Indeed, if we compare the best performing contextual configuration (C-WRI and C-WQN) with the non-contextual counterparts (WRI and WQN), regardless of the adopted representation, it emerges that Contextual eVSM overcomes the baseline in all contextual segments. This improves Adomavicius' results, since their context-aware recommender overcame the baseline in 8 out of 9 contextual segments. Furthermore, results show that the configurations with $\alpha = 0.8$ generally outperform those with $\alpha=0.5$ and $\alpha=0.2$ in terms of F1. This suggests that user preferences, regardless the contextual situation, still play a key role, while the context has to be used to slightly influence the recommendation score computed by eVSM. As regards content representation, results show that the combined use of entity linking and distributional semantics can provide a richer and meaningful representation. Indeed, by comparing entity-based to keyword-based results, it emerges an overall increase of +4% on average (ranging from +1.34% to +6.42%) on 8 segments out of 9. By analyzying the single configurations, it clearly emerges that the use of entity linking algorithms can provide a more precise representation since the accuracy is improved in 72% of the comparisons (65 out of 90) and in 58% with a statistically significant gap (52 out of 90). Generally speaking, the representation combining both DMs and entity linking got the best results in 7 segments out of 9. It is also worth to note that in 5 segments out of 7 the configurations using Quantum Negation got the best results. This suggests that our negation operator that combines into a single representation both positive and negative preferences can provide the best results. Next, we compared the previous results with the best-performing ones of the experiments reported in [2].

The comparison between contextual eVSM using the entity linking algorithm based on Wikipedia and the reduction-based approach proposed by Adomavicius et al. is provided in Figure 4. Results show that our approach outperforms the state of the art algorithm in 7 out of 9 contextual segments. It is necessary a further investigation to understand why our approach is outperformed for the segments THEATER-WEEKEND and THEATER-FRIENDS. Even if the experiment has not been completed with a statistical test, it is likely that the difference between the algorithms is significant since in 4 segments the gap is over 10% in terms of F1-measure. This important result further confirms the validity of the CONTEXTUAL eVSM approach, especially when compared to a context-aware algorithm based on *collaborative filtering*.

Table 1. Results of Experiment 1. Configurations that outperform the keyword-based baseline in terms of F1 in bold. Statistical differences highlighted with (*). The best-performing configuration with a grey background.

	HOME (avg. +3.77%)		FRIENDS (avg. +6.42%)		WEEKEND (avg. +6.03%)	
	Keyword	Entities	Keyword	Entities	Keyword	Entities
WRI	47.62	**56.13(*)**	49.43	**56.17(*)**	51.23	**58.12(*)**
C-WRI-0.2	44.56	**46.62**	44.91	**49.89(*)**	55.1	**57.44**
C-WRI-0.5	48.23	**56.38(*)**	50.54	**56.24(*)**	55.75	**58.36**
C-WRI-0.8	50.61	**56.74(*)**	50.11	**55.68(*)**	52.25	**58.75(*)**
WQN	53.62	**57.53(*)**	53.18	**58.25(*)**	51.36	**+57.63(*)**
C-WQN-0.2	53.37	**54.81**	45.93	**52.82(*)**	48.36	**54.44(*)**
C-WQN-0.5	57.82	**61.96(*)**	50.04	**57.20(*)**	51.51	**59.49(*)**
C-WQN-0.8	58.91	**61.3**	54.39	**58.37(*)**	52.86	**60.39(*)**

	THEATER (avg. +6.49%)		NONRELEASE (avg. +1.51%)		WEEKDAY (avg. -2.75%)	
	Keyword	Entities	Keyword	Entities	Keyword	Entities
WRI	50.91	**56.34(*)**	48.95	**52.16(*)**	52.11	46.4
C-WRI-0.2	52.79	**55.82(*)**	48.24	44.99	47.12	46.42
C-WRI-0.5	53.95	**57.21(*)**	49.05	**53.29(*)**	49.56	46.77
C-WRI-0.8	52.87	**58.11(*)**	52.18	**53.34**	52.14	46.34
WQN	50.71	**56.45(*)**	55.94	54.94	50.54	47.32
C-WQN-0.2	46.65	**54.72(*)**	48.67	45.416	44.71	**46.2**
C-WQN-0.5	51.4	**57.81(*)**	52.55	**57.01(*)**	48.1	48.02
C-WQN-0.8	52.64	**62.16(*)**	56.78	56.24	**53.17**	47.57

	GBFRIENDS (avg. +1.34%)		THEATER-WEEKEND (avg. +3.17%)		THEATER-FRIENDS (avg. +5.22%)	
	Keyword	Entities	Keyword	Entities	Keyword	Entities
WRI	49.53	**50.31**	51.93	51.35	47.57	46.66
C-WRI-0.2	47.28	**48.19**	51.64	**54.64(*)**	46.68	**55.35(*)**
C-WRI-0.5	48.38	**50.72**	54.41	**54.95**	46.56	**55.96(*)**
C-WRI-0.8	**51.5**	49.96	54.89	52.38	45.49	**46.63**
WQN	51.4	49.13	50.79	49.1	48.7	48.63
C-WQN-0.2	43.25	**48.44(*)**	41.31	**54.79(*)**	39.36	**55.37(*)**
C-WQN-0.5	45.1	**50.43(*)**	44.46	**52.85(*)**	41.69	**55.92(*)**
C-WQN-0.8	50.39	48.42	52.26	49.77	45.52	**48.93(*)**

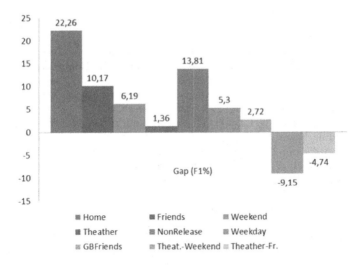

Fig. 4. Results of Experiment 2. The plot shows the gap between CONTEXTUAL eVSM and CF algorithm in terms of F1-measure.

5 Conclusions and Future Work

In this paper we proposed contextual eVSM, a context-aware content-based recommendation framework based on VSM. The original model has been extended by introducing a technique that exploits distributional semantics to build a semantic vector space representation of the context which is used to slightly influence a non-contextual recommendation score. Our novel context-aware technique has been evaluated against several non-contextual baselines, and our approach significantly improved the predictive accuracy of the baselines in most of the experiments. As a future work we will investigate the integration of information coming from the datasets available in the Linked Open Data (LOD) cloud. Indeed, our novel Wikipedia-based representation can be easily mapped to the information stored in the LOD cloud. We will also investigate possible improvements of the current experimental results by implementing some strategies for optimizing parameters in our algorithm, such as α in Equation 2. Finally, we are going to design a user study to investigate the impact of our recommendation framework on real users, in terms of predictive accuracy as well as user-centered metrics, such as novelty, diversity, and serendipity.

Acknowledgments. This work fullfils the research objectives of the projects PON 01 00850 ASK-Health (Advanced System for the interpretation and sharing of knowledge in health care) and PON 02 00563 3470993 project "VINCENTE - A Virtual collective INtelligenCe ENvironment to develop sustainable Technology Entrepreneurship ecosystems" funded by the Italian Ministry of University and Research (MIUR).

References

1. Adomavicius, G., Mobasher, B., Ricci, F., Tuzhilin, A.: Context-aware recommender systems. AI Magazine 32(3), 67–80 (2011)
2. Adomavicius, G., Sankaranarayanan, R., Sen, S., Tuzhilin, A.: Incorporating contextual information in recommender systems using a multidimensional approach. ACM Trans. Inf. Syst. 23(1), 103–145 (2005)
3. Adomavicius, G., Tuzhilin, A.: Context-aware recommender systems. In: Recommender Systems Handbook, pp. 217–253. Springer (2011)
4. Cantador, I., Bellogín, A., Castells, P.: News@hand: A Semantic Web Approach to Recommending News. In: Nejdl, W., Kay, J., Pu, P., Herder, E. (eds.) AH 2008. LNCS, vol. 5149, pp. 279–283. Springer, Heidelberg (2008)
5. Codina, V., Ricci, F., Ceccaroni, L.: Semantically-enhanced pre-filtering for context-aware recommender systems. In: Proceedings of the 3rd Workshop on Context-Awareness in Retrieval and Recommendation, pp. 15–18 (2013)
6. Cohen, T., Widdows, D.: Empirical distributional semantics: Methods and biomedical applications. Journal of Biomedical Informatics 42(2), 390 (2009)
7. Harris, Z.: Mathematical structures of language. John Wiley & Sons (1968)
8. Herlocker, J., Konstan, J.: Content-independent task-focused recommendation. IEEE Internet Computing 5(6), 40–47 (2001)
9. Karatzoglou, A., Amatriain, X., Baltrunas, L., Oliver, N.: Multiverse recommendation: n-dimensional tensor factorization for context-aware collaborative filtering. In: Proceedings of RecSys 2010, pp. 79–86. ACM (2010)
10. Lops, P., de Gemmis, M., Semeraro, G.: Content-based recommender systems: State of the art and trends. In: Recommender Systems Handbook, pp. 73–105. Springer (2011)
11. Mitchell, T.: Machine Learning. McGraw-Hill (1997)
12. Musto, C.: Enhanced vector space models for content-based recommender systems. In: Proceedings of RecSys 2010, pp. 361–364. ACM (2010)
13. Musto, C., Semeraro, G., Lops, P., de Gemmis, M.: Random indexing and negative user preferences for enhancing content-based recommender systems. In: Huemer, C., Setzer, T. (eds.) EC-Web 2011. LNBIP, vol. 85, pp. 270–281. Springer, Heidelberg (2011)
14. Musto, C., Semeraro, G., Lops, P., de Gemmis, M.: Contextual eVSM: A content-based context-aware recommendation framework based on distributional semantics. In: Huemer, C., Lops, P. (eds.) EC-Web 2013. LNBIP, vol. 152, pp. 125–136. Springer, Heidelberg (2013)
15. Narducci, F., Musto, C., Semeraro, G., Lops, P., de Gemmis, M.: Leveraging encyclopedic knowledge for transparent and serendipitous user profiles. In: Carberry, S., Weibelzahl, S., Micarelli, A., Semeraro, G. (eds.) UMAP 2013. LNCS, vol. 7899, pp. 350–352. Springer, Heidelberg (2013)
16. Panniello, U., Gorgoglione, M.: Incorporating context into recommender systems: an empirical comparison of context-based approaches. Electronic Commerce Research 12(1), 1–30 (2012)
17. Rubenstein, H., Goodenough, J.B.: Contextual correlates of synonymy. Commun. ACM 8(10), 627–633 (1965)
18. Turney, P., Pantel, P.: From frequency to meaning: Vector space models of semantics. J. Artif. Intell. Res (JAIR) 37, 141–188 (2010)
19. Widdows, D.: Orthogonal negation in vector spaces for modelling word-meanings and document retrieval. In: ACL, pp. 136–143 (2003)

IntelWiki: Recommending Resources to Help Users Contribute to Wikipedia

Mohammad Noor Nawaz and Andrea Bunt

Department of Computer Science, University of Manitoba, Winnipeg, Manitoba, Canada
{chowdmnn,bunt}@cs.umanitoba.ca

Abstract. We describe an approach to facilitating user-generated content within the context of Wikipedia. Our approach, embedded in the *IntelWiki* prototype, aims to make it easier for users to create or enhance the free-form text in Wikipedia articles by: i) recommending potential reference materials, ii) drawing the users' attention to key aspects of the recommendations, and iii) allowing users to consult the recommended materials in context. A laboratory evaluation with 16 novice Wikipedia editors revealed that, in comparison to the default Wikipedia design, IntelWiki's approach has positive impacts on editing quantity and quality, and perceived mental load.

Keywords: User-Generated Content, Recommendations, Wikipedia.

1   Introduction

User-generated content (UGC) is content generated by people who voluntarily contribute data, information, articles, or media on the web. Despite the explosion of UGC in recent years, the percentage of the population that contributes content tends to remain relatively small. Most community content follows the "1% rule", where approximately 1% of internet users create content, 9% enhance it, and the remaining 90% simply consume it [5], [12]. This participation imbalance is a concern for a number of reasons, including both the amount of work required of contributors to uphold content standards and a potential underrepresentation of the views and interests of a large percentage of the population [12].

While there are many factors that influence participation rates, including community politics [19], a significant barrier to participation is simply the amount of effort required to do so. In particular, in his article on participation inequity in UGC, Nielsen's number one suggestion on how to increase participation rates is: "Make it easier" [12]. This assertion is supported by studies indicating that editing effort can indeed affect participation rates [2], [8], [20].

In this paper, we propose an approach for facilitating contributions to Wikipedia, one of the most widely accessed forms of user-generated content. Like other community content repositories, only a small percentage of Wikipedia users contribute content. For example, in September 2013, Wikipedia had over 500 million unique

V. Dimitrova et al. (Eds.): UMAP 2014, LNCS 8538, pp. 393–404, 2014.
© Springer International Publishing Switzerland 2014

visitors; however, only 0.05% of these visitors made at least one edit and only 0.015% were considered "active contributors" (i.e., with five or more edits) [18], [23].

Prior work suggests that an attribute of Wikipedia articles that makes them particularly difficult to edit in relation to some other forms of UGC (e.g., movie reviews) is the need for background research [20]. To address this challenge, our approach provides users with streamlined access to recommended reference materials -- recommendations that are personalized to the individual article. To illustrate our approach, we designed and implemented the *IntelWiki* prototype, which automatically generates resource recommendations, ranks the references based on the occurrence of salient keywords, and allows users to interact with the recommended references within the Wikipedia editor. A second contribution of this work is a formal laboratory evaluation exploring the potential for our approach to ease the editing burden in comparison to the default Wikipedia editor. Our results indicate that having streamlined access to resource recommendations increased the amount of text participants were able to produce (with time held constant) and that this text was both more complete and more accurate than when using the default editor. Participants also reported experiencing significantly lower mental workload and preferred the new design.

2   Related Work

Prior to describing our approach and its evaluation, we begin by overviewing related work. User-generated content in general and Wikipedia in particular, has been a widely studied phenomenon, including studies on what motivates contributions (e.g, [2], [13]), how editing roles evolve over time (e.g., [17]), and statistical analyses of Wikipedia data (e.g., [9]). We focus our coverage on two areas: systems designed to improve Wikipedia articles, either through completely automated means or by helping potential editors, and systems for helping people choose their editing tasks.

2.1   Enhancing the Text of Wikipedia Articles

The content of Wikipedia articles, and other similar UGC environments, can often be classified into two primary forms: 1) content that is structured, and 2) free-form content. Structured information has a pre-defined schema, such as the information found in a standard Wikipedia article's infobox (see Fig. 1, left). The bodies of the articles contain free-form content, including prose, images, links and references.

A notable example of improving structured Wikipedia content is the Kylin system, which automates the process of creating and completing Wikipedia article infoboxes (e.g., [8], [22]). An evaluation of a mixed-initiative version of Kylin revealed that recommending potential changes to the infoxboxes had positive impacts on both user contribution rates and infobox accuracy [8]. Sharing some similarities with our approach, Weld *et al.* proposed an extension to the system, where the information extraction used to improve the infoboxes is extended beyond Wikipedia articles to the general web [16]. As in our approach, this extension relied on web queries to find

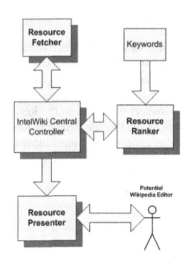

Fig. 1. (Left) Infobox for the Lake category   (Right) The IntelWiki system architecture

useful resources, however, these resources were used by the learning algorithm only as opposed to presented to potential editors. As another example targeted at improving structured Wikipedia content, the WiGipedia tool helps users identify and correct inconsistencies among structured data spread across different articles [1].

Our work focuses on supporting edits to free-form Wikipedia text. In contrast to our approach, which aims to support human editors, most prior work in this area has tried to fully automate the process. For example, Okuoka *et al.*'s system links Wikipedia entries on news events with relevant videos from external sources [14]. WikiSimple takes Wikipedia articles as input and automatically produces articles re-written in simpler grammatical style (to enhance readability) [21]. Finally, Sauper *et al.* proposed a fully automated process for generating a multi-sectioned Wikipedia article [15]. Approaches that leverage human expertise have also been explored, but in the context of corporate wikis, where the focus has been on tools to support knowledge transfer from e-mails to wikis (e.g., [6], [10]).

3   IntelWiki Prototype

Our approach to facilitating user enhancements to free-form text in Wikipedia articles is to help editors locate and interact with relevant Web-based reference materials through article-tailored resource recommendations. To illustrate our proposed approach, we designed and implemented the *IntelWiki* prototype, which recommends pertinent resources to the user and streamlines the process of interacting with these recommended resources. In this section we overview the three main components in IntelWiki's framework (see Fig. 1, right): i) the *Resource Fetcher*, ii) the *Resource Ranker*, and iii) the *Resource Presenter*.

3.1   Resource Fetcher

IntelWiki's Resource Fetcher searches the web for resource material that could help a potential editor enhance a given Wikipedia article. To do so, IntelWiki uses Google's Custom Search Engine (CSE) API, submitting the article title as a search query. From the returned results, the Resource Fetcher then selects the top 60 pages (a configurable parameter) to submit to the Resource Ranker for further processing. From the set returned by the Google CSE, the Resource Fetcher removes any dead links or links to pages that are not easily machine readable (e.g., consist of solely images). These latter types of pages were removed as a simplification for this proof-of-concept prototype -- one could imagine extending this candidate set by embedding more sophisticated document processing capabilities within the system.

3.2   Resource Ranker

The Resource Ranker's role is to assess the suitability of each candidate resource, information that is then used by the Resource Presenter (described next) to emphasize the most promising resources. The Resource Ranker's assessment of suitability involves calculating a relevance score for each resource based on the number of occurrences of "pertinent keywords" within the resource. These relevance scores are then used to re-rank the resources from the ordering initially returned by the Google CSE.

By default, the Resource Ranker uses the article's infobox schema attributes as the set of pertinent keywords. Through experimenting with different article categories, we found that using the complete set of infobox attributes as the pertinent keywords typically provided a more personalized resource ranking than the Google CSE default ranking; however, we also noted the potential for improvement by using a widened set of keywords. Potential additions that we have found to improve rankings include: attribute synonyms, root words, and parts of speech variants, as well as units of measurement. Therefore, IntelWiki allows additional keywords to be specified on a per-category basis (articles in Wikipedia are grouped hierarchically according to category). We envision these tailored lists of keywords could be generated by a Wikipedia administrator, through crowdsourcing techniques, or by training the system to learn pertinent keywords from other (more complete) articles of the same category.

In addition to sharing common infobox schemas, articles in a given category are often very similar in structure. For example, articles in the "Lake" category typically contain sections describing Geography, Climate, History, Ecology and Geology, among others. Therefore, IntelWiki's Resource Ranker has the capability to leverage a keyword-to-section mapping, should one exist, to personalize its ranking of the resources based on the section the user is currently editing. Similar to the set of pertinent keywords, a keyword-to-section mapping could be defined on a per-category basis by a Wikipedia administrator, through crowdsourcing techniques, or through machine learning techniques.

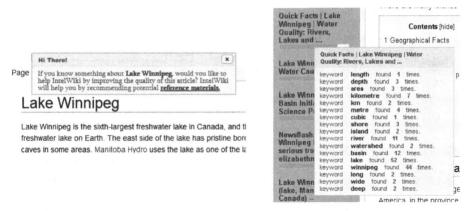

Fig. 2. (Left) IntelWiki's callout. Clicking on "reference materials" will display recommended resources. (Right) A tooltip showing the occurrences of pertinent keywords within the resource.

3.3   Resource Presenter

The IntelWiki system's Resource Presenter makes the set of suggested resources available to a potential editor on demand (see Fig. 2, left). As shown in Fig. 3, when a potential editor asks to view the reference materials, the system adds two additional panes to the regular Wikipedia interface in both viewing and editing modes (shrinking the article to make room). The first is a "Suggested Resources" Pane, which lists the recommended resources. The second is a "Resource Viewer" Pane, which allows users to inspect and consult individual resources in place.

To promote the references that the system believes will be most helpful to the editing task, the Resource Presenter sorts the recommended resources using the relevance scores calculated by the Resource Ranker. Initially (or whenever the user is in the view mode) an article's recommended resources are sorted according to the per-article relevance scores. When the user goes to edit a particular section (i.e., in the edit mode), the list of suggested resources is reordered based on the section-specific relevance scores, if a keyword-to-section mapping exists for the article's category.

The system tries to further support resource selection in two ways. First, it displays the resources' relative relevance assessments (see the green bars in Fig. 2, right and Fig. 3) allowing the users to see which ones the system believes will be most useful. Second, to allow for additional inspection without having to open the resource, when the user hovers over a particular resource, the system displays a tooltip consisting of the keywords found in the resource and their respective frequencies (see Fig. 2, right).

The user can view the contents of a particular resource by either clicking on it or dragging it to the Resource Viewer Pane. To help the users locate relevant information within the resource, the system highlights all occurrences of the pertinent keywords within the resource (as shown in Fig. 3). In our initial design, we experimented with multiple resource viewer panes (up to four); however, pilot participants felt that they consumed too much screen real-estate and were difficult to manage.

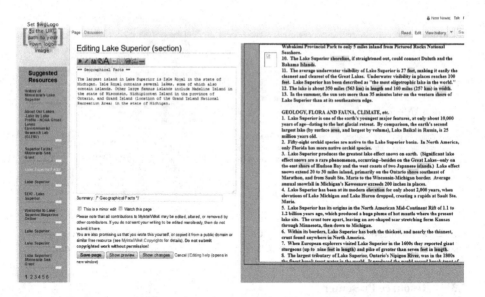

Fig. 3. Editing with IntelWiki Interface, with the "Suggested Resources" Pane (left) and the "Resource Viewer" Pane (right)

4   Evaluation

We conducted a formal laboratory study comparing the IntelWiki system described above to the default Wikipedia editor. The goal of the study was to explore if the IntelWiki system could make it easier for users to edit Wikipedia articles. We leave an assessment of recommendation quality to future work.

4.1   Participants

Sixteen participants completed the study (6 females, mean age 24.4), recruited through on-campus advertising. To ensure access to a wide enough pool, we did not screen according to previous Wikipedia editing experience. Our pre-study questionnaire revealed that all participants were regular Wikipedia visitors, but none had previous Wikipedia editing experience. Participants were provided with a $15 honorarium.

4.2   Design

Interface Type was the primary within-subjects factor with two levels:

1. **IntelWiki:** The complete IntelWiki system described in previous section.
2. **Default:** The Wikipedia Edit Interface plus the Google Search Engine.

Participants completed one task with each interface type (described in the next section). Therefore, task was a within-subjects control variable. Interface and task order were fully counterbalanced to account for potential learning effects.

4.3   Tasks and Procedure

After completing a demographics questionnaire, participants edited the "Geography" section in two articles on well-known lakes (one per condition). From these articles, we removed most of the content in the "Geography" section, leaving only three lines to provide initial guidance. We also removed the articles' infoboxes since they were populated with facts from the original Geography sections. Participants were provided with a list of example of attributes (using geography-related attributes from the infoboxes), but were told to edit the sections as they saw fit. To discourage direct plagiarism, we disabled copying and pasting.

Participants were asked to write the best Geography section that they could within the 25 minutes (i.e., editing time was fixed across all participants). Prior to editing, participants were briefly introduced to the interface in that condition, and completed a short practice task. Immediately following each condition, participants completed a NASA-Task Load Index (TLX) questionnaire [7] to measure their perceived mental workload. The experiment concluded with a post-session questionnaire and a short semi-structured interview. Each session lasted between 75-90 minutes.

In the IntelWiki condition, the system retrieved and assessed the recommended resources using a set of section-specific keywords related to "Geography", which consisted of the relevant infobox attributes and their units of measurement.

4.4   Results

In the analysis below, quantitative dependent measures were analyzed using a Repeated-Measures ANOVA with Interface Type (IntelWiki, Default) as the within-subjects factor. To check for asymmetric learning effects between two conditions, we also included Interface Order (IntelWiki_First, IntelWiki_Second) as a between-subjects factor in the analysis. Error bars on all graphs depict standard error.

Text Volume and Completeness
Since editing time was fixed, we begin by examining text volume. Fig. 4(left) shows that participants wrote significantly more words with IntelWiki (229.9, s.e. 22.7) than with Default (202.8, s.e. 22.4; $F_{1,14} = 5.302$, $p = 0.037$, $\eta^2 = 0.275$).

We analyzed two measures of text completeness by having the first author code the text participants generated for: i) the number of facts described (Fact Count) and ii) the number of facts accurately described (Fact Accuracy). Any distinct piece of information was counted as a fact. A fact was coded as accurate if it i) was related to the topic of the section, and ii) was accurately reported (judged using the original infobox or article when possible, or the participant's source).

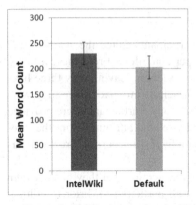
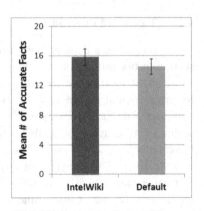
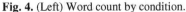

Fig. 4. (Left) Word count by condition.   (Right) Fact accuracy by condition

As shown in Fig. 4(right) and Fig. 5(left), IntelWiki outperformed Default for both text completeness measures. For Fact Count, participants covered 17.8 (s.e. 1.1) different facts with IntelWiki as compared to 16.2 (s.e. 1.2) with Default ($F_{1,14} = 7.304$, p = 0.017, $\eta^2 = 0.343$). Interestingly, there was also a significant Interface Type * Interface Order interaction effect ($F_{1,14} = 6.182$, p = 0.026, $\eta^2 = 0.306$). As illustrated in Fig. 5(middle), the primary benefit of the IntelWiki system came for those who experienced this condition second. Those who edited with IntelWiki first covered roughly the same number of facts in each condition. We suspect that in this latter case, Intel-Wiki helped participants learn what types of facts to describe in the first condition, and that they were able to transfer this knowledge to the second editing task, even though the scaffolding was removed. For Fact Accuracy, Fig. 4(right) shows that participants were significantly more accurate with IntelWiki (15.9, s.e. 1.1) than they were with Default (14.6, s.e. 1.1, $F_{1,14} = 4.520$, p = 0.052, $\eta^2 = 0.244$).

Perceived Mental Workload and Subjective Preference
The results of the NASA-TLX indicate that perceived mental workload was significantly lower (see Fig. 5, right) when using IntelWiki (49.5, s.e. 6.1) than when using the Default interface (66.7, s.e. 3.1, $F_{1,14} = 10.212$, p = 0.006, $\eta^2 = 0.422$). Participants also expressed a preference for its design, with 14 out of the 16 participants preferring the IntelWiki interface over the Default one ($\chi^2=9.000$, p = .003).

Interview Comments
While the above results suggest that IntelWiki's approach improves editing performance and lowers perceived mental workload, it does not isolate the value of its individual components. Therefore, in the semi-structured exit interviews, we elicited participants' impressions of the IntelWiki system, including what they liked and did not like about its approach.

Integrating Editing and Background Research: For the majority of the users who preferred the IntelWiki system, it was for its ability to integrate the two tasks of

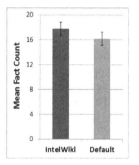 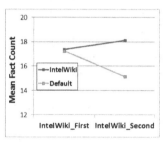 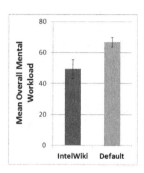

Fig. 5. (Left) Fact count (Middle) The Interface Type * Interface Order interaction effect, and (Right) Cumulative Mental Workload as measured by the NASA TLX

background research and article editing. In particular, participants liked the fact that they did not have to switch windows to consult (or search for) reference material, as the following quote illustrates:

> *I preferred [IntelWiki] because the screen was shared. [...] It gives you the ability to do two things at the same time: go through what you are going through and still edit what you are editing. – P5*

We note that in the Default condition, participants were able to place the windows in any configuration they wished, with the monitor used (23") providing ample space to place the editing and search interfaces side-by-side. When reviewing the session videotapes we found that six participants chose to place their windows in this configuration. An analysis of their data alone suggests that the value of IntelWiki's approach goes beyond integrated editing and resource viewing. For example, even with this small sample size, the difference in Fact Count remained significant ($p = 0.003$), with a trend in IntelWiki's favour for mental workload ($p = 0.051$).

Supporting Resource Inspection and Evaluation: Participants also liked the ability to inspect the recommendations through the tooltips, indicating that they were able to quickly evaluate the suitability of an individual resource:

> *Even before you open the resource in the viewer pane you know what you are expecting to see. When I am searching online [Google text snippets] show me a plethora of mostly useless information that would not directly give you what you are looking for. – P8*

Similarly, participants appreciated the manner in which IntelWiki's keyword highlighting streamlined their search for key information within an article:

> *[Keyword highlighting] was very helpful; didn't have to read the whole page, or even the paragraph, only the lines containing the highlighted words. – P17*

Replacing Independent Search: Most participants responded positively to the notion of system recommended resources, with many commenting that they were relieved of having to do their own searches. For example:

> *[IntelWiki] eliminated any need for [additional searches] because, virtually anything that's needed I think was provided in the [recommended resources] – P12*

As the following quote illustrates, however, not all participants, however, felt that IntelWiki's recommendations were sufficient:

For most of the information I didn't need [Google]. But when I was looking for the "connected rivers", the "river" keyword was listed, but I did not find any information about connected rivers from that resource. So, I searched through Google. – P14

While participants had the option to supplement the recommended resources with external searches, P14 was the only participant to exercise this option (for a single external section). This suggests that when provided with a good set of pertinent keywords, the system is able to retrieve a useful set of resources. However, the above quote also suggests that allowing users to incorporate their own retrieved resources would be a useful extension to the system.

5   Discussion and Future Work

Our proof-of-concept evaluation provides encouraging evidence in favour of IntelWiki's approach. With editing time fixed, participants contributed significantly more text and experienced significantly lower perceived mental workload in doing so. In terms of text completeness, IntelWiki was particularly helpful for participants who experienced that condition second (i.e., after editing with the Default interface), with results suggesting that IntelWiki helped scaffold the editing process. Participants also expressed a strong preference for IntelWiki's design over the status quo.

Having established potential for the general approach, there are a number of promising directions for future research, one of which is assessing the accuracy of the system's recommendations. For "proof-of-concept" evaluation purposes, IntelWiki was provided with a set of hand-crafted section-specific pertinent keywords to help the system rank the resources. Future work could examine the feasibility of using crowdsourcing or machine learning approaches to generate such a list as well as the impact of list accuracy on the utility of the approach. Further evaluations are also needed to explore the relative utility of IntelWiki's different features. Finally, a field deployment would be necessary in order to explore the impact of IntelWiki's support on contribution rates.

Our decision not to screen for Wikipedia editing experience resulted in a set of participants without any Wikipedia editing experience. While this decision was primarily based on pragmatics, studying our approach with this participant group does align with the motivation of improving overall contribution rates by making it easier for newcomers to contribute. Given that IntelWiki's support is for background research as opposed to for wiki-editing mechanics, there is reason to be optimistic that the findings would generalize beyond novice editors. Similarly, to control for participant expertise while still having access to a wide enough participant pool, participants edited articles on topics that they were familiar with, but not for which they were experts. Therefore, exploring the value of the approach with participants with more article-related expertise is another important area of future study. It would also be interesting to examine IntelWiki's impact on editing confidence, given Bryant *et al.*'s finding that novice editors initially edit articles on topics only which they are experts in, but eventually branch out as they gain confidence [2].

There are number of ways that the system could be extended to further personalize its recommendations. One promising approach would be to collect implicit and explicit relevance feedback for the recommended resources and to use this feedback to improve future recommendations. For example, one could image favouring resources previously used to edit other articles of the same category. To collect explicit feedback, editors could be allowed to "vote" on the utility of the different resources. For repeat editors, one could also weight the recommendations towards websites or domains that the editor has frequently consulted in the past.

Finally, it would be interesting to explore the generalizability of IntelWiki's resource recommendation strategy to other environments where background research is often required, such as writing articles/blogs in online communities, or writing research papers/essays using word-processing software. The Google Search technique used to fetch relevant resources could be incorporated directly, whereas developing streamlined queries and pertinent keywords would require further work. Further research would also be needed to determine effective ways to integrate recommendations within these new environments.

6   Summary

We presented an approach to facilitating user contributions to unstructured content within Wikipedia articles. This approach aims to reduce the amount of effort required to contribute to Wikipedia articles by helping users find and consult relevant resource materials. In a formal laboratory evaluation, we found that this approach, embedded in the IntelWiki prototype, affords a number of advantages in comparison to the default Wikipedia editor design. With IntelWiki, participants were able to write more text, describe a larger number of different facts and were more accurate in their descriptions. Subjectively, participants reported experiencing significantly lower mental workload and all but two of the sixteen participants preferred IntelWiki's approach. We have also identified a number of promising avenues of future work including automated pertinent keyword identification, exploring system extensions that leverage relevance feedback, and exploring the impact of the approach on contribution rates.

Acknowledgements. This work was supported by the GRAND Network Center of Excellence and the National Sciences and Engineering Research Council of Canada.

References

1. Bostandjiev, S., O'Donovan, J., Hall, C., Gretarsson, B., Höllerer, T.W.: WiGipedia: A Tool for Improving Structured Data in Wikipedia. In: Proc. of ICSC, pp. 328–335 (2011)
2. Bryant, S.L., Forte, A., Bruckman, A.: Becoming Wikipedian: Transformation of Participation in a Collaborative Online Encyclopedia. In: Proc. of GROUP, pp. 1–10 (2005)
3. Cosley, D., Frankowski, D., Terveen, L., Riedl, J.: Using Intelligent Task Routing and Contribution Review to Help Communities Build Artifacts of Lasting Value. In: Proc. of CHI, pp. 1037–1046 (2006)
4. Cosley, D., Frankowski, D., Terveen, L., Riedl, J.: SuggestBot: Using Intelligent Task Routing to Help People Find Work in Wikipedia. In: Proc. of IUI, pp. 32–41 (2007)

5. Croteau, D., Hoynes, W., Milan, S.: Media/Society: Industries, Images, and Audiences. Sage (2011)
6. Hanrahan, B.V., Bouchard, G., Convertino, G., Weksteen, T., Kong, N., Archambeau, C., Chi, E.H.: Mail2Wiki: Low-Cost Sharing and Early Curation from Email to Wikis. Proc of C&T, 98–107 (2011)
7. Hart, S.G., Staveland, L.E.: Development of NASA-TLX (Task Load Index): Results of Empirical and Theoretical Research. Human Mental Workload 1, 139–183 (1988)
8. Hoffmann, R., Amershi, S., Patel, K., Wu, F., Fogarty, J., Weld, D.S.: Amplifying Community Content Creation with Mixed Initiative Information Extraction. In: Proc. of CHI, pp. 1849–1858 (2009)
9. Holloway, T., Bozicevic, M., Borner, K.: Analyzing and Visualizing The Semantic Coverage of Wikipedia and Its Authors. Complexity 12(3), 30–40 (2007)
10. Kong, N., Hanrahan, B.V., Weksteen, T., Convertino, G., Chi, E.H.: VisualWikiCurator: Human and Machine Intelligence for Organizing Wiki Content. In: Proc. of IUI, pp. 367–370 (2011)
11. Krieger, M., Stark, E., Klemmer, S.R.: Coordinating Tasks on the Commons: Designing for Personal Goals, Expertise and Serendipity. In: Proc. of CHI, pp. 1485–1494 (2009)
12. Nielsen, J.: Participation Inequality: Encouraging More Users to Contribute, http://www.nngroup.com/articles/participation-inequality/ (accessed: October 7, 2013)
13. Nov, O.: What Motivates Wikipedians? CACM 50(11), 60–64 (2007)
14. Okuoka, T., Takahashi, T., Deguchi, D., Ide, I., Murase, H.: Labeling News Topic Threads with Wikipedia Entries. ISM, 501–504 (2009)
15. Sauper, C., Barzilay, R.: Automatically Generating Wikipedia Articles: A Structure-Aware Approach. In: Proc. of ACL and AFNLP, pp. 208–216 (2009)
16. Weld, D.S., Wu, F., Adar, E., Amershi, S., Fogarty, J., Hoffmann, R., Patel, K., Skinner, M.: Intelligence in Wikipedia. In: Proc. of AAAI, pp. 1609–1614 (2008)
17. Welser, H.T., Cosley, D., Kossinets, G., Lin, A., Dokshin, F., Gery, G., Smith, M.: Finding Social Roles in Wikipedia. In: Proc. of iConference, pp. 122–129 (2011)
18. Wikimedia Report Card, http://reportcard.wmflabs.org/ (accessed: December 2, 2013)
19. Wikipedia:Please Do Not Bite The Newcomers, http://en.wikipedia.org/wiki/Wikipedia:Please_do_not_bite_th e_newcomers (accessed: October 7, 2013)
20. Wilkinson, D.M.: Strong Regularities in Online Peer Production. In: Proc. of EC, pp. 302–309 (2008)
21. Woodsend, K., Lapata, M.: WikiSimple: Automatic Simplification of Wikipedia Articles. In: Proc. of AAAI, pp. 927–932 (2011)
22. Wu, F., Hoffmann, R., Weld, D.S.: Information Extraction from Wikipedia: Moving Down The Long Tail. In: Proc of KDD, pp. 731–739 (2008)
23. Zachte, E.: Wikipedia Statistics, http://stats.wikimedia.org/EN/TablesWikipediaZZ.htm#editor_a ctivity_levels (accessed: Deceber 2, 2013)

Balancing Adaptivity and Customisation:
In Search of Sustainable Personalisation in Cultural Heritage

Elena Not[1] and Daniela Petrelli[2]

[1] Fondazione Bruno Kessler, Trento, Italy
not@fbk.eu
[2] Sheffield Hallam University, Sheffield, United Kingdom
D.Petrelli@shu.ac.uk

Abstract. Personalisation for cultural heritage aims at delivering to visitors the right stories at the right time. Our endeavour to determine which features to use for adaptation starts from acknowledging what forms of personalisation curators value as most meaningful. Working in collaboration with curators we have explored the different features that must be taken into account: some are related to the content (multiple interpretation layers), others to the context of delivery (where and when), but some are idiosyncratic ("match my mood", "something that is relevant to my life"). The findings reveal that a sustainable personalization needs to accurately balance: (i) support to curators in customising stories to different visitors; (ii) algorithms for the system to dynamically model aspects of the visit and instantiate the correct behaviour; and (iii) an active role for visitors to choose the type of experience they would like to have today.

Keywords: Personalisation in Cultural Heritage, Sustainability, Customisation, Adaptivity, Personalisation by design.

1 Introduction

In a scenario of digital content delivery for the Cultural Heritage sector, either online or onsite, mechanisms for appropriately adjusting what is presented to the user and how is now seen as a necessity, to accommodate different visit motivations, expectations, and needs [3]. A co-design process where curators, designers and computer scientists work hand in hand is required to guarantee that user-system and personalisation requirements are properly spelt out and that the design of IT solutions meet both the curators and the visitors' needs and expectations.

In the meSch project[1] [8], museum experts and curators are active players of an investigation that aims at designing personalisation technologies that support the tangible and embodied interaction with exhibits and spaces augmented with digital content. Personalised content will be revealed if and when conditions are right, e.g. visitors have reached the right time in the storyline, or a group of them is acting in a certain way, or another smart object is close by. In such a rich scenario, the design of a

---

[1] http://mesch-project.eu/

V. Dimitrova et al. (Eds.): UMAP 2014, LNCS 8538, pp. 405–410, 2014.
© Springer International Publishing Switzerland 2014

component delivering personalisation services across different heritage types needs to face strict sustainability requirements related to: the reusability of the main functionalities in different contexts (e.g. onsite vs. online interaction); portability to different physical sites (e.g. indoor vs. outdoor), hardware devices (e.g. wearables), and different domains; the implementation of relevant forms of personalisation both in content and in interaction; proper support for curators to retain their pivotal role in creating the stories and the multiple layers of interpretation; easy tuning and maintenance.

This paper presents a methodological approach for spelling out the requirements for a sustainable personalisation architecture to support the complex scenario outlined above. It is based on the meSch experience in collaborating with curators and museum experts to understand and shape personalisation in a way that is meaningful to them and to visitors, that is sustainable to implement, and effective in managing the complexity of context-awareness. Section 2 describes how cultural heritage professionals were active players in investigating the meaning of personalisation and the different features that must be taken into account. Section 3 then explains how the output of the co-design process has been translated into requirements for the implementation of a personalisation component, where complementary approaches are adopted to allow for content to be controlled by curators (customisation) and context to be controlled by the system (adaptivity) [7].

2   Personalisation: What Does It Mean for Cultural Heritage?

Personalisation for cultural heritage has been a topic of research for many years [1], however no common understanding is shared across the community on which features should be used and for which aim. To propose a personalisation architecture that can be used for different instantiations of personalised visitors' experiences and heritage types we need first to gain a broad understanding of what personalization of cultural heritage could be. To this aim we conducted two complementary studies and integrated the results to define the requirements for such a generic approach. The first study is a meta-analysis of the literature that classifies the features used in different personalisation systems and which model they feed. The second study is a user-centred qualitative study of what personalisation means for cultural heritage professionals.

2.1   Personalisation: Features in the Literature and Their Use

In order to determine which features have driven research so far, and the computational approaches adopted, an extended reading of the existing literature was undertaken. Milestone works in the field of visitor studies were used as starting point; technical papers describing implemented solutions evaluated with final users in onsite settings complemented and completed the set. Overall 41 features were classified according to the static/dynamic nature of the information and to the subject they refer to such as: (i) the visitor (e.g., age, disabilities, personality [4], background knowledge, motivations, expectations [2], interests [9], visiting style [6], previous visits and available time,…); (ii) the interaction and social context (e.g. location and proximity [5], group social interactions [6], visit history,…); (iii) the environment (e.g., physical layout [5], weather conditions, crowding, noise,…); (iv) the content (e.g., narrative threads, story plot [9], …). In the comparative analysis, for each feature multiple pieces of information were collected across different papers: what the feature is; its possible values; a justification of its relevance in personalisation and the opposite, i.e. why such a feature should be ignored in the actual implementation; a discussion on the suitability of the feature for onsite and online scenarios; technical requirements or possible implementation solutions for computing the feature values at runtime.

The survey showed that usually implemented systems concentrate on the modelling and evaluation of a specific complex feature (e.g., visiting style) or on a subset of easy to model features (e.g., age, stereotypes, location), possibly leaving out other personalisation dimensions highly valued by curators (e.g., motivation for the visit). A clear indication of a strategy for actually prioritising the many possible features when coming to the decision of which personalisation to implement is still missing and, we believe, much needed.

2.2   Personalisation: The Perspective of Cultural Heritage Professionals

To complement the analysis of the literature, we conducted a user-centred qualitative study aiming at understanding what personalisation means for cultural heritage professionals. During a co-design workshop that brought together 10 curators, 7 interaction designers and 8 computer scientists (only 2 with experience in personalisation), we asked the participants to contribute their thoughts on what must be changed in a visit to achieve personalisation. We briefed our participants and explained our aim as to collect the broadest set of personalisation features that could be used to personalise "content" in "context"; we used these two terms to broadly direct participants' thoughts. A total of 176 annotated post-its was collected. The content of the post-its was at different levels of granularity with some very precise features such as 'age' and other much open such as 'no information but emotion'. A thematic analysis was applied to systematically classify the post-its and create an affinity diagram: similar features were aggregated under a single label and a question was used to make the interpretation clearer; groups of labels were then aggregated under the same theme. In this way from a large number of small clusters a total of 20 classes (or themes) were created (8 entries were not classified as they had no similarity with others, such as 'hermeneutics' or 'intended educational goal'); the 20 classes were further aggregated in 3 larger sets that map the Content, the Context and the Visitor, as shown in Table 1. When comparing the two sets of features, literature vs. user-generated, we can see that some occur in both sets such as 'age' or 'short time' or 'interest', but overall there are many more differences than similarities. We explain this by the small number of respondents with experience on personalisation systems (2 people) in the group of 25; for all the other 23 participants it was an exercise of imagination, on "What could personalisation be? How would it manifest itself? What do we need to model?". The result is an unexpected and exciting range of challenges and opportunities.

Table 1. The 3 sets and 20 classes created out of the 176 entries suggested at the co-design workshop. In () the number of occurrences of similar concepts; in '' examples of the entries.

Content	
— Type (11) 'written text', 'spoken text'	— Perspective (9) 'fun vs. information seeking'
— Source (4) 'visitor's generated', 'curator's view'	— Narrative (11) 'stories as multiple connected
— Background (10) 'what is it? How was it used?'	points'
Context	
— Proximity (4) 'what is near?'	— Alone/group (6) 'lonely visitor', 'first date'
— Time/length (5) 'visitor just killing time', 'short visit'	— Environment (9) 'no power', 'no WiFi'
— Visit history (14) 'multiple visits, same museum', 'personal history'	— Devices/technology (11) 'enable digital shadows', 'own device, e.g. phone'
	— Engagement (6) 'touch', 'activating the senses'
Visitor	
— Take away (4) 'collect objects, virtual, physical'	— Mood/emotion (8) 'mood selector, what I want'
— Leave (4) 'leave a message – comment!'	— Social interaction (11) 'who is around?', 'force social interaction'
— Unexpected (7) 'surprise me! Suggest me some content!', 'I believe in coincidence'	— Human body (5) 'age', 'disabled, special needs'
— Me (15) 'personal interest', 'how is the content related to my life?'	— Attention (4) 'current attention span', 'don't distract me too much from the content'

As it could be expected, the larger sets of entry refers to 'me' and the 'visit history', however features generally considered worth implementing in the personalisation literature such as 'visiting style' and 'personality' have not been mentioned at all in our sample. Intriguing is the large number of terms generated that is novel and has never been addressed by implemented personalisation. 'Unexpected' (7) and 'mood' (8) clearly indicate an interest for interactions that are different from what is generally provided by technology designed for cultural heritage, that is to say they point toward emotion rather than information. A similar call for affective engagement is found in other entries such as 'how is this content related to my life' classified as 'me'. From an implementation point of view this affective direction is a serious challenge that, we believe, must be addressed by other means than computation; in our research we use design. The user-generated features also show the importance given to the direct engagement of visitors with objects, that is a new and different take on personalisation for cultural heritage currently seen as a challenge [1].

The three sets of Content, Context and Visitor, point at three major ingredients that shape the visit experience. In meSch, we use these as the building blocks for a personalisation architecture that supports: the curator-supervised customisation of the content and of the overall visitor experience; the system-controlled adaptivity of the content to the context; and forms of visitors' driven customisation [7].

3   Personalisation: How Can It Work?

Via co-design important guidelines for a personalisation architecture were defined.

1) *Prioritize and group features.* Not all the features produce the same benefit, or are easily portable across different settings. Features that are simple to acquire and to model (like age) can in principle be taken as the basis to infer automatically what might be interesting for that user; but the risk is that the corresponding stereotypes oversimplify user needs and preferences with the danger of offering a sub-optimal experience thus diminishing the value of personalisation. It can be more convenient to consider complex features (e.g. visitor motivations or interests for current visit) that are highly valued by curators [3] and have proved to be more effective in representing the visitor's expectations, behaviour, and visiting style, being therefore helpful to model various aspects of personalisation simultaneously.

2) *Keep curators in control of the customization of stories and the experience.* There are aspects of personalisation that curators deem important to be under their control, like the provenance and the type of content used, the multiple layers of interpretation and perspectives available, the type of experiences that relate to their museums mission statements. Heritage already offers personalised content to different visitors (particularly for educational purposes) and this level of control should be maintained if we expect heritage professionals to adopt personalisation systems. They have to be comfortable in building and visualizing the structure of the stories, with the alternative perspectives and thematic threads, and the different levels of detail. Facilities should be available to match the variability in content with the desired interactions with objects/space and social interactions, to shape the intended experience.

3) *Keep the instantiation in context as a separate phase.* Curators need to be relieved from the burden of fine-grained modelling of the visit context and history, with the implementation of automatic adaptivity mechanisms that instantiate the system behaviour properly. By keeping the rules for runtime, context-aware instantiation of adaptivity separated from the structuring of narratives and experiences, it is possible to decouple the curator authoring task from the physical architecture, facilitating the reuse of exhibition templates with different hardware setups. Thus the heritage professionals will focus on the personalisation they are already familiar with (different stories for different visitors) and leave the system to deal with a dynamic context.

4) *Bootstrap by design.* Instead of asking the visitor to fill in questionnaires to match them to a hypothetical interest profile or delaying the personalisation until enough live-data of the visit has been collected, the visitor can be granted an active role in controlling the experience that is delivered. This can be done for example in a purposefully designed 'introduction' section where the visitors are offered multiple experiences (or stories) to sample, thus allowing them to choose the type of visit that best matches their motivations and expectations for the visit. The clear advantage is in avoiding mismatching and building upon a solid foundation (visitor's choice).

4   Conclusion

Shaping personalisation in a scenario of tangible and embodied interaction for cultural heritage involves challenges that go well beyond the requirements of implementing content personalisation for portable mobile guides. Through an inspiring co-design process, we reinforced our belief that there are aspects of personalisation that curators explicitly wish and need to be in control of. The curator-supervised customisation grants more portability across different content domains, as the personalisation component requires a lighter content data model. The system then monitors the state of the context, updates its model, and dynamically adapts whenever multiple options apply. By decoupling the low-level management of the context from the higher levels, we support a more sustainable porting to different hardware configurations. An additional important finding was that interaction design can become a powerful means to get the visitor into the personalisation loop: purposefully designed interactions empower visitors to control their experience, bootstrapping multiple personalisation features at the same time and relieving the system from complex log-based guessing or rigid stereotyping. These requirements are currently being put into action in the on-going implementation of the multilayer personalization component of the meSch system.

Acknowledgements. The research described in this paper is part of the meSch project, Material Encounters with Digital Cultural Heritage. meSch (2013-2017) receives funding from the European Community's Seventh Framework Programme 'ICT for access to cultural resources' (FP7-ICT-2011-9) under the Grant Agreement 600851.

References

1. Ardissono, L., Kuflik, T., Petrelli, D.: Personalisation in Cultural Heritage: The Road Travelled and the One Ahead. UMUAI 22(1-2), 73–99 (2012)
2. Dim, E., Kuflik, T.: Early Detection of Museum Visitors Identities by Using a Museum Triage. In: Herder, E., Yacef, K., Chen, L., Weibelzahl, S. (eds.) Workshop and Poster Proceedings of UMAP 2012, CEUR, vol. 872 (2012)
3. Falk, J.: Identity and the Museum Visitor Experience. Left Coast Press (2009)
4. Goren-Bar, D., Graziola, I., Pianesi, F., Zancanaro, M.: The influence of personality factors on visitor attitudes towards adaptivity dimensions for mobile museum guides. UMUAI 16(1), 31–62 (2006)
5. van Hage, W.R., Stash, N., Wang, Y., Aroyo, L.: Finding Your Way through the Rijksmuseum with an Adaptive Mobile Museum Guide. In: Aroyo, L., Antoniou, G., Hyvönen, E., ten Teije, A., Stuckenschmidt, H., Cabral, L., Tudorache, T. (eds.) ESWC 2010, Part I. LNCS, vol. 6088, pp. 46–59. Springer, Heidelberg (2010)
6. Kuflik, T., Dim, E.: Early Detection of Pairs of Visitors by Using a Museum Triage. In: Proc. of MW 2013: Museums and the Web 2013, Portland, OR, USA (2013)
7. Not, E., Petrelli, D.: Curators in the Loop: a Quality Control Process for Personalisation for Tangible Interaction in Cultural Heritage. In: Berkovsky, S., Herder, E., Lops, P., Santos, O.C. (eds.) UMAP 2013 Extended Proceedings, CEUR, vol. 997 (2013)
8. Petrelli, D., Ciolfi, L., van Dijk, D., Hornecker, E., Not, E., Schmidt, A.: Integrating Material and Digital: a New Way for Cultural Heritage. Interactions 20(4), 58–63 (2013)
9. Pujol, L., Roussou, M., Poulou, S., Balet, O., Vayanou, M., Ioannidis, Y.: Personalizing interactive digital storytelling in archaeological museums: the CHESS project. In: Archaeology in the Digital Era. Papers from the 40th Annual Conference of Computer Applications and Quantitative Methods in Archaeology (CAA 2012). Amsterdam Univ. Press (2013)

Who's Afraid of Job Interviews? Definitely a Question for User Modelling

Kaśka Porayska-Pomsta[1], Paola Rizzo[1], Ionut Damian[2], Tobias Baur[2], Elisabeth André[2], Nicolas Sabouret[3], Hazaël Jones[4], Keith Anderson[5], and Evi Chryssafidou[1]

[1] London Knowledge Lab, Institute of Education, London WC1N 3QS, UK
{K.Porayska-Pomsta,P.Rizzo,E.Chryssafidou}@ioe.ac.uk
[2] Human Centered Multimedia, Augsburg University, 86159 Augsburg, Germany
{damian,baur,andre}@hcm-lab.de
[3] Laboratoire d'Informatique pour la Mécanique et les Sciences de l'Ingénieur,
91403 Orsay, France
nicolas.sabouret@limsi.fr
[4] Laboratoire d'Informatique de Paris 6, 4 Place Jussieu, 75005 Paris, France
hazael.jones@lip6.fr
[5] Tandemis Limited, 108 Blackheath Hill, London SE10 8AG, UK
keith@tandemis.co.uk

Abstract. We define job interviews as a domain of interaction that can be modelled automatically in a serious game for job interview skills training. We present four types of studies: (1) field-based human-to-human job interviews, (2) field-based computer-mediated human-to-human interviews, (3) lab-based wizard of oz studies, (4) field-based human-to-agent studies. Together, these highlight pertinent questions for the user modelling field as it expands its scope to applications for social inclusion. The results of the studies show that the interviewees suppress their emotional behaviours and although our system recognises automatically a subset of those behaviours, the modelling of complex mental states in real-world contexts poses a challenge for the state-of-the-art user modelling technologies. This calls for the need to re-examine both the approach to the implementation of the models and/or of their usage for the target contexts.

1 Introduction

As a domain of interaction, job interviews rely crucially on the participants' mutual modelling of each other's behaviours and mental states. The ultimate goal of a job interview is for the interviewer to ascertain the fit of the candidate to a particular job and, ideally, for the candidate to assess a given company as a possible workplace [1]. Job interviews are often a game of bluff, where personas are adopted by the interactants and where it is normal, even expected, that the display of participants' real emotions may be suppressed [2]. This presents substantial challenges for real-time user modelling: the subtle nature of the behaviours manifested by the interviewees in such contexts makes them difficult

V. Dimitrova et al. (Eds.): UMAP 2014, LNCS 8538, pp. 411–422, 2014.

to detect as well as to interpret in terms of more complex mental states. The interpretation of the observable behaviours in terms of the mental states, such as *stress, boredom* or *hesitation* is important as those states may be indicative of a person's ability to cope with the demands of a given job. The primary challenge, as we see it, is in obtaining a reliable measure of the users' affective states during interactions that could inform the design of our model and/or against which the model could be evaluated. This challenge is well known in the field [3,4].

In this paper we present four studies, which have iteratively informed the implementation of the user modelling tools in the TARDIS project.[1] TARDIS implements a serious game for job interview skills coaching for young unemployed people, aged 18-25. The game is motivated by a growing need for technology-enhanced approaches to helping young people gain skills needed to secure jobs, both because of the marked youth unemployment and the expense associated with traditional methods, such as mock job interviews enactments.

The TARDIS user modelling tools, as well as the serious game more generally, have been described in [5] and [6]. Presently, we discuss some key issues, highlighted through the studies, that relate to finding a balance between the need to detect and interpret target users' subtle behaviours in ecologically valid contexts and the still limited capabilities of the state-of-the-art social cues detection technologies. Our work demonstrates that striving for ecological validity of our models, while highly desirable, further exacerbates the challenges of finding reliable measures of the phenomena of interest.

2 Related Work

Nonverbal behaviours are key in job interviews. For example, [7] found a relationship between audio-visual cues of the candidates and the interview outcomes. [8] studied how the success of simulated job interviews can be predicted from conversational engagement, vocal mirroring, speech activity, and prosodic emphasis. Other researchers have focused on the relationship between interviewers' decision making and the perceived personality of the candidate (measured along the dominance, equivalence and submissiveness dimensions) and the related behaviours [9]. [10] found a negative correlation between the interviewees' performance (interview scores) and trait anxiety, while [11] found a link between high state anxiety and information acquisition and retention, suggesting that anxiety may interfere with the applicant's acquisition and processing of the information presented to them by the recruiters and thus, with their performance. This implies that anxiety regulation is fundamental to candidates' performance in interviews.

Less is known about interviewee's other mental states that may be relevant to achieving success in an interview. Crucially, most of the substantial evidence that links the specific social cues with candidates' traits or states has been conducted in the laboratory settings with university students. While this research is of practical importance to us, a key difference between it and the context of TARDIS is that we aim to define the characteristics of a population which is at

---

[1] http://www.tardis-project.eu

risk of marginalisation, with our technology being designed for use in real-world contexts of youth organisations across Europe. TARDIS' focus, therefore, leads to a need to (a) verify and define further the states and social cues that are pertinent to the contexts of its intended use and (b) identify, implement and test the social cue detection tools that are affordable, robust and least intrusive.

Using signal processing techniques to detect behavioural patterns is not a new idea, e.g. [12]. However, to date, most research focused on a reduced number of modalities to infer user states, such as speech [13] or facial expressions [14]. Relatively little attention has been paid to gestures or postures [15,16]. Furthermore, most work on signal processing is intended for offline analysis, rather than real-time interactive applications. For example, in Batrinca et al.'s [17] system for practicing public speaking, behaviour analysis happens post-hoc and offline, with their system not being able to react to the user's behaviour in real-time.

There are, of course, exceptions, one of which is the MACH job interview simulation system [18], which is able to detect a limited number of social cues in real time, including smiles, audio features and speech. In contrast, our system recognises a much broader range of social cues, including bodily cues, such as expressivity features, gestures and postures, physiological features and eye gaze, although it does not engage in speech recognition [5].

In the remainder of this paper we present the four studies aimed to define job interviews as a domain of interaction, specifically focusing on the evaluation of social cues and mental states for use during interactions in real-world contexts.

3   Manual Annotations of Mock Interviews by Experts

To identify the social cues and hidden mental states displayed by youngsters during mock job interviews, we conducted a study with ten youngsters and five practitioners at a youth association in France. The study's procedure involved one-on-one mock job interviews, all of which were video recorded, followed by semi-structured interviews with youngsters and practitioners, and post-hoc video walkthroughs with practitioners. The semi-structured interviews focused on identifying the youngsters' strengths and weaknesses during each mock interview. The walkthroughs served to identify the social cues observed by the practitioners and the hidden mental states that could be linked to those cues.

The walkthroughs were facilitated by the Elan annotation tool (Fig. 1, left), which allows simultaneous replay of videos and their annotations. During the walkthroughs, the practitioners were asked to stop the videos anytime they observed a critical incident. *Critical incident* was defined as a specific behaviour on the part of the interviewee, e.g. smile, or a set of behaviours, e.g. persistent smiling and gaze averting, that the practitioner thought crucial, in a positive or negative way, to the job interview and its outcome. This procedure allowed for the key behaviours in the given interactions to be identified within exact time frames and to be annotated additionally with the practitioners comments – these were used in further video data analysis by independent annotators.

Three interactions were annotated by the practitioners for social cues with additional comments linking them to specific hidden mental states. This resulted in nineteen individual social cues, as shown on the x-axis of Fig. 1, right. One annotator coded the videos for social cues, using practitioners' walkthrough annotations as exemplars. A second independent annotator verified those annotations, ensuring that all observable behaviours of interest were captured. The inter-rater agreement analysis was not conducted at this point, however the two annotators met to agree the thresholds for annotating social cues including *long silence* (established as ≥ 3 seconds) and *short answer* to questions requiring elaboration (established as simple yes/no answer), as annotating these cues presented the most difficulty for the annotators. The videos were then re-annotated using these thresholds. However, full agreement could not be achieved with respect to the instances of *clear/low voice*. These presented significant problems primarily due to the low quality of the recordings which were taken in a minimally controlled environment of a real youth association, with the normal daily business of the association taking place at the same time, the outside noise often interfering with the recordings. Gaze *saccades* were also extremely difficult to establish through the video analysis: given that the recorded interactions were face-to-face between two humans, achieving an ideal angle of the camera to capture as fine grained detail as the youngsters' eye-gaze shifts proved virtually impossible. While this means that some social cues were hard to identify with confidence through the videos alone, given that TARDIS is intended for use in real youth associations, the need for a careful selection of the social cue sensors along with their set up in real-world contexts was clearly highlighted.

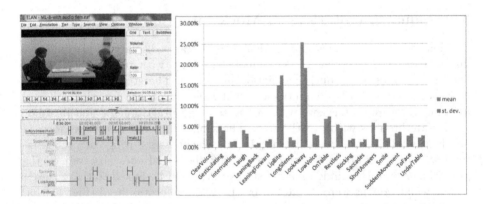

Fig. 1. Human-to-human mock interview with social cues manually annotated (left) and percentages of frequencies of social cues across participants (right)

Eight complex mental states have been identified during walkthroughs, including: (i) stressed, (ii) embarrassed, (iii) hesitant, (iv) ill-at-ease, (v) bored, (vi) focused, (vii) relieved and (viii) relaxed. These mental states have been associated by the practitioners with specific social cues in the videos annotated. For example, observable behaviours such as *looking away, laughter* and *hand-to-mouth*, have been associated with youngsters' *embarrassment*, whereas *restless hands* – with *stress*. The mental states annotations, along with the practitioners' comments provided the basis for further manual annotations of the videos. Two independent annotators coded the video data for the eight mental states. Unfortunately, with Cohen's Kappa below 0.2, the inter-rater agreement was significantly below the level necessary to provide a reliable measure of youngsters' affects that could (a) be generalisable to other youngsters and (b) could serve as a reliable measure against which to evaluate the TARDIS user model directly [3]. Amongst the eight states identified, the greatest source of difficulties amongst the annotators related to the difference between *embarrassed* and *ill-at-ease*, which one annotator found virtually impossible to distinguish. On the other hand, *stress* seemed so ubiquitous that it became at times difficult for the annotators to differentiate it from the other states.

The difficulties in finding a good agreement between mental states annotations are not altogether surprising given that other researchers have reported similar set-backs when trying to establish some ground truth for eliciting emotion recognition models [3]. One typical culprit is the use of labels which are a liability owing to the imprecision of language, with the meaning of a label being typically constrained by context and linguistic repertoire of the labeller [4] - in our case the practitioners. The fact that several practitioners came up with the same labels for the youngsters mental states may be an artefact of their working and training together, which may have resulted in their labelling habits being aligned. Another potential reason for the imprecision of labels may be the fact that they have been provided in French and then translated into English, leaving further scope for linguistic imprecision.

However, the most compelling explanation seems to lie in the great variability in the behaviours manifested by the youngsters (in Fig.1(right), many standard deviations of frequency and duration of the social cues identified are higher than the mean occurrences of those cues), which makes any standardisation of the mental states labelling very difficult. Furthermore, the individual differences between the youngsters' behaviours may represent persistent behavioural traits rather than being dependent on the context of the interaction. For example, one youngster looked away from the interviewer over 250 times in one interview, compared to another two who have only done so 60-100 times, and two others who have never been observed to look away. Similarly, all youngsters seem to lip bite to some extent (10-15 times each), but one youngster did it 80 times in the course of a 20 minute interaction. This suggests that although the practitioners were able to name some of the youngsters' mental states, they did it relative to their individual behavioural habits. The individual differences between the youngsters also suggest that the nineteen social cues may not help us to uniquely identify the specific mental sates without recourse to some qualifying information such as the interviewer's questions, some of which, e.g. questions related to the candidate's weaknesses, may be generally more difficult than other.

A further data analysis (based on one coder's annotations of mental states) seems to confirm the weak discriminative power of the cues identified. Specifically, given that social cues can occur either in isolation or in combination with other cues, we decomposed the social cue data into all groups (defined as any overlap between 2 or more social cues) that occurred across all participants. We then assigned probabilities to each grouping of cues to represent the likelihood that it implies an emotional state. This was done by measuring the duration of each social cue grouping (CG), and the duration of its intersection D_t with the presence of an emotional state (ES), using the following simple formula:

$$P(ES|CG) = \frac{D_t(CG)}{D_t(ES)} \tag{1}$$

Despite there being many groups of cues that were found uniquely or very strongly to imply the presence of a single emotional state, there were many groupings that co-occurred rarely with an emotional state. For example, the combination of *leaning forward* while *looking away* was found to lead to a high probability of *stress* ($P = 0.83$), based on its total occurrence across all annotations of 7.6 seconds and its total co-occurrence with the *stressed* state of 6.3 seconds. However, *leaning back* and *speaking clearly* was found to imply *boredom* with a probability of only $P = 0.01$. Apart from a large number of individual cues (groupings) that correlate weakly with many mental states, many of the groupings occurred only once across all participants, raising a question of the extent to which many of the correspondences are generalisable to other participants and suggesting the need to reduce the number of cues and possibly the mental states modelled to only the key ones. However, the selection of the cues whose detection should be abandoned needs to be done in tandem with the investigations of what social cues are feasible to detect automatically in the job interview contexts.

4   Computer-Mediated Interaction

To ascertain the feasibility of detecting the different social cues during interaction, we conducted a further study with six youngsters and two practitioners in the UK. The study's procedure mirrored that of the study described in Section 3. However, in order to facilitate the use of the automatic detection tools as well as an approximation of the future human-agent interaction, the mock interviews were mediated through a video link, headphones and microphones. The youngster and the practitioner were situated in opposite corners of the same room, back to back (Fig. 4). This arrangement together with the isolating earphones allowed the participants to see and hear each other only through the media link. In addition, a Microsoft Kinect depth sensor was positioned over the monitor facing the youngster. This allowed us to record the participants' audio, video and skeleton tracking data. As well as informing the social cue detection framework in TARDIS, this set-up allowed us to assess the ease and the credibility of a job interview experience delivered via a computer screen and microphone.

The recording of the user's social signals was handled by TARDIS's social cue recognition [19] component which uses the Social Signal Interpretation framework [20]. The system enabled playback of the recorded data and thus, the testing of the behaviour recognisers in an online context even after the studies.

Fig. 2. Computer-mediated interview

Upon analysis of the data, we observed clear indications of (a) what social cues we can feasibly detect during interactions between youngsters and TARDIS and (b) which of these social cues may be the most robust and informative.

To this end, we refined the list of the 19 social cues identified in the previous study: vocal social cues such as *clear/ low voice* proved to be difficult to recognise due to the heterogeneity of the speakers and the physical environments in which the studies took place. Both of these cues rely on audio intensity analysis [17] – a speaker and hardware dependent feature that is highly susceptible to noise (e.g. coughs or voice clearing). Here, cues involving pitch variation, proved more robust. *Gesticulation, restlessness* and *sudden movements*, while correctly recognised by our automatic recognisers real-time and online, had to be joined together due to insufficient accuracy in skeleton tracking. We encountered no issues for turn taking cues such as *interrupting, short answers* or *long silences*, as these mainly relied on the user's voice activity compared to the practitioner's.

While recent advances in the domain of signal processing show that automatic recognition of *laughter* is feasible, this is usually the case for highly expressive forms of laughter [21]. In contrast, our analysis revealed subtle types of laughter, which proved not to be distinctive enough. Similarly, *lip biting, rocking* and *saccades* also turned out to be too subtle for our sensing equipment. To perceive these social cues, we would require more accurate sensors, such as an eye tracker or body worn motion tracking devices (see Section 5), which, apart from being quite expensive, may be too intrusive for some users in our target population.

Data processing also revealed that the recognition of gestures and postures (*lean front, lean back, hand to face* and *look away*) and smiles was possible using the FUBI [22] and SHORE [23] frameworks respectively. Finally, some social cues (*hands on/under table*) had to be eliminated due to the table-less setting of the study, chosen to ensure correct skeleton tracking using the Microsoft Kinect.

5   Wizard of Oz Experiment

The WOZ experiment aimed to (1) identify a combination of sensors that can enhance the recognition of youngsters' behaviours during simulated interviews to enable inferences about the users' internal states, and (2) ascertain any impact of specific types of interview question, i.e. those that might be considered difficult or aggressive, on participant's nonverbal behaviours.

The study involved three participants, who were seated in an armless chair in front of a 40" display with a Microsoft Kinect depth camera situated on top. They wore a headset, eye tracking glasses, a motion tracking glove and SC/BVP sensors on their fingers (Fig.3(a)). From the user's point of view, s/he interacted with a virtual recruiter (VR), which was, in fact, controlled by a human interviewer seated in another room (Fig.3(b)).

All sensors performed flawlessly during the interaction and the recorded data gave us a large amount of information regarding the participants' non-verbal behaviours. In particular, the skin conductance values showed the impact of the interview questions on the user, with the questions, e.g. *'What are your weaknesses?'* or harsh statements, e.g. *'I don't think you are right for this job'* correlating with higher SC values (Fig.4(b)). This suggests a possible relationship between certain types of interview questions and the candidate's emotional states, even though the interviewer posing these questions was a synthetic character.

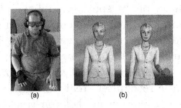

Fig. 3. Participant wearing the study apparatus (a) and images showing a user's point of view (b) including gaze information (green point) captured using the eye tracking glasses.

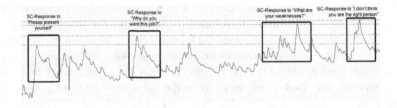

Fig. 4. Skin conductance data of one user. Highlighted areas represent user's SC response to various utterances. The blue dotted lines mark the peaks of each highlighted area.

The gaze cues clearly mark the regions of interest during the interaction. All users focused heavily on the face, in particular the mouth area of the virtual agent, followed by its torso and then, by its hands. The gaze only dropped to the hands when the agent performed a gesture as illustrated in Fig.3(b).

The study also revealed that even with the more challenging scenario, the users still performed very little in terms of physical movements. While this may have also been an effect of the sensing devices worn by the users, the observation is in line with the previous studies reported in this paper.

Additionally, even though the eye tracking data yielded some interesting trends, the eye tracking glasses' high intrusion level combined with their incompatibility with prescription glasses make them ill-fitted for large scale field studies. Given this, we decided to limit the number of sensors for future studies to the following three least intrusive sensors: depth camera, microphone and SC sensor.

6   Self-reports during Human-Agent Interaction

Building on the results of the WOZ experiment, we piloted the use of a pop-up questionnaire with seven French youngsters. The pop-up questionnaire aimed to elicit self-reports from the youngsters about their anxiety levels during their interaction with the TARDIS VR. The youngsters were asked to score their anxiety level on a 1 (not at all anxious) to 5 (extremely anxious) scale. A similar approach has been adopted in [3] to obtain emotional self-reports during the interaction with a tutoring system.

In total 124 scores were obtained against thirty interviewer questions. The questions were asked by two types of VR: (i) an understanding VR, which had a gentle manner and (ii) a demanding VR, which was more aggressive. The 124 scores were grouped according to those two conditions, resulting in 70 scores for the "demanding" and 54 for the "understanding" questions. Owing possibly to the small sample, the statistical analysis did not reveal any significant effects either with respect to the differences in the anxiety means between the two conditions (t-test: $t(122) = 0.71$, one tail $p = 0.23$), or between anxiety vs. questions asked under the three categories: (i) skills needed for the job, (ii) knowledge about the job, and (iii) salary level (ANOVA comparison: $F = 0.11$, $p = 0.89$). Nevertheless, the results shown in Fig.5(left) suggest a possible trend towards youngsters exhibiting trait anxiety, which would be in line with some of the studies reported in Section 2. The results, shown in Fig.5(right) also seem to suggest that some types of interviewer's questions may lead to greater anxiety than others: for example "Elaboration_Jobskills_Understanding" that groups questions about the skills needed for the job in the "understanding" mode, and

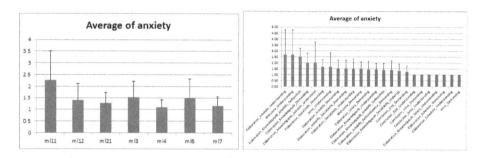

Fig. 5. Self-assessed anxiety means and standard deviations per participant (left) and self-assessed anxiety means and standard deviations per question(right)

"Welcome_Understanding", that groups questions for welcoming the participant in the "understanding" mode show higher anxiety than all the other questions analysed. Unfortunately, the small data sample and the high standard deviations for the several questions, prevent us from drawing definitive conclusions, which means that the results reported can only serve as the basis for further hypothesis generation.

7   Conclusion

In this paper we presented four formative studies which define job interviews as a domain of interaction. Each study contributed knowledge needed for the implementation of the TARDIS' real-time user model in this domain: (1) what social cues and mental states are relevant, (2) what is feasible to detect with non-intrusive technology, (3) what aspects of the interaction cause (detectable) nonverbal behaviours in users, and (4) how to evaluate anxiety.

Although, the studies presented do not offer definitive answers, they do demonstrate the magnitude of the challenge of building adaptive complex systems for real-world use, which, as TARDIS, are based on user modelling, while also having some grounding in the real world. One lesson learnt is that the use of non-intrusive sensors, coupled with the field conditions, and the peculiar nature of this interaction domain where emotional displays seem to be suppressed, lead to a reduced set of detectable cues. To address this requires a careful balancing of what is relevant to model with what is feasible to detect. Our studies suggest that focusing on key social cues, such as voice that can be reliably detected through the sensing technologies, coupled with a focus on state anxiety may be the way forward in this domain. The studies also point to a need for TARDIS to allow for an online initial training phase during which individual users' baseline of social cues can be established to allow for a tailored parameter adjustment based on the frequency of a given users' cues. This points to a continuous model, instead of a category-based one, in which users' behaviours are compared to their typical baseline and where peak behaviours that are likely indicators of corresponding peak internal reactions are identified. A complimentary approach, currently piloted in TARDIS and whose use is motivated directly by the studies reported, involves open user modelling, where the models generated online are displayed to the users who can accept or correct them according to their self-perception. This allows to both validate TARDIS' user models and to foster self-awareness in the youngsters - a pre-requisite job interview skill. Our next studies will assess youngsters' performance in human-human interviews before and after using TARDIS, in a bid to evaluate our modelling tools indirectly within TARDIS.

Acknowledgments. This work was partly funded by the European Commission (TARDIS project FP7-ICT2011-7-288578). The authors are solely responsible for the content of this publication. It does not represent the opinion of the EC, and the EC is not responsible for any use that might be made of data appearing therein.

References

1. Posthuma, R.A., Morgeson, F.P., Campion, M.A.: Beyond employment interview validity: A comprehensive narrative review of recent research and trends over time. Personnel Psychology 55(1), 1–82 (1982)
2. Sieverding, M.: Be cool!: Emotional costs of hiding feelings in a job interview. International Journal of Selection and Assessment 17(4), 391–401 (2009)
3. Conati, C.: How to evaluate models of user affect? In: André, E., Dybkjær, L., Minker, W., Heisterkamp, P. (eds.) ADS 2004. LNCS (LNAI), vol. 3068, pp. 288–300. Springer, Heidelberg (2004)
4. Porayska-Pomsta, K., Mavrikis, M., D'Mello, S., Conati, C., Baker, R.: Knowledge elicitation methods for affect modelling in education. International Journal of Artificial Intelligence in Education 22(3), 107–140 (2013)
5. Porayska-Pomsta, K., Anderson, K., Damian, I., Baur, T., André, E., Bernardini, S., Rizzo, P.: Modelling users' affect in job interviews: Technological demo. In: Carberry, S., Weibelzahl, S., Micarelli, A., Semeraro, G. (eds.) UMAP 2013. LNCS, vol. 7899, pp. 353–355. Springer, Heidelberg (2013)
6. Anderson, K., André, E., Baur, T., Bernardini, S., Chollet, M., Chryssafidou, E., Damian, I., Ennis, C., Egges, A., Gebhard, P., Jones, H., Ochs, M., Pelachaud, C., Porayska-Pomsta, K., Rizzo, P., Sabouret, N.: The TARDIS framework: Intelligent virtual agents for social coaching in job interviews. In: Reidsma, D., Katayose, H., Nijholt, A. (eds.) ACE 2013. LNCS, vol. 8253, pp. 476–491. Springer, Heidelberg (2013)
7. De Groot, T., Janaki, G.: Can nonverbal cues be used to make meaningful personality attributions in employment interviews? Journal of Business Psychology 24, 179–192 (2009)
8. Curhan, J., Pentland, A.: Thin slices of negotiation: predicting outcomes from conversational dynamics within the first 5 minutes. Journal of Applied Psychology 92(3), 802–811 (2007)
9. Schmidt, N.: Social and situational determinants of interview decisions: Implications for the employment interview. Journal of Personnel Psychology 29, 79–101 (1976)
10. Ryan, A.M., Daum, D., Friedel, L.: Interviewing behavior: Effects of experience, self-efficacy, attitudes and job-search behavior. In: Annual Conference of the Society for Industrial and Organizational Psychology, San Franscisco, CA (1993)
11. Barber, A.E., Hollenbeck, J.R., Tower, S.L., Phillips, J.M.: The effects of interview focus on recruitment effectiveness: a field experiment. Journal of Applied Psychology 79, 886–896 (1994)
12. Vinciarelli, A., Pantic, M., Heylen, C., Pelachaud, C., Poggi, F., Errico, A., Schroeder, M.: Bridging the gap between social animal and unsocial machine: A survey of social signal processing. IEEE Transactions on Affective Computing. 3(1), 69–87 (2012)
13. Vogt, T., André, E., Lewis, T., R., Leibbrandt, Powers, D.: Comparing feature sets for acted and spontaneous speech in view of automatic emotion recognition. In: IEEE International Conference on Multimedia and Expo, pp. 474–477 (2005)
14. Zeng, Z., Pantic, M., Roisman, G.I., Huang, T.S.: A survey of affect recognition methods: Audio, visual, and spontaneous expressions. IEEE Trans. Pattern Anal. Mach. Intell. 31(1), 39–58 (2009)
15. Kapoor, A., Picard, R.W.: Multimodal affect recognition in learning environments. In: Proceedings of ACM MM 2005, pp. 677–682 (2005)

16. Kleinsmith, A., Bianchi-Berthouze, N.: Form as a cue in the automatic recognition of non-acted affective body expressions. In: Proceedings of the 4th International Conference on Affective Computing and Intelligent Interaction, Amsterdam, Netherlands. Part I, pp. 155–164 (2011)

17. Batrinca, L., Stratou, G., Shapiro, A., Morency, L.-P., Scherer, S.: Cicero - towards a multimodal virtual audience platform for public speaking training. In: Aylett, R., Krenn, B., Pelachaud, C., Shimodaira, H. (eds.) IVA 2013. LNCS, vol. 8108, pp. 116–128. Springer, Heidelberg (2013)

18. Hoque, M.E., Courgeon, M., Martin, J., Mutlu, B., Picard, R.W.: Mach: My automated conversation coach. In: International Joint Conference on Pervasive and Ubiquitous Computing, UbiComp 2013 (2013)

19. Damian, I., Baur, T., André, E.: Investigating social cue-based interaction in digital learning games. In: Proceedings of the 8th International Conference on the Foundations of Digital Games, SASDG (2013)

20. Wagner, J., Lingenfelser, F., Baur, T., Damian, I., Kistler, F., André, E.: The social signal interpretation (ssi) framework - multimodal signal processing and recognition in real-time. In: Proceedings of ACM MULTIMEDIA 2013, Barcelona (2013)

21. Niewiadomski, R., Hofmann, J., Urbain, J., Platt, T., Wagner, J., Piot, B., Cakmak, H., Pammi, S., Baur, T., Dupont, S., Geist, M., Lingenfelser, F., McKeown, G., Pietquin, O., Ruch, W.: Laugh-aware virtual agent and its impact on user amusement. In: Proceedings of the 2013 International Conference on Autonomous Agents and Multi-Agent Systems, AAMAS 2013, pp. 619–626. International Foundation for Autonomous Agents and Multiagent Systems, Richland, SC (2013)

22. Kistler, F., Endrass, B., Damian, I., Dang, C.T., André, E.: Natural interaction with culturally adaptive virtual characters. Journal on Multimodal User Interfaces 6, 39–47 (2012)

23. Küblbeck, C., Ernst, A.: Face detection and tracking in video sequences using the modifiedcensus transformation. Image Vision Comput. 24(6), 564–572 (2006)

Towards Understanding the Nonverbal Signatures of Engagement in Super Mario Bros

Noor Shaker[1] and Mohammad Shaker[2]

[1] IT University of Copenhagen, Rued Langaards Vej 7, 2300 Copenhagen, Denmark
[2] Independent Researcher, Damascus, Syria
nosh@itu.dk, mohammadshakergtr@gmail.com

Abstract. In this paper, we present an approach for predicting users' level of engagement from nonverbal cues within a game environment. We use a data corpus collected from 28 participants (152 minutes of video recording) playing the popular platform game *Super Mario Bros*. The richness of the corpus allows extraction of several visual and facial expression features that were utilised as indicators of players' affects as captured by players' self-reports. Neuroevolution preference learning is used to construct accurate models of player experience that approximate the relationship between extracted features and reported engagement. The method is supported by a feature selection technique for choosing the relevant subset of features. Different setup settings were implemented to analyse the impact of the type of the features and the position of the extraction window on the modelling accuracy. The results obtained show that highly accurate models can be constructed (with accuracies up to 96.82%) and that players' nonverbal behaviour towards the end of the game is the most correlated with engagement. The framework presented is part of a bigger picture where the generated models are utilised to tailor content generation to a player's particular needs and playing characteristics.

Keywords: Player experience modelling, affect recognition, nonverbal behaviour, affect modelling, facial expressions, neuroevolution preference learning.

1 Introduction

Analysing users' interaction with a digital interface has been the focus of many research studies. One of the main motivations behind investing in this area is to keep the user engaged during the interaction. This direction has drawn significant attention from both the Affective Computing community and Human-Computer Interaction. Motivated by the current trend towards understanding and modelling users' interaction and ultimately generating immersive experience, this paper investigates the relationship between players' nonverbal behaviour during an in-game interaction and their experienced affective states elicited as a result of this interaction. We envision a game where the proposed approach can be employed to effectively capture players' affects as they interact with a game

V. Dimitrova et al. (Eds.): UMAP 2014, LNCS 8538, pp. 423–434, 2014.

and efficiently use this information to alter the content according to a specific player's needs consequently providing a more engaging experience.

In games, such as in many other applications, the engagement value of content is crucial to its success. While players' skill and expertise vary over time, and in order to accommodate for the differences between players in terms of playing characteristics, behaviour and preferences, the game should be able to efficiently detect these differences and automatically adjust its content so that a personalised engaging experience can be created.

In this study we investigate the effectiveness of different visual and facial expression features as indicators of player's level of engagement while playing the popular 2D platform game *Super Mario Bros.* A dataset of 28 subjects was collected for this study and experiments were conducted with several settings to analyse the impact of the feature type, feature extraction and selection on the classification accuracy. Models of player experience are constructed as classifiers and neuroevolutionary preference learning is implemented as a modelling approach.

The main findings can be summarised as follows: (1) players' nonverbal behaviour carries rich information about the interaction experience and consequently they can be used to accurately predict the engagement value of content, (2) the importance of visual cues differs along the game session; players' visual reactions towards the end of the game is found to be the most relevant for predicting engagement.

This paper is structured as follows: section 2 summarises the previous research efforts; section 3 provides detail information about the dataset collected and the tool used; section 4 describes the modelling methodology followed to relate features extracted from players' visual behaviour to reported engagement; section 5 illustrates the different settings for feature extraction and the experiments conducted to construct models of player experience; finally, the experimental results are presented and discussed in section 6.

2   Related Work

There are many studies in the literature dealing with the problem of user state estimation during digital interaction. Recent research in computer vision techniques has discussed a number of methods incorporating notions such as body and head movements [2], eye gaze [10] and facial expressions [9] as indicators of user affective states with varying accuracies depending on the settings, application and the modality used. Furthermore, several psycho-physiological signals such as heart rate and skin conductance are found to correlate with affective states in response to visual stimuli [25,14].

Recently, there has been an increasing attention given to detect users' emotional states while interacting with a game. Players' performance captured through recorded actions and interactions with game events is usually utilised as an indicator of player's affect [18,20,5]. Physiological signals are used in some studies to investigate the relationship between this modality, player behaviour and affects [16,26]. Measuring affect using physiological signals usually requires specialised hardware, which is often expensive and hard to calibrate. As a result, related approaches may be efficient in terms of recognising player affect, but are extremely problematic to deploy in mass scales and for commercial uses. On the other hand, affect estimation approaches based on video sequences taken from low-end cameras utilise hardware that most gamers already possess and do not impose any additional requirements.

The use of verbal and nonverbal affective communication has led to advances in realising real-time multi-modal affective interactions between agents and learners in Intelligent Tutoring System and Learning Companion technologies [4,11]. In games, facial expression has been used for investigating affects with promising results [6,8]. Features extracted from multiple modalities, including players' actions and visual reactions, have been investigated [22,24,1].

The increased diversification of users demographics, needs, skills and preferences has increased the importance of experience personalisation. In the domain of games, player experience modelling [27] studies that rely on single or multiple modalities of user input (see [23,26,15,11] among many) have provided some initial benchmark solutions towards achieving such a goal. The use of computational models of engagement, among other affective states, has been investigated in several studies to predict the appeal of specific piece of content to a particular player [16,26,22,20] .

In this paper, we take a further step in this direction by investigating nonverbal cues extracted through different settings. We build on our previous attempts on modelling player experience [22,24] and we extend it through: (1) investigating new types of visual and facial expression features (while in [22] we experimented with different attributes of the head movement such as the average, fluidity and energy, in this paper we focus on the bias of the head in the x- and y- coordinate, we extract new features related to the eye and the mouth and we utilise several facial expression states); (2) experimenting with different settings for feature extraction and (3) analysing the importance of the portion of the session segment from which the best features can be extracted for predicting engagement.

3   Experimental Set-Up and Protocol

In the following sections we present the procedure followed to collect the dataset and the tool used to process the data gathered.

3.1   Material and Setup

In order to study the relationship between users' interaction within a game environment and their affective states, we conducted a survey experiment where users were asked to play a clone of the popular game *Super Mario Bros* while interaction and self-assessments of a number of affective states were gathered.

The gameplay in our testbed game constitutes of moving the main character, *Mario*, through a 2D environment while collecting rewarding items, killing enemies, and avoiding obstacles. The character can achieve these objectives by doing simple actions such as running, jumping, shooting and ducking. The main goal of the game is to reach the end of the level with minimum lose of lives and maximum number of collected rewards.

The study was conducted in a lab environment in Denmark and Greece. Data was collected from users who played individually in a room where lighting conditions were typical of an office environment and interruption was kept to minimum. The system is composed of a laptop where the software was installed, equipped with a High Definition camera (Canon Legria S11) for video recording. A detailed description of the dataset used can be found in [12,21].

3.2 Study Procedure

For the purpose of this study, data from 28 participants (21 male; player age varied from 22 to 48 years) was recorded. Subjects are seated in front of a computer screen for video recording. Each session consists of playing at least a pair of two games followed by a post-experience game survey design to collect subject self-reports of *engagement*. Self-assessments were collected using the 4-Alternative Forced Choice (4-AFC) questionnaire protocol proposed in [29]. According to this protocol, after completing a pair of two games A and B, the subject is asked to report the preferred game given four options: A is preferred to B; B is preferred to A; both are preferred equally; neither is preferred (both are equally not-preferred). Each participant played three pairs on average resulting in a total of 66 valid pairs and 152 minutes of gameplay. For detailed information about the experimental protocol followed, the reader may refer to [21,12].

3.3 Tools: SHORE Engine

SHORE[1] (Sophisticated High speed Object Recognition Engine) [13] is a recognition engine that enables the detection of objects and faces. SHORE enables feature extraction from both images and videos. The list of features that can be extracted by SHORE includes the position of the face, eyes, nose and mouth, information about whether the eyes or the mouth are open or closed and recognition of facial expressions (the set of recognised expressions includes: happiness, sadness, anger and surprised). All of the above mentioned features can be extracted in realtime. SHORE engine processes a video using 5 frames per seconds. We use the C++ interface of the engine. All the videos recorded were post-processed with the engine to extract visual and facial expression features as will be described in the following sections.

4   Method

The first step towards creating a more engaging experience is to effectively recognise whether the player is enjoying an piece of content. One way to achieve this

---

[1] http://www.iis.fraunhofer.de/de/bf/bsy/fue/isyst.html

goal is to construct models of player experience derived from the in-game interaction where content is annotated with user experience tags. Several machine learning techniques have been utilised to build such models including Support Vector Machine and Bayesian Inference [30]. In a comparison study, Neuroevolutionary Preference Learning (NPL)) [7,30] showed capability of constructing models with accuracies surpass those achieved by the other methods in a similar settings to the one at hand [30]. Therefore in this paper, NPL is used to approximate the function between nonverbal features and reported affective preferences.

In the following sections, we describe the procedure followed to build the player experience models using NPL.

4.1 Feature Extraction

The first step towards understanding the relationship between reported affects and players' nonverbal reactions while interacting with a game is to extract representative features that can be utilised as indicators of players' behaviour in reaction to game events. This work is motivated by previous attempts where expressive nonverbal behaviour is linked to user engagement; namely eye gaze and smiles were found to be correlated with user engagement and interest while interaction with a robot [4,19].

In this study, we track head location and changes in the properties of the eyes and the mouth. More specifically, we calculate the averages and standard deviations of the followings: head position on the $x-$ and $y-$axis, the closeness of the left and right eyes and the openness degree of the mouth (the full list of features and their description are presented in Table 1). We call this set of nonverbal features *visual reaction* features (VR). The use of these features is inspired by earlier work where visual features were found to be related to arousal [3].

Along with VR features, we employ another set of *Facial expression* (FE) features. This set includes the average and standard deviation degrees of the following states: happiness, sadness, anger, and surprise.

When constructing the Player Experience Models (PEMs) we hope that these features will correlate with reported affects, i.e. we aim at exploring content-behaviour relationships that can be utilised to predict players' emotional state of engagement from his/her visual cues. For example, the player might experience a moderate degree of happiness and a steady head movement when the game starts, these states, however, might change during the course of gameplay and a state of surprise combined with a sudden movement of the head might arise as the player encounters an enemy. A game that comprises these two states, among some others, can then be annotated as being highly engaging by the PEMs.

A total of 18 features were extracted (averages and standard deviations of all the above mentioned features) as can be seen in Table 1. We experimented with different settings of the frames from which these features are extracted as will be seen in Section 5.

Table 1. Visual reaction and facial expression features extracted from the data recorded. Average and standard deviation values are extracted for each feature.

Feature	Description
Visual reaction	
h_x	Bias of head location on the x-axis compared to the location of the head in the first frame
h_y	Bias of head location on the y-axis compared to the location of the head in the first frame
$leftEye_c$	Closeness degree of the left eye
$rightEye_c$	Closeness degree of the right eye
$mouth_o$	Openness degree of the mouth
Facial expression	
H	Degree of happiness
S	Degree of sadness
A	Degree of anger
U	Degree of surprise

4.2   Player Experience Modelling

As mentioned earlier, neuroevolutionary preference learning is chosen as a modelling approach in our study. In NPL, a genetic algorithm evolves an Artificial Neural Network (ANN) so that its output matches the pairwise preferences in the dataset. The input of the ANN is a set of extracted features.

As a preprocessing step, all features extracted are uniformly normalised to [0,1] using standard max-min normalisation. These features are then used as inputs for feature selection and ANN model optimisation. The steps followed to construct the models can be summarised as follows:

- Feature selection: We use Sequential Forward Selection (SFS) [28] to select the relevant subset of features for predicting reported engagement [30]. The simplest form of ANN, that is a single-layer perception was implemented to achieve this.
- Feature space expansion: The feature subset derived from the first phase is used as the input to small multi-layer perceptron (MLP) models of one two-neuron hidden layer and SFS selects additional features from the remaining set of features based on their classification accuracy.
- Optimising topology: In the last phase, the topology of the MLP models is optimised. This process starts with a small two hidden-neuron MLP and the network topology gradually increases up to two hidden layers consisting of 10 hidden neurons each. The network that achieves the best accuracy is then chosen as the final model.

The quality of a feature subset and the performance of each MLP is obtained through the average classification accuracy in three independent runs using 3-fold cross validation across ten evolutionary trials. The data was partitioned into folds such that the likelihood of a subject appearing in more than one fold is minimised. We use a population of 100 individuals and we run evolution for 20 generations. A probabilistic rank-based selection scheme is used, with higher ranked individuals having higher probability of being chosen as parents. Finally, reproduction is performed via uniform crossover, followed by Gaussian mutation of 1% probability. All of these parameters were chosen as a result of a tuning process.

5   Experiments

In order to analyse the relationship between the extracted features and players' reported engagement and to investigate the significance of the type of features and the importance of context information, we construct models on three different settings for feature extraction as follows (a summary can be seen in Table 2):

- VR_{all}: The features used as input to these models are VR features extracted from the full sessions, i.e. the average and standard deviation values of all features presented in Table 1 are calculated from all frames for each game played (note that each game session consists of a maximum of three trails). This setting is considered in order to minimise the effect of habituation where the player becomes more familiar with the game over time.
- VR_{events}: As players' expressivity appears to increase during certain events, we considered features extracted during certain gameplay events as described below:

  - When the player loses a life.
  - When the player kills an enemy by stomping on it.
  - When the player starts or ends a critical move: jump, duck, run, and move left or right.
  - When the player interacts with a game object.

  These features are calculated for a period of 3 frames before and after the corresponding events.
- All_{wind}: In this category, VR and FE feature values are calculated from the players' last attempt only in an attempt to minimise the habituation effect. Similar to VR_{events}, the values are considered only when specific game events occur. We also introduced a windowing factor: the last trail is partitioned into three equal-sized windows and the values of all features are calculated from each window separately resulting in a total of $18 * 3 = 54$ features. Three separated models are then constructed for each window permitting investigation of the part of the session that carries the most significant information for predicting reported affective state of engagement. More specifically, the models constructed from information extracted from the first window encompass details about players' behaviour at the beginning of the game and the importance of the initial behaviour and content on the

Table 2. The settings for the three types of models constructed

	Feature extraction frames	Game session	Input features
VR_{all}	All frames	Three trails	VR
VR_{events}	Three frames before and three after specific gameplay events	Three trails	VR
All_{wind}	Three frames before and three after specific gameplay events	Last trail	VR + FE

experienced engagement. The significance of the outcome of the game on the level of engagement felt, however, can be captured through the models constructed from the third window.

6   Results and Analysis

Several models are constructed from the different types of features and the various settings of feature extraction. For each feature input space, models with different subset of features as selected by the feature selection methods are constructed. The models also differ in their complexity as depicted by the various network topologies obtained for the best performing models. Table 3 presents the different models constructed. Each column stands for a model build from a specific set of features (VR, FE or both) as input. The features selected using SLPs and the corresponding best and average performance over 50 runs are presented for each model (row 2-4). The models are further improved by selecting features using simple MLP (rows 5-7). Finally, using the selected subset of features, the models were optimised for best prediction accuracy and the obtained topologies (row 8) and performance are presented (row 9-10). In general, models of very high accuracies are obtained with a performance up to 96%.

As can be seen in Table 3. The best accuracy obtained is the one from the models constructed from the last window in the session using both VR and FE as input features. It is worth noticing however that only VR features are selected with no FE features. These models have a moderate network size consisting of one hidden layer of eight neurons. An interesting observation is that all the features are selected through a single-layer perceptron indicating a simple relationship between the features and the experienced level of engagement. Three features only out of the 18 extracted features are selected, two of which are related to the closeness of the eyes and the third captures the shift of the head along the x-axis. This can be understood as an implicit indication of the importance of the outcome of the game (whether it is winning or losing) which appears to be reflected in players' visual reactions as closing the eyes and posing the head. The results align with our observation of the video recordings which showed a common pattern of closed eyes and head poses when winning and losing. Example instances of such cases are presented in Figure 1.

Players' FE appears to be an important predictor of engagement in the middle of the game. Specifically, the level of recognised happiness and sadness are found to be correlated with experienced engagement.

High prediction accuracies are also obtained when constructing models from VR features only as inputs, both when calculated during specific game events and when all frames are considered. More features and more complex topologies, however, are observed in the latter case.

The worst accuracies obtained are the ones for the models constructed from features from the first window in the sessions. This implies that players' visual reactions at the beginning of the game is trivial for predicting the level of engagement felt compared to their visual behaviour towards the end of the game.

Table 3. Features selected from the set of visual reaction and facial expression features for predicting engagement. The table also presents the corresponding average and best performance values obtained from the ANN models' and the best models' ANN topologies. The ANN topologies are presented in the form: number of neurons in the first hidden layer−number of neurons in the second hidden layer.

	VR_{all}	VR_{events}	All_{wind}		
			1st window	2nd window	3rd window
SLP features	$mouth_o\_avg$ re_c_avg h_y_std	$mouth_o\_avg$ $rightEye_c\_avg$	h_x_avg h_y_avg	$leftEye_c\_std$ H_avg S_std H_std	h_x_avg $rightEye_c\_avg$ $leftEye_c\_avg$
$SLP_{perf}\%$	65.77	64.44	41.21	68.78	70.63
$SLP_{max}\%$	69.69	71.42	48.48	80.30	77.77
MLP features	$rightEye_c\_std$ $leftEye_c\_avg$ h_x_avg	$mouth_o\_std$	S_avg	-	-
$MLP_{perf}\%$	82.12	84.28	60.90	-	-
$MLP_{max}\%$	92.42	92.06	66.66	-	-
ANN Topology	8_2	2_6	6_0	4_0	8_0
$MLP_{opt}\%$	81.57	83.14	62	84.03	86.09
$MLP_{opt\_max}\%$	92.42	93.65	72.72	93.93	96.82

| (a) | (b) | (c) | (d) |

Fig. 1. Example instances from the video recordings of subjects playing the testbed games. (a) and (b) show head pose and eyes condition when winning the game while (c) and (d) corresponds to visual reactions when losing.

7   Conclusions and Future Directions

In this paper we empirically investigated whether users' visual reactions and facial expressions can be efficiently utilised as indicators of engagement when playing a computer game. To facilitate such analysis, a large dataset of video recordings from 58 players playing the 2D game *Super Mario Bros* was collected. The dataset consists of gameplay sessions annotated with players' self-assessment of engagement. Eighteen representative visual reaction and facial expression features are then extracted from the gameplay session for each subject. These features form the input for classifiers that are trained to predict reported engagement from the extracted features. The experiments conducted included several settings for feature extraction, the type of features and the position of the extraction window. The results obtained show that models of very high accuracies (around 96%) can be constructed using visual reaction features. The results also highlight the importance of some of the features compared to others. When studying the best segment for feature extraction that yields the highest accuracy, the results show that the most accurate models can be built from visual reaction features extracted from the last portion of the game. This finding signifies the importance of the content presented towards the end of the game and indicates that the level of engagement felt correlates with the outcome of the game.

Our findings align with studies reported in the literature that concluded that nonverbal channels carry informative affective cues [11,17]. However, although models of high accuracies are constructed, understanding these models is not trivial due to the complex nature of neural networks. Therefore, investigating other, more expressive, approaches such as Bayesian Inference or SVM constitutes an important future direction towards understanding the link between nonverbal behaviour and affects. Moreover, the models built are average models across all participants, therefore it is interesting to investigate whether different results could be obtained after clustering players according to their expressiveness and/or demographics .

The study presented in this paper is the first step towards generating user-adapted content. The player experience models constructed can be ultimately used to predict the appeal of a piece of content to a specific player given her visual behaviour. Based on this information, adjustments can be made to the content in real-time so that the game will become more engaging.

Another future direction is to investigate the use of fused features from multiple modalities such as features representing content and players' in-game actions. Previous attempts showed that models constructed from fused features are usually more accurate than those built from a single modality [22,24,16,1].

References

1. Abadi, M.K., Staiano, J., Cappelletti, A., Zancanaro, M., Sebe, N.: Multimodal engagement classification for affective cinema. In: Humaine Association Conference on Affective Computing and Intelligent Interaction, pp. 411–416. IEEE (2013)

2. Asteriadis, S., Tzouveli, P., Karpouzis, K., Kollias, S.: Estimation of behavioral user state based on eye gaze and head poseapplication in an e-learning environment. Multimedia Tools and Applications 41(3), 469–493 (2009)
3. Caridakis, G., Castellano, G., Kessous, L., Raouzaiou, A., Malatesta, L., Asteriadis, S., Karpouzis, K.: Multimodal emotion recognition from expressive faces, body gestures and speech. In: Artificial Intelligence and Innovations 2007: From Theory to Applications, pp. 375–388. Springer (2007)
4. Castellano, G., Pereira, A., Leite, I., Paiva, A., McOwan, P.W.: Detecting user engagement with a robot companion using task and social interaction-based features. In: Proceedings of the 2009 International Conference on Multimodal Interfaces, pp. 119–126. ACM (2009)
5. Conati, C., Maclaren, H.: Empirically building and evaluating a probabilistic model of user affect. User Modeling and User-Adapted Interaction 19(3), 267–303 (2009)
6. Mello, D., Craig, S.K., Graesser, S.D., Multi-method, A.C.: assessment of affective experience and expression during deep learning. Int. J. Learn. Technol. 4(3/4), 165–187 (2009)
7. Fürnkranz, J., Hüllermeier, E.: Pairwise preference learning and ranking. In: Lavrač, N., Gamberger, D., Todorovski, L., Blockeel, H. (eds.) ECML 2003. LNCS (LNAI), vol. 2837, pp. 145–156. Springer, Heidelberg (2003)
8. Grafsgaard, J.F., Boyer, K.E., Lester, J.C.: Toward a machine learning framework for understanding affective tutorial interaction. In: Cerri, S.A., Clancey, W.J., Papadourakis, G., Panourgia, K. (eds.) ITS 2012. LNCS, vol. 7315, pp. 52–58. Springer, Heidelberg (2012)
9. Ioannou, S., Caridakis, G., Karpouzis, K., Kollias, S.: Robust feature detection for facial expression recognition. Journal on Image and Video Processing (2) (2007)
10. Jennett, C., Cox, A.L., Cairns, P., Dhoparee, S., Epps, A., Tijs, T., Walton, A.: Measuring and defining the experience of immersion in games. International Journal of Human-Computer Studies 66(9), 641–661 (2008)
11. Kapoor, A., Burleson, W., Picard, R.: Automatic prediction of frustration. International Journal of Human-Computer Studies (8), 724–736 (2007)
12. Karpouzis, K., Shaker, N., Yannakakis, G.N., Asteriadis, S.: The platformer experience dataset. IEEE Transactions on Computational Intelligence and AI in Games (2014)
13. Küblbeck, C., Ernst, A.: Face detection and tracking in video sequences using the modifiedcensus transformation. Image and Vision Computing 24(6), 564–572 (2006)
14. Lisetti, C.L., Nasoz, F.: Using noninvasive wearable computers to recognize human emotions from physiological signals. EURASIP Journal on Applied Signal Processing 2004, 1672–1687 (2004)
15. Mandryk, R., Inkpen, K., Calvert, T.: Using psychophysiological techniques to measure user experience with entertainment technologies. Behaviour & Information Technology (2), 141–158 (2006)
16. Martinez, H., Yannakakis, G.: Mining multimodal sequential patterns: A case study on affect detection. In: Proceedings of the 13th International Conference in Multimodal Interaction, ICMI 2011, Alicante. ACM Press (November 2011)
17. McDaniel, B., D'Mello, S., King, B., Chipman, P., Tapp, K., Graesser, A.: Facial features for affective state detection in learning environments. In: Proceedings of the 29th Annual Cognitive Science Society, pp. 467–472 (2007)
18. Pedersen, C., Togelius, J., Yannakakis, G.N.: Modeling player experience for content creation. IEEE Transactions on Computational Intelligence and AI in Games 2(1), 54–67 (2010)

19. Peters, C., Asteriadis, S., Karpouzis, K., de Sevin, E.: Towards a real-time gaze-based shared attention for a virtual agent. In: Workshop on Affective Interaction in Natural Environments (AFFINE), ACM International Conference on Multimodal Interfaces, ICMI 2008 (2008)

20. Shaker, N., Yannakakis, G.N., Togelius, J.: Towards Automatic Personalized Content Generation for Platform Games. In: Proceedings of the AAAI Conference on Artificial Intelligence and Interactive Digital Entertainment, AIIDE (2010)

21. Shaker, N., Asteriadis, S., Yannakakis, G.N., Karpouzis, K.: A game-based corpus for analysing the interplay between game context and player experience. In: D'Mello, S., Graesser, A., Schuller, B., Martin, J.-C. (eds.) ACII 2011, Part II. LNCS, vol. 6975, pp. 547–556. Springer, Heidelberg (2011)

22. Shaker, N., Asteriadis, S., Yannakakis, G.N., Karpouzis, K.: Fusing visual and behavioral cues for modeling user experience in games. IEEE Transactions on Cybernetics 43(6), 1519–1531 (2013)

23. Shaker, N., Togelius, J., Yannakakis, G.N., Weber, B., Shimizu, T., Hashiyama, T., Sorenson, N., Pasquier, P., Mawhorter, P., Takahashi, G., Smith, G., Baumgarten, R.: The 2010 Mario AI championship: Level generation track. IEEE Transactions on Computational Intelligence and Games (2011)

24. Shaker, N., Yannakakis, G.N., Togelius, J.: Crowd-sourcing the aesthetics of platform games. IEEE Transactions on Computational Intelligence and AI in Games (2013)

25. Soleymani, M., Lichtenauer, J., Pun, T., Pantic, M.: A multimodal database for affect recognition and implicit tagging. IEEE Transactions on Affective Computing 3(1), 42–55 (2012)

26. Tognetti, S., Garbarino, M., Bonanno, A.T., Matteucci, M., Bonarini, A.: Enjoyment recognition from physiological data in a car racing game. In: Proceedings of the 3rd international Workshop on Affective Interaction in Natural Environments, pp. 3–8. ACM (2010)

27. Yannakakis, G.N., Togelius, J.: Experience-Driven Procedural Content Generation. IEEE Transactions on Affective Computing (2011)

28. Yannakakis, G.N., Hallam, J.: Entertainment modeling through physiology in physical play. Int. J. Hum.-Comput. Stud. 66, 741–755 (2008)

29. Yannakakis, G.N., Maragoudakis, M., Hallam, J.: Preference learning for cognitive modeling: a case study on entertainment preferences. Trans. Sys. Man Cyber. Part A 39, 1165–1175 (2009)

30. Yannakakis, G.N., Maragoudakis, M., Hallam, J.: Preference learning for cognitive modeling: a case study on entertainment preferences. Trans. Sys. Man Cyber. Part A 39, 1165–1175 (November 2009)

Towards Personalized Multilingual Information Access - Exploring the Browsing and Search Behavior of Multilingual Users

Ben Steichen[1], M. Rami Ghorab[2], Alexander O'Connor[2],
Séamus Lawless[2], and Vincent Wade[2]

[1] Department of Computer Science, University of British Columbia, Vancouver, Canada
[2] Centre for Next Generation Localisation, Knowledge & Data Engineering Group,
School of Computer Science & Statistics, Trinity College Dublin, Ireland
steichen@cs.ubc.ca, {rami.ghorab,seamus.lawless,alex.oconnor,
vincent.wade}@scss.tcd.ie

Abstract. The shift from the originally English-language-dominated web to-wards a truly global *world wide web* has generated a pressing need to develop novel solutions that address *multilingual user diversity*. In particular, many web users today are polyglots, i.e. they are proficient in more than one language. However, little is known about the browsing and search habits of such users, and even less about how to best assist their multilingual behaviors through appropriate systems and tools. In order to gain a better understanding, this paper presents a survey of 385 polyglot web users, focusing specifically on the relationship between multiple language proficiency and browsing/search language choice. Results from the survey indicate that polyglot users make significant use of multiple languages during their daily browsing and searching, and that contextual factors such as language proficiency, usage purpose, and topic domain have a significant influence on their language choice and frequency. The paper provides a detailed analysis regarding each of these factors, and offers insights about how to support multilingual users through novel *Personalized Multilingual Information Access* systems.

Keywords: Personalization, Multilingual Information Access, User Study.

1 Introduction

A key challenge for information access systems lies in their ability to tailor the retrieval, composition, and presentation of heterogeneous information to diverse user needs, abilities, and preferences. In particular, with the unrelenting rise in global web usage, such systems increasingly need to cater for a growing variety of user language skills and preferences. For example, recent statistics from Internet World Stats[1] indicate that 45% of Internet users are now from Asia, and that there will soon be more native Chinese speakers on the web than native English speakers. An important

---

[1] www.internetworldstats.com/stats.htm

V. Dimitrova et al. (Eds.): UMAP 2014, LNCS 8538, pp. 435–446, 2014.
© Springer International Publishing Switzerland 2014

development related to this diversification is the fact that users themselves are becoming increasingly polyglot, i.e. people are increasingly proficient in more than one language. For example, statistics about language education in the European Union show that on average 94.6% of secondary education pupils now learn English in general programs, and 64.7% learn two or more languages[2]. This trend is equally evident throughout the developing world, and it is estimated that there are many more people who know English as a second language than there are native speakers[3].

Despite this continuous development towards global polyglotism, information access systems generally ignore their users' multiple language abilities and preferences. For example, in order to access information in multiple languages, users typically need to switch between different versions of an information portal, or are required to conduct separate searches for each of their languages. Our research advocates for novel solutions that support a user's multilingual abilities and preferences through *personalized* language support. In order to build such systems and tools, it is necessary to understand and model the different user aspects and contextual factors of multilingual web use. For example, while users are increasingly multilingual, it is not known whether they actually feel the need to make use of their multilingual skills for daily web browsing and searching. Likewise, there are no studies investigating if users exhibit the same interests and preferences across each of their languages.

This paper aims to tackle these open issues via the following research questions:

- **RQ1**: To what extent do polyglots use multiple languages to browse and search the web?
- **RQ2**: How are language choice and usage frequency affected by the user's proficiency in different languages?
- **RQ3**: How are language choice and usage frequency affected by usage purpose and topic domain?

Through a detailed analysis of a survey involving 385 polyglot participants, this paper is able to uncover the complex relationship between the various user and contextual factors, thereby providing valuable insights for designing and building novel *Personalized Multilingual Information Access (PMIA)* systems.

2   Related Work

The goal of our research is to design information access systems that tailor to each individual user's language abilities, as well as to any other user characteristics (e.g. culture, domain expertise) and contexts (e.g. intent, topic) that influence what and how information should be retrieved and presented. Our work thereby lies at the intersection of *Personalized Information Access* and *Multilingual Information Access*.

Personalized Information Access (PIA). PIA systems are exhibited in several areas in the literature, such as Web search [1], eLearning [2], and news dissemination [3].

---

[2] epp.eurostat.ec.europa.eu/statistics_explained/index.php/
Foreign_language_learning_statistics

[3] www.britishcouncil.org/learning-research-english-next.pdf

A key component of these systems is the user model [4], which is used to represent information such as the user's prior knowledge, interests, personal preferences, or demographics (e.g. location, language, etc.). By automatically capturing and storing such information through a variety of interaction and data representation methods [5], PIA systems are able to adapt both the type of content presented to the user, as well as the way in which content is presented, thereby increasing user satisfaction and efficiency when interacting with the system [6].

The user models in these PIA systems typically represent user information in a monolingual fashion, thus not taking into account the various language abilities and preferences of polyglot users. By contrast, our research argues for the development of *PMIA* systems, which, in addition to modeling and adapting to the various aspects typically addressed in PIA systems, should take into account each user's language-dependent abilities, preferences, and interests.

Multilingual Information Access (MLIA). In the field of Information Retrieval (IR), the majority of research involving multiple languages has been concerned with the notion of *Cross-language Information Retrieval (CLIR)*, i.e. retrieving relevant information (documents) in languages that are different from the query language [7]. *MLIA* takes a step further by additionally investigating how to present this information and how to make it more accessible to users from different linguistic/cultural backgrounds [8]. This involves, but is not limited to, the following three aspects: (1) investigating ways to improve the tools and techniques for Cross-/Multilingual Information Retrieval, such as enhancing query translation/disambiguation [9, 10] and enhancing Machine Translation [11]; (2) investigating improvements to the user interface [12, 13] and (3) gaining a better understanding of multilingual user search behavior and how users interact with information on the web. The study reported in our paper particularly contributes to this third aspect of MLIA, by investigating the specific browsing and search behavior of polyglot users.

In relation to this aspect, the authors in [14, 15] investigated the connection between content creation (amount of content available in different languages) and content consumption (the number of web users who correspond to those languages). They also analyzed the logs of a multilingual website with the objective of investigating the behavior of users from different linguistic backgrounds. By contrast, our paper investigates the degree to which polyglot users generally browse and search the web in multiple languages. In addition, we examine this behavior with respect to detailed aspects pertaining to the users' language proficiency, the type of content they seek/consume in each language, and the frequency by which they seek/consume it.

Most similar to our work, the study carried out in [16] adopted a qualitative approach to exploring how monolingual and multilingual users in university communities (in the UK and Spain) search for information using one or two languages in the digital libraries domain. While their results provided some initial qualitative insights into multiple language usage (e.g. students from social science and linguistics are most inclined to search across multiple languages), we extend this work in a number of ways: (1) the participants of our questionnaire are significantly more diverse in terms of occupation and countries of origin/residence; (2) we have a larger sample of multilingual participants and the number of languages they speak (up to 4 languages per user); (3) we consider general web browsing and web search; and (4) we adopted both qualitative and detailed quantitative approaches to be able to quantify *the degree to which multiple languages are currently used by polyglots*, and *for what purpose* (including, for example, correlations between a user's proficiency in each language and the frequency by which users browse/search for content in each language, etc.).

3   Methodology

In order to explore the online behavior of polyglot users, we designed a questionnaire focusing specifically on their multilingual browsing and search language choices and frequencies. The first part of the questionnaire consisted of a set of questions about participants' demographic information, (e.g. age, occupation, country of origin/residence), as well as their respective language skills. Specifically, we asked users (i) to name and rank the languages they are most proficient in (up to a maximum of 4 languages), and (ii) to indicate their proficiency in each of them on a scale from 1 ("basic understanding of the vocabulary and grammar") to 5 ("native proficiency"). The second part then focused on participants' multilingual *browsing* and *search* behavior. We first asked participants to indicate whether they use *only one*, *several*, or *all* of their languages to browse and/or search the web. Following this, participants indicated specifically for each language *how often* they use the language for browsing/searching, as well as *for what purpose/topics* they use this language (both using predefined purpose/topic domain categories and free text responses).

The online questionnaire was distributed widely using international mailing lists, as well as several social media channels. Participants were required to be proficient in at least two languages, with one of them being English. This allowed us to analyze the particular importance of English, given that it represents the most popular foreign language in the world[4], and continues to have the largest percentage of web content[5].

4   Results

In total, 448 participants took part in the survey, of which 385 participants completed both parts. We first provide the general demographics of this participant population (section 4.1), followed by a detailed analysis of their multilingual browsing and search frequency (4.2). We then investigate the impact of language rank/proficiency (4.3), followed by the impact of browsing/search purpose and topic domain (4.4).

4.1   Participant Demographics

The majority of participants were either in the age groups of 18-24 (26.75%) or 25-34 (52.73%), and there was a slightly higher percentage of male participants (55.84%) compared to female participants. Given the distribution of the survey through several academic mailing lists, there was a relatively high number of participants who are currently in an academic occupation (e.g. student, professor, researcher – 55.84%).

---

[4] http://www.ethnologue.com/
[5] http://w3techs.com/technologies/overview/content_language/all

There was a large variation in terms of participants' geographical and linguistic backgrounds, with a total of 68 different countries of origin, 32 different countries of residence, and proficiencies in 61 different languages. All 385 participants were at least bilingual, and many of them were also proficient in a third language (61.56%) and even a fourth language (27.01%).

In terms of first ranked language, i.e. the language that a participant had ranked as their most proficient language (hereafter: L1), there were a total of 34 different languages. For their second (L2), third (L3) and fourth (L4) ranked languages there were 35, 33, and 28 different languages respectively. The most common languages for L1 were Arabic (31.69%), English (24.68%), and Chinese (8.57%), for L2 the dominant language was English (69.35%), and for L3/L4, the most common languages were French (31.65% for L3, 28.85% for L4), German (12.66% for L3, 13.46% for L4), and Spanish (9.28% for L3, 10.58% for L4).

4.2   Multilingual Browsing and Search Frequency (RQ1)

Overall, we found that the vast majority of polyglots make use of multiple languages when looking for information on the web. In particular, only 14% of users indicated that they use *only one* of their languages for browsing, whereas 42.34% indicated that they use *some* of their languages, and 42.86% saying that they use *all* of their languages. Similarly, only 17% of users indicated that they use *only one* language with general web search engines, 38.70% use *some*, and 42.86% use *all* of their languages.

In addition, we were also interested in comparing the particular behaviors of participants who had/had not specified English as their L1. As shown in Figure 1, the proportion of participants' browsing/searching in *only one* language is much bigger for English L1 users (32.63% for browsing, 40% for searching) compared to non-English L1 users (7.93% for browsing, 10% for searching).

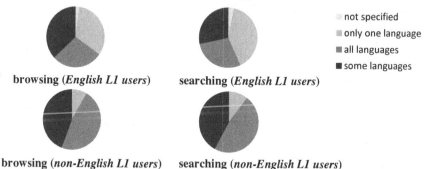

browsing (*English L1 users*)   searching (*English L1 users*)

not specified
only one language
all languages
some languages

browsing (*non-English L1 users*)   searching (*non-English L1 users*)

Fig. 1. Multilingual browsing and searching behavior for *English L1 participants* and *non-English L1 participants*

This indicates that users who ranked English as their first language are less inclined to browse/search in other languages, possibly due to English serving their information needs for both work/study and personal-related information (see section 4.4 for more details). Nonetheless, the very high overall percentage of users browsing and searching in multiple languages indicates that there is indeed a great opportunity to provide new solutions that specifically support multilingual browsing and searching.

An additional trend that can be observed in Figure 1 is that the proportion of users *browsing* in multiple languages is slightly larger compared to *searching*. When analyzing the open-text comments of the survey, we found that a number of participants indicated that their proficiency in certain languages (particularly in L3 and L4) is only good enough for browsing websites (or sometimes just watching videos), but not for expressing their information needs in search queries in those languages. Furthermore, some participants mentioned that the unavailability of supporting input facilities, such as localized keyboards, is the reason why they would use a certain language less frequently when searching the web (regardless of their language proficiency).

4.3   Overall Impact of Language Rank/Proficiency (RQ2)

In addition to the overall browsing and search frequencies of polyglot users, we were interested in the more detailed relationship between language rank, language proficiency, and browsing/search frequency. To this end, we analyzed pairwise correlations between each of these factors using Spearman's rank correlation coefficient.

As to be expected, language rank (1,2,3,4) and proficiency (5,4,3,2,1) were strongly (negatively) correlated (correlation -0.795, p<.000). Interestingly, we found that for their second ranked language, many participants still indicated very strong proficiencies, with 85% of L2 proficiencies being 4 or higher. However, we found that L3 and L4 proficiencies were generally much lower for our participant population.

When asked to specifically indicate how often they use each of their languages, we found that the majority of participants use L1 and L2 'every day' (frequency code *4* in Figure 2 – 63.45%) for browsing (71.61% for L1, 70.34% for L2) and searching (63.44% for L1, 66.58% for L2), or at least 'a few times a week' (freq. *3*). By contrast, third and fourth ranked languages are used considerably less frequently, with more participants indicating usage of 'only a few times a month' (freq. *2*), 'a few times a year' (freq. *1*), or 'no use' (freq. *0*).

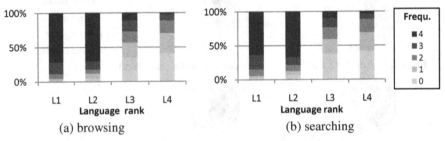

(a) browsing   (b) searching

Fig. 2. Frequency of use from 0 (no use) to 4 (daily use), split by language rank

Nonetheless, these high overall frequencies confirm and further quantify the results in section 4.2, revealing that polyglots make significant use of more than one language when browsing and searching the web. In particular, given that the first and second ranked languages are both used on a daily basis, there is a tremendous opportunity for information systems to incorporate support for multilingual online behavior.

An additional analysis of browsing/search frequency with respect to language proficiency revealed that there is a significant drop-off when proficiency becomes too low. For example, as shown in Figure 3, the majority of polyglots do not use a language at all if they only have basic proficiency in the language (i.e. proficiency level 1). Note, however, that this result does not mean that users would not be interested in searching for information in these languages, but rather that assistive features such as translation support might help alleviate user difficulties. Also, this trend is again more pronounced for *search frequency* compared to *browsing frequency*.

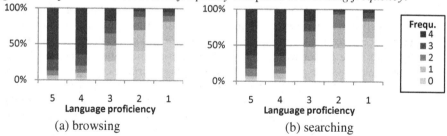

(a) browsing   (b) searching

Fig. 3. Frequency of use from 0 (no use) to 4 (daily use), split by language proficiency

4.4   Impact of Purpose, Topic Domain, and Additional Factors (RQ3)

In addition to general usage frequencies, we were interested in investigating the reasons for choosing particular languages for web *usage* (note that in this section we use the term *usage* to include both browsing and searching). As mentioned in section 3, we asked users to indicate their usage reasons in both free text form, as well as using predefined categories, which included several options for *purpose* (choice of 'Work/Study', 'Personal', 'Other', 'No use') and *domain topics* (choice of 18 topic domains – based on taxonomy categories from the Open Directory Project[6]).

Purpose. When asked to indicate if they used their languages for *work/study*, *personal*, and/or *other*, we found that participants often gave different answers depending on language ranking (see Figure 4).

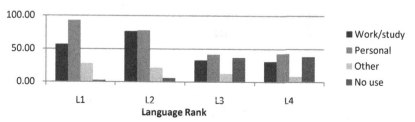

Fig. 4. Language use depending on purpose

In particular, we found that L1 is used by almost all participants for *personal* purposes (93%), but significantly less for *work/study* (56.62%). By contrast, L2 is used by many participants for *work/study* purposes (76.62%), and less frequently for *personal* purposes (compared to L1). For L3 and L4, we found a significant increase in *no use* responses, as well as a slight trend towards more *personal* use than *work/study* use for these languages. When analyzing the free-text responses of participants, we largely confirmed these quantitative results, with many participants indicating that L1 is used particularly often for finding information regarding their country of origin

---

[6] http://www.dmoz.org/

(which may or may not be the current country of residence), as well as for communicating with friends and family on social media.

In addition to these cumulative statistics, we investigated the degree to which users selected the same purpose for multiple languages. We first ran several Fleiss' Kappa [17] analyses (using the tool described in [18]) to measure the overall purpose 'agreement' between a participant's languages. Results from this analysis showed a particularly poor agreement for bilingual users for *work/study* (κ=-0.326). This means that if such users use L1 for work/study-related material, they often do not use L2 for this purpose (and vice-versa). For other user groupings/purposes, we generally found slightly higher agreement, albeit still within the regions of 'poor' to 'slight'. In order to delve further into the specific language relationships, we ran Spearman's correlation analyses across all language rank pairs and for each of the purposes. Results from these analyses confirmed some of the trends from the agreement analysis, for example showing a statistically significant negative correlation (r=-.367, p<.01) between L1 and L2 for work/study, i.e., confirming that users who use L1 for *work/study* generally do not use L2 for work/study, and vice versa. However, we did not find such negative correlations for *personal* purposes, indicating that searching for this type of information in one language does not imply that a user would not use other languages for this. Interestingly, we found that for L3 and L4, there were statistically significant positive correlations across all purposes, meaning that users who are proficient in 4 languages often use their third and fourth language in a similar fashion.

Lastly, to analyze the particular role of English, we split participant responses depending on whether the response relates to the use of *English* or a *Non-English* language. As shown in Figure 5, English is almost always used for work/study purposes, regardless of whether it is a user's L1 (96.84% indicate *work/study* use) or L2/L3/L4 (95.44% indicate *work/study* use).

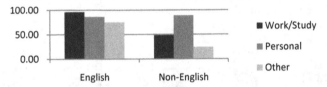

Fig. 5. Frequency of use depending on purpose, for English (left) and Non-English (right)

As to be expected, we found that English is also very popular for *personal* purposes when it is a user's L1 (93.68% of English L1 users indicating *personal* use), and it also appears to be frequently used (*83.16%*) when it is a user's L2/L3/L4. For Non-English languages, however, we found that users are much more inclined to use them for *personal* use compared to *work/study*. In particular, while 97.10% of participants with a non-English L1 indicated that they use L1 for *personal* information, only 45.65% said they would use it for *work/study*. Similarly, the results for non-English L2/L3/L4 show that if web users are proficient in multiple languages other than English, they predominantly use these for *personal* purposes. This was also confirmed by open-text answers, as well as the responses regarding domain topics (discussed next).

Domain Topics. In addition to general browsing and search purpose, we investigated the range of topic domains that users would look for in each of their languages. In line with our previous findings on overall frequency, participants selected on average 9.63

topics for L1 and 10.18 topics for L2, but only 5.13 topics for L3 and 4.00 topics for L4, i.e. users generally selected around double the topic domains for both L1 and L2 compared to L3 and L4. However, there were also some noticeable differences between L1 and L2, as shown in Figure 6. In particular, L1 is strongly used for local information/news and politics, whereas L2 is used particularly for business, technology, and education. This finding was also further confirmed in open-text answers, such as participants who currently live abroad indicating that they use their L1 to stay in touch with their home country by following local news and local politics.

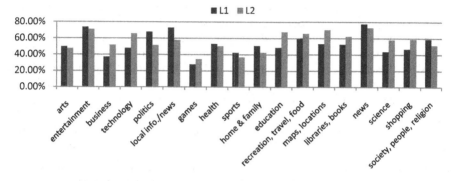

Fig. 6. Topic domain choices for L1 and L2

To further investigate this, we examined the difference between English and all other languages. Results showed that, while English is generally used more frequently across all topics, Non-English languages are particularly used for issues relating to local and personal topic domains. For example, Figure 7 shows the topic differences for participants who had a Non-English L1, and English as either L2, L3, or L4.

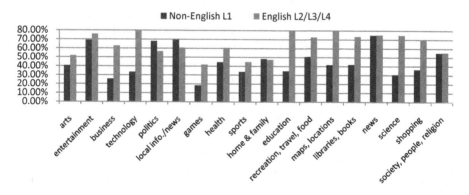

Fig. 7. Comparison of topic domains for participants with Non-English L1

As shown in this figure, the topics that were particularly frequent for users' Non-English L1 were politics, local information/news, home & family, as well as society, people and religion. By contrast, topics such as business, technology, science, and education were strongly biased towards English, despite this not being participants' first ranked language. Interestingly, shopping-related information is also more frequent in English, possibly due to a greater choice of e-commerce sites in English.

Lastly, as with the general usage purpose analysis, we also ran agreement and correlation analyses for all topic domains, in order to see if users selected similar topics across their languages. While the agreement analysis across all languages generally found only poor to slight agreement (i.e. suggesting that users generally use different languages for different topics), the detailed correlation analyses for each language pair and topic domain indicated that the various relationships are much more nuanced. In particular, for the language pair L1-L2, we found statistically significant positive correlations for the topics 'arts', 'entertainment', 'politics', and 'society, people, religion' (each with p<.01). This means that users use *both* L1 and L2 for information relating to these topics. By contrast, we found statistically significant negative correlations for the topics 'technology', 'education', 'maps, locations', and 'science' (each with p<.01), meaning that participants would generally only use one of the two languages for these topics. For the language pair L3-L4, we found that they are almost always positively correlated, confirming that tri-/quadrilingual users generally use their third and fourth language for similar topics. As with L1-L2, for the remaining language pairs we found both positive and negative correlations depending on the topic domain, confirming again that multiple language choice is not only dependent on multiple language proficiency, but also on the user's topic of interest and purpose.

Additional Insights. Participants' open-text answers revealed that two common reasons for choosing a language were 1) a natural personal preference depending on the topic (e.g. personal information in one's mother tongue) and 2) content availability (regardless of whether they use the language frequently or not). For the latter, many participants felt that content availability strongly depends on the topic they are browsing/searching, e.g. English for scientific papers, Japanese for Manga, Arabic for religious texts, etc. Conversely, some participants noted that they do not use a particular language - even if it is their strongest language in terms of proficiency - because they perceive a significant lack of content for that language.

For L2/L3/L4, we also found that participants' web usage sometimes stems from their desire to learn or practice their foreign language skills, as well as for particular language learning purposes such as obtaining translations. Furthermore, participants who currently reside in a country other than their country of origin indicated that they use their native language for the purpose of maintaining their proficiency in it.

5   Discussion and Conclusions

The goal of our survey was to investigate the extent to which polyglots use multiple languages for browsing and searching the web (RQ1), as well as how this behavior is affected by level of proficiency (RQ2), usage purpose, and topic domain (RQ3). This section concludes the paper with key findings to each of these questions, and provides recommendations for building novel PMIA systems.

RQ1. Our results show that the vast majority of polyglots frequently browse and search in multiple languages. In particular, we found that most users' first two languages are often used together on a daily basis, meaning that there is a great opportunity for novel solutions that specifically support multilingual web usage. For example, while multilingual users currently need to specify their information need separately for each of their languages, novel systems could take into account a user's multiple proficiencies and potentially (depending on the purpose and topic) adaptively retrieve and present relevant information in multiple languages.

These results also mean that for users who are proficient in English as a foreign language and who are thus able to leverage content in English, they still make extensive use of their first language (that is not English). This shows that the combination of growing English language user proficiency and continued English content dominance does not justify the provision of tools and services that ignore a user's various language skills and preferences. On the contrary, it means that information access systems should adaptively retrieve and present information in multiple languages.

RQ2. Responses show that as long as users possess sufficient proficiency in a language, they make use of it for regular browsing and searching. Conversely, we found that a major inhibiting factor for not using a language is indeed proficiency, and that this particularly affects searching more so than browsing. This indicates that there is a great opportunity to apply multilingual information access techniques for users who, despite having basic proficiency in a language, cannot fully leverage this language due to insufficient skills for web searching. In particular, such techniques could be applied in a personalized manner, by tailoring the amount of support (e.g., for query generation, result translation, etc.) to each user's specific abilities and preferences. For example, when retrieving information in multiple languages, and knowing that a user's behavior in a particular language is limited to watching videos (due to lack of reading/writing skills), a system could retrieve only audio/visual materials for this language. Likewise, textual results for a user's weaker languages could contain easier access to translation tools, in order to allow a user to still retrieve and consume relevant textual information in this language.

RQ3. Crucially, results from the survey show that language choice and frequency strongly depend on usage purpose and topic domain. This signifies an opportunity for developing novel solutions that not only support multiple user languages, but that also provide *personalized* support across different user interests and preferences. For example, a PMIA system could re-rank results according to a user's particular preferences in the current query language, or it could adaptively retrieve results from an additional language that is often selected by the user for the current search topic. In order to implement such solutions, there is a need to develop novel multilingual user models, which, in addition to a user's proficiency, keep track of user interests and preferences for each of the user's multiple languages.

Lastly, the development of such PMIA systems gives rise to a number of additional research challenges and opportunities, particularly regarding multilingual interfaces, i.e. how to best display and interact with multiple languages. To this end, in our future work we aim to compare the relative affordances and drawbacks of different multilingual interface designs, including, for example, faceted interfaces, merged ranked lists, or multilingual aggregate search.

Acknowledgements. This research is supported by the National Research Fund Luxembourg and cofunded under the Marie Curie Actions of the European Commission (FP7-COFUND). The research is also supported by the Science Foundation Ireland (Grant 12/CE/I2267) as part of the Centre for Next Generation Localisation at Trinity College Dublin.

References

1. Vallet, D., Cantador, I., Jose, J.M.: Personalizing web search with folksonomy-based user and document profiles. In: Gurrin, C., He, Y., Kazai, G., Kruschwitz, U., Little, S., Roelleke, T., Rüger, S., van Rijsbergen, K. (eds.) ECIR 2010. LNCS, vol. 5993, pp. 420–431. Springer, Heidelberg (2010)
2. Brusilovsky, P., Millán, E.: User models for adaptive hypermedia and adaptive educational systems. In: Brusilovsky, P., Kobsa, A., Nejdl, W. (eds.) Adaptive Web 2007. LNCS, vol. 4321, pp. 3–53. Springer, Heidelberg (2007)
3. Billsus, D., Pazzani, M.J.: Adaptive News Access. In: Brusilovsky, P., Kobsa, A., Nejdl, W. (eds.) Adaptive Web 2007. LNCS, vol. 4321, pp. 550–570. Springer, Heidelberg (2007)
4. Gauch, S., Speretta, M., Chandramouli, A., Micarelli, A.: User profiles for personalized information access. In: Brusilovsky, P., Kobsa, A., Nejdl, W. (eds.) Adaptive Web 2007. LNCS, vol. 4321, pp. 54–89. Springer, Heidelberg (2007)
5. Ghorab, M.R., Zhou, D., O'Connor, A., Wade, V.: Personalised Information Retrieval: survey and classification. User Model. User-Adapt. Interact. 23, 381–443 (2013)
6. Steichen, B., Ashman, H., Wade, V.: A comparative survey of Personalised Information Retrieval and Adaptive Hypermedia techniques. Inf. Process. Manag. 48, 698–724 (2012)
7. Nie, J.-Y.: Cross-Language Information Retrieval. Morgan and Claypool Publishers (2010)
8. Peters, C., Sheridan, P.: Multilingual information access. In: Agosti, M., Crestani, F., Pasi, G. (eds.) ESSIR 2000. LNCS, vol. 1980, pp. 51–80. Springer, Heidelberg (2001)
9. Gao, W., Niu, C., Nie, J.-Y., Zhou, M., Hu, J., Wong, K.-F., Hon, H.-W.: Cross-lingual query suggestion using query logs of different languages. In: Proc. 30th Int. Conf. on Research and Dev. in Information Retrieval (SIGIR), pp. 463–470 (2007)
10. Cao, G., Gao, J., Nie, J.-Y., Bai, J.: Extending query translation to cross-language query expansion with markov chain models. In: Proceedings of the Sixteenth ACM Conf. on Information and Knowledge Management. pp. 351–360 (2007)
11. Magdy, W., Jones, G.J.F.: An efficient method for using machine translation technologies in cross-language patent search. In: Proceedings of the 20th ACM Int. Conf. on Information and Knowledge Management. pp. 1925–1928 (2011)
12. Amato, G., Cigarrán, J., Gonzalo, J., Peters, C., Savino, P.: MultiMatch – Multilingual/Multimedia Access to Cultural Heritage. Research and Advanced Technology for Digital Libraries, pp. 505–508 (2007)
13. Petrelli, D., Levin, S., Beaulieu, M., Sanderson, M.: Which user interaction for cross-language information retrieval? Design issues and reflections. J. Am. Soc. Inf. Sci. Technol. 57, 709–722 (2006)
14. Berendt, B., Kralisch, A.: A user-centric approach to identifying best deployment strategies for language tools: the impact of content and access language on Web user behaviour and attitudes. Inf. Retr. 12, 380–399 (2009)
15. Kralisch, A., Berendt, B.: Language-sensitive search behaviour and the role of domain knowledge. New Rev. Hypermedia Multimed. 11, 221–246 (2005)
16. Clough, P., Eleta, I.: Investigating Language Skills and Field of Knowledge on Multilingual Information Access in Digital Libraries. International Journal of Digital Library Systems (IJDLS) 1, 89–103 (2010)
17. Davies, M., Fleiss, J.L.: Measuring Agreement for Multinomial Data. Biometrics 38, 1047 (1982)
18. Geertzen, J.: Inter-Rater Agreement with multiple raters and variables, https://mlnl.net/jg/software/ira/ (retrieved January 31, 2014)

Graph-Based Recommendations: Make the Most Out of Social Data

Amit Tiroshi[1,2], Shlomo Berkovsky[1,3], Mohamed Ali Kaafar[1],
David Vallet[1], and Tsvi Kuflik[2]

[1] NICTA, Australia
[2] University of Haifa, Israel
[3] CSIRO, Australia

Abstract. Recommender systems use nowadays more and more data about users and items as part of the recommendation process. The availability of auxiliary data, going beyond the mere user/item data, has the potential to improve recommendations. In this work we examine the contribution of two types of social auxiliary data – namely, tags and friendship links – to the accuracy of a graph-based recommender. We measure the impact of the availability of auxiliary data on the recommendations using features extracted from both the auxiliary and the original data. The evaluation shows that the social auxiliary data improves the accuracy of the recommendations, and that the greatest improvement is achieved when graph features mirroring the nature of the auxiliary data are extracted by the recommender.

Keywords: Graph-based recommendations, feature extraction, social data, music recommendations.

1 Introduction

The popularity of Web-based recommender system has led to the development of a spectrum of recommendation techniques. Most of them exploit, in a canonic form, three information entities: users, items, and feedback of users for items. Numerous prior works have shown that the accuracy of the generated recommendations improves when the representation of these entities is enriched by *auxiliary* external data, such as user's demographic data, item domain knowledge, or information on the recommendation constraints [2]. This finding was validated across a variety of recommendation techniques, application domains, and types of auxiliary data that can be used by the recommender.

Here, we investigate the exploitation of an auxiliary data originating from an online social networking system in a graph-based recommender. The choice of the social auxiliary data is driven by the abundance and ease of access to social data. Nowadays, it is common for users to have accounts on a social network (often, on more than one), to express their opinions, stay in touch with contacts, and share content of interest [5]. All this information can be captured and mined, and potentially serve as the source of a rich auxiliary user information for the

V. Dimitrova et al. (Eds.): UMAP 2014, LNCS 8538, pp. 447–458, 2014.

recommender [7,10]. Specifically, we leverage two types of social auxiliary data: (i) free-text tags assigned by users to content items, and (ii) online friendship links established between the social network users.

The focus on graph-based recommendations is also natural. In previous works, graph-based representation of the recommender data was shown to successfully encapsulate the relationships between the entities and to facilitate the generation of accurate recommendations [15,16]. It also allows for automatic extraction and population of graph-based features, which further improve the recommendation accuracy. Hence, our goal in this work is to study how the inclusion of auxiliary tags and friendship link data, along with the graph features extracted from this data, affects the accuracy of the graph-based recommender.

To answer this question, we use a publicly available data extracted from the music Web-site Last.fm.[1] The dataset consists of 1,892 users and 17,632 artists, whom the users tagged or listened to. That is, every user-artist pair is accompanied by the by the set of tags assigned by the user to the artist and by the number of times the user listened to the artist. Every user tagged or listened to, on average, 98.56 and 49.06 artists, respectively - and, vice versa, every artist was tagged or listened by 14.89 and 5.26 users, respectively. The dataset also contains information regarding 12,717 friendship links established between users on Last.fm. We represent this data as a graph, where the users, artists, and tags are the nodes, and 'listens' and 'friend' relationships are the edges. The assigned tags are reflected in the graph by the user-tag and tag-artist edges (see schematic diagrams in Figure 1).

We experiment with four graph schemes, where the tag, friendship, or both tag-and-friendship auxiliary data is included. For each schema, we extract and populate two sets of graph-based features. The first refers to a subset of *basic* features that can be extracted only from the original user, item, and feedback entities, disregarding the inclusion of the auxiliary data. The second is the *extended* set of features, where the basic features are augmented by a set of new features that mirror the nature of the included auxiliary data. We feed these features into a Gradient Boosted Decision Tree classifier [8] to predict withheld listening numbers, and recommend the top-ranked artists to users.

The evaluation highlights two key findings. Firstly, we show that the inclusion of auxiliary tag and friendship data improves the accuracy of the generated recommendations, whereas the inclusion of both achieves the greatest improvement. We also observe that the information encapsulated in the user friendship links turns to have more influence on the recommendations than the artist tagging information. Secondly, we show that features, which were conceived in a way that reflects the very nature of the auxiliary data being used, yield substantially more accurate recommendations.

2   Methodology

The effect of social auxiliary data on a graph-based recommender entails two questions: (i) what data is included in the graph representation, and (ii) which

---

[1] http://www.last.fm, Last.fm – Listen to free music and watch videos.

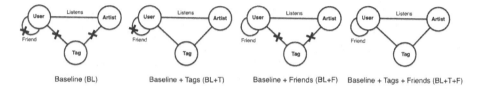

Fig. 1. Four schematic graph model

graph features are extracted and populated. We describe the methodology for graph-based data representation and feature extraction in the sections below.

2.1 Graph Models

The canonic Last.fm data used by graph-based recommender uses three entities: users, artists, and feedback (in this case - number of listens). The users and items are represented as the graph nodes, whereas the number of listens is expressed through the label of the edge between the two nodes. We use four different graph models, which use different types of social auxiliary data: no auxiliary data (denoted as baseline, BL), user-artists tags data (BL+T), user-to-user friendship links (BL+T), and both the tag and friendship data (BL+T+F). The graph models are illustrated in Figure 1.

When the auxiliary tag data is included, the free-text tags are also represented as the graph nodes. This way, a user-artist tag is converted into two edges: between the user and the tag, and between the tag and the artist. When the auxiliary friendship data is included, bi-directional edges between the nodes of users who friended each other are established. Finally, the inclusion of the tag and friendship data at the same time augments the baseline graph with the tag nodes, user-tag edges, tag-artists edges, and user-to-user edges.

2.2 Feature Subsets

Given the above graph-based representation of the data, we extract and populate a set of graph features. Some of these features can be populated directly from the data, e.g., number of artists listened by a user, number of users who listened to an artist, average number of listens for all artists listened by a user, and so forth. Other features inherently rely on the graph-based representation, e.g., node degree centrality, average neighborhood degree, PageRank score, and clustering coefficient. Intuitively, these features are not populated from the data, but rather quantify the importance of nodes in the graph-based representation of the data. Note that these features can be populated both for the user and artists nodes, and we refer the reader to [16] for an elaborate discussion of the graph features that can be extracted and populated.

We differentiate in our work between two groups of features. The *basic* features are extracted from the graph-based data representation only and disregard the unique nature of the social auxiliary data. For example, consider the PageRank score feature. The value of this feature for a given user node can be populated regardless of the auxiliary data. Including the friendship edges will clearly affect the value of this feature, but it can still be extracted and populated for the four graph models. We denote by F the set of basic features, e.g., F_{BL+T} is the set of basic features extracted from the graph-based representation of data augmented by user-artist tags.

The set of *extended* features includes, on top of the above-mentioned basic features, also new features that mirror the nature of the included auxiliary data. For example, consider a feature defined as "the ratio of user's friends, who also listened to a certain artist." This feature leverages the very notion of friendship between two users, on top of only considering the presence of a new edge between the two nodes in the graph-based representation of the data. We denote the set of extended features by $\hat{F}$, e.g., $\hat{F}_{BL+T+F}$.

We would like to highlight the dual impact of the *new* features $\hat{F} \setminus F$. These features can be populated using the auxiliary data only, as this data does not exist in the BL graph model. In the first instance, the mere presence of these features in the recommendation process may affect the accuracy of the graph-based recommender. However, the inclusion of the auxiliary data and the augmentation of the graph-based representation with the new nodes and edges, may affect the values of the basic features in F and, indirectly, also affect the recommendation generation process. We will investigate this duality in the experimental part of the work.

3   Experimental Setting

3.1   Dataset

We use a publicly available dataset extracted from the Last.fm music Web-site and used in [3]. The dataset contains 1,892 users and 17,632 artists, whom the users tagged and/or listened to. The dataset also contains social information regarding the friendship links established between Last.fm users. There are overall 12,717 such bidirectional friendship links. There are in total 11,946 unique tags in the dataset, which were assigned by users to artists 186,479 times. Each user assigned on average 98.56 tags, 18.93 of them being distinct. Each artist was assigned with 14.89 tags on average, 8.76 of them being distinct.

A brief characterisation of the dataset is shown in Figure 2. We first observe in Figure2(a) the distribution of the number of friends per user. We note that the average number of user-to-user edges in the BL+F model is low, which is illustrated by the vast majority of users having less than 10 friends, and about half of users having less than 4 friends. Nevertheless, friendship-based features prove to be important for the recommendations, as per the next section. Intuitively, the existence of the friendship edge between two users can be a good indicator of similar tastes, and as such, friendship-based features are expected to affect the recommendation process.

In Figure2(b), we show the distribution of the average number of tags each user shares with other users. This is presumably an indicator of the connect-

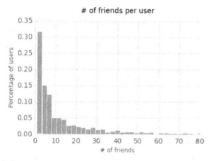

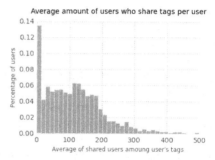

(a) Distribution of the number of friends per user

(b) Distribution of the average number of tags shared with other users

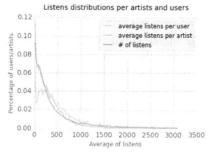

(c) Distribution of the average number of listens per user/artist and overall

Fig. 2. Data characteristics

edness of users in the BL+T graph. We observe that, on average, a user tag is found redundant across a non-negligible set of other users. In essence, many tags are used by a significant portion of users, while only 13.5% of tags do not propagate in the graph. In Section 4, we show that this feature is amongst the most important features extracted from the auxiliary tag data.

Lastly, we measure the distributions of the number of listens per artist, user, and in total. We observe that the overall and per artist distribution are highly similar. The user-based distribution resembles the same behaviour, but, as expected drops faster. This aligns with the intuition that the number of users who listen to several hundreds of artists is smaller than the number of artists who are listened by several hundreds of users [11].

3.2 Prediction and Metrics

We perform a 5-fold cross validation in which 5 different training sets are created. We prune users with less than 5 ratings to ensure that every user has at least one rating in the test set and four training ratings. For each training fold, we create a graph for each graph model outlined in Figure 1. Each graph generates the set of basic features, as well as a different set of extended features associated with the auxiliary data being included. The generated features are used as the input for a linear regressor, trained to predict the number of listens for a given user-artist pair. We use the Gradient Boost Decision Tree regressor, which is often used for general classification and prediction problems [8].

In order to evaluate each graph model and its associated features, we measure the performance of the regressor in predicting the number of listens and in ranking the artists. For each user, we create a candidate set of artists by picking 10 artists out of the true set of top-50 artists listened by the user and complementing these by randomly chosen artists. For example, candidate set of 100 artists includes 10 artists listened by the user and 90 random artists.

Then we use the regressor to predict the number of listens for each artist in the candidate set, rank the set accordingly, and compute precision at 10 (P@10) for every user, as the performance metric [13]. That is, we compute the intersection between the top-10 artists in the predicted ranked set and the real 10 artists listened by the user that were included in the candidate set. Finally, we average P@10 across all the test set users. This evaluation method is known as *top-n recommendations* [6], and is applied to evaluate recommenders that use implicit factors, e.g., number of views or behavior logs.

4 Results

As outlined in Section 2, social auxiliary data allows for different representations of the graph model, which, in turn, offer new possibilities for the extraction and population of graph features. In this section, we first study the impact of such auxiliary data and the corresponding features on the accuracy of graph-based recommendations. Then, we analyze the difference between the recommendations generated using the basic and the extended set of graph features.

4.1 Auxiliary Data as a Source of Graph Features

In this experiment, we observe the performance of the recommender when using the extended set of features, i.e., both basic and new features, as extracted and populated from the four graph models. Figure 3 shows the P@10 values averaged across all test set users, as obtained for the BL, BL+T, BL+F, and BL+T+F graph models, while the candidate set size varies from 50 to 150 artists. The boundaries of the boxes denote the 25th and 75th percentile of P@10, and the average P@10 is marked by the dots inside the boxes.

First, we clearly observe that the inclusion of the social auxiliary data of either the artist tags or friendships links substantially improves P@10. When both the tags and friendship links are included in the BL+T+F model, we observe the highest average P@10 across all the candidate set sizes. The improvement with respect to the BL model that includes no auxiliary data is statistically significant, ranging from 70% for candidate set size of 50 to 84% for candidate set size of 150. Note that a modest improvement (2.9% for candidate set size of 50 to 9%

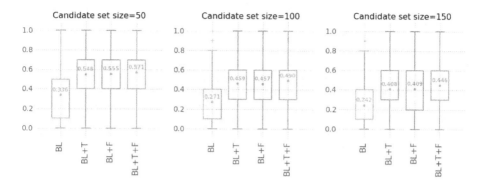

Fig. 3. Average precision for the four graph models and varying candidate set size

for candidate set size of 150) of the BL+T+F model with respect to the best-performing model that included either the tag or the friendship data. This shows that including both types of social auxiliary data further improves the accuracy of the recommendations.

Notably, the BL+T and BL+F models obtain very similar P@10 scores across all three candidate set sizes, showing the positive effect of the inclusion of the auxiliary data. However, as noted in Section 3.1, the tag data includes more than 186K user-artist tags, whereas the friendship data consists of only 12K user-to-user links. The observation that the obtained precision is similar indicates that a single user friendship link is more influential than a single artist tag and yields a greater improvement in the recommendation accuracy.

We observe a drop in the obtained P@10 scores when the size of the candidate set increases. This is expected, as the selection of top-10 listened artists out of a set of 150 candidates is inherently harder than out of 50 candidates only. Nevertheless, the drop in accuracy is smaller than one may expect. Specifically, P@10 of the BL+T+F model drops by 14% when the size of the candidate set is doubled from 50 to 150, and by 22% when it is tripled to 150.

To assess the fluctuations in the accuracy of the graph-based recommender, we measure the precision scores obtained for various users. In Figure 4-left, we plot the average P@10 obtained for all the users having a certain number of friends. The regression line shows that P@10 increases with the number of friends, i.e., users who established many friendship links with other users get more accurate recommendations than those who established a few. A strong positive correlation of 0.82 is observed between between the number of friends of a user and P@10 achieved for the user.

No dependency is observed is a similar experiment referring to the number of tags a user assigned. Hence, we turn to the popularity of the assigned tags. Figure 4-right shows the P@10 of a user as a function of the average popularity of tags used by the user, i.e., average number of other users who used these tags. As shown by the regression line, P@10 increases with the popularity of the used tags, although in this case the correlation is weaker, 0.29. Note that

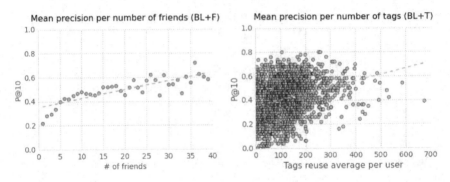

Fig. 4. Precision vs. number of friends (left), and average popularity of tags (right)

the precision obtained for users with non-popular tags fluctuates all over the precision spectrum. This suggests that the dependency between the number and popularity of tags, and the accuracy of recommendations is harder to establish.

4.2   Basic and Extended Feature Set

We turn now to the analysis of the performance of the basic and extended features sets extracted from various graph models. For each graph model, we compare the average P@10 of the predictions generated using the extended feature set $\hat{F}$ with the one generated using the basic feature set F. The candidate set size is fixed in this experiment to 50. The results of the comparison are shown in Figure 5, where the solid boxes denote the extended feature set $\hat{F}$ and the dotted boxes - the basic set F. Note that the comparison is impossible for the BL graph model, since no auxiliary data is included there and $\hat{F} = F$.

It can be observed that the extended feature sets outperform the basic ones across the boards. The improvement contributed by the new features $\hat{F} \setminus F$ is

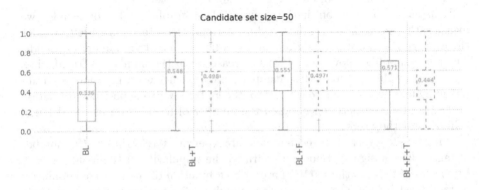

Fig. 5. Precision of the extended (solid boxes) vs the basic (dotted boxes) feature set for the four graph models

Table 1. Feature importance rankings for the four graph schemes

F_{BL}		$\hat{F}_{BL}$	
#1 user_avg_nei_degree	(100%)	user_avg_nei_degree	(100%)
#2 user_pagerank	(56%)	user_pagerank	(56%)
#3 artist_pagerank	(50%)	artist_pagerank	(50%)
#4 user_clustering_coef	(49%)	user_clustering_coef	(49%)
#5 artist_degree_centrality	(47%)	artist_degree_centrality	(47%)

F_{BL+T}		$\hat{F}_{BL+T}$	
#1 artist_pagerank	(100%)	fraction_of_shared_neighbours	(100%)
#2 user_avg_nei_degree	(96%)	fraction_of_shared_tags	(27%)
#3 user_pagerank	(87%)	user_avg_nei_degree	(18%)
#4 artist_degree_centrality	(79%)	user_clustering_coef	(17%)
#5 user_clustering_coef	(57%)	user_pagerank	(17%)

F_{BL+F}		$\hat{F}_{BL+F}$	
#1 user_clustering_coef	(100%)	fraction_of_shared_neighbours	(100%)
#2 artist_pagerank	(73%)	fraction_of_shared_friends	(36%)
#3 user_pagerank	(65%)	user_pagerank	(23%)
#4 artist_degree_centrality	(58%)	user_clustering_coef	(20%)
#5 user_degree_centrality	(53%)	artist_degree_centrality	(16%)

F_{BL+T+F}		$\hat{F}_{BL+T+F}$	
#1 artist_pagerank	(100%)	fraction_of_shared_neighbours	(100%)
#2 user_pagerank	(81%)	fraction_of_shared_friends	(41%)
#3 user_avg_nei_degree	(70%)	fraction_of_shared_tags	(18%)
#4 user_clustering_coef	(68%)	user_clustering_coef	(12%)
#5 user_degree_centrality	(46%)	user_avg_nei_degree	(11%)

comparable for BL+T and BT+F models (10% and 12%, respectively), while it is substantially higher for the BL+T+F model (29%). This clearly shows that extracting features that reflect the nature of the included auxiliary data and enriching the set of basic features is beneficial, as this improves the accuracy of the recommendations. It should be noted that some improvement is observed also for the basic feature set F, but this improvement can be leveraged if the new features $\hat{F} \setminus F$ are extracted and populated.

We note that out of the three graph models with the basic feature set, the lowest P@10 is achieved, somewhat surprisingly, by F_{BL+T+F}. That is, although $\hat{F}_{BL+T+F}$ is superior to $\hat{F}_{BL+T}$ and $\hat{F}_{BL+T}$ (see Figure 3), in the case of basic feature sets we observe that F_{BL+T} and F_{BL+T} both outperform F_{BL+T+F}. We conjecture that including both types of social auxiliary data but not extracting and populating the new features leads to redundancy in the graph and degrades the performance of the recommender.

Related to this is the analysis of most important features in each feature set. A by-product of the Gradient Boost Decision Tree is the feature importance ranking, which communicates the the contribution[2] of every feature in the set to correct predictions of the user-artist number of listens. Table 1 compares the 5 most important features along with their importance scores, for the four graph models. Like in Figure 5, the basic and the extended feature sets are identical for the BL model.

---

[2] Note that the importance values of the features shown in Table 1 do not sum up to 100%. Instead, the importance of the top feature is marked as 100% and the importance of other features is scaled with respect to this top feature.

Note that the most important features in the extended feature sets of all three graph models are new features that are extracted from the auxiliary data. The $fraction\_of\_shared\_neighbours$ feature denotes the ratio between the number of nodes that are common neighbours (both tags and friends) of the user and artist and the overall number of neighbors. This feature is further broken down into $fraction\_of\_shared\_friends$ and $fraction\_of\_shared\_tags$. The first feature is steadily selected by the Gradient Boost Decision Tree as the most important feature, and it is accompanied by the ratio computed for the tags and friends in the BL+T and BL+F models, respectively. In the combined BL+T+F model, both features are selected, but the importance of the ratio for friends is higher than for tags, which aligns with our earlier observation that the auxiliary friendship data is more influential than the tag data.

As the new features from the $\hat{F} \setminus F$ set are selected as the most important features, other features from the basic set are pushed down the list. However, in all three models, the basic features included in top-5 list of the extended feature set were also present in the top-5 list of the basic set. This experiment highlights our observation regarding the importance of the extraction of the new features for the graph-based recommendation process.

5 Related Work

There are multiple works in the field that evaluate the contribution of social links to popular personalisation and recommendation techniques, such as collaborative and content-based filtering [12,4,10]. A hybrid recommender system that combines tags and social links was evaluated by Guy et al. in [10]. The authors compared the hybrid approach to stand-alone approaches that solely use only social links or tags, and it was found that the hybrid approach significantly outperformed others. A user study discovered that recommendations generated by the hybrid approach were regarded by users as the most interesting. Our work reaffirm their findings and shows the superiority the graph the exploits both the tag and friendship social auxiliary data.

Along similar lines, Freyne et al. developed a personalized model for recommending social network news updates [7]. The model combined in a linear manner the quantified strength of user-to-user online relationships with the observed importance of network activities for the user. Their strength of user-to-user relationship encompassed the activity of the two users, as well as their direct and indirect (through common friends) interaction. The model was evaluated in a user study and was found to accurately recommend relevant social network updates, to assist users in establishing and maintaining friendships, and to boost contribution of user-generated content. Recent reviews of additional works that leverage social data for the purpose of recommendation generation can be found in [9], [14], and [1].

In [12], Konstas et al. developed a graph-based approach based on random walks for generating recommendations over social datasets, among them Last.fm (this was a proprietary dataset, and not the publicly accessible one used in our work). The reported results showed an improvement in recommendations when using the random walk approach in comparison to the baseline standard collaborative filtering. The optimizations in that work surrounded a single graph algorithm, random walk with restarts, and its parameters, such as the walk restart. In our work, random graph walks with static parameters are represented by the PageRank score feature. We extend the work of Konstas et al. by considering a broader range of graph features and evaluating the basic and extended feature set on four graph models. We also provide insight on the most important individual features.

In our own previous works we studied the performance of graph-based recommendations and graph features in various scenarios [15,16]. We used graph features in two different domains: for business recommendation and for interest recommendation. In both use-cases, the graph features were found to have a positive impact on the prediction accuracy. The difference between the graphs and features in this work with respect to our previous works lays in the availability of social auxiliary data, which introduces new graph features, affects the existing features, and imposes a new type of relatedness between the graph nodes. Also, the friendship data connects nodes from the same type (user-to-user edges), thus, extending the bipartite user-item graph. In this work, we used a different machine learning technique and evaluation metric to generate the predictions, showing that the effect of graph features holds also for Gradient Boost Decision Tree and ranking-based tasks.

6   Conclusions

In this work we studied the effect of inclusion of social auxiliary data on graph-based recommendations. We discovered that the inclusion of both the tags assigned by users to items and of the friendship links established between users contributes to the accuracy of recommendation. The impact of the friendship data was found to be stronger than of the tags data, while the strongest impact was observed when both types of auxiliary data were included.

Following these observation, we thoroughly investigated the need for extracting new features, which mirror the nature of the included data. We assessed the contribution of these features and conclude that the greatest improvement in the accuracy of the recommendations is achieved when the inclusion of the auxiliary data is complemented by the extraction and population of the new features. Overall, our work shows highlights the benefits offered by the graph features to recommender systems.

This work raises several challenging questions that we leave for the future. One question pertains to leveraging the content of the tags for enriching the graph structure. For instance, multiple tags assigned by a user (or to an artist) may convey a similar message. We would like to analyse the textual content of the tags and establish graph links between similar tags. We will then study the impact of these links on the accuracy of the generated recommendations.

Another question deals with the importance of specific values of the features. In here, we measured the importance of the extracted features. It may turn out, for instance, that although the importance of a feature is low, the importance of specific values of the feature is high. For example, consider the importance of listening to a popular mainstream artist versus of listening to a niche punk band. We will develop models that identify these important values and exploit them for the recommendation purposes.

References

1. Abel, F., Herder, E., Houben, G.-J., Henze, N., Krause, D.: Cross-system user modeling and personalization on the social web. User Model. User-Adapt. Interact. 23(2-3), 169–209 (2013)
2. Berkovsky, S., Kuflik, T., Ricci, F.: Cross-technique mediation of user models. In: Wade, V.P., Ashman, H., Smyth, B. (eds.) AH 2006. LNCS, vol. 4018, pp. 21–30. Springer, Heidelberg (2006)
3. Cantador, I., Brusilovsky, P., Kuflik, T.: Second workshop on information heterogeneity and fusion in recommender systems. In: RecSys (2011)
4. Cantador, I., Konstas, I., Jose, J.M.: Categorising social tags to improve folksonomy-based recommendations. J. Web Sem. 9(1), 1–15 (2011)
5. Chen, T., Kaafar, M.A., Friedman, A., Boreli, R.: Is more always merrier?: A deep dive into online social footprints. In: WOSN, pp. 67–72. ACM (2012)
6. Cremonesi, P., Koren, Y., Turrin, R.: Performance of recommender algorithms on top-n recommendation tasks. In: RecSys, pp. 39–46 (2010)
7. Freyne, J., Berkovsky, S., Daly, E.M., Geyer, W.: Social networking feeds: recommending items of interest. In: RecSys, pp. 277–280 (2010)
8. Friedman, J.H.: Greedy function approximation: A gradient boosting machine. Annals of Statistics 29, 1189–1232 (2000)
9. Groh, G., Birnkammerer, S., Köllhofer, V.: Social recommender systems. In: Recommender Systems for the Social Web, pp. 3–42. Springer (2012)
10. Guy, I., Zwerdling, N., Ronen, I., Carmel, D., Uziel, E.: Social media recommendation based on people and tags. In: SIGIR, pp. 194–201 (2010)
11. Haupt, J.: Last.fm: People-powered online radio. Music Reference Services Quarterly 12(1-2), 23–24 (2009)
12. Konstas, I., Stathopoulos, V., Jose, J.M.: On social networks and collaborative recommendation. In: SIGIR, pp. 195–202 (2009)
13. G. Shani and A. Gunawardana. Evaluating recommendation systems. In *Recommender Systems Handbook*, pages 257–297. 2011.
14. Shapira, B., Rokach, L., Freilikhman, S.: Facebook single and cross domain data for recommendation systems. User Modeling and User-Adapted Interaction 23(2-3), 211–247 (2013)
15. Tiroshi, A., Berkovsky, S., Kaafar, M.A., Chen, T., Kuflik, T.: Cross social networks interests predictions based ongraph features. In: RecSys, pp. 319–322. ACM (2013)
16. Tiroshi, A., Berkovsky, S., Kaafar, M.A., Vallet, D., Chen, T., Kuflik, T.: Improving business rating predictions using graph based features. In: IUI, pp. 319–326. ACM (2014)

Fast Incremental Matrix Factorization for Recommendation with Positive-Only Feedback

João Vinagre[1,2], Alípio Mário Jorge[1,2], and João Gama[1,3]

[1] LIAAD - INESC TEC, Porto, Portugal
[2] Faculdade de Ciências, Universidade do Porto, Portugal
[3] Faculdade de Economia, Universidade do Porto, Portugal
joao.m.silva@inescporto.pt, amjorge@fc.up.pt, jgama@fep.up.pt

Abstract. Traditional Collaborative Filtering algorithms for recommendation are designed for stationary data. Likewise, conventional evaluation methodologies are only applicable in offline experiments, where data and models are static. However, in real world systems, user feedback is continuously being generated, at unpredictable rates. One way to deal with this data stream is to perform online model updates as new data points become available. This requires algorithms able to process data at least as fast as it is generated. One other issue is how to evaluate algorithms in such a streaming data environment. In this paper we introduce a simple but fast incremental Matrix Factorization algorithm for positive-only feedback. We also contribute with a prequential evaluation protocol for recommender systems, suitable for streaming data environments. Using this evaluation methodology, we compare our algorithm with other state-of-the-art proposals. Our experiments reveal that despite its simplicity, our algorithm has competitive accuracy, while being significantly faster.

1 Introduction

The purpose of recommender systems is to aid users in the – usually overwhelming – choice of items from a large item collection. Collaborative filtering (CF) is a popular technique to infer unknown user preferences from a set of known user preferences [11]. This set can be conceptually laid out in a user-item matrix, where each cell represents the known preference of a user for an item. CF algorithms analyse this matrix and try to "guess" missing values – typically the vast majority. Recommendations are then produced by extracting the best "guesses" and making them available to the user.

The ultimate task of any recommender system is straightforward: recommend items to users. Depending on the type of feedback users provide, this problem can be formulated in two ways: rating prediction and tem prediction. In a rating prediction problem the main task is to predict missing values in a *numeric* user-item ratings matrix. This is a natural formulation when quantified preferences – ratings – are available, and the problem is most naturally seen as a regression task. However, some systems employ positive-only user preferences. These systems are quite common – e.g. "like" buttons, personal playlists, shopping history, news reading, website logs. In these cases, numeric ratings are not

V. Dimitrova et al. (Eds.): UMAP 2014, LNCS 8538, pp. 459–470, 2014.

available. The user-item matrix can be seen as a boolean value matrix, where *true* values indicate a positive user-item interaction, and *false* values indicate the absence of such interaction. In systems with positive-only feedback, the task is to predict unknown *true* values in the ratings matrix – i.e. item prediction –, which can be seen as a classification task. This distinction has implications not only in the algorithms' mechanics but also in evaluation protocols and metrics.

Our work is focused on the item prediction problem, for two main reasons. First, while relatively few online systems have an implemented numeric rating feature, while most systems have some kind of positive-only feedback – e.g. web page visiting logs, customer buying history, click streams, music listening, event participation. Algorithms for rating prediction are not directly applicable in these cases. Second, while the majority of published research focuses on algorithms for rating prediction, some issues related with the specific properties of positive-only feedback remain unexplored. These properties encompass the absence of negative feedback, the inherent subjectivity of implicit ratings and the requirement for specific evaluation measures [12,17].

1.1   Incremental Learning

If we look at ratings data in a real world system, it is reasonable to approach it as a data stream: ratings are continuously being generated, and we have no control over the data rate or the ordering of the arrival of new ratings [8]. Ideally, algorithms that learn from data streams maintain predictive models incrementally, requiring a single pass through data.

Research in incremental CF is not abundant in the literature. Incremental neighborhood-based CF is presented in [18] and further studied in our previous work [16,25]. One first solution for incremental matrix factorization is presented in [22], where the authors use the Fold-In method [4] to incrementally update the factor matrices. In [24] an incremental method to update user factors is proposed, by using a simplified version of the batch process. An incremental algorithm for ranking that uses a selective sampling strategy is proposed in [7]. Two incremental methods using Stochastic Gradient Descent (SGD) are evaluated in [15]. Our work differs from the aforementioned for the following. First, we are solving item prediction problems and second, our proposed evaluation methodology is substantially different (see Sec. 5), since we use a prequential approach to measure the algorithms' evolving accuracy.

Starting with a simple iterative SGD algorithm, we adapt its mechanics to work incrementally using only the currently available observation. We show experimental results that indicate that the predictive ability of our proposed incremental algorithm is competitive with state of the art proposals. We also describe our novel experimental setup specifically designed for streaming user feedback.

The remainder of this paper is structured as follows. In Sec. 2 we introduce the basics of modern MF algorithms for CF. Sec. 3 describes an incremental version of the batch algorithm. Some evaluation issues are discussed in Sec. 4. Results are presented and discussed in Sec. 5. Finally we conclude in Sec. 6.

2   Matrix Factorization for CF

Over the last decade several Matrix Factorization (MF) algorithms for CF have been proposed, and were greatly popularized by the Netflix Prize competition [3]. So far, MF methods have proven to be generally superior to other alternatives, in terms of both predictive ability and run-time complexity.

Matrix Factorization for CF is inspired by Latent Semantic Indexing [6], a popular technique to index large collections of text documents, used in the field of information retrieval. LSI performs the Singular Value Decomposition (SVD) of large document-term matrices. In a CF problem, the same technique can be used in the user-item rating matrix, uncovering a latent feature space that is common to both users and items. As an alternative, optimization methods [2,9,19,24] have been proposed to decompose (very) sparse ratings matrices. Supposing we have a ratings matrix R, the algorithms decompose R in two factor matrices A and B that, similarly to a classic SVD, cover a common latent feature space. Matrix A spans the user space, while B spans the item space. Given this formulation, a predicted rating by user u to item i is given by the dot product $\hat{R}_{ui} = A_u.B_i^T$.

Training is performed by minimizing the L_2-regularized squared error for known values in R and the corresponding predicted ratings:

$$\min_{A.,B.} \sum_{(u,i)\in D} (R_{ui} - A_u.B_i^T)^2 + \lambda(||A_u||^2 + ||B_i||^2) \tag{1}$$

In the above equation, D is the set of user-item pairs for which ratings are known and λ is a parameter that controls the amount of regularization. The regularization term $\lambda(||A_u||^2 + ||B_i||^2)$ is used to avoid overfitting. This term penalizes parameters with high magnitudes, that typically lead to overly complex models with low generalization power. The most successful methods to solve this optimization problem are Alternating Least Squares (ALS) [2] and Stochastic Gradient Descent (SGD) [9]. It has been shown [9,19] that SGD based optimization generally performs better than ALS when using sparse data, both in terms of model accuracy and run time performance.

Given a training dataset consisting of tuples in the form $< user, item, rating >$, SGD performs several passes through the dataset – iterations – until some stopping criteria is met – typically a convergence bound and/or a maximum number of iterations. At each iteration, SGD sweeps over all known ratings R_{ui} and updates the corresponding rows A_u and B_i^T, correcting them in the inverse direction of the gradient of the error, by a factor of $\eta \le 1$ – known as step size or learn rate. For each known rating, the corresponding error is calculated as $err_{ui} = R_{ui} - \hat{R}_{ui}$, and the following update operations are performed:

$$\begin{aligned} A_u &\leftarrow A_u + \eta(err_{ui}B_i - \lambda A_u) \\ B_i &\leftarrow B_i + \eta(err_{ui}A_u - \lambda B_i) \end{aligned} \tag{2}$$

One obvious advantage of SGD is that complexity grows linearly with the number of known ratings in the training set, actually taking advantage of the high sparsity of R.

Algorithm 1. BSGD - Batch SGD

Data: $D = \,<u, i, r>$
input   : $feat, iters, \lambda, \eta$
output: A, B

init:
> for $u \in \mathtt{Users}(D)$ **do**
>> $A_u \leftarrow \mathtt{Vector}(size : feat)$;
>> $A_u \sim \mathcal{N}(0, 0.1)$;
>
> for $i \in \mathtt{Items}(D)$ **do**
>> $B_i \leftarrow \mathtt{Vector}(size : feat)$;
>> $B_i \sim \mathcal{N}(0, 0.1)$;

for $count \leftarrow 1$ **to** $iters$ **do**
> $D \leftarrow \mathtt{Shuffle}(D)$;
> for $<u, i, r> \in D$ **do**
>> $err_{ui} \leftarrow r - A_u.B_i^T$;
>> $A_u \leftarrow A_u + \eta(err_{ui}B_i - \lambda A_u)$;
>> $B_i \leftarrow B_i + \eta(err_{ui}A_u - \lambda B_i)$;

This method – Algorithm 1 – has first been informally proposed in [9] and many extensions have been proposed ever since [19,14,24,21].

3   Incremental Matrix Factorization for Item Prediction

As stated in Sec. 1 we are focusing on item prediction problems. In item prediction, the ratings matrix R contains either *true* values – for positively rated items – or *false* values – for unrated items. One important consideration is that a *false* value in R may have two distinct meanings: the user either dislikes (negative preference) or did not interact with that item (unknown preference). In our current work, we assume that *false* values are missing values – as opposed to negative ratings. In practice, this assumption has two main consequences. First, the sparsity of R is maintained because only positive ratings are used for training. Second, all *false* values for each user are valid recommendation candidates. Another possible approach is to use some criterion to discriminate between negative and missing ratings within the *false* values. This technique has been shown to improve accuracy in some cases [17], however it typically requires batch data pre-processing, which is not viable in a data stream environment.

3.1   Incremental SGD

The optimization process of Alg. 1 consists of a batch procedure, requiring several passes – iterations – through the dataset to train a model. While this may be an acceptable overhead in a stationary environment, it is not acceptable for streaming data. As the number of observations increases and is potentially unbounded, repeatedly revisiting all available data eventually becomes too expensive to be performed online.

We propose Alg. 2, designed to work as an incremental process, that updates factor matrices A and B based solely on the current observation. This algorithm, despite its formal similarity with Alg. 1, has two fundamental differences. First, the learning process requires a single pass over the available data. Note that in Alg. 2, at each observation $< u, i >$, the adjustments to factor matrices A and B are made in a single step. One other possible approach is to perform several iterations over each new observation, with potential accuracy improvements, at the cost of the additional time required to re-iterate. Second, no data shuffling – or any other pre-processing – is performed. Given that we are dealing with positive-only feedback we approach the boolean matrix R by assuming the numerical value 1 for *true* values. Accordingly, we measure the error as $err_{ui} = 1 - \hat{R}_{ui}$, and update the rows in A and B^T using the update operations in (2). We refer to this algorithm as ISGD.

Algorithm 2. ISGD - Incremental SGD

Data: $D = \{< u, i >\}$, a finite set or a data stream
input : $feat$, λ, η
output: A, B

for $< u, i > \in D$ do
    if $u \notin \text{Rows}(A)$ then
        $A_u \leftarrow \text{Vector}(size : feat)$;
        $A_u \sim \mathcal{N}(0, 0.1)$;
    if $i \notin \text{Rows}(B^T)$ then
        $B_i^T \leftarrow \text{Vector}(size : feat)$;
        $B_i^T \sim \mathcal{N}(0, 0.1)$;
    $err_{ui} \leftarrow 1 - A_u.B_i^T$;
    $A_u \leftarrow A_u + \eta(err_{ui}B_i - \lambda A_u)$;
    $B_i \leftarrow B_i + \eta(err_{ui}A_u - \lambda B_i)$;

Since we are mainly interested in predicting good recommendations, we order candidate items i for each user u using the function $f_{ui} = |1 - \hat{R}_{ui}|$, where $\hat{R}_{ui}$ is the non-boolean predicted score. In plain text, we order candidate items by descending proximity to value 1.

4   Evaluation Issues

Classic evaluation methodologies for recommender systems begin by splitting the ratings dataset in two subsets – training set and testing set – randomly choosing data elements from the initial dataset. The training set is initially fed to the recommender algorithm to build a predictive model. To evaluate the accuracy of the model, different protocols have been used. Generally, these protocols group the test set by user and "hide" user-item interactions randomly chosen from each group. These hidden interactions form a holdout set. Rating prediction algorithms are usually evaluated by measuring the difference between predicted ratings and hidden ratings. Item recommendation algorithms are evaluated by matching recommended items with hidden items.

The main objective of these protocols is to simulate user behavior in lab conditions. Regarding this, some limitations need to be pointed out:

- Dataset ordering: randomly selecting data for training and test, as well as random hidden set selection, shuffles the natural sequence of data. Algorithms designed to deal with naturally ordered data cannot be rigorously evaluated if data are shuffled;
- Time awareness: shuffling data potentially breaks the logic of time-aware algorithms. For example, by using future ratings to predict past ratings;
- Online updates: incremental CF algorithms perform online updates of their models as new data points become available. This means that neither models or training and test data are static. Models are continuously being readjusted with new data;
- Session grouping: most natural datasets, given their unpredictable ordering, require some pre-processing to group ratings either by user or user session in order to use offline protocols. As data increases in size, it eventually may become too expensive to group data points;
- Recommendation bias: in production systems, user behavior is – expectedly – influenced by recommendations themselves. It is reasonable to assume, for instance, that recommended items will be more likely to be interacted with than if they were not recommended. Simulating this offline usually requires complicated user behavior modeling which can be expensive and prone to systematic error.

These limitations, along with other known issues (see [13]), weaken the assumption that user behavior can be accurately modeled or reproduced in offline experiments. Nevertheless, offline evaluation still provides a useful tool. In [23] some clues are provided on how to solve some of these problems.

5   Evaluation and Discussion

Given the problems listed in the previous Section, we propose a prequential approach [10], especially suited for the evaluation of algorithms that deal with data streams. The following steps are performed for each observed event $< u, i >$, representing a positive interaction between user u and item i:

1. If u is a known user, use the current model to recommend N items to u, otherwise go to step 3;
2. Score the recommendation list given the observed item i;
3. Update the model with the observed event;

4. Proceed to the next event in the dataset;

This protocol provides several benefits:

- It allows continuous online monitoring of the system's predictive ability;
- Online statistics can be integrated in algorithms' logic – e.g. automatic parameter adjustment, drift detection, triggering batch retraining;
- In ensembles, relative weights of individual algorithms can be adjusted;
- The protocol is applicable to both item prediction and rating prediction.

In an offline experimental setting, an overall average of individual scores can be computed at the end – because datasets are in fact finite. For a recommender running in a real-world setting, this process allows us to follow the evolution of the scores throughout the experiment by keeping a statistic of the score. Thereby it is possible to depict how the algorithm's performance evolves over time. In Sec. 5.2 we present both the overall average score and complement it with plots of the evolving score using a simple moving average.

We compare the overall accuracy of four algorithms, using the datasets described in Sec. 5.1. To avoid cold-start issues – which are not the subject of our research – we perform an initial batch training of the algorithms using the first 20% data points in each dataset. The remaining data is naturally used for incremental training. Five algorithms are tested: our incremental SGD algorithm (ISGD), Bayesian Personlized Ranking MF (BPRMF) and its weighted variant WBPRMF [20] and the incremental version of the classic user-based nearest-neighbors algorithm (UKNN), described in [16].

Parameters for all algorithms are independently tuned for each dataset. Because cross-validation is not applicable with streaming data, we use the same evaluation protocol adopted for the presented experiments, but evaluating only on the initial 20% of data of each dataset.

5.1   Datasets

We use four distinct datasets, described in Table 1. All datasets consist of a chronologically ordered set of pairs in the form $< user, item >$. Music-listen and Lastfm-600k consist of music listening events obtained from two distinct sources, where each tuple corresponds to a music track being played by a user. We removed unique occurrences of $< user, item >$ pairs, since these probably do not reflect a positive interaction. Music-playlist consists of a timestamped log of music track additions to personal playlists. MovieLens-1M is well known dataset[1] consisting of timestamped movie ratings in a 1 to 5 rating scale. To use this dataset in an item prediction setting, since we intend to retain only positive feedback, movie ratings below the maximum rating 5 are excluded. Lastfm-600k consists of the first 8 months of activity observed in the Last.fm[2] dataset originally used in [5]. Both Music-listen and Music-playlist are extracted

---

[1] http://www.grouplens.org, 2003
[2] http://last.fm

Table 1. Dataset description

Dataset	Events	Users	Items	Time frame	Sparsity
Music-listen	335.731	4.768	15.323	12 months	99,90%
Lastfm-600k	493.063	164	65.013	8 months	99,11%
Music-playlist	111.942	10.392	26.117	45 months	99,96%
MovieLens-1M	226.310	6.014	3.232	34 months	98,84%

from the Palco Principal[3] website, a social network dedicated to non-mainstream music enthusiasts and artists.

One particular consideration about Music-listen and Lastfm-600k is that they contain repeated events – in music listening, users listen to their favorite music tracks more than once. Most systems do not recommend items to a user that already knows them, except in very specific applications, such as automatic playlist generation. For this reason, we skip the evaluation of these points. However, we do consider them to update the models, in order to better reflect a real world scenario.

5.2   Results and Discussion

Table 2 lists overall results, including the average incremental update times. We express accuracy using recall@N at cut-offs $N \in \{1, 5, 10\}$. Recall yields 1 if item i is within the N first recommended items, and 0 otherwise.

From the observation of results, we begin by pointing out that ISGD is from 2 to over 25 times faster – depending on the dataset – than the second faster algorithm, while having comparable accuracy. With Music-playlist and even more with Lastfm-600k, ISGD shows to be superior in both accuracy and processing time. With Music-listen, ISGD's accuracy only falls below the classic UKNN, which is well over 2.000 times slower. The worst relative accuracy obtained by ISGD is with Movielens-1M, performing under all other algorithms. In terms of speed, however, ISGD still performs many times faster than all three alternatives.

One relevant observation is that the relative accuracy between algorithms is highly dependent on the dataset. With Music-listen and Movielens-1M, the neighborhood algorithm is the most accurate, whereas with Lastfm-600k and Music-playlist ISGD performs best. Exclusively regarding MF algorithms, ISGD outperforms the two BPRMF variants with all datasets except Movielens-1M.

Overall results are possible to obtain in offline experiments, given that datasets are finite. However, in an online environment – like production systems – these results can only be interpreted as a snapshot of the algorithms' performance within a predefined time frame. One valuable feature of our adopted evaluation protocol is that it allows the monitoring of the learning process as it evolves over time. To do that, we need to maintain statistics of the outcome of the predictions.

---

[3] http://www.palcoprincipal.com

Table 2. Overall results. Best performing algorithms are highlighted in bold for each dataset. Update times are the average value of the update time for all data points.

Dataset	Algorithm	Recall@1	Recall@5	Recall@10	Update time
Music-listen	BPRMF	0,003	0,016	0,028	0,846 ms
	WBPRMF	0,012	0,037	0,056	1,187 ms
	ISGD	0,017	0,044	0,061	**0,118 ms**
	UserKNN	**0,038**	**0,101**	**0,139**	328,917 ms
Lastfm-600k	BPRMF	<0,001	0,001	0,003	28,061 ms
	WBPRMF	<0,001	0,002	0,003	29,194 ms
	ISGD	**0,012**	**0,027**	**0,034**	**1,106 ms**
	UserKNN	0,001	0,004	0,006	290,133 ms
Music-playlist	BPRMF	<0,001	0,009	0,020	1,889 ms
	WBPRMF	0,011	0,038	0,057	2,156 ms
	ISGD	**0,060**	**0,136**	**0,171**	**0,949 ms**
	UserKNN	0,033	0,095	0,132	190,250 ms
Movielens-1M	BPRMF	0,012	0,045	0,080	0,173 ms
	WBPRMF	0,013	0,050	0,084	0,229 ms
	ISGD	0,007	0,028	0,050	**0,016 ms**
	UserKNN	**0,018**	**0,066**	**0,110**	84,927 ms

We study how the algorithms' accuracy evolves over time by depicting in Fig. 1 a moving average of the recall@10 metric.

The plotted evolution of the algorithms with each dataset generally confirms overall results, however more information becomes available. For instance, although the overall averages of ISGD and UKNN are relatively close with the Music-playlist dataset, Fig. 1 c) shows that these algorithms behave quite differently, starting with a very similar accuracy level and then diverging substantially, starting near the 40.000th data point. With this dataset, all algorithms except ISGD deteriorate over time. With Lastfm-600k and Music-playlist – Figs. 1 b) and c) –, ISGD clearly outperforms the other algorithms. For these datasets besides obtaining better aggregated scores, ISGD seems to take a clear advantage of the incremental learning process, yielding increasingly better results. With Music-listen – Fig. 1 a) – the user-based neighborhood algorithm achieves considerably better scores than all others and ISGD is the second best performing. With Movielens-1M – Fig. 1 d) –, all algorithms share a similar evolving pattern.

We also conducted statistical significance tests between ISGD and the other algorithms for every dataset, using the signed McNemar test over sliding windows [10] of the same size as the ones used for the moving averages used in Fig. 1, with a significance level of 1%. For the sake of space, we omit the details about these tests since we found that the diferences visible in Fig. 1 are statistically significant for all tested cases except for the following two:

1. ISGD vs WBPRMF with Music-listen – Fig. 1 a). Here significant difference is not detected for over 55% of the experiment. In less than 12% of the datapoints – and only in the first 30.000 –, ISGD is significantly worse than

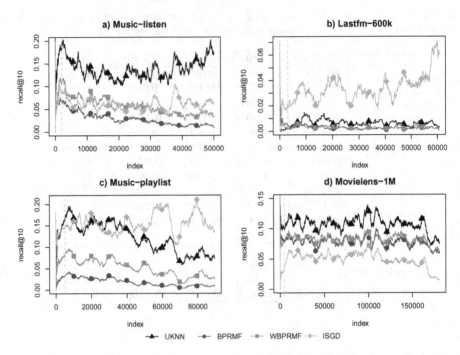

Fig. 1. Evolution of recall@10 with four datasets. The plotted lines correspond to a moving average of the recall@10 obtained for each prediction. The window size n of the moving average is a) $n = 2000$, b) $n = 3000$, c) $n = 5000$ and d) $n = 5000$. The first n points are delimited by the vertical dashed line and are plotted using the accumulated average. Plots a) and b) do not include repeated events in the datasets.

WBPRMF. In more than 28% of the experiment – mainly after the 30.000^{th} data point – ISGD is better than WBPRMF.

2. ISGD vs UKNN with Music-playlist – Fig. 1 c). In the first half of the dataset, ISGD is alternately significantly better, significantly worse or with no significant difference from UKNN. In the second half of Music-playlist, ISGD is significantly better than UKNN.

The online monitoring of the learning process allows a more detailed evaluation of the algorithms' performance. Figure 1 reveals phenomena that would otherwise be hidden in a typical batch evaluation. We consider that this finer grained evaluation process provides a deeper insight into the learning processes of predictive models.

The variability in the results suggests that some characteristics of the datasets – for instance, sparsity, length, user-item ratios or user/item frequency distributions – are somehow determinant in the relative performance of different algorithms. However we were not yet able to correlate meta-data characteristics with the algorithms' ability to produce good models.

6   Conclusion and Future Work

In this paper, we propose a fast matrix factorization algorithm that is able to deal with a stream of positive-only user feedback. To effectively evaluate CF algorithms in a streaming environment, we also propose a prequential evaluation framework that monitors algorithm accuracy as it continuously learns from a data stream. We use this protocol to compare our algorithm to other incremental algorithms for positive-only feedback. Results suggest that our algorithm, while being faster, has competitive accuracy. We further notice that our evaluation method allows for a finer grained assessment of algorithms, by being able to continuously monitor the outcome of the learning process.

The analysis of results motivates future work towards a better understanding of the effects of dataset properties, such as sparseness, user-item ratios or frequency distributions, in the predictive ability of different algorithms. We are also researching the convergence between the predictive abilities of incremental and batch variants of matrix factorization algorithms.

Acknowledgements. Project "NORTE-07-0124-FEDER-000059" is financed by the North Portugal Regional Operational Programme (ON.2 - O Novo Norte), under the National Strategic Reference Framework (NSRF), through the European Regional Development Fund (ERDF), and by national funds, through the Portuguese funding agency, Fundação para a Ciência e a Tecnologia (FCT). The first author's work is funded by the FCT grant SFRH/BD/77573/2011. The authors wish to thank Ubbin Labs, Lda. for kindly providing data from Palco Principal.

References

1. Proceedings of the 8th IEEE Intl. Conference on Data Mining (ICDM 2008), December 15-19, 2008, Pisa, Italy. IEEE Computer Society (2008)
2. Bell, R.M., Koren, Y.: Scalable collaborative filtering with jointly derived neighborhood interpolation weights. In: ICDM. pp. 43–52. IEEE Computer Society (2007)
3. Bennett, J., Lanning, S., Netflix, N.: The netflix prize. In: In KDD Cup and Workshop in conjunction with KDD (2007)
4. Berry, M., Dumais, S., O'Brien, G.: Using linear algebra for intelligent information retrieval. SIAM review pp. 573–595 (1995)
5. Celma, Ò.: Music Recommendation and Discovery - The Long Tail, Long Fail, and Long Play in the Digital Music Space. Springer (2010)
6. Deerwester, S.C., Dumais, S.T., Landauer, T.K., Furnas, G.W., Harshman, R.A.: Indexing by latent semantic analysis. JASIS 41(6), 391–407 (1990)
7. Diaz-Aviles, E., Drumond, L., Schmidt-Thieme, L., Nejdl, W.: Real-time top-n recommendation in social streams. In: Cunningham, P., Hurley, N.J., Guy, I., Anand, S.S. (eds.) RecSys. pp. 59–66. ACM (2012)
8. Domingos, P., Hulten, G.: Catching up with the data: Research issues in mining data streams. In: DMKD '01: Workshop on Research Issues in Data Mining and Knowledge Discovery (2001)

9. Funk, S.: http://sifter.org/~simon/journal/20061211.html (2006)
10. Gama, J., Sebastião, R., Rodrigues, P.P.: Issues in evaluation of stream learning algorithms. In: IV, J.F.E., Fogelman-Soulié, F., Flach, P.A., Zaki, M.J. (eds.) KDD. pp. 329–338. ACM (2009)
11. Goldberg, D., Nichols, D.A., Oki, B.M., Terry, D.B.: Using collaborative filtering to weave an information tapestry. Commun. ACM 35(12), 61–70 (1992)
12. Hu, Y., Koren, Y., Volinsky, C.: Collaborative filtering for implicit feedback datasets. In: ICDM [1], pp. 263–272
13. Kohavi, R., Longbotham, R., Sommerfield, D., Henne, R.M.: Controlled experiments on the web: survey and practical guide. Data Min. Knowl. Discov. 18(1), 140–181 (2009)
14. Koren, Y.: Factorization meets the neighborhood: a multifaceted collaborative filtering model. In: Li, Y., Liu, B., Sarawagi, S. (eds.) KDD. pp. 426–434. ACM (2008)
15. Ling, G., Yang, H., King, I., Lyu, M.R.: Online learning for collaborative filtering. In: IJCNN. pp. 1–8. IEEE (2012)
16. Miranda, C., Jorge, A.M.: Incremental collaborative filtering for binary ratings. In: Web Intelligence. pp. 389–392. IEEE (2008)
17. Pan, R., Zhou, Y., Cao, B., Liu, N.N., Lukose, R.M., Scholz, M., Yang, Q.: One-class collaborative filtering. In: ICDM [1], pp. 502–511
18. Papagelis, M., Rousidis, I., Plexousakis, D., Theoharopoulos, E.: Incremental collaborative filtering for highly-scalable recommendation algorithms. In: Hacid, M.S., Murray, N.V., Ras, Z.W., Tsumoto, S. (eds.) ISMIS. Lecture Notes in Computer Science, vol. 3488, pp. 553–561. Springer (2005)
19. Paterek, A.: Improving regularized singular value decomposition for collaborative filtering. In: Proceedings of KDD Cup and Workshop. vol. 2007, pp. 5–8 (2007)
20. Rendle, S., Freudenthaler, C., Gantner, Z., Schmidt-Thieme, L.: Bpr: Bayesian personalized ranking from implicit feedback. In: Bilmes, J., Ng, A.Y. (eds.) UAI. pp. 452–461. AUAI Press (2009)
21. Salakhutdinov, R., Mnih, A.: Probabilistic matrix factorization. In: Platt, J.C., Koller, D., Singer, Y., Roweis, S.T. (eds.) NIPS. MIT Press (2007)
22. Sarwar, B.M., Karypis, G., Konstan, J., Riedl, J.: Incremental SVD-based algorithms for highly scalable recommender systems. In: Fifth International Conference on Computer and Information Technology. pp. 27–28 (2002)
23. Shani, G., Gunawardana, A.: Evaluating recommendation systems. In: Ricci, F., Rokach, L., Shapira, B., Kantor, P.B. (eds.) Recommender Systems Handbook, pp. 257–297. Springer (2011)
24. Takács, G., Pilászy, I., Németh, B., Tikk, D.: Scalable collaborative filtering approaches for large recommender systems. Journal of Machine Learning Research 10, 623–656 (2009)
25. Vinagre, J., Jorge, A.M.: Forgetting mechanisms for scalable collaborative filtering. J. Braz. Comp. Soc. 18(4), 271–282 (2012)

When the Question is Part of the Answer: Examining the Impact of Emotion Self-reports on Student Emotion

Michael Wixon and Ivon Arroyo

Learning Sciences and Technologies. Social Sciences and Policy Studies Department
Worcester Polytechnic Institute

Abstract. A variety of methodologies have been put forth to assess students' affective states as they use interactive learning environments (ILEs) and intelligent tutoring systems (ITS), such as classroom observations and subjective coding, self-coding by students after replays, as well as self-reports of student emotion as students are using the learning environment. Still, it is unclear what the disadvantages of each methodology are. In particular, does measuring affect by asking students to self-report alter student affect itself? The following work explores this question of how self-reports themselves can bias affective states, within one particular tutoring system, Wayang Outpost.

Keywords: affect, assessment, modeling of emotions.

1 Motivation

Several methods have been proposed to measure how students feel as they interact with digital learning environments. This data has been used to research how to facilitate learning by enhancing students' positive valence affective states, mitigate potentially harmful negative valence affective states such as boredom [1, 2], and explain the complex relationship between frustration/confusion and learning [3, 4]. In pursuit of these goals, emotion assessments are collected to generate affect models and classifiers that may be used to automatically predict students' emotions within the digital learning environment.

The first step in developing these automated detectors is to establish a "ground truth" label of affect that a detector can approximate. There are several different methodologies to obtain such "ground truth" label. A large body of work in affect detection utilizes videos of students' facial expressions with posterior coding by students themselves, for posterior detection through behaviors such as gaze tracking, and galvanic skin response sensors [5-6]. Another approach is BROMP, which employs specially trained observers to identify students' affective states through unobtrusive observations and inter-rater reliability of observers to establish construct validity [8,9]. Finally, students may self-report their emotions as they are learning, to obtain "ground truth" labels of student affective states [7].

We have employed this third method of self-report. Specifically, our approach has been minimally invasive, similar to the concurrent forced-response technique [10] which uses Likert scales in between problems [11]. Our endeavors to be minimally invasive by placing our self-reports between problems and furthermore by not requiring responses, are meant to avoid the pitfalls that come the interruptions to

V. Dimitrova et al. (Eds.): UMAP 2014, LNCS 8538, pp. 471–477, 2014.
© Springer International Publishing Switzerland 2014

students' work that self-report necessitates. Prior work has found that interrupting students during primary tasks can cause an increase in annoyance [12], and it is our hope that judicious use of self-reports will mitigate effects such as these. Nonetheless, there are still concerns that even unobtrusively collecting self-report data may influence a student's affective state [10].

Our most troubling evidence of self-report negatively impacting student affect, although anecdotal, comes from our own data collections. In a prior study, after students were asked to give a self-report of their affective state, they were asked to explain their self-report. Student responses included "[I am frustrated] Because you keep asking me if I am frustrated." Such responses were rare, but might indicate a larger unreported trend. So we resolved to quantitatively address concerns with self-reported affect influencing students' affective states.

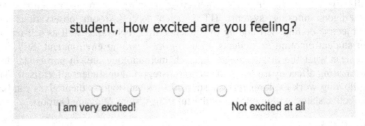

Fig. 1. Emotion Question that appears on average every 5-7 minutes on average. "student" is replaced by the student's first name. "Why is that?" question (not shown) allows students to expand on their reasons for their rating.

2   Method

Participants. Participants consisted of two hundred and ninety five (295) students, 7th, 8th, 9th and 10th graders from three semi-rural area schools in Massachusetts from several studies involving the Wayang Outpost math tutoring system, in 2009. Students used the tutoring system for several days (3-5 days) during 1-2 weeks.

Wayang Outpost. Wayang Outpost is a mathematics ITS which covers K-12 material such as number sense, pre-algebra, algebra, geometry. Wayang Outpost[1] adapts content presented to students depending on mastery learning. It emphasizes scaffolding students through multimedia hints and pedagogical agents also known as "learning companions" who provide both motivational and cognitive support [13]. Affective measures for self-report were selected based on prior work used to model a range of various emotional states during learning [14]: Confidence/Anxiety (bipolar scale), Excitement (unipolar), Frustration (unipolar), and Interest/Boredom (bipolar scale), that overlap with metrics from the Theory of Achievement Emotions [19].

Overview of Analyses. We performed three levels of analysis, each with finer granularity than the previous one. First, we examined the correlation between the affective state reported by a student to the total number of self-reports a student was

---

[1] http://wayangoutpost.com

asked so far, while controlling for time in tutor session. We expected that this analysis might reveal a relationship between sheer quantity of self-reports and student affective state. Second, we examined the correlation between affective self-reports and the interval of time that had passed since the last self-report. This analysis was also correlational and similar to the first one, except that total self-reports was now replaced with "time since last self-report". Finally, we examined changes in students' affective states at an even finer grain size: from one problem to the next. We used predictive models of affect for this analysis, which allowed us to understand the affective state of individual students at any math practice problem. We considered the difference in emotional state between a pair of problems preceding a self-report as a control condition, and compared this general trend to the difference between the problem preceding a self-report and the problem following a self-report. The next section describes our results.

Predictive Models. The affect detectors were trained under five fold batch student-level cross validation using simple linear regression in Rapidminer 5.0 [15]. Post-hoc discretization (i.e. survey responses and predictions 1 to 2 are negative affect, 3 is neutral affect, and 4 to 5 are positive affect) was employed to obtain weighed Cohen's Kappa [16] values measuring agreement between actual self-report and prediction. Results of these detectors are in Table 1. We concede that the performance of these detectors is poorer than the typically accepted Cohen's Kappa of 0.4; however, generally accepted Kappas in sensor-free affect detection tend to be lower than Kappas detected for other constructs [9,17].

Table 1. Affect Detector Performance

	Confidence	Excitement	Frustration	Interest
Pearson's R for Continuous Prediction	0.404	0.224	0.372	0.232
Kappa for Discretized Classification	0.200	0.151	0.173	0.100

Additionally, due to its sensitivity to affect as a continuous rather than binary variable this detector suffers a handicap: it is more difficult to select affect correctly due to chance (e.g this detector which distinguishes between "bored", "neutral", and "interested" and may be outperformed by a detector which need only distinguish between the binary "bored" vs "not bored"). The affect model generates a prediction of each of each affect after each solved problem. Details on how similar models are created, which relies on a classifier based on linear regression, may be found in [18].

3   Results

First Analysis. This analysis measured the correlation between self-reported affect and the number of times a student had been asked to self-report on any affect so far, for each of our four emotions while controlling for "time in session" to account for any changes in affective state that might be due to fatigue. We obtained only one near significant correlation between frustration and requests for self-report. This correlation was negligible ($r=0.043$, $p=0.108$, df=1408).

Second Analysis This analysis examined how the spacing between requests for self-report influenced students' self-reported affect. This is possible because while reports were set to happen at intervals of 3-5 minutes, Wayang Outpost would "wait" until the student had finished the actual math problem. Thus, the correlation between the interval of "time since last self-report" and self-reported affect were considered, while controlling for overall "time spent in the tutoring session". We found a negligible relationship between "time since last self-report" and change in interest (r=-0.074, p=0.011, df=1185).

Third Analysis. In the last analysis, we considered the change in affect from one problem to the next. Here we looked at the problems which are adjacent to self-reports in order to get a better idea at how self-reports influence affect, within a small window of time. For this analysis, we were able to estimate affective states for problems where affect was not self-reported by using our predictive models of affect. The models predict a student's affect given information from pretest surveys and their log files. Since our prior analyses had shown little to no change in affect due to self-report, we used our models to detect change in affect between two problems that have no self-report between them (e.g. between Time1 and Time2 as displayed in figure 2) as compared to the change in affect between two problems that did have a self-report between them (e.g. between Time2 and Time3). These time and self-report immediately follow one another which minimizes the chance of other intervening events influencing our effects.

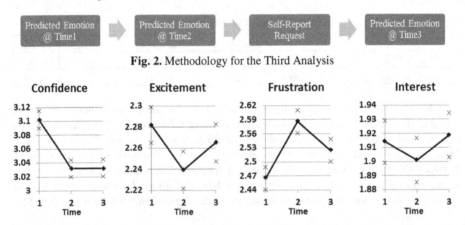

Fig. 2. Methodology for the Third Analysis

Fig. 3. Predicted Affect at Each Time (Paired Samples T-Test shows significant difference in affect p < 0.05 between Times 1 & 2 and 2 & 3 for all. Self-Report Occurs between Times 2 & 3, but not 1 & 2. 95% Confidence Interval denoted by Xs. N = 2878 for Confidence, Exceitment & Interest. N = 3001 for Frustration).

Figure 3 illustrates how students' affect changes between problems when there is no intervening self-report (Time 1 to Time 2) and how their affect changes when there is an intervening self-report (Time 2 to Time 3). The changes we have detected in affect here seem negligible given that students typically respond on a Likert scale from 1 to 5. Our analyses have been ordered in progressing sensitivity, examining information at smaller and smaller grain size. At the individual problem level we have detected a negligible, but consistent effect. With no intervening self-report students' affect states appear to become very slightly more negative (i.e. confidence, excitement, and interest decrease while frustration increases). However, with an intervening self-report the valences of students' affective states become more positive (excitement and interest increase while frustration decreases). While the change in affect appears to be negligible in magnitude it is statistically significant at a large sample size (Paired sample T-Tests indicate $p < 0.05$ for all cases when comparing each affect at Time 1 to Time 2, and Time 2 to Time 3).

4   Discussion

Most of the results of the first two analyses aren't significant. We are certainly not proving the null here that self-reports do not impact student affect, but we are addressing that concern that self-reports may influence students' affective state. In this way, it is our belief that these results are a valuable contribution to researchers modeling affect using self-report measures.

However, the data of the third analysis indicates that self-report appears to have an small but positive effect on the valence of the affects measured herein, from activity to activity. To the extent that the question is part of the answer, it seems to be a positive part, improving students mood as compared to not intervening. This may be due to the system exhibiting some degree of empathy with the student, which has been shown to improve students' overall mood [20]. Another possible reason for this positive effect is that students have the possibility of venting any negative affect, not only through the actual scale but also through the "Why is that?" text box that accompanies the question. This change from negative affective trends (before the self-report) to positive affective trends (after the self-report) are causing an oscillating effect, which is harder to see in the more global first two analyses we report on.

A major weakness of this work is that it treats affective reports as independent when many of them may come from the same student. While these results appear indicate a small and overall positive effect of self-report on students' affect they of course do not preclude large or negative effects of self-report on students' affect in different environments or with distinct samples of students. It is our hope that the analytical methods outlined in this work may serve as a means of easily checking on the effects of self-report confounds in other learning environments.

References

1. D'Mello, S., Person, N., Lehman, B.: Antecedent-Consequent realtionships and Cyclical Patterns between Affective States and Problem Solving Outcomes. In: Dimitrova, V., Mizoguchi, R., du Boulay, B., Grasser, A. (eds.) Artificial Intelligence in Education. Building Learning Systems that Care: from Knowledge Representation to Affective Modelling, pp. 57–64. IOS Press (2009)
2. Pekrun, R., Goetz, T., Daniels, L., Stupnisky, R.H., Raymond, P.: Boredom in achievement settings: Exploring control–value antecedents and performance outcomes of a neglected emotion. Journal of Educational Psychology 102(3), 531–549 (2010)

3. Baker, R.S.J.D., D'Mello, S.K., Rodrigo, M.M.T., Graesser, A.C.: Better to Be Frustrated than Bored: The Incidence, Persistence, and Impact of Learners' Cognitive-Affective States during Interactions with Three Different Computer-Based Learning Environments. International Journal of Human-Computer Studies 68(4), 223–241 (2010)
4. Gee, J.P.: Situated Language and Learning: A Critique of Traditional Schooling. Routledge Taylor & Francis, London (2004)
5. D'Mello, S., Graesser, A.: Multimodal Semi-Automated Affect Detection from Conversational Cues, Gross Body Language, and Facial Features. User Modeling and User-Adapted Interaction 20(2), 147–187 (2010)
6. D'Mello, S.K., Picard, R.W., Graesser, A.C.: Towards an Affect-Sensitive AutoTutor. Special Issue on Intelligent Educational Systems IEEE Intelligent Systems 22(4), 53–61 (2007)
7. Arroyo, I., Woolf, B., Cooper, D., Burlesom, W., Muldner, K., Cristopherson, R.: Emotion sensors go to school. In: Dimitrova, V., Mizoguchi, R., Du Boulay, B., Graesser, A. (eds.) 14th International Conference on Artificial Intelligence In Education, IOS Press, Amsterdam (2009)
8. Ocumpaugh, J., Baker, R.S.J.D., Rodrigo, M.M.T.: Baker-Rodrigo Observation Method Protocol (BROMP) 1.0. Training Manual version 1.0. Technical Report. EdLab, Ateneo Laboratory for the Learning Sciences, New York, Manila (2012)
9. Baker, R.S.J.D., Gowda, S.M., Wixon, M., Kalka, J., Wagner, A.Z., Salvi, A., Aleven, V., Kusbit, G., Ocumpaugh, J., Rossi, L.: Sensor-free automated detection of affect in a Cognitive Tutor for Algebra. In: Proceedings of the 5th International Conference on Educational Data Mining, pp. 126–133 (2012)
10. Porayska-Pomsta, K., Mavrikis, M., D'Mello, S., Conati, C., Baker, R.S.J.D.: Knowledge Elicitation Methods for Affect Modeling in Education. International Journal of Artificial Intelligence in Education 22(3), 107–140 (2013)
11. Conati, C.: How to Evaluate a Model of User Affect? In: André, E., Dybkjær, L., Minker, W., Heisterkamp, P. (eds.) ADS 2004. LNCS (LNAI), vol. 3068, pp. 288–300. Springer, Heidelberg (2004)
12. Bailey, B.A., Konstan, J.A.: On the need for attention-aware systems: measuring effects of interruption on task performance, error rate, and affective state. Computers in Human Behavior 22, 685–708 (2006)
13. Woolf, B.P., Arroyo, I., Muldner, K., Burleson, W., Cooper, D., Dolan, R., Christopherson, R.M.: The Effect of Motivational Learning Companions on Low Achieving Students and Students with Disabilities. In: Aleven, V., Kay, J., Mostow, J. (eds.) ITS 2010, Part I. LNCS, vol. 6094, pp. 327–337. Springer, Heidelberg (2010)
14. Kort, B., Reilly, R., Picard, R.W.: An affective model of interplay between emotions and learning: reengineering educational pedagogy-building a learning companion. In: Proceedings of the IEEE International Conference on Advanced Learning Technologies, pp. 43–46 (2001)
15. Mierswa, I., Wurst, M., Klinkenberg, R., Scholz, M., Euler, T.: YALE: Rapid Prototyping for Complex Data Mining Tasks. In: Proceedings of the 12th ACM SIGKDD International Conference on Knowledge Discovery and Data Mining (KDD 2006), pp. 935–940 (2006)
16. Cohen, J.: Weighted kappa: nominal scale agreement with provision for scaled disagreement or partial credit. Psychological Bulletin 70, 213–220 (1968)
17. Pardos, Z.A., Baker, R.S.J.D., San Pedro, M.O.C.Z., Gowda, S.M., Gowda, S.M.: Affective states and state tests: Investigating how affect throughout the school year predicts end of year learning outcomes. In: Proceedings of the 3rd International Conference on Learning Analytics and Knowledge, pp. 117–124 (2013)

18. Arroyo, I., Cooper, D.G., Burleson, W., Woolf, B.P.: Bayesian Networks and Linear Regression Models of Students' Goals, Moods, and Emotions. In: Handbook of Educational Data Mining. Chapman & Hall/CRC Data Mining and Knowledge Discovery Series (2010)
19. Arroyo, I., Shanabrook, D., Woolf, B.P., Burleson, W.: Analyzing Affective Constructs: Emotions, Motivation and Attitudes. In: International Conference on Intelligent Tutoring Systems (2012)
20. Nguyen, H., Masthoff, J.: Designing empathic computers: the effect of multimodal empathic feedback using animated agent. In: Proceedings of the 4th International Conference on Persuasive Technology (2009)

Enhancing Exploratory Information-Seeking through Interaction Modeling

Kumaripaba M. Athukorala

Helsinki Institute for Information Technology HIIT,
Department of Computer Science, University of Helsinki

Abstract. With the explosive growth of information available in the web, locating needed and relevant information remains a difficult task, whether the information is textual or visual. Although information-retrieval algorithms have improved greatly in retrieving relevant information, exploratory information-seeking still remains difficult due to its inherently open-ended and dynamic nature. Modeling the user behavior and predicting dynamically changing information-needs in exploratory search is hard. Over the past decade there has been increasing attention on rich user interfaces, retrieval techniques, and studies of exploratory search. However, existing work does not yet support the dynamic aspects of exploratory search. The objective of this research is to understand how user interaction modeling can be applied to provide better support in exploratory information-seeking.

Keywords: User Modeling, Exploratory Search, Scientific Information-Seeking.

1 Introduction

Search can be broadly divided into two types: known-item search, where the user has a specific search result in mind, and exploratory search, where the goal is ill-defined and changes as the search progresses [1]. Traditional information retrieval techniques concentrate mostly on known-item search. Exploratory search, is becoming more important as the web has become a major source for learning and discovery [2].

Exploratory information-seeking is known to be complex and hard to support due to its inherently open-ended and dynamic nature [3]. It arises in situations where there is a need to find information from a domain in which we have a general interest but not specific knowledge [1]. Exploratory search has also been defined based on the distinct characteristics in the search process such as submitting tentative queries, selectively seeking and passively obtaining cues about the next steps, and iteratively searching with evolving information-needs.

Success in search is determined by how well the search results match the user's information-needs. However, in exploratory information-seeking the user knowledge and information-need change as the search progresses. Therefore, the search queries that a user generates also change and predicting the relevance of results to the constantly evolving information-needs is a challenge.

V. Dimitrova et al. (Eds.): UMAP 2014, LNCS 8538, pp. 478–483, 2014.

The information retrieval community attempted to support exploratory search by employing techniques such as results clustering [4], relevance feedback [5], and faceted search [6]. However, these techniques are cumbersome to use and cannot capture the evolving user knowledge and interests in exploratory search [7]. A response from the machine learning community has been to apply various reinforcement learning methods to allow for better user modeling over a search session through trading off between the exploration and exploitation [8]. However, for these methods to work successfully in real life systems a good understanding of user behavior in various type of searches is necessary in order to initialize the system in accordance to user needs as well as to set various parameters of the underlying algorithm(s) to fully reflect the cognitive behavior and expectations of the user. Hence there is a need for techniques to model the evolving information-needs and knowledge of the user. The main purpose of this research is to build interaction models that allow information retrieval systems to infer the state of exploration from observable aspects of user interactions.

2   Research Goals

The primary goal of this research is to enhance exploratory information-seeking. We are approaching this problem by constructing user models from observable user behaviors.

In this research we are particularly interested in the information-seeking behaviors of academics, because exploration of unfamiliar topics is one of the most common purposes of scientific searches [9] and if experienced information-seekers such as researchers have problems with exploratory search, then it implies a more sever information-seeking problem for the rest of the users. Therefore one of the contributions of this research is an exploratory study of the information-seeking behaviors of academics.

Another contribution is a prototype application for scientific information-seeking. This prototype application demonstrates how to integrate existing machine learning solutions such as reinforcement learning with interactive interfaces to construct a user model, visualize it, and get user feedback on the model. As a part of this research we conduct user studies to evaluate our prototype search tool with existing information-seeking systems.

An important contribution of this research is a model of dynamic parameters of exploratory search such as the user knowledge and interests. We investigate the possibility to develop a formal mathematical model to infer the state of exploration from observable aspects of user behavior, namely search result viewing and selection actions. We expect these observable behaviors to reflect the changes in user knowledge and interests, which supports the information-retrieval systems to estimate whether the suggested results are relevant to the current user interests and knowledge. We also investigate the predictive power of this model through user studies.

The main contributions we aim to achieve can be summarized as follows.

1. Exploratory study of scientific information-seeking behaviors of academics
2. Prototype exploratory search tool for scientific information-seeking
3. A formal mathematical model to predict state of exploration from observable aspects of user behavior
4. Evaluate the user interaction model by incorporating our model in running IR systems.

3 Progress Made to Date

To begin this research, it is essential to understand what sort of problems exist in exploratory information-seeking. To this end, we conducted a study to investigate how academics search for scientific information and what challenges they face. This was a mixed method study involving interviews, diary logs, user observations, and a survey. The findings suggested that exploring unfamiliar research areas was one of the most common purposes of scientific information-seeking and it is the most difficult task to perform. We published these useful findings [9] and it inspired us to focus on scientific information-seeking.

The next step involved implementing a novel system that addresses the existing problems of exploratory information-seeking. In exploratory search, users have no clear goals. Therefore, it is essential to design visualizations of the information space to help the users to make sense of the topic they are searching. User modeling is crucial to understand the constantly evolving information-needs of the user. It is also essential to allow the user to correct the system generated user model. To these ends, we designed a novel interactive visualization as in Figure 1. We named this prototype application SciNet. In SciNet, the user can perceive the state of user model through the interactive visualization and provide feedback by moving keywords. The reinforcement learning algorithm dynamically adjusts the user model according to user feedback and balances exploitation (more specific subtopics) and exploration (alternative topics). SciNet is the first system to combine reinforcement learning with an interactive visualization to guide users through unfamiliar information spaces. We further designed user studies to compare SciNet with two baselines: SciNet excluding interactive user modeling and a real world baseline (Google Scholar). The results show that SciNet helps users to more effectively find relevant, novel and diverse results. We published these findings in the ASIST 2013 conference and we won the best paper award at the International Conference on Intelligent User Interfaces (IUI 2013), a premier venue for this kind of research [10].

Our next task was to contribute a formal mathematical model that allows an IR system to infer the state of exploration. The model is expected to predict if the suggested search results, queries, or keywords are too specific versus too broad to the user's information-need as exploration progresses. Combining insights from research into exploratory search and from Information Foraging Theory (IFT) [11], the model assumes that the number of search results that a user selects can be expressed as a function of the number of search results seen by the user, and that this follows a natural logarithmic distribution. We experimentally evaluated this model through a controlled user study. The findings of this research is currently under review at SIGIR 2014 conference.

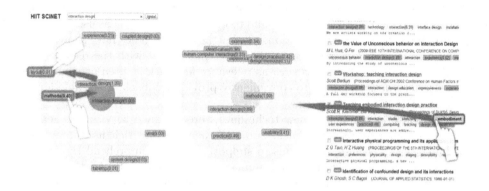

Fig. 1. Interactive radar visualization contains a set of exploratory and exploitative keywords retrieved by the reinforcement learning algorithm. User can indicate an increased importance of the keyword "methods" by moving it towards the center of the exploratory view and indicates a reduced importance of the keyword "layout" by moving it outside. User can also move more interesting keywords from the list of documents. The keywords explicitly manipulated by the user are colored in orange. In the second iteration (right), new keywords and documents have been predicted by the system.

4   Future Contributions

An important future challenge is to investigate in a real exploratory information-seeking scenario the performance of the formal mathematical model that we developed to predict the specificity of search results. We have already conducted a preliminary classification study which found that a system using only a simple classifier can obtain informed estimates on the specificity of a query while the user is interacting with its results. In the future we will incorporate our model in a running IR system and further validate it's usefulness in enhancing performance of exploratory search tasks.

Another interesting opportunity is to employ the model outside the scientific information-seeking scenario. In the future we will investigate the possibilities to apply our model to general exploratory search tasks.

5   Related Work

Over the past decade researchers from, among others, IR, HCI, and cognitive science communities have made many attempts towards improving exploratory search by developing retrieval techniques and user interfaces, as well as conducting studies to understand user behaviors.

In the context of information retrieval techniques, existing contributions can be categorized as relevance feedback based retrieval [5], faceted search [6], and result clustering [4]. But evidence from user studies later show that results clustering and relevance feedback based methods are rarely used due to high cognitive overload of selecting relevant results and providing feedback, and the problem of context traps [5]. Faceted search is found to be overly demanding as users have to go through a large number of options [6]. Furthermore, studies have shown that exploratory search requires more active user engagement with the results [12]. The lack of success of systems such as relevance feedback is often attributed to user interface designs failing to conveniently provide feedback at suitable levels of granularity [6].

In response, a number of new techniques were designed to visualize search results and capture user feedback. Some of them include rich user interfaces combined with learning algorithms to support users to comprehend the search results [13], and visualization and summarizing of results [14]. All these solutions are giving users more control yet without taking the moment-by-moment information-needs of the user into consideration [15].User modeling is essential for this purpose.

User behavior in exploratory information-seeking is studied with intents: predicting cognitive styles [16], identifying search and query formulation strategies [17], and constructing user models to predict the domain knowledge [18]. Early studies showed emergence of different search strategies depending on the users familiarity with the topic. Important results include users spending more time evaluating unfamiliar topics than familiar ones [18], domain knowledge and experience with a search tool impact search behavior [19], and that search strategies change over time when domain knowledge increases [20]. Existing models are useful in customizing results according to user preference [21] and knowledge, they however, do not capture situations where domain experts search information in narrower sub-fields of a familiar domain. Information Foraging Theory (IFT) provides several quantitative models of user search [11], yet existing work on IFT does not consider the effect of evolving user knowledge and queries. Overall, behavioral studies clearly point to the dynamic nature of the exploratory information-seeking process and the effect of prior knowledge on users' search strategies, which lends support to the assumptions behind the models we develop in this research. Our aim is to design user models that predict moment-by-moment information-needs of the user through observable user behaviors to improve the performance of retrieval algorithms.

References

1. White, R.W., Kules, B., Drucker, S.M.: Supporting exploratory search. J. Comm. ACM 49(4), 36–39 (2006)
2. Teevan, J., Alvarado, C., Ackerman, M.S., Karger, D.R.: The perfect search engine is not enough: a study of orienteering behavior in directed search. In: CHI, pp. 415–422 (2004)

3. Marchionini, G.: Exploratory search: from finding to understanding. J. Comm. ACM 49(4), 41–46 (2006)
4. Ferragina, P., Gulli, A.: A personalized search engine based on Web-snippet hierarchical clustering. J. Software: Practice and Experience 38(2), 189–225 (2008)
5. Kelly, D., Fu, X.: Elicitation of term relevance feedback: an investigation of term source and context. In: SIGIR, pp. 453–460 (2006)
6. Yee, K.P., Swearingen, K., Li, K., Hearst, M.: Faceted metadata for image search and browsing. In: CHI (2003)
7. Ruotsalo, T., Athukorala, K., Glowacka, D., Konyushkova, K., Jacucci, G., Kaski, S.: Supporting Exploratory Search Tasks with Interactive User Modeling. In: AGM of Assoc. Inf. Sci. Tech. (2013)
8. Karimzadehgan, M., Zhai, C.: Exploration exploitation tradeoff in interactive relevance feedback. In: CIKM, pp. 1397–1400 (2010)
9. Athukorala, K., Hoggan, E., Lehtio, A., Ruotsalo, T., Jacucci, G.: Information-seeking behaviors of computer scientists: Challenges for electronic literature search tools. In: AGM of Assoc. Inf. Sci. Tech. (2013)
10. Glowacka, D., Ruotsalo, T., Konyushkova, K., Athukorala, K., Kaski, S., Jacucci, G.: Directing exploratory search: Reinforcement learning from user interactions with keywords. In: IUI (2013)
11. Pirolli, P., Card, S.: Information foraging in information access environments. In: CHI, pp. 51–58 (1995)
12. Hearst, M., Elliott, A., English, J., Sinha, R., Swearingen, K., Yee, K.: Finding the flow in web site search. J. Commun. ACM, 42–49 (2002)
13. Chau, D.H., Kittur, A., Hong, J.I., Faloutsos, C.: Apolo: making sense of large network data by combining rich user interaction and machine learning. In: CHI, pp. 167–176 (2011)
14. Käki, M.: Findex: search result categories help users when document ranking fails. In: CHI, pp. 131–140 (2005)
15. Teevan, J., Alvarado, C., Ackerman, M.S., Karger, D.R.: The perfect search engine is not enough: a study of orienteering behavior in directed search. In: CHI, pp. 415–422 (2004)
16. Saito, H., Miwa, K.: A cognitive study of information seeking processes in the www: the effects of searcher's knowledge and experience. In: WISE, pp. 321–327 (2001)
17. Payne, S.J., Howes, A.: Adaptive interaction: A utility maximization approach to understanding human interaction with technology. In: Synt. Lec. Hum.-Cent. Inf., pp. 1–111 (2013)
18. Holscher, C., Strube, G.: Web search behavior of internet experts and newbies. J. Computer Networks 33(1), 337–346 (2000)
19. Vakkari, P., Pennanen, M., Serola, S.: Changes of search terms and tactics while writing a research proposal: A longitudinal case study. Inf. Proc. Manag. 39(3), 445–463 (2003)
20. Wildemuth, B.M.: The effects of domain knowledge on search tactic formulation. J. Assoc. Inf. Sci. Tech. 55(3), 246–258 (2004)
21. Kelly, D., Teevan, J.: Implicit feedback for inferring user preference: a bibliography. In: SIGIR, pp. 18–28 (2003)

Hybrid Solution of the Cold-Start Problem in Context-Aware Recommender Systems

Matthias Braunhofer

Free University of Bozen-Bolzano, Bozen-Bolzano, Italy
mbraunhofer@unibz.it

Abstract. A challenge of Context-Aware Recommender Systems (CARSs) is the cold-start problem, i.e., the usual poor recommendation of new items to new users in new contextual situations. In this research, we aim at solving this problem by developing a switching hybrid CARS, which exploits different context-aware recommendation techniques, each of which has its own strengths and weaknesses, and switches between these techniques depending on the current recommendation situation (i.e., new user, new item and/or new context).

Keywords: Context-aware recommender systems, cold-start problem, switching hybrid systems.

1 Introduction and Motivation

Cold-start is an important and challenging problem for Recommender Systems (RSs). It is generated when a new user or a new item is introduced into the system but the system does not have enough information (e.g., ratings, purchasing records, browsing history) about the user or item to provide the new user with accurate recommendations or to reliably recommend the new item to any user.

Overall, while there is a substantial amount of research on cold-start in traditional RSs [13], only little research has been conducted on cold-start in Context-Aware Recommender Systems (CARSs). In CARSs, the cold-start problem becomes even more challenging, since it does not suffice to have enough ratings for users and items; the systems must have collected a sufficient number of ratings in the various contextual situations as well (i.e., new context problem). For instance, imagine that a CARS for places of interest (POIs) collected from the users many low ratings for a mountain hiking route during rainy weather, but no rating for the same route during a great sunny day when the route is expected to be highly attractive. Then, the route would erroneously not be recommended to any user in a sunny day.

Having new users, new items and new contextual situations is in fact the normal situation of any CARS at the beginning of its operational life, and practicality requires that a CARS must be relevant from the beginning of its deployment, to ensure users' and providers' loyalty. A crucial question is therefore how accurate context-aware recommendations can be produced in the various cold-start situations. That is the question that this research work tries to address.

V. Dimitrova et al. (Eds.): UMAP 2014, LNCS 8538, pp. 484–489, 2014.

2   Problem Statement, Research Goals and Hypotheses

In this work, we deal with cold-start situations occurring in CARSs. In particular, we consider the following:

- *New user problem*: The new user problem occurs when a new user is added to the CARS and there is not enough information about the user's preferences to make a good suggestion.
- *New item problem*: The new item problem refers to new items introduced into CARSs that can not be recommended until some users have rated it.
- *New context problem*: The new context problem denotes the impossibility to accurately recommend items to users under new contextual situations.
- *Mixtures of the above mentioned problems*: This situation reflects the problem of making relevant recommendations given any possible combination of the previously mentioned elementary/pure cases.

We hypothesise that the above mentioned problems can be addressed by adaptively selecting a recommendation technology among a range of solutions. This can be implemented with a hybrid approach and in particular with a switching technique. A switching hybrid CARS algorithm seems to be a promising and intuitive solution in order to cope with the cold-start problem, as it assumes the existence of several different recommendation algorithms with significantly different performances, which is likely to be the case across the individual cold-start situations. Consequently, the ultimate goal of this research is the design and development of a switching hybrid CARS that exploits different context-aware recommendation techniques, and switches between these techniques depending on the current (cold-start) situation. Switching hybrid CARSs is a new, challenging topic, since it requires to determine the exact switching criterion, which in turn requires to understand the individual strengths and weaknesses of the constituent recommendation techniques in different recommendation situations but also under different levels of data sparsity.

3   Related Work

In spite of the importance of the cold-start problem for CARSs, only little research has been conducted specifically on this subject. One approach to the cold-start problem is to try to acquire additional information about the users, items or contextual situations. The problem, however, is that acquiring such information usually requires some additional effort from the users and/or service providers of the RS. It can be obtained, for instance, by employing an Active Learning (AL) strategy [9] or a cross-domain recommendation technique [10]. Another alternative, which inspired our work, is to exploit a set of metadata describing the users and items (e.g., demographics and item descriptions), and to utilise them in a hybrid CARS in order to overcome the new user and new item problem, respectively [18]. A particular hybridisation method is the switching hybridisation method proposed in [8] and [5]. It selects and applies the best performing recommender from among multiple recommenders based on the current recommendation situation, and hence can avoid problems specific to one recommender (e.g., the new item problem of a collaborative RS by switching to a content-based recommender).

Instead of acquiring new preference data, one can try also to better process the existing preference data. An example of such approach can be found in [19], where the authors present a novel recommendation algorithm, called Differential Context Weighting (DCW), that alleviates the context sparsity problem caused by the standard, reduction-based approach [1] by exploiting weighting vectors and similarity of contexts in order to weight the contribution of individual contextual factors and ratings in the rating prediction algorithm, respectively. Another similar example, which we have evaluated and tested in our work, is Semantic Pre-Filtering (SPF) [7]. SPF is a contextual pre-filtering method that tries to overcome the new context problem by using, in the recommendation process, not only contextual ratings that exactly match the target context but also those that were provided in semantically equivalent contexts.

4   Overview of the Proposed Approach

Related work shows that there is no universal solution to all types of cold-start problems in CARSs. All the proposed approaches have different strengths and weaknesses, and are able to solve different sub-problems of the cold-start problem. Therefore, in our research, we propose to combine the benefits of these existing approaches into one hybrid solution, and more precisely a switching hybrid approach. Switching hybrid CARSs are adaptive in the sense that they can switch between recommendation techniques using some criterion, hence making efficient use of the strengths and weaknesses of the considered RSs. Although switching hybrid RSs as an approach to overcoming the cold-start problem in traditional RSs have been proposed before [8,5], to the best of our knowledge they have not yet been applied to CARSs. As a consequence, there does not exist an explicit reference model for switching hybrid CARSs, and thus it is necessary to design such a system from the ground up.

To achieve this, we have first identified candidate CARS algorithms that are hypothesised to address specific aspects of the cold-start problem. For instance, demographic-based CARSs use socio-demographic attributes such as age, gender and region, and hence are able to learn the users' preferences, also when no or only few ratings for those users are available [14]. Analogously, content-based approaches rely on textual item descriptions as well as item features, and are capable of recommending items not yet rated by any user [15]. And finally, there exist some recommendation algorithms that try to make better use of available contextual information by exploiting context hierarchies (e.g., Saturday → weekend) or similarities (e.g., rainy ≈ snowy), which often allows to generate accurate recommendations even under unrated contexts [19,7]. Following these ideas, we have tested the recommendation algorithms listed below. Some of these are new and have been developed by us, while others have been published in the research literature before.

- **MF.** MF denotes the context-free matrix factorisation model proposed in [11] that we used as a baseline.
- **CAMF-CC.** This model is a variant of Context-Aware MF (CAMF) [3] that extends MF by incorporating baseline parameters for each contextual condition and item category to model how the ratings of items belonging to a specific category deviate due to the contextual conditions.
- **Category-based CAMF-CC.** Category-based CAMF-CC is a novel variant of CAMF-CC that we have designed. We hypothesise that it is specially useful in addressing the new item problem since it incorporates additional sources of information about the items (e.g., category or genre information).
- **Demographics-based CAMF-CC.** This is another variant of CAMF-CC that we propose for tackling the new user problem by profiling users in terms of known user attributes (demographics), such as gender, age group, personality traits, and so on.
- **SPF.** SPF is a contextual pre-filtering approach proposed in [7], which uses a local MF model trained on the ratings tagged with a target contextual situation and other similar situations to compute rating predictions for that specific target context. We conjecture that SPF will better perform in cold-start situations because it is able to reuse ratings tagged with contexts that, notwithstanding they are syntactically different, they actually influence in a similar way the users' ratings.

To evaluate the cold-start performance of the above mentioned algorithms, we executed an offline experiment using two datasets: STS (South Tyrol Suggests), containing 2,422 contextually-tagged ratings for places of interest (POIs) collected in about one year of activity of our STS app [6,9], and LDOS-CoMoDa [12], containing 2,296 contextually-tagged ratings for movies. Our offline experiment followed a five-fold cross-validation strategy where we measured the models' Mean Absolute Errors (MAEs) by identifying and predicting those ratings in the test sets that were coming from new users, new items and new contextual situations, respectively. According to our definition, users, items or contextual situations were new if they had at most n ratings in the training set, with n ranging from 0 to 10. Compared to the previously proposed evaluation techniques [16,17], we believe that our experimental procedure more closely matches a realistic scenario where the RS encounters a cold-start situation and is requested to compute a prediction given the full set of the ratings available at that point in time.

5   Results Obtained Up to Date

The main results obtained up to date indicate the following:

- **New Users.** In the new user situation, we were able to prove our conjecture by observing a good performance of demographics-based CAMF-CC on both datasets, especially for user profiles containing a low number of ratings (i.e., up to 4 ratings for both STS and CoMoDa). This changes as soon as more ratings are available in the user profile. Then, the incorporation of user attributes (i.e., demographics) into the CAMF-CC prediction model becomes less useful, and the demographics-based CAMF-CC model is again outperformed by the other tested CAMF-CC variants.

- **New Items.** Under the new item scenario, we found category-based CAMF-CC to be very effective, outperforming all other considered algorithms over all tested item profile sizes. This proves our hypothesis that category-based CAMF-CC successfully addresses the new item problem, which is due to the fact that it incorporates also the item category (genre) information, and hence can produce reasonably accurate item profiles also for new items given that other items belonging to the same category (genre) have obtained a few ratings.

- **New Contextual Situations.** Finally, for the new contextual situation scenario, we observed all context-aware recommendation algorithms to be more accurate than the baseline MF model, with the best being SPF for STS and category-based CAMF-CC for CoMoDa. We did not observe any consistent significant differences between SPF and the various CAMF variants. Therefore, our hypothesis that SPF is especially useful for the new context situation can not be supported.

6   Future Work

As future work, we plan to first continue our offline experiments, trying to better separate the elementary cold-start cases from the mixtures of elementary cases. Secondly, it is necessary to assess the performances of our tested CARS algorithms on additional datasets (e.g., MovieLens, LibraryThing) and to compare them with other CARS algorithms (e.g., DCW [19], item splitting [4], user splitting [2]). Thirdly, we will design and develop the switching hybrid CARS algorithm based on the results from the offline experiments. Finally, we plan to integrate the developed switching hybrid CARS algorithm into our STS server so that we can perform a live user study and compare the users' perceived recommendation quality of our proposed algorithm against another state-of-the-art CARS algorithm (e.g., CAMF-CC or SPF).

References

1. Adomavicius, G., Sankaranarayanan, R., Sen, S., Tuzhilin, A.: Incorporating contextual information in recommender systems using a multidimensional approach. ACM Transactions on Information Systems (TOIS) 23(1), 103–145 (2005)
2. Baltrunas, L., Amatriain, X.: Towards time-dependant recommendation based on implicit feedback. In: Workshop on Context-Aware Recommender Systems, (CARS 2009) (2009)
3. Baltrunas, L., Ludwig, B., Ricci, F.: Matrix factorization techniques for context aware recommendation. In: Proceedings of the Fifth ACM Conference on Recommender Systems, pp. 301–304. ACM (2011)

4. Baltrunas, L., Ricci, F.: Experimental evaluation of context-dependent collaborative filtering using item splitting. In: User Modeling and User-Adapted Interaction (to appear, 2014)
5. Billsus, D., Pazzani, M.J.: User modeling for adaptive news access. User Modeling and User-Adapted Interaction 10(2-3), 147–180 (2000)
6. Braunhofer, M., Elahi, M., Ricci, F., Schievenin, T.: Context-aware points of interest suggestion with dynamic weather data management. In: Information and Communication Technologies in Tourism 2014, pp. 87–100. Springer (2013)
7. Codina, V., Ricci, F., Ceccaroni, L.: Local context modeling with semantic prefiltering. In: Proceedings of the Seventh ACM Conference on Recommender Systems, pp. 363–366. ACM (2013)
8. Ekstrand, M., Riedl, J.: When recommenders fail: predicting recommender failure for algorithm selection and combination. In: Proceedings of the Sixth ACM Conference on Recommender Systems, pp. 233–236. ACM (2012)
9. Elahi, M., Braunhofer, M., Ricci, F., Tkalcic, M.: Personality-based active learning for collaborative filtering recommender systems. In: Baldoni, M., Baroglio, C., Boella, G., Micalizio, R. (eds.) AI*IA 2013. LNCS, vol. 8249, pp. 360–371. Springer, Heidelberg (2013)
10. Enrich, M., Braunhofer, M., Ricci, F.: Cold-start management with cross-domain collaborative filtering and tags. In: Huemer, C., Lops, P. (eds.) EC-Web 2013. LNBIP, vol. 152, pp. 101–112. Springer, Heidelberg (2013)
11. Koren, Y., Bell, R.: Advances in collaborative filtering. In: Recommender Systems Handbook, pp. 145–186. Springer (2011)
12. Košir, A., Odic, A., Kunaver, M., Tkalcic, M., Tasic, J.F.: Database for contextual personalization. Elektrotehniski Vestnik 78(5), 270–274 (2011)
13. Lam, X.N., Vu, T., Le, T.D., Duong, A.D.: Addressing cold-start problem in recommendation systems. In: Proceedings of the 2nd International Conference on Ubiquitous Information Management and Communication, ICUIMC 2008, pp. 208–211. ACM, New York (2008)
14. Lee, J.S., Lee, J.C.: Context awareness by case-based reasoning in a music recommendation system. In: Ichikawa, H., Cho, W.-D., Satoh, I., Youn, H.Y. (eds.) UCS 2007. LNCS, vol. 4836, pp. 45–58. Springer, Heidelberg (2007)
15. Musto, C., Semeraro, G., Lops, P., de Gemmis, M.: Contextual evsm: A content-based context-aware recommendation framework based on distributional semantics. In: Huemer, C., Lops, P. (eds.) EC-Web 2013. LNBIP, vol. 152, pp. 125–136. Springer, Heidelberg (2013)
16. Park, S.-T., Chu, W.: Pairwise preference regression for cold-start recommendation. In: Proceedings of the Third ACM Conference on Recommender Systems, pp. 21–28. ACM (2009)
17. Rendle, S., Schmidt-Thieme, L.: Online-updating regularized kernel matrix factorization models for large-scale recommender systems. In: Proceedings of the 2008 ACM Conference on Recommender Systems, pp. 251–258. ACM (2008)
18. Woerndl, W., Brocco, M., Eigner, R.: Context-aware recommender systems in mobile scenarios. International Journal of Information Technology and Web Engineering (IJITWE) 4(1), 67–85 (2009)
19. Zheng, Y., Burke, R., Mobasher, B.: Recommendation with differential context weighting. In: Carberry, S., Weibelzahl, S., Micarelli, A., Semeraro, G. (eds.) UMAP 2013. LNCS, vol. 7899, pp. 152–164. Springer, Heidelberg (2013)

Improving Mobile Recommendations through Context-Aware User Interaction

Béatrice Lamche

Technische Universität München,
Boltzmannstr. 3, 85748 Garching, Germany
lamche@in.tum.de
http://www11.in.tum.de

Abstract. Mobile recommender systems provide personalized recommendations to help deal with today's information overload. However, due to spatial limitations in mobile interfaces and uncertainty of the user's preferences in the beginning, the improvement of the user experience remains one of the main challenges when designing these systems and has not been investigated thoroughly. This paper describes the aim and progress of the author's PhD studies on the user interaction, usability and accuracy of mobile recommender systems. The approach aims to combine different user interaction methods with context-awareness to allow user-friendly personalized mobile recommendations.

Keywords: mobile recommender systems, user modelling, context-awareness.

1 Motivation

Mobile phones are more and more used for information access. Due to corresponding technological developments in this area, the amount of information and online services increases. Hence, it becomes more and more difficult for mobile users to filter the necessary information to make a decision. Recommendation techniques are widely used to improve the usability of mobile systems. Although lots of research has focused on web-based recommender systems, mobile systems reveal additional challenges related to human-computer interaction issues that have not been researched thoroughly: First, supporting input and interaction capabilities on mobile devices to elicit user preferences is extremely difficult because of their spatial limitations in the user interface (e.g. small keypads and screens). Secondly, users might be unable to formulate explicit queries and prefer being involved in an *exploratory* process due to their uncertainty at the beginning of the recommendation session. Thirdly, since the user is on the move, connectivity problems might occur and the user's attention span is limited as well [1]. I aim to investigate the possibility to consider different forms of mobile context and user interaction techniques to enhance the system's accuracy and at the same time the usability. A mobile shopping recommender is chosen as

V. Dimitrova et al. (Eds.): UMAP 2014, LNCS 8538, pp. 490–495, 2014.
© Springer International Publishing Switzerland 2014

application, because particularly for exploratory scenarios such as going shopping without having a specific item in mind, a system that adapts to consumer preferences constitutes a domain that is largely unexplored in the literature.

2   Background and Related Work

Context plays an important role regarding the perception of the usefulness of an item for a user [2]. [3] define a recommendation process that integrates context. They distinguish between a user's *short term* (STM) and *long term* memories (LTM). STM stores explicit or implicit ratings for items from the active interaction. LTM stores preference models within specific contexts, derived from previous user interactions with the system. Contextual cues are used to retrieve relevant preference models from LTM that belong to the same context as the current interaction. This information is merged with the current preference model stored in STM for generating context-aware recommendations [3].

However, the proposed framework is very general and does not emphasize how it can be applied in a mobile scenario. First of all, mobile recommender systems face a different context than web-based systems that has to be treated differently. [2] divides mobile context into four sub-categories: *physical context* (e.g. location, time, weather), *interaction media context* (e.g. the device used to access the system and the type of media that is being interacted with), *modal context* (e.g. the user's intention, mood, experience) and *social context* (e.g. people that surround the user). A concept for the generation of mobile recommendations should include these four different types of context.

Moreover, the efficient presentation of mobile recommendations is difficult due to spatial limitations in mobile interfaces. Interactive interfaces have to be designed to support the elicitation of the user's preferences.

[1] also emphasizes that mobile recommendations have to be presented in a transparent and easily understandable way and suggests the automatic generation of explanations. However, this topic hat received very few studies so far.

For the purpose of delivering accurate recommendations, the recommender system needs to learn about the user. This is a difficult task since the user is often uncertain of her/his preferences, in particular in an exploratory scenario where the user does not know exactly what she/he is searching for (e.g. looking for an open restaurant or shop). Moreover, due to a limited attention span and spatial limitations in mobile interfaces, the user might be unable to formulate explicit search queries. *Conversational* or rather *Critiquing recommender systems* aim at solving this problem. Once a set of recommendations has been issued, it will involve the user in an ongoing conversation and solicit a user critique through ratings to again issue an improved set. Instead of having to specify exact values or sift through categories, users can simply state their current preference, e.g. "show me more trousers, but not in this color" [4]. Especially for the elicitation of the user's preferences for mobile devices [5] suggest the concept of conversation-based *Active Learning* but without investigating the mobile application area further. By starting with general recommendations, the system narrows down the user's interests through eliciting critiques until the desired item is obtained. In contrast to other existing systems, even new users receive recommendations right from the beginning. The user can always interrupt this process when distracted and only simple interaction methods such as rating a specific item feature are needed to exercise a critique [5].

The underlying user model plays an important role of a recommender system. In order to provide personalized mobile recommendations even in the cold start phase, a user modelling approach based on *stereotypes* seems to be a promising approach [6]. In particular in the fashion domain, most people can be associated with a specific style that barely changes (e.g. *casual* vs. *elegant*), so that stereotypes can be easily predefined and an already existing user data base is not required. New users will be initially assigned to different stereotypes to receive personalized recommendations right from the beginning.

3   Statement of Thesis or Problem

The literature review has shown that very little research has investigated the development of a concept which describes the overall recommendation process of context-aware and user-friendly mobile recommender systems. Based on the previous considerations, I developed a conceptual framework for the generation of context-aware mobile recommendations shown in *figure 1*. It adapts the idea of [3] to distinguish between a short term and a long term memory. However, I define the short time memory as an instance that stores the overall mobile *context* (consisting of the modal, physical, social and media context). This context is used to update the long term memory (here defined as the *user model*) after each interaction. The user model also includes the user profile, since this is data that is constant (such as the user's nationality, gender and date of birth). The information of the user model is then used in conjunction with the context as input for the Active Learning algorithm that generates the recommendations. The recommendations will be presented in an understandable and transparent

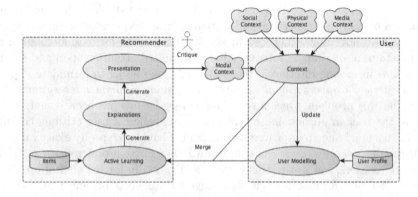

Fig. 1. A conceptual framework for the generation of mobile recommendations

way, so that the user can criticize them efficiently, which in turn updates the modal context. For this purpose, suitable explanations have to be generated and presented. Throughout my research, I am conducting a series of user studies for a shopping scenario to validate the individual components of the framework.

4   Research Goals and Methods

This dissertation project aims at developing a conceptual framework that describes all necessary steps that need to be implemented when designing an efficient context-aware mobile recommender system out of a human-computer interaction perspective. As shown in *figure 1*, the framework consists of five building blocks that require further research: *Active Learning, explanation, presentation, context* and *user modelling*. All of these building blocks will be evaluated separately, both theoretically and empirically. For each experiment, I will develop a prototype so that the theoretical considerations can be evaluated within a user study. The outcome of each of the experiments will iteratively extend parts of the framework for mobile context-aware recommendations. The individual five building blocks of my conceptual framework will be investigated over the time of my Ph.D. project within sub-projects and combined in a final evaluation. As a result, I will propose an evaluated framework consisting of concrete presentation guidelines, efficient algorithms and suitable user modelling approaches that supports developers to improve mobile recommendations by maintaining usability.

5   Dissertation Status

I have already reached several steps towards the overall thesis goal of developing a conceptual framework for the generation of context-aware recommendations in mobile scenarios. In the first part of my Ph.D. thesis I focused on the *Active Learning* building block of my conceptual framework (see *figure 1*). For this purpose, I investigated different Active Learning strategies suitable for mobile recommender systems. I developed a mobile shopping recommender application (see *figure 2*) which uses a conversation-based Active Learning strategy, which involves the user in a cycle of updating displayed recommendations based on her/his critiques on features of those items until a satisfactory item is found and selected. Feature critiques are differentiated into positive ('like') and negative ('dislike') feedback enabling the system to decide whether to further *refine* the selection by showing more similar items or to *refocus* and show a more diverse set of items. The logical critiquing-process is illustrated in *figure 3*. Results of the user study show that conversational Active Learning improves the user experience and diversity-based information retrieval is preferred to similarity-based in a mobile exploratory context regarding accuracy, effort and the intention in returning to the system. Moreover, a solely similarity-based approach is worse in recovering from focusing on the wrong area of the item space and requires more effort from the user for correction. The concept behind, the implementation and evaluation of the application will be published in [7]. The developed application illustrated in *figure 2* serves as a basis for the development of future prototypes.

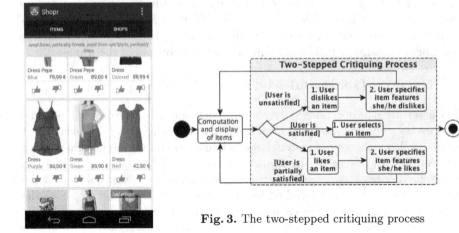

Fig. 3. The two-stepped critiquing process

Fig. 2. The main view of the smartphone application

Regarding the *User Modelling* building block of *figure 1*, I have recently also developed a smartphone application that compares a mobile shopping recommender system using a stereotype-based user model with one without a specific user model. The application computes the likelihood of each stereotype based on the user's age and profession. I moreover take the taste of music into account, since studies found out that it is highly related to the individual fashion style [8]. Each stereotype has been given a weight for all available age groups, jobs and music styles. The stereotype algorithm iterates through all stereotypes available and adds up the likelihood that this stereotype has for each of the properties age, job and music. Images representative for the three stereotypes that had the highest likelihood are then presented. As soon as the user selects the preferred stereotype, stereotype-based recommendations are calculated and presented. A following user study proved that a user model based on stereotypes generates better results than a recommender without a user model. Moreover, stereotype-based user models allow the generation of personalized recommendations right from the beginning.

Right now, I focus on the *presentation* building block of the framework (see *figure 1*). For this purpose, I first conducted an online survey which investigated the three key interaction activities between the user and the system: the initial preference elicitation process, the presentation of the resulting recommendations set and the preference feedback process. Results include that users like giving feedback by rating stars, wish to see multiple recommendations in a list and prefer answering questions as preference collection method. These findings were then implemented in an interactive smartphone app. The evaluation resulted in deriving nine guidelines for a more satisfactory interaction with a mobile shopping recommender system, followed by the finding that contextual change heavily influences participants' choice of their favorite interaction method.

In the future, I plan to investigate how *mobile context* such as current temperature, the user's distance to the shops, taken pictures and knowledge about surrounding people can be used to generate more accurate recommendations. Until now, I also haven't answered the research question how to automatically generate *explanations* for mobile recommender systems. The main challenges consist of generating understandable recommendations for a small display size and also give the user the opportunity to interact with these. Finally, I will implement the conducted results in a matured prototype to evaluate the overall framework in a large-scale user study.

6 Expected Contributions

The expected outcome of my dissertation project will provide findings about how to improve the user experience of mobile recommender systems by the application of traditional human-computer interaction methods. Therefore, expected contributions will be fivefold: (1) Concrete guidelines for the design of interactive mobile recommender user interfaces; (2) Detailed understanding of how explanations should look like and how they can be generated automatically; (3) Evaluation of different Active Learning strategies and concrete suggestions for their application depending on the specific scenario; (4) Proposal of a suitable user model for mobile recommender systems based on stereotypes; (5) Better understanding of mobile context and how it can be used to improve mobile recommendations. The final evaluated conceptual framework should give mobile recommender system developers an understanding of how to generate user-friendly and accurate recommendations in mobile scenarios. With this knowledge, mobile recommender systems can be developed more quickly and successfully.

References

1. Ricci, F.: Mobile Recommender Systems. Information Technology & Tourism 12(3), 205–231 (2010)
2. Ricci, F.: Contextualizing Useful Recommendations. In: UMAP 2012 (2012), http://www.inf.unibz.it/~ricci/Slides/Context-UMAP-2012-Ricci.pdf
3. Anand, S.S., Mobasher, B.: Contextual Recommendation. In: Berendt, B., Hotho, A., Mladenic, D., Semeraro, G. (eds.) WebMine 2007. LNCS (LNAI), vol. 4737, pp. 142–160. Springer, Heidelberg (2007)
4. Mcginty, L., Reilly, J.: On the Evolution of Critiquing Recommenders. In: Recommender Systems Handbook, pp. 419–453. Springer US (2011)
5. Rubens, N., Kaplan, D., Sugiyama, M.: Active Learning in Recommender Systems. In: Recommender Systems Handbook, pp. 735–767. Springer US (2011)
6. Rich, E.: User Modeling via Stereotypes. Cognitive Science 3(4), 329–354 (1979)
7. Lamche, B., Trottmann, U., Woerndl, W.: Active Learning Strategies for Exploratory Mobile Recommender Systems. In: Proc. Decisions@CaRR workshop, 36th European Conference on Information Retrieval, Amsterdam, Netherlands (2014)
8. Na, Y., Agnhage, T.: Relationship between the preference styles of music and fashion and the similarity of their sensibility. International Journal of Clothing Science and Technology 25(2), 109–118 (2013)

Personalized Cultural Heritage Experience Outside the Museum: Connecting the Museum Experience to the Outside World

Alan J. Wecker

University of Haifa, Israel; University of Trento, Italy
ajwecker@gmail.com

Abstract. Museums, as cultural heritage sites, have long been a primary showground for the exploration of new technologies. Recent new directions for research in this field, have concerned themselves with 1) expanding the on-site visit with prior and post experiences, primarily at a desktop computer at home, but not necessarily; 2) expanding the visit from a onetime experience to an experience that may repeat itself multiple times over a lifetime, including the reuse of personal information elicited from experience gained onsite (e.g. a user model) for providing personalized experience at multiple sites. The proposed third new direction for research in this field, the one which is focused on is: examining how to enhance other experiences outside the museum site, based on experiences at the museum site. By doing this one can begin to connect our cultural heritage experiences to our "daily" lives.

Keywords: Lifelong User Modeling, Context, Mobile Guides, Opportunity Management.

1   Statement of Problem

The research problem (question) I aim to focus on and begin exploration of is:

How can we apply technology, enhanced with accumulated experiences at cultural heritage sites (e.g. museums), to identify and exploit opportunities for delivering personalized content to users in settings external to such sites (e.g. archeological sites, historical houses, etc…)?

This question can be broken down to more specific questions based on the three processes:

1. How can cultural heritage opportunities be identified and exploited, taking into account context and personal characteristics?

2. When an opportunity presents itself (a.k.a. opportunity exploitation); how can relevant content (informative, emotional, and social) be identified/found/selected?

3. How can this content (personalized) be delivered and presented within the context of the specific user?

V. Dimitrova et al. (Eds.): UMAP 2014, LNCS 8538, pp. 496–501, 2014.

2   Context and Motivation

The focus is on personalization as "product customization based on deep models of users' needs and behaviors". Personalization is deemed by many [1], [3], [4], [8], [14], though not all [7], [15], as a key factor in the success of such objectives. My proposed new direction for research in this field is examining how to enhance other experiences outside the museum site, based on experiences at the museum site. By doing this I can connect our cultural heritage experiences to our "daily" lives. In our common global melting pot, cultural heritage experience can help one carve out a unique personal identity.

From my research on example scenarios emerge three processes which are the three research themes which I aim to further examine: 1) identification of contextual opportunities outside the museum site, which are suitable to present cultural heritage information (primarily from museums, that the user has visited or may visit in the future), 2) selection of material which may interest the user in this particular contextual opportunity 3) delivery of such material given the context (devices, displays) and user preferences (user profile).

Each of these areas has a critical aspect that relates to HCI. These include cognitive, user modeling, and user interface design aspects. Results from the cultural heritage domain may be applicable to other domains or generalized.

3   Expected Contributions

In [8], a list of major research challenges for museums and lifelong cultural heritage was presented. Relating links to the rest of the user's life was presented at the hardest level of challenge. What is proposed is to start to find the paths and partial solutions to the challenges of representation, maintenance and reasoning with lifelong user models in the field of cultural heritage in order to link museum visits to other facets of the cultural heritage experience. The artifacts that will be developed will serve to further research in this important area, and collection of data will further the field of lifelong cultural heritage.

I aim to contribute, as part of my research to the following areas:

- The use of personal, emotional and social artifacts (as opposed to institutional or static web artifacts) for content selection. This has the potential to connect the visitors to their cultural heritage on a different level than intellectual. In addition, I aim for progress on questions of what spheres of social influence should be used.
- Life "wide" processes with data coming from multiple sites over periods of time. Part of the solutions involves research into how to develop lifelong user models. This includes changes to the model over time, where such a model should be held (client/server), who owns the model and how scrutable is it.

4   Progress

Based on my literature survey (extensively written up in my approved thesis proposal), I have initial definitions of what constitutes opportunities, content selection and contextual delivery. In addition I have identified a preliminary list of potential contextual and user model constituents for each of the three processes. These are to be written up and submitted to a workshop or doctorial colloquium or workshop for feedback. In addition a preliminary version of this proposal, presenting the challenge at hand and identifying the three processes, was presented as a position paper at PATCH 2013 and as a poster at UMAP 2013 [17].

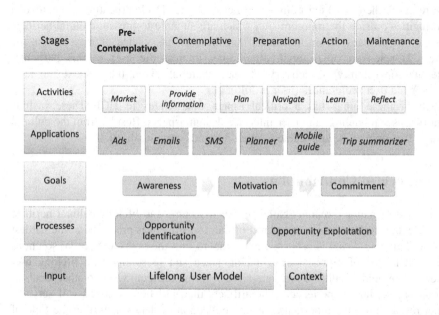

Fig. 1. Theoretical Model

I have begun to develop a theoretical framework (Figure 1) of how, where, why and what happens, or should happen during the attempt to engage visitors at a Cultural Heritage Site in order to encourage them to visit related cultural heritage sites; which we now briefly describe. Using Dubin's methodology we use concepts (in **bold**), instances (or examples in *italics*) and describe in words the relationships between the concepts. I start by borrowing concepts from the health coaching field (summarized in [13]), thusly; we have five **stages** of visitor engagement: *Pre-contemplative, Contemplative, Preparation, Action, and Maintenance*. In each stage, dependent on the stage we attempt to do a number of **activities**: such as *market, provide information, plan, navigate, and reflect*. Each of these activities is realized and supported by one or more **applications**: (*ads, emails, sms, planner, mobile guide, trip summarizer, etc...*). Each one of these activities attempts to accomplish one or more **goals** (or determinants as called in [13]) such as: *Awareness, Motivation, and*

Commitment. These goals are accomplished by the following **processes**: *Opportunity Identification and Opportunity Exploitation.* **Opportunity Identification** uses **context** (*infrastructural, spatial, temporal, task, social* [18]) to trigger an exploitation which makes use of **the User Model** (*Context preferences, Content preferences, Format Preferences, Social preferences, demographic data and social network data*)[6]. **Exploitation** is based on *determining an interrupt/communication scheme, picking content, picking a media format and presenting it to the user in a coherent way.* The last one "presenting it in a coherent way" is a potentially complex task and consists of: how to realistically tailor the presentation, connect it to previous cultural experience, and utilize the user model.

In addition I use the info flow from Knowledge Management: i.e. I gather all sorts of **data** at the various stages (*Surveys/Questionnaires, Explicit Remarks, Observed Behavior, Recorded Behavior, Social Interactions, Feedback*) to construct **information** (*Context Preferences, Content Preferences, Format preferences, Social Networks*). This information in turn is used to create a *User Model* which together with *context information* can create **actionable knowledge** which can lead to opportunity identification and exploitation.

5   Related Work

In this sub-section I review systems and projects which are close to my goal of examining lifelong systems to connect the indoor and outdoor experiences in addition to items described in the Background section. Though today I know of no personalized mobile guides which connect the indoor and outdoor cultural heritage experiences I will examine related personalized outdoor guides and guides with reusable user models and other similar features to my proposed research.

- The PUP museum guide [16] creates outdoor city tours based on the CHIP museum guide methodology (ontology, user models, etc.) [2]. The user model can be reused from one application to another thus addressing the cold start problem. The system uses the same user models for indoors and outdoors addressing our concerns of interoperability between indoor and outdoor models. This is preliminary work where they explored the potential of the CHIP technology to support both scenarios. In addition the authors discuss the future addition of contextual items such as time of day, hours of operation, and weather.
- The CULTURA project [5]aims at providing personalized access to digitalized collections. They use a four phase approach of guide, explore, suggest, and reflect [5]. This four phase approach allows them to cater to different levels of expertise and interests. While this project concerns itself with a high degree of personalization, the project does not concern itself with connecting various experiences and its focus is on digitized cultural heritage collections. However their four phase approach should be applicable and beneficial for my scenario.
- In the SUMI project, lifelong user modeling (LUM) was examined with emphasis on interoperability, scrutability and privacy [10], [11], [12]. This was not connected to a cultural heritage application, but was meant as first step towards an infrastructure. He also examines the use of social network and e-commerce sites to enhance LUM [9].

- Another project that has bearing on my work is Google Field Trip[1], which is an application which provides local sites that match a user's interest. From the description in the App Store[2]:

  o *Field Trip is your guide to the cool, hidden, and unique things in the world around you. Field Trip runs in the background on your phone. When you get close to something interesting, it pops up a card with details about the location. No click is required. If you have a headset or bluetooth connected, it can even read the info to you.*

  o *Field Trip can help you learn about everything from local history to the latest and best places to shop, eat, and have fun. You select the local feeds you like and the information pops up on your phone automatically, as you walk next to those places.*

  o *The hyperlocal history experts of Arcadia and Historvius will unveil local lore in places you never expected. Trend-setting publications like TimeOut, Thrillist, Food Network, Zagat, and Eater will point out the best places to eat and drink. Experts at Sunset, Cool Hunting, WeHeart, Inhabitat, and Remodelista will guide you to the latest unique stores and products. Atlas Obscura, Dezeen and Daily Secret help you uncover hidden gems no matter where you are. Songkick and Flavorpill guide you to local music.*

They use three different modes of frequency (frequent, occasional, on request) to update users about possible opportunities. Differences between my proposal and Field Trip are 1) an emphasis on the cultural heritage domain 2) the concept of connecting items seen in museums with outdoor sites. The later difference holds true for other state of the art outdoor applications and distinguishes my research.

Acknowledgments. My advisors: Dr Tsvi Kuflik and Prof Oliviero Stock.

References

1. Ardissono, L., Kuflik, T., Petrelli, D.: Personalization in Cultural Heritage: The Road Travelled and the One Ahead. User Modeling and User-Adapted Interaction 22, 1–27 (2011)
2. Aroyo, L.M., Stash, N., Wang, Y., Gorgels, P., Rutledge, L.: CHIP demonstrator: Semantics-driven recommendations and museum tour generation. In: Aberer, K., Choi, K.-S., Noy, N., Allemang, D., Lee, K.-I., Nixon, L.J.B., Golbeck, J., Mika, P., Maynard, D., Mizoguchi, R., Schreiber, G., Cudré-Mauroux, P., et al. (eds.) ASWC 2007 and ISWC 2007. LNCS, vol. 4825, pp. 879–886. Springer, Heidelberg (2007)
3. Asif, M., Krogstie, J.: Research Issues in Personalization of Mobile Services. International Journal of Information Engineering and Electronic Business (IJIEEB) 4, 1 (2012)

---

[1] http://www.fieldtripper.com

[2] https://play.google.com/store/apps/details?id=com.nianticproject.scout

4. Bohnert, F.: Personalising the Museum Experience. In: Pervasive User Modeling and Personalization (PUMP 2010), p. 33 (2010)
5. Hampson, C., Bailey, E., Munnelly, G., et al.: Dynamic Personalisation for Digital Cultural Heritage Collections (2013)
6. Heckmann, D., Schwartz, T., Brandherm, B., Schmitz, M., von Wilamowitz-Moellendorff, M.: GUMO – The General User Model Ontology. In: Ardissono, L., Brna, P., Mitrović, A. (eds.) UM 2005. LNCS (LNAI), vol. 3538, pp. 428–432. Springer, Heidelberg (2005)
7. Kramer, J., Noronha, S., Vergo, J.: A User-Centered Design Approach to Personalization. Commun ACM 43, 44–48 (2000)
8. Kuflik, T., Kay, J., Kummerfeld, B.: Lifelong Personalized Museum Experiences. In: Proc. Pervasive User Modeling and Personalization (PUMP 2010) (2010)
9. Kyriacou, D.: Enriching Lifelong User Modelling with the Social E-Networking and E-Commerce "Pieces of the Puzzle" (2009)
10. Kyriacou, D.: A Scrutable User Modelling Infrastructure for Enabling Life-Long User Modelling. In: Nejdl, W., Kay, J., Pu, P., Herder, E. (eds.) AH 2008. LNCS, vol. 5149, pp. 421–425. Springer, Heidelberg (2008)
11. Kyriacou, D.: Life-Long User Modelling. A progress report submitted for continuation toward a PhD. Southampton, UK (2007),
http://citeseerx.ist.psu.edu/viewdoc/summary
12. Kyriacou, D., Davis, H.C.: Moving Towards Life-Long User Modeling, 647-648 (2008)
13. Mogles, N., Klein, M., Wissen, A.: An Intelligent Coach for Therapy Adherence: Development and Preliminary Validation. IEEE Pervasive Computing (2013)
14. Pechenizkiy, M., Calders, T.: A Framework for Guiding the Museum Tours Personalization, pp. 11–28 (2007)
15. Shneiderman, B., Plaisant, C.: Designing the user interface, 5th edn. Addison-Wesley, Reading (2009)
16. Stash, N., Veldpaus, L., De Bra, P., et al.: Creating Personalized City Tours using the CHIP Prototype (2013)
17. Wecker, A.J., Kuflik, T., Stock, O.: Personalized Cultural Heritage Experience Outside the Museum (2013)
18. Wigelius, H., Väätäjä, H.: Dimensions of context affecting user experience in mobile work. In: Gross, T., Gulliksen, J., Kotzé, P., Oestreicher, L., Palanque, P., Prates, R.O., Winckler, M. (eds.) INTERACT 2009. LNCS, vol. 5727, pp. 604–617. Springer, Heidelberg (2009)

Personality Profiling from Text and Grammar

William R. Wright

University of Hawai'i at Mānoa, Honolulu, USA
wrightwr@hawaii.edu

Abstract. Personality assessment can be used to predict subjects' use of products and services, thriving in academic programs, and performance in work environments. To avoid the costs and inconvenience of administering personality questionnaires, researchers have inferred author personality from their writings. Extending such methods will enable marketing, interface adaptation, and a variety of data mining applications. The proposed program of research examines elements of syntax, addressing the following questions: does authors' usage of English grammatical structures reflect their personalities? What methodology extracts and predicts personality from grammar usage? Key to this approach is the use of locally defined grammatical structures as described by Part of Speech n-grams.

Research Question. Given similar circumstances, individuals behave in ways that differ between them, and the differences persist over time. Verbal behavior, specifically, communicates something about author personality, age, gender, geography, and social relationship to audience, cf. [15]. Personality questionnaires predict performance in various significant settings, allowing the actors to adjust accordingly. Beyond the traditional personality questionnaires, researchers have developed techniques to infer personality from digitized records of individual behavior—predominantly digitized text [18], [14], [8].

Personality as described by the Five Factor Model of Personality subsumes significant differences in mature human behavior described by the following categories, called *dimensions* because they are assessed on a numerical continuum [10]: **Extraversion:** Retiring vs. sociable, **Agreeableness:** Irritable vs. good natured, **Conscientiousness:** Careless vs. careful, **Neuroticism:** Calm vs. worrying, **Openness:** Conventional vs. original. [4] presented 3 key studies that confirmed the generality of the model.

To predict personality, researchers generally extract bag of words features and features measuring word sentiment and other word categories that are correlated with the personality of a writer [3], [13]. Although such features are highly predictive of personality within a given study sample, only a limited subset both endure the passage of time and remain useful amongst geographically diverse participants. For more robust personality prediction, there is a need to identify additional language features that reflect writer personality. The choice of grammar is a matter of style: two authors making the same assertions *prima facie* about objects and events may express themselves in radically different ways.

V. Dimitrova et al. (Eds.): UMAP 2014, LNCS 8538, pp. 502–507, 2014.

The ensuing question is then twofold: (1) Does authors' usage of English grammatical structures reflect their personalities? (2) What methodology extracts and predicts personality from grammar usage?

Motivation. Personality assessment can be used to predict subjects' use of products and services, thriving in academic programs, and performance in work environments. Some such applications have been realized–companies employ personality questionnaires for personnel selection, and dating websites use personality assessment for purposes of assessing compatibility between users. However administering the personality questionnaires is often impractical and costly. Also, the possibility of dissimulation threatens the validity of self-report questionnaires, e.g. in the case of medical school applicants [5] or others [2].

Lately researchers have conducted experiments to infer author personality from text corpora posted by the public on the Internet, such as on social network websites, blogs, and reviews of products or services, as well as from other offline sources [18]. Extending such methods promises to make possible new marketing, interface adaptation, and a plethora of data mining applications. The methods proposed by this research program are also readily transferrable to psychopathology inference useful in criminal investigation, cyber security, antiterrorism and counterintelligence, especially when the subjects are deceptive.

Anticipated Contributions. Previous work attends to the *semantics* of digitized writing, identifying word-level features predictive of personality–yet with room for improvement. This research explores *syntax* much further than before. The anticipated contributions are as follows: (1) Identify grammatical structures whose presence predicts author personality, (2) Report the features identified, and investigate whether there are any shared across populations diverse by age and geography, (3) Produce and compare predictive models with and without the newly discovered features, (4) Given the syntactic features discovered, offer some unifying insight about their relationship with personality, (5) Offer a rigorous, maximally language independent method that accomplishes all of the above.

Perhaps this work will uncover some valuable features that are applicable to different populations of varying age and geography. At a minimum it will offer a way to discern how participants in a social group express their personalities.

Progress Made to Date. We have conducted an exploratory study of essays and personality scores of 2,588 university students (thanks to James W. Pennebaker for the data) and submitted it for publication by UMAP 2014. Features extracted include word sentiment, Bag-of-Words, and POS n-grams. After dividing the participants into two classes of equal size for each personality dimension (one class consisting of those above the median score, and the other half consisting of those below), we trained SVM's with and without the POS n-grams to predict the personality classes. In the presence of the POS n-gram features, test accuracy during 5-fold cross validation on the binary classification task improved for all personality dimensions except Extraversion, assuming a significance level of 0.0001. Figure 1 includes binary and 3 class results.

The study contributed a successful method to build a successful personality classifier, including feature extraction and selection. We introduced the use of POS n-grams to predict authors' Five Factor personality, and demonstrated that those features significantly improve personality classification accuracy. Finally, to inform others attempting to build a personality predictor, we reported the best of the individual features for each personality dimension.

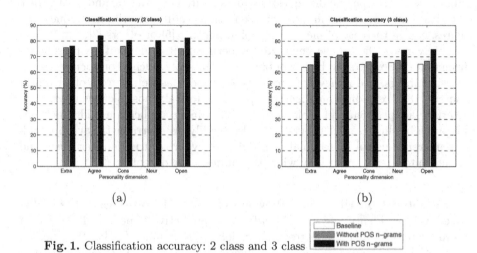

(a)   (b)

Fig. 1. Classification accuracy: 2 class and 3 class

Proposed Approach. The proposed method extracts predictive features from texts written by authors of known personalities. The personality scores are the labels for supervised learning to create binary classifiers as discussed above. We give particular attention to the grammatical features that we wish to test for personality inference. The process is then: (1) Collect multiple samples from diverse populations—text corpora and personality questionnaire scores; (2) Extract features from author text; (3) Perform feature selection; (4) Train and test predictive models, with and without the grammatical features; (5) Identify and explain any helpful features held in common across samples.

Plan of Further Research. Besides the data that I have already located for the exploratory study, I plan to examine public web forum postings. I will administer an online personality questionnaire to participants using items from the IPIP [7]. Their motive for involvement is their personality scores, which I will provide upon completion of the questionnaire. In the event that the number or incidence of the features I extract from this data are insufficient, I will consider alternative data sources.

Text features will be extracted using pre-existing tools when possible, selected according to their accuracy and reputation. Previously I have used [17] for POS tagging, but I am open to other tools. Of particular interest to me are the grammatical structures that the POS n-grams represent. POS n-gram extraction is a fast and highly accurate technique, hence my preference. Due to the results of the exploratory study I am optimistic about the usefulness of these features: for example Extraversion scores correlated with the POS n-gram (**ADV ADJ to**) collocation, wherein adverbs modify adjectives. Table 1 shows some specific instances of this form, wherein writers employ "so" and "extremely" as intensifiers. This example suggests that gregarious extraverts are apt to drive their point home by piling on modifiers, rather than by careful verb choice. In the event that the localized POS n-grams feature set does not offer features that are useful across populations, I will consider other parsing methods such as a chunking parser that identifies noun phrases, prepositional phrases, etc. Then I could also extract the size and order of sentence components as features.

Discourse analysis suggests that when building a model of personality, it is appropriate to extract such features as speech acts (as did [16]) and any other features that may indicate personality such as: the number of participants in a dialogue, chronology and time of day, turn taking (e.g. comparing latency of responses), and variety in the language employed by an individual in various situations. This variational analysis is performed with attention to structure in these variations, e.g. one person varying language whenever interacting with another specific individual. This could reveal something about the personality of either of the two individuals. Finally, if possible it may be worthwhile to consider that the lexical proximity and topical context of some words affects their significance, for example "Louisiana" and "hurricane" signals a discussion of a specific disaster rather than of hurricanes in general.

As [6] did, I would like to extract the frequencies of hapax legomena and hapax dislegomena (words appearing just once or twice in a document). Phrase chunking and clause boundary detection and classification are of interest. Finally, extra vs. intra-sentence anaphora antecedents, and even references to antecedents in others' writings during a dialogue are of interest. The Information Gain technique (or perhaps another) will generate a reduced set of relevant features for training. If there data is sufficient, I will perform feature selection on a holdout set to mitigate overfitting.

Empirical trials will demonstrate the significance of the new features by actually creating and comparing pairs of models that predict personality: one including the (new) features of interest as input, and the other without. This will also allow me to compare the models with the state of the art and with the test-retest reliability of the underlying personality test. The metric will be relative information between each feature and personality, or, to repair its inadequacies, a multivariate derivation thereof. Besides SVM's, I plan to compare other classifiers and regression techniques such as Naive Bayes, Nearest Neighbor (NN), logistic regression, and decision trees. In the end, I will report the best predictive features and offer some insight as to why they reflect personality.

506 W.R. Wright

Table 1. POS *n*-gram examples

Ex.								
(1)	I	am	so	excited	to	be	done with	school!
			ADV	**ADJ**	**to**			
(2)	It's	so	funny	to	me	.		
		ADV	**ADJ**	**to**				
(2)	After a busy and funfilled weekend it is extremely boring to sit in front of a computer							
				ADV		**ADJ**	**to**	

Related Work. There is no illusion that language use and personality are static over a person's lifetime. On the contrary, both are well known to change over time. Nevertheless, a growing body of work shows that some aspects of language use reflect personality, which encourages ongoing investigation of the connection between grammar and personality. Besides a study of transcriptions [9], most efforts are focused on English writing, with a few exceptions (e.g. Chinese and Dutch). Pennebaker and King [13] pioneered this area; also they contributed growing and very useful corpus as well as the use of word categories such as sentiment to extract features significantly correlated to personality. Pennebaker found, among other correlations, that Extraverts tend to use positive emotion words (*happy*, *good*), and those high on Neuroticism the first person singular (*I*, *me*).

Later computer scientists directed Machine Learning techniques to such features to predict personality [1]. They continue to publish the results of applying these methods to diverse study groups. Among the studies, most of them offer results of the binary classification task, but Mairesse [9] is the only one I have found offering regression results. In general they employ single-word features such as word sentiment and bag-of-words, although [12], employed lexical *n*-grams as features and outlined their feature selection strategies. The same author suggested in the context of a broader study of 105 university student authors [11] that POS *n*-grams reflect personality. Although the incidence of any POS feature was no more than 10 for any personality High/Low/Medium class, [11, Table 10], the *n*-grams they discuss beg further investigation.

Roshchina et al. suggested the application of a pre-trained model offered by the authors of [14] to build a recommender system that guides the user to hotel reviews written by people with similar personalities. Research continues to the present; notably [15] predicted personality given bag-of-words features extracted from postings of 75,000 Facebook users.

Background. I have passed my PhD Qualifying Exam, finished a literature review, and am currently preparing a dissertation proposal. I have completed coursework in Natural Language Processing and in Machine Learning.

References

1. Argamon, S., et al.: Lexical predictors of personality type. In: Proceedings, Interface and the Classification Society of North America (2005)
2. Furnham, A.F.: Knowing and faking one's five-factor personality score. Journal of Personality Assessment 69(1), 229–243 (1997)
3. Golbeck, J., et al.: Predicting personality from twitter. In: 3rd International Conference on Social Computing, pp. 149–156. IEEE (2011)
4. Goldberg, L.R.: "An alternative" description of personality: the big-five factor structure. Journal of Personality and Social Psychology 59(6), 1216 (1990)
5. Griffin, B., Wilson, I.G.: Faking good: self-enhancement in medical school applicants. Medical Education 46(5), 485–490 (2012)
6. Hirst, G., Feng, V.W.: Changes in Style in Authors with Alzheimer's Disease. English Studies 93(3), 357–370 (2012) ISSN: 0013838X
7. International Personality Item Pool, http://ipip.ori.org
8. Kosinski, M., et al.: Private traits and attributes are predictable from digital records of human behavior. Proceedings of the National Academy of Sciences 110(15), 5802–5805 (2013)
9. Mairesse, F., Walker, M.: Words mark the nerds: Computational models of personality recognition through language. In: Proceedings of the 28th Annual Conference of the Cognitive Science Society, pp. 543–548 (2006)
10. McCrae, R.R., Costa, P.T.: Validation of the five-factor model of personality across instruments and observers. Journal of Personality and Social Psychology 52(1), 81 (1987)
11. Oberlander, J., Gill, A.J.: Language with character: A stratified corpus comparison of individual differences in e-mail communication. Discourse Processes 42(3), 239–270 (2006)
12. Oberlander, J., Nowson, S.: Whose thumb is it anyway?: classifying author personality from weblog text. In: Proceedings of the COLING/ACL Conference, pp. 627–634. Association for Computational Linguistics (2006)
13. Pennebaker, J.W., King, L.A.: Linguistic styles: language use as an individual difference. Journal of Personality and Social Psychology 77(6), 1296 (1999)
14. Roshchina, A., et al.: User Profile Construction in the TWIN Personality-based Recommender System. In: Sentiment Analysis where AI meets Psychology (SAAIP), p. 73 (2011)
15. Andrew Schwartz, H., et al.: Personality, Gender, and Age in the Language of Social Media: The Open-Vocabulary Approach. PloS One 8(9), e73791 (2013)
16. Shen, J., Brdiczka, O., Liu, J.: Understanding Email Writers: Personality Prediction from Email Messages. In: Carberry, S., Weibelzahl, S., Micarelli, A., Semeraro, G. (eds.) UMAP 2013. LNCS, vol. 7899, pp. 318–330. Springer, Heidelberg (2013)
17. Toutanova, K., et al.: Feature-rich part-of-speech tagging with a cyclic dependency network. In: Proceedings, Conference on Human Language Technology, pp. 173–180. Association for Computational Linguistics (2003)
18. Wright, W.: Literature Review, http://www2.hawaii.edu/~wrightwr/WilliamWright_literature_review.pdf (Online; accessed March 2, 2013)

Author Index

Author Index